FINANCIAL SERVICES IN INDIA

Dr. V. A. AVADHANI

M.A., Ph.D. (Neb), M.A., LL.B., C.A.I.I.B.

* RETIRED ADVISER IN THE RESERVE BANK OF INDIA
* FORMER DIRECTOR OF RESEARCH IN BOMBAY STOCK EXCHANGE
* FORMER ADVISER IN HYDERABAD STOCK EXCHANGE
* VISITING FACULTY IN A NUMBER OF MANAGEMENT COLLEGES

Himalaya Publishing House

ISO 9001:2015 CERTIFIED

First Edition : 2009
Second Revised and Enlarged Edition : 2010
Third Revised and Enlarged Edition : 2015
Edition : 2019
Edition : 2024

Published by : Mrs. Meena Pandey
for **HIMALAYA PUBLISHING HOUSE PVT. LTD.,**
"Ramdoot", Dr. Bhalerao Marg, Girgaon, **Mumbai - 400 004.**
Phone: 022-23860170/23863863, Fax: 022-23877178
Email: himpub@bharatmail.co.in; **Website:** www.himpub.com

Branch Offices

New Delhi : "Pooja Apartments", 4-B, Murari Lal Street, Ansari Road, Darya Ganj, New Delhi - 110 002. Phone: 011-23270392, 23278631; Fax: 011-23256286

Nagpur : Kundanlal Chandak Industrial Estate, Ghat Road, Nagpur - 440 018 Phone: 0712-2738731, 2721215

Bengaluru : Plot No. 91-33, 2nd Main Road, Seshadripuram, Behind Nataraja Theatre, Bengaluru - 560 020. Phone: 080-41138821; Mobile: 09379847017, 09379847005

Hyderabad : No. 3-4-184, Lingampally, Besides Raghavendra Swamy Matham, Kachiguda, Hyderabad - 500 027. Phone: 040-27560041, 27550139; Mobile: 09848130433

Chennai : No. 34/44, Motilal Street, T. Nagar, Chennai - 600 017. Mobile: 09380460419

Pune : First Floor, "Laksha" Apartment, No. 527, Mehunpura, Shaniwarpeth (Near Prabhat Theatre), Pune - 411 030. Phone: 020-24496323/24496333

Cuttack : Plot No. 5F-755/4, Sector-9, CDA Markat Nagar, Cuttack - 753 014, Odisha. Mobile: 09338746007

Kolkata : 3, S.M. Bose Road, Near Gate No. 5, Agarpara Railway Station, North 24 Parganas, West Bengal - 700 109. Mobile: 09674536325

DTP by : Sudhakar Shetty

Printed by : Geetanjali Press Pvt. Ltd., Nagpur. On behalf of HPH (P).

PREFACE TO THIRD REVISED EDITION

The present revision is a thorough updating of all facts and figures, keeping the basic framework intact. In all discussions, the conceptual side was kept in mind, before setting out the practical and operational aspects. The coverage is comprehensively wide from the Basics to High Tech Services in the 21st century.

The Financial Services, including banking and non-banking services are the fastest growing sectors now. The recent boom of 2004-08 and in I.T. on the stock market was led by banking sector, followed by other services. The economic and financial reforms are continued with renewed vigour with emphasis on infrastructure, which is the backbone of the economy. For this and other reforms, the role of financial services cannot be overemphasised.

This book is sweepingly wide, covering as it does, the financial architecture including the Regulatory Authorities like RBI, SEBI, IRDI, etc., financial and non-financial intermediaries in the financial markets, along with a discussion on the markets, ranging from the call money market of one day, to insurance market of lifetime saving and investments and the players in the markets and the retail investors who are all covered in this book.

The theory and practice are juxtaposed to be useful to students in the real world. The analysis is kept simple and lucid for the average students to grasp the basics of the subject. As the reforms are a continuous process and developments in policy changes are taking place daily, the *Daily Financial Press* is an added advantage to the students of this subject.

The coverage of the book is so wide that it can be adopted for many subjects in Finance and Commerce streams and for both graduate and undergraduate courses in universities and colleges in India. Both domestic and foreign markets are covered as also banking and non-banking financial services and the related markets. The Financial Services, Financial Markets and marketing of these services have all found a place in this book. It can be used for many competitive examinations in the area of finance at the Central and State level.

The revised book is more student friendly and hopefully it continues to receive the patronage of the students and faculty alike for many subjects in the finance area. It has to be admitted that there are many repetitions and overlappings in many chapters which was necessitated to make each chapter self-contained and it is to the advantage of the readers to concentrate only on chapters in which their interest lies.

The author gratefully acknowledges the help and co-operation of Faculty and the Himalaya Publishing House, in this venture.

AUTHOR

CONTENTS

PART VI

FINANCIAL MARKETS IN INDIA

INTRODUCTION

The objective of this introduction is to provide an overview of the book and throw light on the inter-linkages of Parts and the subjects covered. Sequentially, the book sets out the treatment of the whole gamut of financial activities from the short end of the spectrum to the long end of the financial system and the foreign sector and its inter-linkages to the domestic sector.

The ongoing reforms in the economy and in the financial system emphasise two things, among others — firstly there is need for an integrated teaching material in the finance area suitable to the Indian context and secondly there is greater need now than ever before for giving the material a practical bias. Such a book should satisfy the majority of the universities in their effort to revise the syllabuses for a strong applied component in them. Accordingly, I started by referring to the syllabuses in the Finance area of most of the Universities in South India, which were easily available to me. In trying to adopt these topics, the present book became a comprehensive compendium covering both the short end and the long end of the financial system in India, encompassing the RBI and its area of hegemony and the SEBI and its tutelage. The object of this book is to integrate various sub-sectors of the financial system in the treatment on the one hand and on the other, present a coverage of the finance area suitable to both the Finance and Marketing students. Thus, there will be a proper and much needed synthesis of the finance and marketing streams in the Business teaching in Management schools. The design of this book is such as to give a comprehensive coverage of financial markets and marketing; it will encompass finance markets, financial institutions, financial systems, comprising both banks and non-bank financial institutions, financial services and marketing of financial services.

Accordingly, Part I deals with the financial system and its linkages with the real system which includes production and marketing of production or output. RBI as the leader of the financial system finds a place in this part along with the genesis of the system, namely, savings and investment and their multiplier role for the growth of the economy and the financial system, which are inter-linked. Finance is seen as an input in the productive process here.

Part II starts with the RBI as the watchdog of the economy and the financial system and deals with RBI as the central bank of India and its role and functions, its organisations and structure, etc. RBI is the currency authority which provides cash which is the source of all liquidity and constitute the brick-layers of the financial system. RBI is also the banker to banks and as such, this part deals in two separate chapters — Commercial Banking and Banks as Intermediaries. The latest trends in banking such as, Telebanking, electronic funds transfer, e-banking, etc., find a place in this part which also discusses the credit cards as a supplement to cash and as an important component of the financial system in India.

Part III analyses the non-bank finance companies, which have grown in importance since the reforms started in 1991-92 and now constitute a major component of the financial system, posing serious threat of competition to the banking system. First, an overview of the NBFCs is given, followed by trends and growth of NBFC services. This part also deals with some of the major financial organisations like merchant banks, mutual funds and venture capital funds.

The core part of the book is contained in Part IV, which presents an analysis of the financial services provided in India. It should however be noted that the services of stock brokers and security firms are dealt with in Part VI and those of portfolio managers in Part VII and of foreign exchange dealers in Part VIII. The more important financial services covered in Part IV are lease, hire-purchase and housing, creding rating, registrars' functions, underwriting services, marketing of new issues, custodial services, factoring and forfaiting and insurance services.

SEBI and its reforms are covered in Part V. This part deals with SEBI and Investor protection, Functions of SEBI, Institutional Structure of the capital market and reforms and the state of the capital market in India. Here emphasis is on the developmental and regulatory role of the SEBI and its area of jurisdiction, namely, the capital market.

Part VI deals with the second important core part of the book, namely, the financial markets in India, their operations and institutions. The markets covered in this part are the New Issues market, Money market, stock market and Government securities market. Among the stock markets, the regular stock exchanges, OTCEI and the NSE are covered. Trading in the money market, stock market and Government securities market are discussed in more detail. Securities trading regulations, instruments of issue and trading and functional aspects of these markets also find a place in this book. The theme of this part is to unveil the instruments of trading, trading operations, institutions involved, mechanics of operations, etc.

Part VII is an adjunct to the Part VI which deals with major financial markets. This part deals with the market indicators, yields, and returns on various instruments in the market, investment and portfolio management and the services related to the portfolio management in India. In particular, this section contains security market indicators which help investment activities, interest rate theory and structure which reflect the yield pattern on the basis of which trade take place in the markets, and basics of the portfolio management services in India.

In the fast changing scenario of the Indian economy, with deregulation, competition, free market orientation, and globalisation, inflows and outflows of funds increased and FFIs and FIIs have started operations in the Indian financial markets. As such, the importance of the foreign sector has grown in its role and its activity. With the adoption of the current account convertibility in 1994, Indian funds started flowing out subject to some limits and foreign funds increased in their inflow for direct investment and portfolio investment in India. It is in the above background, that the importance of PART VIII dealing with the International markets has to be visualised. This part discusses the operations in the Foreign exchange markets and Euro-currency markets and the instruments and institutions involved are set out with particular reference to trading activities, covering the export and import trade, investment and hedge operations, forward trade and trading in the derivatives. This part also covers the exchange risk management which has grown in operational importance due to freer trade and payments and larger risks. Lastly, the remaining exchange controls operated by the RBI and ADs are set out in this part.

PART I

FINANCIAL SYSTEM

FINANCIAL SYSTEM AND REAL SYSTEM

1

Economic Activity

The object of all economic activities is to promote growth of income and output leading to rising standards of living. Basically, economic activity involves production, consumption, saving, accumulation and distribution and the productive process constitutes the axle of the wheel of economic activity. The productive process involves pumping in of inputs to produce certain outputs. The relationship between the inputs and outputs is called technology. Given the state of technology, the actual relation between any given inputs and outputs can be represented by an input-output matrix. Broadly, these inputs can be categorised into (*a*) factoral inputs such as labour, land, capital and entrepreneurship, (*b*) physical inputs which include the supply of raw materials and spare parts and (*c*) financial inputs such as money and near money assets. The payments to the factorial inputs for the services rendered are in the form of wages, rent, interest and profit made out of the value added which is equivalent to the value of output minus the value of material inputs. Thus in any productive system, we can increase the output by increasing either inputs or improving the state of technology, viz., the input-output relation.

Accounting of Economic Activity

Under the modern system of accounting of all activities in the economy, viz., wealth, income, production, consumption, saving, investment and financial flows, etc., there is again admixture of the real variables with money variables. These are explained in terms of what is called social accounting which comprises the National Income Accounts (current account) dealing with output and income, the National Balance Sheet (capital account) comprising the national balance sheet of assets and liabilities, which in turn leads to the Flow of Funds Accounts relating to the financial flows between the sectors, and lastly the input-output relations (real productive process). The basic objective of social accounting is to explain the inter-relationship between different sectors of the economy in terms of current and capital account, in real sector and in the financial sector.

Financial Inputs

It is the inter-relationship between the real sector and the financial sector that is an important part of the productive process because finance is an important input and many times a scarce input. Traditionally, finance was not considered a separate input until finance theory became well developed. Today, in the subject of Financial Management, finance occupies an important place as an input in every economic activity. The forms which financial inputs take are money and near money assets including deposits with banks, investments in shares, debentures and Government securities etc.

In the traditional theory, finance was supposed to take the form of either circulating capital or fixed capital and the concept of **finance** as distinct from **capital** was not well conceived and developed. In modern theory, finance is different from capital. While the former relates to money and near money assets which have separate identity and marginal satisfaction to the holders, capital relates to the physical plant and capital goods such as machinery, etc., which are capable of further production. In the portfolio approach of Tobin and others, economic units are found to hold some amount of money and near money, which implies that they yield some satisfaction. The satisfaction or utility arises out of the Keynes' famous theory of motives for transactions demand, precautionary demand and speculative demand for money. The so-called Friedman's monetarist theory postulates that money and near money assets are part of the asset portfolio of the economic units, constituting the asset demand for money.

Growth in incomes can take place through growth in investment which in turn depends upon savings in the economy. Bulk of the investment takes place, particularly in India in the business sector and the Government sector which are mainly the deficit sectors. The surplus sectors which have some savings are the household sector and the foreign sector. The role of the financial system comes in here for the purpose of mobilising the surplus savings of the household and foreign sectors for channeling them into deficit sectors, viz., the Government and business sectors. The business sector comprises a number of sub-sectors, viz., corporate business, non-corporate business, financial institutions, etc. The flow of savings into investment is aided by the Financial System comprising financial institutions. Savings can be converted into circulating capital and fixed capital — circulating capital for the purpose of operations of the company or business and fixed capital for the purpose of producing further output.

Interactions between Real and Financial Sectors

The operations in the real sector would produce the real output of goods and services leading to real incomes depending upon the three categories of inputs referred to earlier: (*a*) factoral inputs (*b*) physical input or material inputs and (c) financial inputs.

While the factoral inputs come from various sectors in the economy and mostly from the household sector, physical inputs come from the real system and the financial inputs from the financial system. The real output is equal to the real income and this provides necessary physical inputs in the productive process.

In the process of production, goods and services are produced and the total value of this output is the Gross Domestic Product. It has two aspects, viz., income and expenditure. The income aspect shows that a part of the output is used for consumption purposes and a part is saved. Savings are used for further investment or hoarding. The expenditure side shows the spending on investment and on the real goods and services consumed. The savings component from the income side is equal **ex-poste** with investment on the expenditure side. The equality is brought about through the intermediation of the financial system which also brings about the transformation of savings into investment. This is supply side of the financial inputs, referred to earlier. Whether spent on consumption goods or spent on investment goods, the expenditure side has to be equal to the income side as they are two sides of the same coin and what is saved is disposed of in two forms, viz., hoarding and investment. If we discard the possibility of hoarding and deal only with inventories, all savings will equal investment either in inventories or fixed capital assets.

Inventories are here understood in the sense of desirable holding of stocks for the purpose of further production. In a closed economy, excluding the foreign sector, the interaction between the real sector and the financial sector can be represented in the following diagram:

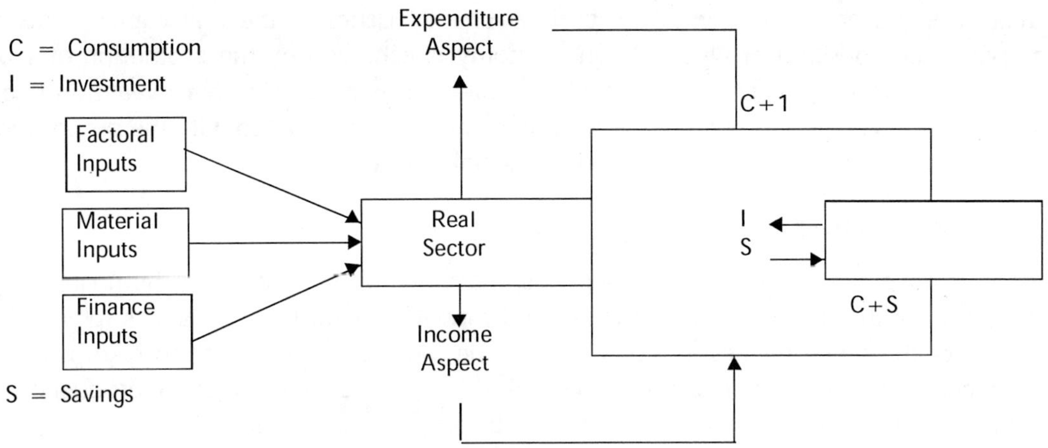

Fig. 1.1

In the real world, inter-connections between the two sectors are so intimate that it is difficult to distinguish them. We are so used to expressing everything in money terms that the distinction between real and money goods and services is lost. Once this distinction is borne in mind, at least conceptually, it is not difficult to see their inter-connections. Briefly the financial system provides money and monetary assets and transforms the savings into investment for the real sector, while the real system provides the savings to the financial system. There is a demand for and supply of physical goods and services in the real sector, which in turn depends on the demand for and supply of financial assets in the financial sector. The equilibrium in one rests on the other. The demand for money as a medium of exchange and a measure of value competes with the demand for any physical commodity in the real sector, as money is like any other commodity. Secondly, this demand is inter-dependent on the demand for real goods in the sense that the latter are measured and exchanged through money. Similarly, money in its function as a store of value equally competes with either physical assets or financial assets representing the real sector and financial sector respectively.

Functions of the Financial System

This leads us to the questions: what is the financial system and what are its functions? The financial system regulates dealings between various economic units including individuals and institutions in money and money assets including all I.O.U.s (Promissory notes). Before the introduction of money as medium of exchange, the economy ran on a barter basis, *i.e.,* exchange of goods for goods. It was only with the use of money as an intermediary in the transactions that the financial system emerged in the modern sense.

The financial institutions constituting the financial system have normally two important functions in money economy, *viz.,* (1) to act as intermediaries for the mobilisation of savings through offer of financial assets of various maturities and qualities and allocation of these savings in various channels of investment, and (2) to arrange for the creation and distribution of money and credit.

In developing countries, the financial system has another and more important function of promoting growth in the economy. Investment in an economy takes the form of either inventories or fixed capital assets. The growth of fixed capital formation is necessary for the development of the economy. The types of financial assets provided by the financial system would influence the types of capital formation in the economy and *vice versa.* Thus, the economic development of a country depends *inter alia* on the growth of the financial system. The larger the proportion of financial assets to real assets, the greater is the scope for development because, as referred to earlier, growth in the economy requires, adequate investment which only the financial system can facilitate. Finance is an important input in the productive process and as such developed financial system is an important pre-requisite for economic growth.

The financial system should have proper width and resilience so that the rate of growth of the financial assets and their structure are in tune with the optimal characteristics of the real capital stock needed for growth. The optimal composition of wealth in an economy is achieved by the promotion of such financial assets as provide incentives to savers and the public to hold a growing part of their wealth in financial form. The rate of savings and the rate of growth in the economy are highly correlated with the proportion of savings held in the form of financial assets relative to non-financial assets.

Economic Growth and Financial System

The economic development of a country depends, *inter alia,* on the growth of the financial system. The larger the proportion of the financial assets (money and monetary assets) to real assets (physical goods and services), the greater the scope for economic growth in the long run. For growth to take place, investment is necessary which flows from the financial system. Besides, as a scarce factor of production in the less developed countries (LDCs), finance has a crucial role to play in these economies.

The growth objective of the financial system is to achieve the structure and rate of growth of various financial assets and liabilities in consonance with the optimal characteristics of real capital stock. The more efficient composition of real wealth is obtained through the promotion of such financial assets which provide incentives to savers and the public to hold a growing part of their wealth in financial form. Increasing rate of savings correlates well with the increase in the proportion of saving held in the form of financial assets relative to tangible assets.[1] There is a direct correlation between growth of the economy and the growth of the financial assets. Investment in the real sector depends on the functioning of the financial sector, as the latter collects and channels savings into investment which is necessary for growth. It would be pertinent to note here that economic growth is a function of the level of investment, capital-output ratio and the state of technology. Given the state of technology and capital-output ratio in each activity of productive process, the level of investment determines the increase in output of goods and services and incomes in the economy.

There is another aspect of the financial system which is relevant to growth, namely, the absorption of liquidity and its use for productive purposes. A well developed financial system with adequate institutions would not only promote savings but encourage these savings to flow into financial assets as against physical assets. The flow of liquidity into physical assets such as gold, silver, real estate and commodities — particularly the sensitive commodities of a speculative nature — would feed inflation while the same flowing into financial assets is not only non-inflationary but would aid growth in the economy and reduce inflationary pressures. In LDCs with inadequate and underdeveloped financial systems, increasing government deficits and growing liquidity could not be absorbed in the financial system and this leads to the well known phenomenon of money chasing goods and to investment in unproductive physical goods and assets feeding further inflation.

Financial System in the LDCs

The introduction of money as a medium of exchange has involved the substitution of money economy for barter economy. Increasing monetisation in the economies of LDCs notwithstanding, there is still a subsistence sector, where money does not enter into transactions. Within the monetised sector of the economy, money and monetary assets play an important part and constitutes the elements of the financial system.

The monetised segment of the economy in the LDCs is covered by the financial institutions which are either in the organised sector being controlled and regulated by the Central Bank of the country, or in the unorganised sector which is more or less outside the purview of the Central Bank. The Central Bank as the

1. H. T. Patrick, "Financial Development and Economic Growth in Underdeveloped Countries", *Economic Development and Cultural Change,* Vol. 14, No. 2, Jan. 1966.

head of the financial system, is a regulator and controller of the financial system. But in some countries, monetary institutions such as the indigeneous bankers and moneylenders and some non-monetary financial institutions such as Chit Funds, and Nidhis fall outside the control of the Central Bank. Thus, in most less developed countries, there is some component of the unorganised sector in the financial system. One of the problems of the Central Bank in the LDCs is to integrate both the organised and unorganised segments of the financial system.

Components of the Financial System

The financial markets have two components — the short-term and the long-term — called the money market and the capital market respectively. Money and near money assets traded in financial markets are of varying degrees of liquidity. The money market comprises the group of connected sub-markets, which deal in money and monetary assets of short-term nature and of more liquid character, such as call money, treasury bills and bills of exchange. The capital market consists of a number of term lending institutions which borrow and lend for long-terms and deal in near money assets of lower liquidity, such as equity, debentures, Government debt, and private debt. The nature of the financial system is determined by such variables as the nature and the number of financial assets, the volume of trading in these assets, etc.

Types of Financial Institutions

The money and capital markets have two types of institutions: (*i*) monetary institutions, which include the Central Bank, commercial and co-operative banks, etc., and (*ii*) non-monetary institutions which comprise the savings banks, savings and loan associations, development banks, mutual funds and investment companies, etc.

The liabilities created by former category constitute money either in the form of currency or deposit money. These institutions are not only intermediaries; their liabilities are in the form of time deposits, shares, bonds, debentures, etc., which constitute the near money assets. While the former influences the quantity of money (M) as well as the velocity of circulation (V) the latter influences only the velocity.

The distinction between money and near money assets is getting blurred, as they are increasingly substituted one for the other. There is a wide spectrum of liquid assets which are dealt with in the financial markets. It is overall liquidity in the economy, and not just money supply which is important for the purpose of monetary policy and the impact on the economy.[2] It is being increasingly realised that non-monetary financial institutions influence the purchasing power through their effect on the velocity of circulation of money.

Classified by the nature of their activities, these financial institutions fall broadly under the following heads:

1. Carry institutions, which earn their income from carrying their assets. Examples are commercial banks, co-operatives banks and development finance companies.
2. Turnover institutions, which are intermediaries earning their income from buying and selling financial assets. Examples are investment companies and mutual trust companies.
3. Brokerage institutions, which do not carry or purchase and sell on their own account, but act simply as agents for the buyers and sellers of the financial assets. Examples are the various brokers' firms in the stock exchange and commodity exchange.

Role of Financial Institutions in the LDCs

The major function of the financial institutions, whether short-term or long-term, is to provide the maximum financial convenience to the public. This can be done in three ways: (*i*) promoting the overall

2. Radcliffe Report on Monetary Policy in U.K. (1959).

savings of the economy by deepening and widening the financial structure; (*ii*) purveying the existing savings in a more efficient manner so that those in great need, from the social and economic point of view, get priority in allotment; and (*iii*) creating credit and deposit money for facilitating the transactions of trade, production and distribution in the economy.

Gurley and Shaw[3] have argued that during the past century and a half, there is a secularly rising ratio of financial assets to real assets, and this is directly correlated with the development process. This is a corollary to the extension of the principle of division of labour to investment and financial intermediation.

There is also a felt need for diversification of financial instruments based on the principle of product differentiation to cater to varying tastes and habits of saving and investment groups. Diversification is one of the ways of promoting saving and investment in the economy. Not only should the funds available for development increase to cater to the growing needs of industry, trade and agriculture but there should also be an increasing variety of forms that the savings can take to satisfy the varying asset preferences of different classes of savers. The former relates to the supply aspect and the latter to the demand aspect.

The argument that it is not economical for the LDCs to set up a number of institutions to specialise in various functions is valid up to a point, particularly in the initial stages of growth. After this point, the advantages gained outweigh the diseconomies of scale.

This is not to argue, however, that institutions should be set up without the felt need for them. There are two schools of thought in this connection. One school believes that such institutions would grow on account of felt needs, called demand following institutions. The other school believes that such financial services are to be made available in the hope of generating or anticipating a demand for such services. Patrick[4] believes that in actual practice, there is likely to be an interaction of supply-leading and demand-following phenomena in many LDCs before sustained industrial growth gets under way. Supply-leading may be able to induce real innovation and new entrepreneurship and as the process of real growth gets under way, supply-leading forces are replaced by demand-following financial responses.

As noticed above, in the LDCs, there is a need for a sound financial infrastructure comprising diverse financial institutions and assets for promoting development. The financial institutions raise the level of savings, by activating the idle funds and allocating the scarce capital more efficiently among the various alternative investments. They do ensure that no worthwhile project suffers for lack of funds, if found feasible on all other grounds. This is known as the **finance function.** Secondly, they have a **developmental function** in that they tend to promote the spirit of enterprise and risk taking, by encouraging the managerial and entrepreneurial talents in the economy. They have a third function in furnishing the technical consultancy services to the entrepreneurs. This is called the **technological function.**

In addition to the three main functions referred to above, they help the special needs of particular geographical areas or certain segments of the economy. Actually it is only for the purpose of catering to the special needs of certain geographical areas or particular segments of the economy or of industry that specialised financing institutions are more desirable. These institutions help the process of shifting resources away from certain sectors to others and encouraging some activities and discouraging others on the basis of national priorities.

Burdened with such diverse functions these financial institutions find it hard to grow on their own. It would therefore be necessary for the Government or the Central Bank of the country to take the initiative and develop these institutions. Besides, in early stages of development, the low incomes of people lead to low voluntary savings, necessitating the bulk of capital formation to take place in the Government sector.

3. J. G. Gurley and E.S. Shaw, "Financial Development and Economic Development", *Economic Development and Cultural Change*, Vol. 15, No. 3, April 1967.
4. H. T. Patrick, "Financial Development and Economic Growth in Underdeveloped Countries", *Economic Development and Cultural Change*, January 1966.

In addition to budgetary surpluses and profits of the public sector undertakings, the Government can mobilise additional savings for investment through intermediation of its financial institutions. It would therefore be necessary to encourage or set up even the supply-leading type of financial institutions in the developing countries, on top of the demand-following pattern of institutions. These financial institutions are variously called development corporations, development banks, development finance companies, etc. These institutions have taken forms so diverse in ownership, management, resources and functions that despite frequent similarity of the formal titles, they have very little resemblance to each other.[5] The degree of specialisation or diversification varies from country-to-country and institution-to-institution.

Long-term financial institutions may be basically of two types: primary and secondary. Primary financial institutions raise the bulk of their resources from the original savers, *viz.*, households, business, etc. In India, Unit Trust of India and Life Insurance Corporation are examples of this type — the former raising funds by sale of units and the latter through insurance premiums. The secondary institutions depend for the bulk of their resources on the primary institutions, banks, the Central Bank and the Government. Examples of this category in India are Industrial Finance Corporations, SFCs, etc. The main function of this category is to purchase primary securities from ultimate lenders.

The financial system has to perform the basic function of matching the needs and preferences of the lenders and borrowers in the market. These will affect the saving and investment activity of all sectors in the economy. The households are the net savers, either voluntarily or involuntarily.

Business borrows more than it lends, not only for fixed capital investment, expansion, diversification, etc., but also due to lags between expenditure and receipts. Intermediation should ensure that business and the Government who are net borrowers would get their requirements in right amounts and at the right time. Business has sometimes an excess of idle balance which financial institutions attract and utilise profitably. Governments borrow not only for their developmental work but also to meet the time lags between payments and receipts as their inflows and outflows do not synchronise in quantity and time.

Promotional Role of the Financial System

These mutual interactions between the financial and real system may take promotional or developmental forms. It is in this context that the development role of the financial system is to be emphasised.

This role assumes two forms: innovation and promotion, which are inter-related. The innovatory role relates to the creative activity of these institutions. Thus, dynamisms as well as creative imagination can be in both the assets and liabilities side of the activities of financial institutions. This takes the form of improving the quality of assets as well as showing new and more profitable activities or keeping pace with the developmental priorities of the Government.

This creative element in the case of commercial banks can be seen in the Lead Bank Scheme, financing of neglected sectors, opening of branches in the rural areas, etc. The creative role in the case of development banker takes the form of a critical examination of the appraisal and follow-up actions including the application of social cost and benefit analysis. The development banker follows sound appraisal techniques including the economic and financial tools both from the point of view of the company as well as the economy. The industrialist finds a contractive partner in the banker who will help him in improving his project plan and prospects of investment.

The financial institutions by virtue of long experience, expertise and information, which they acquire during the course of their project appraisal are in a better position to play the promotional role in the economy. Firstly, they can share their expertise with their clients and improve the project preparation, plug up the loopholes in their schemes and advise them on improving project prospects as well as on the new areas they can explore. Secondly, these institutions have established their own training institutions or schools as in

5. William Diamond: "Development Finance Companies" — *Fund and Bank Review,* June, 1965.

the case of IFC (Management Development Institute) and ICICI (Institute of Financial Management) etc. Thirdly, they are instrumental in setting up consultancy companies, accounting firms, leasing companies and industrial estates, etc. The I.D.B.I. with the help of other institutions have set up at State levels various consultancy service centres. Iran and Greece have also set up similar institutions. Fourthly, development bankers can share their experience with the Government in the formulation of their financial policy as their experience with projects and project implementation would help the Government. Their day-to-day market knowledge about the demand pattern, export market, etc., would also enable the development bankers to advise the Government.

Financial institutions can also undertake what William Diamond calls "directed efforts" in the sense that the efforts are directed toward achieving the specific objectives of the Government which of course change from time-to-time. Thus, when the Government's intention was to encourage small and cottage industries, development bankers geared themselves to this task. When development bankers are directed to give priority to development of backward areas, concessional finance as well as special efforts are made to encourage entrepreneurship in the backward areas.

The creation of enterprise is, no doubt, costly and expensive and the return will be delayed and meagre. But these are the risks which are to be undertaken along with the financial and moral implications of it. The banks will have to carry in its capital structure such burdens of risks sometimes unrewarding until they reach a stage when they can be passed on to the public. This is the cost of promotion which the development banks have to undertake.

✠ ✠ ✠

RESERVE BANK AND FINANCIAL SYSTEM

2

Introduction

The components of the Financial System are: (*i*) the apex institution, namely, the RBI, (*ii*) the organised sector and (*iii*) the unorganised sector. The RBI is centre piece of the financial system and by virtue of its being a central bank of the country is banker to Government, banks and other financial institutions. The RBI's link is traditionally with the short-term market although it has various connections with the long-term market also by virtue of its promotional and developmental role in the latter. It is also the note issue authority, currency manager and foreign exchange controller.

Organised vs. Unorganised Markets

The term 'organised market' refers to regular financial institutions organised on modern lines such as commercial and co-operative banks and various non-banking financial institutions like I.F.C., I.C.I.C.I., etc. The organised market has two components: short-term and long-term called money market and capital market respectively.

Short-term market comprises (*i*) commercial and co-operative banks, (*ii*) call money market, (*iii*) bill market, (*iv*) collateral loan market, and (*v*) short-term gilt-edged market and a host of other sub-markets.

The long-term or capital market, has many sub-markets: new issues market, stock market, private loan/ bond market, Govt. loan/bond market, etc. There are two apex institutions for term lending set up by the RBI: IDBI and NABARD, one for industries and the other for agriculure. Besides there are also all-India financial corporations and State financial corporations, land development banks, share brokers, stock market operations, etc. Allied to these markets is the bullion market which provides a bridge between the financial markets and commodity markets. There are a few specialised institutions in the capital market, *viz.*, ICICI, IFCI, IIBI, NHB, SFCs, SIDC's, etc. in addition to LIC, UTI, GIC Investment companies, Insurance companies and other financial institutions.

The unorganised market refers to the indigenous system of financial institutions such as rural and urban moneylenders (agricultural moneylenders and professional moneylenders), indigenous bankers like Multanis, Shroffs, Marwaris, Chettiars, etc. In fact, there are a number of such unorganised markets, relative to these various classes of bankers, because their practices and methods of operation vary. Similarly, there are various bazar interest rates in the unorganised market relating to the transactions put through in these markets. These interest rates are generally higher than those in the organised market. Besides in the unorganised sector, there is no distinction between the short-term and long-term segments and between production and consumption finance. There is also a high degree of oligarchy in these markets, each with a group of clients and partly competing and partly non-competing among themselves. The degree of control by the RBI on these markets, unlike on the organised markets, is indirect and remote. The linkages between organised and unorganised markets are also tenuous. These and other aspects of the financial system are discussed in the chapter on money markets.

Role of Central Bank

The role of Central Bank is basically different in the developing countries from that in the developed countries. Normally, the Central Bank performs only regulatory role in the context of the socio-economic and structural framework in the economy. In a developing economy, however, the Central Bank often faces the difficulty of lack of an adequate infrastructure and developed money and capital market. It is left to the Central Bank therefore, to build up the financial infrastructure and undertake promotional work for development of the money and capital market.

Measures to develop the capital market should aim at a general encouragement of appropriate economic and financial environment and specific measures to deepen and widen the financial base. The financing of investment requirements of underdeveloped sectors involves a type of work different from that of the Central Bank. Hence, the Central Bank has to set up separate financial institutions, specialised for the purpose, with special skills and know-how. Thus, the function of Central Bank in developing countries can be classified as *regulatory, promotional and financing* (including refinancing).

The Central Bank has to fill up the felt needs in the financial field as and when they arise. It could be a gap in the supply of finance or lack of certain financial institutions or inadequacy of demand itself which can be tackled by supply-leading institutions. Thus, the existing institutions may be inadequate to meet the additional demand or they may be ill-equipped to meet certain new demands for financial services. The Central Bank may have to be geared for promoting economic development through filling up the gaps.

The Central Bank, in addition to direct financing or refinancing, helps fostering new institutions by (*i*) participation in the equity and bonds (subscription to capital), (*ii*) making available loans, advances and discounts of a medium-term and long-term nature, and (*iii*) guaranteeing certain minimum dividends on the investments made in the shares and debentures of financial institutions by the public. If the Central Banks do not wish to get involved in long-term finance, they may set up separate apex institutions for the purpose. Thus, in India, the Reserve Bank has set up an Agricultural Refinance and Development Corporation as the apex institution for term lending to agriculture which later became NABARD and an Industrial Development Bank of India for lending to industry. RBI has also set up DICGC, NHB, etc., for specific purposes.

Due to the low level of savings in the LDCs, the Government and the Central Bank in these countries assume a special role in capital formation. The Government has to raise public debt not only to meet their expenditure but to finance investment through financial institutions, both in the private and public sectors. The Central Bank in its turn has to ensure that there is a ready market to buy and sell in Government securities so as to safeguard their liquidity and adopt a suitable debt management policy[1] for the purpose.

As the Central Bank is responsible for fostering new institutions it finances, it is necessary sometimes to own these institutions partially or wholly. Thus, in the financial field, public, private and joint sectors have been evolved both in short-term and long-term categories. The ownership of financial institutions becomes a variable to be reckoned with in the financial field. In a paper on development banking prepared for the MIT

1. E. Nevin, *Capital Funds in Underdeveloped Countries,* MacMillan & Co., 1963.

by Nyhart and Roberts[2] it was shown that what the development institutions do is more important than the type of ownership of the institutions from the point of view of economic development. It was argued that the institutional variables such as public, private and mixed neither explain the high and the low return of the development banks nor of their performance. Similarly, the contribution of the financial institutions to the economic development is not judged merely by the total amount of finance but by the totality of the services rendered. Roberts[3] has shown that public development banks in India, Iran, Pakistan and the Philippines have been more efficient than private ones in terms of operating costs and profits, and the public development banks have turned out far better performance in terms of profitability of their investments. However, in view of the market imperfections and structural rigidity in the developing countries private profitability and social profitability do vary widely and institutions cannot be judged by the profitability of loans. But it became necessary for many Central Banks to involve themselves in actively owning and participating in the activities of the financial institutions because of the need for promoting such institutions and the difficulty of securing certain institutional services in the private sector.

Money and Capital Markets

The Indian money market in organised sector is insulated from the money markets abroad due to the prevailing exchange controls in India and the absence of free inflow and outflow of funds.

The core of the Indian money market is the inter-bank call money market where the lenders and borrowers are mostly the banks. In addition, the UTI and the LIC, Mutual Funds and many others also enter this market as suppliers. The funds dealt with are the over-night money or money up to a fortnight. There is no true market for bills, neither commercial and treasury, nor is there any acceptance business. Some of the bills are not genuine trade bills. Treasury bills are sold on tap and auction by the RBI on behalf of the Government and the main buyers are commercial banks.

The capital market comprises several institutions, such as the stock market where old securities are dealt with, new issues market where new capital is raised and bullion exchange where gold and silver bullion is purchased and sold. The gilt-edged market has special characteristics in that it can be both short-term and long-term; also this market is narrow and the main holders are commercial banks and other financial institutions. There were many developments in policy which promoted this market due to financial reforms since 1992.

RBI and the Financial System

The Reserve Bank is the centre piece of the financial system and is the apex institution in the money market. It is concerned with the efficient and smooth functioning of the financial system. The Reserve Bank keeps a watch on the developments and disturbances, both of daily and seasonal nature, in the financial system. It provides liquidity to the system with a view of facilitating the smooth functioning of the system and controlling it. The flow of liquidity is controlled through money supply changes, reserve requirements of banks, open market purchases and sales of Government securities, etc. The cost and availability of credit is also regulated by suitable monetary policy. The Reserve Bank can influence the operations in the financial system through not only the liquidity flows, but also through regulation of the banking system, of bank loans, bank holdings of liquid assets, interest rates, public deposits with banks and non-bank financial institutions, etc.

In India, the money market and the capital market are not properly developed. The link between these two segments as well as between the organised and unorganised sectors is tenuous. The RBI has in the past attempted to link the unorganised and organised sectors in a systematic way, but even now the dichotomy

2. J.D. Nyhart and P.E. Roberts, *Development Banking: Return Performance of 186 Development Finance Institutions,* M.I.T. Working Paper, Series No. 396-69 (Cambridge, Massachusetts, May 1969).
3. Paul E. Roberts, "The Issue of Public and Private Development Banking: Reply", *Economic Development and Cultural Change,* January, 1974.

between these two sectors continues to exist. There is inadequate integration, cohesion and specialisation among the components in the financial system. The saving and banking habits are underdeveloped with the result that the operation of the monetary policy in the financial system becomes less effective throwing greater burdens on the Reserve Bank.

Interest Rate Structure

The interest rate is the price paid on the borrowing of money. Different interest rates prevail for different maturities of financial assets. In India while usurious rates of interest prevail in the unorganised sector, those in the organised sector are determined partly by the Reserve Bank and the Government and partly by the interaction between demand for and supply of funds in the system.

Because of the poor linkage between the different sub-markets in the organised sector, the Reserve Bank's interest rate policy is not as effective as it should be and the impact of any change in the bank rate does not percolate quickly and effectively into other sub-markets of the financial system. Similarly the structure of interest rates for various maturities of assets, etc., does not lead to an orderly arrangement. After the economic and financial reforms were started in 1991-92, the interest rate policy has become more flexible and partially market-oriented.

RBI as the Leader

The preamble to the Reserve Bank of India Act says that the main function of the Bank is to regulate the issue of bank notes and keeping of reserves with a view to securing monetary stability in India and generally to operate the currency and credit system of the country to its advantage. Thus it is not only a banker to the Government, but also a banker to the commercial banks, co-operative banks and other financial institutions, in which capacity the Reserve Bank grants accommodation and keeps the reserves of these institutions.

The Bank has also an important role to play statutorily on the maintenance of the external value of the rupee in view of the close inter-dependence of international trade and finance and national economic well-being. The Bank has been entrusted with the custody of the country's international reserves and also represents the Government at the I.M.F. and operates exchange control and other restrictions on foreign payments and receipts.

It would thus appear that the Reserve Bank's functions can be set out in terms of the various contact points it has with the economy: (*i*) Government finance, (*ii*) finance to banking sector and thus to the private sector of the economy, (*iii*) finance to foreign sector, and (*iv*) finance to non-banking financial sector. The Reserve Bank as the apex institution in the financial system is the source of all currency and credit in the economy by virtue of its being the creator of currency and also the custodian of the reserves of the commercial and co-operative banks.

The operations of the RBI influence the economy and are influenced by the economy in the sense that it is environment and the context which shape the policies of the Bank and the policies of the Bank have in turn their impact on the economy. The interactions between the RBI and the economy can be set out in terms of the changes in its assets and liabilities. The liabilities of the RBI give rise to changes in reserve money which produce a multiplier effect on the actual changes in money supply. The assets of the RBI explain the factors influencing the changes in liabilities and thus of reserve money. (See Table).

Table 2.1: RBI: INTERACTIONS AND INTERCONNECTIONS OF THE RBI WITH THE ECONOMY

Sectors of the Economy Influencing	*Liabilities Side*	*Assets Side*	*Sectors of the Economy Influenced*
Govt. sector	Deposits of Government	Loans and advances to Government	Government sector
Private and business sector	Deposits of banks	Loans and advances to financial sector	Bank and non-bank financial sector
Private and foreign sector	Other deposits	Merged in other assets	All sectors
All sectors (Households in particular)	Other liabilities (Notes in circulation)	Investments (*a*) In Government securities (*b*) In Private assets (*c*) In Foreign assets Other assets	 Government sector Private sector Foreign sector

The Reserve Bank's main activities in relation to these sectors can be classified under a finance function and a regulatory function. There is also a third function, *viz.,* a development function with reference to the financial system. As a regulator of the financial system, the Reserve Bank would need a well-developed and well-organised financial system in which its actions could percolate from one segment to the other easily and quickly with the result that its control could become effective. It would thus be in the interest of the Reserve Bank's control that it should help develop an integrated and cohesive functional system, mature in all respects, *viz.,* in respect of the institutional structure, the instruments traded and the interest rates in the economy. It should also ensure that credit gaps, both geographical and functional, are duly filled up. These credit gaps may be in the short-term or the long-term credit-end. The Reserve Bank has not only a stake in the short-term money market but also long-term money market; its actions percolate to the long-end in view of the various direct controls that it operates. The Reserve Bank has a responsibility to the public through the maintenance of monetary and price stability, and to trade and industry through the availability of sufficient liquidity in the system.

RBI and Banks

As regards its regulatory role, the Reserve Bank controls and regulates the activities of the commercial banks in terms of the Banking Regulations Act, 1949. These regulatory provisions were extended to co-operative banks in 1966 in terms of the Banking Laws (Application to Co-operative Societies) Act, 1965. To protect the interests of the depositors, the Bank had set up the Deposit Insurance Corporation in 1962 to insure the deposits of the public and infuse confidence in the banking system. The Bank had acquired powers to effect compulsory amalgamation of banks with a view to weed out the weak and sick units and to control the management and other aspects of operations of banks including loans, advances, investments, etc.

In respect of its promotional role, let us take the commercial and co-operative banks or short-term financial institutions, which are also part of the organised financial system. To bring about a wider diffusion of the benefits of banks, they were exhorted to open branches in rural and underdeveloped regions and to lend to neglected, weaker and underprivileged regions and to lend to neglected, weaker and underprivileged sections of the population. The scheme of social control of banks and the subsequent nationalisation of the 19 major banks were aimed at these promotional objectives. The lead bank scheme of allotting each of the districts to one or more of the banks for the purpose of development of these regions is yet another example of the promotional role of banks. Mention may also be made here of the promotional aspects of encouragement and concessional refinance from the RBI for priority sector lending by banks as well as the credit authorization scheme which requires prior sanction for lending to bigger industrial houses, which has since been withdrawn.

✠ ✠ ✠

SAVINGS AND INVESTMENT FOR GROWTH

3

How do Savings Emerge?

Savings are excess of income over expenditure for any economic unit. Thus S = Y–E where S is savings, Y is income and E is expenditure. Secondly, excess funds or surplus in profits or capital gains are also available for investment. Thus, $S = W_2 - W_1$ where W_2 is wealth in period 2 and W_1 is wealth in period 1 and the difference between them is capital gains or losses. Thirdly, investment is also made by many companies and individuals by borrowing from others. Thus the Corporate Sector and Govt. Sector are always net borrowers, as they invest more than their savings. Thus, S = B – L where "B" is borrowings and "L" is lendings. Savings can be positive or negative.

Why do People Save?

Saving is abstaining from present consumption for a future use. Savings are sometimes autonomous coming from households as a matter of habit. But bulk of the savings come for specific objectives, like interest income, future needs, contingencies, precautionary purposes, or growth in future wealth, leading to rise in the standard of living, etc.

Impact of Inflation

All investments lose in value due to inflation or rise in prices leading to depreciation of the value of rupee. When the rate of inflation is about 10%, the real value of money is lost by 10% every year. The investors have therefore to protect themselves from this loss of real values of their assets by proper Investment planning and by securing returns, higher than the inflation rate.

Some investments give only income like bank deposits, P.O. Certificates, Company deposits, etc. Some assets show capital appreciation if they are shares in companies or bullion, land and buildings. Some are safe and liquid, like the investments in Govt. securities, bonds of P.S.Us, etc. A few investments like Indira Vikas Patra are easily transferable and marketable. So also the shares and securities, listed and traded on the Stock Exchanges. But all the above investments do not satisfy all the needs and objectives of investors, referred to later, including securing a hedge against inflation. All objectives of income, capital appreciation, safety, marketability and liquidity as also hedge against inflation can be secured only by proper investment in *corporate securities.* The chart below shows the real rates of return on all investments, which are mostly negative since 2003-04.

Table 3.1: INVESTOR'S CASH PLANNING CASH VERSUS OTHER ALTERNATIVE ASSETS (DATA FOR 2014)

Asset Class	*Proportion Held By Average Household**	*Nominal Return*	*Real Return*
Cash	10.0	0%	–8%
Bank Deposits	56	S.B. 4%	–4.5%
		F.D. 4%-10.25%	1-2%
Insurance	16.4	Estimated	
Pension funds, P.F.s etc.		at 3 to 5%	
(LIC, GIC, UTI, HDFC, etc.)	14.6	**	–3.0%
Company Deposits	1.9	10%-14%	6%
Company Shares and Debentures	1.5	Variable	–
Claims on Government	1.2		
Post Office Deposits	6.5	Maximum rate	1-2%
Postal Certificates, etc.	2.6	of 9%	
Gold and Silver, etc.	Not available	14% to 20%	6 to 12%
UTI Units and MF Schemes	0.4	9.5 - 12%	up to 4%

* As percentage of total financial savings. Inflation rate is assumed at 8%, although the actual rates may be around 5 to 6.5%.

** P.F. and Pension funds have a nominal rate up to 9% and real rate may be negative sometimes.

(The data are as per the latest RBI Publications. Totals do not add up due to others not included in Table).

For Household Sector

The following assets have shown the proportions shown against them in 2013-14.

(1) Cash and Bank deposits	70%
(2) Life and other Insurance items	10%
(3) P.F. Pension Fund	10%
(4) Shares & debentures	09%
(5) Claims on Government like P.O. Savings media	01%
	100%

The poportion are rough and ready measures of the actuals. This may differ from time-to-time and year-to-year. As such, the above data have to be read with caution.

Investment Activity

At the outset any study on Investment Activity should start with the question of what is investment. It means many things to many persons. If one person has advanced some money to another, it may be his loan which may be considered his investment for a return. If a person has purchased one kg of gold for the purpose of price appreciation or a consumer durable like washing machine for the flow of services, it is his investment. If he purchases an insurance plan or a pension plan, it is an investment. Thus, there are various types of investments, for various persons.

For the individual, it is the exchange of the money or cash for a future claim on money or the purchase of a security of a promise to pay at a later date along with a regular income as in the case of a share, bond, debenture, etc. For the issuer of security, it is the use of money for fixed capital equipments, working capital or any other productive activity. Sometimes, it is also a service like consultancy, construction, hotel or hospital and services in future, as in the case of consumer durables.

What is Investment Activity?

Investment activity includes buying and selling or trading in the above claims on money and/or promissory notes. An investment for one may be disinvestment of another as in the case of stock market trading or may be a fresh investment in a new issue. In the New Issue Market, one can only buy securities. Investments can also be made in non-marketable securities or instruments or other avenues.

All purchases of securities are thus investments although for the economy as a whole, some investments are offset by corresponding disinvestments. There are two terms which are relevant for this context, namely, Gross and Net Investments. Gross are total investments made from all sources by an economy or a single economic unit. Net investments are those which are Gross investments, minus disinvestments for an economic unit. Gross Assets and Investments minus Depreciation for the economy or a company or Corporate Sector or Govt. Sector, is net Investment, which is termed as net Capital formation.

Savings and Investments

Some investors are also savers but all savers cannot be good investors, as investment is a science and an art. Savings are sometimes autonomous and sometimes induced by the incentives like fiscal concessions or income or capital appreciation. The number of investors is about 50 to 100 million out of a population of more than 1.2 billion in India. During the year 1999-2000, as one SEBI study has shown 7.66 million new Indian households are estimated to have invested in the markets for the first time. Savers come from all classes except in the case of 26% of the population who are below the poverty line. The growth of urbanisation and literacy have activated the cult of investment. More recently, since the eighties the investment activity has become more popular with the change in the Govt. policies towards liberalisation and financial deregulation. The process of liberalisation and privatisation was accelerated by the Govt. policy changes towards a market-oriented economy, through economic and financial reforms started in July 1991.

Objectives of Investors

(*a*) Income

(*b*) Appreciation of Capital

(*c*) Safety

(*d*) Liquidity

(*e*) Hedge against inflation.

The mix of these objectives may also depend on the timeframe of his investment.

(*a*) Short-term/day-to-day trading gains.

(*b*) Short-term capital appreciation up to one year (short-term capital gains).

(*c*) Long-term appreciation of 1 to 3 years (long-term capital gains) and more.

Investment preferences of public may be set out in terms of their savings for:

(*a*) Transactions purpose (for daily needs or regular payments).

(*b*) Precautionary purposes (for contingencies or special needs).

(*c*) Speculative or asset purposes (for Capital gains and building of assets).

Investment for Consumption and Business

The income is divided into two components, namely, consumption and investment. The amounts not consumed are saved and invested. But investments are also useful for present and future consumption in the case of consumer durables, cars, gold and silver, etc. But investments generally promote larger consumption in future as they lead to more income and larger capital appreciation in the years to come.

Some investments in business are used in trade and transport and other services. Thus, doctors, lawyers, traders, etc., spend money for making investments for their business, which lead to further consumption or income.

Investment and Speculation

Purchase of assets like shares and securities can be for either investment or speculation or for both. Investment is long-term in nature, while speculation is short-term. Investment aims at income and normal long-term capital growth while speculation aims only at short-term trade-gains through buying and selling. Investment is less risky and speculation is more risky.

Basically, both aim at income and capital appreciation. But the difference is in motives and objectives. All investments are risky to some extent but speculation is most risky as it involves short-term trading, buying and selling which may lead to profits sometimes and losses at other times.

Investment Opportunities

Investment avenues are multifold and each has its own risk-return characteristics. Riskless investments in the common parlance are bank deposits, Govt. securities, bonds of Govt. and semi-govt. bodies, post office savings schemes, P.O. deposits, etc., Provident funds and pension fund schemes, Insurance for life, endowment, accident, etc. The details are discussed in another chapter.

Financial Investments vs. Physical Investment

Many savers will have their first preference for physical investments which are less productive and rarely income earning. Such investments are in consumer goods — non-durables or durables, gold, silver, cars and antiques and 'Curios'. These are satisfying the immediate consumer needs, for comfort, luxuries, social status, ego satisfaction, etc. Some investments of physical nature are more in real estate, land, buildings, etc. Some of them if rented out to others give income and sometimes capital appreciation also, if the location is at good places or commercial areas. Similarly, gold, silver and other metals, diamonds, and antiques may present capital appreciation, without giving any regular income. Some investments are for social status and prestige as gold, diamonds, jewellery, etc.

Bank Deposits

Commercial and cooperative banks accept deposits from public in the form of current account which bears no interest, savings accounts which bear interest at 4% per annum, and fixed deposits of varying maturities from 15 days to 5 years. The interest rates will vary from bank-to-bank but the ceiling rates are fixed by the RBI. These deposits are also insured with the Deposit Insurance and Credit Guarantee Corporation. Besides the operation of the banks, being regulated and inspected by RBI, the deposits kept with them are supposed to be safer and risk free. Although the returns are lower, the risk is also lower and risk averse investors will prefer investments in these avenues.

Next to keeping in cash most savings generally flow into some form of the bank deposits. The average households in India keep about 10% of their savings in financial form in cash and nearly 55% in bank deposits of various forms. But these avenues of investment give a return which is zero in the case of cash or a return less than or equal to the inflation rate of about 8% per annum. (average of last decade)

Savings and Investment which are promoted by the capital market are the basis of capital formation and economic growth in the country. As such it is necessary to present at the outset the inter-relation between savings and investment and growth in relation to the financial system in the process.

Structure of the Economy

The Indian Economy has undergone vast changes since planned development was initiated in 1951. Early in the fifties, total domestic savings as a percentage of GDP was hardly 5% and rate of growth of GDP was around 3%.

The structure of Indian economy in 1951-52 showed that the shares of the primary sector, secondary sector and tertiary sector were 56%, 17%, and 27% respectively. The primary sector consists of Agriculture, Forestry, Fishing, Mining and Quarrying. The secondary sector comprises Manufacturing, Construction, Electricity, etc. The tertiary sector encompasses the rest of the economy, *viz.,* Transport, Communication, Trade, Finance, Real Estate, and Other Services. By the end of the Seventh Plan (1990-91), after four decades of planning, agriculture accounted for 35% and manufacture and construction sector for 26% and the tertiary sector accounted for the rest (39%). By 2010-11, the importance of the services sector has gone up further to around 66% while that of primary sector fell to 14% and industry to 20%.

It would thus be seen that the importance of agriculture has gone down from 56% to 14% while the significance of manufacturing and services has gone up significantly over the planned period mainly due to shifts of resources from the primary sector to other sectors of the economy and in particular the services sector. The saving rate continued to be 32 to 34% of the GDP during the first decade of 21st century while the same in fifties was only 10%.

What is Growth Process?

The economic performance is reflected in the growth of income or GDP and growth refers to a rise in output and incomes. The rate of growth of income and the distribution of income are the factors which influence the savings and are a function of the growth process. As the economy develops, production of goods and services would increase, leading to a rise in their consumption and the standard of living of the people. The growth of the economy involves a rise in incomes of the people, but development is a wider term, which includes both growth and qualitative improvement in the standard of living of the people and a better distribution of incomes. Development thus involves a rise in the level of income and better distribution and higher standard of living in general through growth plus socio-economic changes.

Role of Savings

Growth is a function of savings and investment in the economy, which along with the capital-output ratio determines the level of income. By increasing investment in fixed assets, plant, machinery, etc., capital formation rises which results in a rise in output depending on the capital-output ratio. The latter is a ratio of output to capital employed in any industry or productive activity. The total capital-output ratio for the economy, speaking in macro terms, and the total volume of investment in the economy would determine the growth of output and incomes. Thus, output (O) is a function of investment (I) and capital-output ratio (K); $O = f(I,K)$. Thus, $DO = f(DI, DK)$ where Ds are incrementals and DK is marginal capital-output ratio, defined as DO/DI, namely, a rise in output resulting from a given incremental capital used in the productive process. The average capital-output ratio and incremental capital-output ratio are the two ratios to be looked into for the multiplier process to work from investment to income or output. Crudely expressed, if investment rises by 12% and capital-output ratio is 4:1, then the income would rise by 3% ($12 \div 4$). These ratios vary from industry-to-industry, sector-to-sector and activity-to-activity. Similarly, the savings ratio and investment ratio also vary in each of the industries and units, and among the various sectors.

In India, the net savers are the household sector whose savings are higher than their investment, leading to their positive contribution of savings in the economy. On the other hand, business and Government sectors are negative savers in that their investment is higher than the savings leading to a net negative contribution to the savings of economy. The foreign sector also contributes to net savings due to a larger inflow of funds through commercial borrowings and other forms of capital inflows.

Other Factors in Development

Another factor which influences the standard of living of the people is the rate of inflation which is measured by the rate of rise of prices, namely, wholesale prices or consumer prices (WPI or CPI for industrial workers). A rise in prices leads to the lowering of the value of money and its purchasing power, which in turn leads to the lowering of consumption basket of goods and services. This results in a lower standard of living of the people, other things remaining the same. The distribution effects of inflation are also adverse to the development process. Some income groups gain at the expense of others and the saving capacity may go down for the bulk of the population which are marginal savers.

Savings and investment not only depend upon income, but on its distribution among the population. The level of income in real terms is what matters for the standard of living of the people and this in turn depends on the distribution of income and the rate of inflation in the economy. So investment and income are to be looked into from the point of view of the inflation rate in the economy, namely, in real terms rather than in nominal terms. The other factor is the poverty ratio, which connotes the number of population below a level of minimum subsistence. The lower the poverty ratio, namely, if the proportion of those below the minimum subsistence level of income is lower, the better is the performance of the economy, as it shows a rising standard of living of the people.

The rate of savings also depends on the structure of the economy. As noticed above, agriculture used to dominate the Indian economy with a share of 56% of total national income in terms of output and nearly 70% of employment in terms of population. The saving potential of these people is low as agriculture used to be mainly for subsistence rather than for commercial and marketing purposes. This proportion of agriculture to GDP declined to around 36% at the end of the seventies by expansion of the industry and services sectors. In the early 21st century agriculture accounted for about 14-15% of total income of the people although about 60% of the population still depend on agriculture either directly or indirectly. This shows that there has been a considerable widening of the base of economic activity into industry and services. Growth process leads to shifts in the structure of the economy from the primitive agriculture to modern capitalistic production in industry and services sectors. The savings have also increased enormously and that investment has also accelerated. The fall in the contribution of agriculture is not good by itself. There is a larger scope for technology and the induction of corporation and growth of productivity.

Financial Intermediation

The development process involves a larger role of financial intermediation and shifting of savings away from investment in physical assets to investment in financial assets. The financial intermediation not only promotes savings *per se* but leads to the process of shifting resources from less productive activities or underproductive activities to more productive activities. Not only the total quantum but the distribution of investment in the economy as between the various activities and sectors is relevant to the growth process. These factors can be effectively influenced by the financial institutions, namely, banks, UTI, LIC, IDBI, ICICI, etc., through their lending operations. The degree to which these institutions can influence the investment and productive activity depends *inter alia* on the depth and sophistication of the financial system and its structure. Thus, the variety of instruments available for investment and trading, the specialisation among institutions and the range of their services and a host of other factors influence the productive activity and growth process. The sophistication in the financial structure depends on the degree of financial intermediation. In India, the financial system has been developing rapidly in the last two decades and the proportion of financial savings has been growing. Thus, savings in financial form of the household sector has increased from around 30% of the total in the fifties to 53% in recent years. As a proportion of GDP total savings of household sector is about 24% at present, of which that in physical form is 11.7% and that in financial form is 11.8%. The gross investment (GDCF) rate was 35% in 2012-13, while the gross domestic savings rate was around 31%.

Links of Real Economic System and Financial System

There is a continuous interaction between the financial system and the real economic system. The flows of funds in the form of savings and investment emanate from the financial system and promote production of goods and services in the real sector, leading to a rise in output and incomes of the people. The role of the financial system is thus to promote savings and investment in the economy and to enlarge these resources flowing into the financial assets, which are more productive than the physical assets. Even among financial assets, some are more productive than others and a proper financial intermediation and sophistication in financial services would promote larger production of goods and services in the economy. The financial system thus has an important role to play in the productive process and in the mobilisation of savings and their distribution among the various productive activities. The stock and capital markets have a significant role to play in this context because they are part of the financial system. They promote *inter alia* a larger mobilisation of savings by facilitating investment in financial assets such as shares, debentures, securities, etc., and a greater degree of liquidity is imparted to the existing investments by facilitating the purchase and sale of existing securities through the secondary market (*viz.*, stock market). They also provide encouragement to the listing of the shares of companies which facilitates their trading and the valuation of their assets by virtue of a quotation on the stock exchange, and help them to raise further resources, if need be. These institutions promote the expansion of the new issues and in the raising of larger resources in the capital market through widening the base of trading, increase in the number of instruments for savings and investment and through widening the network of saving mobilisation efforts. The recent increase in the financial institutions such as leasing and hire-purchase and Housing Finance companies, merchant banks and mutual funds also helped to increase the degree of specialisation in the financial structure. New instruments of trading such as participation certificates, certificates of deposits, and Flexi-bonds are being experimented in the money and capital markets which have widened the scope of financial services and sophistication in India.

Savings Rate

The Central Statistical Organisation (CSO) has defined savings as the excess of current expenditure over income and is a balancing item on the income and outlay accounts of producing enterprises and households, Government administration and other final consumers. In simple words, savings are the excess income over expenditure of the economic units. For the purpose of estimating domestic savings, the economy in a closed set up has been divided into three sectors: household sector, private corporate sector and public sector. The savings at household sector, which account for the bulk of savings, are measured by the total of financial savings and savings in physical assets. The savings in financial form include savings in currency, bank deposits, non-bank deposits, life insurance funds, provident and pension funds, claims on Government, shares and debentures, units of UTI and trade debts. Of these, currency and deposits are voluntary savings and motivated by transactions and precautionary motives and are governed by interest income and other incentives. The savings in life insurance, provident and pension funds are contractual savings governed by precautionary and contingency motives. The claims on Government are compulsory deposits, tax credits and investments in Government bonds, etc. The savings in the form of units, shares and debentures, etc., are all voluntary savings and are used for investment in the business sector, directly or indirectly. The savings in postal investments are claims on the Government which are voluntary. The above are the gross savings against which should be set off the financial liabilities such as borrowings by them from the Government, business sector and other sectors of the economy. The flow of *net* savings in financial form is a relevant variable for influencing the growth process in the economy. The foreign sector is the fourth sector in an open economy contributing net savings.

The gross savings of the household sector constituted around 22-24% of the GDP in recent years. Of these more than 50% is in physical assets and the rest in financial form in the early years of 21st century. The savings in physical form include agricultural implements, tools, tractors, consumer durables, gold, silver, etc., among the rural households, and such items as real estate, buildings, durable goods, gold, silver, etc. among all households. The savings in physical form are less productive, while savings in financial form are more productive in various degrees depending on the efficiency of their use.

Household Savings

The savings of the economy are mostly concentrated in the household sector in recent years. For example, more than 100% of the domestic savings have originated from the household sector in 1988-89 due to negative savings in the public sector and insignificant savings in the private corporate sector in terms of percentages to the GDP. In 2005-06, the same proportion has come down to around 70% due to better performance of public sector, and private corporate sector.

The savings in the household sector are mobilised directly in the form of units of the Unit Trust, premiums to the LIC and other insurance companies, contribution to pension funds, provident funds, etc., which are contractual forms of savings. Savings in the form of currency and deposits with commercial and co-operative banks are direct voluntary savings in financial form. Indirect investments from the household sector are investments in the secondary markets through purchases of shares and debentures, etc., by banks and financial institutions. The investments through provident fund and pension fund, UTI, etc., of household sector are also indirect investments. Investments in the new issues market are direct investments in the corporate sector by the households. At present, the direct investment in the corporate sector in the form of shares and debentures including UTI and mutual funds accounts for about 4 to 6% of the total financial savings of the household sector. Some forms of holding savings particularly in the form, of currency are barren and unproductive while some are less productive, such as those in real estate or buildings, in the sense that there will be no further production of goods and services. There is a large scope in our economy not only to raise savings in financial form but also to increase the investment in shares and debentures through shifts of assets held by the household sector and investments to more productive forms available to savers in the form of larger capital formation.

Shifts within Industrial Sector

Growth process involves structural shifts in the economy as between agriculture and industry and in favour of the latter, which was reported earlier. More importantly, within the industrial sector, there have been shifts over the long run in favour of the organised manufacturing activity and from consumer goods to capital goods and consumer durable goods. The base of industrial structure has been widened and many new industries have been added in India after the initiation of the planned process. Among the various industries, production in mining, oil exploration and gas products, etc., has been increased significantly both in quantitative terms and relative terms in India. The unregistered manufacturing sector, particularly small-scale sector accounted for about 8% of the NDP while registered manufacturing activity constituted 13% of the NDP. It is no doubt true that the growth of modern large-scale industry under the planned process has reduced the importance of the unorganised small sector. But even so, the unorganised small sector now accounted for around one-third of the total industrial production. This shows that this sector still occupies an important position in the Indian Industry.

The other main features in the structure of the Indian economy are a larger rise in the shares of transport, communications, energy, banks and insurance, which shows that the role of infrastructural industries in the economy has increased significantly. Besides, the share of public administration and defence has also grown over the past few decades, partly due to the increase in the role of the public sector in the economy and partly due to the expansion of the Government activities in providing infrastructure and other services. The role of services sector has vastly grown over the last decade, as referred to earlier.

Lead and Lag Industries

Among the industries, there are some as lead sectors and others as lag sectors. The savings and investment flowing into the lead sectors result in accelerated growth while those in the lag sectors may have less dynamic effects. Some of the lead sectors also called "sun-rise industries" are electronics, I.T, computers, multi-media, chemicals, communications and hi-technology industries. The future growth prospects of the economy depend on these industries, some of which have high capital-output ratios. The secondary market trends, the share prices and market capitalisation would depend more upon these industries in future.

Public Sector Enterprises

The various five-year plans laid emphasis on capital-intensive industries *vis-a-vis* wage goods industries. The result is that there was scarcity of many consumer items while utilisation of capacities in capital-intensive industries like steel, coal, electricity, etc., was poor and capital was used most inefficiently. Large capital investment in the public sector has taken place over the past many years with the result the underproduction and underutilisation of capacities exist in these industries. There was continued low productivity and low profitability of a majority of the public sector undertakings like coal, steel, electricity, and Railways. This shows the wrong usage of scarce capital and the need of the hour is to increase productivity.

In the business sector, many public undertakings have negative savings due to the high capital intensity, high borrowing costs, and low earning potential. The managements in many of these public sector undertakings are inefficient and less dynamic and their contribution to the total profits and retained earnings is so small that they cannot meet their capital expenditure from their own resources. The budget allocation for investment has been withdrawn recently, with the result that they have to depend on public borrowing. This is particularly true in the case of Railways, Food Corporation of India and a number of State Electricity Undertakings. Capital formation in these undertakings is poor, in view of their low profits and poor internal accruals.

Paradox of High Savings and Low Growth

In India, we have the paradox of a high savings rate and a low growth rate in the economy. With a savings rate of 22-24% and investment at 24%-26% the economic growth has averaged at around 4-5% during the eighties and nineties This is explained by a high capital-output ratio in the Indian economy at around 4.5:1. The Seventh Plan projections were based upon a capital-output ratio of around 4.5 and savings rate of around 21-23%. The capital-output ratio was only 3.2:1 in the First Plan period, which has gone up to a high of 5.7:1 during the Fourth Plan but has since declined to 4.5 in the Seventh Plan period as per the estimates of the Planning Commission. The Tenth Plan has assumed a capital-output ratio of 4.1:1. This should give an average rate of growth of economy of around 8% in the Tenth Plan. The actual achievement was about 6%.

The Seventh Plan gave an average rate of growth of around 5% and the Eighth Plan a rate of growth of around 5.5%. A rate of growth of this order is necessary to increase the standard of living of people because there is a continuous growth in the population at a rate of about 2% per annum. In the fifties and sixties, for example, when the average rate of growth of incomes was around 3.5% and the population growth at more than 2%, there was hardly enough growth in the *per capita* incomes of the people (namely, at 1.5%). During the period 1951-90 the annual rate of increase in *per capita* income at this level of 1.5% compares very badly with the most developing Asian countries. This should be attributed to inadequate savings potential of the public sector undertakings and poor capital formation in the private corporate sector and low productivity of the factors, say of capital and technology.

Role of Private Corporate Sector

It was seen earlier that the performance of the private corporate sector and public sector in generating savings was poor. The reasons for poor performance of the public sector have been explained above. The performance of the private corporate sector has also been disappointing in so far as its contribution to raising the Indian savings rate is concerned. In spite of five decades of development and a significant rise in manufacturing output, the contribution of savings of the private corporate sector to total domestic savings was about 1-2% on an average. This compares very badly with the performance in developed countries where the corporate sector's retained earnings constitute a significant proportion of the total savings in the economy.

The reasons for poor savings by the corporate sector in India are many. Firstly, they place undue reliance on the loan capital due to the low level of owned resources. Besides, the share of profits in factory incomes has declined or did not rise as fast as the incomes out of interest. Secondly, a significant portion of the business in India is done by the unincorporated enterprises and partnership concerns, whose profits are reflected in income and savings of the household sector and not in the corporate sector. Thirdly, the taxation policy in the corporate sector encourages the use of loan capital by companies and the dividend policy does not encourage the accumulation of retained earnings.

Conclusions

As referred to earlier the savings rate of the household sector at around 22% of GDP over the last few years has been stagnant mainly due to increased inflation rates and a tapering off of the level of growth of savings. This stage of growth is called "low level equilibrium trap". Even so, the rate of growth of around 5.5% over the first four decades of planning should be considered as a good achievement by the Indian planners. During the more recent period of Tenth Plan 2002-07 the rate of growth was 8 to 9%. Besides, the other achievements of planning in India are rapid growth in the public sector and a mixed economy with a contribution of public sector of around one-fourth of the total production. The basic and capital goods industries which were well developed since the Second Five Year Plan have led India into one of the leading industrial producers in the world with a diversified industrial base and structure. It should also be noted that India has developed a high level of infrastructural facilities such as transport, communications, irrigation, etc., and entered into a number of high-technology industries like computers, satellite communication and non-conventional energy and nuclear energy. The commendable performance of these industries, particularly transport, communications, tourism, media, energy, etc., have helped the industrialisation process in India. During the second half of nineties, the growth of infrastructure industries was stagnant. Even so these achievements are in no way insignificant and can be attributed mainly to the growing role of financial intermediation in India during eighties and nineties. In recent years, more varieties of financial institutions have come up like Venture Capital Funds, factoring agencies, securities firms, etc., and more categories of investment avenues, due to the ongoing financial reforms.

✠ ✠ ✠

FINANCIAL SYSTEM — INTERMEDIATION

4

As opposed to financial activity, the real system deals with the production, distribution and consumption of goods and services. The introduction of money as a medium of exchange for goods and services, measure of value of the goods and services in the real system and a store of value of these in the real system. Financial system refers to the activity relating to the provision of the above services in terms of money and facilitates activity in real system. When we have the growth of financial system, providing inputs to productive activity, we have the growth of savings and investment and economic development. Financial sector provides inputs in the form of cash credit and assets in financial form necessary for production in real system. Finance is the lubricating mechanism for economic activity to run its cycles.

Financial sector provides *inter alia,* the following essential services for the real system to function and grow:

(1) Economic growth and development depends on savings and investment which is the role of the financial system to mobilise and channel savings into investment and capital formation.

(2) Capital formation is the basis for economic growth and under the capitalistic system of production, this plays a major role.

(3) Financial system promotes the liquidity in the system and allocation and reallocation of savings and investment into various avenues of economic activity is facilitated.

(4) Financial system serves a most crucial function of intermediation, between savers and investors and among various avenues of investment and between real activity in physical form and financial activity in the form of providing a means and a medium of exchange.

(5) As a store of value, the command on future goods and services is secured by financial assets such as bank deposits, company deposits, and corporate and Govt. securities. Money as a store of value leads to financial assets and wealth and according to Friedman school of thought, money is held in the form of financial assets and constitutes the Asset Motive for money. The first and most vital function of money is to serve as a medium of exchange and a measure of value. Here the objective is to use money for transactions and precautionary purposes. The second and equally important function of money is the store of value function, as per Keynes' Analysis. But Milton Friedman and

his followers have converted this store of value function into asset function. The speculative motive of holding money in terms of Keynes' motives of holding money will now be analysed in terms of asset motive as money is a form of wealth and holding money in one's portfolio increases the wealthiness of the individual.

The above analysis conclusively proves the crucial role that financial system plays in functioning of real economy and for the growth of the economic activity. The sophistication and growth of intermediation role of financial system and the growth of financial assets in the economy are the *sine-qua-non* for the smooth functioning of the economy and growth of economy through rise in GDP and the rate of growth of GDP and of per capita incomes measuring the standard of living of people.

Financial Intermediation

The role of financial institutions is to provide intermediation between financial and real sectors and savers and investors and promote capital formation and economic growth. The study of the national balance sheet shows that over any period, how the ratio of financial assets to total assets has been growing. This ratio is one of the indicators of economic growth. Over the planned period in India, this indicator has been rising, as reflected in the ratio of financial assets to total domestic assets excluding land. This was mainly due to rapid rise in financial assets, attributed to expanded role of public sector during 1950 to 1990 and large capital investments in capital intensive projects. But more importantly there was more active financial intermediation and widening and deepening of the financial system in terms of range of financial instruments and magnitude of funds raised. During nineties and later, the importance of financial sector increased due to ongoing economic and financial reforms, privatisation, deregulation and globalisation.

Ratios of Financial Intermediation

The ratio between direct debt issued by non-financial institutions and indirect debt issued by financial institutions is called financial intermediation ratio. But the ratio of total debt to total investment activity is the financial inter-relations ratio. These ratios indicate the extent of the role played by financial institutions in the economy, in terms of the services they render. The specialisation in savings and investment activity is indicated by the growth of financial inter-relations ratio, namely, total financial issues to total physical asset formation (investment).

The following are the indicators which are more frequently used to assess the role of financial institutions and their services for the growth of economy.

Some Financial Indicators

(1) Indirect issues of financial institutions to non-financial sector

(2) Issues of non-financial sector

(3) Issues of rest of the world

(4) Total Issues = (1) + (2) + (3)

(5) Total physical assets formation (investment)

(6) Financial inter-relation ratio = (4) ÷ (5)

(7) Investment financed by the financial institutions = (1) ÷ (5)

(8) Financial intermediation ratio (1) ÷ (2)

(9) New issues ratio = (2) ÷ (4).

Savings mobilisation and promotion of investment are functions of the stock and capital markets which are a part of the organised financial system in India. The objective of all economic activity is to promote the well-being and standard of living of the people, which depends on the income and distribution of income in terms of real goods and services in the economy. The production of output, which is vital to the growth process in the economy, is a function of the many inputs used in the productive process. These inputs are material inputs (in the form of physical materials, *viz.,* raw materials, plant, machinery, etc.), human inputs (in the form of labour and enterprise) and financial inputs (in the form of capital, cash and credit). The easy availability of financial inputs promotes the growth process through proper co-ordination between human and material inputs.

The financial inputs emanate from the financial system, while real goods and services are part of the real system. The interaction between the real system (goods and services) and the financial system (money and capital) is necessary for the productive process. Trading in money and monetary assets constitute the activity in the financial markets and are referred to as the financial system.

What Constitutes Financial Activity?

The term "liquidity" is used to refer to cash, money and nearness to cash. Money and monetary assets are traded in the financial system. Thus provision of liquidity and trading in liquidity are the major functions of the financial system. While cash creation is the function of the RBI, credit creation is done by banks and claims on money or monetary assets are dealt in by financial institutions including the RBI, banks and term-lending institutions. These institutions are all a part of the financial system.

Besides, the financial system is also geared to the mobilisation of savings and channelisation of these savings into productive activity. Through appropriate differentials in the rate of return and other incentives, funds flow from less productive to more productive activities. These flows of funds are facilitated by the efficient functioning of the financial system.

Sector-wise, government and business sectors are the major borrowers whose investment is always greater than savings. On the other hand, in India the household and foreign sectors are the net savers, with savings exceeding investment. The financial system provides the intermediation between savers and investors and helps the process of specialisation and sophistication in the financial infrastructure, leading to greater financial development which is a pre-requisite for faster economic development.

RBI and the Financial System

The original source of liquidity in the economy is the Reserve Bank of India. As a controller of currency and credit and creator of currency, the Reserve Bank is the central piece of the financial system. As a banker to the banks, the Reserve Bank controls the credit and banking system including the financial institutions. These are altogether called the organised sector of the financial system.

The functions of RBI with respect to the financial system are: (i) provision of finance and refinance and control of the liquidity in the economy to keep monetary stability and to maintain foreign exchange stability; (ii) regulation of banking and financial institutions for protecting the interest of the public and for monetary and foreign exchange stability; and (iii) development of sound financial system by strengthening the institutional structure and by promoting saving and investment in the economy.

Money Market

An important segment of the financial system is the money market which refers to all transactions in near money such as short-term claims on banks, financial institutions and corporate sector. It is a market for short-term monetary assets or claims on money. The duration should normally be less than one year. These include transactions in inter-bank call money (Call money market) and treasury bills issued by the government and commercial bills issued by the private corporate sector (Bills Discount market). The money market is the short-term wing of the financial system dealing in claims on money of a short-term nature, say, of a few days to a few months. Next to the currency, the most liquid assets are the short-term claims or call money of a duration of up to 15 days. The bills, both of the government and the private corporate sector, may run for three to six months. But all these instruments would generally be of a few days to one year and fall into the category of short-term monetary instruments. The intercorporate funds market is also a part of this market which conducts the borrowing and lending operations among the corporate units in the private sector. The banks, financial institutions and companies operate in these markets and effect purchase and sale transactions in these near-money assets.

The commercial paper (CP) issued by companies for raising short-term working capital is being developed in India. The participation certificates (PC) issued by banks and financial institutions, the deposit certificates (CD) issued by banks and factorisation bills are the other instruments. The institutions operating in these markets are banks, development finance companies like the LIC, UTI, GIC, etc., and other financial institutions. In the inter-bank money market, however, only the LIC and UTI have been permitted to operate in addition to banks. In 1990, the GIC, IDBI, NABARD, Mutual Funds and other financial institutions have also been permitted to operate. In April 1991, the RBI allowed the entry of any mutual fund and any entity with bulk lendable resources of ₹ 20 crore and above as also the Money Market Mutual Funds to enter the call money market. This market is being developed in India by the establishment of Discount and Finance House by the Reserve Bank in April 1988, in collaboration with the financial institutions.

The money market is developing at present. The qualities of a developed money market such as cohesion, integration of sub-markets, specialisation in various categories of business and openness to foreign forces are absent in India. There is no secondary market for many instruments like Treasury Bills, Commercial Bills, CPs and CDs, etc. Recently, schemes for the development of secondary market in commercial paper and for trading in certificates of deposits and participation certificates have been initiated by the RBI.

Characteristics

The money market establishes the link between the RBI and banks and the policy of RBI is felt in this market first before it percolates to other markets. The inter-bank market matches the deficits and surplus of banks; SBI and foreign banks are the major players in this market. This market provides an important area or venue for central bank intervention in the economy. It is also a place to secure the short-term requirements of banks and FIs. This provides a link between the cash and near-money assets and to long-term wing of the capital market. Operations in this market extend to dealings in UTI units, PSU Bonds, and short-term bonds of semi-government and government sector, etc.

Discount and Finance House

The Discount and Finance House of India (DFHI) was set up in April 1988, in accordance with the recommendations of the Working Group on Money Market under the chairmanship of Shri N. Vaghul. The paid-up capital of ₹ 100 crore was contributed jointly by the RBI (₹ 51 crore), public sector banks (₹ 33 crore) and financial institutions (₹ 16 crore). The aim of DFHI is to deal in short-term money market instruments with the primary objective of imparting improved liquidity to such instruments.

The functions of DFHI are as follows:

1. Discount/purchase, etc., of 91 day Treasury bills and 364-day treasury bills;
2. Discounting and rediscounting of short-term commercial bills for banks and financial institutions; and
3. Participation in the inter-bank call money market, both as lender and borrower, subject to the regulations of Indian Banks Association and the RBI.

The sources of finance are as follows:

1. Paid-up capital of ₹100 crore;
2. Credit limits of ₹200 crore with public sector banks; and
3. Back up refinance lines from the RBI.

Operations of DFHI

The DFHI purchases and sells Treasury Bills of 91 days, and 364 days. Continuous bid and offer rates are maintained. The yields to investors varied from 9 to 14% depending on the conditions in the market. It is the vehicle of operations of RBI in the money market.

The DFHI rediscounts from the banks commercial bills at the going market rates; also purchases and sales are carried out and bid and offer rates are quoted. It also operates in the inter-bank call money market, both as lender and borrower.

Stock Market

An important component of capital market is the stock market. In the stock and capital markets, there are various types of term-lending institutions, all-India and state financial corporations and finance companies and development corporations, which deal in money and debt claims. The trading in debt claims of a medium and long-term nature can be classified into those of the government sector and of the private sector. The securities of government are traded in the stock market as a separate component, called gilt-edged market. The securities of the government sector include those of the Central and State Governments, local bodies, semi-government bodies and those guaranteed by the government. These securities may have a maturity running up to 25 to 30 years. In this market, there are again three types of securities — short, medium and long-dated government securities, depending upon the maturity period.

Another component of the stock exchange deals with trading in corporate shares, equities, and preference shares which are forms of raising funds of an ownership category. When these equities are floated to the public for the first time by the companies as shares, they constitute the new issues market, which is a component of the capital market. Besides, there are also further issues which are floated by the existing companies for additional capital for expansion, modernisation, etc. The new issues and further issues are the claims of the public on the corporate sector. The claims on the private corporate sector can also take the form of preference shares which are also of ownership category. There are also securities of a debt nature such as bonds/debentures and the companies may borrow from the public directly by raising deposits. These are of various maturities extending up to 3-5 years in the case of company deposits and 5 to 7 years in the case of debenture. Debentures may be convertible or non-convertible, depending on the availability of option for conversion into equity. Similarly, preference shares may be cumulative or non-cumulative depending on the provision for accumulation of dividends or not. More recently, convertible preference shares and debentures are also permitted, which can be converted into equity shares at a later stage. An instrument permitted by the Government since 1985 but which has not become popular is the cumulative convertible preference share (CCP) which is not only cumulative with respect to payment of arrears of dividends but also convertible into equity after 3 to 5 years. These shares carry a fixed rate of dividend of 10% until conversion. A number of new instruments have also been introduced and referred to later.

Financial Institutions

The various financial institutions which trade in these stock and capital markets are all-India financial institutions like IFC, ICICI and IDBI and various SFCs, for which the apex institution is the IDBI which has now become universal bank. Institutions which issue primary securities to collect the savings from the public directly are UTI, GIC, LIC, etc. They collect savings of the public directly in the form of units or premiums.

These are called investment institutions. Over the years, some public sector banks such as SBI, Indian Bank, Bank of India, Canara Bank, etc., have started their mutual funds, as also the LIC and GIC. These are also part of the stock and capital markets. These institutions trade and invest in these markets. The securities traded by them may be the claims of the government or of the private corporate sector. The all-India institutions and state financial institutions like the ICICI, IFC or SFCs, etc., raise resources directly from the public in the form of deposits or by issues of bonds/debentures. They may also borrow from the banks and other financial institutions as also from the RBI. These are called Development Corporations. The uses of their funds are investments in corporate shares, securities and bonds/debentures and loans and advances to corporate units. More recently, a number of new finance companies have cropped up, namely, lease finance, housing finance, etc. The range of instruments offered to the public has accordingly widened and the capital market has been deepened and broadened enormously in recent years.

Savings and Investment

The household sector is the major saver in India and contributes to the bulk of the total savings that flow into financial assets which may take any of the forms of currency, deposits with banks and companies, PF, insurance and corporate shares, bonds, etc.

In addition to providing liquidity to investments, the stock and capital markets promote mobilisation of savings and channelise them into investment. As already referred to, the major borrowers are government and business sectors in the economy, which invest more than they save. The net savings flow from the household and foreign sectors. The financial system helps the process of institutionalisation of these savings for promoting investment and production in the economy. The financial intermediaries play a crucial role in the process in the stock and capital markets in India. The importance of underwriting of shares and stock-broking activities of brokers and dealers is to be appreciated in this context, as brokers are financial intermediaries like banks and financial institutions.

Interest Rate Structure

The interest rates paid on these various securities are fixed by the government and the RBI. The bank rate and other interest rates as applicable to the banks are fixed by the Reserve Bank and the others by the government in consultation with the RBI. In India, the interest rates are partly administered and all the rates in the organised financial system are controlled. The peculiar feature of the structure is that interest rates neither reflect the free market forces nor do they reflect the scarcity value of capital in the economy. Most of these rates are determined by government and RBI on an *ad hoc* basis, in tune with the exigencies of monetary and credit policy or fiscal policy. Normally, interest is a reward for risk and return for abstaining from present consumption. In India, certain priority sectors like borrowings by the government and operations of agriculture, exports and other priority sectors are financed at concessional rates on considerations other than risk/return. More recently, there has been some deregulation of the financial system and many interest rates have been freed from controls. These and other details are discussed in a separate chapter.

The interest rates on company deposits are now freed which were earlier fixed by the govt. Certain returns like those in National Saving Certificates of the government also carry fixed interest rates in addition to certain tax exemption and other fiscal benefits. The criteria of fixing these rates differ from their nature and from instrument to instrument. The interest rates on 364 days Treasury bills introduced in the recent reforms of 1986-87 are determined by auctions and expected to reflect the free market forces. The coupon rates on govt. loans were already revised upwards in the early years of the nineties to be more realistic and market-oriented. Although almost all the interest rates in India are fixed, the interest rate policy is operated in a flexible manner so as to reflect the emerging conditions in the economy.

Reference may be made here to the relevant recommendations of the Chakravarthy Committee to review the working of the monetary policy (RBI, 1985). This report highlighted the need to bring the interest rates nearer to the free market rates and to fix them at levels of positive return in real terms adjusted for inflation. Debentures are the corporate debt just as deposits are, but while debentures are mostly secured, deposits are not. Some of the debentures are convertible into equity shares, called convertible debentures. The interest rates offered on them are lower than on non-convertible debentures. The interest rates on debentures are allowed to be fixed by the companies depending on the free market forces. The inter-bank call rate had a ceiling of 10%, which was removed in May 1989. The short-term deposit rates of banks vary and the maximum rate payable by banks on deposits is now freed for deposits of above one year.

Under the ownership category of capital, there are equity and preference shares. The interest rate on preference shares is fixed by the government at 14% while the returns on equity depend on the dividends declared by the company and the operational performance of the corporate sector. All these categories of securities are of a long-term nature and are basically the claims of the public on the government or the corporate sector.

Some of these are quoted and traded in the market while others are not. Of those quoted, a few are more actively traded than others. The trading on the stock exchanges is called the secondary market, while the primary market refers to the issue of new securities to the original savers, *viz.*, the households, trusts, charities, corporate entities, non-corporate enterprises, government, etc.

Capital Market

As referred to earlier, in the category of financial institutions, there are some which issue primary securities. Besides the corporate sector which issues primary securities in the form of new issues and further issues and public deposits, there are also financial institutions like LIC and GIC, which sell insurance certificates for collecting the savings from public directly. They also collect the premiums and mobilise savings of the public. These funds are mobilised for channeling them ultimately into the stock and capital markets.

The public sector units and the government are in fact the largest borrowers in the primary market. Many public sector undertakings like Railways, SAIL, FCI, banks etc., are now directly issuing shares and bonds to the public. Similarly, UTI also issues certificates and other unit schemes leading to mobilisation of savings directly from the public. The units of UTI as well as the certificates of LIC, GIC, etc., are all part of the capital market transactions of mobilising savings directly from the public. The Mutual Funds floated by some public sector banks and more recently by private sector also raise funds directly from households and invest them in turn in the primary and secondary market in shares, debentures, bonds, deposits, etc., of the companies or in government securities floated from time to time. The financial institutions like ICCI, IFC, etc., also issue bonds in the market to raise funds for their operations. In the case of primary market, the institutions may underwrite or make direct subscription to the new issues or further issues of the corporate sector. The brokers, banks and the financial institutions referred to above are all intermediaries operating in the primary and secondary markets.

In the primary market, the brokers act as underwriters, managers, registrars and even merchant bankers to the new issues. In the secondary market, the claims of a long-term nature of one year and above are traded both on spot or forward basis. This trading imparts liquidity to investments and thus promotes savings and investment. These financial institutions can only change the velocity of circulation of money (cash and credit), while dealing in the primary and secondary markets, but the banks can influence both creation of money and its velocity.

The RBI has linkages with banks and other financial institutions through its control and finance functions and provision of cash and currency. Besides, the money market trades in claims on money of varying maturities of a few days to a few months. The trading in the money claims is what constitutes the financial system, controlled by the RBI and is called the organised financial system. Banks have linkages with both brokers and dealers in securities through the credit limits granted to them and through their operations in the primary and secondary markets.

Unorganised Financial System

In India, we have an unorganised financial system which is not amenable to control by the Reserve Bank directly. In this system, there are a number of moneylenders, traders, landlords, who lend money to the public and indigenous banks who also accept deposits from them. There are also private finance companies, Nidhis, chit funds and host of other unincorporated bodies whose activities are not amenable to the financial discipline of RBI. Some State Governments have passed legislation to control them, but not effectively operated. But some activities like deposit taking activities, the maturity and interest rates on their deposits, etc., are controlled by the RBI and the Central Government. In this system, claims on money are traded, bills of exchange are discounted, monies lent, advances made and a host of other transactions take place in money and near money assets. The rates of interest may vary from 20% to even 100%, depending upon the stringency in the market. There are links between the organised system and unorganised system in the form of credit limit sanctioned to the moneylenders, brokers and finance companies by the commercial and co-operative banks. In this process, both commercial and co-operative banks play an important role as the links between these two segments of the financial system. The RBI control on co-operative banks is partial and limited. The RBI however, controls the acceptance of deposits and interest rates thereof of financial companies, while those of other companies are controlled and regulated by the Registrar of Companies and Company Law Board (CLB).

Bullion Market

In the last resort, gold, silver, bullion and even real estate can also be considered as monetary assets in the long spectrum of liquidity as people prefer to hold them as alternatives for company deposits, debentures, etc., in the organised sector. It would thus appear that the spectrum of liquidity is very wide spreading from cash/currency of the Reserve Bank to long-term securities, shares, etc., which are not easily realisable and even to monetary metals like gold and silver. The bullion market is thus an adjunct of the capital market in the sense that funds which could not be deployed in the capital or stock market may sometimes flow into the bullion market and *vice versa.* In the overall financial system, the money market, capital market and bullion market are closely linked and the flow of funds in either direction is possible as between them.

Charts 4.1 to 4.7 depict a schematic presentation of the financial system in India.

WHAT IS FINANCIAL SYSTEM?

A. ORGANISED MARKETS

RBI	BANKs AND INTER-BANK	MONEY MARKET STOCK AND CAPITAL	BULLION MARKET

B. UNORGANISED MARKETS

1. INDIGENOUS BANKERS
2. MONEYLENDERS
3. PAWN BROKERS
4. TRADERS, LANDLORDS, ETC.

Chart 4.1 Schematic Presentation of the Financial System in India

WHAT CONSTITUTES FINANCIAL SYSTEM?

A TRADING IN LIQUIDITY

CASH	CREDIT	LENDING AND BORROWING	CLAIMS OF MONEY	SHORT-TERM LONG-TERM
RBI	BANKS	BANKS AND AND FINANCIAL INSTITUTIONS	FINANCIAL SYSTEM AND CAPITAL MARKET	MONEY MARKET STOCK AND CAPITAL MARKET

B. MOBILISATION OF SAVINGS AND PROMOTION OF INVESTMENT

	SECTORS	S/1	MARKETS
NATIONAL SAVINGS AND FLOW OF INVESTMENT	HOUSEHOLD SECTOR	S > 1	PRIMARY MARKETS
	FOREIGN SECTOR	S > 1	ALL MARKETS — NEW ISSUES AND CAPITAL MARKET
	BUSINESS SECTOR	I > S	PRIMARY AND SECONDARY MARKETS
	GOVT. SECTOR	I > S	STOCK MARKETS — GILT-EDGED MARKETS

S : SAVINGS I : INVESTMENT

Chart 4.2

FINANCIAL SYSTEM — BUSINESS SECTOR

SECTOR		NATURE OF ASSETS	MARKETS
BANKS F.I.s	S = I	BORROWINGS EQUITY SHARES PREFERENCE SHARES CUMULATIVE DEBENTURES — SECURED AND UNSECURED — CONVERTIBLE AND NON-CONVERTIBLE	STOCK MARKET (TRADING IN OLD SECURITIES)
GOVERNMENT SECTOR	I > S		
FOREIGN SECTOR	S > I		
HOUSEHOLD SECTOR	S > I	PUBLIC DEPOSITS NEW ISSUES FURTHER ISSUES PURCHASE OF OLD SECURITIES	CAPITAL MARKET (BORROWING, DEPOSITS, ISSUE OF NEW SECURITIES)

Chart 4.3

FINANCIAL SYSTEM — GOVERNMENT SECTOR

RBI	CREATION OF MONEY —	*AD HOC* TBs	MONEY MARKET
BANKS & F.I.s	LENDING LENDING AND INVESTMENT	TBs (91 DAYS) TBs (364 DAYS) SHORT-TERM ADVANCES	LENDING AND INVESTMENT (FOR PUBLIC SECTOR UNDERTAKINGS)
RBIs, BANKS FIs, CORPORATE SECTOR, PFs, etc.	INVESTMENT IN GOVT. AND SEMI-GOVT. SECURITIES	SHORT-TERM MEDIUM-TERM LONG-TERM (OLD AND NEW SECURITIES)	STOCK AND CAPITAL MARKETS

T.B. = TREASURY BILLS

Chart 4.4

A. SEGMENTS OF MONEY MARKET

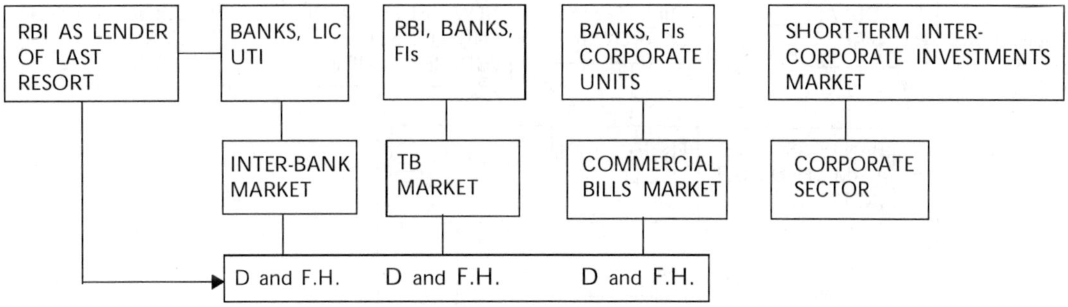

B. SEGMENTS OF CAPITAL MARKET

APEX BODY	INSTITUTIONS		OPERATING MARKETS	
SEBI as regulator	IDBI IFCI ICICI BANKS SFCs DEVELOPMENT AGENCIES PFs	LIC UTI GIC FINANCE COMPANIES INVESTMENT COMPANIES BROKERS	NEW ISSUE MARKET — SECURITIES MARKET — DIRECT BORROWING — FROM BANKS — FROM PUBLIC DEPOSITS — OTHERS	INITIAL ISSUES FURTHER ISSUES TRADING —

Chart 4.5

INTER-CONNECTIONS
SEGMENTS OF MONEY MARKET

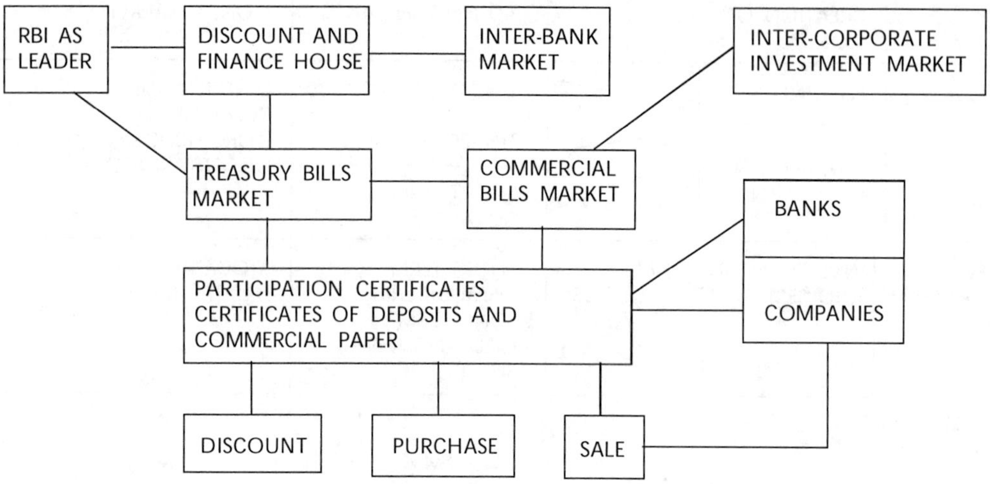

Chart 4.6

INTER-CONNECTIONS
SEGMENTS OF CAPITAL MARKET

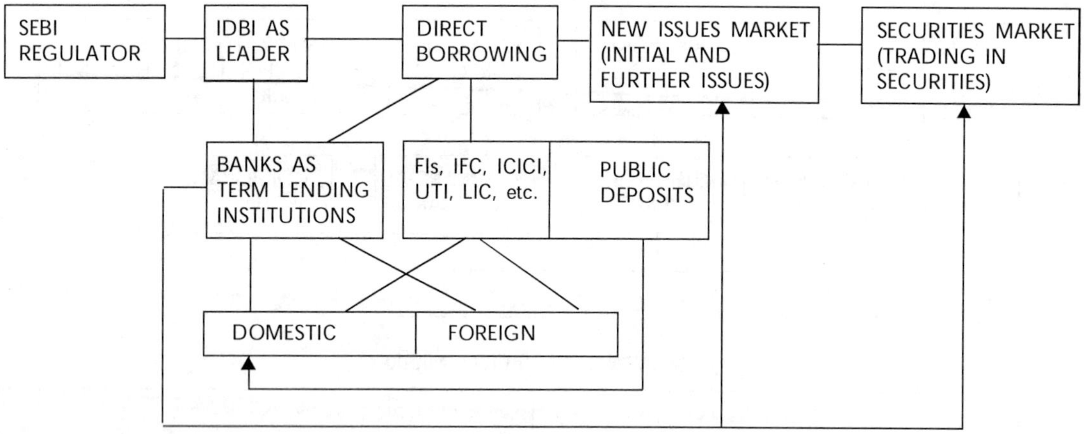

Chart 4.7

✠ ✠ ✠

PART II

RBI AND BANKING SYSTEM

RESERVE BANK AS CENTRAL BANK OF INDIA

5

The essence of central banking is discretionary control over the monetary system of the economy. Since money has become the medium of exchange, the monetary system has come into prominence and the role of the central banker has become crucial. Central bank as an apex institution in the banking and financial system of the country shoulders partially the responsibility for the management of the economy. This role depends on the system of the government, the stage of economic development, the organisation of the financial markets and a host of other factors.

A central bank has to function in the environment in which it is placed and the forces — economic, social and political — which operate on it. Most of the functions of the central bank have been evolved historically as a result of the responses of the central bank to the various forces operating on it. These responses are discretionary and as such central banking is an art.[1] The forces that operate and the environment it faces are different from central bank to central bank. Thus, the central banking in developing countries is different from that in developed countries in the sense that the totality of forces that operate on the central bank in developing countries is different from that in developed countries. The financial system is undeveloped or underdeveloped or developing; there are inadequate financial institutions, insufficient mobilization of savings, problems of development, lack of integration of various financial markets and so on. The central bank has to face and tackle these problems as they emerge from time to time, irrespective of the fact whether it is a private central bank or a government-owned central bank.[2]

The central bank is a banker's bank and, as a consequence of this, keeps the balances of commercial banks. The latter are supposed to channel their credit and other activities in the directions set by the government for development. It is in this context that the central bank comes into the picture to ensure that banking activities support the development programmes in the economy. In some developing countries such as India and Pakistan, the central banks help identification and filling up of the credit gaps. In some others like Malaysia and Thailand, the commercial banks are given the option of investing a specified portion of their reserves in some industries whose development the authorities wish to encourage. The central banks of a few countries such as Finland and Colombia have even invested a part of their funds in industrial concerns in whose development the authorities are vitally interested.

1. See R.S. Sayers, *Central Banking after Bagehot* (Oxford University Press, London).
2. H.V.R. Iyangar, *Role of Central Banking Authority and Commercial Banks in a Planned Economy,* 1968.

Objectives of Central Bank@

The objectives of the central bank are broadly:

(1) to maintain the internal value of the nation's currency;

(2) to preserve the external value of the currency;

(3) to secure reasonable price stability; and

(4) to promote economic growth with rising levels of employment, output and real income.

These objectives are common to all countries, developed or developing. More relevant to the developing countries are those of economic growth and price stability which means that the central bank should strive to achieve economic growth with reasonable price stability.

Within the framework of the above objectives, the functions of central bank in the developing countries may be classified into two categories: (1) traditional functions; and (2) developmental functions. The traditional functions and developmental functions are discussed below.

Traditional Functions

It is no doubt true that the traditional functions of a central bank are to act as a lender of last resort, as a banker to banks and to the government and as a note issue authority. Finance and regulation are crucial to these functions. For example, the preamble to the Reserve Bank of India Act, 1934 states that the objective of setting up of the Bank is "to regulate the issue of Bank Notes and the keeping of reserves with a view to securing monetary stability in India and generally to operate the currency and credit system of the country to its advantage". All central banks carry-out the management of note issue, act as a banker to the banks, a banker to the government and a custodian of the foreign exchange reserves of the country. Ancillary to these functions the central bank helps in the clearance of cheques, remittances of funds and distribution of coins and currency, regulation of the banking system, management of foreign exchange, etc.

The statutes governing the central banks in developing countries are generally framed on the same lines as those in developed countries. In addition, these central banks are equipped with more legal powers and a wider variety of tools to operate in view of the underdeveloped nature of the markets in which they operate. The result is that the central bank in a developing country has a wider range of instruments to control and regulate the banking system. Besides, the governments of developing countries have assumed responsibility for economic development and the old 'independent' central bank has given place to a new concept of 'government-dominated' central bank. This has resulted in the involvement of the central bank in a wide variety of tasks which the government would normally undertake on its own. Besides, the central bank operates in the background of underdeveloped financial system which reduces the efficacy of its policy instruments. This places an additional responsibility on the central bank to develop the financial system of the country. The developmental functions of the central bank have thus been built up over a period of time on the basis of the above rationale.

Developmental Functions

The developmental functions[3] may be broadly classified into two types:

1. those to increase the volume of investment and change the pattern of financial flows for the purpose of promoting investment and output; and
2. those to promote a balanced and viable financial system in the economy.

@ V.A. Avadhani, "Theory and Practice of Central Banking in India", 1979. Somaiya Publications.

3. Al Kral, "The Role of a Central Bank in a Developing Economy", in *International Seminar on Banking and Development,* RBI (1970).

Under the first, the central bank is faced with the shortage of capital and savings and pursues a suitable monetary policy for the purpose of promoting savings and the proper channeling of those savings into investment. The monetary expansion by the central bank has to be attuned to the needs of monetisation in the economy and the increase in the real output which is expected through a rise in the volume of investment. The central bank should bring about monetary expansion adequate for growth and the desired level of economic activity, keeping in view the likely trend of conversion of barter economy into money economy and maintenance of adequate demand for output. At the same time, the central bank should ensure that monetary expansion should not go unbridled leading to an inflationary spiral. The monetary policy should be geared to promoting real savings in the economy and not lead to inflation. The central bank should also ensure that all priority sectors and neglected segments of the economy would get adequate resources for investment. Besides, the central bank should manage the public debt of the government in such a way as to ensure the success of the government financing at low interest rates, at the same time keeping interest rates attractive enough for increased savings in the economy.[4]

Development depends not only on the total volume of investment but also on the distribution of that investment. The central bank has then a unique responsibility for the resources mobilisation for the planned development and for the proper and efficient allocation of the investment funds. Not only the regional and sectoral development has to be evenly distributed through proper distribution of credit, but the very banking habit and the availability of banking services should be brought to the door of all people in the country.

The central bank has for its main function the provision of finance and refinance. Flow of capital into and out of the country is another facet of the provision of finance and capital information in the country. Exchange control is therefore, a normal adjunct of the credit control. Although management of external value of the currency is one of the traditional functions of the central bank, there is a developmental aspect of it arising out of three reasons: First, developing country is a poor earner and its earnings fluctuate widely and terms of trade tend to move against it. Thus the external factors tend to percolate into the economy which the central bank should endeavour to offset. Secondly, the inadequate foreign exchange reserves tend to make the country depend on foreign capital inflow which adds to the central bank's and the government's responsibility for foreign debt servicing and management of foreign assets and liabilities. Thirdly, development efforts necessitate imports larger than exports and trade controls along with exchange controls are to be geared for development. Exchange control and its use for development are again a responsibility of the central bank. Control aspect was replaced by Management aspect in the financial reforms initiated since 1992.

Role of Selective Controls

There is greater scope for the operation of direct and selective controls in developing countries than in developed countries. In developing countries, stocks, shares and consumer durable goods which are subject to speculative hoarding and price fluctuations are generally subjected to selective controls. It is an important aspect that the selected commodities of mass consumption sensitive to speculative hoarding and undue price fluctuations should be controlled through proper selective controls on credit. The Reserve Bank of India thus operates a wide network of selective controls designed to regulate the flow of bank funds to the selective sectors of the economy. These are referred to in a later chapter. These controls are necessary due to the structural inadequacies and lack of proper integration between sectors. The limitations of the general controls of monetary policy in a developing country are well-known. The bank rate and interest rates are, for example, inadequate to regulate expenditures in general due to insufficient responsiveness of investment to interest rates and the existence of a large non-monetised sector in the economy. The direct and selective controls produce a better and quicker effect in these countries.

4. L.V. Chandler, *Central Banking and Economic Development,* University of Bombay, 1962.

Use of "price" as an incentive or disincentive is yet another device resorted to by the central banks.[5] Thus, in many developing countries there is a multiplicity of interest rates for varying purposes and the more beneficial and desirable economic activities enjoy relatively lower rates as in the case of exports, agriculture, etc. The higher rates are charged on those advances which are to be discouraged, such as on trade and against commodities subject to selective controls.

Strengthening the Institutional Structure

In India there are serious gaps in the institutional structure for mobilisation of savings, a large segment of unorganised money market, inequitable distribution of credit and inadequate development of banking habits.

Under the second category of developmental functions, the central bank has to provide for setting up of new institutions, a wider spread of the bank offices, and more equitable distribution of credit. The central bank may also expand the organised sector of the money market through such schemes as the Bill Market Scheme and reduce the influence of the moneylenders and indigenous bankers who are in the unorganised sector in the country. It is also the responsibility of the central bank to broaden the market for government securities and maintain orderly conditions in that market.

One of the important duties of a central bank in a developing country is to build up the existing institutions or to initiate new ones which are needed and suitable to the socio-economic and political set-up in the country. The central banks may thus be associated with the general purpose development banks as in Thailand, Nigeria and Colombia or with specialised category of development institutions for industry and/or agriculture as in the case of India, Pakistan, Greece, Turkey, Philippines, etc.

The institutional structure for mobilisation of savings has various gaps in the developing countries. The existing agencies are inadequate and new institutions have to be created for the purpose. Thus the Reserve Bank of India has promoted agricultural financing through co-operatives. The Reserve Bank has also established apex institutions for term lending to industry and agriculture, *viz.*, Industrial Development Bank of India and Agricultural Refinance and Development Corporation, later replaced by National Bank for Agriculture and Rural Development, respectively. The Regional Rural Banks and Local Banks are the more recent additions to the structure of banking. The commercial banks are themselves encouraged to lend medium-term both to industry and agriculture. The Reserve Bank has also given a re-orientation to commercial banks' lending policies, from security-orientation to production-orientation. It has also helped in the setting up of various other institutions in the capital market such as the Industrial Finance Corporation — an institution for the provisions of industrial finance at all-India level and of various State Financial Corporations for the State level industrial finance and UTI for promotion of savings and investment. The Reserve Bank is helping these institutions through contributions to their equity, bonds and by granting loans, to augment their base of financial resources.

Yet another developmental function is training of the banking personnel. The central bank of a developing country has a responsibility for creating a cadre of trained and capable banking personnel in the country. In India, the Reserve Bank took up the responsibility for training the personnel or commercial and co-operative banks since as early as 1954. This was the first unique example of a developmental function, undertaken by a central bank in a developing country in this line. The Reserve Bank has not only established a Bankers' Training College for training bankers but took the initiative in setting up of the National Institute of Bank Management for training, research and consultancy in banking.[6] It has also set-up an Institute of Development and Research in Banking Technology to promote I.T. in banking, in Hyderabad.

5. A.F.W. Plumptre, "The Role of Central Banks in Developing Countries", in *International Seminar on Banking and Development*, Reserve Bank of India, 1970.
6. Govt. of India, *Report of the Banking Commission* (1972), pp. 357-365.

Impact of these Functions on the Economy

As a traditional function, the central bank acts as the banker to the banks which involves its interaction with the financial system; acts as the banker to the government and manager of the government debt, which results in its relations with the government sector; acts as the regulator of the foreign exchange, which produces its inter-relations with the foreign sector; acts as a sole authority for the note issue which brings it into close relationship with the whole economy including the business sector and the government sector. All these sectors together constitute the economy, which implies that the activities of the central bank impinge on a whole economy. Thus the central banker is vitally concerned with the macro-economy as much as the various sectors individually.

In the non-traditional functions of the central bank, which involve the promotion of a sound and viable financial system and growth of savings and capital formation in the economy, there are various promotional activities which the central bank undertakes particularly in developing countries. This will involve the central bank in the process of economic growth, through the total quantum of liquidity flowing in the economy and the cost of such liquidity, *viz.*, the structure of interest rates, etc. It will thus be seen that the central bank is very much concerned with economic growth in its non-traditional functions, just as in the case of traditional functions it is concerned with the functioning of the economy.

There is another aspect which should be noted in the functioning of the central bank, *viz.*, the interaction between the central bank and the economy, the details of which will be referred to in a latter chapter. To put it briefly, the central bank not only influences the real economic system but is also influenced by the latter. In the various sources of its inflow and outflow, namely, assets and liabilities, we will see a reflection of the activities of the central bank in relation to various sectors of the economy. The central bank in turn can influence the various developments in the economy through its policies, such as monetary and credit policy, foreign exchange policy, debt management policy, etc.

A major source of savings in a developing economy is the household savings. Traditionally, these household savings are kept in the form of currency, deposit money, insurance, provident funds, pension funds, etc., in various quantities depending on the asset preferences of the public. There is a leakage of these savings into unproductive assets such as gold, jewellery and real estate. The central bank in its promotional activities has a responsibility to the nation in promoting real savings in the economy and channeling them into productive investments. Although there are limits to its policy instruments in the form of practical difficulties in influencing the real savings, the central bank can promote savings as already referred to in the following ways:

(*i*) It can increase the variety of financial instruments which are attractive enough for the public to hold, or save.

(*ii*) It can strengthen the institutional structure and diversify the financial system, so as to promote the growth of financial assets *vis-a-vis* the real assets, which is an indicator of development.

The central bank influences the savings and investments through a variety of measures other than monetary policy as the Reserve Bank of India has done. There is the new banking policy, shifting emphasis from security-oriented lending to production-oriented lending and filling up the credit gaps and institutional gaps, infusion of confidence in the deposits of the banks through the Deposit Insurance Scheme, promotion of middle and low income savings through various unit schemes of the Unit Trust of India, spread of the banking habit through a proper branch licensing policy, and integration of various sub-markets into the financial system through such schemes, as Bill Market Scheme, etc.

On the financial side of planning, the central bank of the country has a role in proper planning of the resource mobilisation, allocation of resources and management of the government debt. The central bank in developing countries generally plays a secondary role to the government, in advisory capacity on financial matters and planning. There is thus an interaction between central banking functions on the one side and all government activities on the other. As referred to earlier, in its various functions, the central bank deals with the various sectors of the economy, *viz.*, household, business, government and foreign sectors and there are interactions between these sectors and the central bank in almost all the daily operations of the central bank. On top of this, the central bank's activities influence the various economic developments through its policies, *viz.*, monetary and credit policies, banking regulation policy, foreign exchange policy, and debt management policy. In the operation of these policies, the central bank has to co-ordinate with the various economic policies that the government operates. In this context, it should be mentioned that although the Reserve Bank of India should act as adviser to the government, many times, the government became the adviser to the RBI and its independence was in doubt. Thus, although on the conceptual side, the central bank is the centre piece of the financial system, on the operational side it is the centre piece of the whole economic system and there are intricate mechanisms which connect the central bank to the real economic system.

RBI as Leader in Financial System

Conceptually, a distinction is made between the real sector and the financial sector of the economy. The real sector refers to the production of goods and services in a physical sense, while the financial sector refers to the demand for and supply of money, near-money assets and the whole spectrum of financial assets. These two sectors are inter-related and the equilibrium in the one is dependent upon that in the other. Money and near-money are demanded for their functions as medium of exchange, measure of value and store of value of goods and services in the real sector for consumption and investment purposes which, in turn, depends, upon the availability of money and near-money from the financial sector. Thus, the demand for goods and services in the real sector is for consumption and investment purposes which, in turn, depends, upon the availability of money and near money from the financial sector. Thus, the demand for and supply of goods in the real sector will depend upon the conditions in the financial sector and the demand for and supply of money and financial assets in the financial sector depend on the conditions in the real sector. It is in this sense that real and financial sectors are inter-related. The financial system offers a wide variety of financial assets with different maturities and refers to the functioning of the financial sector comprising the financial institutions.

Functions of the Financial System

The financial system provides various financial assets of short-term and long-term nature, referred to later in the chapter. The major functions of the financial system are the following:

(*i*) to act as intermediaries for the mobilisation of savings, provision of financial convenience to the public and the allocation of investment funds to various uses;

(*ii*) to facilitate creation and distribution of credit and money; and

(*iii*) to promote economic growth with a more balanced regional and sectoral distribution of funds, particularly to the underprivileged and the poorer sections of the society.

In developing countries, the most important function is promotion of development in the economy. Development is a function of investment which takes the form of either inventories or fixed capital assets. The larger the fixed capital formation, the greater is the development in the economy. The types of financial assets provided by the financial system would influence the types of capital formation in the economy and *vice versa*. Thus, economic development of a country depends *inter alia* on the growth of the financial system. The greater the proportion of financial assets, the greater is the scope for development because, as referred to earlier, to facilitate growth in the economy, there should be adequate investment which only the financial system can provide. Finance is an important input in the productive process and, as such, a developed financial system is an important pre-requisite of growth. The financial system should have proper characteristics, such as width and resilience, so that the rate of growth of the financial assets and their structure are in tune with the optimal characteristics of the real capital stock needed for growth. The optimum composition of wealth in an economy is achieved by the savers and the public to hold a growing part of their wealth in financial assets which provide incentives to savers and the public to hold a growing part of their wealth in financial form. The rate of savings and the rate of growth in the economy are highly correlated with the proportion of savings held in the form of financial assets as compared to the non-financial assets.

Types of Financial Institutions

The financial system comprises various types of institutions which can be classified under the following heads and was discussed in detail in an earlier chapter:

1. Carry institutions which earn their income from the financial assets they are carrying. Examples are commercial banks, co-operative banks and development finance companies.
2. Turnover institutions which are intermediaries earning their income from buying and selling financial assets. Examples are investment companies and mutual trust companies.
3. Brokerage institutions which do not carry or purchase and sell on their own account, but act simply as agents for the buyers and sellers of the financial assets. Examples are the various brokers' firms in the stock exchange and bullion exchange.

Characteristics of the Financial System

In most of the developing countries, there is a large component of subsistence sector where money does not enter into the transactions and the financial system does not encompass these transactions, wherein goods are exchanged for goods and payments are made in kind. There is, however, a monetised sector, where money is used as a medium of exchange, side by side with the subsistence sector. In the developed countries, monetised sector is more extensive and all pervading. In the developing countries, within the monetised sector there are again two components: (1) organised sector and (2) unorganised sector. In the organised sector, there are again two components: (*i*) short-term and (*ii*) long-term. While the short-term market is called money market, the long-term market is called capital market. The institutions in the organised sector can be classified into two broad categories:

(*a*) Monetary institutions can create or destroy money. These institutions include the RBI, commercial and co-operative banks and Regional Rural Banks.

(*b*) Non-monetary institutions which cannot create money but can borrow and lend money and near-money assets. These institutions include development finance companies, the Unit Trust of India, Mutual Funds, investment companies, etc.

While the former can create liabilities in the form of money, either as cash or demand deposits, the latter are mere intermediaries between savers and investors. The latter can activate idle balances with the public and mobilise the unused savings and channel them for active circulation and investment, thereby increasing the velocity of circulation of money.

The unorganised sector comprises indigenous bankers and moneylenders both in urban and rural areas. While indigenous bankers accept deposits as well as lend, moneylenders only lend to parties in need of funds and mostly for consumption. In addition, there is an important component of the unorganised sector which is in the form of private deposits accepted by firms, companies, etc., from the public. The sources of funds for the indigenous bankers are partly their own deposits and partly borrowed funds from commercial and co-operative banks in the organised sector. For the moneylenders, the source is normally their own money supplemented by occasional borrowings from their friends and relatives. There is, however, no clear demarcation between short-term and long-term finance in this sector.

In the organised sector, the short-term component, namely, the money market, comprises various sub-markets, *viz.*, call money market, bill market, collateral loan market, treasury bill market, etc. The institutions in the short-term market are the commercial banks and co-operative banks.

Unorganised Money Market in India

Indigenous banker is defined as any individual or firm which, in addition to making loans, also receives deposits and deals in hundis or bills. A moneylender is defined as any individual or firm who makes loans but does not receive deposits or deal in hundis. The distinction between moneylender and indigenous banker revolves around three factors: *(i)* acceptance of deposits, *(ii)* dealing in hundis, and *(iii)* the magnitude of capital invested — the indigenous banker invests a larger amount of capital in the business than the moneylender. These distinctions were referred to by the Central Banking Inquiry Committee (1929), the Reserve Bank of India in their Committee on Rural Credit Survey[7] and some Provincial Banking Inquiry Committees.

Moneylenders cannot create credit or provide a medium of exchange. They only lend whatever resources they have got. Indigenous bankers accept deposits and advance loans and, in the process provide a medium of exchange through bills in a limited sense. They discount bills or hundis with commercial banks which might in turn be discounted with the Reserve Bank.

The unorganised market consists of basically indigenous bankers and moneylenders — multanis, shroffs, pawnbrokers, merchant bankers, chits etc. The trader or big farmer may as well be the moneylender. Moneylending has been mixed-up with other activities of business and is not generally kept separate from them. The defects of the indigenous financial system are broadly the following:

(1) Usurious rates of interest which are sought to be regulated by various State Usurious Loans Act;

(2) Lack of proper accounting and bifurcation between banking and non-banking;

(3) Lack of significant deposit business and discount market for their bills or hundis; and

(4) Lack of leadership and co-ordination in their activities.

In the unorganised market, there is no free and full information and no free flow of funds. Loans are granted without collateral or securities. Short-term loans are rolled over and no maturity pattern exists. Loans are granted on a personal basis. There is no distinction between short-term and long-term loans and loans are sometimes paid in commodities. Interest rates are highly individualised, vary from lender to lender and borrower to borrower and mostly usurious, varying from 20% to 100%. It is difficult to replace the moneylenders and indigenous bankers because they serve a unique function of supply of funds in an easy and facile manner or an individual or a personal basis with minimum formalities. The moneylenders are easily accessible, informal, quick in the disposal of loans and have their own mode of recovery.

The links between the organised and unorganised markets are tenuous and shaky. Within the organised sector, the linkage works through the city shroffs supplying funds and goods on credit to the town merchant banker who, in turn, supplies to the village merchants and moneylenders. The borrowers approach the moneylenders and indigenous bankers and take credit from them with or without collateral in villages, towns and cities. The moneylenders and indigenous bankers may, in turn, borrow from the co-operative and commercial banks. Some big commercial banks, including the State Bank of India, keep on the approved list the names of indigenous bankers[7] who satisfy certain requirements regarding financial standing, number of years in the banking business, and the proper introductions through approved parties. These bankers on the approved list are given credit limits up to which they can borrow from the commercial banks.

R.B.I. and Indigenous Bankers

The Reserve Bank has tried overtime to link the indigenous bankers with organised sector. The major hurdle in its effort lies in their combining money lending with trading and other activities which is not acceptable to the Reserve Bank. Besides, there are professional moneylenders and non-professional

7. The Rural Credit Survey Committee of the Reserve Bank of India observed: "From analysis of the circumstances, it is clear that the village moneylenders are an indispensable element in the financial system of the country though their reserves are limited and methods antiquated". (Volume II, Pages 133/134).

moneylenders, and some of them have no proper licences. It is difficult to locate various moneylenders and identify their activities.

The Reserve Bank tried to bring indigenous bankers into its fold through its various efforts in 1937, 1941 and 1951 but with very little success. As early as 1937, the Reserve Bank had offered to bring the shroffs and other indigenous bankers under its control by offering some incentives. Following Central Banking Enquiry Committee Report, the Reserve Bank had laid down the following conditions for linking them with the organised sector:

(1) The banker should have a minimum working capital of at least ₹10 lakh and a standing of over five years.

(2) The banker should keep a proportion of capital and deposits with the Reserve Bank.

(3) The banker should bifurcate banking from non-banking business which would have to be given up later.

These conditions were not acceptable to the indigenous bankers and the community of shroffs. The Reserve Bank had again tried in 1941 to attract the shroffs by liberalising the conditions referred to above. The Reserve Bank agreed not to insist on immediate shedding of non-banking business, if other conditions were complied with and non-banking and banking business were bifurcated. Again, the Reserve Bank failed to get any response from the indigenous bankers.

Old Bill Market Scheme

The Reserve Bank introduced a Bill Market Scheme in 1952. Under this scheme, the Reserve Bank made advances to scheduled banks in the form of demand loans, against the promissory notes supported by usance bills or promissory notes of their constituents. This would enable the banks to get advances from the Reserve Bank on the basis of time promissory notes of their constituents. The banks had, of course, to certify that such notes have arisen after bona fide credit transactions (including indigenous banker's hundis). The Reserve Bank agreed to bear half the cost of the stamp duty incurred in converting the demand bills into time bills. This scheme had been changed from time to time and in 1954, it was extended to all scheduled banks and the minimum limit of total advances was ₹10 lakh and the minimum of each individual bill was ₹50,000. In 1956, the concession of the stamp duty was partly withdrawn and in 1958, the scheme was extended to export bills on an experimental basis. Although this scheme was intended for all types of bills, including the indigenous bills, there was very little recourse to this Bill Market Scheme at that time in respect of the indigenous bills.

The Bill Market Scheme had its own limitations. Thus, it made no provision for the indigenous banker's hundis in particular. The Reserve Bank had not accepted the recommendations of the Shroff Committee which had suggested that the indigenous banker's hundis should be made eligible for borrowing from the banks. The commercial banks would, therefore, lend to indigenous bankers out of their own resources but could not use those hundis for rediscount with the Reserve Bank. Besides, the market in bills was also not a genuine bill market, the reason being that the bills were more accommodation bills rather than trade bills and it is difficult to distinguish between these two.

New Bill Market Scheme

The Reserve Bank had introduced a new Bill Market Scheme in 1970 with a view to tiding over the difficulties experienced in the earlier Scheme. This market is a means of development of credit market with bills as instruments and a means of borrowing from the Reserve Bank. The Reserve Bank had agreed to rediscount bills with a maturity of only 90 days, although the bills may have maturity originally of 30 days to 120 days. Some banks may discount bills of up to 180 days but hold them for some time before they can be rediscounted with the Reserve Bank. Although the banks have allotted these bills to first-class parties, some banks have made arrangements with the buyer through the seller to ensure that one of them takes the responsibility for making payments on due date. If the bill has the acceptance of a licensed scheduled bank on behalf of the buyer and/or seller, the bill is treated as good for the purpose of discounting. Where the acceptance is given by the buyer alone, many banks would ask for the usual security.

The Reserve Bank of India had offered to rediscount the bills from licensed scheduled banks in their Regional Offices at Mumbai, Kolkata, New Delhi and Chennai. The banks have left the business of discounting to either regional offices or head office. Some of the banks are also doing resdiscounting themselves if they have surplus funds, at rates slightly lower than that of the Reserve Bank. The rediscounting with other parties is a good development from the point of view of developing a subsidiary market in bills. In such cases, the discounting bank takes full risk and gives unconditional guarantee to pay the bill to the party with whom they are rediscounting. This has two advantages: firstly, the bank gets a lower rate than the Reserve Bank rediscounting rate and secondly, once market for rediscounting is developed, the banks may not be entirely dependent upon the Reserve Bank.

This rediscounting by the private customers is a development which is akin to the participation certificates of banks or financial institutions. The bills can be rediscounted by any private party or a financial institutions or a bank, whereas a participation certificate is a deposit/loan by one financial institution to another financial institution. While the banks with surplus funds can transmit their funds to the banks in need of funds, this can take the form of participation certificate which is another source of funds for banks. Under the New Bill Market Scheme, many banks are able to offer bills for rediscounting with the Reserve Bank. With a tight credit position, the banks find it convenient to borrow from the Reserve Bank. There has been considerable increase in the volume of bills handled by the banks under this account and there was also an increase in the volume of bills rediscounted with the Reserve Bank under the New Bill Market Scheme. The banks have now been using this type of business as an additional source of Reserve Bank finance for them. The Bill Market is now developed through commercial bills, allowed to be issued by corporates which is referred to in later chapters.

Money and Capital Markets

The Indian money market is less insulated from the money markets abroad due to the prevailing liberalisation in India and the absence of many controls on inflow and outflow of funds. The core of the Indian money market is the inter-bank call money market where the lenders and borrowers are mostly the banks. The UTI and the LIC and many large FIs and MFs are allowed to this market. The funds dealt with are the overnight money and funds up to seven days. There is no true secondary market for bills, either commercial or government, nor is there any acceptance business in India. Most of the bills are not genuine trade bills. Treasury bills are sold on tap by the RBI on behalf of the government and the main buyers are commercial banks.

In the long-term section of the organised sector, namely, the capital market, there are a number of institutions such as stock market where the old securities are dealt with, new issues market where new capital is raised, bullion exchange where gold and silver bullion are purchased and sold. The gilt-edged market has a special characteristic in that it includes both short-term and long-term. This market is also narrow and the main holders are commercial banks and other financial institutions. There are a number of specialised financial institutions in the capital market. Some of these institutions are Industrial Finance Corporation, Industrial Credit and Investment Corporation, Provident Funds, Pension Funds, State Financial Corporations, State Development Corporations, etc.

RBI and the Financial System

The Reserve Bank is the centre-piece of the financial system and the apex institution in the money market. It is concerned with the efficient and smooth functioning of the financial system. The Reserve Bank has to keep a watch on the developments both of daily, and seasonal nature, in the financial system. It provides liquidity with a view to facilitating the smooth functioning of the system and controlling it. The flow of liquidity is controlled through money supply changes, reserve requirements of banks, open market purchases/ sales of government securities, etc. The cost and availability of credit is also regulated by suitable monetary policy. The Reserve Bank can influence the operations in the financial system through not only the liquidity flows, but also through regulation of banking system, of bank loans, bank holdings of liquid assets, interest rates, public deposits with banks and non-banks, etc. As referred to earlier, the RBI has three types of functions in relation to the financial system — (*a*) Financial, (*b*) Regulatory and (*c*) Developmental.

In India, the money market and the capital market are not properly developed. The link between these two segments as also between the organised and unorganised sectors, is poor. The RBI has in the past attempted to link unorganised and organised sectors in a systematic way, but even now the dichotomy between these two sectors persists. There is inadequate integration, cohesion and specialisation among the components in the financial system. The savings and banking habits are underdeveloped with the result that the operation of the monetary policy becomes less effective, throwing greater burden on the Reserve Bank.

Interest Rate Structure

Interest is the price paid for borrowing money or finance. Interest rates exist for each of the various maturities of financial assets. These interest rates are determined partly by the Reserve Bank and the government which fixes them, and partly by the interaction between demand for and supply of funds in the system.

While usurious rates of interest prevail in the unorganised sector, the interest rates in the organised sector are controlled by the Reserve Bank. But because of the poor linkage between the different sub-markets in the organised sector, the Reserve Bank's interest rate policy is not as effective as it should be and the impact of any change in the Bank rate does not percolate quickly and effectively into other sub-markets of the financial system. Similarly, the structure of interest rates for various maturities of assets does not reflect on orderly arrangement.

The interest rate structure in any economy depends upon the stage of development of the financial system, maturities of the financial assets, the linkage between the sub-markets, and the inter-relationship between these markets. The difference between the interest rates on instruments of various maturities is based upon the principles of risk and return. While the return for abstinence remains constant, the element of risk varies from maturity to maturity, from one financial instrument to another and from borrower to borrower. The interest rates may also vary due to oligopolistic elements in the market and the imperfections in the financial system. Thus, even in the organised sector some rates are controlled and others free and some low and others high. The interest rates of bank deposits, as controlled by the RBI are now giving negative real rates to the savers. There are many such weaknesses in the present policy, despite its flexibility.

Interest rates are important factors which influence relative attractiveness of saving and investment. They can influence the rate of growth in the economy by attracting funds into banks in the form of deposits and to the government for larger public developmental expenditure, and by discouraging uneconomical use of credit and ostentatious consumption expenditure by the public. Interest rates also influence the pattern of distribution of income in the economy; those with access to credit are the more well-to-do, and low rates would benefit them at the expense of millions of small savers who contributed those funds.

The Reserve Bank influences the structure of interest rates in a variety of ways, such as:

1. Changes in Bank rate at which bills and other acceptable paper are discounted by the RBI.
2. Fixation of minimum and maximum lending rates for banks along with the maximum deposit rates changes in CRR, SLR, open market operations, etc.
3. Changes in treasury bill rate.
4. Call money rates are influenced by changes in variable reserve ratios and refinance policy of the RBI through Repos and Reverse Repos and credit policy of the RBI.

5. Yields on government securities and the rates on comparable maturities of private securities are affected indirectly by the open market purchases and sales by the RBI.

Latest Trends

The Reserve Bank as well as the financial system have gone through far-reaching changes in the new millennium. Following the deregulation measures initiated due to the Narasimham Committee (1991) recommendations. The decade of nineties has seen many changes in the financial system.

1. The control and regulatory aspects were drastically curtailed.
2. Greater freedom and autonomy to banks were given with larger discretionary powers.
3. Interest rate policy became more market-oriented, less controlled and more flexible.
4. The money market was reformed to have greater depth and width. The number of players and instruments traded were both widened and strengthened.
5. The gilt-edged market was made more active as part of the wholesale debt segment in the Stock Exchange and a retail market in government securities is being developed.
6. The Reserve Bank became more autonomous and less dependent on the government for policy initiatives and for operation.
7. Rupee was allowed to freely fluctuate and current account controls were removed and some initiatives were taken towards less capital account controls.
8. Financial markets have been kept open to foreign capital inflow and foreign expertise.
9. Controls of procedural nature were reduced and discretionary controls were removed.
10. The Reserve Bank was strengthened in its control on non-bank financial companies and its regulatory role was extended to the whole financial system.

The latest position in regulatory aspect of the RBI has some weaknesses like insufficient regulation of co-operative urban banks leading to liquidation of many such banks, improper licensing policies in respect of co-operative urban banks and branch network changes of commercial banks and regulation of non-bank Finance Companies and lack of proper coordination with the concerned agencies in respect of such regulation of co-operative urban banks and non-bank Finance Companies. The insurance of all deposits with non-bank Finance Companies is also being contemplated for which legislation is expected to be changed. Many reforms are yet to be implemented in this respect.

✠ ✠ ✠

RBI – ORGANISATION AND FUNCTIONS

6

Introduction

The Reserve Bank of India was set-up in 1935 as a Private Shareholders' bank. It was nationalised in January 1949 by the passage of the Reserve Bank (Transfer to Public Ownership) Act of 1948. As a result, all the paid-up capital of the Bank of ₹ 5 crore, has since been held by the Central Government, which may from time to time give such directions to the Bank, as it may, after consultation with the Governor of the Bank, consider necessary in the public interest. Subject to such directions (under Section 7 of the R.B.I. Act), the general superintendence and direction of the affairs of the Bank are vested in the Central Board of Directors.

History of Central Banking in India

The history of central banking in India may be briefly reviewed here.

In 1835, a uniform currency was established whereby the silver rupee was adopted as the standard coin for the whole of British India. Afterwards, the presidency banks were established which acted as bankers to the East India Company and had the right of note issue in their respective presidency towns. In 1862 the right of note issue by private banks was taken over by the government and currency was issued by the government, but the government balances were, however, left with the presidency banks thus originating the idea of central banking in India.

India was on a silver standard since 1835 with the passage of the Silver and Gold Coinage Act, but due to difficulties following the fall in the price of silver in 1870, attention shifted to a Gold Exchange Standard. The idea of a central bank gained support during this period, to make the gold exchange standard work. But the idea was not pursued further until 1913, when Keynes wrote: "The governments have taken over so many of the functions of a central bank that they cannot wisely neglect the rest".[1] The need for the early establishment of a central bank was emphasized by him before the Chamberlain Commission (1913). But with the outbreak of the First World War, the idea was again shelved.

The Imperial Bank of India was established with amalgamation of three presidency banks in 1921. This Bank was recognised as a semi-public institution with provision for some control by the government in its

1. J.M. Keynes, *Indian Currency and Finance*, 1913.

administration. The banking business of the government and the management of public debt were vested in this Bank. In the central banking tradition, the Bank was to play the role of a bankers' bank and yet carry on the commercial bank's business which it had inherited from the Presidency Banks. It had thus started performing the central banking function except in that it was not permitted to deal in foreign exchange and was not given the power of note issue. The banking field soon got into trouble as the joint stock banks refused to approach the Imperial Bank as lender, guide and friends while it was competing with them in their business.

It was in this background that the Hilton-Young Commission recommended the establishment of a central bank in the country (1926). The Commission pointed out the inherent weakness of a system in which the control of currency and credit was in the hands of two distinct authorities, and suggested the setting up of a new central bank, divesting the Imperial Bank of its central banking functions. Following the recommendations of the Commission, a Bill was introduced for setting up on the Reserve Bank but it could not be passed due to the opposition on the legislature. But the Report of the Central Banking Enquiry Committee (1931) re-emphasized the need for setting up of the Reserve Bank of India and the Bill was resuscitated and enacted in 1934.

As originally set up, it was a private shareholders' bank with a share capital of ₹5 crores. To make it a public institution, there was a nominal government contribution to share capital and the government retained some powers over the working and operations of the Bank.

Statutory Central Banking Functions of the Reserve Bank of India

In the Reserve Bank of India Act of 1934, as amended up to date, Chapter 3 lays down the central banking functions as follows:

1. Firstly, the Bank has to accept monies for the account of the Central Government and to make payments from the amounts standing to the credit of its account and to carry-out its exchange remittances and other banking operations, including the management of public debt. In return, the Central Government entrusts the Bank with its money, remittances, exchange and banking transactions and also deposits free of interest all its cash balances.
2. Secondly, the Bank may, by agreement with the government of any State, undertake all its money remittance, exchange and banking transactions in India, including in particular the acceptance as deposit, 'free of interest', of all its cash balances with the Bank and the management of the public debt of and issue of any new loans by that State.
3. Thirdly, the Bank shall have the sole right, to issue bank notes in India and also agency right to issue and distribute the currency notes of the Government of India on behalf of the latter. The Central Government shall not issue the one rupee notes directly but only through the Reserve Bank.
4. Bank notes are of the denominational values of two rupees, five rupees, ten rupees, fifty rupees, one hundred rupees, five hundred rupees and thousand rupees.[2] These notes are of unlimited legal tender at any place in India and are guaranteed by the Government of India. The two and five rupee notes were replaced gradually by coins of the same denominations. It is expected that ten rupee coins will also be issued. The earlier notes continued to be legal tender.
5. The Bank buys from and sells to any authorised dealer at its offices, viz., Mumbai, Kolkata, Delhi or Chennai, foreign exchange in minimum amounts equal to ₹2 lakh at such rates of exchange and on such terms as may be determined by the government having regard to its obligations to the IMF with respect to the rate of exchange.
6. The Bank shall keep the cash reserves of scheduled banks at a rate of 3% of total demand and time liabilities in India which may be increased up to 15% by the Bank. The Bank may also impound such

2. Thousand rupee notes and above denominations were demonetised in January, 1978. As part of the Financial reforms and in keeping with the needs of trade and industry thousand rupee notes were again monetised late in the nineties.

additional amounts out of the incremental deposit liabilities in India which may be increased up to 15% by the Bank. The Bank may also impound such additional amounts out of the incremental deposit liabilities as it may think proper at any time. All scheduled banks shall submit a weekly statement of the selected assets and liabilities at the close of business on each Friday, under Section 42(2) of the Reserve Bank of India Act. This section was amended by the Banking Laws (Amendment) Act 1983, whereby the banks are required to file fortnightly returns instead of weekly returns, which shall be the basis for determining the cash reserves ratio, referred to above.

7. The Bank may grant loans, advances against approved government or Trustee securities or rediscount bills of exchange.

Policy Making — Central Board

The Reserve Bank of India is administered by a Central Board of Directors which consists of twenty directors, including the Governor and two or more Deputy Governors. There are four Directors deputed by Central Government from the four Local Boards referred to below under Section 8(1)(b). The Central Board will also have ten directors nominated by the Central Government representing various economic and functional interests and professional expertise in the country under Section 8(1)(C) of the RBI Act. Besides, there will also be a government official nominated by the Central Government, usually a Secretary of the Ministry of Finance.

The Governor and Deputy Governors are full-time officers of the Bank and are appointed by the Central Government for a period not exceeding five years at a time. They are paid salaries as fixed by the Central Board of Directors. The Deputy Governors and the government official, are not entitled to vote normally although they are members of the Central Board. Any Deputy Governor however, may be entitled to vote provided he is authorised by the Governor in writing to act on his behalf and vote for him at a meeting. The directors appointed from the Local Board shall hold office during their tenure with the local Boards. A director appointed to represent the professional and functional interests may hold office for a fixed period of four years. A retiring director is eligible for re-nomination if he is not otherwise disqualified.

Under Section 30 of the R.B.I. Act, the Central Government has powers to supersede the Central Board of Directors, if the Bank fails to carry-out any of the obligations imposed on it by the Act. The Central Government may entrust these functions to any agency that it may think proper.

Local Board

The Local Boards are constituted for each of the four regional areas, viz., Delhi, Kolkata, Chennai and Mumbai, representing respectively the Northern area, Eastern area, Southern area and Western area. The members of the Local Boards are appointed by the Central Government to represent as far as possible the territorial and the regional economic interests, the co-operative banks and indigenous banks, etc. The Local Boards function under the direction of the Central Board. The members of the Local Boards are appointed for a period of four years by the Central Government, to represent the local interests. There are normally five such members on each of the Local Boards. The members elect a Chairman from among themselves to chair the deliberations of the Local Board. The Local Boards may meet as often as desired by the Central Board and may discuss the matters referred to it specifically by the Central Board. There has been certain delegation of powers from the Central Board to the Local Boards and the advice of the Local Boards is sought on some items of expenditure within certain limits and also on certain matters relating to the opening of branches of co-operative banks. The Local Boards play only an advisory role to the Central Board. There has been greater delegation of powers to Local Boards in 1984 in regard to advice on local matters, agricultural and industrial problems, branch licensing, urban co-operative banks, credit policy, etc.

Committee of the Central Board

As a matter of practical convenience, there is a Committee of the Central Board consisting of the Governor, Deputy Governors and Directors representing the interests of the area in which the meeting is held (who are five in number in Mumbai). This Committee meets once a week, normally on Wednesday, at the office of the Bank where the Governor has his Head Quarters, to attend to the regular current business of the Bank. Executive Directors of the Bank may attend these meetings as special invitees.

Disqualifications

A member of the Local Board or Central Board is disqualified to be a member if he is a salaried government official other than a Secretary, or has been declared insolvent, or is an officer of a bank or a banking company, or is found to be a lunatic or of unsound mind. A director who absents himself without prior leave from the Central Board, for any three consecutive meetings, can be removed from office by the government and is not eligible for reappointment. Besides, no two persons who are directors of the same firm or company or are connected by agency business to the same firm or partners in the same firm, shall be Directors of the Central Board or Local Board at the same time. Any casual vacancy in the Central Board or the Local Board is filled by the Central Government after considering the recommendation of the Central Board in this behalf. A person nominated for a casual vacancy may officiate during the unexpired portion of the term of his predecessor.

Branches and Sub-offices

The Governor and Deputy Governors of the Reserve Bank have their Head Office at Mumbai. The four Regional Offices of the Bank are in Mumbai, Kolkata, Chennai and New Delhi. Besides these Regional Offices, the Bank has set up branches/sub-offices in various States, in keeping with the requirements of the public and expanding activities of the Bank. Such branches are presently at 13 centres, namely, Ahmedabad, Bangalore, Bhopal, Bhubaneswar, Chandigarh, Gauhati, Hyderabad, Jaipur, Jammu, Kanpur, Nagpur, Patna, and Trivandrum. Besides there are 6 sub-offices at Lucknow, Belapur, Dehradun, Panaji, Raipur and Kochi. At the Regional Offices, almost all the Departments of the Bank are functioning, except those connected only with the internal administration of the Bank, referred to later, while in branches only selected main departments of the Bank operate, depending on the needs of the localities. Although the Central Offices of all the Departments are located at Mumbai, the Central Office of the Department of Financial Companies (DFC) was located at Kolkata. Of the branches, referred to above, full-fledged Issue Dept. Offices are located only at Ahmedabad, Bangalore, Bhubaneshwar, Gauhati, Hyderabad, Jaipur, Kanpur, Chandigarh, Nagpur, Patna and Trivandrum.

Internal Administration

The Governor as Chairman of the Central Board of Directors is also responsible for the internal administration of the Bank, subject to overall guidance of the Central Board. The Governor and Deputy Governors act on behalf of the Central Board and take decisions on internal administrative matters subject to the overall approval of the Board. As the Central Board meets quite infrequently and even the Committee of the Central Board meets once in a week, certain routine day-to-day matters are looked into by the Governor and Deputy Governors assisted by Executive Directors and Chief Officers of the Departments. The Regional Directors are in charge of Regional offices and branches.

Departments of Central Office of the RBI

There are nearly 25 departments of the central office which can be classified on the basis of their functions and operations in addition to those which are purely for internal administration. Those purely for internal administration are ***Customer Service Dept., Dept. of Administration and Personnel Management,***

Dept. of Expenditure and Budgetary Control, Human Resource Management Dept. and Premises Dept. and ***Inspection Dept.*** and ***Information Technology Dept., Management and Dept. of Communications.***

As against purely internal departments, there are a number of functional depts. As a banker to the banks and the govt., there are ***DBOD, DBS, Dept. of Govt. and Bank Accounts.*** As a regulator of the non-bank financial system, there are departments of ***Financial Markets, and Non-banking Supervision, Urban Banks Dept., and Dept. of Payments and Settlement.***

As a banker to the govt., there is ***Secretary's Dept. to keep Liaison with the Govt., and Internal Debt Management Dept. and Dept. of Govt. Accounts as part of the Dept. of Govt. and Banks Accounts, and Rashtrabhasha Dept. These departments are subject to change from time to time.***

As a currency authority with the power of note issue, it has Department of ***Currency Management.*** As controller of ***Foreign Exchange there is Foreign Exchange Dept., and Dept. of External Investments and Operations.***

As per the RBI Act, the Bank has a responsibility for agricultural finance and rural development for which it has a ***Rural Planning and Credit Dept.***

As Policy Making Departments, mention should be made of the Dept. of Economic and Policy, Research and Monetary Policy Dept., and Dept. of Statistical Analysis and Information Management, Legal Department.

The functional and operational departments are overlapping, but they are all started and operated as per the statutory obligations of the RBI as per the RBI Act, BR Act and FEMA and Government Guidelines.

As referred to earlier there are three categories of Departments at the Central Office, *viz.*, (*i*) those relating to the internal administration, (*ii*) those relating to functional or operational aspects of the Bank and (*iii*) those relating to policy or advisory matters. Of the former category, the most important departments are the Department of Administration and Personnel Management, and the Department of Expenditure and Budgetary Control. As a result of the reorganisation of these Departments in March 1981, the following new Departments have been set up:

(1) The Department of Administration and Personnel Management comprising the Staff Division, Administration Division, Vigilance Cell and Hindi Division under the charge of the Chief Manager. This Dept. looks after the staff matters — postings, transfers, promotions, confirmations, training, recruitment, discipline, information and documentation, vigilance and propagation of Hindi in the Bank, etc.

(2) A customer service department was set up to look after complaints from customers and Human Resources Development Department for the staff welfare schemes. There is also an Administration Wing under the charge of a Chief Officer. This Department is entrusted with the policy matters relating to staff, industrial relations, dealings with Associations and Unions, periodical reviews of staff policies, recruitment, posting, transfers, staff welfare measures, etc. This Department was once a part of Department of Administration and Personnel Management.

(3) The Department of Currency Management under the charge of a Chief General Manager looks after the work of planning the requirements of currency and coins for the country, arranging for their issue and distribution, withdrawal and destruction of soiled or mutilated notes, maintenance of currency chests, small coin depots and other matters relating to currency notes.

(4) The Department of Expenditure and Budgetary Control under the charge of a Chief General Manager is entrusted with the preparation of the Bank's Budget, appraisal and review of budgetary operations, control of expenditure, provident, pension and guarantee funds, housing loans to staff and other establishment matters.

(5) The Department of Govt. and Bank Accounts under the charge of the Chief General Manager deals with all matters relating to accounts of Banking and Issue Depts., preparation of weekly, half-yearly and yearly accounts, management of Clearing Houses and audit. Matters relating to Foreign Accounts, namely, those of

foreign Central banks, IMF, etc., Govt. Accounts, Govt. Debt Management and custody of Foreign Govt. securities, etc., is now looked after by Dept. of External Investments and Operations.

The other Departments, dealing with purely internal administration of the Bank are the Premises Dept., Inspection Dept., Legal Dept., Information Technology Dept. and the Bank's Services Board. The Premises Dept. is in charge of the construction and maintenance of office buildings, residential buildings for the staff and training establishments, etc. The Inspection Dept. is entrusted with inspection of various offices and branches of the Reserve Bank at periodic intervals. This Dept. examines the workloads, adequacy of staff, systems and methods followed by various depts. and offices of the Bank. The Regional Audit Cells located at big centres supplement the Inspection Dept's work by continuous scrutiny of accounts and surprise checks at various centres. The Legal Dept. advises the Bank on all legal matters including the interpretation of various statutes in the Bank's day-to-day operations with the Govt. the commercial and co-operative banks and others. The Information Technology Dept. is purely for internal administration of the Bank and for advising the Bank on Computerisation systems and methods with the objective of improving the productivity and efficiency and lowering of the costs.

Functional and Policy Departments

The Functional Depts. of the Bank at the Central Office are formed on the basis of the major functions of the Bank, namely, keeping Government and bank accounts, currency management, Government borrowing supervision of banks, and their operations, inspection, audit, etc. The Advisory Depts. are the Secretary's Dept. and Rural Planning and Credit, Dept. of Economic and Policy Research and Department of Statistical Analysis and Information Management and Monetary Policy Department, etc. These Advisory Depts. are mostly concerned with policy matters, economic and statistical intelligence and analysis and advice.

The Secretary's Dept. keeps a liaison with the Central and State Governments, performs the secretarial functions to the Central Board of Directors and Committee of the Central Board and is concerned with the policy matters relating to the floatation of Central and State Government loans, co-ordination of market borrowing programmes of various financial institutions, Treasury bills, sanction of ways and means, advances to the Central and State Governments and conduct of open market operations of the Bank, investment of surplus funds of the Governments, etc.

The Rural Planning and Credit Department is responsible for credit planning and formulation of credit policy relating to commercial banks, authorisation of borrowing limits to banks and administration of Rediscount and Refinance Schemes of RBI. The department advises on policy matters in co-ordination with Dept. of Banking Operations and Development and the Dept. of Economic Analysis and Policy. The Rural Planning and Credit Dept. (RPCD) is the counterpart of the DBOD for credit policy, planning and banking development in respect of agricultural credit and co-operative banking. The RPCD has been started in 1979 in tune with the growing importance of co-operative credit and agricultural finance and the need to co-ordinate the policy matters in respect of the operations of the various Depts. of the Bank and the agencies dealing with agricultural credit. NABARD was set up in 1982 and RPCD co-ordinates with the NABARD on matters of Rural Credit. NABARD has replaced the earlier ARDC, which was set up by RBI for the refinance of Agricultural Credit.

The Department of Economic and Policy Research is entrusted with advisory functions of the Bank in all policy matters for which purpose it keeps an expert staff for conducting research and analysis and for maintaining a vigil on the economic developments at home and abroad and be available for consultation with the Planning Commission and Central and State Governments on matters relating to banking, finance and exchange control and policy aspects of the Bank. The work of the Dept. comprises certain items of fundamental and operational research and others of routine reporting and information to the top executives of the Bank. The Dept. of Statistical Analysis and Information Management (DSAIM) collects, compiles and analyses the statistical information and data on banking and financial matters in particular and of the economy in general. The DEPR as well as the DSAIM are responsible for bringing out the more important publications of the Bank such as Report on Currency and Finance and Monthly Bulletins. The DEAP is also responsible for a number of other publications of the Bank, including the Bank's Annual Report.

The Functional and Operational Depts. at the Central Office level are the Department of Banking Operations and Development (DBOD), Department of Banking Supervision (DBS), Urban Banks Department (UBD), Rural Planning and Credit Dept. (RPCD) Foreign Exchange Department (FED) and Department of Financial Markets, Inspection Department and Department of Non-banking Supervision, Internal Debt Management Department, etc. These departments are subject to change depending on the needs and the workload involved and expertise required.

The Department of Government and Bank accounts deals with all accounts of the Government, Central and State and those of the Banks who keep their reserves with the RBI under CRR or otherwise. The Foreign Exchange Dept. (FED) is entrusted with the operational aspects of the Foreign Exchange Management Act 1999 and shoulders the responsibility for the administration of Exchange Management in India. The work of this Dept. also includes sanction of foreign exchange for various purposes, travel and other payments, exports and other receipts, loans and overdrafts in foreign currencies, foreign currency and non-resident accounts, etc. The FED undertakes inspections of foreign exchange departments of authorised dealers in collaboration with the DBOD. Dept. of External Investments and Operations is entrusted with the task of Management of Foreign Investments and forex reserves.

The DBOD administers the Banking Regulation Act and the Reserve Bank of India Act insofar as they relate to the commercial banks. It is entrusted with the supervision, control and development of commercial banking system. Its main functions relate to granting of licences for opening of a branch/bank, operation of various credit schemes of the Bank in relation to commercial banks, rendering advice and assistance to banks on amalgamations, mergers, liquidations, appointments to top executive positions in banks, etc. There is a separate Inspection Department which looks after inspection of all banks, in addition to the Dept. of Banking Supervision and the Department of Non-banking Supervision.

The Industrial and Export Credit Dept. (IECD) has been carved out from the erstwhile Industrial Finance Dept. which used to look after the operational and organisational aspects of the SFCs, inspection of SFCs and of administration of Credit Guarantee Scheme on behalf of the Govt. of India for small-scale industries. The inspection of SFCs was passed on to the IDBI while the credit guarantee work was handed over to the Deposit Insurance and Credit Guarantee Corporation set up in April 1978, combining the work of deposit insurance and credit guarantee. Besides, the IECD has now taken over from the DBOD, the credit authorisation scheme and monitoring of big borrowal accounts and other policy matters relating to industrial credit.

Effective from May 11, 1981, the Department of Industrial and Export Credit (IECD) was entrusted with the responsibility of co-ordinating the policy of Industrial Development Bank, term lending institutions and commercial banks for various aspects of the flow of credit to the large and medium industries and organised trade. Some of the existing functions of Department of Banking Operations and Development (DBOD) have been transferred to the IECD, namely, the operation of Credit Authorisation Scheme, credit to sick industries, export credit and the work of the Committee of Direction.

In the process reorganisation of RBI during 1992-96, BFS was set to supervise the financial system supported by a separate Dept. of Supervision and Inspection and Dept. of Information Technology for computerisation of important operational Departments and overhaul of systems and procedures.

The DBOD has, on the other hand, taken over from the IECD, the work relating to development of small-scale industries, District Industries centres and decentralised sectors. The earlier work of DBOD, namely, inspection and regulation under the Banking Regulations Act, Priority Sector lending, etc., was continuing with this Dept. A separate Dept. of Information Technology was set up in Jan. 1995 and Dept. of Management Services was closed and some of its functions were passed on to Dept. of HRD. There is also a Financial Markets Department to look after policy matters relating to F.I.s at the central office level. These departments have since been reorganised and renamed with some changes in functional coverage. The IECD was merged with DBOD. The above treatment is only illustrative and not complete or exhaustive.

The various categories of Priority Sector lending were redefined by the Working Group on the Modalities of Implementation of Priority Sector lending and new 20-point programme. The new categories brought under Priority Sectors are housing finance, consumption finance and indirect loans to State sponsored organisations assisting the weaker sections. The earlier categories which continue to be in the Priority Sectors are the agriculture small-scale industries, Industrial Estates, Road and Water Transport operators, Retail trade and small business, professional and self-employed persons and education. Effective from February 14, 1981, a new definition of the SSI units was accepted for purpose of Priority Sector lending, namely, all units with plant and machinery valued up to ₹20 lakh (as against ₹10 lakh earlier); in the case of ancillary units, the comparable value was raised to ₹25 lakh (from ₹15 lakh earlier) and in the case of tiny units, the comparable value was raised to ₹2 lakh (from ₹1 lakh earlier).

The Agricultural Credit Dept. (ACD) was one of the original departments of the Bank, set up statutorily. This Dept. maintained expert staff for the study of questions relating to agricultural credit provision of finance to co-operative credit movement, co-ordination of Bank's activities in the field of agricultural credit with those of State Co-op. Banks and other institutions engaged in agricultural credit and co-operative credit movement. It collaborated with the Central and State Govts. and other bodies engaged in strengthening of the co-operative credit structure so that the co-operatives would be able to meet all the credit requirements of the agriculturists and the cottage and small-scale industries in the co-operative sector. With the extension of the Banking Regulation Act, 1949 to co-operative banks in 1966, this Dept. was entrusted with the task of administering the provisions of that Act insofar as they relate to the co-operative banks. Broadly, this Dept'.s functions related to sanction of limits to co-operative banks, co-ordination between commercial and co-operative banks in the provision of agricultural finance, inspection, licensing, administration of Banking Regulation Act, package credit and operation of other schemes of agricultural credit, supervision and control on land development banks, etc. Most of this work was taken over by the ARDC later on and the Rural Planning and Credit Dept in RBI co-ordinated the Policy aspects of Rural Credit.

As an adjunct to the ACD, the Reserve Bank has sponsored the Agricultural Refinance Corporation in July 1963 which has been renamed as Agricultural Refinance and Development Corporation in 1978. The main objective of the Corporation was to help augment the resources available for medium and long-term finance for agriculture. Although it was originally started as a refinancing agency at the apex level comparable to the Industrial Development Bank of India for industrial finance, it has taken up developmental work to a greater extent particularly since 1978. The refinancing is done through commercial and co-operative banks or land development banks. Besides, direct finance is also provided to federations, co-operative societies and some agencies for medium and long-term agricultural schemes, including animal husbandry, dairy, pisciculture and poultry farming. With effect from July 12, 1982 the functions of ACD and ARDC were taken over by the National Bank for Agriculture and Rural Development (NABARD). Up to June 1982 ARDC functioned as a Corporation subsidiary to Reserve Bank of India. The management of the ARDC was vested in a Board of Directors with one of the Deputy Governors of the Reserve Bank as the Chairman and the Managing Director was appointed from the officers of the Reserve Bank.

Consequent on the transfer of Agricultural Credit Department and Agricultural Refinance and Development Corporation to the National Bank for Agriculture and Rural Development, the Reserve Bank of India has set up a new Department of Rural Planning and Credit with effect from July 12, 1982. The functions of this Department are broadly the implementation of the Lead Bank Scheme, priority sector advances and Special Programmes for weaker sections, Integrated Rural Development Programme, 20-Point Programme, etc. Compliance with the various sections of the Reserve Bank of India Act of 1934 and Banking Regulation Act of 1949, insofar as they relate to the State and Central Co-operative Banks, Regional Rural Banks as well as submission of various statutory returns, licensing of branches or banks in the co-operative fold, control and regulation of interest rates on deposits and advances, etc., continue to be the responsibility of the RBI in respect of Urban Co-operative Banks and Salary earners' societies.

Regional Offices

At the Regional Office level, the major departments are Banking and issue Departments which are counterparts of the Central Office Depts. of Govt. and Bank Accounts and of Currency Management. The Banking Dept. has four major offices under it, *viz.*, Public Accounts Dept. dealing with the Govt. Accounts, Public Debt Office, connected with the Govt. Debt. Securities Dept., responsible for the custody and servicing of Govt. Securities and the Deposit Accounts Dept. connected with the maintenance and upkeep of the Bank Accounts and other accounts. The Issue Department at Regional Office level is connected with the Department of Currency Management at the Central Office level. The Issue Department is divided into General Department and Cash Department. The General Dept. arranges for supply of notes from Govt. of India Presses, which are dispatched to the Currency Chests, and looks after maintenance of assets of the Dept. against note issue and currency circulation accounts, cancellation of notes, verification, re-issue, claims, etc. The Cash Department looks after cash transactions and actual remittances of cash and accounts between Bank and Currency Chests.

These Regional Office Departments are mainly concerned with the implementation of the policy matters decided upon at the Central Office. Thus, in the Banking Department, the PAD and PDO have their policy matters decided at the Secretary's Dept. and Central Debt Section of the Dept. of Govt. and Bank Accounts. Similarly, DAD operates under instructions from the Central Office, DBOD and RPCD. In the issue Dept., the Currency Officer and Treasurer are in charge of General Department and Cash Department respectively and report to the Chief General Manager of the Dept. of Currency Management. The Manager is in charge of the Banking Department and reports to the Chief General Manager of the Department of Administration. The Chief General Manager was designated as Regional Director is also the Secretary of the Local Board and the President of the Local Clearing House. The operations in the Clearing House are conducted by the Reserve Bank in some centres under the control of the Banking Department. The Operational and Functional Departments, *viz.*, FED, DBOD and RPCD have their Regional Offices in almost all centres. The Estate Department in the Regional Offices is linked to the Premises Department at Central Office level. Similarly, the Audit Cells at Regional Office report to the Inspection Department at Central Office. The Research Sections located in the Regional Offices are attached to the Department of Economic and Policy Research and are now full-fledged Departments. The DSAIM has also set up its regional offices at Kolkata, Delhi and Chennai in 1985.

The Department of Non-banking Companies now called the dept of non-banking supervision was set up in March 1966 with its Central Office at Kolkata to administer the powers conferred on the Reserve Bank under Chapter III-B of the RBI Act. This chapter empowers the Reserve Bank to control the deposits accepted by non-bank financial companies and undertake regulation of deposit business and related business of non-bank financial companies. The DNBC collects information on the deposits accepted by non-bank financial and non-financial companies and undertake inspection of non-bank financial companies. The object of this control is to ensure that the monetary policy is not defeated by the deposit business of non-bank financial and non-financial companies. The DNBC work is taken over by the Dept. of Non-banking Supervision at the Central office level and has regional offices in the name of Dept. of Non-banking Supervision, for inspection and audit of the NBFCs.

Distribution of Responsibility

The four Deputy Governors are assisted by six Executive Directors and the Chief Officers of the various Departments. The responsibility for the various Departments is distributed among the Deputy Governors and Executive Directors.

This distribution of functions and their numbers are subject to changes from time to time depending on the exigencies of the requirements of the Bank.

Hierarchy and Nomenclature

In the order of hierarchy, the Deputy Governors come next to the Governor and Executive Directors next to the Deputy Governors. Below the Executive Director is the Chief General Manager and Regional Directors. The various departmental heads, namely, the Chief General Manager, rank in the order of their seniority. The offices and branches are now headed by Regional Directors.

The administrative set up in each of the departments varies significantly. Below the Chief Officer there may be an additional Chief Officer in some Departments. In the order of rank, the Joint Chief Officer and the Deputy Chief Officer come in that order followed by Assistant Chief Officers and Banking Officers or Accountants. The nomenclature of these various cadres vary from department to department. Thus, in specialised departments like the DEAP and DSAIM hierarchy the nomenclatures are slightly different; there is a Principal Adviser followed by a number of Advisers, Directors, Asst. Advisers and Research Officers in that order.

RBI AS NOTE ISSUE AUTHORITY (ISSUE DEPT.)

Principles of Note Issue

There are two principal schools of thought concerning the issue of currency, namely, currency school and the banking school. Under the Bank Charter Act of 1844, in U.K., the principle of note issue was based upon the currency school. Prior to that, there were a number of bank failures leading to the dishonour of notes issued by some of the banks in U.K. It was, therefore, felt that all notes issued should be backed by gold by the issuing banks. The currency school favours rigid controls on note issue and a 100% backing for all notes. On the other hand, the banking school holds that note issue should be flexible, expanding and contracting with the requirements of the economy.

Under the Bank Charter Act, the currency school has been given the pre-eminent position in order to obviate the failure of banks. Under the Act, the Bank of England's work has been divided between two departments: Issue Department and the Banking Department. While the Issue Department has the sole responsibility of note issue, the Banking Department is concerned with the maintenance of the accounts of banks and arranging their banking activities. A small fiduciary issue of notes was permitted without any backing but rest of the notes had to be fully backed by gold. Subsequently, the fiduciary limit had been raised from time to time, enabling expansion of currency in tune with the requirements of the economy. The subsequent enactments in U.K., such as the Currency and Bank Notes Act of 1928, 1939 and 1954 raised the fiduciary limit. The Bank of England was given powers to alter it with the consent of the Treasury. Since then there has been almost every year an increase in the fiduciary issue and the Bank was never under constraint with regard to its issuing powers.

Reserve Bank as the Currency Authority

The Reserve Bank of India Act of 1934 empowers the Reserve Bank to be the sole note issue authority in India (under Section 22 of the Act). Reference was made earlier to the historical evolution of the note issue authority of the Central Bank in India. However, one rupee notes/coins and coins of smaller denominations are issued by the Government under the Indian Coinage Act. The distribution of all coins, including one rupee notes, is undertaken by the Reserve Bank under the Act (Section 38). One and half-rupee coins are legal tender upto ₹10 and coins of smaller denominations are legal tender up to ₹1.

Following the practice of the Bank of England, the Reserve Bank of India is also constituted of two departments, *viz.*, Issue Department and the Banking Department. Issue Department is in charge of the issue of currency, while the Banking Department performs the function of a banker to banks, banker to the Government, etc. The three main functions of the Issue Department are: (1) issue of currency; (2) maintenance of the Currency Chests; and (3) facilitating the seasonal adjustment of the currency in circulation.

Traditionally, the assets of the Issue Department are kept separate from those of the Banking Department. The assets of the Issue Department normally consist of gold coins and bullion, foreign securities, rupee coins and Government of India Rupee Securities. Although bills of exchange and promissory notes are eligible to be the assets of the Issue Department, they are not held so far by the Department because of the absence of a developed bill market in the country. The Act originally provided for a proportional reserve system whereby 40% of the notes issued has to be backed by gold coins/bullion, and sterling securities (foreign securities). The remainder, namely, 60% should be backed by rupee securities. In view of the importance of sterling and because of its predominant position in foreign exchange reserves of the country at that time, sterling was the main asset held for issue of currency. Statutorily the Reserve Bank was obliged to maintain exchange parity with the sterling. This was the result of India being a member of the British Empire and consequently, of the sterling area. After attainment of Independence, however, the reserves have been diversified to include other currencies also.

The Reserve Bank of India Act has been amended in 1956, 1957 and 1968, in respect of this requirement of backing of currency in circulation. In 1956, the minimum reserve system was introduced whereby ₹515 crore were to be in the form of gold bullion and coin. The amendment of 1957, however, reduced the minimum reserves to ₹200 crore of which gold coin and bullion would not be less than ₹115 crore. The holding of foreign securities was reduced to ₹85 crore only and the balance could be held in the form of rupee securities. The provision with regard to foreign securities could be suspended by the Bank with the prior sanction of the Central Government for a period of six months in the first instance which could likewise be extended for periods of three months at a time subsequently. Now the backing for currency is nominal and its acceptance is now backed by the Government guarantee.

Originally the value of gold coin and bullion held by the Reserve Bank was put at ₹40 crore and gold was valued at ₹21.24 per tola. In 1949, price of gold was put at ₹62.50 per tola and the adjustment in the book of accounts of the Reserve Bank under this new valuation was done in 1956.

The gold holdings were again revalued in 1969 following the amendment of the Act in 1968. The new value of the gold was ₹98.44 per tola corresponding to 0.118489 grammes of fine gold per rupee. Now the gold holdings are valued at international market prices.

Provision of Currency Chests

Currency chests are repositories of currency and coins to be kept at various places in the country as extension of the Issue Department of the Reserve Bank. The currency chests are maintained at the various offices of the Issue Department of the Reserve Bank, at the State Bank and its subsidiaries which are the agents of the Reserve Bank in this connection, and also at the Government treasuries and sub-treasuries at district and taluka headquarters. More recently, some of the public sector banks have also been provided with the currency chests. The basic objectives of a currency chest are to facilitate quick dispersal of currency and coins to various distant places, to facilitate remittances to banks and the public, economising the available cash by banks and Governments so that they can do business on a minimum cash basis and also to enable the public to exchange currency for coins and *vice versa* and to exchange higher denomination notes with notes of lower denomination. The State Bank of India and its subsidiaries take responsibility for safeguarding the currency chests maintained in their premises, while the State Government ensures the safeguarding of the currency chests with the treasuries and sub-treasuries.

Implications of Currency Chest Operations

The currency chests are, as pointed out earlier, the extended arms of the Issue Department. Any currency and coins deposited in the currency chest would tantamount to contraction of currency with the public. Similarly, any disbursal of currency and coins out of the currency chest would amount to expansion of currency in circulation. In the case of rupee coins and rupee notes, they are also assets of the Issue Department of the Reserve Bank of India. A deposit of rupee coins and rupee notes in the currency chest increases the amount of coins forming part of the reserve of the Issue Department. An exchange of currency for coins in the currency chests would tantamount to a reduction in the assets of the Issue Department and a simultaneous contraction of currency in circulation. A simultaneous deposit of notes into currency chest against the withdrawal of rupee coins and notes would lead to a reduction in the amount of the notes in circulation and a corresponding reduction in the assets of Issue Department.

In addition to the above functions, the Issue Department also makes adjustments for seasonal fluctuations in the currency requirements of the public. India being an agricultural country, there are basically two seasons — busy season and slack season. The busy season coincides with the harvesting and movement of crops, starting with November and ending in April. This would lead to expansion of currency requirements of the public. But during the off season of the agricultural operations, known as slack season, which starts with May and ends in October, the currency expansion would be smaller and there would be return flow of funds to the banking system. In India, currency still constitutes 55-60% of the total money supply in circulation (M_1). Because of the changes in the currency component following the seasonal variations in its demand there will be seasonal variation in money supply. Nowadays, the importance of the seasonality in currency in circulation has dwindled following the fall in the value of agricultural product in the total value of the GNP.

Mechanics of Expansion and Contraction

The mechanics of expansion and contraction of currency by the Issue Department may be briefly noted here. This will apply both to the seasonal contraction and expansion of the currency as well as to day-to-day fluctuations in the notes issued by the issue Department. The traders and members of the public withdraw money in cash, currency and coins from the banks; the banks, in turn, draw upon their cash balances with the Reserve Bank or borrow from the Reserve Bank. This would lead to changes in the cash held by the Banking Department of the Reserve Bank as well as the balances held by the banks with the Reserve Bank. When the balances held by the Banking Department decline below what is considered as a minimum requirement for day-to-day working, the Banking Department will, in turn, transfer some of the eligible securities held in its investment portfolio to the Issue Department in exchange for cash. The Issue Department would be able to use the eligible assets from the Banking Department as backing and expand the currency to meet the increased demand for currency by the public. This is the process by which an increased demand for currency by the public is met by the Issue Department of the Reserve Bank of India and the notes in circulation expand.

A corresponding process takes place when notes in circulation contract. The public, traders, industries, etc., payback to the banks their borrowings or keep their excess money with the banks, who, in turn, transfer these excess balances to the Banking Department of the Reserve Bank either by repayment of their borrowings or purchase of Government securities from the Reserve Bank or keep excess reserves with the Bank. As cash balances with the Banking Department of the Reserve Bank increase beyond the accepted normal requirements for banking purposes, the Banking Department would, in turn, transfer these excess funds to the Issue Department and take in exchange rupee securities and foreign securities held in the Issue Department. As a result of this, the cash balances of the Banking Department will decline and the volume of their eligible assets in their investment portfolio will increase. Correspondingly, in the Issue Department, the assets eligible for issue will also decline leading to a contraction of currency with the public. Thus, basically the Issue Department expands and contracts currency in tune with the requirements of the public through the Banking Department of the Reserve Bank. Although the bifurcation between the Issue and Banking Departments is anachronistic, it is justified on the basis of accounting convenience. Even in U.K. where it has no significance and the Radcliffe Committee (1959) favoured the discontinuance of this division, it is still maintained in the Bank of England for the same reason of accounting simplicity.

RESERVE BANK'S CONTROL OVER COMMERCIAL BANKS

The Reserve Bank's Control over banks is comprehensive and extends to all their activities. The important activities of commercial banks are acceptance of deposits, purveying credit to the various sectors of the economy such as industry, trade and commerce, agriculture, small industries, etc., providing remittance facilities, cheque collection, etc. The banks also perform an important function of transacting foreign exchange business, financing exports and imports, making remittances abroad, providing forward cover, buying and selling foreign currencies, etc. The Reserve Bank's control over the banks starts from their inception and ends with their liquidation. The nature and degree of control and the extent of the regulation varies from business to business of the bank and from time to time.

Broadly, RBI's control can be classified under two heads — general banking and foreign exchange business. The regulation of general banking is under the Banking Regulation Act of 1949[3] and that of foreign exchange business under the Foreign Exchange Management Act of 1999.

Reserve Bank's control over commercial banks has been statutorily provided for under the RBI Act, 1934 and Banking Regulation Act, 1949. In order to appreciate the Reserve Bank's control over the banking system, it would be apt to set out at first the broad framework of the Indian banking system at present.

With the setting up of the RBI, the commercial banks which used to finance industry and trade have come to be classified into two groups, scheduled and non-scheduled banks. Scheduled banks are those which are listed in the Second Schedule to the RBI Act and as per Section 42(6) (a) of the RBI Act should have a paid-up capital of ₹ 5 lakh and above, must be a company as defined in the Companies Act, 1956 and its affairs must have been conducted in a manner not detrimental to the interests of the depositors. With effect from March 1966, State Co-operative Banks and Central Co-operative Banks and with effect from February 1976 Regional Rural Banks were also eligible for inclusion in the list of scheduled banks.

Non-schedule banks are those which are not so listed in the Second Schedule to the RBI Act. While scheduled banks are enjoined to maintain minimum balances with the RBI, called cash reserve ratio, the non-scheduled banks are only required under Section 18 of the B.R. Act to keep such balances in cash with themselves, or with the RBI or SBI or its subsidiaries. Scheduled banks enjoy certain rights of "lender of last resort" accommodation from the RBI in return for the compulsory reserves kept with the RBI. Under Section 24 of the Banking Regulation Act, both scheduled and non-scheduled banks have to maintain in India, in addition to cash reserve ratio, liquid assets in the form of cash, gold, unencumbered approved securities up to an amount of not less than 25% of their total demand and time liabilities. In addition, the foreign banks are required to maintain in India, assets which are not less than 75% of their demand and time liabilities in India, under Section 25 of B.R. Act.

The Reserve Bank as the banker and the controlling authority of banks, has to ensure that the above provisions and other regulations under the Banking Regulation Act are complied with by banks. The adoption of a policy of social control over banks in 1967 and nationalisation of the 14 major Indian scheduled commercial banks in July 1969 have changed the banking scene and imposed new responsibilities on the RBI for not only control and regulation of banking but for development of the system on the right lines for accelerated growth of the economy. Further six more scheduled commercial banks were nationalised in April 1980 bringing the total number of banks in the Public Sector to 28 accounting for about 80 per cent of total deposits and credit of all commercial banks.

Developmental Function

The Reserve Bank pursued a policy of development of banking in its branch licensing policy, control over management and methods of operation by laying down guidelines for a proper production-oriented

3. The provisions of this Act were extended to co-operative banks on the same basis as the commercial banks with effect from March 1966 by the Banking Laws (Application to Co-operative Societies) Act, 1965.

lending instead of erstwhile security-oriented lending. The Bank had encouraged the opening of more semi-urban and rural branches and helped the growth of cheque habit and monetisation in those areas, as part of its licensing policy. In its control over banks' deposits and lending operations, the RBI has channeled the banking growth in the right directions so as to promote lending to erstwhile neglected and weaker sections of the population, neglected segments and sectors of the economy and to borrowers who have had no access to banking facilities before.

The RBI had set up the Deposit Insurance Corporation in 1962 as its wholly-owned subsidiary to insure the bank deposits up to a limit so as to provide a measure of protection to depositors and ensure confidence of the public in keeping their deposits with banks. This had contributed to the stability and growth of the sound banking system without failures of and run over banks.

In 1968, the Deposit Insurance Corporation Act of 1961 was amended to extend the scheme of deposit insurance to State and central co-op. banks. As and when the State Govts. have passed the enabling legislation to amend their State Co-op. Laws, the Corporation has extended the benefits of deposit insurance to co-op. banks in the respective States.

Among other developmental aspects of RBI's functioning, mention may be made of education and training of banking personnel of commercial and co-op. banks. The Bank has set up the Bankers' Training College in 1954 in Mumbai to impart training in practical banking to officers of commercial banks and the College of Agricultural Banking in Pune in 1969 to impart training to the managerial staff of the co-operative institutions. The Bank had also taken the initiative in setting up the National Institute of Bank Management (NIBM) in 1969. The Institute has the financial support of the Govt., RBI, SBI and other commercial banks and is designed to promote training of higher executives of banks, research in banking industry and consultancy to individual banks, in their problems of recruitment, lending and other areas. It has also set up a centre for Advanced Financial Learning, Mumbai for Promoting training and Research in Advanced Financial Problems. The RBI has also set up an Institute for Development and Research in Banking Technology in Hyderabad for promoting computerisation and Information Technology in banking.

The RBI was also promoting the collection, pooling and dissemination of credit information among banks since 1962 under an enabling amendment under Chapter III A of the RBI Act, 1934. The information is in respect of secured and unsecured limits granted beyond certain limits by banks to individual parties, collected and disseminated on a confidential basis. This service promotes the growth of banking on sound lines, helps the co-ordination of banking practices and reduces the risks of lending.

Banking Regulation

The control on general banking is under various heads referred to below:

(i) Regulation regarding paid-up capital and reserves: Minimum paid-up capital for a bank is laid down at ₹5-10 lakh depending upon the nature of the bank — whether it is national or regional and whether it has a branch in a metropolitan area. Reserves are to be built at the rate of 20% of the profits of the bank. The private sector banks licenced to be set up since 1995 are expected to have a minimum paid-up capital of ₹100 crore.

(ii) Opening of branches: Not only is a licence required for starting banking business but also for opening branches and changing location. There are some regulations governing the granting of licences for opening branches in metropolitan, urban, semi-urban and rural areas, under the Branch Expansion Programme and under usual commercial considerations. Banks are now free from the branch licensing requirement.

(iii) Control over management: In respect of the twenty nationalised banks, the Chairman and Board of Directors are appointed by the Central Government and there is a nominee of the Reserve Bank on the Board. The members of the Board of Directors are chosen to represent various interests such as commerce, industry, agriculture, depositors, employees, etc. In respect of private sector banks, the Reserve Bank is vested with

powers of approval and review of appointment and removal of the Chairman, Directors, Chief Executive Officers, Auditors, etc., and their remuneration and terms of appointment. The Chief Executive of the bank cannot be a person who is insolvent, lunatic or of moral turpitude. The Managing Director or the Chairman cannot hold office for more than 5 years at a time. The bank cannot have a Director who is also a Director of another company engaged in other business or vocation. The Director of a bank cannot also be a Director of a company having an aggregate voting right in excess of 20% of the total voting rights of the shareholders.

(*iv*) *Control over methods of operation and inspections:* Regular inspections are carried out by the Reserve Bank to ensure that the banks conduct their business of banking in the prescribed ways and not to the detriment of the interests they are expected to serve. Inspections are supported by follow-up action as also by calling for statistical returns and necessary information from the banks. The inspections may relate to the adequacy of capital, eligibility for licence, opening of branches, amalgamation, suspension of business and compromise or arrangement. There are various types of inspections — to examine systems and procedures, to assess the financial position, or to make surprise checks on the working of branches centre-wise or for any other *ad hoc* purpose. The Reserve Bank aims at inspecting every branch of commercial banks at least once in three years. Banks are not permitted to carry on any trading activities or acquire any immovable property not required for their own use. Similarly, banks are not permitted to hold shares in any company exceeding 30% of the total paid-up capital of the company or of the bank whichever is lower. The Reserve Bank can issue instruction regarding the management of the banks, the maintenance of accounts or the policy to be followed for any of the advances made by the bank. Banks are advised to have manpower planning and development and are required to submit periodical reports indicating the progress in this direction. They are also required to keep a record of all applications for advances from the priority sectors, which have been rejected. Banks are advised to streamline the procedures and to set up vigilance cells to weed out all corrupt practices. More recently, the banks have been instructed to improve the Customer Service and pay greater attention to better housekeeping so as to eliminate frauds and to improve the quality of the information system and bank data. The government policy as enunciated by the Banking Department from time to time was to tone up the administration in banks, improve the staff discipline and provide better customer service to the public by resorting to computerisation to the extent possible. The clearing house operations in some centres have already been computerised and the banking operations which can be mechanised are recommended to be fed to the computer.

(*v*) *Deposits:* Maximum interest rates on deposits are fixed by the RBI. Deposit Insurance Corporation insures the deposits of the public with banks upto ₹ 1 lakh per account. Overdue deposits and non-operative accounts are reported to the RBI by the banks.

(*vi*) *General advances and selective advances: The* rates of interest charged on general advances are fixed by the RBI at a minimum or a maximum as well as for selected commodities subject to selective controls. These rates vary from time to time and are controlled by the Reserve Bank. These controls have been relaxed very much on both advances and deposits and banks are given powers to fix their own rates of deposits based on their costs, during the economic and financial reforms initiated in 1991-92.

(*vii*) *Advances to priority sectors:* The priority sectors are defined as agriculture, small business, small industries, retail traders, road and water transport operators, self-employed, and education. A minimum proportion of advances are required to flow to the priority sectors as part of the banking policy and the fortnightly statements from scheduled banks should contain data on advances to priority sectors.

(*viii*) *Advances to small industries:* These are covered under the Credit Guarantee Scheme of the Credit Guarantee Organisation. Banks are encouraged to finance small-scale industries on the basis of these guarantees.

(*ix*) *Export financing:* Export Credit and Guarantee Corporation covers the risk of the exporter and banks can take advantage of this in providing larger finance. The Reserve Bank provides refinance at a concessional rate for export credit which will not count for the purpose of discretionary refinance at penal rates.

(*x*) *Voluntary and compulsory amalgamation:* The banks may voluntarily amalgamate if one of them is weak and unable to compete with other banks. Voluntary amalgamations are to be made with the approval of the Reserve Bank. It is the Bank's policy to permit schemes of arrangement instead of forcing the bank into liquidation, as the depositors will benefit more by the former. The Reserve Bank may also force a bank into compulsory amalgamation with another bank or apply to the Central Government for the grant of a moratorium on the bank or apply to the High Court for winding up of the business and shift over to non-banking business by transferring its assets and liabilities of the banking business to another bank. It is also within the power of the Central Government to acquire any banking company in the interest of the depositors if the management is recalcitrant in following the instructions of the Reserve Bank of India.

(xi) Liquidation: The Reserve Bank's prior permission is required for voluntary winding up of a banking company which is granted only if the company is in a position to pay in full all its debts to the creditors as they accrue. Otherwise, the Reserve Bank may *suo motu* or at the direction of the Central Government, make an application for the winding up of a banking company, under certain conditions. The Bank may also supervise the proceedings of liquidation of a bank and expedite the same in the interests of the public. It may appoint an official liquidator who may submit periodical returns on the position of the bank under liquidation.

Banking Laws (Amendment) Act, 1983

In the matter of RBI control on commercial banks, mention may be made here of the recent amendments to the RBI Act and the Banking Regulation Act, by the passage of Banking Laws (Amendment) Act, 1983. The Sections 42 and 43 of the RBI Act were amended so as to require the scheduled banks to submit fortnightly returns instead of weekly returns which came into force from the end of March 1985 and to ensure that the average daily balances to be maintained by the banks under CRR and SLR are based on the average daily balances held at the close of business on each day of the fortnight. Provision was also made for imposing severe penalties for non-compliance with the above liquidity requirements.

By an amendment to the Banking Regulation Act, the RBI is empowered to appoint a chairman of a private bank when the office has fallen vacant and the continuation of such vacancy is not in the interests of the bank. The RBI's permission is required to change the maximum number of directors of a private bank. A limit of 8 years was put on the tenure of directors of a banking company.

The banks are now empowered to form subsidiaries to carry on any business approved by the RBI, such as leasing business under Section 6 of the BR Act. The amendment also empowers the RBI to raise the maximum statutory liquidity ratio that the banks have to maintain up to 40% and to call for daily returns from any bank on any specific matter or to carry-out the scrutiny of the affairs of a bank any time in addition to regular inspections under Section 35 of B.R. Act. The amendment provides for nomination facilities for deposit accounts, articles under safe custody, lockers etc. The definition of deposit was widened so as to include any receipt of money by way of deposit, loan or any other form and put a limit to the number of depositors in respect of individuals, firms or unincorporated associations accepting deposits from public.

Section 18 of BR Act was amended to provide that every banking company not being a scheduled bank shall maintain by way of cash reserves in India an amount equal to not less than 3% of demand and time liabilities in India as on the last Friday of the second preceding fortnight and the monthly return should show the amounts so held on alternate Fridays during the month.

Section 20 was amended to preclude a bank from granting a loan or advance to a company or its subsidiary or its holding company in which the director of the bank is a director, managing agent, manager or employee or in which he holds a substantial interest.

A new Section 21(A) was added to BR Act to the effect that transactions between a banking company and its debtor shall not be questioned in a Court of Law on the ground that the rate of interest charged by the bank is excessive.

Draft legislation is under consideration of the Government on matters relating to granting more powers and greater flexibility in operations and in particular provide for regulation and supervision by the RBI on the payments and settlement system in India. A Board for this purpose is expected to be set up. A draft bill on the Credit Information Bureau is on the anvil and when passed will enable the setting up of companies on credit information for collection of the information from the banks and transmit the same to other banks. The dissimination of credit information among the banks quickly and easily is the objective of this proposal.

SELECTED READINGS

1. The Reserve Bank of India Act, 1934.
2. The Banking Regulation Act, 1949.
3. The Foreign Exchange Regulation Act, 1973.
4. The Foreign Exchange Management Act, 1999.

✠ ✠ ✠

RESERVE BANK AND ITS ROLE

7

The earlier chapter on the Reserve Bank mainly dealt with the organisation and central banking functions in general. The present chapter supplements its role, specifically with reference to India. Some duplication is thus unavoidable but this recap is maintained to benefit the students at the risk of repetition.

The central bank is the apex institution in the banking and financial system. It is established mainly with a view to control and regulate the monetary and credit system in the country. It is a banker to banks and, in this context, a lender of last resort to the banks and other financial institutions. In all the countries, it is a banker to government. It is also an adviser to the government on financial matters and arranges for the issue of loans and acts as an underwriter to the government borrowing programme. The central bank is thus established to play a pivotal role as the head of the banking industry.

Being the currency authority, it has the monopoly of note issue given to it by the law of the country or by the sovereign power of Parliament. As a banker to banks, it is the custodian of their cash balances and is a lender of last resort to help banks in times of financial need. As a corollary to these functions, the central bank is also the controller of foreign exchange and regulator of the external value of the currency. It has the responsibility to the nation to keep the internal value of the currency stable to be achieved by price stability.

A Brief History

The first central bank to be established was the Bank of England which was set up in 1694 for advancing money to the government. In exchange, it was given the sole monopoly of note issue. These were the first two functions for which central bank was set up in many countries of the world. Then the English central bank, *i.e.,* the Bank of England, came to act as the lender of last resort. Thus, the Bank of England was the pioneering central bank of the United Kingdom. It was responsible for the creation of central banks in other countries. The countries to follow the footsteps of the Bank of England were Sweden (The Risks Bank), Netherlands, etc. Almost every country in Europe, some Eastern countries and a few African countries have established their central banks by the end of the 19th century. In the USA, the Federal Reserve Act was passed in 1913, and thereafter the Federal Reserve Banks were established. The Federal Reserve Board which has been established to co-ordinate their activities serves as the U.S. "central bank".

In India, the Reserve Bank of India which is the Indian central bank was established in 1935 under the R.B.I. Act, 1934, initially for regulating the issue of bank notes and keeping of reserves with a view to securing monetary stability in India and generally to operate the currency and credit system of the country to its advantage.[1] The bank was nationalised on 1st January, 1949.

There is a Central Board of Directors to manage the affairs of the Reserve Bank. The Board consists of *(a)* a Governor and not more than four Deputy Governors to be appointed by the Central Government, *(b)* four Directors to be appointed by the Central Government, one each from the four Local Boards, *(c)* ten Directors to be nominated by the Central Government, and *(d)* one government official to be nominated by the Central Government. There are four Local Boards for each area, *viz.*, Western, Eastern, Northern, and Southern.

Objectives

The objectives of Reserve bank were set out earlier but can be summarised as follows:

(1) to maintain the internal value of the nation's currency;

(2) to preserve the external value of the currency;

(3) to secure reasonable price stability; and

(4) to promote economic growth with rising levels of employment, output and real income.

These objectives are common to all countries, developed and developing. More relevant to the developing countries like India are those of economic growth and price stability in these countries.

Within the framework of these broad objectives, the central bank operates. In order to enable it to achieve these objectives, it is empowered with some authority and given some instruments of control and operations. The most important of such instruments are the monetary and credit policies which will be discussed in a later chapter.

The preamble to the Reserve Bank of India Act, 1934 states that the objective of setting up of the RBI is "to regulate the issue of bank notes and the keeping of reserves" which implies that the objectives of currency issue and controlling of banks by acting as a lender of last resort are important.

The traditional functions are those which are operated traditionally by all the central banks and in particular those in developed countries. The non-traditional functions are developmental functions operated in particular in developing countries and designed to increase the volume of investment in the economy or change the pattern or direction of financial flows for the purpose of promoting more productive deployment of funds and growth of the economy or those designed to promote a balanced and viable financial system in the economy.

(a) Traditional Functions

The traditional functions are as follows:

(i) To Act as a Note Issue Authority: The central bank along with the government has generally the monopoly of note issue according to which, currency notes are printed and issued by the central bank. It also regulates the issue and circulation of the notes in the country as per the requirements of the economy.

(ii) To Act as Banker to Government: The central bank advices the government on financial matters, distributes as its agent the coins and one rupee notes issued by the Central Government, provides for receipts and payments through the cheque facility to the government, keep its current account balances, etc. As a banker to government, the central bank underwrites its borrowing programme, provides loans and advances or other short-term facilities and even creates currency to meet the deficit of the Central Goverment in their

1. Preamble to the R.B.I. Act, 1934.

budget through the mechanism of what is called creation of *ad hoc* securities which is tantamount to deficit financing.

(iii) To Act as Banker to Banks: The central bank keeps the custody of cash reserves of commercial banks,[@] regulates their business, provides the necessary guidance and financial support in times of need and controls their activities.

(iv) To Act as Lender of Last Resort: This implies that the central bank lends to banks and other financial institutions in times of need or during financial emergencies. Thus, it provides finance or refinance facilities to banks as and when needed against the deposits they keep with the former. In other words, it accommodates commercial banks when they are short of funds.

(v) To Act as a Clearing Bank: Being the custodian of cash reserves of commercial banks, the central bank performs this essential function as a clearing house. Cheques drawn on different banks and collected by various commercial banks are exchanged at the clearing house. Banks receiving net credit are credited with the same in their accounts with the central bank and the accounts of those with net debit are debited. Actual cash is not exchanged. Besides this advantage, there is a saving of time, labour and cost in settling inter-bank claims at the clearing house.

(vi) Ancillary Functions: These are providing remittances throughout the country, clearance of cheques, distribution of coins and currency, regulation of the banking institutions or banking business of non-banking institutions, collection and publication of financial statistics, and dissemination of this data and information.

(vii) To Act as a Custodian of Foreign Exchange Reserves: In this function, the central bank keeps custody of gold and foreign exchange reserves of the country, operates the exchange management system and maintains a stable external value of the currency. All foreign inflows and outflows and various items of receipts and payments as appearing in the balance of payments of the nation are controlled and supervised by the central bank.

(viii) Controller of Credit: The central bank's fundamental objective is to maintain price stability. For this, it controls the expansion and contraction of credit by the commercial banks. A number of credit control weapons are used for this purpose.

(b) Developmental Functions

The governments of developing countries and particularly India have assumed responsibility for economic development and socio-economic reforms. This responsibility was also shouldered by the central bank as the old concept of "independent central bank" has given way to the concept of "government-dominated central bank". This has involved the central bank in a wide variety of developmental functions of the government. Besides, as the central bank in developing countries has to operate in an environment of underdeveloped financial system with a large component of unorganised financial system, it has to perforce promote the institutional structure and develop a balanced and viable financial system in the economy. As a consequence of the above factors, the central bank has voluntarily and under government influence undertaken a number of developmental functions which are briefly set out below:

List of Developmental Functions

(*a*) Promote savings through a proper interest rate policy and a wide spectrum of savings instruments and to deepen and to widen the financial architecture and fill in institutional gaps.

(*b*) To improve the monetisation in the economy with a view to bringing the whole of the barter economy and the unorganised system into the fold of organised financial system. This comprises banks, financial institutions and developmental agencies which are amenable to control and regulation by the government and the RBI.

@ Here Commercial Banks, Co-operative Banks, Industrial Development Banks and NBFCs, etc., are included.

(*c*) To ensure the flow of adequate credit to the neglected sectors of the economy and sections of the population, such as agriculture, SSIs and scheduled castes and scheduled tribes, etc.

(*d*) To improve the allocation of funds to the underdeveloped regions and states so as to achieve a more balanced economic development of the country.

(*e*) To promote the cheque habit and banking facilities of people so as to promote the increased role of the banking system and lead to larger monetisation of the economy.

(*f*) To take banking to the doors and the underprivileged and provide them with credit support from banks so as to improve their employment opportunities and earning potential with a view to bring the development results to the poor.

(*g*) To operate exchange management in the interests of growth of the economy and to conserve the limited foreign exchange reserves of the nation.

(*h*) To arrange credits from the IMF and IBRD (the World Bank) or other foreign agencies so as to fill up the gap in the availability of foreign resources for the country's development programmes.

(*i*) To provide training of banking personnel by setting up training institutions, for helping the banks to run on efficient lines and dissemination of banking technology and development of research.

The above are some of the more important functions of a developmental nature, performed by a central bank. It will thus be seen that the role of the central bank is both regulatory and developmental. In fact, the role of the central bank can be briefly summarised as follows:

1. Provision of finance and refinance to the commercial and co-operative banks, government and financial institutions.
2. Provision of currency and coins adequate for the economy to carry on business, industry and commerce.
3. Regulation and control of banks, non-bank finance companies and other financial institutions.
4. Development of financial system and promotion of the growth process in the economy.

Objectives of Credit Control

Modern economies are all based on money, which consists of both cash and credit. Cash can be created by only the Reserve Bank, while credit can be extended by banks. Since such credit creation can be both excessive and deficient as compared to the requirements of the economy, some control on them is exercised by the central bank of the country, which is the monetary authority, the apex bank and banker to banks. The need for credit control was explained by De Kock by saying that credit has "come to play a predominant part in the settlement of monetary and business transactions of all kinds and thus to represent a powerful force for good or evil".

The objectives of credit control are as follows:

1. Stabilisation of prices without inflation and deflation by adjusting credit creation to the needs of the economy.
2. Keeping the exchange rates stable through a proper adjustment of credit creation to the inflows and outflows of funds and sterilisation of excess inflows and outflows.
3. Stabilisation of short-term money markets by the central bank through its influence on cost and availability of credit.
4. Promotion of economic growth by making credit available for all productive activities and controlling it for non-productive activities.

Instruments of Credit Control

The operation of credit control is through various instruments of policy. These instruments are classified into quantitative or general controls and qualitative or selective controls.

Quantitative or general controls are:

(A) Bank Rate Policy.

(B) Open Market Operations.

(C) Variable Cash Reserve Requirements and Liquidity Requirements.

(D) Quantitative Credit Limits and other Direct Credit Controls.

Selective Controls are:

(*i*) Variation in margin requirements, and interest rates on selected commodities subject to speculation.

(*ii*) Consumers' Credit Control and control on quantum of flow of funds to stock and commodity markets.

Selective credit controls are controls on consumer credit or credit flowing into the various sectors of the economy or for various purposes and against various securities or commodities.

General Controls vs. Selective Controls

(1) While general controls aim at influencing the economy in general uniformly in respect of all economic variables, selective controls attempt at regulating some selected sectors of the economy or credit against particular commodities which are subject to speculation or other manipulations and malpractices.

(2) Quantitative or general controls affect the credit creation only indirectly by changing the capacity of commercial banks to create extra credit in the economy which they can do by giving loans, buying or selling of securities and various other assets, etc. Qualitative or selective controls directly attack the banks' credit creation by regulating and diverting its flow into desirable channels from undesirable or unproductive uses.

(3) The general or quantitative credit control weapons can control only the total volume of credit in the economy and not its use, whereas selective controls, as we shall discuss later in this chapter, control the quality of credit given by the commercial banks.

The central bank through those controls ensures that bank advances flow into certain desirable channels of productive activity, such as agriculture, manufacturing of essential goods, growth of essential services such as public transport, house construction for the masses, etc. The central bank attempts to prohibit, directly the use of bank funds for unproductive and speculative activities, and to restrict the use of advances for production of undesirable goods.

(4) Traditionally, quantitative weapons of credit control were in much use in the past, whereas during the last three or four decades, more attention is paid by the various central banks of the world to the use of selective controls both in developed and less developed countries. The main reason for this change is the failure of the traditional quantitative controls in achieving price stability, economic growth and full employment.

Other Controls

In addition to general and selective controls, central banks also use direct controls, moral suasion and others to influence the credit by banks and other financial institutions and to make them follow certain policies or priorities in lending.

Impact on Cost and Availability

The general and selective controls influence the cost and availability of credit. To be specific, bank rate and control on other interest rates would have their impact on the cost of credit. The reserve requirements, namely, the cash reserve ratio of banks and other quantitative limits to bank credit, would control the availability of credit. Open market operations would influence both the availability and cost of credit. Some policy tools such as statutory liquidity ratio (SLR) would influence the flow of credit sectorally as between the government sector and other sectors. The setting of targets segment-wise and sector-wise was also aimed. For, in a developing economy like India control on both volume and direction of credit flows is necessary as the total volume of credit is limited and it has to be used in the most productive and socially desirable directions, suitable to the emerging situation in the economy. Thus, food and export credit are given priority by the RBI in its policy directives.

Monetary Policy and Economic Variables

In broad terms, monetary policy should also aim at a desirable level of monetary growth. In India, the existence of unorganised and subsistence sectors and a vast parallel economy necessitates a constant adjustment of the monetary policy to the changing economic scenario.

Besides, it is generally assumed in any discussion on monetary budget and in monetary policy that the velocity of circulation of money remains constant. But in India with frequent shifts of public preferences from cash to deposit money and *vice versa* and as between black economy and organised economy, there are frequent fluctuations in the velocity of money.

Promotional Role

The credit policy instruments are operated to take care of the various aspects of policy, namely, regulatory role, promotional role and social service obligations of the banks. In respect of the promotional role and social service obligations of banks, the central bank has been promoting banking habit by increasing the spread of bank branches geographically and filling up the credit gaps. In the promotional role, many policy schemes are operated by banks to promote credit flows to the neglected sectors and segments of the economy and to fill up the credit gaps, namely, institutional, sectorial and geographical credit gaps. These are particularly relevant to the developing countries.

Developmental Role

Under developmental role, the credit policy is geared specially in developing economies for the purpose of ensuring proper credit allocation sectorally. The credit policy is actively pursued in these countries to achieve social objectives and planned priorities. As market forces might not achieve the desired flow of funds, the planned levels of flow to various sectors and industries are sought to be secured by the credit allocation by the central bank, followed by monitoring of credit flows by its credit planning and policy and other policy schemes are geared to the productive use of credit, proper allocation of scarce resources, geographically and sectorally as per planned priorities of the government and social objectives of planned development of the economy.

A. BANK RATE AND INTEREST RATES

What is a Bank Rate?

Bank rate is the standard rate of discount charged by the central bank of the country to eligible parties. It is the minimum official rate at which the central bank rediscounts first-class bills of exchange from the discount houses and commercial banks. By bank rate policy, we mean the terms and conditions under which the money market can have temporary access to the central bank in the form of discounts or rediscounts or secured advances. This policy would influence both the cost and availability of credit. The cost is the interest rate of commercial banks and the market rate of interest, both of which are influenced by changes in the bank rate. The availability of credit is influenced by appropriate changes in the conditions under which the central bank provides credit to commercial banks such as difficult access or easy access. Thus, raising of the bank rate makes credit dearer through more or less equivalent changes in the commercial bank's interest rate and in the market rate of interest rate and *vice versa.*

Thus, the bank rate policy has the following effects:

(1) Commercial banks find it difficult (when the bank rate is raised) or easy (when the bank rate is reduced) to approach the central bank for loans, which limits or increases their ability to create credit respectively.

(2) Commercial banks are expected to raise their rate of interest (when the bank rate is raised) or reduce it (when the bank rate is reduced). This affects the market rates of interest accordingly. The credit either becomes dearer or cheaper as the case may be. Accordingly, there are anti-expansionary or pro-expansionary effects on credit creation.

Modus Operandi of the Bank Rate

The immediate effect of a change in the bank rate is to change the banks' deposit/lending rates as the banks depend on the central bank for finance and refinance and its rate of advance sets the pace for the market rates of interest. By an increase in the bank rate, the deposit rates increase, leading to larger mobilisation of deposits and these can be used for lending but at higher interest rates; borrowing is discouraged. Thus, the borrowing and lending rate of banks and along with them, those related to non-bank financial institutions would rise. Since loans to customers would be dearer for investment, their demand for credit will decrease while the supply of credit will increase. Profit expectations would go down and lower investment leads to a downward movement of the economy as a whole. On the other hand, a fall in the bank rate would lead to opposite effects and would result in an upward movement of the economy through a rise in investment and aggregate demand in the economy.

In India the bank rate is defined in Section 49 of the Reserve Bank of India Act as the rate at which the Reserve Bank is prepared to buy or discount bills of exchange or other commercial papers eligible for purchase under the Act. This in effect is the lending rate of the RBI, at which it provides the lender of last resort facility to the banks. Banks and financial institutions in India get refinance or finance under the RBI Act, at bank rate, mainly against eligible bills or securities, namely, treasury bills or Government securities.

Interest Rate Policy in India

The RBI has been operating the interest rate policy in a flexible manner in tune with the development requirements of the economy. The bank rate is its standard rate of discount or advance to both banks or financial institutions. It provides refinance to banks at varying rates, depending upon the purpose and security under Section 17 of the RBI Act. Although the bank rate is its standard rate, it is not applicable to all lending by the RBI. Similarly, banks' borrowing and lending rates have been fixed by the RBI within a broad spectrum, from a low rate of 4 per cent for DRI loans to weaker sections to a maximum lending rate of 17 per cent for general purposes. There are multiplicity of rates to suit the needs of sectorial development and to meet the socio-economic obligations of the government. Some rationalisation of these rates is also attempted to the RBI in tune with the recommendations of the Chakravarthy Committee referred to later. The discount and rediscount rates on bills, government borrowing rates, etc., have been revised recently to bring them in line with the more realistic market-oriented rates.

The bank rate fixed by the RBI in 1990-91 was 10 per cent per annum and has since been brought down by stages to 6% p.a. by 2004-05, but has been raised steeply to 9% in 2010-11 to induce a reduction in expenditure and control inflation, particularly food inflation. It now stands at 9% in 2015.

Refinance Rates

There are many rates of refinance charged by the RBI for its financial accommodation to banks, depending upon the purpose and/or security. While the standard lending rate is the bank rate, there are special rates or refinance for lending against export bills or against banks' food credit. There are also other rates for standby refinance and discretionary refinance provided by the RBI. The net effective rate of refinance provided by the RBI is, therefore, different from the bank rate. The Repo rate is the prevailing rate of RBI by which the RBI controls the call money and short-term rates, and Repo deals are referred to later.

Importance of Bank Rate

Bank rate is the leader among interest rates and sets the pace for other rates. Any change in it indicates a change in the central bank policy. Bank rate and changes in interest rates are the major instruments of monetary policy, which are activated in India since 1996, and are now operated in a flexible manner.

In India, due to the needs of cheap government finance and developmental needs of the economy, bank rate changes have been kept to the minimum, while other refinance rates have been changed, depending on the requirements of the economy.

Impact of Bank Rate Policy

Bank rate influences the economy both on the domestic and external fronts. On the domestic front changes in bank rate affect investment and income in the economy through corresponding changes in interest rates. In particular, the holding of inventories (stocks) and fixed assets formation are influenced by changes in interest rates and these in turn influence investment and income in the economy.

On the external front, bank rate changes influence the inflow and outflow of funds of both short-term and long-term nature, namely, those for speculative and investment purposes. But in India due to the prevailing all-pervading exchange regulations, these external effects are limited for all practical purposes.

Limitations of Bank Rate Policy

The efficacy of the bank rate policy would depend on the following factors:

1. Link with market rates of interest: The link between the bank rate and other interest rates should be strong and close so that changes in the bank rate would lead to consequent changes in the other interest rates in the economy. If the markets are not close and integrated, this would not be possible.

2. Extent of cash reserves: If there are excess reserves with the banks and there is no need to borrow from the central bank, then the bank rate changes would not percolate to other segments of the money market and its effectiveness will be limited.

3. Interest elasticity of investment: If the interest elasticity of investment is low and the demand for bank credit is interest inelastic, interest rate policy or bank rate changes would not affect significantly the real economic variables such as investment, income and employment.

4. Flexibility in cost and prices: For the bank rate policy to work effectively, there should be flexibility in cost and prices and interest cost should be a significant variable in the cost of production of industries.

5. Business psychology: For effectiveness of the bank rate policy, particularly in a period of depression, it should be capable of influencing the business psychology on which investment outlays would depend generally. As the bank rate cannot influence this psychology in depressed conditions, it is said that the bank rate policy may work during an inflationary period but not at times of depression.

6. Extent of money market development: For the bank rate policy to work, there should be a developed bill or money market, in which the central bank operates. In the absence of eligible bills for discount or because of an undeveloped money market as in India, the efficiency of bank rate policy will be limited.

Efficacy of Bank Rate Policy in India

(*i*) The efficacy of bank rate policy in India is limited because of the multiplicity of refinance rates and the relative low elasticity of savings and investment to interest rates. This is due to the fact that the bulk of investment in India is in the public sector and by the government.

(*ii*) As an indicator of the policy, the bank rate is, harbinger of changes in credit policy. It no doubt influences the cost and availability of bank funds. So far as the organised financial sector is concerned, changes in other interest rates follow the changes in the bank rate. In India, deposit rates and lending rates of banks, including the various rates charged by banks on loans for different purposes, are controlled by the RBI. The interest rates charged by financial institutions and post offices are fixed by the government in consultation with the RBI. The short-term and long-term rates and whole spectrum of interest rates change in tune with the bank rate. But in India these changes are not autonomous as all rates are fixed by the RBI and the government and simultaneous changes take place in the whole spectrum of interest rates. But the effect of these changes on the economy is limited to their impact on the organised financial system.

(*iii*) Bank rate influences the willingness and ability of banks to lend due to change in policy and consequently, the level of inventory holdings and investment in the economy are affected.

On the whole, the bank rate policy is of limited significance and more so in developing countries, mainly due to the absence of conditions in the real world which make it effective. But a change in bank rate is an official indicator of the change in the credit policy of the central bank and the business conditions would be affected broadly by this change in policy. As the bank rate policy is of limited significance, the central banks all over the world operate this policy along with other policies to make its effects felt on the economy in general. In brief, the bank rate is a nominal rate of RBI refinance in India and it has only a psychological effect on the markets. The effective rate is set by the Repo and Reverse Repo rates in India as announced by the RBI from time to time in its policy statements.

B. OPEN MARKET OPERATIONS (OMO)

Open market operations are an important instrument of monetary policy and refer to the purchases and sales by the central bank of Government securities, treasury bills, gold, foreign exchange, etc. In India, Section 17 of the RBI Act authorises the Reserve Bank to purchase and sell Government securities — Central, and State — and those fully guaranteed by the Central Government. At present, the RBI puts through the transactions only in Central Government securities. The reasons for this are as follows:

(*i*) These securities have the highest degree of liquidity and easily marketable.

(*ii*) These are held by the Reserve Bank in its own investment account and also by the banks and financial institutions which facilitates the Reserve Bank's operations in these securities on a daily basis.

(*iii*) There is a ready market for them in major cities in terms of quotations of prices, yields, etc.

Objectives

The objectives of open market operations are as follows:

(*i*) to improve the efficiency of monetary policy by influencing the availability of funds which is done by increasing and decreasing the liquidity of banks and to influence the pattern of yields and interest costs through the yields on Government securities.

(*ii*) to maintain a stable yield pattern in the market and to avoid undue fluctuations in prices and yields of Government securities.

(*iii*) to assist the debt management policy of the RBI so as to facilitate the government's floatation of new loans under their borrowing programme and the financing of the government by the RBI.

Advantages

The advantages of open market operations over other monetary policy instruments are as under:

(1) These can be operated on a daily basis and as and when desired.

(2) These operations are flexible in that the purchases and sales can be reversed at short notice and the quantum of operations can be varied quickly.

(3) Their influence on the cost and availability of funds is quick and direct. The availability of funds is influenced by RBI purchases of Government securities, whereby cash or reserves are supplied to the banks and their funds are augmented. The reverse process takes place when open market operations result in sales of Government securities by the RBI, leading to loss of reserves or cash with the banks.

Mechanism of Open Market Operations (OMO)

When open market purchases are made by the central bank, it will lead to the issue of cheques by the central bank on itself, which are credited to the accounts of sellers, namely, banks or the public who are dealing with the central bank. This will increase available cash reserves with banks which enables them to expand credit and money supply. This may lower the interest rates for two reasons. Firstly, the central bank's purchases by themselves may push up the prices of Government securities which would lower the yields and hence interest rates. Secondly, the expansion of credit would increase the supply of credit and with the given demand at that time, the interest rates will fall. Thus, the central bank buys securities in the open market to encourage credit expansion.

The opposite effect would follow when the central bank sells the securities. The banks and public who buy the securities would pay cheques to the central bank which would lead to a contraction in credit extended by banks and in money supply. This may also raise rates in the economy for similar reasons explained above. Thus, the central banks sells securities in order to reduce the capacity of the commercial banks to create credit.

Limitations of OMO

There are many limitations to these operations in India which are briefly set out below:

1. Captive nature of the market: The major limitation to the successful operation of the open market purchase and sale is the lack of a proper developed bill market or a Government securities market. For example, in India, there is no bill market and the Government securities market is a captive market and not well developed.

2. Dependence on public response: These operations depend on the willingness of banks and the public to do business with the central bank but in a depression when the central bank wishes to buy securities and pump in money, there may be very few to respond because for the depressed psychology in business and the difficulty of banks to lend.

3. Dependence on banks' habit of keeping excess reserves: Banks should be prepared to lend to the full extent of the excess cash reserves to the public and the public should be willing to borrow, in order to make the effect of OMO to be felt on the economy. The banks in India are used to keep excess reserves with the result that their dependence on the RBI is less.

4. Dependence on the holdings of the central bank: This policy is also limited by the central bank's holdings of securities to sell freely and its ability and willingness to incur losses sometimes on the value of its assets, due to lowering of the security prices for sale.

5. Offsetting factors like outflow of funds: The importance of open market operation is limited, if there are offsetting conditions like outflow of funds when the central bank buys securities for expansion of credit or if the velocity of circulation falls with every increase in credit and money supply.

6. Countervailing operations of banks: The central bank's operations should not be nullified by the countervailing operations of commercial banks by their initial purchases and subsequent rediscount of the same with the central bank.

7. Disturbance to market conditions: The operations of central bank may disturb the pattern of yields and market structure which will make difficult the fresh floatation of loans by the government. For this purpose, the central bank has to operate in such a manner as not to disturb the market conditions but groom the market at the time of new loan floatations. Grooming refers to maintaining an orderly yield and price structure and providing funds to banks by buying maturing securities, so that they can buy the new loans floated.

Open market operations are effective in developed countries to strengthen the bank rate policy. The bank rate affects indirectly by raising interest rates. While the OMO influence directly both short-term and long-term rates as the central bank's operations may extend to both short- and long-term securities, the bank rate influences only short-term rates. Thus when the bank rate is raised, the central bank may sell securities in the market and *vice versa.* Besides the OMO are flexible and operated on a daily basis. They can be used to stabilise the market and assist government's borrowing programme when necessary. Thus both the bank rate and OMO are complementary and are operated jointly to make the monetary policy effective.

Efficacy of OMO in India

In India, the efficacy of OMO is limited for the following reasons:

(*i*) The market for government loans is limited and captive in the sense that banks and financial institutions hold the bulk of Government securities.

(*ii*) The secondary market, namely, trading in old securities, is almost negligible due to the captive nature of the market.

(*iii*) The range of instruments and institutions operating in the market is narrow.

(*iv*) The structural rigidities and loosely-knit market segments lead to lower efficacy.

(*v*) The proportion of government debt (securities) in which the RBI operates is small with the result that their effect is negligible.

Policy of OMO in India

In India, OMO are undertaken not so much for monetary policy purposes but for debt management. The market for Government securities in which the RBI operates is captive market and hence its effect is limited to influence the cost and availability of credit. The OMO are used to stabilise yields, groom the market to facilitate redemption of maturing loans and issue of new loans by the government. The RBI operations result mostly in net sales to provide funds to the government but not in support of the monetary policy. In effect, the OMO in India are not used so much for monetary policy as for the support of the government debt management policy.

Traditional Instruments of Policy and Developing Countries

The traditional instruments of central bank, namely, the bank rate and open market operations, are less effective in India for the purposes intended for in developed countries. The bank rate in India is a notional leader to indicate the direction of change and the stance of monetary policy. But it is not the real effective rate as there is a wide spectrum of refinance rates applicable for various purposes. This weapon is also not relevant for all purposes as concessional refinance rates are available for exports, food procurement operations and other selected purposes. The average cost of refinance to banks would vary from bank to bank and from time to time and is not represented by the bank rate.

To repeat, the open market operations are not used as an instrument of monetary policy in India as there is not real wide-based market in Government securities. Open market operations are conducted as a tool of debt management policy for facilitating orderly movement of yields and for successful implementation of the borrowing programme of the government and not so much as an instrument of monetary policy.

Open market operations refer to direct purchases and sales of approved securities and bills by the central bank on its own initiative to control credit. These purchases and sales are made in treasury bills, Government securities, commercial bills, and even gold in some countries. In practice, in most countries, these operations are confined to government bonds or securities of both short-term and long-term nature.

C. VARIABLE RESERVE RATIO

Objectives

The variable reserve ratio is a device used by the central banks, in their capacity as bankers' bank, to make commercial banks keep a minimum proportion of their deposits as balances with the central bank. These proportions are fixed by law in some countries and by custom in other countries. The power to vary these proportions is given to the central bank as part of the credit control measures.

Mode of Operation

As a banker to banks, the central bank lends, as a lender of last resort in times of need, to commercial banks, to help them tide over their temporary liquidity problems against the minimum balances to be kept with it. This proportion of balances kept by banks with the central bank is variable and this is an instrument to influence the cost and availability of bank credit.

If this proportion is raised, the available resources (cash reserves) with banks to lend will be lower and hence there will be a contraction of credit and the costs of credit would rise. On the other hand, if this reserve ratio is lowered, banks will have excess reserves and there can be expansion of credit, leading to a lowering of costs of credit.

To give an example, if the commercial banks have deposits of say ₹100 crore and the minimum reserve ratio is 10 per cent then the banks have to keep ₹10 crore with the central bank. If this ratio is raised to 15 per cent, ₹15 crore will have to be kept with the central bank, lowering its available funds to lend from ₹90 crore to ₹85 crore which reduces the credit given to the public. If, on the other hand, this ratio is lowered to 5 per cent, funds available with banks will rise to ₹95 crore and their lending capacity will increase to that extent. Thus variations in the required reserve ratio would lead to changes in the lending capacity of banks and in their credit expansion through multiplier effect.

Comparison with Other Instruments

This instrument of variable reserve ratio is more effective than the bank rate and open market operations. While the bank rate can influence credit costs, OMO can affect both cost and availability of credit. But their effects are less certain and indirect. The effects of OMO are more direct and immediate on the banks and as a result their influence on the real economy can also be quicker and more effective. The instrument of reserve requirements is not dependent on the market forces or market conditions, as in the case of bank rate or open market operations. As such, it is a superior and more powerful weapon in the armoury of the central bank, as it affects the bank's ability to lend directly and immediately in a clear-cut manner.

Limitations

Despite its efficacy as an instrument of credit control, variable reserve ratio suffers from various limitations in actual operation. The major limitations are set out below:

1. Bank's habit of keeping excess reserves: This instrument will be ineffective if banks are in the habit of keeping excess reserves with themselves so that even if the central bank raises the required ratio, their lending operations are not affected.

2. Bank's unwillingness to approach the central bank: If banks follow their own independent policies and they do not have to approach the central bank for funds, the instrument of variable reserve requirements will not become effective, as banks can then raise funds from abroad or from other sources.

3. Demand for credit is out of its purview: This instrument may not be effective, as it cannot influence the demand for credit but only its supply, and if the demand is not very elastic, the public may not borrow even if the banks are willing to lend their excess balances.

4. Cumbersome and inconvenient: This instrument is cumbersome and inconvenient for administration and as such it cannot be used frequently and on a daily basis.

5. This method of credit control is discriminatory as it affects different banks differently without any adjustment of allowance for the individual position of banks.

6. It adversely affects the psychology of banks and borrowers, as their prior plans for credit needs will be upset by sudden changes in the reserve requirements, which bring about major changes in the credit availability. Besides, this policy cannot be used for small adjustments in the supply of credit or to bring about marginal effect on bank's lending position.

The variable reserve ratio is an instrument which is more effective than bank rate or open market operations in monetary management. Its effects are more direct and quick so far as the changes in monetary variables like cost and availability of credit are concerned. But its effect on real economic variables like investment, income and employment are not certain as these depend on the relative elasticities and responsiveness of the relevant variables. This instrument suffers from a number of limitations and cumbersome in operation. Thus, it can be concluded that no single instrument of monetary policy is adequate and a co-ordinated use of all instruments is necessary. The use of these instruments should also depend on the prevailing circumstances and the targets aimed at. We may conclude by quoting what De Kock had said that while variable reserve ratio is "A very prompt and effective method of bringing about the desired changes in the available supply of bank credit, it has some technical and psychological limitations which prescribe that it should be used with moderation and discretion and only under obviously abnormal conditions".

Reserve Requirements in India

There are two types of legal requirements for banks in India namely: *(i)* Cash reserve requirements under Section 42 of the RBI Act, and *(ii)* Statutory liquidity requirements under Section 24 of the Banking Regulation Act.

Cash Reserve Ratio (CRR) in India

As regards cash reserves, the minimum cash reserve ratio (CRR) to be kept by banks with the RBI in the form of cash balances is variable between 3 per cent and 15 per cent of the demand and time liabilities of banks. The power to vary this ratio is given to the RBI under the Act for its credit control purposes.

Besides when the acquisition of fresh deposits is uneven as between banks, the RBI has powers to impose an additional reserve requirement variable up to 100 per cent of incremental deposits, subject to an overall ceiling of 15 per cent of the total demand and time liabilities for any bank. The RBI, however, pays interest on these additional deposits over the minimum of 3 per cent at a rate to be fixed by it. Under the financial reforms, initiated since 1992, and as per the Narasimham Committee Reports, the CRR as brought down from 8% in 2000 to 4% by end-2004, and it stood at 4.75% in April 2012.

Objectives of CRR in India

The power to vary the CRR was designed to control the banks' liquidity by the RBI and for ensuring, at the same time, the liquidity and solvency of individual banks. The RBI provides refinance and acts as a lender of last resort to banks on the basis of the reserves kept by banks with it. This measure promotes the confidence of the public in the banks as the RBI is expected to support these banks in times of need by finance and refinance to tide over their financial problems.

Besides, the liquidity position of banks can also be controlled by this measure, as an increase in CRR from 10 to 15 per cent for instance immobilises the additional 5 per cent of deposits of banks from their use for loans and investments. The CRR is 4% as at end 2014.

At the same time, the assurance that the RBI helps the banks in times of need, obviates any possible liquidity crisis or loss of public confidence in banks.

Statutory Liquidity Ratio (SLR)

Under the second legal requirement called the statutory liquidity ratio (SLR), banks have to maintain liquid assets in the form of excess cash, gold, treasury bills, unencumbered Government securities, etc., of a minimum of 25 per cent of total net demand and time deposit liabilities, exclusive of the balances to be maintained with the RBI under the above CRR provision. This minimum ratio of 25 per cent can be varied up to 40 per cent of the deposit liabilities. This power to vary the SLR is also given to the RBI under its credit control measures.

This would imply the RBI has power under CRR and SLR to control the liquid assets of banks up to a maximum of 55 per cent (CRR up to 15 per cent and SLR up to 40 per cent) of bank deposits. But now the SLR is 25% of NDTL since early 2005, but lowered to 24% from December 2010 and to 23% from August 2012 and it stood at 22% as at end 2014..

Objectives of SLR in India

The objective of SLR is to enable the RBI to control the liquidity of banks in total and of individual banks separately and to curb the excessive expansion of credit not justified by the real economic trends or normal inventory norms of borrowing companies which depend upon bank credit for their working capital. The individual bank's solvency and liquidity is also protected by this measure. Besides, this measure controls the directional flow of bank funds as between sectors. As the funds kept under SLR are mostly invested in treasury bills and Government securities, any rise in SLR would increase the flow of funds to the Government securities, and any decrease in SLR would increase the funds available to the private sector. The present SLR holdings of both Commercial and Co-operative banks in India is 38.5% of total deposit liabilities as in 2004-05, which is in excess of the requirement.

Penal Provisions for SLR and CRR Defaults

As the banks have been found to be defaulting in keeping these rates of CRR and SLR, the RBI has been given powers by the passage of Banking Laws (Amendment) Act, 1983 to impose stringent penalties on shortfalls in CRR and SLR. Since then, the RBI started charging penal rates of rediscount or refinance to those banks in default. As resort to participation certificates (a form of short-term borrowing from financial institutions) by banks has been found to be defeating the monetary policy, these certificated borrowings have been treated as deposits for the purposes of CRR and SLR. The non-resident deposits and foreign currency deposits have also been subject to the CRR and SLR by the RBI.

The instrument of reserve requirements acts directly on the quantum and flow of credit. Its effect is immediate and straightforward. In an economy like India, where the financial structure lacks integration and depth, such direct controls have been found to be more effective. Among the various policy instruments, available to the RBI, CRR and SLR are more frequently used at the present time to control the bank's liquidity and expansion of bank credit with a view to curbing the inflationary pressure.

As part of banking reforms, following the Narasimham Committee Report 1991-92, the SLR was kept at the lowest level of 25%, while the CRR was operated on many occassions. As at end June 2008, the CRR was kept 8.25%, but lowered to 6% from April 2010.

D. QUANTITATIVE CREDIT LIMITS

Among the policy instruments used by the RBI to control credit, quantitative ceilings are also important. These ceilings are fixed by the RBI in respect of refinance limits to individual banks. Thus, the normal facility of automatic borrowings from the RBI has been restricted to 1 or 2 per cent of the demand and time liabilities of banks.

The quantitative limits apply to all banks together as well as to individual banks in respect of refinance. There are limits in the form of ceilings or floors to bank credit, sector-wise or segment-wise. Thus credit ceilings are imposed on banks in respect of their financing of foodgrains procurement, financing of stocks and shares, purchase of commercial crops such as jute, cotton, etc. There are, however, floorings fixed in respect of bank credit to priority sectors such as agriculture, small-scale industry, *etc.,* where there is a minimum level of bank credit to flow at 40 per cent of gross bank credit.

Minimum levels are also fixed for advances to weaker sections, *viz.,* scheduled castes, scheduled tribes etc., under the various developmental and promotional schemes operated by the banks. In the case of selective credit controls referred to below, bank credit ceilings are imposed bank-wise, region-wise and party-wise.

SELECTIVE CREDIT CONTROLS

Theory of Selective Credit Controls

Selective credit controls are qualitative in nature and affect the distribution and direction of credit flows. The rationale of selective credit controls lies in their ability to influence the cost and quantum of credit flows to selected segments, sectors or borrowers in the economy. General credit controls affect all borrowers and the entire economy alike without discrimination. When the objective of policy is to encourage or discourage flows to particular sections of people or sectors of the economy such as consumer credit or credit against foodgrains, only selective controls can be used. Such commodities or sectors may be sensitive to pressures of demand more than others, leading to a price rise or inflation or they may be less essential for consumption. These may also be subject to hoarding and speculation which are to be discouraged, without affecting the general flow of credit in the economy.

The special advantages of selective controls are as follows:

1. They affect the targets direct and straight, instead of in a round about or indirect way as in the case of general controls.
2. They can influence the cost, total quantum and individual limits of credit etc.

3. They can affect both borrowers and lenders in their capacity to lend and capacity to borrow.
4. Although their immediate effect is on the sectors targeted, the overall credit is also affected thereby.
5. The social goals of encouraging desirable consumption and discouraging undesirable consumption can be achieved by these controls.
6. Selective and qualitative effects on lending and credit flows in the economy can be secured by these controls.

Objectives of Selective Controls

1. To prevent undesirable use of credit: To prevent or reduce the flow of credit to socially or economically undesirable lines of activity and to encourage those that are desirable. For example, these controls are useful to discourage the consumption of less essential goods like consumer durables in times of inflation or for stock market operations.

2. Prevent hoarding of essential goods: To discourage the flow of credit to commodities or sectors which are price sensitive or in short supply and subject to hoarding and profiteering like edible oils or foodgrains.

3. To encourage credit for desirable uses: To encourage the flow of credit to preferred sectors of the economy whose growth helps the development of the economy like lending to agriculture or to small-scale industries which provide employment and income to a large proportion of population.

4. To encourage exports: To help correct the balance of trade imbalance by encouraging the flow of credit to exports and discouraging it for imports. The export-oriented industries may be given larger credit at cheaper rates and export bills may be discounted or rediscounted at concessional rates, while charging higher rates for import bills.

5. To curb excessive expenditure on consumption: These controls can be used to curb excessive consumer expenditure through controls on consumer credit and raising the cost of borrowing such credit.

6. To discourage speculative activities: Speculative activities can be curbed by imposing controls on lending against shares, debentures, commodities, gold and silver, etc., which are particularly relevant when the economy is in inflationary phase.

7. To control hire-purchase credit: These controls can be extended to credit advanced by hire-purchase or housing mortgage companies or other private non-banking financial institutions.

Methods of Selective Controls

The following are the methods of using selective controls:

1. Variation in Margins: The central bank is given powers to fix margins or vary them for all or any categories of advances. By such variation in margins, the loan value of any given collateral securities is increased or decreased to suit the requirements of the economy or the concerned industry or commodity. Thus if the margin is 20 per cent and the value of collateral pledged or mortgaged with the bank is ₹100, then the loan value is ₹80. If the margin is raised to 40 per cent by the central bank, then it will reduce credit to such borrowers, as the loan value will be only ₹60 as against ₹80 earlier.

This is a direct and effective method of controlling the quantum of credit flow. This is useful to discourage speculation and reduce the inflationary pressures. This can be used against any commodity or borrowers without affecting other commodities or borrowers. This is easy to administer and enforce. This will affect both lenders and borrowers alike and both demand and supply of credit are regulated.

Its only disadvantage is that it discriminates and is considered arbitrary. It can be defeated in its objective if the borrower borrows and diverts the credit for some other purpose.

2. Consumer Credit Regulation: Many industrialised countries and India only have made provision for financing the purchase of consumer durables to encourage the concerned industries. Under this system, the buyer pays only a small part of the total price as *down payment* and the balance is financed by the hire-purchase companies or commercial banks or some non-banking financial institutions which undertake such transactions. Many consumer products like T.V., refrigerators, washing machines, cars, etc., are purchased by this method. Even houses are purchased under this system. In times of inflation there is a tendency for this type of finance to go up. If the central bank so desires to reduce this type of credit, it may resort to selective credit controls in the form of consumer credit regulation.

To curb an excessive rise in consumer credit, the central bank can impose the following types of restrictions:

(*a*) To reduce the overall quantum of credit flowing in this direction, bank-wise, or party-wise credit may be fixed in absolute terms or as a percentage of total credit. In such cases, commercial banks may be directed to stop such advances or reduce the quantum of credit depending on the needs of the economy.

(*b*) To raise the margins payable by the purchasers, which are also called down payments in cash by the purchasers: These are varied as a proportion of the total value of the product. When down payments are increased in proportionate terms, the required credit granted by banks will be lower. The same objective can be achieved by raising the margins to be kept by banks. Thus if the margin requirement is raised from 20 per cent to 40 per cent, the loan component of the total cost of say ₹100 would fall from ₹80 to ₹60. In some cases like shares, whose purchases are to be discouraged for controlling speculation, the margins may be as stiff as 50 per cent.

(*c*) Another method to curb consumer credit is to reduce the period of maturity of loan or repayment period. If the repayment period is lowered from, say 10 years to 5 years, many borrowers will be discouraged because of the increased liabilities involved in repayment of the credit. If, on the other hand, if it is to be encouraged, the maturity period can be raised from 10 years to 20 years.

(*d*) Under selective credit controls, the cost of credit can be raised by asking the banks to charge penal rates on consumer credit. Thus, if the rate is raised from the normal lending rate of 17 per cent to 20 per cent for consumer credit, many of the borrowers may be discouraged to resort to this type of credit. This will lower the quantum of credit flowing in this direction and reduce the excess demand in the economy.

3. Rationing of Credit: Rationing of credit is done by allocation of credit to various uses by the central planning authority. In totalitarian system like the erstwhile USSR, this method of credit control was in operation. Credit rationing may take *inter alia* two major forms: *(i)* Variable portfolio ceiling. This is the ceiling of aggregate portfolios of banks as fixed by the central bank and this sets a limit to the banks' advances and loans. *(ii)* Variable capital assets ratio: This prescribes the minimum capital to be held as a ratio to total assets, by the bank. In many countries this power to change this rate is exercised by the government or monetary authority. Recently, major developed countries like the USA and Japan have raised the capital requirements of their banks operating in the international markets. India has also followed suit in this regard in respect of foreign branches of Indian banks as well as for Indian banks and fixed the minimum capital adequacy norm as recommended by the Basel Agreement.

4. Issue of Directives: In recent years, credit control measures are issued in the form of directives to commercial banks, particularly those relating to selective controls. Thus if the central bank wishes to influence the directional flow of credit to some selected sectors like the agricultural sector, they issue directives to this effect. Similarly, many measures of credit control are implemented as directives to banks by the central bank. These may take the form of oral or written statements or appeals and warnings by the executives of the central bank to the executives of commercial banks. Some examples of this in India are the directives issued to banks for priority sector lending and lending to scheduled castes and scheduled tribes, etc.

5. Moral Suasion: Moral suasion is general persuasion and request by the central bank to the commercial banks. Many policies are implemented by the central bank with their power of friendly contacts and persuasion over banks. Sometimes, personal appeals of chief executives of the central bank will have a good psychological effect and may be implemented. In cases where there are only a few commercial banks and the contacts between the central bank and commercial banks are close, this method of credit control would work. It is generally appreciated as more democratic and as such banks comply with them. Examples of moral suasion in the case of India are found in the credit budget discussions of each bank with the central bank which will be referred to later. This instrument was commended by Chandler and is used extensively in developed countries.

6. Direct Action: This refers to direct action taken by the central bank against any bank or all banks in pursuit of its objectives of policy. Thus, the central bank may set ceilings on all discounts or charge penal rates to any bank or banks who do not follow its directives or refuse the lender of last resort facility to such recalcitrant bank. Examples of direct action in India are found in the fixation of ceiling for rediscounts for the major banks and fixation of limits for the participating banks in the consortium lending by bank as in the case of financing of cotton and jute procurement operations or of the FCI operations and charging penal rates to banks with CRR or SLR defaults. This instrument is effective no doubt but it is considered crude and cumbersome in its operations and undemocratic in nature. But it is most effective as an instrument of credit control.

Limitations of Selective Controls

Selective controls are considered by many economists as undemocratic and undesirable forms of interference in the credit system. They restrict the freedom and choice of borrowers and lenders. They are cumbersome and difficult to administer. On the other hand, they produce an immediate and direct effect on the cost and availability of credit and are dependable. Selective and qualitative effects can be brought about without affecting the economy in general.

The limitations of selective controls are as follows:

1. These restrictions can be evaded if the loans meant for one purpose can be used for other purposes by the borrowers. Thus loans taken for genuine productive purposes can be used for undesirable purposes by borrowers like hoarding of the sensitive commodities.
2. The banks can defeat the purpose of these controls by giving loans on clean basis or against some other securities not subject to selective credit controls.
3. Malpractices can be resorted to in the valuation of security or assets used for bank lending and observance of margins.
4. These controls are not applicable to non-banking financial institutions in respect of their advances for consumer durables, hire-purchase, etc., and hence their effects are limited on the real economy.

Despite the limitations in respect of their effects and cumbersome nature of these controls, they are useful as a part of the tools of monetary management. They are used in advanced countries to control credit to selected sectors like hire-purchase or shares and securities. In developing countries, they are used more extensively along with other general controls to influence the sectoral flow of credit, discourage some forms of lending and encourage others to suit the requirements of the economy.

SELECTIVE CONTROLS IN INDIA

The objective of these controls is to discourage some forms of activity while encouraging others. Examples of such controls are in respect of bank credit flowing to foodgrains, raw cotton, raw jute, oils, oilseeds, sugar, gur, khandsari, etc. Selective controls are used in India mostly in respect of agricultural commodities which are subject to speculative hoarding and wide price fluctuations.

Role of Selective Controls

These are adjuncts to the general controls and make them more effective. In economies which are less developed and financially less sophisticated as in India, the efficacy of general controls like the bank rate and open market operations is limited due to structural and institutional inadequacies and bottlenecks. In such an environment, selective controls and quantitative controls have a greater role to play as instruments of credit policy than general controls like the bank rate, interest rates and open market operations.

Objectives

In India, selective controls are used to prevent speculative hoarding of commodities of mass consumption and raw materials. They are designed to control the flow of credit to these sensitive commodities and thus control the price movements indirectly. By regulating the flow of bank credit for purchasing and holding such commodities, their prices can be influenced through the demand side. These controls are expected to correct imbalances between demand and supply in respect of commodities in short supply.

Legislative Sanction for Such Controls

Extensive powers have been given to the RBI under Sections 21, 35A and 36 of the Banking Regulation Act to control bank advances or any other matter of banking business. The RBI can give directives to banks regarding the management of the bank, its policies, and the purposes for which advances may or may not be made, the margin to be kept, quantity of advances, the rate of interest to be charged, securities to be accepted or not accepted, etc.

Framework of Such Controls

The broad framework of selective controls in India consists of the following:

(*i*) fixation of party-wise and bank-wise, quantitative ceilings of credit for each commodity. The basis may be outstandings at a point of time or the peak reached during a base year and ceilings are fixed as percentage of the base levels.

(*ii*) imposition of minimum margins for advances against each commodity.

(*iii*) fixation of minimum rates of interest.

(*iv*) prohibition of grant of credit against book debts and clean credits.

(*v*) restriction on advances against shares and debentures and quantitative ceilings on bank credit against private securities and against public sector bonds, etc.

Despite restrictions in some categories of advances, encouragement is also given to advances in backward regions, and to scheduled castes, scheduled tribes, weaker sections of the society, etc. Exemptions from selective controls are given for warehouse receipts for co-operatives, for export production and for marketing societies etc. Encouragement is also given to processing and manufacturing units but not for distribution or hoarding, under the selective credit controls.

Moral Suasion

As discussed earlier, moral suasion is also an instrument of monetary and credit policy. This refers to the use of influence and persuasion by the central bank on the member banks. Very often the top executives of the central bank can influence the executives of individual banks in their meetings on what policies to be followed and what not and impress on the banks the priorities to be followed by them.

As credit is becoming more selective and individualised, there is a greater dependence on moral suasion by the RBI, particularly since the latter started credit planning exercises in the eighties. The RBI has been holding credit budget discussions with individual banks on their credit plans and budgets and on their resource mobilisation and credit deployment plans. During these discussions, the RBI generally impresses on the individual banks their order of priorities and what it expects from the banks in respect of policies to be pursued or directional flow of credit to the various sectors and the broad order of magnitude.

Credit Budgets

As referred to earlier, the RBI discuses with the major scheduled banks their credit budgets regularly and provides credit policy guidelines for them individually.

During the credit planning and budgeting discussions, the RBI used moral suasion as an instrument of credit policy. Besides, in the seasonal credit policy statements made by the RBI twice a year, some of the guidelines are in the form of moral suasion rather than based on legal sanction. With the nationalisation of banks in 1969 and 1980, there was concentration of the banking business in about 15 banks and moral suasion has become more effective since then through the discussions that the RBI would have with the top executives of these banks. Some of the RBI guidelines regarding what banks should do or should not do are thus in the form of advices rather than legal imperatives. These advices and guidelines can be considered as examples of moral suasion in India. Some of the measures of credit control in the category of moral suasion are also given orally.

Monetary Targeting in India

A major instrument of monetary policy used by the RBI since 1986 is monetary targeting. This involves the fixing of the target growth rate of money supply, consistent with the expected growth in output and prices. Other policy tools are operated in tune with the objective of achieving this target of growth rate of money supply through proper growth of reserve money for which RBI is responsible. It tries to co-ordinate the monetary and fiscal policies, as created money or reserve money of the RBI depends on the government borrowing policy and hence the fiscal policy and reserve money are the basis for the increase in money supply in any year. This target is so fixed that it would meet the genuine needs of the economy and yet curb excessive rise in liquidity which will lead to inflation or price rise.

Thus, the control on rates of growth of money supply in relation to fluctuations in output is considered to be the proper method to influence the course of prices. The demand for money provided convenient starting point for fixing what is a desirable order of increase in money supply in the context of expected growth in real income.

Influence of Real Variables

As non-monetary factors also play an important role in influencing the price variations in India, these are also taken into account on any yearly basis while determining the tolerable limits to monetary expansion for the purpose of monetary targeting exercises which the RBI undertakes. At present, these monetary targeting exercises are done by the RBI in a flexible manner, taking into account the emerging situation and contingent factors emanating from the non-monetary sector. This is what the Chakravarthy Committee Report called "monetary targeting with a feedback, which enables changes in the targets to be made in the light of emerging trends in output and prices". (1985)

Stance of Credit Policy in India

The stance of credit policy up to 1951 was one of continuation of cheap money policy dictated by war-time reconstruction and rehabilitation of industries. The subsequent changes were necessitated by the need for planned development in the economy. The period up to 1971 was characterised by a moderate degree of inflation and the tenor of monetary policy was anti-inflationary. During this period, bank rate was changed five times upwards from 3 per cent to 6 per cent and once downwards from 6 per cent 5 per cent. During the period 1968-70, the need to stimulate the economy necessitated the stance of monetary policy to be reflationary. The bank rate was lowered and refinance conditions were liberalised. The RBI used Ledger Adjustment Facility (LAF) to make needed adjustments in the liquidity position of banks. This is a refinance in addition to OMO of the RBI and operation under type of Market Stabilisation for grooming the market for the government borrowing programme and it is a type of refinance facility.

Latest Trends in Credit Policy

The subsequent period was marked by a more active pursuit of interest rate policy. From 1971 to date the bank rate was raised four times from 5 per cent to 10 per cent and the tenor of monetary policy turned to be one of extreme caution. The control over lending and borrowing rates of banks was initiated in the sixties and minimum and maximum lending rates were fixed for various categories of lending since 1969. Deposit rate of banks were also regulated and fixed by the RBI to ensure a reasonable margin between the borrowing and lending rates of banks and to eliminate wasteful price competition among banks. Bank rate was activated again since 1996 as part of financial reforms, and it is now kept at 6% since 2003 up to date.

Frequent Use of Direct Controls

The refinance policy RBI was used frequently to influence both the cost and availability of credit to the banks. The scheme of refinance and rates charged varied from time to time but more active use of this instrument was noticed particularly in the seventies and eighties. The RBI has been operating a scheme of discretionary refinance and quantitative ceilings on refinance along with the existing framework of concessional refinance facilities for food procurement, export credit, etc.

Since 1975, there were quick and drastic changes in the monetary policy instruments due to the sharp increases in liquidity in the economy consequent on the increase in RBI credit to government. Some of the years witnessed a setback in the growth rate of real output, failure of monsoons affecting agricultural production and structural rigidities, shortages and inadequate infrastructural growth. It was in this context that active use of quantitative restrictions on credit was resorted to in respect of selected sensitive commodities (under selective credit controls) along with general quantitative ceilings and sectoral targets. More frequent use of CRR and SLR was also made during this period.

Recent Reforms

Following the recommendations of the Chakravarthy Committee, for reorganisation of interest rate structure to be in tune with the market forces a new 182-day treasury bill was started with an interest rate to be determined through auctions. The rise in interest rates on Government securities since 1981 and the restructuring of the maturity pattern of deposits of banks are also in the direction of a more flexible interest rate policy and are designed to make them more realistic and market-oriented. To bring about greater conformity between the debt management policy and monetary policy, the coupon rates on Government securities have been raised gradually since 1981 to a maximum of 11.5 per cent with a view to making interest rates in India realistic to represent the true cost of credit. Thereafter, following the financial reforms and pursuit of flexible interest rate policy, these rates as also the bank rate were brought down in stages.

The other instruments of credit policy operated during the seventies and early eighties were more quantitative in nature. The most widely used instruments are Cash Reserve Ratio and Statutory Liquidity Ratio which are both quantitative in nature and constitute the first and second line of defence respectively. The SLR is also used for setting aside the required credit allocation to the government sector in the form of banks' investment in Government securities. Quick and frequent changes were made in these two instruments during the nineties and later. Besides, incremental CRR and SLR on FCNR and NRE deposits were also imposed during this period.

Selective credit controls were another instrument very actively used during the eighties to control the flow of credit to selected commodities subject to speculative hoarding. These aim at regulating the quantum of credit flowing to these segments with a view to ensuring that bank credit is not used for speculative hoarding of these commodities. These are operated through the fixation of margins, party-wise and bank-wise, fixation of quantum and through minimum rates of interest to be charged on credit. Since 1985, there has been a rationsalisation of these controls with a view to simplifying their structure and operation.

Credit controls in India were more frequently used in the seventies and eighties due to the emergence of inflationary pressures and larger recourse to deficit financing and borrowing by the government. These controls were made an instrument in larger allocation to the government sector and rationing of credit to the private corporate sector and other segments of the economy. Certain sectors like agriculture, SSIs, small traders and transport operators, and exporters, etc., have, however, received priority treatment. Greater use is also made of direct controls and quantitative credit measures like variable reserve requirements during the latest period. During nineties, reforms in the banking and financial sector led to greater autonomy to banks and less regulation, but monetary policy was actively pursued. Interest rate policy is to make it market-oriented and flexible. From 1999 onwards, the interest rates and bank rate were lowered to promote trade and industry. Financial markets and debt markets were promoted. There was widening and deepening of the markets and deregulation and market-oriented forces were allowed to operate more freely. Foreign investment in private banks was allowed up to 49%, which was raised to 74% in 2005.

✠ ✠ ✠

COMMERCIAL BANKING

8

Introduction

In this chapter, a brief account is given of what is banking, traditional and modern functions of banks, the role of banks in the economy, deposit mobilisation and various forms of lending, etc. Then the principles of banking such as efficiency, liquidity and profitability, etc., are discussed. Recent innovations and non-banking services undertaken by banks in India are set out at the end.

In the very concept of banking, there is the principle of trust or confidence as the public keep their funds in trust with banks. This confidence along with the practices of banking gives banks the power to create credit as the cheques drawn on them constitute deposit money and these are accepted by the public in their transactions in substitution for cash or currency. Banks are monetary institutions as they have the power to create, expand or contract credit.

Definition of Bank

In the words of Sayers, a bank

"*is an institution whose debts are widely accepted in settlement of other* people's debts to each other."

In the Banking Regulation Act of 1949, banking is defined as–

"*accepting for the purpose of lending or investment of deposits of money from the public repayable on demand or otherwise and withdrawable by cheque, draft, order or otherwise.*"

The critical determinants of what a bank is are thus:

(*i*) the acceptance of deposits from the public,

(*ii*) making loans and advances and

(*iii*) in the process of the above transactions, create credit which is a part of the total money in the economy.

There are also other definitions of commercial banks by many writers. All of them convey more or less the same understanding of what is a commercial bank. It is worthwhile to quote in particular the more comprehensive definition of Findlay Shirras.

> *"A banker or bank is the person, firm or company, having a place of business where credits are opened by the deposit of scores of money or currency subject to be paid or remitted upon drafts, cheques or orders or where money is advanced as loans on stocks, bonds, bullions and bills of exchange and promissory notes are received for discount and sale."*

FUNCTIONS OF BANKS

There are various types of banks, namely, commercial banks, co-operative banks, regional rural banks, local area banks and development banks. In India, the oldest bankers were merchant bankers or trader banks. Even though banking in India is of hoary antiquity, modern banking has been started only after the entry of the East India Company into India for trading purposes. The setting up of joint-stock banks with limited liability on Western lines was a feature of the 19th century and early 20th century.

Primary or Traditional Functions

The major functions of commercial banks are:

(*i*) acceptance of deposits,

(*ii*) creation of credit,

(*iii*) lending and

(*iv*) transferring of money and other related activities like — safe custody bills discounting, foreign remittances, etc.

The banks accept deposits of various categories and make loans and investments for commercial and business activities. The banks also create credit for the purpose of lending to industrial/commercial activities, individuals and consumers as also the government and the corporate sectors.

Credit creation is, thus, an important function of banks. These created deposits are called 'secondary money' while primary deposits are those mobilised directly from the public. The deposit money, either primary or secondary, is part of the money supply in the economy. Cheques drawn on deposit money are accepted and circulated among the public. The acceptance of deposit money through cheques depends on the public confidence in banks and the creditworthiness of the banks.

Ancillary Functions

The banks render many other ancillary services such as remittance of funds or transfer of money from one place to another or from one party to another through mail, telex, telegrams and cables. The banks also provide the mechanism for clearance and collection of cheques. The banks operate as agents and trustees for managing the property affairs of their customers. They also provide safe custody for the valuables of the customers. The agency and trustee business, safe custody, etc., are all incidental to the main activity of the banks.

Secondary or Incidental Functions

Banks perform a number of functions incidental to their major activities of saving mobilisation and purveyors of credit. These functions of modern commercial banks may be set out as follows:

(*i*) Transfers of funds and remittance facilities.

(*ii*) Cheque clearances and collection of money.

(*iii*) Agency and trustee business for customers.

(*iv*) Safe custody of valuables.

(*v*) Merchant banking and underwriting business with respect to new issues of companies.

(*vi*) Provision of market intelligence, technical and financial constancy services.

(*vii*) Making portfolio management for customers and arranging the investment of funds for the corporate and non-corporate clients.

(*viii*) Financing of import-export business.

(*ix*) Issue of foreign letters of credit and doing foreign exchange business.

The last two functions have become major functions of banks in view of the importance of foreign trade.

Core Functions of Banks

As noticed above, the definition of banking itself suggests two functions of banks, namely, *(a)* acceptance of deposits of money from the public and *(b)* lending or making advances to the public or making investments in selected assets, as approved by the principles of banking which will be referred to later. These two core functions are discussed in detail below:

Acceptance of Deposits — Source of Funds

Banks accept money from the public in various forms, which constitute borrowing by banks. As these are the funds owed by banks to outsiders, they are shown as liabilities in the balance sheets of banks. The other sources of funds for banks are borrowing from the Reserve Bank of India and financial institutions, other banks and from abroad.

Individuals, households and corporate and non-corporate business units, government and other agencies keep their surplus funds with banks for reasons of safety, security and convenience. Sometimes, the public are activated to keep funds with banks for meeting any contingencies and emergencies or as a matter of precaution. Some of the inflows of deposits into the banks are governed by the motive of earning interest income on these funds.

Types of Deposits

(i) Current Accounts: If these deposits are kept in current account with banks, they can be withdrawn at any time and in any amount, but they do not bear any interest income to the account holder. These accounts are, therefore, mostly held for business transactions by companies, institutions, governments and individuals for the purpose of facilitating their receipts and payments. These funds are meant mainly for transaction purposes.

(ii) Savings Accounts: The second form of deposits kept with banks is the savings accounts. These accounts facilitate mobilisation of savings of the public, both for the purpose of facilitating their transactions and for earning on income in the form of interest. These accounts serve both transactions and precautionary purposes. There are some restrictions on their operations, such as keeping a minimum balance in these accounts, limits to the number of cheques that can be drawn or in the amounts that can be withdrawn at any one time or during a period of time. Savings deposits carry a rate of interest on their outstandings.

(iii) Fixed Deposits: The third form of keeping money with banks is fixed deposits which are also called "term deposits". A number of variants of term deposits are notice deposits, recurring deposits, etc. These deposits are for varying periods of time, from a notice period of seven days to a fixed period of one to five years. As these deposits cannot normally be withdrawn until maturity, banks can fully use these funds for their operations and these deposits carry higher rates of interest, depending on the maturity period. These deposits mostly serve as a store of value for future uses. These are also called time deposits.

Uses of Funds

As the basic purpose of commercial banking is to do the business of lending and is based on profit motive, banks do not keep idle the funds mobilised by them as deposits, but lend for various purposes and in various forms. All these constitute the assets of the banks in its balance sheet. As these funds are all public money, certain principles of prudent lending are followed by banks on their own as well as under guidelines from the monetary authority, or the central bank of the country, which in India is the Reserve Bank of India (RBI). These principles are safety, liquidity, solvency and profitability, which will be discussed later.

Cash

As a first safety valve, a certain proportion of the deposits is kept as cash in vaults with banks themselves. Generally, this proportion is 1 to 2 per cent of the total deposit funds. Besides, under the guidelines from the RBI, a minimum cash ratio, varying from 3 to 15 per cent of their deposit liabilities, is kept by banks with the RBI in the form of balances.

Liquid Assets

As a second line of defence for safety and liquidity, banks also keep a certain proportion of their deposits in the form of liquid assets to ensure that the need for liquid funds is met in the event of any contingencies. There is a statutory requirement under the Banking Regulation Act of 1949 that a minimum, varying from 25 per cent to 40 per cent of total deposit liabilities in India, is to be kept in the form of liquid assets, namely, cash, gold, treasury bills, Government securities and other approved trustee securities. This cash should be in excess of the minimum cash reserves, referred to above.

Loans and Investments

After the above requirements are met, the remaining funds are distributed in the form of loans to and investments in the various sectors of the economy. The loans and advances are mostly to the corporate sector, businessmen and individuals while investments in bonds, shares, etc., are in the securities of the government, financial institutions, corporate entities, etc. There are certain prohibited or restricted items of investment, namely, in real estate, buildings, bullion, etc., except those required for their own use and business.

Forms of Lending

Banks follow various forms of lending which are discussed below:

(i) Overdraft Facilities: Companies, firms and businessmen are given facilities of overdrafts on their current account with banks. This would mean that all debit balances in the current accounts of clients are treated as loans to them. These overdrafts are secured by pledge of goods in process or those stored in the godowns. Some clients are provided with demand draft facility which is tantamount to drawing on the bank in excess of their funds. These can be clean or on personal security or against pledge/mortgage of goods or property, or titles of property.

(ii) Cash Credit Facility: The banks permit, up to a certain limit, drawing on a borrowal account in the form of cash credit. The limits are fixed on the basis of expected cash accruals of the company and/or on the security of goods pledged to the bank, in accordance with their schedule of production or sales. As this is a provision of credit against cash accruals, this form of lending is known as cash credit.

(iii) Direct Loans or Advances: Some parties are given a fixed quantum of loan outright for the purpose of acquisition of some fixed assets or for the core part of the working capital (minimum inventories) required for the business of the company. These loans are for a fixed period with fixed terms of interest and repayment. These may also be secured by some assets of the company.

(iv) Bills Discounting and Purchase: The banks undertake to purchase or discount bills of exchange arising out of sale or business transactions for their customers. This process puts the borrower in funds for the interim period between the sale of goods and the realisation of the sale proceeds. The banks charge commission and interest on these funds against bills, up to their maturity period and/or up to the realisation of funds from the buyer. These bills may be inland bills or foreign bills. The bills for the financing of foreign trade are called foreign trade bills.

(v) Term Loans: Banks also provide term loans for varying periods of time, extending up to 7 years. Although these are long-term loans and bank funds are of short-term nature, these are permitted under prudent banking principles, as these are necessary for business concerns as a complement to the short-term working capital loans which banks normally give. These are mainly for acquisition of fixed assets or for the core part of the working capital.

Principles of Banking

Prudent banking principles are generally followed in the above transactions of lending by banks in view of the fact that their funds are all public funds. Solvency and liquidity of their funds are the basic tenets of lending by banks. A proper assessment of the creditworthiness and credit needs of the borrower is, therefore, necessary and banks follow these credit norms.

Firstly, banks lend mainly for holding inventories or stocks and for short-term, as their deposits are mostly of short and medium-term nature.

Secondly, although banks are lending term finance for the acquisition of fixed assets for medium-term up to 7 years these advances are kept to the minimum and on a sharing basis with the financial institutions such as the IFC, LIC, etc. This form of lending, already discussed earlier, is meant for the acquisition of fixed assets, expansion and modernisation of plant, etc.

Thirdly, banks ensure the security of their advances by proper mortgage of immovable or movable property even after their assessment of production schedule, for the liquidity and creditworthiness of the borrower.

Fourthly, banks avoid lending against landed property, real estate or risky or speculative ventures, with a view to keeping to the minimum the risks involved in lending.

The basic tenets or principles of banking are discussed below:

(a) Profitability and Liquidity: Each bank is motivated by the commercial consideration of profit, and maximisation of profit is the basic objective, subject to the constraint of the banking regulations imposed by the Reserve Bank of India/government and the liquidity and solvency criteria imposed by rules of prudent banking. The requirements of profitability and liquidity are the opposing claims which the banker has to balance.

The safety and solvency of bank's funds is essential as confidence of the public in banks depends on this. The solvency in turn depends on liquidity of bank's funds. Here liquidity means easy realisability of funds, convertibility of assets into cash and marketability of the investments made by the bank.

There are a number of constraints on the banker, such as the environment he faces, the customers approaching the bank and their requirements and the socio-political background in which they operate. For example, in Islamic countries where payment of interest is prohibited, banking has adjusted itself to a system of profit-sharing with borrowers in lieu of charging interest. Similarly, in communist and socialistic countries, where all banking is State-owned and State-operated, profit motive is subordinated to the basic principle of service and accounting and planning on behalf of the State. Banks in these countries have been tuned to using interest rate mechanism and profit principle only for accounting purposes. But these are the things of the past, as almost all countries are now having market-oriented economies.

(b) Solvency and Efficiency: Efficiency of a bank depends on the security of its funds, which in turn rests on the capital adequacy and its profitability. Efficiency also reflects the productivity of banking operations in the sense that the cost of operations is to be minimal for the given level of business or output of banks. This in turn depends on the productivity of labour and their efficiency, as labour is the major input in banking service.

Quick and prompt service and low cost of operations reflect the efficiency of banks which also determine their profitability. To serve as a hallmark of solvency, banks should also have adequate capital. The capital or owned funds of banks consist of paid-up capital and reserves and as observed by the Banking Commission in its Report (1972), *such capital funds are primarily meant as a reassurance to the banking public and the supervising authorities that the bank is in a position to withstand whatever strains may be placed upon it* (p. 297). These owned funds act mainly as a buffer against the risk of liquidation of the bank (because of lack of liquidity to repay depositors) and against possible losses that the bank may incur in its transactions.

(c) Costs and Returns: Profitability is to be studied in relation to costs and returns on deposits, advances and other items of balance sheet. While deposits and other forms of borrowing (other than owned funds) attract interest on them, the assets in the form of advances, investments, etc., earn a return in the form of interest received. The differences between interest received and interest paid is the spread on these items. The greater the spread, the greater is the profitability of banks. Besides, there are other services such as remittances, DD/TD, etc., rendered, safe custody, agency functions, etc., which have both a cost and a return. The difference between them is the net profit for the bank. Profitability of a bank's operations depends on a host of such factors.

ROLE OF COMMERCIAL BANKS

Banks are both manufactures of money and purveyors of money. In this context, banks play an important role in the economy. Their role can be set out under the following heads:

(1) Mobilisation of Savings: Economic development depends on the available savings and investment in the economy. By mobilisation of deposits, banks collect savings from the public which in turn are lent for investment when they purvey credit to various sectors of the economy.

(2) Facilitate Commerce and Trade: Finance is important for trade and commerce and banks provide funds for facilitating these activities in the economy.

(3) Balanced Regional Development: In tune with the policy of the government to have more balanced development of the economy, the banks do promote lending and investment in those regions or parts of the country which are less developed and thus banks promote social objectives.

(4) Provision of Finance to Backward Communities and Neglected Segments of Society: This is another important contribution of commercial and co-operative banks in India. They provide loans at concessional rates to scheduled castes/scheduled tribes and weaker sections of the society, as per the guidelines of the government.

(5) Development of Agriculture and Other Priority Sectors in the Economy: The banks give special treatment in their lending operations to some priority sectors in the economy, such as agriculture, small-scale industries (SSIs), retail trade, small borrowers, self-employed persons, etc., so as to facilitate their growth and provide productive employment in the economy. Exports are also a priority sector which banks help in various ways.

Recent Innovations in Banking in India

After nationalisation of major banks in India in 1969 and 1980, a number of socio-economic obligations have been thrust on the banks. These are:

(*i*) Minimum targeted lending to priority sectors such as agriculture, SSIs, road and water transport operators, small business, retail trade, etc.

(*ii*) Lending to weaker sections of society, scheduled castes, scheduled tribes, etc.

(*iii*) Lending under poverty alleviation and employment generation schemes.

(*iv*) Lending to hitherto neglected sections of society under various schemes, such as the 20-Point Programme, Differential Rate of Interest Scheme, etc., which are all merged as lending to the economically backward population, and weaker sections of society.

Thus, banks have been acting as instruments of socio-economic justice to help in the redistribution of income to the poorer and weaker sections of society in India. They have been undertaking innovative schemes of helping debt-ridden tenants and farmers, riot-hit victims and people affected by natural calamities, such as drought, floods, etc., The banks have also been instrumental in implementing the socio-economic policies of the government and in financing their expenditure plans, so that they bring the benefits of economic development to all classes of public in India.

Non-banking Business of Banks

After the passage of the Banking Laws Amendment Act, 1983, banks have started entering new lines of activity, which are not of banking nature. These non-banking activities are also called "non-funded business" of banks. These are briefly set out below:

(*i*) Setting up Mutual Funds, Hire Purchase Subsidiaries, etc., to undertake investment on the stock exchanges, contribute to shares and debentures of companies and to become members of the stock exchanges for trading on the markets and to undertake hire purchase business.

(*ii*) Setting up subsidiaries or holding companies to do leasing or lease finance business.

(*iii*) Providing factoring services to customers by acting as factorisation agents to take risk in the collection of funds, without recourse, from the buyer firms.

(*iv*) New instruments of trading among banks have been developed such as participation certificates, commercial paper and certificates of deposits for the purpose of mobilisation of funds by companies, banks and financial institutions. Participation certificate is a certificate of lending or share in lending through deposit of funds by one financial institution or bank with another. Certificates of deposit are also similar instruments of borrowing issued by banks to raise funds from individuals, companies and financial institutions for the purpose of promoting lending of a short-term nature up to a maximum period of one year.

The commercial paper is an instrument of borrowing by companies of standing and creditworthiness directly from the money and capital markets or the working capital purposes rather than from the banks. These can be issued to individuals, companies, financial institutions, etc.

WHAT IS UNIVERSAL BANKING?

The RBI constituted a working group under the Chairmanship of Shri S.H. Khan, the then Chairman of the IDBI in 1997 to review the role, structure and operations of Development Financial Institutions (DFIs) and commercial banks and bring about harmonisation in their roles. The Khan Working Group (KWG) had submitted its report in May 1998. The report recommended progressive move towards Universal Banking by both DFIs and commercial banks, so that in future there would be only two categories of financial intermediaries, namely, banks and non-bank financial companies. The DFIs which have not moved towards universal banking would be categorised as NBFCs. In the interim, the DFIs would be permitted to move through their own departments or through subsidiaries to move into banking.

Earlier, the Narasimham Committee II, in its report submitted in April 1998, observed that DFIs in India following the trends in European countries should convert themselves into banks and be subject to the same discipline of regulatory and prudential norms as applicable to commercial banks.

The RBI, following the recommendations of these two committees, prepared a discussion paper on universal banking, whereby the DFIs can be expanding into banking services by mergers and acquisitions for inhouse banking services or through a subsidiary within a time frame of 5 years. They should continue to provide long-term capital however to small and medium sized companies for sometime until the long-term debt market develops fully. The DFIs would have thus the freedom to become full banks with universal banking practices or continue as NBFCs, if not competent to convert themselves into banks.

The discussion paper on Universal Banking by the RBI envisaged the following architecture for the financial sector in the years to come:

(1) The international experience and domestic requirements should guide both banks and DFIs to develop into universal banking agencies, subject to RBI regulations.

(2) After a transition period of say 5 years, there should be only banks and NBFCs.

(3) During the transition period, the special role of DFIs is provision of long-term finance and to become only banks or to be restructured as NBFCs.

(4) A corporate form of organisation is recommended for mergers, acquisitions or for diversification into banking activity or to meet the evolving situations.

(5) The supervisory functions have to be delinked from the refinancing institutions like IDBI/RBI.

(6) The ownership role of IDBI should be transferred to Government of India so that RBI would focus on its regulatory role.

(7) Each DFI whether private or public has to work at its own path of transition with the RBI being available for guidance and consultation only.

(8) Various efficiency issues pertaining to each organisation have to be addressed individually by banks or DFIs and they should be encouraged to chalk out their own path of evolution within a timeframe according to their own capabilities and expertise.

Thus, the IDBI and ICICI, which were DFIs were converted into universal banks, in the latter half of nineties. These banks are following the international practices of merging banking — both for the short-term and long-term markets and integrating commercial banking with development banking.

THEORY OF BANKING
(Liquidity and Profitability)

Introduction

The concepts of liquidity and profitability are explained with reference to the balance sheet items of the bank. Liquidity and profitability are principles of sound banking. As referred to earlier, liquidity refers to nearness to cash or easy convertibility into cash, while profitability refers to the net return on the funds as reflected in the earning minus expenses per each unit of bank's funds.

CONCEPT OF LIQUIDITY

Liquidity has various facets. A bank is said to be liquid when it is able to meet all its current liabilities of demand nature. It is the ability of the banker to pay deposits on demand. The first type of liquidity is deposit liquidity which refers to the bank's ability to meet its deposit liabilities or demands for cash as they arise.

The Second type of liquidity is loan liquidity which is bank's capacity to meet all the legitimate credit requirements of its customers. The higher the deposit liquidity, the lower is the possible loan liquidity, as the bank's capacity to meet the customer's loan requirements would be reduced, the greater is the drain of cash to meet the deposit liquidity.

Deposit Liquidity

The deposit liquidity depends on the composition of deposits and the stability of these deposits. The larger the demand component of deposits, the greater is the need for deposit liquidity as the demand for conversion into cash would be larger. Similarly, the larger the instability of deposits, owing to the fluctuating nature of amounts due to the public, the greater is the need for deposit liquidity. If the need for deposit liquidity is greater, the bank has to keep more of its funds in cash or short-term assets like treasury bills, commercial paper and inter-bank loans.

Loan Liquidity

Loan liquidity depends upon the loan requirements of bank's customers. To some extent, the bank can influence this by its lending policy. If the likely rise in loan demands is expected to be higher than the likely rise in deposits, the bank has to keep more of its funds in short-term assets to meet the increase in loan demands.

The overall liquidity requirement of a bank is thus, dependent upon the nature of their deposits and loan demands. The pattern — seasonal and cyclical — of the bank's liquidity requirements would determine its asset pattern.

The excesses or shortfalls of liquidity of any one bank are corrected by lending to or borrowing from other banks and financial institutions. For the banking system as a whole, the only source of liquidity is the central bank of the country.

Measurement of Liquidity

(a) Cash-to-deposits ratio (cash reserve ratio): This is the ratio of cash with itself and balances with the RBI to total deposits. The higher this ratio, the better is the bank's ability to meet demand deposit obligations.

(b) Cash plus liquid assets to deposits ratio (liquidity ratio): This is also called the liquidity ratio, which measures the solvency of the bank. The liquid assets are the cash in excess of the required cash ratio, investments in treasury bills, Government securities and other approved trustee securities which are short-term in nature and easily marketable and shiftable to other banks and the RBI. This ratio measures the overall liquidity position of the bank and its capacity to meet current liabilities of short-term nature, as they arise.

(c) Loan to deposit ratio: This ratio is the proportion of loans to total deposits. In India, it is called the 'credit deposit ratio'. The higher this ratio, the lower is the liquidity position of the bank.

Solvency of the Bank

The concepts of solvency and liquidity go together. Any bank should not only be liquid but solvent to retain the confidence of its depositors. If the bank suffers from loss of confidence, there will be a run on the bank by its creditors and the bank would be declared insolvent if it is unable to meet all the liquidity requirements of the public. But the bank is solvent so long as its total assets are larger than total liabilities and paid-up capital and reserves are greater than zero.

The solvency of the bank would, therefore, depend on its paid-up capital and reserves which includes its profits or losses and market value of its assets. If a bank is incurring losses continuously and its asset values are falling due to capital losses incurred in the sale of its long-term assets its capital and reserve can be wiped out and it may become insolvent.

PROFITABILITY

The liquidity requirements are not the only consideration of the bank. The solvency is also important and it also depends upon its profits and reserves as seen above. Profits are also required to meet the demands of shareholders for dividends. The bank can increase its earnings by having more of loans and investments of long-term nature. These are less liquid than short-term assets like treasury bills, commercial bills, etc., but the latter are less income-earning.

Thus idle cash earns no income. Inter-bank loans, treasury bills and other short-term investments would earn some interest but lower than on loans and investments of longer maturities.

The least profitable is cash which is most liquid.

The most profitable earning asset is long-term loan which is least liquid.

Thus, liquidity and profitability criteria are inversely related and have opposing claims on the banks.

Liquidity vs. Profitability

The business of a bank is to maximise profits consistent with its maintaining a minimum level of liquidity as required for its structure of assets. Thus, the bank has to choose a portfolio of assets, satisfying the opposing claims of liquidity and profitability. Stated in simple terms a proper balance has to be struck between cash plus other liquid assets and income-earning assets so as to satisfy both the criteria of liquidity and profitability. These two principles can be diagrammatically represented as follows:

The cash income-earning assets combination which a bank has chosen is its portfolio. The maturity structure of its portfolio depends on both these criteria. The higher the maturity pattern, the higher is the income-earning capacity of the portfolio, but lower is its liquidity. A higher proportion of cash can only be held at the expense of some income-earning assets.

In the Figure 8.1, liquidity is represented on the *Y*-axis and earning capacity on the *X*-axis. At the portfolio point of *M* on the *AB* line, which is the locus of various combinations of cash and earning assets, OY_1 of cash is held as against OX_1 of earnings assets. If the cash requirement is lower, and cash held is reduced to OY_2, then the income earnings assets can be increased to OX_2 which makes the bank more profitable. Thus, the lower the cash held, the greater is the profitability and *vice versa*. The optimum portfolio point may be *Q* or any other point on the *AB* line, depending on the bank's assets and liabilities and its management policy.

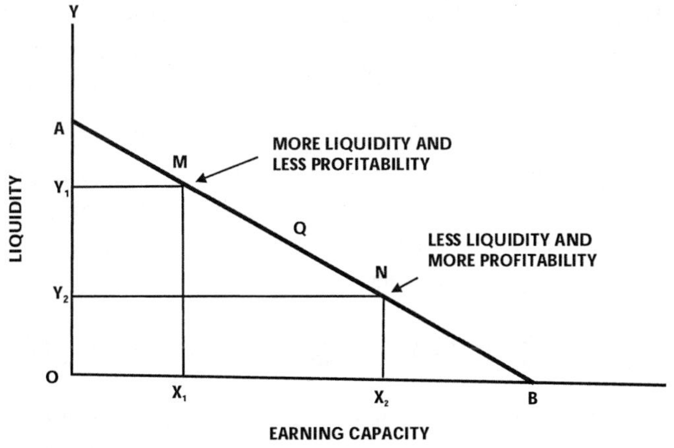

Fig. 8.1 Profitability and Liquidity of Assets

Balance Sheet Analysis

Let us analyse the balance sheet items from the point of view of liquidity and profitability of a bank. For this purpose, a simplified balance sheet giving the main items of a typical Indian bank is presented below:

BALANCE SHEET OF BANK 'A'	
Liabilities	*Assets*
1. Paid-up capital and reserves 2. Aggregate deposit liabilities 3. Borrowings from banks and RBI 4. Other liabilities	1. Cash on hand and with RBI 2. Money at call and short notice 3. Bills discounted, etc. 4. Investments in Treasury Bills, Government and other securities 5. Bank credit-loans and advances 6. Other assets, premises, etc.

Leaving aside owned funds in the form of paid-up capital and reserves, the main item on the liabilities side is aggregate deposits. Borrowings from banks, RBI, etc., constitute a small proportion of the total. For the banking system as a whole, the only major source of funds is deposits, which has been discussed in detail earlier.

Liquidity and Profitability of Each Item

Taking the assets side, the concepts of liquidity and profitability can be analysed in respect of each of the items. The qualities of assets to be looked into in this regard are the following:

(a) Asset Liquidity: The liquidity concept applied to an asset refers to its ability to be converted into cash promptly without loss of capital value. This depends on its marketability and maturity period. The greater the marketability, the easier it is to convert an asset into cash. The shorter the maturity, the smaller is the capital loss in such conversion.

(b) Risk: There are various types of risk related to loans and investments, of which, credit risk and interest risk are critical. Credit risk may arise out of the inability of the borrower to repay the loan on maturity. Interest risk reflects the possible decline in market prices of investments, resulting from a rise in interest rates. This leads to loss in capital value of assets.

Credit risk is more prominent in lending to the private corporate sector, although interest risk is also present in respect of investments in their bonds and securities. The investments in Government securities, etc., are, however, more prone to interest risk than to credit risk.

(c) Net Return or Income: Another criterion for assessing an asset is its income or earnings capacity. Net return represents gross earnings minus costs. Every earning asset has an interest income and a cost associated with the original cost of raising funds and servicing of the loans and investments or administrative expenses. The level of expected net return depends on the interest rates on these loans or securities and also on the possible capital gains or losses on the sale of securities or on realisation of funds.

(d) Tax Laws: A further variable which influences the bank's investments is the tax laws. Taxation may affect both interest income and capital gains/losses in the form of income taxes or taxation on capital gains. Any tax-free bond or security may, therefore, be more attractive to the bank earning. Thus, in India, banks prefer investments in Government securities for their high yields and tax-free public sector bonds, but not so much the taxable private sector bonds or securities.

SELECTION OF ASSET PORTFOLIO

In the selection of asset combinations by bank, the criteria of liquidity and profitability are in conflict with each other. An optimal combination is the desired portfolio for a bank which minimises the liquidity risk, given a level of profitability, or maximises earnings and profitability, given a level of liquidity risk.

Cash in Vaults

First to meet the immediate liquidity needs, banks keep a minimum proportion of deposits as cash in vaults or with the RBI. These are not income-earning but satisfy the liquidity criterion fully.

Short-term Liquid Assets

As a second line of defence, banks hold some liquid short-term assets which are income-earning and not barren like cash but earning less than loans and investments. These liquid assets are money at call and short-notice, investments in treasury bills, commercial bills and short-term Government securities. These are all of short maturity and earn some interest for the bank but more importantly, they can be converted into cash with the least cost and loss of time; so they satisfy partly the liquidity criterion and partly the profitability criterion.

Long-term Liquid Assets

The last category is long-term investments in Government securities, private corporate securities and loans and advances to business, industry, trade, etc. These are the least liquid due to their long maturity periods, possible loss of capital values, high risks involved and poor marketability in respect of some of them. But they are also high-income earning assets with the maximum returns coming from this category to the bank.

The greater the risk, the greater is the return and profitability but lower is the liquidity. Thus, in the balance sheet of a bank, the most profitable assets are bank credit, loans and advances, bills purchased and discounted, investments in Government and semi-Government securities and private corporate securities.

Assets are to be arranged in the descending order of liquidity (most liquid first and then less liquid) and in the ascending order of profitability (least profitable first and most profitable at the last) and a proper selection of portfolio is to be made.

CREDIT CREATION BY BANKS

We will discuss, in this part, the most important function of banks, namely, credit creation. The concept of credit creation, the role of reserve base in the process and mechanics of credit creation are described, followed by an explanation of the multiple creation of credit by the banking system as a whole.

Banks — Purveyors of Credit

The banks are monetary institutions in the sense that they can create, expand or contract money in the form of credit. As observed by Sayers, "Banks are not merely purveyors of money but also in an important sense, manufacturers of money".

Credit creation is possible because of the confidence that the public have in banks and in their creditworthiness. If cheques on banks are accepted in lieu of cash and are circulated freely, these serve as money. The cheques on bank deposits are bank's I.O.Us (I owe you). It is a liability of the bank to the public and a promise to pay. As the public are willing to accept and deal in these I.O.Us of banks or cheques drawn on them, these deposits of banks serve as money.

Credit creation is possible due to the confidence of the public in banks and in their creditworthiness. If cheques on banks are accepted in lieu of cash and are circulated freely, these serve as money. The cheques on bank deposits or their payments are bank's I.O.Us (I owe you). It is a liability of the bank to the public and promise to pay. As the public are willing to accept and deal in these I.O.Us of banks or cheques drawn on them, these deposits of banks serve as money. Cheques are to be discussed with their checks and balances. They are next to cash for the purpose of liquidity, but as good as money as long as they are accepted by public in lieu of cash. This is true in developed countries, where most payments and receipts are in cheque form.

Credit cards and plastic money is a replacement or equivalent to credit or overdrafts of the issuing bank. This is also equivalent to credit creation.

CONDITIONS FOR CREDIT CREATION

Bank's ability to create credit, therefore, depends on the following conditions:

(*a*) Public should be willing to accept and deal in cheques or deposit money and there is a demand for credit from the public.

(*b*) Public demand for cash for their requirements should remain stable or constant.

(*c*) There should be availability of excess reserves with banks, under the reserve ratio system in which they operate.

(*d*) The banks should be willing to lend all the excess reserves with them motivated by commercial and profit considerations.

While (*a*) and (*b*) depend on the habits of the public which are relatively stable, (*c*) and (*d*) relate to the monetary and banking policy and depend on the RBI and banks. Given the legal reserve system, when the banker lends his excess reserves or invests them in assets, he creates deposits which constitute money or created credit.

Primary and Derivative Deposits

Banks have two types of deposits, namely,

(*i*) primary deposits and

(*ii*) secondary deposits, also called derivative deposits.

Primary deposits arise from the placement of savings of the public with the banks in the form of savings accounts, current accounts, fixed deposits, etc. These funds are used by banks for their activities of lending and investment. But they also create deposits in the process of performing their functions of making advances. Suppose Bank A makes an advance in the form of overdraft or cash credit, a current account is created which constitutes the derivative deposit. These overdraft accounts, cash credit and advance accounts are forms of creating credit and constitute the secondary deposits or derivative deposits.

Concept of Credit Creation

Banks create deposit money when they sanction a loan or make an investment. Thus, loans create deposits, on which borrowers can draw cheques. Thus, if A is given a loan of ₹ 1,000 by Bank B, this is done by Bank B through a cheque or draft on itself for ₹ 1,000 or an account is opened in the name of A with Bank B and ₹ 1,000 is credited to this account. If a cheque or draft for ₹ 1,000 is given, the borrower A keeps it with Bank B or any other bank and the money is still with the banking system as a whole, until this deposit money is converted into currency or cash.

Besides, a loan is given against some assets or security. These assets are wealth in liquid form. As such banks create money against a potential or existing wealth or assets and not out of nothing.

Deposit Money

The deposit money which the banks create is in the form of credit or loan extended by them. These deposits are called "derivative" or "secondary" deposits, as compared with primary deposits, which arise when a saver keeps his surplus cash with the banks.

In the case of primary deposits, the savings of the public mobilised by banks and their role is passive. But in the case of derivative deposits, or deposit money the bank's role is active. This deposit is created by the bank when it has sanctioned a loan to the customer. The money is credited to the customer's account. The customer has not deposited his savings into it. This is created by the action of the bank in granting him a loan.

These created deposits are claims against the bank and cheques can be drawn on them and hence, forms part of the total deposit money. It is also not possible to distinguish derivative deposits from primary deposits in actual practice and hence both serve as money.

Role of Reserves

The role of reserves in credit creation should also be explained here. The reserves or reserve base, as is often called by the central bank, consist of cash with the banks plus balances kept with the central bank as part of the credit control policy. These reserves constitute the basis for creation of credit by banks.

In banking practice, it is found that out of ₹100 created deposits, only a proportion of it, say, 10 per cent, is being demanded in cash by the public. The banks therefore keep only ₹10 as cash for ₹100 of credit extended by them with which they can meet the cash requirements of the public.

Legal Reserve Requirement (Cash Reserve Ratio)

In some countries, there is a legal reserve requirement of, say, 5 per cent or 10 per cent as the case may be, that the banks have to keep with themselves or with the central bank of the country. It is only the central bank which can create cash or reserve base and the banks operate on the required reserve ratio as laid down by the central bank. The cash reserve ratio is the ratio of reserves (cash with the banks and balances with the central bank) to the deposits which the banks have to maintain in the interest of safety and liquidity of bank funds.

Let us assume that the central bank has laid down a reserve ratio of 10 per cent and ₹100 crore (cash) are created by the central bank, all of which are kept by the public with the commercial banks. Then the balance sheet of all commercial banks taken together shows the following changes. The other items of balance sheet do not change and hence are not shown here.

Liabilities	₹	*Assets*	₹
Deposits	+ 1,000 crore	Cash reserves Loans and investments	+ 100 crore + 900 crore
	Total ₹ 1,000 crore		Total ₹ 1,000 crore

(Deposits of ₹1,000 crore above consist of primary deposit of ₹100 crore and the derivative deposits of ₹900 crore resulting from loans given and investments made.)

For ₹10 of primary deposits or the additional reserves, ₹90 of additional deposits can be sustained with a reserve ratio of 10 per cent. The total deposit resulting from the initial cash deposit of ₹100 crore is ₹1,000 crore. How this is possible is explained below:

CREDIT CREATION EXPLAINED

Each bank lends all its resources based on the prudent principles of banking, *viz.*, solvency, profitability, etc. Thus, Bank A has made a loan of ₹90 to a party on the basis of some deposits of ₹10 from the public. The consequent cheques in the balance sheet of Bank A, on the basis of *ceteris paribus* principle, can be shown as follows:

CHANGES IN BALANCE SHEET OF BANK A			
Liabilities		*Assets*	
Deposits	+ ₹ 100	Cash	+ ₹ 10
		Loan	+ ₹ 90
	Total ₹ 100		Total ₹ 100

The deposits of public are liabilities of the bank while its loans to the public are its assets. If the deposits increase by ₹100, the loans have also risen by ₹100 and money with the public has increased to that extent. As the balance sheet has to balance between assets and liabilities, the contra entries are passed. When the loan is repaid, the assets are reduced and bank's I.O.Us are lower and money is reduced. What happens is that when the loan is repaid, the derivative deposit of ₹90 which was created by the bank while giving the loan gets automatically cancelled.

Bank's Investment

The bank can increase the supply of money through credit creation. It creates a deposit in its book when it purchases securities by creating the seller's account or advances a loan by giving an overdraft. In these cases, the banker shows an increase in deposits without a corresponding inflow of cash. This deposit resulting from lending transactions or buying of securities is money created by banks. Thus, every loan creates a corresponding deposit. In the case of investment in Government securities, when the seller's account with Bank A is credited and no cash is withdrawn, the transaction can be represented in the balance sheet of Bank A as follows:

CHANGES IN BALANCE SHEET OF BANK A			
Liabilities		*Assets*	
Deposits	+ ₹ 100	Cash	+ T 10
		Investment	+ ₹ 90
	Total ₹ 100		Total ₹ 100

In this case, there is an increase in deposits and hence in money due to creation of credit by the bank. What is true of purchase of securities is true of the acquisition of any asset by the bank as the corresponding liabilities have to increase. These liabilities of banks are money in the hands of the public to the extent that can draw cheques on the bank.

Bank's Profit Motive

If there is any chance, banks would increase their assets which are income-earning and these would lead to an increase in the quantity of money. The larger the investment in assets, the larger is their earnings and larger their profits. But the increase in assets would also lead to a rise in costs and risks either through the needed borrowing or due to the administrative and incidental expenses. The banks make their net profit by the difference between the average rate of interest they pay on their liabilities (*i.e.*, on primary deposits) and the average rate of return they earn on their assets, after providing for their incidental and administrative expenses.

Limits of Profitability

Although profitability criteria would induce the banker to create credit to the maximum extent possible, his actual capacity is limited by various regulations of the government and the central bank with regard to lending and investment referred to earlier. More importantly, banks will be restrained in credit creation for the fear of risk of conversion of credit into cash by the public. The bank has to keep a minimum cash (called the Cash Reserve Ratio) with itself to meet the demand for cash by the public at any time. If these needs are not met, there will be a run on the bank for conversion of all deposits into cash and the bank will become insolvent.

As a second line of defence, banks keep some funds in near liquid assets such as treasury bills, call money with other banks or Government securities, etc. The cash is the most liquid but it is barren as it is not interest bearing. The near liquid assets are earning some interest but their earnings are lower than on loans and investments. Thus, the banker has to sacrifice some high-earning assets and higher profitability for low earning assets in the interests of liquidity and solvency.

MULTIPLE CREATION OF CREDIT

Although each bank can lend only the funds it has got, multiple creation of additional credit is possible if we take the banking system as a whole. This can be explained under the following assumptions:

Firstly, banks should be prepared to lend on the basis of required reserves to the full extent of their excess reserves.

Secondly, the public should be willing to leave their funds with the banking system rather than hoard the currency and accept the cheques in settlement of debts rather than demand cash from banks.

These conditions presuppose that banks are solvent and creditworthy and the public have confidence in the bank's ability to pay cash when demanded.

The credit system in most countries is based on a reserve base. The principle involved in banking is that confidence is the basis of credit creation and that only a small proportion of bank's I.O.Us (i.e., derivative deposits) would be converted into cash, while the bulk of the money would be kept in the form of deposit money with banks. That small proportion of bank's liabilities which would be kept in the form of cash (currency and coin issued by the government or the monetary authority is called the reserve base, which has been explained earlier.)

Mechanics of Multiple Creation

Multiple creation of credit can be explained as follows:

Let us take all the banks, A to Z. Let Bank A get additional reserves in the form of primary deposit in cash of ₹ 1,000 from any public member, who wants to keep his cash deposit with Bank A. Then the balance sheet of Bank A would show the following changes on the assumption that the banks keep a cash reserve ratio of 10 per cent of total deposits existing.

BANK A — BALANCE SHEET CHANGES			
Liabilities		*Assets*	
Deposits	+ ₹ 1,000	Reserves	+ ₹ 100
		Loans and Investments	+ ₹ 900

Out of the additional reserves inducted into the banking system, Bank A has kept ₹ 100 as reserves and lent ₹ 900 to the public. As the cash reserve ratio is assumed at 10%, for every additional deposit of ₹ 1,000 with a bank, ₹ 100 are immobilised as reserves and ₹ 900 are lent out on the assumption that there is continued demand for credit.

Out of ₹ 900 lent out by Bank A to the borrower, let us assume that the whole amount is deposited in Bank B. This becomes a primary deposit for Bank B. Then following the above argument, ₹ 90 (10% of the additional deposit) will be kept as reserves and the rest, *viz.*, ₹ 810 will be advanced by Bank B. The balance sheet of Bank B will show the following changes:

BANK B — BALANCE SHEET CHANGES			
Liabilities		*Assets*	
Deposits	+ ₹ 900	Reserves Loans and Investments	+ ₹ 90 + ₹810

The additional credit of ₹810 from Bank B will be kept with say Bank C. A similar expansion of credit takes place by Bank C to the extent of ₹729 (90% of ₹810). This system of credit expansion takes place in all the banks, whenever their deposits keep on rising. This leads to a possible expansion of credit by the whole banking system by a multiple of the original deposit over a period of time. Thus, taking the credit expansion in various rounds the total expansion will be a multiple of the original expansion. If the reserve ratio is 10 per cent, then the multiplier is 10 under the above assumption and the total deposits will be ₹10,000. If the primary deposit is ₹1,000 the created deposits are ₹9,000 as explained below:

In the table below, the additional deposits and additional loans created in the various rounds are shown and multiple creation of credit is explained.

Table 8.1 PROCESS OF MULTIPLE EXPANSION OF CREDIT

(Assumption: Reserve requirement 10%)

Round of Credit Creation from Bank to Bank	*Initial Cash Deposit*	*Cash reserve Maintained 10%*	*Loans/Investments in (₹)*
1st Round (Bank A)	1,000.00	100.00	900.00
2nd Round (Bank B)	900.00	90.00	810.00
3rd Round (Bank C)	810.00	81.00	729.00
4th Round (Bank D)	729.00	72.90	656.10
5th Round (Bank E) and so on	—	—	—
Total Deposits	10,000.00	1,000.00	9,000.00

$$\text{Total Deposits} = 1{,}000\ [1 + (9/10)^1 + (9/10)^2 + (9/10)^3 + (9/10)^4 \ldots.]$$

$$= 1{,}000\ (1/1\text{-}9/10) = 1{,}000\ (1/1/10) = 1{,}000 \times 10 = 10{,}000$$

$$\text{Multiplier} = \frac{\text{Total additional deposits}}{\text{Original additional deposits}} = \frac{10{,}000}{1{,}000} = 10$$

The multiplier can be represented by a formula as follows:

$$\Delta D = \Delta R\ [1/1-(1-r)] = \Delta R\ [1/r]$$

where ΔD is change in deposit money, ΔR is the increase in reserves and r is the reserve ratio. Then, the multiplication factor is $1/r$. If r is 10 per cent, then $1/r = 1/10 \times 100 = 10$ which is the multiplier.

Assumptions

(1) Implicit in the above analysis is the assumption that there is no leakage of funds from the banking system into cash or hoarding outside the banking system.

(2) Besides, it is also assumed that the public are willing to borrow from the banks and the demand for bank credit exists.

(3) The banks in turn are willing to lend to the full extent of excess reserves and do not keep any reserve unutilised. As the banks are motivated by profit and commercial considerations, they generally lend to full extent of their excess reserves. But in times of depression or sluggish business conditions, the demand for credit may fall and banks may have excess reserves which they use for less profitable purposes as in investments in treasury bills or Government securities.

(4) It is assumed that the banks maintain a certain cash reserve ratio (CRR), *e.g.,* 10 per cent as in the above example. This assumption shows that the process of credit expansion is not unlimited. It is limited by CRR.

(5) It is also assumed that the central bank's credit control policy is given and stable.

Table 8.2 **MULTIPLE EXPANSION OF CREDIT IN INDIA**
(How much money is created by commercial banks in India)) outstandings (` crore)

Year at end March	*Cash with banks and bankers' deposits with RBI, resulting from primary deposits*	*Total demand and time deposits resulting after the multiple expansion of credit process*	*Additional money including that created by banks*
1980 81	5,007	38,335	33,328
1986-87	15,555	1,02,724	87,169
1996-97	53,195	5,22,995	4,69,800
2003-04	1,13,246	15,75,143	14,61,897
2006-07	1,96,330	30,24,606	28,28,276
2009-10	3,65,812	47,52,456	43,86,644
2012-13	3,75,174	74,29,532	70,54,358

The above table shows that the commercial banks in India create additional deposits through their lending operations and buying of securities and other assets.

Table 8.3 shows the details of credit expansion of scheduled banks in India in terms of outstandings. The data are classified into various types of loans, inland, and foreign bills purchased and discounted by banks which are different methods of extending credit by banks to the public.

Table 8.3 **CREDIT BY SCHEDULED/COMMERCIAL BANKS IN INDIA**
Amounts Outstanding (` crore)

Year	*Loans cash credits overdrafts*	*Inland bills*	*Foreign bills*	*Total*
1985-86	51,032	3,807	1,228	56,067
1986-87	57,978	3,752	1,578	63,308
1987-88	69,534	4,068	1,934	75,536
1990-91	1,05,982	5,711	4,609	1,16,302
2003-04	6,80,740	58,813		7,39,553
2006-07	19,17,260	48,341	40,730	20,06,331
		89,071		
2009-10	33,07,469	1,89,585		34,97,054
2013-14	59,94,098		4,39,090	59,94,696

Controversy on Bank's Credit Creation

There is a controversy on whether banks can create credit or not. It is said that the banks can lend no more than what they borrow (i.e., their deposits) as they are strictly limited in their operations by the amount which the depositors think fit to leave with them. This would imply that no credit can be created by banks on their own initiative but if the depositors prefer to leave all their cash with banks, then the latter may create credit. Thus, the banks depend on the depositors for the initiative and willingness to leave cash with them.

Since each bank can lend only the resources it has got, it is true to say that any single bank by itself cannot create credit. But if all banks are taken together and if the amounts withdrawn from one bank are kept in another bank and the public habits are such that they do not prefer to hold cash much in excess of the minimum and most of the transactions are put through the banks then the banks can and do create credit. In fact, the controversy between Dr. Walter Leaf and Dr. Hartly Withers is about the process of initiating credit creation — whether by depositors or banks. It will be more realistic to say that the co-operation of both the banks and the public is required for credit creation.

MONEY IS NOT CREATED OUT OF THIN AIR — CROWTHER'S VIEW

Credit is not created out of thin air. Banks are not magicians. Deposits are the basis of loans, advances and investments of banks. The primary deposits are used as backing for extending credit by the commercial banking system, but no individual bank alone can create credit by a multiple. When any bank lends, a new deposit is created. But when obtaining credit, the customer has to keep with the bank some assets as security. These assets are wealth in less liquid form. Thus, banks convert wealth (less liquid assets) into the most liquid asset (money) in the form of loans and advances.

As banks extend money against wealth in the form of assets, it is aptly observed by Crowther that the bank "does not create money out of thin air, it transmutes other forms of wealth into money".

Even where personal loans are given without any tangible security, the personal worth of the borrower in the market is an intangible asset which is converted into loans, *i.e.,* bank deposits. Thus, when banks create money, what they do is simply convert less liquid assets into the most liquid one, that is money.

LIMITATIONS OF CREDIT CREATION

The banks do not have unlimited power to create credit. Their power is limited by certain factors referred to below:

(1) Liquidity Preference of the Public: The availability of excess cash reserves with banks and the public's willingness to keep their money with banks without withdrawing as cash would facilitate the creation of credit. If the liquidity preference of public is very high and the proportion of cash to total money supply is also high, then the bank's ability to create credit will be limited.

(2) Cash Reserves Ratio: The cash reserve ratio which is the ratio of cash reserves kept by banks to total deposit liabilities will also limit credit creation. If this ratio as required by law or by the monetary authorities is high, the ability to create credit will be low as a larger proportion of cash has to be kept for a given amount of deposits which reduces their lending ability.

(3) Availability of Securities: Another factor which limits their credit creation is the availability of borrowers with productive schemes or creditworthy securities so that banks can lend against them. In other words there should be borrowers who are eligible or creditworthy to borrow from the banking system.

(4) The Central Bank's Credit Control: Most important limitation to credit creation comes from the central bank. Thus, the central bank can increase or decrease the cash reserve ratio which decreases or increases the power of credit creation. The power of the central bank to create cash and pump in more or less of it would also influence the credit creation. Besides, the overall tenor of the credit policy in the form of interest rates, open market operations, etc., would also affect the extent of credit creation by banks.

(5) Leakages or Withdrawals of Deposits in Cash: There may be leakages in the credit creation process such as cash withdrawal and hoarding by the public or the practice of keeping excess reserves with banks or idle cash balances with the public, etc.

All the above factors influence the extent of credit creation by banks and the actual credit created by banks at any time is the result of a host of such factors.

MEASURES OF FINANCIAL SERVICES (BANKS)

The services sector in India contributes more than half of the GDP of the country, as per the C.S.O. estimate for the latest years based on constant prices. This contribution may be expected to grow in years to come. In view of this critical role of services, it becomes necessary to prepare indices of the value added from the various segments of financial sector, in particular as in the case of banks, NBFCs, Finance Corporations, etc. The financial services in the form of intermediation constitutes about 16% of the value added from the total services sector. The growth and changes in its composition have to be measured to assess the impact of the reforms, for which there should be some measures of their output or sales and costs.

Limitations of the Data

There are many limitations in compilation of any measure. Many financial services are jointly produced and prices and costs for them are not separately allocatable. Some financial services, for example, cheque collection of S.B. accounts holders appears to be free in nature. Some services as those of Merchant bankers, lead managers, etc., are clubbed together and charged in lump sum. Many bankers include charges, in the interest rates they charge for loans, advances, discounts, etc., which means that there are some implicit charges and some explicit charges. The examples of implicit charging is in loan intermediation, which is the major source of profit of commercial and cooperative banks.

The examples of explicit charging is in provision various auxiliary services by banks in the form of investment advice, tax consultancy and instalment payments, currency exchange, etc. The output of the former is measured by the formula of interest payments minus interest received or the spread between the return on funds and cost of funds. The latter, namely, explicit services are charged in the form of fees, commissions, discounts, etc., as in the case of sale of DD, P.O., Discounts and Bills Receivables, bills for collection, cheque forms issued, collection of outstation cheques, etc.

The System of National Accounts (SNA), 1993 recommended the use of financial intermediation services, indirectly measured (FISIM). The SNA has defined the FISIM "as the total property income receivable by financial intermediaries minus their total interest payable, excluding the value of any property income receivable from the investment of their own funds, as such income does not arise from financial intermediation".

Of the total services sector, financial sector contributes about 17.4% of GDP in terms of value. While service sector has been growing at a rate of 9.2%, financial sector is also growing at around the same rate of 9.9% in the year 2010-11.

Thus their total output is equal to FISIM plus the value of services for which an explicit charge is made by banks and Financial institutions. Again the components of FISIM are: (*i*) Intermediate consumption by enterprises (*ii*) Final consumption by households and (*iii*) Exports to non-residents. Certain parts of interest payments have to be allocated as payment for services. Notionally the benchmark for calculating the above excess is the risk free rate or internal rate of return. The allocation of interest payments for loans, advances, etc., and that for services implicit will be based on the excess of actual rates of interest and the reference rate such as risk-free rate or T.B. Rate or the Bank Rate of RBI. The data on the following items are to be compiled for the purpose:

(*a*) Charges on various services of banks separately, compiled from their basic accounts.

(*b*) Fees for auxiliary services like portfolio management, consultancy, tax payments, etc.

(*c*) Total intermediary charges to be decomposed into those for capital borrowed and those for services.

(*d*) Calculation of turnover of each of the sub-sectors of the services sector along with the cost per unit (account or voucher) and price relatives weighted by the turnover is needed per each of the units in the services sector.

(*e*) The quantity relatives, cost relatives and turnover weights are to be calculated for current savings and term deposit accounts separately.

(*f*) Similar data on credit items such as those granted to Industry, Trade SSI, Agriculture, Consumption or personal loans, etc., have to be compiled and tabulated for the above purpose of arriving at the quantity.

(*g*) Similar data as above are to be compiled for other services, rendered by banks.

Measures Adopted by National Accounts

The measurement of national output of the banking services is difficult due to lack of specific input output relationship and overlapping inputs into a given output and multiplicity of products from a given input mix. These are both implicit and explicit services, rendered to a wide varieties of customers, depositors, creditors, debtors, loanees and a host of other categories. In some cases, services are rendered at no cost or subsided costs and in other cases the fees or charges are higher than the estimated costs. Thus keeping a large number of small accounts is burdensome in costs for the entries to be passed and vouchers to be entered and cheques cleared, etc. A small number of large accounts, on the other hand, may earn a handsome net gain to the banker. This net gain or profit is measured by the deferential in interest received on loans and advances and interest paid to depositors. These costs explicit or implicit vary from bank to bank and suffer from computational difficulties and subjectivity. They are also relative to time and place.

The system of National Accounts has therefore followed the indirect method of measurement. Certain parts of Interest Payment are allocatable to services rather than the capital lent. There is thus need for reclassification of the receipts as well as payments under heads of (*i*) Factor payments and (*ii*) Service charges. Flexibility and discretion in allocation under the above heads are also necessary. A reference rate like that of bank rate or notional transfer rate is adopted for calculation of excess over the interest component.

Costing in Banks

The costing of various services in banks was conducted at the instance of IBA and RBI. Banks are urged by some researchers to use the average number of deposit and loan accounts serviced per month per employee as a measure of productivity. On the other hand, some banks have adopted the measure of financial services sold by a bank as represented by the money balances of various products.

Due to lack of precise measures of costs and prices of banking services, some proxies like vouchers passed, or accounts maintained or balances kept in accounts, etc., are used. Assuming no change in labour productivity in the banking sector, outputs of services by banks are measured by some researchers by extrapolating benchmark value of services by the value and quality of services per person employed. Some others used the same method by taking the value and quantity per single unit of deposits of ₹ 100 or so. While the first is factor related to labour, the latter is factor related to capital employed in the bank. In the case of the latter, the value of activity is measured by taking the ratio of each of the activities as proportion to the aggregate deposits. In the literature on the subject three different approaches are discernible: (1) Asset approach, (2) value added approach and (3) user cost approach.

Asset Approach

In the asset approach, the activities to be measured will be taken as financial outputs such as credit loans, bill discounting, investments, etc., whereas liabilities are the financial inputs. As the banks buy and sell funds, the borrowing of funds is input while lending of funds is output. Asset approach concentrates on the use of funds which are outputs of the banks. This is similar to intermediation approach which is more generally accepted or the services approach used in the National Accounts literature.

Value Added Approach

This is frequently used as a measure of labour productivity in banking sector, in that it takes into account all output characteristics in both assets and labilities sides. Under this approach, any banking service or activity, that absorbs sometime and labour or real resources are used is considered as output. Others are inputs or intermediate products in the process.

The categories which have substantial value added, as judged by the use of an external source, be it labour, capital or any other input and the cost involved in such services are considered as outputs. The example of outputs are number loan and deposit accounts or amounts or balances involved in monetary terms, number of vouchers passed, receipts and withdrawals in different accounts or any other activity indicators or transaction measures. Here each of these transactions or activities is weighted by the costs of making the transaction or activity, to arrive at the index — real or nominal of the bank value added output, of the banks.

The costs are difficult to calculate due to difficulties of segregation of inputs as well as outputs which are clubbed together. The prices are implicit in the interest received or fees charged. The use of weights through costs is also a problem in this approach. In the present day computerised operations in banks, the labour measure of product or output per labour loses much of the significance and this approach becomes less attractive to that extent.

User Cost of Financial Products

Hanlock, Fixler and a number of other researchers have advocated this approach as appropriate to banking services. In this approach, each financial product is assigned a category of either input or output, depending on the role of the product in the bank's own operations. A product is a financial output, when its economic return is positive and as a financial input when its economic return is negative. The determining factor is the relationship between the holding revenue or cost and the opportunity cost of money. The sign of the product user cost determines the status of the financial product, whether it is output or input. If user cost for the bank is negative then it means that it receives a net return and it is a financial output. If on the other hand, if the user cost is positive, then it is a financial input. This is the basis of input and output classification, on both the assets and liabilities sides. Thus deposit accounts can be both an input and output, depending on whether it adds to the costs or to revenue on a net basis. Similar is the case with the loan account or bill discounts or any other activity of the bank.

Measures of Prices and Output by Banks

The services of banks relate to the following three categories: (1) depositors (2) debtors or borrowers from banks and (3) customers, other than the above two categories (others). In respect of all these categories, the costing is difficult, as there is no acceptable measure for real rate of interest and nominal rate of interest. Therefore pricing is a relative term and so is the problem of defining the output of the banking sector. In the present day of banking scenario in India, with some activities being computerised, while still others are handled by physical labour, it is difficult to disaggregate the data on cost per unit of service and pricing of them. Similarly, the return for capital advanced and the return for the other services included in making advances cannot be disaggregated easily.

In the above scenario, we measure the quantity of intermediation services as the total number of accounts of different types. The weights to be attached to these data are to be based on the cost of that instrument. Alternatively, we can use the number of vouchers produced as the quantity and cost of it compiled. Weights can also be based on turnover of accounts, namely, the number of debits and credits passed or the total number of entries in the accounts.

Index Computation

The present data in the banking sector are not amenable to a classification on a clear-cut basis of the price and output data for the purpose of calculation of an index for either price or output. There is need for additional data reclassification of the data and homogenisation of the data, across the country uniformly and for the whole banking sector.

The OECD countries and other developed countries are developing reliable indicators for the service sector on a monthly basis as also on an yearly basis. In most cases, the recommended indicator is the turnover of the different sub-sectors within the services sector and in particular for the banking sector. In India such Indices on prices and output of the banking sector can be worked out and presented by such Apex organisation as RBI, or IBA or NIBM. At present such data as required can be derived from the books of banks and collected on a regular basis. As most of these data are on an annual basis, an attempt can be made for the presentation of annual series of such indices, for the time being. At present, no such indices are available in published data.

BANKS AS INTERMEDIARIES

9

Banks are the oldest and most important intermediaries in the financial system. They are short-term institutions, borrowing from the public up to 3 to 5 years and lending to govt. private and corporate sectors for short-term working capital or current expenditure and for term loans for project finance.

Their sources of funds and their uses of funds are as shown below:

Current accounts are deposits from corporates and business executives with facility for overdrafts if necessary. They do not carry any interest. Savings accounts are for individuals, HUFs partnerships, etc., in the household sector, and do not carry any overdraft facility but carry a modest interest rate of say 4%. Both accounts are eligible for credit card facility and 24 hour banking and electronic mode of transfers, banking operations and customer services. Term deposits are for maturities from 15 days to 5 years at present.

Sources	*Uses*
Deposit from public	Cash credit
Current deposits	Loans and Advances
Savings deposits	Overdrafts
Fixed deposits	Term loans
Borrowings from banks	Packing credit
Inter-bank deposits	(for domestic and foreign business)
Inter-bank borrowings	Bills purchased and
Borrowings from F.I.s	Discounted
Borrowings from RBI	Inland
Borrowing from abroad	Foreign
(Nostro Accounts)	Investment in
Paid-up Capital/Reserves	Approved securities
	Other corporate shares and securities
	Fixed Assets.

Banking Structure in India

Reserve Bank is the Apex Bank and the Central Banking Authority in India. It is the regulator of all banks and non-bank finance companies and controls all their activities through the credit and monetary policy. Of the banking sector, the most important segment is Scheduled Commercial Banks who are included in the Second Schedule to the Banking Regulation Act. This is done by some criteria like a minimum net worth and some minimum balances to be kept with RBI, in addition to conducting affairs of the bank, not detrimental to the interests of depositors.

Scheduled banks include both commercial and co-operative banks and both are entitled to some facilities with the RBI. Besides, scheduled commercial banks include both Indian and foreign banks and Indian scheduled banks include the following categories. Some local area banks were also licensed to operate in the specified areas during 1999-2000. There are now only a few of them stilll operating (4).

- (1) Public Sector Banks
  - SBI and Subsidiaries
  - Nationalised Banks
  - Regional Rural Banks
- (2) Private Sector Banks
  - Old Pvt. Sector Banks
  - New Pvt. Sector Banks
- (3) Foreign Sector Banks
  - Offices
  - Branches

As regards the co-operative banks, there are 93,550 primary agricultural co-operative banks (PCBs), of which only 31 are scheduled PCBs; there are 366 central co-operative banks as at end June 2012. There are 1,606 co-operative urban banks and 51 scheduled State co-operative banks as at end 2013. There are 82 PCBs as at end March 2007.

Table 9.1 **BRANCH NETWORK — COMMERCIAL BANKS**

	1990-94	*1996-97*	*2000-01*	*2004-05*	*2006-07*	*2010-11*
Metropolitan / Port Towns	6113	7,587	8,180	8,934	11,826	14,742
	(10.2)	(11.9)	(12.5)	(13.3)	(16.6)	(21.3)
Urban Areas	7613	9,298	10,045	10,937	12,792	16,007
	(12.7)	(14.6)	(15.4)	(16.3)	(17.9)	(23.2)
Semi-urban Areas	11,265	13,641	14,328	15,035	16,214	17,638
	(18.7)	(21.5)	(21.9)	(22.4)	(22.6)	(25.5)
Rural areas	35,113	33,008	32,773	32,212	30,639	20,773
	(58.4)	(52.0)	(50.2)	(48.0)	(42.9)	(30.0)
Total	60,101	63,534	65,326	67,118	71,471	69,160

Note: Figures in brackets are percentages to total.

Rural areas still predominate in the branch network, despite the closing of some loss making branches more recently between 1990-91 to 2006-07. With the freedom given, to banks to open or close branches and dispensation with the branch licensing by RBI, many banks have reshuffled the locations of many branches to improve their viability and profitability. This pattern of branch network is not found in the case of foreign banks which confined mostly to Metropolitan/Port towns and many private sector banks particularly those newly opened after the reforms were started in 1992.

AS ON LAST FRIDAY OF MARCH 2006 OWNERSHIP OF DEPOSITS

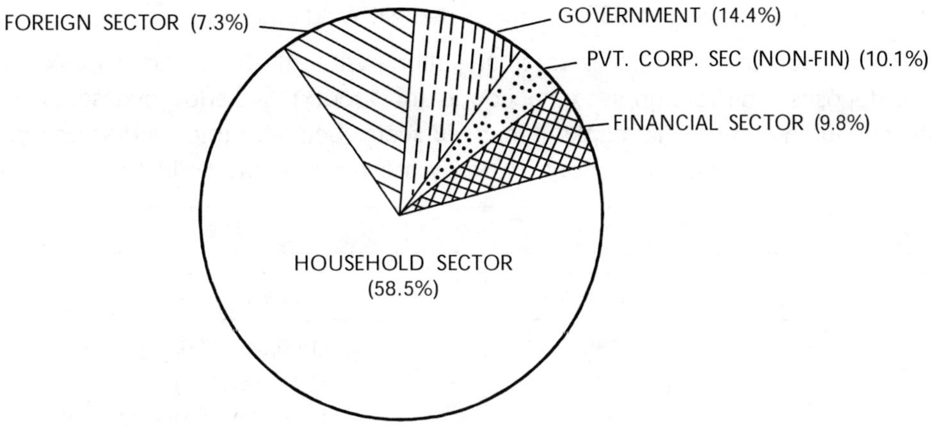

As seen from the above chart, the ownership of deposits is in the hands of household sector who are the real savers and whose savings at the national level, as percentage GDP was about 23-24% and as percentage of total national savings it was around 70% as in 2011-12.

Table 9.2 **OWNERSHIP OF DEPOSITS AS ON MARCH 2010**

Sector	(₹ crore)	%age of total
1. Government sector	6,55,091	13.5
2. Private Corporate Sector (Non-financial)	7,13,696	14.8
3. Financial Sector	4,82,043	10.0
4. Household Sector	28,04,875	58.0
5. Foreign Sector	1,80,657	3.7
6. Total (Grand)	48,36,362	100

Source: RBI Bulletin, Nov. 2011.

The total deposits (total of demand and time) given by 15% in 2010-11. The contribution of the term deposits in the total incremental deposits was the highest at 52% followed by savings deposits and current deposits in that order. The household sector continued to be the largest contributor to aggregate deposits during the past four decades. The share of the foreign sector was the smallest in most of the years. According to the type of accounts, savings accounts are the leaders at 31%, followed by current accounts at 19% and term deposits at 15.8% in 2009-10.

Deposit Structure

Aggregate deposits of scheduled commercial banks stood at ₹15,75,243 crores as at end March 2004. Demand deposits comprising current deposits plus chequable portion of the savings deposits stood at ₹2,25,022 crore accounting for 14% of aggregate deposits. Time deposits comprising the fixed deposits notice deposits and non-chequable portion of saving deposits worked at for the rest, namely, 83%. Total credits to total deposits stood at 55% and investment deposit ratio was 45% as at end March 2004. For example,

Households are the major contributors to the deposits of banks. About 88% of savings deposits and 68% of fixed deposits are accounted for by households. Households are responsible for the bulk of the ownership of aggregate deposits.

Population group-wise classification shows that among current accounts, about 54% of total current account funds are accounted by metropolitan centres. Metropolitan and urban centres together accounted for 54% of the total savings account funds and 63% of fixed deposit funds.

Bank group-wise data shows that SBI and its associates along with all public sector banks accounted for about 85% of the total deposits. The foreign sector accounts for about 11% and govt. sector for about 9% of total deposits of all scheduled commercial banks. Financial sector being an intermediary only, its accounts are not significant; although they account for about 7% they are not real savers in the economy.

Table 9.3 *(in ₹ crores)*

	Savings deposits	*Aggregate deposits*
2005-06	5,75,130	21,09,049 (3.6)
2006-07	6,71,425	26,11,933 (3.8)
2007-08	7,72,282	31,96,939 (4.1)
2008-09	9,00,967	38,34,110 (4.2)
2009-10	11,36,676	44,92,826 (3.9)
2010-11	13,77,238	52,07,969 (3.8)
2011-12	15,39,180	59,09,080 (3.5)
2013-14	2,00,5469	77,05,560

Savings deposits of commercial banks are assumed to be primary deposits or savings of the public. But aggregate deposits include all types of deposits primary savings, credit created by banks and business overdrafts, etc.

The relationship between them will roughly indicate the extent of created money to primary savings deposited in banks. This relationship appears to be stable at 4 times roughly in all the years studied.

This is only a hypothetical illustration and as data is overlapping, no firm conclusions can be drawn.

Population Group-wise Deposits — An example

Although rural areas account for bulk of the branches of about 50%, in terms of total deposits, they do not contribute more than 15% of the deposits. Both in terms of savings Accounts and fixed deposits, their share less than 15% to 20%. Metropolitan branches, although accounting for about 17% of the total branches, the deposit mobilisation by them accounts for about 35-40% of the total deposits of all branches. The mobilisation of deposits in the rural and semi-urban areas is however growing over years. Even so, the mobilisation of deposits by urban and metropolitan centres workout to about two-thirds of the total deposits. This is seen from the chart below:

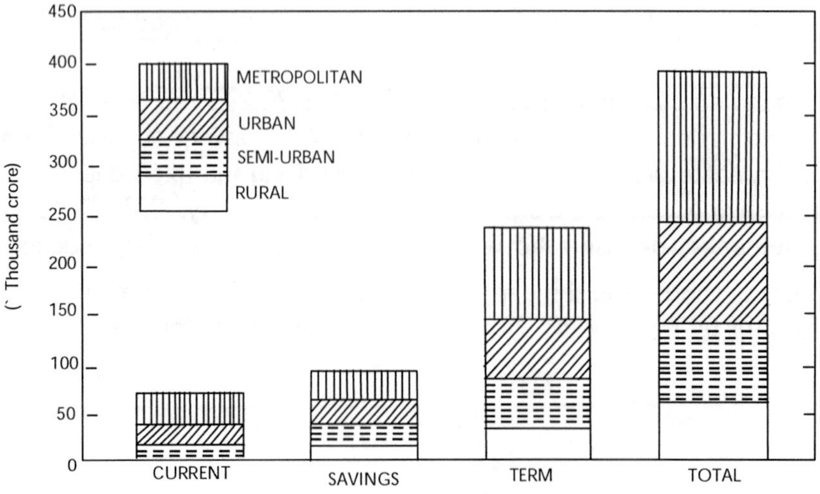

POPULATION GROUP-WISE DEPOSITS OF SCHEDULED COMMERCIAL BANKS

SECTORAL DEPLOYMENT OF BANK CREDIT

(in ₹ crores)

	Outstanding at end March			
	1995-96	*2006-07*	*2010-11*	*2013-14*
Gross Bank Credit	2,31,860	18,41,878	39,42,083	59,94,098
Public Food Procurement Credit	9,791	35,967	64,283	98,477
Priority Sector	73,329	6,32,647	12,39,386	18,78,100
Industry (Small, medium and large)	93,053	6,91,483	16,20,848	98,479
Trade/Wholesale Trade	11,980	1,08,041	1,03,584	N.A.
Other Sectors(Housing, Consumer Durables)	43,707	4,35,503	9,32,637	N.A >
Export Credit	29,590	1,04,926	61,940	48,313
Net Bank Credit (Non-food)	2,22,069	17,95,357	36,67,354	58,95,619
Priority Sector Credit as Percentage of Net-Bank Credit	33.0%	35.2%	33.8%	34%
Export Credit as Percentage of Net Bank Credit	13.3%	5.4%	1.7%	0.9%

Source: RBI, Trend and Progress of Banking 2006-07.

Net bank credit excluding food credit rose by nearly 8 times during the decade 1995-06 to 2006-07. Bulk of the rise was due to Industry and services. Export credit rose by only 3½ times and priority sector credit rose by much more by 8 to 9 times, on tune with the rise in net bank credit in total. Export credit fell in 2010-11 due to global recession and slow rise in exports.

Special Credit Policy Measures (2001)

This policy statement of April 2001 is special in that it came after a series of scams in the Capital Market and bank's involvement in lending against shares to stock brokers and serious irregularities in the operations of GTB and Madhavpura Mercantile Co-op. Bank, etc. These policy measures are briefly set out below:

(1) Prudential norms for urban co-op. banks were tightened. They are debarred from equity lending and loans against shares and capital market operators.

(2) A new supervisory body for co-operatives is proposed.

(3) To improve the risk profiles of NBFCs, a new Act is proposed to be brought out and tightened their Asset Liability Management System.

(4) Banks are now free to lend below prime lending rate to eligible corporates. Exposure to group companies was brought down from 50% to 40% of bank's capital and for individuals from 20% to 15% of bank's capital.

(5) No CRR on inter-bank deposits to encourage the development of Term money market. The minimum tenure of Term deposits is reduced to 7 days.

(6) To improve the working of the Call market, non-banks are to be phased out of the market and banks are advised to reduce reliance on Call money borrowings.

(7) 14 days and 182 days Treasury bills are withdrawn leading to more concentration on 91 days and 364 days Treasury bills in the market.

RBI Norms for New Banks

In January 2001, RBI came out with new guidelines for setting up of new banks. Firstly, the minimum net worth requirement of ₹ 100 crore for private banks was hiked to ₹ 200 crore. Secondly, an opening has been given for NBFCs of high net worth and good track record to convert themselves into regular banks. It is necessary for promoters to have a minimum net worth of ₹200 crore to set up a bank, but they should raise it to ₹300 crore in three years. They should have NPAs of less than 5% and capital adequacy requirement (CAR) of above 12%. Tripe 'A' credit rating is also needed.

Corporates will not however be permitted to set up banks, irrespective of their networth. Only NBFCs have been given entry into banking. These new banks can have headquarters anywhere in India. The promoters should hold a minimum of 40% of the capital. Corporates have been permitted to invest upto a maximum of 10%, which applies to all inter-connected companies within the same business group. The new banks cannot set up a subsidiary or Mutual Fund during the initial three year period.

The newly licensed banks will have to observe all existing priority sector requirements and prudential norms. Additionally, they should commit to having 25% of their branches in rural and semi-urban areas. NRIs are also allowed to pick up their equity stake up to 40% of the total.

RISK MANAGEMENT IN BANKS

Risk	*How Managed*
(I) *Credit Risk* On Balance sheet — Domestic and Foreign of Balance sheet	Lending operations. General Appraisal, Domestic Credit Administration, Overseas Credit Administration
(II) Interest Rate Risk Mismatched position Dealing in P.S.U. Securities in Investment Account	A.L. Management overall market operations — Norms; Trading Norms; Investment (Non-trading A/c), Fund Management (Non-trading A/c)
(III) Foreign Exchange Risk	Overall market operations limits; Trading Norms; Investment A/c. Fund Management, Exchange control, RBI-reporting.
(IV) Liquidity Risk	Overall Trading and Investment Risk Management and non-Trading Fund Management
(V) Operation Risk (VI) EDP Risk (VII) Systemic Risk	Business operations; EDP Risk Management

Safeguards against Risk

International Guidelines and RBI Guidelines

Limits Sanctioning and Trading

Internal Inspection and Audit

RBI Inspection and Audit (D.O.S. of RBI)

Reporting to the RBI.

Control on Banks

The regulatory framework for banks by the RBI was liberalised in stages, following the recommendations of Narasimham Committee on financial reforms. The licensing of branch location or branch expansion or contraction was removed. Despite the removal of control, the major portion of commercial bank branches are in the rural areas (40 to 50%) followed by semi-urban areas (22%), urban areas (16 to 23%) and metropolitan centres (13 to 20%). Foreign banks have branch network of 175, of which 99% are in metropolitan and uraban areas. At the other extreme, out of a total 14,460 branches of nationalised banks, 98% of the branches are in rural and semi-urban centres. During the period 2004-05 to 2010-11, many non-viable branches in rural areas were closed.

Some controls on deposit interest rates and lending interest rates were removed by stages over the period 1992-98. The cash reserve Ratio and statutory liquidity ratio which are controls on banks' cash balances with RBI and their investments in Govt. securities are reduced by stages so as to free the banks' precommitted funds with a CRR of 10% and S.L.R. of 25%; only 35% of incremental deposits of banks are precommitted. But out of the remaining 65% of deposits, nearly 40% (or 26% of the deposits) are tied to make advances to priority sector even now. These include advances to agriculture, SSIs, small traders, Transport operators, self-employed, weaker sections, etc. As in June 2014, CRR stood at 4% and SLR at 22% and priority sector advances as varied from bank to bank, although the guideline is 40% of the NDTL.

The other committed bank funds are for the purpose of growing food credit to government and semi government agencies like FCI and for export credit (around 8% of total bank credit). The funds left over for granting commercial credit on a discretionary basis would workout to around 25 to 30% of total credit granted by banks.

Refinance by RBI was also rationalised and only export credit refinance is provided at present. Refinance Liquidity Adjustment Facility (LAF) advances against Treasury bills and Govt. securities, etc., was discontinued but the facility of Repos through DFHI and STCI has filled in the gap for resources from RBI to the banking system. The Bank rate on Reverse Repo Rate is made flexible and operative through necessary changes from time to time and effective April 1997, General Refinance facility was provided at bank Rate up to the 1% of each bank's fortnightly average outstanding aggregate deposits, for the first four weeks followed by Bank rate plus one percentage point for the refinance for the second block of four weeks. As at early 2007, the descretionary refinance by the RBI is provided as LAF at Reverse Repo Rate, which is the same as the Bank Rate (6%). As in June 2011, Repo Rate was 8% and Reverse Repo rate was 7%.

Interest rate changes are also made more frequently to suit the conditions in the economy. Government securities are issued at market determined rates and on an auction basis. The bank rate and prime lending rate are made lead rates of the RBI and banks respectively and banks are free to fix their own prime lending rates [PLR] based on the RBI bank rate and interest rates on deposits.

Reforms in Banking Sector

Reforms in banking sector were started after Narasimham Committee on financial Reforms (1991) has made its recommendations, most of which were accepted.

During 1992-93, insurance sector reforms were started with the setting up of the R.N. Malhotra Committee. Similarly, reforms in the financial sector regarding NBFCs were initiated with the setting up of a committee under the chairmanship of A.C. Shah.

Lending rate structure of banks and financial institutions was rationalised. Banks are now subject to single ceiling rate for domestic deposits. Capital adequacy ratio of 9% and income recognition norms and classification of assets and provisioning norms were introduced. Export credit target was fixed at 10% of bank credit in 1992-93 which was raised to 12% in 1995-96 and later left to market forces. Interest tax on export credit was withdrawn in 1993.

In 1993-94, full provisioning of non-performing assets (NPA) was introduced. Special recovery tribunal was set up for recovery of bad debts of banks. SBI became the first PSB to access capital market for securing the recapitalisation of the bank. Select FIs have been allowed to borrow from the term money market for 3 to 6 months. The ceiling on bank's investment in P.S.U. bonds was withdrawn and banks are now free to decide on the level of inventory and receivables to assess the credit requirements of its customers. Department of supervision (DOS) was set up in RBI for inspection of banks on a more regular basis and a Board of Financial Supervision (BFS) was started in November 1994 to take over supervisory functions on All-India financial institutions and also to decide on policy matters regarding financial supervision of banks and non-banks. Later in 1997-98, D.O.S. was split up into two separate departments — one for supervision of banks and the other for Non-bank Finance Companies respectively. The nationalised bank namely, New Bank of India was merged with PNB in 1993-94 and the latest mergers are that of South Gujarat Local Area Bank with the Bank of Baroda and Global Trust Bank with the Oriental Bank of Commerce since 2004-05.

In 1994-95 private sector banks were licensed for the first time since reforms started and six new private sector banks commenced operations. 49 regional rural banks were taken up for restructuring and revival. Banks were allowed to fix their own PLRs, based on the bank rate and Bank deposit rates. Banking Companies Act was amended in 1994-95 to allow nationalised banks to access capital market.

In 1995-96, private sector mutual funds were allowed into the Call Money Market and Money Market Mutual funds were licensed to operate in Money Market. Bridge loans, barred after M.S. Shoes Case in 1996, were again allowed since 1997-98.

Refinance against Government securities which was allowed from 1992 was withdrawn in 1996-97. Only Export Refinance is however permitted to be given to banks by the RBI. Banks which were advised to stand away from secondary market since 1995-96 were given entry and financing of brokers and against shares and debentures was allowed up to a limit of 5% of bank's incremental deposits since 1997-98. Banking Ombudsman scheme was introduced for better customer service in 1995 and in as many regions as,14, this authority of Ombudsman was nominated, by July 1997. Nationalised banks are given more authority and CMD and EDs were allowed to sanction proposals up to a ceiling. The banks have started getting connected to the Internet and Banknet for quicker customer service and transfer of funds through electronic network in 1996. Standalone ATMs have been permitted and 24-hour banking has been started by some banks at a few branches.

In 1997, cooperative banks were allowed to participate in leasing and hire-purchase activities. The cash reserve ratio (CRR) and S.L.R. on inter-bank liabilities were removed. The licensing and registration with RBI by NFBCs and their regulation by the D.O.S. of RBI was started. Capital adequacy norms and prudential norms were imposed in NBFCs. A committee for supervision of NBFCs was set up in 1996-97.

Bank rate was activated as a signal of interest rate changes by RBI in 1997 and bank deposit rates were freed for medium and long-term deposits. Banks are given greater freedom to fix their own interest rates on deposit, and lending, subject to one or two limits fixed by the RBI.

Banks' lending in the form of cash credit component was reduced to 40% of maximum permissible bank finance (MPBF) and loan component was increased 100% with a view to discipline the utilisation of bank credit. *Ad hoc* credit units can be granted after the utilisation of cash and loan components. The corporate borrowers are allowed to make issues of commercial paper to cover the extent of cash credit component. This ratio of 40% is to be reduced year after year to make it zero. Already by October 1996, the cash credit component was reduced to 25% of MPBF. The issue of commercial paper was delinked from cash credit component and independent of MPBF with the result that it standsalone without any bank support or guarantee and is to be judged by investors on their own merits and that of the issuing company.

As regards the bank's investment portfolio, the ratio of permanent and current categories was set out at 60 : 40 for the year 1995-96 and at 50:50 for the year 1996-97. This was followed by further reduction of the permanent category so that the principle of marking to the market value of the whole investment portfolio would be followed by the public sector banks. All private sector banks have been asked to mark the whole investment portfolio to the market value, from the beginning itself. By now, all banks follow the same practice.

Another development in 1996-97 is the sanction by the RBI for the Private Sector local banks to be set up. By end March 1998 some four such banks were granted licence in principle to be set up. The Central Budget continued to provide some amounts for recapitalisation of PSBs. Some ₹850 crore were provided in 1995-96 and ₹909 crores in 1996-97 for this purpose. Similarly, the government took upon itself the capital restructuring of RRBs which have got net worth eroded by non-performing assets.

For IL/HP as well as Loan and Investment Companies, which comply with RBI norms and registered with RBI, the ceiling interest on deposits accepted by them was 15%. Similarly, the Mutual Benefit Finance

Companies or Nidhi Companies are also subject to a ceiling interest rate on deposits at 15% since July 1996 which was reduced to 14% early in 2001. All NBFCs registered with RBI have to be compulsorily credit rated and observe the norms for income recognition and provisioning for NPAs.

The recent reforms, effected since 1992 in the banking sector are briefly set out below:

1. Interest Rate Deregulation both in respect of deposits and advances.
2. Bank rate is made flexible and intended to reflect the refinance rate of RBI as well as the benchmark rate for all other interest rates in the banking and financial sector.
3. CRR and SLR were drastically cut down with the result that banks are left with a larger discretionary funds for lending on commercial lines and improve the profitability of banks.
4. Although the govt. continued to provide some budgetary allocation for capital restructuring of banks, they are now allowed to access the capital market funds directly.
5. New private sector banks have been licensed to start business and were asked to maintain 100% provision by marking to market value their investment portfolio.
6. Capital adequacy, income recognition and provisioning for bad and doubtful debts.
7. Improve the loan delivery system by increasing the loan component of Maximum Permissible Bank Finance (MPBF), which will ultimately replace the cash credit system.
8. Greater autonomy for PSBs to operate as commercial lines and increase their profitability.
9. Net interest spread of scheduled banks (interest income minus interest expended) has been showing a rise due to these reforms of the banking system. It was around 4 percentage points in 2007-08.

Telebanking and Electronic Banking

By telebanking, a customer can access the information about his account through a telephone call and by giving the coded personal identification number (PIN) to the bank branch. This facility is made available by some banks like SBI, Indian Bank, Andhra Bank etc., to selected branches of theirs. The information that is given is in respect of the last three transactions of that account, account balance and account statement.

Another facility is automatic withdrawals and transmission of the cash balance data and other information about an account in a number of branches of a bank in a consolidated form through fax or telex. The use of e-mail service for data and information transmission has been adopted by same banks. The electronic display of information in an instantaneous manner through satellite communication system and transfer of funds through the same channel for inter-branch and inter-bank adjustment and clearance of cheques, drafts, etc. has been started already.

BANKING PAYMENT GATEWAY

Payment Gateway

A payment gateway is third party network that acquires the transaction from an e-commerce portal and processes it through the banking or credit card system. It serves as a link between the banking network and the internet, as the public will have no access into the banking network.

Payment gateway acts as an intermediary for effecting transaction between the merchant and the bank's payment processing system. It translates the internet messages into other message formats (like Visa Net) that are used for the authorisation and settlement of merchant transactions.

All payment gateways are based on secure electronic transaction (SET)– Technology for ensuring the security and privacy of financial transactions on the internet. It was supported by Mastercard, Visa, Microsoft, Netscape and others.

Payment Service

A payment service is internet banking provided by a bank on a portal site of a merchant. Payment service is vendor and bank specific. Payment gateway is different in that it provides linking several banks together and is a general service to all banks. It takes a transaction, then certifies it and routes it after securing it with encryption. It also manages the translation and decryption.

What is SET? (Secure Electronic Transaction)

SET is an encryption technology that helps protect the transfer of payment information over the internet. It uses advanced security technology which allows cardholders to make secure payments to merchants on the internet.

E-Commerce and Payment Gateway

In India payment services are provided by ICICI Bank, HDFC Bank and Satyam. But nobody has yet started the payment gateway as at end March 2000.

In 2003-04, the RBI has started a payment and settlement system, referred to below:

Consumers interact with the e-commerce site only. They do not come in direct contact with the payment gateway. When they submit the credit card number, this information is forwarded to the payment gateway which completes the transaction. The e-commerce sites are required to have an agreement with bank and the payment gateway provider to access these services. The e-commerce sites do not come to know about the credit card authentification and information on customers. This ensures risk-free payment mechanism and obviates any misuse of this information.

Payment gateway enables banks to allow real-time transactions from one account to another and from one bank to another. It helps merchants doing online business to focus on their products and customers rather than on the payment mechanism. The payment gateway enables secure, fast and standardised e-commerce and e-business. It improves trade turnover and bank transactions are facilitated.

COMPONENTS OF E-BANKING

The various components of e-banking are already available in banking sector. Many banks have been using e-banking components in isolation. What is wanted is that banks must gear up to create e-banking environment by using the required components in an integrated banking software. E-banking software has to be integrated in a manner that it helps monitoring assets and liabilities, their movements and analysis of profit and loss and balance sheet details. The system should help tracing cash flows, control and monitoring of all key parameters of banking including NPAs. Banks have to use integrated banking software technology for all their uses and achieve integration of their activities bank-wise and of all banks together in the banking system.

This integrated e-banking scenario at macrolevel is presented in this Chart.

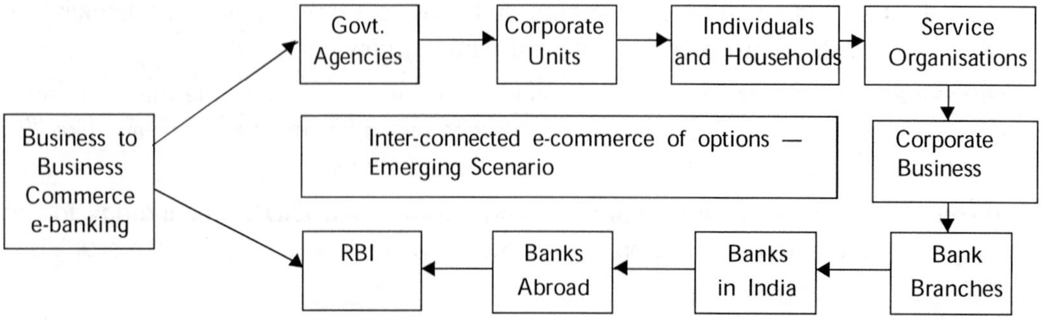

The interconnections of the banking sector involve:

(1) Commerce — business to business — involving payments on bank branches.

(2) Bank-wise integration.

(3) All Banking Sector integration.

(4) Receipts and payments and settlements.

(5) Funds Transfer electronically.

Electronic Payment and Settlement System

The RBI has announced in 2004 that they would set up a board for payment and settlement systems (BPSS), which would lay down the policies for regulation and supervision of settlement systems, comprising of both domestic and cross-border systems. The Real Time Gross Settlement System (RTGS) was implemented by the RBI since March 2004. The RTGS provides for an electronic based settlement of inter-bank and customer based transactions. This system has about 100 participants, comprising of scheduled commercial banks and primary dealers, with an average daily turnover of ₹ 24,000 crore. By the year end of 2006-07, the coverage is expected to be 32,768 branches all over the country.

This RTGS System is fully integrated with the accounting system of the RBI and other systems. It is a single all-India system, with payments being settled transaction by transaction, in an irrevocable manner in real time. It is a safe and secure system which uses the digital signatures and PKI based encryption.

It has many advantages. It provides intra-day collateralised liquidity support for member banks to meet mismatches of funds flows; it is a risk free funds transfer in quickest time, for both banks and customers apart from providing for a more efficient funds management of the treasuries of banks.

The Special Electronic Funds Transfer (SEFT) System operating since April 2003 from Mumbai covers about 29 banks and 2312 branches situated in 127 cities across the country. Both debit cards and credit cards are growing indicating the increasing acceptance of electronic mode of funds transfer, necessitating a regulatory and supervisory body in the form of BPSS, proposed by the RBI, referred to above.

The value of transactions through retail electronic payments methods stood at ₹ 11,945 crore in 2010-11 registering a growth of 61% on top of a growth of 35% in the proceeding year. This value rose to ₹ 31,877 crore in 2012-13.

Progress of I.T. in Banking

The Reserve Bank has taken the lead to propagate the I.T. tools in banks both for better customer service and improved efficiency and profitability in banks. Two decades back, the major initiative was taken by RBI in introducing mechanized cheque clearing facility through Magnetic Ink Character Recognition (MICR) technology. This led to faster and safer cheque clearing through networking in banks. Next, banks have computerized their accounts at head office and branches stagewise during the nineties, with the result that there was better customer service and facilitated the accounting of all transactions of customers.

During the later half of nineties, the RBI has introduced the Negotiated Dealing System (NDS) for screenbased trading in Government securities. During this period, Electronic Clearing System (ECS) and Electroic Funds Transfer (EFT) and Special Electronic Funds Transfer (SEFT) were also implemented for safe, secure and quick modes of transfer of funds across banks, agencies and places. The Real Time Gross Settlement (RTGS) was introduced for online settlement of inter-bank funds transfer resulting in risk-free real time settlement of funds flows. The growth of ATM and sharing of ATM by a group of banks through networking and compatible computerization systems in banks was also achieved. This led to intra-bank and inter-bank networking in banks and their branches resulting in "Anywhere" "Anytime" banking in selected banks and selected branches. With *e-banking*, many banking transactions can be made from home, through the internet, without visiting a bank or a branch. This led to Mobile Banking.

The growth of *Master Card* and *Smart Card*, etc., led to growth of plastic money without the need for currency, economising the cash and reducing the costs of currency management. The introduction of Online Accounting System (OLTAS) facilitated electronic transmission of tax related information from banks to tax information network (TIN) of Income Tax Dept.

The RBI has also facilitated through its IDRBT, the introduction of safe and efficient communication network among banks through Indian Financial Networks (INFINET) for funds and non-funds information flows and safety of these transfers is secured by Public Key Infrastructure (PKI) which is the latest state-of-Art in I.T. The security and reliability of I.T. and e-banking is sought to be achieved.

Electronic Card Business

The latest craze in banking using electronic media is internet banking. By visiting, the website of each bank, one can enter his key password and know the account balance and even pass his own credit and debit entries. Such internet banking facility is opened up by GTB, in December 1999. This means that you can do your banking through your personal computer sitting at home. Banks may soon allow zero balance savings accounts through internet facility only; also that will obviate the need for bank clerks to pass entries and maintenance of books of account. Each account holder maintains his own account in the website of the bank by opening up your passbook page. Banks have been asking for a minimum balance in saving accounts to cover costs of accounting fixed costs of rent, electricity, furniture, paper, clerical time, etc.

While customers can now make only balance enquiries, download statements and open fixed deposits over the net. They will soon be able to carry-out all their transactions over the net, and visiting a bank branch would then become needless. Similarly, the increasing use of ATMs, and their installation in offsite areas by banks will also do away with personal visits to bank branch. The number of ATMs by the Public Sector Banks is growing and stood at 6,748 at the end March 2004 and 16,329 at end March 2007. The number of ATMs as end-March 2011 stood at 74,505 and 1,14,014 at end March 2013. The number of Debit Cards issued in 2013 was 4,69,000 crore while the same for credit cards was 39,700. But the value of transactions was highest for credit card at ₹ 1,23,000 crore which the same for debit cards was ₹ 74,300 crore for 2012-13. As compared with this, all bank branches were slightly higher at 89,622 in 2013-14. Debit cards are growing faster than credit cards. Many banks are joining with others to share the ATMs to reduce the workload and inter-operability among these clusters is forwarded by National Financial Switch (NFS).

The credit card base in India has grown from the level of 3.5 million in 1999 to 11 million by end-October 2004. The plastic money is expected to account for 15% of all transactions in India by a decade next from just 1% at present. That means that the use of cash will come down further. The debit cards will outdo credit cards in numbers, but credit cards are expected to account for a lion's share of business transactions in the current millennium.

In the years to come, mobile phones will drive banking transactions. These mobile phones will be equipped with smart cards that are embedded with banking and other information. Instead of going to the bank ATM, all you do is to punch up your bank account through your cell-phone. ATM then loads the card up with whatever sum you wish to add to it and the smart card automatically deducts the amount of cash purchase. It is also possible to make enquiries on balance in the account and transfer of funds from one account to another through your mobile phone. This mobile phone banking facility is yet to come but the mechanics of linking the banking with the cell-phone is being worked out.

Already the linking of banking with the internet is completed. Then banks can be interconnected branch-wise and bank-wise, through the internet facility, which was done already by some banks like OBC. The increase in the installation of teller machines for all branches is the first step for the electronic banking facility.

The use of e-mail for banking will open up the gates for internet banking. The next step in the smart banking by the use of cell-phones, where banking will be on the wheels and mobile. As these facilities will increase the volumes of turnover of credits and debits in banks and increase in transactions electronically, but lower the need for paper currency.

Web-based Banking Solutions

Citibank has launched in January 2000 two new web-based corporate banking solutions in India, namely, speed-collect 2000 and city commerce. These two products provide their corporate customers with essential link in the present day e-commerce environment — online information, financial settlement and reconciliation. Speed collect 2000 is an extension of the Citibanks' cash management product, which can now be accessed by customer through a regular internet browser. Citi commerce is a seller centric e-commerce solution, which links corporates with their dealer network.

ICICI Bank is another private bank which is a leader in providing internet banking facilities to its customers. It is the first bank to provide credit card to its customers through a tie up with visa which enables the customer to see the transaction details and make card payments over the internet. It promotes the website commerce and links it with bank payments through the credit card. It is the final link in the bank's chain of personal products, that were launched over the last three years. It is a coherent strategy of leveraging technology and existing customer base to increase its market share in e-commerce.

The e-commerce has come to stay and increase in volumes and gateway providers help the linkage of banking to the merchant business and trade. The internet banking will revolutionise banking in India. Cell-phones help this growth by linking the satellite communications with internet banking. These new financial products will grow in the years to come.

Virtual Banking

Virtual banking refers to the provision of banking and related services through extensive use of information technology without direct recourse to the bank by the customer. The practices of banks have undergone significant changes in the nineties due to economic and financial reforms and the introduction of electronic technology in banking. The shift is to strengthen the customer relationship, improve the quality of service and move towards "relationship banking" to face increasing competition.

The origin of virtual banking in developed countries can be traced back to the seventies with the installation of Automated Teller Machines (ATM). Due to growing competition among the banks in the world, there has been quick transformation of the network of services provided by banks through the I.T.

The principal types of virtual banking services are the Automated Teller Services, shared ATM networks and electronic funds transfer 24-hour banking, phone banking, smart cards and stored value cards had introduced internet and intranet banking. The concept of physical branch banking gave place to provision of services electronically.

The financial benefits of virtual banking services are manifold. Firstly, virtual banking has the advantage of having a lower cost of handling a transaction. Secondly, there was an increased speed of response to customer requirements. Thirdly, there was a widening and deepening of the services provided to customers like electronic transfer of funds. Fourthly, there was an improvement in quality of services in terms of speed, time and facility. Fifthly, the existing staff can provide a larger volume of services and reduced the staff costs. The potential for service and sophistication in service has been increased by virtual banking.

Mobile Banking

Mobile banking is next alternative to normal internet banking. This can be done by the use of the cell-phone users using a secret code for operating on their accounts. They can access information on the closing balance, latest entries of debits and credits. The cell-phone banking help the customer with access to business with consolidated position of various accounts in any number of branches of that bank, wherever it has accounts. Due to computerized information, one all-India number is available to any depositor and borrower and he can use this number and after presenting the secret code, he can access the information that he wants. Banks can receive orders of debits in favour of another accounts holder giving his number of his bank or order the debit entries or similarly pass credit entries in a similar fashion.

It may take some more time before the modalities can be worked and MoU can be worked out between the Mobile phone operators and the networking system and the banking system. All banks have to be fully computerized for this purpose and there should be one number with nine digit or ten digits, for each account holder applicable to that bank where he has account or where he is a borrower.

With huge increase in the cell-phone users and their continued growth, the potential for the use of the mobile phones is great for facilitating banking services without the need to visit the branches and waiting for hours. In the rural and semi-urban areas, there is a larger increase in the cell-phone users for whom this service is particularly useful to bring banking to their doorsteps. There is need for networking co-ordination and banks have to enter a MoU with the cell phone service providers. There should be provision for securing the highest level of secrecy of account numbers with no possibility of hacking and encryption of the signature of the parties. These will work like the smart cards for the specified purposes of banking in the case of banks with provision for this type of banking.

One thing has to be made clear that mobile banking is not the same thing as house to house service or home banking service. Some banks are already providing home banking services in a limited way say for cash or cheque deposit or with cash withdrawals, subject to certain conditions.

e-banking — RBI Regulation

RBI was concerned with the growth of e-banking since 2001, accompanied by large-scale usage of plastic money which may influence the effectiveness of monetary policy. The working group set up by RBI on internet banking submitted its report in July 2003. The group's recommendations relate to technology and security issues, legal basis, and regulatory issues to preserve the role of money as a unit of account and protect the efficacy of monetary policy through regular reporting of monetary statistics on the use of e-money.

The RBI guidelines on "Risks and controls in computers and telecommunications" are applicable to internet banking. As regards legal basis, the IT Act of 2000 and subsequent amendments granted explicit recognition to electronic payment mode. The RBI is faced with the technical security issues which include designating a network and database administrator, information systems auditing, logical access control technique and the use of public key infrastructure (PKI) technology.

There is a risk of a run on e-money system depending on the ability of the system to detect the trends, foreseeing the weak spots in cryptography based security system and problems of backup facilities in networked payment products. These is need for safeguards against anti-competitive and anti-trust practices. Outsourcing, disclosures, customer education and contingency planning, etc., are to be taken care. Several sub-border issues and law enforcement issues are to be part of effective regulation of e-banking in India.

✠ ✠ ✠

CREDIT CARDS IN INDIA (Plastic Money)

10

Many Indian and foreign banks have issued credit cards to its customers. The issuing bank will have a tie-up with a number of establishments ranging from 10 to 12 lakh inclusive of hotels, hospitals, shops and departmental stores, which will honour the credit cards. This issuing bank will provide this facility of credit cards to those having a regular monthly income beyond a limit, creditworthiness, judged by their wealth and income, and business executives and their top brass. The bank takes a risk in that cardholder is given a credit facility to repay within 30 to 45 days and there is a possibility of default risk.

Commercial banks in India, starting with many foreign banks have started issuing those cards since the beginning of eighties. The use of credit card substitutes and replaces the use of cash. It increases the money on hand and accelerates the velocity of money to the extent that idle money is activated for purchase of goods and services. As the credit card gives the overdraft facilities and additional borrowing power, it can supplement the existing money supply and economise the use of cash, which has wear and tear risk.

Progress of Credit Card Business

The number of members using it and the number of establishments honouring this credit card after joining the scheme have increased vastly over the past few years. Since then, Indian banks have joined with international banks to provide this credit card facility on a worldwide basis, or at selected international centres.

As per the latest data available for March 2014, the number of cards launched by banks rose to 776 million. At end-March 2012, the number was only 648 million. Sixteen banks were issuing credit cards as part of their tie-up arrangements with the existing banks in business, the details of the terms of issue and the participating members and establishments honouring the credit cards changed from bank to bank. The number of banks issuing cards vastly increased, with SBI, ICICI and Citibank accounting for the bulk of Credit/Debit cards issued in recent years.

Related Services (Electronic Banking)

As regards electronic banking service to customers, electronic clearing service (ECS or credit clearing service) has become operational at the four metropolitan centres service 1996. It has since been extended to four non-MICR centres, namely, Ahmedabad, Bangalore, Hyderabad and Pune. In addition, ECS (Debit clearing) is in operation in many metropolitan centres for collection of telephone bills. Similarly, the payment of electricity bills to the utility companies in some centres is being, brought under the purview of ECS.

IBA (Indian Banks Association) has sponsored the Shared Payment Network System (SPNS) in addition to a large network of ATMs, POS terminals and cash dispensers connected to a Central Host to provide extended hour electronic banking service to customers for transacting on the network. The SPNS provides the services like deposit withdrawal of cash, balance enquiry, printing of statement of account request for cheque book, standing instructions, POS facilities, etc. Payment and settlement systems are varying from bank to bank. To have a central clearing, National Settlement System (NSS) was started from April 2005, by the RBI. Real Time Gross Settlement System is already in operation by the RBI with some participants.

Debit Card

Use of paper money is replaced by plastic money. The future will see the electronic money clearance of all receipts and payments on a daily basis, through satellite networking. Already electronic transfer of money is taking place and electronic debits and credits through an electronic code displaying plastic card.

Firstly Citibank has issued debit cards. Many banks including SBI, SBH Indian Bank, etc., have issued ATM cards through which 24-hour banking can be done at specified branches. The ATM cards will allow you to withdraw at specified branches through debit to your savings or current accounts, by use of this Automatic Teller Machines. Here electronically your card is identified by code number and your account is debited and money is handed over to you.

Debit card is more advanced than ATM card in that it can be used at specified retail or departmental stores also in addition to specified bank branches. It can be used to make payments by use of the debit card which automatically debits your account in the specified bank. Here your drawal is on your own assets or money, whereas in the credit card, it provides a borrowing limit against which you can draw and pay interest and other charges on the use of this facility to withdraw up to a limit. If you have own assets or a share portfolio with the bank, you can have an overdraft account against them which means that you can use your own money rather than bank money through the debit card.

RBI is encouraging shared ATMs among banks to reduce competition and costs. The latest ATM network announced in 2005 is independent ATM network run by a standalone I.T. company supported by participating banks.

RBI's Directive on Debit Cards

In November 1999, the RBI has put additional restrictions on the issue of debit cards by banks. The RBI has barred banks from tying up with non-bank entities and to use such cards to withdraw cash/make deposits from points of sale. It has also imposed existing reserve requirements on smart card balances. These deposits and withdawals of cash tantamount to the acceptance or creation of deposits through the route of Debit/Smart Cards. Banks have to get their Board's approval for issue of these cards and have to advise the RBI about the details of the operations, the terms and conditions of the Debit/Smart Card Scheme, as submitted to their Boards and the latter's approval. Risk management is an issue on which RBI has issued directives for banks issuing these cards. In June 2005, the RBI directed the banks to bring more transparency on the terms of issue and card users have access to relief through Ombudsman of banks.

Electronic Card

The Master Card issued by Citibank is being converted into electronic cards. Through an electronic tape, it records all transactions done through it and can be used only in places and branches where electronic scan and identification is possible. The plastic money leaders, Mastercard has launched an electronic card, which is claimed to be the first of its kind in India. The waiting time of customers is reduced by this. The card can be accepted at points of sale with electronic authorisation terminal. The electronic programme offers Indian consumers the flexibility, designed to work at all points of sale with this facility and gives added convenience of a new payment product and financial facility for easy transactions.

Debit Cards vs. Credit Cards

The spending power depends on the drawing capacity, which in the case of debit card is your own assets with the bank. But in the case of credit card, it allows a borrowing power on the bank, for which you have to pay some charges or fees.

Both credit cards and debit cards complement each other and are precursors to the electronic card which may be the gold card, which consolidates all your cash accounts in various branches of a bank, connected through the bank internet and allows you to manage your payments most economically in tune with your receipts and promotes efficient cash management. Debit card allows you to draw on your existing assets and deposits with the bank while the credit card allows you to draw on the bank up to your creditworthiness. If you are averse to be a borrower, debit card has an advantage to you. Here there is no risk of overspending, as you can spend what you have. In the case of credit card, borrowing is possible and you pay interest on the overdrawn amount. Debit card does not involve any interest payment or cost to the holder.

There was an increasing usage of plastic money in the form of these cards since their inception in 2000 and the volume of transactions and the value has shown an increasing trend.

If you carry the debit card, then there is no need for carrying cash or even travellers' cheques. Debit card is as good as money in the accounts with your bank. Credit card has the additional advantage of your overdrawing if necessary; payments and made by the bank to the extent of your purchases and if they exceed your limit, you pay interest on the excess amount. The debit cards are now increasingly used for purchase transactions in addition to drawing cash from ATMs. Credit cards outstanding amount, equivalent to advances stood at ₹1,96,200 crore as at end March 2013.

Key to Opening up of the Treasury

Credit cards are the key to the opening of bank accounts for daily payments by the cardholders. It enables the cardholders to have overdraft facilities ranging from ₹2,000 to ₹10,000 depending upon the creditworthiness of the party.

Credit card is a substitute for cash which can be used by selected customers of banks issuing the cards for their use for payments for goods and services. Many company executives, businessmen and high and middle income individuals are found to be eligible member customers of banks for issue of these cards.

These plastic cards will have the photo identity and his signature embossed on the card. It will also have the issuing bank's name and validity period of the card. The bank issuing the credit card knows the customer well and his creditworthiness.

The eligibility for getting the credit card from the issuing bank depends on the following factors:

1. He should have a savings, or Current Account with the Bank.
2. His annual or monthly income are regularly received and credited to this Bank Account.
3. His Assets and liabilities are known and reported to the Bank.
4. He is considered creditworthy upto a limit depending on his income, assets and expenditure.

The eligible member will be asked to fill in an application form giving the details of Account Number, name and address, income, wealth and status and an evidencing statement of his income/wealth, etc.

Arrangements with Banker

The customer provides the details of his assets, expenditure, salary income and other income, his dependents and his estimated expenditure and required overdraft facility. The Bank grants credit card subject to some rules and guidelines to the customer. He has to keep his drawal upto the limit and pay interest at stipulated rate and clear the overdraft within 30-45 days, along with interest and charges, if any. The cardholder is also given a cheque book which he can use for payment to establishments which joined this scheme and accept credit cards for any payments. The signature on the credit card can be verified with that on the cheque and honoured by proper recording of the credit card number on the back of the cheque. These cheques can be issued up to the limits of overdraft given by the Bank. The Bank gives monthly statements and records, the extent of the utilisation of overdraft by him, and due date for repayment of overdraft with interest etc. The card invariably contains the following details.

Name of the account holder/cardholder, his photo, his specimen signature and the signature of the sanctioning authority of the Bank. The extent of overdraft limit, interest rate and other terms are made known to the cardholder at the time of issue and the use of credit or debit card is subject to these terms and conditions.

There are different types of cards with different features. Some are for domestic use and others for both domestic and international use. The terms of issue also vary from bank to bank. These cards are called Gold Card, Visa Card, Mastercard, Citi Card, etc., depending upon the issuing bank. Some credit cards are more popular like those of Grindlays, Citibank and American Express. Among the non-bank institutions which issue credit cards mention may be made of the Thomas Cook, Merbank, etc. The RBI has issued a directive prohibiting the issue of credit cards by non-banking companies in India.

How they Benefit the Bank?

1. This will increase the credit granted by the Bank and its reputation with the public.
2. It will lead to growth of its interest income and total return to funds.
3. The business establishment which accepts these cards also give some incentive or commission to the Bank, by which the Bank gains.

How they Benefit the Cardholder?

1. They give credit up to a limit sanctioned just through the show of his card and his signature on it.
2. They get some period of 30 to 45 days to clear the outstanding overdraft.
3. They can avoid carrying cash and the risk of its loss.
4. They earn a status symbol to the holder.

Banks have to bear some risk similar to unsecured debt. They may have a problem of non-payment or delayed payment of overdraft amount. The Bank also suffers the risk of uncertainty of payment and the time of payment.

When banks found that they have surplus funds and the industry offtake has fallen as in 1980s, they resorted to consumer finance, durable goods hire-purchase, etc. It was in such periods that credit cards have become a venue for banks to lend to individuals. Auto finance to business and households and personal loans to individuals is another area which has grown in 1990s, similar to credit cards in 1980s. By end March 2013, banks' credit card advances, outstanding stood at ₹1,22,000 crore, as against only ₹18,200 crore, at end March 2007. By 2010-11, the value of electronic transactions through credit cards was ₹1,22,000 crore. But the same for debit cards was only ₹7,720 crore.

The number of credit cardholders and the participating business establishments, hotels, etc., have also increased enormously over years to run into some million. Some Indian banks like Andhra Bank and Canara

Bank have entered into agreements with some international banks and agencies to have internationally acceptable credit cards, which are particularly useful to businessmen, export traders and foreign trade agencies, visiting many foreign countries.

Credit Cards — Drivers for Growth

By about 2006-07, there were 22 million credit cards in India but the numbers of debit cards were far higher at 70 million. Since then, the number of credit cards are growing at a rate of only 28% and number of debit cards are growing at a faster rate of 41%. But the volume and value of transactions done by the credit cards is increasing at a faster rate than that on debit cards. As at end March 2010-11, there were 18 million credit cards as against 227 million debit cards.

The drivers for growth of the credit cards are the following:

1. Rising consumerism and increasing urbanization in India along with the growth rare of GDP at around 8%-9% in the recent past.
2. Increasing number of the upper and middle income groups.
3. Economic reforms and trend to globalization leading to exposure to foreign influences.
4. Improved payment and settlement systems and clearing systems.
5. Competition and lower costs.
6. Computerisation and automation and the increased use of ATMs.
7. Demonstration effect of foreign forces on the Indian habits and customs.
8. Co-branding and tie-ups between issuing banks and companies selling consumer durables and non-durables and departmental stores, etc.

Agricultural Credit Cards

Some top ranking agriculturists and cultivators were given credit cards by 21 public sector banks. These cards were given to them after they produced documentary evidence of land owned by them, cultivated by them and their titles and other details. These cards are meant to facilitate quicker and easier flow of credit to agricultural sector which is a priority sector, as per the guidelines of the government. The agricultural credit cards business is encouraged by the RBI and the government. The Andhra Bank is an example for issuing the Kisan Credit Cards liberally.

A passbook and credit card are provided to the selected agriculturists whose credentials are well established. Passbook contains all the details of the holdings of the agriculturist, the annual output, income and other sources of income, if any, etc. Such passbook evidencing the ownership of land, and the extent of ownership, expected crop income and other income will help the bank to decide on the extent of the credit that can be given to them.

These schemes of credit cards are not very popular with middle and low income groups. Income tax difficulties and high interest rates charged by banks and some rigorous terms as to the repayment of overdraft facility have led to less popularity of these credit cards in recent years. But credit cards as a source of extending credit to individuals and households has come to stay and credit cards should be counted as part of the total bank credit and money supply in the economy.

Visa and Master Cards

In the credit card world, there are market leaders, namely, Visa and Master Card issuers. Master credit card base was larger at 1.97 million as at end Dec. 1999, as against Visa Card base of 1.91 million. But in 1999, Visa's base grew by 68%, while the Master Card's base was up by only 10%. After 2000, other credit cards began to be issued which made Visa and Master Cards redundant, in India.

Master Card was the first payment service provider to bring debit card to India. During 1999, however Visa International has surpassed the performance of Master Card. People are spending more on Visa Card. Volumes had risen by 57% to $616 million in 1999 in the case of Visa Card. While the same rose by 5% to $481 million in the case of Master Card. The average card spend was higher at $392 in the case of Visa Card, while it was only $256 in the case of Master Card. The market share of Visa (Visa International) was 58% in 1999, which is expected to go up by 66% in the next few years. There is neck to neck competition between Visa International and Master Card issued in their Indian operations.

The Tables below present the supporting data on electronic payments in the credit card business in India, during 2003-04 and 2009-10. This is only for illustration.

Electronic Fund Transfer (EFT) and special EFT and card based systems (Credit Card, Debit Card, ATM and Smart Cards) are increasing in usage in the years 1999 to 2012. SEFT system was introduced from April 2003, with the settlement being centralised at Mumbai, and provides for the same day funds settlement. SEFT has participants of 29 banks with 2,312 branches situated in 127 cities across the country. The SEFT system facilitated the operation of T + 2 settlement system by the capital market.

Table 10.1 **RETAIL ELECTRONIC PAYMENT SYSTEMS (RECORD OF CASHLESS TRANSACTIONS)**

(number in lakh and amounts in ₹ crore)

	Total Electronic Payments		*Total ECS Credits*		*Total ECS Debits*	
Year	*No.*	*Amount*	*No.*	*Amount*	*No.*	*Amount*
2003-04	1669.55	52142.78	203.00	10,228.00	79.00	2,253.58
2004-05	2289.04	108749.83	400.51	20,179.81	153.00	2921.24
2005-06	2850.13	146382.68	442.16	32,324.35	359.58	12986.50
2006-07	3787.09	235693.12	690.19	83,273.09	752.02	25440.79
2007-08	5353.09	1041991.93	783.65	7822.22	1271.20	974.87
2008-09	6678.24	500321.79	883.94	489.37	1600.55	669.76
2009-10	7182.16	688009.54	981.30	11,761.3	1492.00	6952.40
2012-13	86600.00	199300.00	1950.00	177100	3312.00	1083.00

Source: RBI Trends and Progress of Banking.

ESC Credits and Debits (Table 10.1) grew up to 2006-07 but fell later in terms of values but not in terms of number of transactions.

Table 10.2 **MICRO CENTRES (MICRO CHEQUE CLEARANCES)** *(` million)*

Year	*No.*	*Amount*
2003-04	–	–
2004-05	2029.8	8,62,937
2005-06	2375.9	12,79,394
2006-07	3131.1	18,35,942
2007-08	1481.0	1,33,960
2008-09	11,638.2	1,04,082
2009-10	11497.1	85,315
2013-14	1267.0	93,438

Table 10.3 **RETAIL ELECTRONIC TRANSACTIONS (Value in Percentages)**

		2011	*2013*
Credit Card	–	*16%*	*27.3*
Debit Card	–	*3%*	*39.1*
EFT	–	*35%*	*29.9*
ECS Credit	–	*33%*	*3.6*

Table 10.4 ELECTRONIC FUNDS TRANSFER

(number in lakh and amounts in ₹ crore)

Year	Electronic Funds Transfer		Card Payments			
			Credits		Debits	
	No.	Amount	No.	Amount	No.	Amount
2003-04	8.19	17,124.81	1001.79	17,662.72	375.57	4,873.67
2004-05	25.49	54,601.58	1294.72	25,686.36	415.32	5,361.04
2005-06	30.67	61,288.22	1560.86	33,886.47	456.86	5,897.14
2006-07	47.76	77,446.31	1695.36	41,361.31	601.77	8,171.63
2007-08	133.15	1,40,326.00	228203.00	50,985.00	883.06	12,521.00
2008-09	321.61	2,51,956.00	259561.00	65,356.00	1276.54	18,547.00
2009-10	27.02	2,68,600.00	23424.00	61,824.00	1701.00	26418.00
2011-12	2,261.00	17,00,350.00	3199.00	96,613.00	3275.00	53432.00
2012-13	1,259.00	93,43,800	127.00	17,713.00	76500.00	10,83,100

Source: RBI Monthly Bulletins.

Electronic Funds Transfer increased by 14.7 times over the period 2004 to 2009. Card payments by credit cards increased by 3.7 times, while the same by debit cards grew by only 3.8 times. The value of transactions was almost the same in respect of debit cards growth as in respect of credit cards.

It will be seen from the above Tables that the plastic cards have gained significant acceptance by the public replacing and economising the use of paper money. The relative growth of debit cards is more than credit cards in terms of numbers. ATM cards are also growing in popularity and to regulate the growth of them, the RBI has advised the banks to share the ATM networks instead of proliferating the clusters. The number of ATMs by public sector banks was as high as 74,505 as at end March 2011 and 69,652 at end March 2013 and cards issued have also grown to 1,14,014 as in March 2013.

The RBI initiated measures to regulate and supervise these systems to ensure the financial integrity of electronic money issues and the security of their operations. These initiatives were referred to in the last chapter under e-banking. To facilitate the apex level, inter-systems connectivity, the National Financial Switch (NFS) System was established by banks and the RBI has set up a national clearing system and a Board for their Supervision and Regulation.

Smart Card

The Smart Card is a relative newcomer in the retail payment system. It is a e-money with a huge potential usage. It has an integrated circuit with a microprocessor chip, embedded in it, which gives it wide capacity in performing many calculations, more fast and accurately than an accountant. It does maintain records, statements and acts as an electronic purse, storing e-money. It is usable for drawing cash and making payments with automatic facility of keeping accounts of balances of the party.

During a loading operation, the deposit account of cardholder is debited and credit is given to a centralised card account. In Europe, banks generally issue these cards but in the U.S.A., non-banks also issue these cards. The issuers, must have a strong and efficient supervisory system to reduce the systemic risks. It is not yet introduced widely but is in an experimental stage in India; SBI and Canara Bank are involved in a project in Mumbai conducted by IIT at Powai.

The project has used the Smart Card mode of receipts and payments for IIT with a centralised account keeping system. To start with, the efficacy of this system was tested without imposing any service charges or membership fees and given incentives to potential users to give confidence to the participants of the financial system about its efficacy and secrecy after incorporating necessary security features in the system.

RBI and Credit Card Business

The RBI has announced in June 1988 that banks are allowed to undertake credit card business either independently or in tie-up arrangement with other card issuing banks without prior approval of the RBI. However, banks desirous of setting up a separate subsidiary for credit card business will require prior approval of the RBI.

In October 1998, SBI has set up a subsidiary for carrying on its credit card business under the names of SBI Credit and Payment Services Pvt. Ltd. (SBICPS), jointly with the GE Capital Corporation of U.S.A., with a paid-up capital of ₹ 100 crore of which the share of SBI is 60%. The State Bank of India launched as credit card with Visa International in 1999 and had a base of 3-4 lakh cards by middle of 2000.

Amex had for long concentrated on corporate cards but had entered into mass market of individual cards in 1999. The introduction of a Global Card and reward points in 1999 had acted as a catalyst to growth in card spends. Annual card sales volumes, began to increase vastly during 1999-2007. After recording a growth of 23% in 1998, volumes doubled to ₹ 7,000 crore in 1999-00 and further to ₹ 10,000 crore in 2000-01. The data for later years is given in the above tables. The reasons for faster growth in recent years are attributed to increase in the number of banks, participating in this business and their aggressive sales strategies, involving special incentives to encourage the use of plastic money.

Plastic Money

As per the latest RBI study, the number of debit cards far exceeded the credit cards. As on March 2007, the number of total cards swelled to 24.58 crore, of which about 10 per cent are credit cards and the rest are debit cards. But the value of transactions done through credit cards is five times more as compared to the value of transactions carried out by the debit cards. Banks are issuing at a rate of 20 lakhs cards per month, of which the majority are the debit cards. As regards the smart cards, only a handful of banks have issued smart cards numbering around 3 lakh with outstanding value of ₹ 1,000 crore.

The reasons why debit card is more attractive is that it is very similar to the ATM card with no charges and no service tax. In ATM, cash from branch window is replaced by machine window without the need for any service provider. The man is replaced by machine with greater convenience and efficiency and promptness. The only requirement is customer education and literacy in banking. It has the same facilities as debit card and hence the attractiveness of debit card in comparison with the credit card which has attached service charges and interest charges. Both have their own advantages and disadvantages and the their usage depends on the needs of the customer.

It can thus be concluded that the ATM, debit card and credit card have their own role to play in the spread of banking services and in saving the use of bank branches' manpower and in providing better service to the customer. They economise the use of currency notes.

ATMs have become more attractive to customers and most banks have been providing the services of ATMs. Debit cards serve the same purpose of replacing the cash with the plastic money for transactions with the merchant establishments, supermarkets and departmental stores. But the report of the RBI states that the use of the debit card is more for getting the cash instead of using it as plastic money direct for payments in the stores for transactions purposes.

Conclusion

To sum up, increasing acceptance of plastic company has become a source of income to banks and facilitate the public transactions. The currency management is made easier and costs lower. It economises the use of currency and increases the bank credit and money supply with public. The banks and public both stand to gain by the usage of plastic money.

There are disadvantages also, which are now the concern of the RBI. The security and secrecy of the data on the one hand the prevention of frauds and the possible run on e-money are the major problems of banks and the RBI. The use of plastic money raises many questions on technical security, control and audit systems, most favoured technology to detect frauds and operational problems, foreseeing and plugging the weakspots of the cryptography based system. The legal aspects are partly taken care by the I.T. Act of 2000, but there are many issues which the RBI and government are concerned with the present context, such as inter-connectivity of systems, clearing and settlement of e-transactions and a Supervisory and Regulatory Board. The I.T. Act 2000 has to be amended to plug in the loopholes in cryptography, encryption, national settlement and clearing systems, etc. At macro level, credit card transactions add to creations of bank money and whether it is an addition to bank money or substitution of plastic money in lieu of deposit money is not clear. It is no doubt true that the use of currency is replaced by use of plastic money, but further implications of this have to be empirically proved to draw any conclusion.

✠ ✠ ✠

PART III

NBFCs AND THEIR SERVICES

NBFCs — AN OVERVIEW

11

During the 1980s, the importance of the NBFCs was not significant with hardly a total number of NBFCs at 7063 in 1981. At present they are reported to have gone to about 40,000. The main categories of Joint Stock Companies working as NBFCs were as follows:

Finance Cos. — Public Ltd. / Private Ltd.

Non-financial Cos. — Public Ltd. / Private Ltd.

Nearly 85-90% of the companies are of the non-financial category, some of them accepting deposits.

The various categories of finance companies are shown in the chart I. The more important of them are shown below:

1. Hire-purchase Finance Companies
2. Equipment Leasing Companies
3. Loan Companies
4. Investment Companies
5. Housing Finance Companies
6. Mutual Benefit Finance Companies
7. Insurance Companies and Stock Broking Company
8. Miscellancous non-banking companies

Residual categories are those other than the above categories, as defined by the Non-banking Financial Companies (RBI) Directions (1997) and the Miscellaneous Non-banking (RBI) Directions (1997). These directives were issued under the RBI Amendment Act, 1997. The power to regulate the NBFCs, was given to RBI, in terms of Chapter III B of the RBI Act. The Miscellaneous Non-banking Company is one, conducting Chits and Kuris, and organises the collection of funds from subscribing members in instalments with a definite timeframe and each one of them is eligible for drawing the prize amount decided by tender, or lots or in any sequential order as in the case of Nidhis.

Chart 1

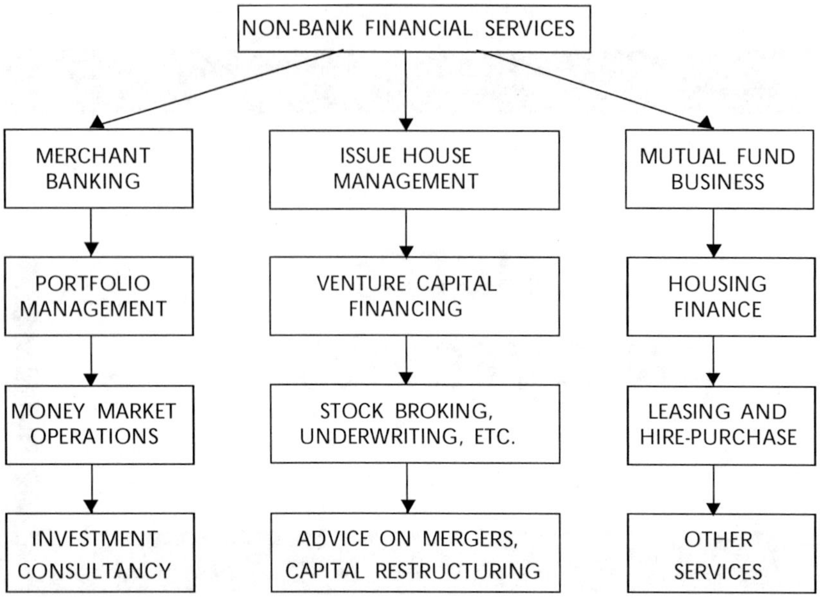

Other services include loan and investment companies, insurance, microfinance companies and other miscellaneous functions of a residuary nature, Chit funds, Kuris, etc.There are seven primary dealers, dealing in money and capital markets and seven FIs being regulated by the RBI, like NABARD, Exim Bank, IFC, NHB, etc.

By 2005, the number of NBFCs have been reported to have gone up to 38,050, as against 25,085, just before reforms started in 1991. During the last one-and-half decades, the number of NBFCs mobilising deposits have increased by 5 times and more. The rate of growth of deposits of NBFCs is however higher at 50% to 120%, and particularly so in the category of exempted deposits. The NBFC's registered with RBI stood at 13,261 which declined to 12,968 at end June 2007.

The number of Joint Stock Companies, both financial and non-financial are in lakh. Of those working, only 3 to 4% are reporting to the RBI. Incidentally all NBFCs, with ₹ 50 lakh and above of net worth should be registered with RBI and submit provisional and regular returns. The registration was made compulsory which was completed by 7th July, 1997. Of the total number working 16% are the financial companies and of the total submitting returns to RBI nearly 78-80% are financial companies only. The total NBFC, accepting deposits and reporting to RBI stood at 12,409 in 2011.

The growth of leasing and hire-purchase companies and their deposits was faster during the recent past. They also borrow from the banks larger amounts than any other category of NBFCs. Their larger reliance on banks, instead of mobilising resources of their own has been a cause of concern to the RBI. Many of the finance companies having more than ₹ 50 lakhs of NOF have not yet got registered with the RBI and their credit rating is not obtained and published as required by the RBI guidelines. Only 13,671 Non-bank finance companies are registered with RBI; of which 584 have submitted regular returns and only a few of them have secured and filed their credit rating. A number of NBFCs have been found to be non-variable by RBI. Some operating NBFCs have closed down on their own and RBI has cancelled licence for some. Deposits of financial companies stood at around 40% of the aggregate deposits of all Non-banking sector. The aggregate deposits of all Non-bank corporate sector worked out to around 2% of the aggregate deposits of banking sector as in 2005, due to closure of many deposit taking NBFCs and the data relates to only regulated NBFCs.

Reforms of Non-bank Finance Companies (NBFCs)

Since the financial reforms were started in July 1991, the importance of NBFCs has grown enormously and they are also subject to financial sector reforms. Narasimham Committee (1991) on financial Reforms recommended that these companies should also be brought under the fold of regulations of the RBI and be subject to the Prudential norms as in the case of commercial banks. A committee or working group under the chairmanship of A.C. Shah was set up by the RBI in May 1992 on the various aspects of working of NBFCs.

Shah Committee Report

The major recommendations of A.C. Shah Committee were as follows:

1. Only those NBFCs with net owned funds (NOF) of ₹ 50 lakh and above should be regulated by the RBI, after being registered and licensed by them.
2. Uniform regulations for all finance companies to be imposed and enforced by the RBI, through their returns submitted to RBI.
3. Regulations should extend to not only the deposit acceptance but to their asset side as well as credit concentration, investment profile, and capital adequacy on the risk assets as in the case of banks, regulation of all deposits including those of exempted categories.
4. As in the case of banks, prudential norms for income recognition, transparency of accounts and provisions for bad and doubtful debts, etc., are to be prescribed.
5. Interest rates on their deposits accepted should be 2 or 3 percentage points above those of commercial banks. Deposits for periods ranging from 12 months to 84 months only are allowed to be accepted by them.

Exempted Deposits as per RBI Guidelines

These include the following categories:

(*a*) Money received from Central and State Govts.

(*b*) Money received from foreign govt./foreign authority

(*c*) Borrowings from banks and FIs

(*d*) Inter-corporate borrowings

(*e*) Money received from shareholders and directors, including private companies

(*f*) Security deposits

(*g*) Advances against orders

(*h*) Secured and conversible debentures

(*i*) Money received for subscription to new issues pending allotment for Bridge finance.

(*j*) Money received in Trust/or in Transit

(*k*) Amounts relating to Conventional Chits of the above *(b)*, *(c)* and *(h)* were not treated as exempted since April 1993. So also the money received for directors and shareholders *(e)* and Inter-corporate deposits *(d)* were also regulated since 1993.

Reforms

A board for financial supervision was set up by RBI, with an Advisory Council to strengthen the supervision of banks and FIs. The reforms or NBFs started with the recommendations of Narasimham Committee (1991) urging the inclusion of the NBFC sector and its integration into the organised financial system. These recommendations received a further boost from the similar observations of Shah Committee on NBFCs (1992). Further reforms were started since 1993, based on the recommendations of the above Committees, in the direction of better regulation of their deposit acceptance, provision for bad and doubtful debts and risk weighted capital adequacy of 8% to be achieved by March 1996.

The above recommendations are being implemented. The interest rates on their deposits are freed in 1996. All exempted categories of deposits like I.C.Ds, monies received from directors and shareholders and the debentures or secured bonds, issued to public by mortgage of immovable property which were not part of regulated deposits before were brought under regulation.

Liquidity Requirements

Hire-purchase and equipment leasing companies will be required to maintain liquid assets at 10% of deposits, of which 5% should be in govt., Semi-govt. and govt. guaranteed bonds. The residuary non-banking companies will have to keep 10% of their deposits in govt. and govt. guaranteed bonds within 70% limit on investments in approved securities.

Ceiling on Deposits

The ceiling imposed by the RBI on acceptance of deposits are related to the NOF of the company in the following manner:

Category of NBFCs — As % of NOF (Net Owned Funds)
Loan and Investment Cos = 40%
Hire-purchase and Leasing Cos = 10 Times the NOF
Housing Finance Cos 10-15 Times of NOF

Exempted Deposits – Items included

Three additional items of deposits have been included in the total exempted deposits from 1993. These are the:

(*a*) Borrowings from banks and specified F.I.s.

(*b*) Monies received through issue of secured or convertible debentures.

(*c*) Borrowings from foreign govt. or foreign sources.

Regulated deposits are the following:

(*a*) Deposits from the public for 12 months to 84 months.

(*b*) Deposits guaranteed by directors.

(*c*) Unsecured debentures.

(*d*) Deposits received from the company's shareholders.

RBI Package for NBFCs (July 1996)

First of all the interest rate ceiling on deposits and on the quantum of deposits was removed in July 1996, as part of this package, in respect of those NBFCs which are registered with the RBI, and they also comply with all the requirements of the RBI guidelines such as securing a credit rating.

The overall ceiling of 10 times the net owned funds (NOF) for EL and H.P. companies which are registered with RBI and not credit rated would stand as it is. For others the ceiling will continue to apply as also the sub-ceiling of ICDs for 12 months and less at two times the NOF would also remain. The overall ceiling on deposits was reduced from 10 to 7 times the NOF in respect of registered EL and HP companies which are registered with the RBI but not credit rated, and not met the prudential norms. But for those NBFCs,

(EL and HPs) which are unregistered the ceiling on deposits quantum was reduced from 10 to 5 times the NOF and the limit for ICD not exceeding 12 months is being brought down from two to one time the NOF. These measures are effective from July 1996.

Registered loan and investment companies which comply with the credit rating requirement and also prudential norms will be allowed to accept up to two times NOF instead of one time the NOF. Separate ceiling of two times the NOF for ICD will remain unchanged. Those who satisfy the requirement of credit rating but not prudential norms, the ceiling limit on deposits was retained at one time of NOF for them with however two times the NOF for ICDs.[@]

For unregistered L and I companies, the ceiling limit on deposits will be 15% for deposits from shareholders and 25% of NOF for public. The limit separately given for ICD is reduced from two times to one time of NOF. But for registered L and I companies complying with neither credit rating requirement, nor prudential norms is being reduced from one time of NOF to 15% for deposits from shareholders and 25% of NOF for deposits from public. The separate ceiling for ICD at two times the NOF will remain unchanged.

The deposit acceptance is for one year to five years. The ceiling of interest rate will be applicable until the NBFC has applied on a specified format to the RBI and got the certificate to the effect that it is registered and complied with all the requirements of the RBI guidelines on credit rating and prudential norms.

Liquid Assets

The liquid requirement for all NBFCs which comply with the requirements of RBI was also reduced from 15% of deposits to 12½%. This is also effective from the date they secure the certificate from the RBI to that effect. Besides the 12½% requirement, the stipulation that at least 10% of the deposits to be maintained in Central and State Government securities will not apply. All the registerred L and I, companies and F and HP companies not satisfying the guidelines of RBI on prudential norms and credit rating will continue to be governed by the stipulation of 15% of deposits to be invested in govt. (Central and State) and govt. guaranteed security and bonds. All unregistered NBFCs and Loan and Investment companies will continue to maintain liquid assets to the extent of 75% of their deposits as hitherto.

It was also provided that RBI may issue certificates to all those who satisfy the requirements, in order to avail of the benefits of relaxation. The NBFCs have to apply to the Concerned Regional Office of Dept. of Supervision, namely, Dept. of Non-banking Supervision with all formats duly filled and necessary information supplied to the RBI. The first certificate will be valid for one year and position will be viewed year after year.

The overall ceilings exempt the following categories:

(1) optically convertible debentures with option open to both issuer and the holders of the debentures.

(2) debentures issued with pre-determined terms and conditions of conversion with option.

The reduction in the limits is made applicable from July 25, 1996. These companies would have to bring down their limits to newly stipulated levels within six months. Slowly, the NBFCs who do not adhere to all the directives of the RBI, would progressively face reduction in the limits for acceptance of deposits from the public and shareholders and a day will come when they will be barred from acceptance of deposits from any body, as per the RBI stipulations.

Khanna Committee Report

Non-banking finance and non-finance companies raised ₹17,352 crore through fixed deposits in 2010, when the new issue market and stock market are both in highly depressed conditions. Among such companies, finance companies like integrated finance (₹13,000 crore), Bajaj capital (₹1,000 crore) and Kotak Securities (₹1,000 crore) raised the largest amounts during the years. The amount raised in 2010-11 was ₹11,964 crore.

@ ICDs are inter-corporate deposits.

FDs are unsecured debt and investors put in their funds in known companies and local firms. The risk is high but the rates of return in the form of interest rates, discounts, cash commissions, etc., are also high. The returns are reported to have ranged from 15% to 20% in many cases and the credit ratings of these varied from single A to Triple A. The Khanna Committee set up in April 1995 has recommended (Jan. 1997) that the operations of NBFCs be brought into the overall framework of Monetary and Credit Policy of RBI. There are 41,361 companies in the category of NBFCs, at end August 1995 and by end 1996, they might have gone up to 60,000. Only 10,000 companies are furnishing returns to RBI, as required by govt. guidelines of 297 deposit taking companies, only 217 NBFCs have reported in time in 2011.

The Khanna Committee recommended greater control on NBFCs by amendment to Chapter III B of the RBI Act, compulsory registration, investment norms and creation of Reserve Fund, etc. Onsite inspection of such large number of companies may be difficult and has to be supplemented by offsite surveillance system through assessment of their policies, procedures, compliance with guidelines, asset quality, capital adequacy and provisioning requirements. The RBI was expected to coordinate with other regulatory agencies of NBFCs like SEBI and Dept. of Company Affairs and make one shot affair of examination and inspection for and of spot examination of their operations and greater control and regulation of their activities.

Details of Recommendations on Non-bank Finance Companies

Their deposits were ₹56,559 crore at end March 1994 and their rate of growing was fast both in number and the amount of deposits raised. A committee, headed by Shri Khanna was asked to examine the feasibility and desirability of regulating these NBFCs (Jan. 1997). The definition of agregate deposits of NBFCs was changed in 1997 as referred to earlier and RBI Amendment Act, 1997 was passed with greater power of control on NBFCs as at end March 1999, public deposits with reporting NBFCs stood at ₹20,429 crore which accounted hardly for 3% of deposits with all banks, which was brought down to 1.6% by end 2004. By end March 2011, public deposits of all NBFCs stood at ₹41,062 crore which is roughly one per cent of aggregate deposits of scheduled commercial banks. The interest rate ranged from 10 to 12.5%.

The committee's main recommendations may be set out as follows:

1. Capital adequacy norm of 8% to be made applicable to NBFCs, over the next two years.
2. A separate suitable legislation which was passed later in the place of chapter III B of RBI Act, 1934 covering the entire regulatory framework for NBFCs by the RBI.
3. Balance sheets of NBFCs should be the same as submitted to the RBI observing the prudential norms, income recognition guidelines, etc., of the RBI.
4. RBI should publicise the norms of NBFCs which have not complied with the regulatory framework of RBI. They should be banned from carrying on financial business and from acceptance of deposits from public.
5. RBI should set up an in-house market intelligence outfit to collect information on activities of NBFCs, interact with the representatives of NBFC associations, examine the observance of RBI guidelines, the interest rates offered and terms of offer of deposit acceptance and on-site inspection and reporting the same to the RBI and scan the credit rating published by the credit rating agencies, etc.

Importance of NBFCs in India

There are more than 40,000 non-banking finance companies, big and small and reporting and non-reporting. Of these registered with the RBI were only about 13,000. Of these there were about 362 companies reporting to RBI at end March 2007, and having the total deposits of ₹24,665 crore, constituting about 1% of aggregate deposits of the Scheduled Commercial Banks as at end March 2007. Next to banks, they have the largest network for deposit mobilisation and collection of savings of the public. These deposits include both regulated deposits and exempted categories of deposits. Not to allow them to compete with banks, the

RBI has not allowed them to have savings accounts and time deposits of less than six months and in some cases not less than one year. They offer higher interest rates and offer incentives to savers and use the services of brokers and agents which are not allowed in the case of banks. As opposed to these advantages enjoyed by non-banking companies, banks enjoy the benefit of higher credibility, safety and liquidity. Banks can offer less risk, cheque drawing, collection and other facilities to savers. Weighing both banks and non-banking companies, it was found that the growth rate of deposits of non-banking companies is faster than of banks, particularly during the few years (up to) 1997, when the financial reforms and liberalisation have attracted both foreign and domestic companies to expand their activities and NBFCs have been brought under the control of RBI.

During 1992-97, the number of finance companies rose faster due to free entry into the capital market and liberalised conditions of financial markets, free market economy and various financial and economic reforms undertaken by the govt. Due to the mushroom growth of finance companies, there were many instances of failures of these companies to repay deposits as in the case of CRB caps, Aneja group, Lloyds group, Nagarjuna group, etc. This has shaken the confidence of investors and forced the govt. to take some measures.

In the above context, the govt. promulgated an ordinance for amending the RBI Act, 1934 in January 1997. This gave greater powers to RBI to control and regulate the NBFCs and unincorporated bodies. Many Nidhi companies were also closed or were in difficulties of liquidity and repayment of deposits. They were asked to achieve a ratio of net owned funds to deposits not exceeding 20 times the NOF, in respect of only the incremental deposit liabilities over the level of January 15, 1997. This led to further reduction of NBFCs and the amount of their deposits.

The Residual Non-banking Companies like Peerless are exempt from these provisions, of control, as imposed by the RBI. Housing Finance Companies were exempted from all the provisions of Chapter III B of RBI Act, as amended in January 1997. They are expected to be regulated by a separate authority, namely, National Housing Board (NHB). Accordingly, the HFCs were not required to apply for a certificate of registration from the RBI as provided for in Section 45IA of the RBI Act.

The January 1997 ordinance was replaced by the RBI Amendment Act in March 1997. Effective April 1, 1997, the RBI controls on the NBFCs became effective. No new NBFCs can be operative without RBI prior registration. Existing NBFCs were required to get themselves registered before July 8, 1997. All NBFCs with less than ₹25 lakh were given 3 years time to reach that level of ₹25 lakh. Those companies with NOF of ₹25 lakh and above have to register with the RBI. As at end June 2004, 38,050 companies have applied for registration, of which only 13,671 NBFCs were registered. Unincorporated bodies like Margadarsi cannot accept deposits. Those NBFCs not registered with RBI cannot also accept deposits from public. NBFCs have to maintain liquid assets of not less than 50% of their deposits or any higher rate up to 75% of deposits as may be announced by the RBI. Every NBFC would create a reserve fund and transfer to it at least 20% of its net profits every year before declaring a dividend.

The RBI has imposed some guidelines on their disclosures, prudential norms on income recognition, accounting standards provisioning for bad and doubtful debts, credit concentration on family concerns, etc. Those which are credit rated after RBI registration and observe prudential norms were exempted from any limits of bank credit access. The percentage of liquid assets to be maintained by unregistered loan and investment companies will be 10% by April 1, 1998, as against the then current limit of 5%. Other NBFCs, which are maintaining 10% limit so far will have to maintain a higher ratio of 15% from April 1, 1998.

The RBI removed the ceiling on bank credit laid down for all registered NBFCs engaged in principal business of equipment leasing, hire-purchase, loan and investments since May 1999.

RBI Directives to NBFCs

In January 1998, the RBI has announced a series of measures to protect the interests of depositors and public from any unhealthy practices by NBFCs. These measures apply to those NBFCs accepting deposits from public while the others will be supervised by RBI in a limited manner.

Firstly, the NBFCs, not having Net Owned Funds (NOF) of ₹25 lakh atleast will not be allowed to raise funds from public in the form of deposits and they cannot be registered with the RBI. For new NBFCs to be registered with the RBI, their NOF should not be less than ₹2 crore. Secondly, Mutual benefit financial company can only accept deposit from shareholders and members in the form time deposits. No brokerage or commission can be paid by them and they cannot issue any advertisement or hoarding, inviting deposits from any source. Thirdly, there is a credit rating requirement for all NBFCs and the amount of deposit that can be raised is linked to it, as shown below:

Credit Rating	*Deposit limit for Equipment Leasing and Hire-purchase companies*	*Loan and Investment Companies*
AAA	3 times their NOF	2 times their NOF
AA	2 times their NOF	1 time their NOF
A	1 time	0.5 time

NBFCs having credit rating less than 'A' cannot raise deposits from public. The NBFCs are subject to a ceiling interest rate of 16% per annum, later brought down to 11%, brokerage of 2% uniformly for all maturities from 1 to 5 years and incur expenses by way of reimbursement up to a limit of 0.5% of deposits collected. Besides NBFCs, accepting deposits will be required to submit to RBI annual statutory returns and financial statements. Their deposits should be of duration of 1 to 5 years only.

Approved credit rating agencies and the minimum rating symbol are as shown below:

Name	*Minimum Rating*
(*a*) Credit Rating Information Services of India Ltd. (CRISIL)	FA
(*b*) Investment Information and Credit Rating Agency of India Ltd. (ICRA)	MA
(*c*) Credit Analysis and Research Ltd. (CARE)	CARE A(FD)
(*d*) Duff and Dhelps Credit Rating India Pvt. Ltd.	Ind A

Prudential Norms

The NBFCs including the Residuary Non-banking Companies accepting public deposits will be required to comply with all the prudential norms, which include the following:

Income Recognition Norms

All lease rentals and hire-purchase instalments due for 12 months and above (instead of 6 months as applicable before), will be treated as (NPA) in the case of lease and hire-purchase companies.

Capital Adequacy Norms

All NBFCs, registered with RBI accepting public deposits, capital adequacy norm has been raised from the present level of 8% to 10% by March end 1998 and 12% by March end 1999. For all NBFCs, incorporated after April 1999, the minimum required NOF was raised to ₹2 crore, in 1999.

Credit/Investment Concentration Norms

Any credit to a single borrower or a group of borrowers at 15% and 25% of the owned funds remains unchanged. Investment concentration norms have been modified. Thus investment in any single company and in any single group of companies should not exceed 15% and 25% respectively. The composite limits of credit and investment by an NBFC in a single entity and single group of companies have been fixed at 25% and 40% of NOF respectively.

The NBFCs have been prohibited to grant any loan against security of its own shares. Those which were issued before January 1998 should not be renewed and no fresh loans can be granted.

The NBFCs which are accepting deposits are required to submit to RBI half-yearly returns on observance of prudential norms, certified by their auditors. The scope of auditor's certificate is widened to include certain aspects of supervisory concerns relevant to RBI and to ensure correct reporting of data. The investment companies, holding not less than 90% of their assets being the securities of their group/holding/subsidiary companies and not accepting public deposits are exempted from the prudential norms.

The liquid asset requirement will be applicable to public deposits only. The ratio of liquid assets to public deposits shall be 12.5% from April 1, 1998 and 15% from April 1, 1999. The deposit taking companies are held responsible for correctness of their statements and declare that they are complying with all the requirements of the RBI.

The NBFCs, not accepting public deposits, to be eligible for exemption from the RBI guidelines, should get their Board of Directors pass a resolution that they will not accept any public deposits. The classification of these companies (NBFCs) into leasing, Hire-purchase investment, etc., companies is left to the discretion of the RBI and is based on the criteria that not less than 60% of its assets and not less than 60% of its income are derived from any one of these activities.

RBI Directions on Prudential Norms

These are called "Non-banking Financial Companies Prudential Norms (Reserve Bank) Directions, 1998, issued under the powers conferred by Section 45JA of RBI Act. These will be applicable to those NBFCs, having NOF of more than ₹ 25 lakh and accepting deposits.

These directions provide for income recognition, asset classification, weightage of risk to risky assets, credit conversion factors for off Balance Sheet items and concentration of credit/investment, etc.

Income recognition shall be based on recognised accounting principles. Income on NPA shall be recognised only when it is actually realised. Income from dividend on shares and units of Mutual Funds shall be taken into account only on cash basis. Only in the case of govt. bonds or PSU Bonds, the interest and repayment can be taken an accrual basis.

Investments are to be classified into current and permanent as in the case of banks. Current investments have to be valued at cost or market value, whichever is lower. Appreciation and depreciation have to be netted only in each category separately. Unquoted investments like shares, preference shares should be valued at cost or face value whichever is lower. NBFCs not holding public deposits need not submit liquid assets return. These accepting deposits are allowed to keep 5% of it in the form of unencumbered term deposits with scheduled banks.

Provisioning Requirements

The asset classification is the same as for banks, namely, standard and sub-standard assets, doubtful assets and loss assets. The provisions to be made for these assets are as follows:

Loss Assets: The entire amount is written off and 100% of the value is provided.

Doubtful Assets: 100% provision to be made to the extent of the provision not covered by realisable securities.

Period for which the asset has been considered not realisable	*% of the provision*
Up to one year	20%
One to three years	30%
More than three years	50%

Sub-standard Assets: A general provision of 10% of total outstandings.

Requirement as to Capital Adequacy

Every NBFC shall maintain a minimum capital ratio consisting of Tier I and Tier II which shall not be less than

10% on or before, March 31, 1998

12% on or before March 31, 1999

of the aggregate risk weighted assets and of risk adjusted value of off Blalance Sheet items. Tier II capital shall not exceed 100% of Tier I capital.

RISK WEIGHTAGE ON ASSETS

Weighted Risk assets on balance sheet items	*Percentage weight*
Cash and Bank balances including fixed deposits, CDs, etc.	0
Investments in Govt. securities	2.5%
Shares/debentures/units of mutual funds, Commercial paper/corporate bonds	100%
Stock on Hire (net book value)	100%
Inter-corporate loans/deposits	100%
Fully secured loans/advances	0
Loans to staff	0
Other secured loans/advances considered good	100
Bills purchased/discounted	100
Others	100
Assets leased out	100
Premises, fixtures, fittings	100
Other assets like TDS, Advance Tax, Interest due on govt. debt	0

Concentration of Credit/Investment

No NBFC shall lend to any single borrower exceeding 15% of its NOF and to any group of borrowers exceeding 25% of its NOF. No NBFC shall invest in shares of another company exceeding 15% of its NOF and to any single group of companies exceeding 25% of NOF. No NBFC shall lend and invest together in any company exceeding 25% of the latter's NOF and to any single group of parties exceeding 40% of the latter's NOF. The investment in bonds/debentures for the above purpose should be treated as loan and not investment. The off balance sheet exposures shall be converted into credit risk by applying the conversion factors, as given below:

The face value of each of the following items requires to be multiplied by the relevant conversion factor to arrive at risk adjusted value of off balance sheet items. The aggregate shall be taken into account for reckoning the minimum capital ratio. This shall have to be again multiplied by the risk weight of 100.

Nature of the item	Risk weight
Financial and other Guarantees	100
Shares and debentures, underwriting	50
Partly paid shares/debentures	100
Bills discounted/rediscounted	100
Lease contracts entered into but yet to be executed	100
Other contingent liabilities	50

Cash margins/deposits shall be deducted before applying the conversion factors. After applying the conversion factors, the total risk weighted capital ratio has to be calculated.

Auditor's Report

Every auditor of a NBFC is governed by the directions given by the RBI, under Sub-section (1A) of Section 45 IA of RBI Act.

The Auditor's report, should contain, in addition to the requirements under Section 227 of the Companies Act, the requirements as given in the RBI directions. The auditor's report shall contain *inter alia* the information on the following points also:

1. In the case of all NBFCs, whether the company is registered under Section 45 IA of RBI Act, and whether it has received any communication from RBI about the grant of or refusal of certificate of Registration.
2. In the case of NBFCs, accepting public deposits, whether the company's public deposits including unsecured, non-convertible debentures/bonds, from its shareholders and from others are within the limits set by the provisions of Non-banking Finance Companies (RBI) Directions 1998.
3. In the case of a NBFC, which is an investment company, not accepting public deposits and which has invested not less than 90% of its assets in the securities of its Group/holding/subsidiary companies as long-term investments, the auditors will have to state whether the Board of Directors have passed a resolution for the non-acceptance of public deposits and whether in fact they raised any public deposits, whether the company has identified the group/holding/subsidiary companies and whether the cost of investments made in the group is not less than 90% of the cost of total assets.

The auditors should also state the reasons for unfavourable or qualified statements in their report.

RBI REGULATION

NBFCs and RNBFCs

The RBI deregulated the interest rate structure for NBFCs after 1999. This means that there will be no 10% floor interest for public deposits raised by RNBFCs and 15% interest rate ceiling for NBFCs. This proposal is in tune with the RBI's overall policy to move towards a deregulated interest rate regime.

Till recently, NBFCs who have been adopting prudential accounting norm of income recognition and asset classification and maintaining the stipulated 10% of SLR and getting their fixed deposits rated were allowed by the RBI to offer a return of over 15% on deposits, which was 12.5% as in 2010-11.

Insurance Cover of NBFC Deposits

With as much as nearly ₹4 thousand crore of deposits, at end March 2011, including only regulated working to a few lakh crore of deposits of NBFCs (non-bank non-financial companies) accepting deposits from the public deposits, constituting 70% of aggregate deposits of scheduled commercial banks, the need for protecting the investors of these deposits became very critical for maintaining the public confidence in the financial system. The possibility of failures of banks and NBFCs is there and more so in the present environment of deregulation and free market economy. Many NBFCs like CRB Caps, Hoffland, Aneja, Lloyds Finance, GVK, etc., have found themselves in a financial crisis and could not repay the deposits at all or at the proper time. The RBI has taken measures in 1996 and 1997 by asking such companies to stop accepting fresh deposits.

The RBI has recommended to the Centre a separate deposit insurance institution to avoid risks of bank failures and run on NBFCs. Both banks and NBFCs need deposit insurance protection. However to ensure that presence of deposit insurance does not prompt them to take unwarranted risks, proper measurement of risk taken by them and adoption of risk based insurance pricing are necessary and also for enforcing proper risk weighted capital adequacy requirements, based on the risk profile of both banks and NBFCs. The premium charged by the insurance organisation should be related to risks taken by the banks and NBFCs.

Rationalisation of Norms

The Reserve Bank of India announced rationalisation of some of the regulations and other measures as applicable to non-banking finance companies (NBFCs) and residuary non-banking companies (RNBCs), in June 2000.

The changes made are: Provisioning norms in respect of lease and hire-purchase assets have been rationalised to encourage NBFCs to continue to extend the facility against second-hand assets as part of their contribution of the economic development of the country.

The NBFCs may obtain and keep on their records a copy of the passport, ration card, election ID card, and identification by an existing depositor as an evidence for identification of new depositors.

Residual non-banking companies have been permitted to make investment in mutual funds schemes approved by the Securities and Exchange Board of India along with the schemes of Unit Trust of India. The floor ceiling on interest rates payable by these companies has also been lowered down by two percentages points.

The NBFCs have been permitted to accept deposits from the relatives of the directors subject to adequate disclosure to the depositors in this regard, outside the purview of the public deposits.

The formats of all the statutory returns to be submitted by the non-banking financial companies, nidhis, residuary non-banking companies and chit fund companies for their reporting in quarterly, half-yearly and annual returns, as applicable, under the RBI regulations have been rationalised with a view to ascertaining supervisory information from the returns to the extent possible and for facilitating electronic processing of these returns to the extent possible to enable the bank to take expeditious steps to address the concerns wherever necessary.

The RBI has also advised all the registered NBFCs to brand their Certificates of Registration by the words as 'deposit taking companies' or 'non-deposit taking companies' so as to avoid any possible mis-representation by any company registered as a non-public deposit taking company and accepting public deposits. The bank has further advised that public deposits should be accessed only by those NBFCs which have been specifically permitted to accept public deposits and RNBCs.

Recent Policy Measures

1. Quarterly reporting of NBFCs, not accepting deposits but having assets size of ₹500 crores and above.
2. Snap inspection and regular inspections for the Registered NBFCs by the RBI.
3. Streamlining of the returns on Asset Liability Management and capital market exposure.

4. Alignment of interest rate with those of banks, with a ceiling of 11% and floor rate of 5%.
5. Prudential norms of banks to be applicable to NBFCs as also a capital adequacy norm of 8% to 10% on risk weighted assets.
6. Application of prudential norms for exposure to infrastructure projects and nomination facilities for depositors.
7. 'Know your Customer' guidelines applied to commercial banks are enforced on NBFCs also.
8. Allowing NBFCs to take up insurance business.
9. Issuance of guidelines for securitisation companies and reconstruction companies.
10. Liberalisation of bank finance to NBFCs, and slow phasing out of public deposits with a view to make NBFCs depend for their resources on owned funds and access to capital market.

✠ ✠ ✠

GROWTH OF NON-BANK FINANCIAL SERVICES

12

Introduction

The securities scandal of 1991-92 and of 2001 emanating from the financial services has thrown light on the vulnerability of the banking sector to any lapses on the part of the non-bank financial sector. The portfolio management services, mutual fund and merchant banking services of banks and their subsidiaries have all become vulnerable to any developments in the non-banking sector. Similarly, the non-bank and non-financial sector, the capital and money markets have all become equally susceptible to any weaknesses and malpractices of other sectors including the banking sector. This was due to better financial integration since 1992 reforms were initiated. The equity boom and the new issue buoyancy in 1992 and the subsequent burst and the prolonged bearishness in these markets have confirmed the increasing vulnerability of these sectors *inter se*. The operations of mutual funds, investment banks etc., have led to greater volatility of stock markets and emphasised the destabilising linkages between the money market and securities market operations and the stock markets. The stock brokers have played a role in these operations and this again underlines the need for forging better relations and healthy traditions and enforcing a code of conduct on bankers and brokers alike. It is this fact, that has led to the emerging importance of overseeing such non-banking financial operations of banking subsidiaries and those of private sector.

Linkages between Bankers and Brokers

Stock brokers are financial intermediaries like bankers, who are now providing various categories of non-bank financial Services. The relations of brokers and bankers are age-old and linkages are broadly provision of:

1. Limits or advances against securities.
2. Banker to act as clearing bank for brokers.
3. Bankers' operations in money market and brokers' role in the process.
4. Bankers' operations in portfolio management and brokers' role in the process.
5. Approved brokers also operate in the Government securities market.

6. In the capital market, underwriting of new issues is done by bankers and brokers and sub-underwriters for bankers.
7. Collecting bankers, co-ordinating bankers, merchant bankers have to work in close co-ordination with brokers acting as underwriters or doing marketing of new issues.
8. Brokers act as conduit pipe for flow of NRI funds to banks and their use for capital and stock market investments.

It will thus be seen that bankers and brokers have to work in close co-ordination with each other in money market, Government securities market and capital market. If this nexus is misused as in the recent past through irregular and unauthorised means then the public, investors and depositors suffer. Healthy practices and observance of a code of conduct on their part are therefore extremely necessary.

In the emerging scenario, of financial and economic reforms with increasing financial deregulation and industrial liberalisation, the role of the financial sector in the private enterprise economy is growing. The financial services sector has thus emerged as the fastest growing sunrise industry in the country. The largest rise in prices of listed companies on the stock markets over the last year was in the financial sector. The future income and employment growth in this sector has vast potentiality. There is a discernible trend that the economic reforms in India initiated since July 1991, are in the direction of greater role for private enterprise, private capital, increasing reliance on public savings and on the capital market. The government, banks, financial institutions etc., have to compete with corporate and business sector for public funds in the capital market. Besides, competition and efficiency will thus be the prime movers in the future in the economic and corporate performance. For this purpose, the role of stock market will increase to be a true reflector of the state of the economy and of the fundamentals of the corporate sector.

INSTITUTIONS IN THE NON-BANK FINANCIAL SECTOR

The following categories of institutions are having operations with an impact on the financial markets, and provide non-bank financial services:

(*a*) Banks (public, private and foreign), requiring better supervision and regulation of their main operations of deposit mobilisation and credit allocation.

(*b*) Financial institutions — all-India and State level — some of whose operations go beyond their ken, namely, lending, borrowing and having developmental and regulatory functions and even investment operations in the capital market.

(*c*) Subsidiaries of banks and financial institutions like venture capital funds, merchant banking, housing finance, mutual funds, portfolio management, investment finance, leasing finance, leasing and hire-purchase factoring, bill financing, etc.

(*d*) Private sector investment and finance companies, FFIs and FIIs brokers, investment consultants, underwriters, portfolio managers, registrars, etc., who are playing an increasing role in the financial sector and hence their activity has become focal point of attention of the authorities, namely, SEBI, RBI and the government.

The importance of finance companies in raising resources directly from the public has been increasing. Of the deposits raised by companies, the proportion raised by finance companies is about 35% and the rest is by non-finance companies. The government have recently permitted banks and financial institutions to raise resources from the public directly as bonds or debt and in some cases even as equity. The SBI was thus in a position to borrow funds as equity directly from the public while the necessary legislation has to be passed in respect of other public sector banks allowing direct access to capital market. Although this relates to the banking sector, this has implications for non-bank financial operations in the capital market.

The recent RBI directive opening up the entry into banking sector for the private enterprise helps in the toning up of the banking sector through better competition and efficiency in allocation of resources. The insistence of minimum paid-up capital of ₹ 100 crores and a capital adequacy norm of 8% would definitely tone up the financial system.

In the non-bank financial sector also reforms were introduced to remove the ceiling of interest rate on debentures at 15% lowering of the maximum rate of interest payable on deposits accepted by them to 11%, etc. Besides, foreign financial institutions, pension funds, etc., were already permitted to operate in the Indian capital market. Foreign investment limit was raised to 51% and FERA was diluted to facilitate foreign capital inflows and outflows and foreign collaboration agreements, etc. The abolition of CIC, free entry into the capital market, freedom to issue fresh capital issues to the public, free market pricing of shares for issue along with the liberalisation of industrial policy and other economic reforms have all boosted the prospects of capital market and the scope for such non-bank financial services has increased.

FINANCIAL SECTOR VS. NON-BANK FINANCIAL SECTOR

The weaknesses of banks in terms of low competitive efficiency, productivity and low profitability of their assets have forced banks to enter into new pastures of non-bank financial services, such as leasing, hire purchase, leasing finance etc., since the early eighties. The Chakravorthy Committee (1985) and Narasimham Committee (1991) have unhesitatingly recommended the need for market oriented financial system where banks and non-bank financial institutions can function with greater autonomy, accountability and efficiency. The lending and borrowing rates and other interest rates, operational practices and risk coverage are all expected to be in conformity with market forces.

As regards non-bank financial services, the Narasimham Committee has recommended that all the institutions involved in the capital market like merchant bankers, mutual funds and other agencies like brokers, registrars, collecting bankers, printers, etc., should operate on sound lines, within a framework of regulatory system of the SEBI with a view to promoting better investor protection and widen the pool of savings and investment. The Committee was of the view that there should be prudential guidelines blending greater freedom to operate with adequate precautions to regulate if necessary the agencies operating and practices of their operations.

Surveillance of SEBI

As per the Narasimham Committee, the SEBI should not get involved in day-to-day functioning of the market or of exchange authorities nor should they exercise any discretionary controls wielded by the CCI (Controller of Capital Issues).

In actual practice, the SEBI controls through their guidelines became all purvasive involving all agencies, or intermediaries in the capital market. The control of stock exchanges and brokers was intensified and was made stronger than ever before. The spirit of market-oriented reforms was sacrificed in the name of investor protection and the regime of all comprehensive controls became the order of the day once again. Starting with licensing and registration of all players a regulatory system with the rules and regulations governing them and a code of conduct for each category of players is being enforced. This was made necessary by the fears of misuse of liberalisation and financial deregulation initiated by the economic reforms since July 1991.

Almost all the capital market reform measures intended to achieve a blending of market freedom and better regulation of the market for investor protection based on prudential guidelines have been implemented. A Presidential Ordinance promulgated on January 31, 1992 accorded statutory status as an autonomous body to the SEBI to protect investors' interest in securities, to promote the development of the capital market and to regulate the working of the market including the stock exchanges. Subsequently, the SEBI bill was passed by the Parliament giving official recognition, effective March 31, 1992, to the organisation as a surveillance body.

SEBI has been vested with wide-ranging powers to oversee constitution as well as the operations of mutual funds including presentation of accounts, following the decision to allow the entry of private sector and joint sector mutual funds. Secondly, all stock exchanges in the country have been brought under the control and annual inspection regime of SEBI for ensuring orderly growth of the stock market and investor protection. Thirdly, with the repealing of the Capital Issues Control Act, 1947 in May 1992, SEBI has been made the regulatory authority in regard to the new issue activities also.

SEBI has issued a series of guidelines covering different aspects of its jurisdiction and responsibility which would have, in their totality a significant bearing on the future development of the capital market. SEBI's guidelines cover: (*i*) Lead managers/merchant bankers concerned with prospectus, issues and portfolio management (including the terms and conditions of the contract), (*ii*) Mutual funds and each of their constituents, namely, sponsors, trustees, asset management company (AMC) and custodian, including the formation of the AMC, (*iii*) Stock exchanges including stringent regulations to curb the practice of insider trading, and (*iv*) Compliance by issuers of capital and intermediaries with norms regarding proper disclosure and investors' protection which *inter alia* cover promoters' contribution, pricing of issues, credit rating of debt instruments, monitoring of issue proceeds of large issues and stipulations regarding underwriting and minimum subscription.

Financial Services of Financial Institutions

The variety of financial services now provided by the All-India Financial Institutions have widened into a broad spectrum of activities. In addition to normal project financing, loan syndication, they operate equipment leasing, equipment procurement, equipment credit, instalment credit, supplier's credit, buyer's credit, finance to leasing and hire-purchase schemes, etc. The IDBI's Bills Rediscounting Scheme also helps in financing the indigeneous manufacturers of machinery and capital equipment by getting the money through discounting the bills with his banker while the banker in turn gets rediscounting facility from IDBI. The purchaser is enabled to repay the cost over a number of years. This helps the growth of sales of manufacturers and also the users of capital equipment, machinery, plant etc.

Forfaiting is another source of finance developed by banks for export and import trade and to cover credit risk. Under this for consideration of having received the full payment immediately by the exporter he surrenders to the forfaiter all his rights to receive the consideration price from the buyer at a future date. The period of finance may be for three to seven years. The political and transfer risks in addition to credit risks are borne by the forfaiter.

Factoring is another service of non-bank financial nature. Banks like SBI, Canara Bank, etc., have set up subsidiaries for such services. Such services are available since 1991 to business concerns through purchase of their book debts and receivables. The services include administration of clients' sales ledger, collection of debts, covering of credit risk, etc. This helps the cash generation against receivables and helps the process of production and distribution of goods. Asset reconstruction companies are set up to take over the NPAs of banks and FIs.

Types of Non-bank Financial Services

1. Merchant Banking and New Issue Marketing.
2. Underwriting and Loan Syndication.
3. Bill Discounting and Money Market Operations.
4. Housing Finance.
5. Lease and Hire Purchase Financing.
6. Venture Capital Funds.
7. Investment Financing.

8. Investment Consultancy and Advise.
9. Mergers, Acquisitions, Amalgamations.
10. Capital Restructuring, Revaluations and Designing Capital Structure.
11. Portfolio Management Services.
12. Corporate Asset Management Services.
13. Technical Consultancy and Project Preparation.
14. Project Appraisal and Feasibility Studies.
15. New Issue House Services.
16. Guarantees and Underwriting including Registrar's Services.

Growth of Non-bank Financial Services

The role of banks in non-bank financial services began to grow from the time of the amendment to the Banking Regulation Act in 1983. Many merchant banking divisions and mutual funds were set up by the public sector banks since then. Banks began to increase their non-bank and non-funded business which are called financial services. More recently some more developments took place to expand the scope for such services: (1) Keeping open Indian capital market to foreign financial institutions and overseas corporate bodies to invest in India. (2) FERA dilution to encourage both the inflow and outflow of funds and foreign investment in India, some of which might flow into the stock and capital markets. (3) Opening up mutual fund business and even banking to the private sector. Already a number of private sector companies/firms are engaged in financial services, such as investment financing, hire-purchase, mortgage financing and housing finance, etc. Private sector was permitted to set up mutual funds, banks and financial institutions. Financial deregulation, freeing of interest rates on debentures, banks' lending rates and their practices, etc., has helped the growth of the financial sector. Today the emerging trends in this finance sector are as follows:

1. Faster rate of growth made it a sunrise industry.
2. Deregulation and liberalisation of procedures, reduction in government redtape and discretionary controls and revolution in information technology and in communication led to globalisation of financial markets.
3. Interlinkages between all segments of financial sector began to grow faster and deeper.

RESERVE BANK OF INDIA (Amendment) ACT, 1997

The main features of this amendment are set out below:

Registration of all existing NBFCs with a net worth of ₹ 25 lakh is made compulsory and those with net worth of less than ₹ 25 lakh have been given three year time period to bring up the network to the minimum level of ₹ 25 lakh. No unregistered NBFC was allowed to operate after July 1997.

The Act clearly defined an NBFC and institutions carrying on agricultural or industrial activity are excluded from this definition. NBFCs have to maintain liquid assets in specified securities on a daily basis at the rate of 15% of their deposits as at the end of the last quarter effective from April 1998. They have to create a Reserve Fund and transfer to it not less than 20% of their net profit to the reserve fund every year. All the guidelines given from time to time by the RBI have to be observed, failing which they would be penalised and even file a petition for winding up.

Nomination facility is available for all depositors in NBFCs. The CLB can adjudicate and pass orders in case of arrears/non-payment of deposits by them.

Unincorporated bodies engaged in financial activity cannot accept deposits from April 1, 1997. They cannot advertise for attracting deposits. These bodies, like the NBFCs subject to penalisation for any non-compliance with directives or orders. Both the RBI and CLB have jurisdiction on them and their orders are binding on them.

With a view to tighten regulation of the activities of NBFCs, and improve the financial health of the economy, the government promulgated an ordinance in January 1997, bringing about comprehensive changes in the provisions of chapters IIIB, and V of the RBI Act, 1934. The ordinance was replaced by an amendment to the RBI Act, relating to acceptance of deposits by unincorporated bodies.

Under the Act, registration with RBI is compulsory for all NBFC's operation in India. Any new NBFC cannot operate if its NOF is less than ₹ 2 crore and is not registered with RBI. The NBFCs have to maintain liquid assets of not less than 15% of their deposits and not more than 25% of their deposits. The Reserve Bank was authorised to issue directives relating to disclosures, prudential norms of income recognition, accounting standards, provisioning for bad and doubtful debt, concentration of credit or loans, capital adequacy and treatments of Non-performing Assets (NPAs). The NBFCs with NOF of ₹ 2 crore and above and registered with RBI are made eligible to do and undertake insurance business from the year 2000.

✠ ✠ ✠

MANAGEMENT OF FINANCIAL SERVICES

13

Introduction

The basic principles of management by objectives hold good for capital market management also. The objectives of management in financial services are efficiency in service, cost-effectiveness and profitability. This is a service industry where quality counts more than quantity. In this process, costs and profitability cannot be sacrificed. In the name of social obligations, banks have sacrified the productivity and profitability which should not happen for non-bank finance companies.

Thus management in capital market requires a combination of talents in finance area and marketing area and in personnel management (HRD). The knowledge required for this purpose is sought to be covered in this book in a basic but exhaustive manner.

This book is intended for those students of management who have some exposure to both finance and marketing or are students of MBA. As an area of specialisation with employment orientation and practical bias, the subject of capital market management is ideally suited to MBA students or finance students. This gives an exposure to practices and procedures in capital market and the institutions and agencies operating in it.

Capital market deals with arranging for loans, raising of funds, dealings in capital and securities which are claims on money. But being a service-oriented market, human element or management component is an all important and vital part of its operations.

Objectives of Management

The management of all capital market institutions should aim at quality of service, timeliness and efficiency, cost control and profitability. The above objectives can be achieved through collaborative efforts of a host of intermediaries like merchant bankers, underwriters, registrars, brokers, etc. The managers of these agencies have to bear a vital responsibility and should have *inter alia* the expertise in human relations and personnel management and co-ordinate the activities of various experts and teams in their activities.

Besides, in this service industry, of non-bank financial activity, men and human relations matter, in addition to practices and procedures. In addition to men, the other inputs that management deals with are money, monetary instruments, capital, plant and machinery involved in projects of companies, etc. The sinews of all industrial activity being finance and financial services, the management in capital market assumes vital importance to the economy. Besides, the fastest growing industry in the years to come is financial services and the largest scope for employment and self-employment lies in this line.

It is thus important for the capital market and for the economy to know who are the future managers heading these institutions and how competent are they. The managers of these finance companies, mutual funds, merchant banks, etc., are so far bankers, CAs, and finance graduates, etc., but a new professional breed of capital market managers through MBA in capital market is the need of the hour. It is for this breed of professionals that this book is meant for.[@]

Fine Tuning Managers to Financial Services: Timeliness

Any manager or management graduate will not fit into the area of capital market. The work involved is a combination of practical and theoretical ideas put into a capsule of sale of services. It thus requires all the management tools plus something more — a practical bias, a bent of mind and a behaviour. All the institutions in capital market are service oriented related to money, and finance. But more importantly a knowledge of law, marketing and rules and regulations a time schedule to follow as per rules and result-oriented actions are needed.

Decision Making

Capacity to take decisions and right decisions, and in time is an essential part of capital market management. After gathering information, classifying and analysing the data and information which is fast growing and put them into alternatives available, he has to chose the one with least cost, timely and most profitable. The manager has to help the companies save time and money to be able to stand competition.

Analytical Power

Corporate data is plenty and information flows in like Niagara falls and it is the manager's competency to pick up the correct information, analyse it and come to correct conclusions. Investment analysis and market analysis requires an expert financial manager.

But the suitable manager for capital market should combine in himself the expertise involved in the following areas:

(*a*) Personnel management with a special bent for co-ordination of expert manpower with capacity for better human relations.

(*b*) Finance management with an expertise in analysis and interpretation of financial data of companies.

(*c*) Expertise in law and practices of capital market and knowledge of rules and regulations relating to the capital market institutions, including SEBI and RBI.

(*d*) Marketing management with a flair for sales promotion to meet the competition of other institutions and increasing the market share in the services rendered by him.

(*e*) Knowledge of banking law, rules and practices relating to the money market to enable him to make proper investment management in the money market, which is closely connected to capital market.

(*f*) Knowledge of all non-bank financial services rendered by these institutions and laws and regulations relating to them as they are all inter-related, as hire-purchase, lease finance, venture capital, and expertise in dealing in such diverse areas.

(*g*) Knowledge of I.T. Rules and Law and the application of computerisation and I.T.

[@] V.A. Avadhani, "Capital Market Management", Himalaya Publishing House.

PRINCIPLES OF MANAGEMENT

Right Person in Right Place

The leader makes all the difference. It is the management talent to pick the right persons to be leaders in each division/department. The leader should be able to think, plan and execute the plan promptly and cost effectively. To keep ahead of competitors, he has to keep contact with information sources of competitors, make the "SWOT" (Strengths, Weaknesses, Opportunities and Threats) analysis and to see the strengths and weaknesses of staff and use the manpower resource optimally. Effective communication, good drafting, creativity and innovation are the qualities of good managers.

The leaders or top management have to set the goals for each department and plan to make it a profit centre. Targets and responsibilities are earmarked for each team who along with leader will achieve the optimum results with limited resources in terms of inputs and finance. Actual activity-wise responsibilities are set for each man and team.

Men are the best assets. The manager has to manage them effectively.

1. Encourage capable and committed men.
2. Train the less capable ones and motivate uncommitted men.
3. Develop self-management ideas and help them to be cultivated by delegation of authority and responsibility.

Time is another valuable asset. Time is money. Develop a sense of timeliness. Good management has time sense and plans all activities in a time bound fashion.

Quality counts in any activity and counts more in services. Competition in services takes the form of quality differences, in addition to pricing and charges.

Finance

The manager has to use "miserly" principle of economising in all possible ways, but should not be pound foolish and penny-wise. The management has to find methods of growing two blades of grass where only one blade grows. He has to use innovative ideas to save on costs and money.

Management of Men

1. Make them thinkers, innovators and motivated.
2. Manage them well by encouraging but not criticising, by correcting but not by humiliating.
3. Motivated and committed people, even if they commit occasional mistakes are assets to a firm.

Management of Time

1. Eliminate time spent on inessentials.
2. Reduce time spent on less-essential and have the capacity to discriminate between the essentials and non-essentials.
3. Plan the time daily, weekly and monthly.
4. Time and objective fulfilment have to be synchronised.
5. Delegate authority and activity so as to optimise time.

Right management means getting the job done in time and efficiently and not doing everything himself.

Management of Money

Finance is a scarce resource. It has alternative uses in daily transactions in working capital investment for raw-materials and inventories and fixed capital investment in buildings, plant, machinery, etc. The sources of finance are many, namely, borrowing from banks, FIs, and other companies. Capital can be raised from capital market, from public as equity (ownership) or bonds and debentures (debt). Even foreign capital market is now open to companies with credit standing. Each of these methods has its own cost — in the form of raising the money, servicing it and repayment of it. Even for equity which need not be repaid it has a cost in the form of expected yields in the minds of investors, based on what they get in other and similar companies.

Thus, the manager has to weigh these costs and design a capital structure with the least cost combination of these components. Being scarce resource, even cash has a cost in the form of alternative income lost. Thus, management of cash in an optimal manner involves some talent in reducing costs and increasing profitability, for which the manager is responsible. Thus management of finance is vital responsibility of manager in all financial services. Capital market management gives crucial role to this job.

Interviews and Plant Visits

Managers in capital market require to meet people, in different grades and levels. Communication, clarity of thinking and analytical power, arduous homework and ability to deal with different types of people differently and with tact would be the needed qualities of manager. He has to visit factory managers, go around the sites of plant, visit the various departments, communicate with collaborators, suppliers, distributors, etc. This is particularly important for project appraisal, investment analysis and research in broker firms.

Managers have to have a team spirit, capacity to get along with equals, superiors and subordinates and ability to communicate effectively and elicit the right information. The work involves the co-ordination with various experts, solicitors, accountants, auditors, finance managers, technicians, engineers, etc. Being equals, the team requires the managers who possess leadership qualities to throw their innovative and creative ideas into action and lead the team of experts. Interviewing and meeting people and asking right questions to elicit correct information are the arts of a manager in capital market.

Specialities in Capital Market Management

One might ask that what has been discussed is relevant to any effective manager. Then what is so special about capital market management? Everybody agrees that bank management is a speciality and there are special examinations of professional competence conducted by the Institute of Bankers and IBA. There are professional organisations like NIBM, B.T.C., IDRBT and other training institutions of public sector banks. If banking is a specialised service regulated by Banking Law and Practice and RBI Act, non-banking financial services are more specialised as they are governed by a variety of Acts, such as Companies Act, S.C.(R) Act, Indian Contract Act, SEBI Act, etc. Besides, the expertise needed here is more diverse, as the functions carried on by them are many and inter-related such as activities in stock market, new issues market, gilt-edged and money markets, foreign exchange market, etc.

Capital market management involves various disciplines, much more than in banking. For example, various laws, requires legal expertise; funding business requires banking knowledge; hire-purchase and leasing requires a different expertise. Mutual funds, brokerage firms, portfolio managers and a host of other agencies require knowledge and expertise in personal management, marketing management, funds management, investment management, etc.

In short, capital market management is different and more specialised than banking. It requires a different cadre of specialists to man the increasing work of financial institutions. It is more practical and operational and the expertise needed is different.

Outlook

This book gives the background information for managers in capital market to function more effectively. The basic principles of management are assumed to be known to readers. On this premise, what is presented in coming pages is only the superstructure, involving the capital market institutions, operations and practices. The word "Capital Market" is used in a wide sense including new issues market, stock market, money market, Government securities market etc. The information about these markets and their operations would hopefully sharpen the tools of management as they are down to earth practical and operational.

MONEY AND CAPITAL MARKET MANAGEMENT

Capital market refers to the market for raising of financial resources by the business enterprises, firms, government, semi-government bodies, PSUs and other organisations. Definitionally, the market comprises some who demand and others who supply these resources. The methods of raising these resources are:

(*a*) from the public,

(*b*) from the banks and financial institutions, and

(*c*) from foreign sources.

Leaving aside the foreign sources, the two major categories are Indian public and Indian banks and FIs, — one directly from source of savings and others indirectly through the financial intermediaries.

Marketable Instruments

1. issue of securities, negotiable and transferable,
2. issue of promissory notes, evidencing debt, transferable and negotiable,
3. issue of certificates, non-transferable by endorsement,
4. borrowing through letters of credit or against securities, non-securitised debt, non-transferable, and non-negotiable.

The first two categories of debt/ownership capital would give rise to marketable securities and hence to traded instruments. The market arises out of these instruments. Once we identify the securities which are transferable by endorsement and hence marketable we have the market. The non-marketable private securities or securities of private limited companies are outside the purview of this study.

CAPITAL MARKET STRUCTURE

An important segment of organised financial system comprises of the new issues market and stock market. The term capital market is a wide term encompassing all long-term claims of moneylendings and borrowings. It thus includes all term lendings by banks and financial institutions and long-term borrowings from foreign markets and new issues by companies and raising of all resources from public through issue of new securities, deposits, loans, etc.

As the chart below shows, capital market includes issues of two major categories — marketable and non-marketable, whether marketable or not, these are issued by government and government departments, companies, PSUs, Mutual funds, UTI, etc. LIC and GIC, sell policies and collect savings from public, which are not marketable. The other non-marketable securities or claims are issued by post offices, as savings certificates, deposit receipts, etc., non-securitised loans and advances of banks and financial institutions, deposits with banks and companies and securities of private limited companies and finance company deposits/ loans, chit funds, etc. The marketable securities are issued through new issues market and are traded through the stock market.

The contributors to new issues are promoters, collaborators, if any, employees, NRIs, banks, FIs, mutual funds and the public at large. The players through whom these issues are managed are mainly merchant bankers, registrars, brokers, mutual funds, etc., which are dealt with in detail in other chapters. The ancillary functions and complementary to the above are those of underwriters, collecting bankers, printers, advertising agents, etc. The main players in the stock market, namely, brokers, investment consultants, portfolio managers, investment managers etc., are also discussed in later chapters.

The capital market study should really encompass both the marketable and non-marketable segments. In view of the fact that demand and supply forces and trading activity is confined only to the segment of marketable securities, this book is using the term "Capital Market" in the sense of marketable securities. Thus more prominent issuers of such securities are public limited companies and government and the more popular instruments traded in the market are equity, debentures, bonds etc., which are discussed in this book. UTI and mutual fund schemes being popular for trading, they are also dealt with. Briefly the major players — instruments and activity in capital market are covered from the point of management.

Issuers of Securities

The players in the market vary from one segment of the market to another. There are a number of segments in the securities market, depending upon the nature of activity.

(*a*) Corporate securities,

(*b*) Government securities,

(*c*) Securities/instruments of P.S.U.,

(*d*) UTI and mutual fund schemes.

Once we identify the marketable securities, we have a recognised market for them, controlled and regulated by the SEBI and the government. The market structure of such regulated market segments is as follows:

MARKET STRUCTURE

New Issues Market	Stock Exchanges	OTCEI	NMS**
↓	↓	↓	↓
New issues of new companies, further issues of existing companies	Trading in existing issues from companies with paid-up capital of above ₹ 5 crores	Trading in existing issues from companies with paid-up capital of ₹ 30 lakh and above upto ₹ 300 lakh and even up to ₹ 25 crore and above	National Stock Exchange — Trading Money Market, Debt Market and Equity Market

Indian capital market is in an infant stage and as such the structure of the market as well as architecture are yet to be developed. The players are limited as also the instruments traded.

Capital raised in the capital market is of various maturities, depending upon the objectives of borrower. Thus, funds may be required for working capital or short-term accommodation or for project finance, expansion, modernisation and diversification, etc. The funds flowing into the market may therefore be in the form of cash, credit and savings and meet the requirements of cash, liquid funds or medium and long-term capital assets.

Cash and credit are parts of money and these are provided by the government, RBI and banks and are used for purchase/sale of securities, borrowing/lending. Savings are income minus expenditure of individuals,

** National Stock Exchange for developing national market system.

households, companies and any other bodies, corporate or non-corporate and these funds are used for purchase of securities or lending for any purpose to borrowers or companies or any other issuer of securities.

If it is cash flowing in or credit is extended, management of money becomes the basic objective of both issuer of security and the purchaser of security. The chart below shows the institutional role in money management — namely, RBI, government banks, financial institutions, etc.

MONEY MANAGEMENT

Cash	Credit	Savings
↓	↓	↓
RBI and Government	Banks and FIs	Public and Households

Basis of Markets

Markets emerge out of the need for funds or demand for money. Those who spend more than their income need to borrow to meet their expenditure. Similarly, some economic units and deficit units and sectors in the economy invest more than they save and hence have to borrow. Money or capital is lent by the surplus units and deficit units borrow from the former, as shown below.

Surplus Units/Sectors	Deficit Units/Sectors
Households S > I Foreign Sector S > I	or S < I Government/ Semi-govt. Sectors/Business Sectors
Net Savings	Net Investment

Lending Units	Money Flow ⟶ Securities Flow	Borrowing Units
Saving Units	⟵	Spending Units
S = Savings	⟶	I = Investment

These money flows and securities flows lead to demand and supply forces in the capital market. The functional basis of the market is thus the conversion of money into securities and *vice versa.* This in turn results in the use of savings for investment, activisation of idle or dormant savings into active money or increase in the velocity of circulation of money. Capital market structure is depicted in Fig. 13.1.

The functional basis of markets is thus seen in the mobilisation of savings for investment and their relocation from less productive to more productive activities, increase in both savings and investment in the economy and to improve productivity of capital by activating the idle balances and increasing the velocity of circulation of money and credit and their use for productive purposes. These trends will lead to increased output of goods and services in the economy and larger industrial growth.

The functional basis is aided by the legal provisions in the Companies Act and S.C. (R) Act, making securities, shares, etc., movable property, transferable by endorsement and marketable. The provision of listing of shares on the stock exchange provides for a marketplace and trading in these securities.

Avenues of Investment

Savers channel their investment into various categories of avenues, depending on the characteristics of these avenues and their own asset preferences.

Chart 13.1 CAPITAL MARKET STRUCTURE

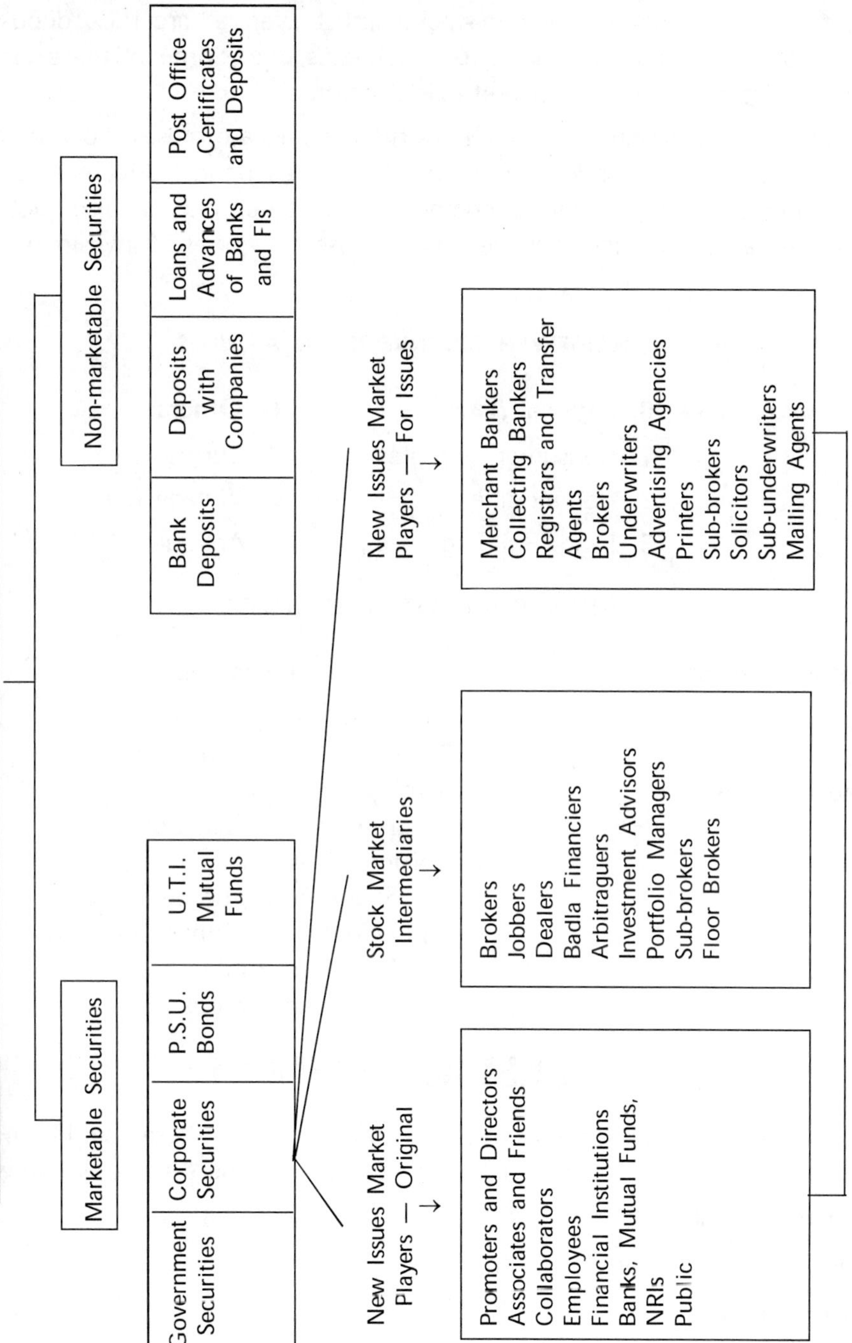

These avenues may be classified into two broad categories:

(*a*) Non-Financial (Physical) Avenues.

(*b*) Financial Avenues.

Under the category of physical assets there are investments in gold, silver, bullion, diamonds, physical commodities, housing and others. Detailed list of them is given in the accompanying chart.

In the case of financial avenues, the non-stock market avenues are P.O. deposits, certificates, bank deposits, insurance policies, annuities, mutual fund schemes, etc. Some of these are non-transferable by delivery and endorsement and hence no market exists for them.

The category of financial investments which are marketable, are mostly stock market investments such as in corporate securities, equity and preference shares, debentures, bonds, Government and semi-Government securities and P.S.U. bonds. Some mutual fund schemes, UTI schemes, etc., are also quoted on stock exchanges and are marketable. The accompanying chart depicts all these categories of investment avenues available for savers in India.

NON-FINANCIAL INVESTMENT AVENUES

A. Precious Metals and Stones	B. Physical Assets	C. Others
1. Gold	1. Consumer Durables	1. Curios
2. Silver	2. Commodities	2. Vintage Cars
3. Diamonds	3. Land, Buildings, etc.,	3. Antiques

FINANCIAL INVESTMENT AVENUES

A. Non-stock Market Avenues

1. Postal Savings
2. Bank Deposits
3. Company Fixed Deposits
4. Insurance Policies, Life, Accident, etc.,
5. Annuities
6. U.T.I. — Units/Schemes
7. Mutual Fund Schemes

B. Stock Market Avenues

1. Gilt-edged Securities — State/Central Governments
2. Semi-government Securities and P.S.U. Bonds
3. Corporate Securities —
   (*i*) Shares-equity-bonus-Rights
   (*ii*) Debentures, Convertible and Non-convertible
   (*iii*) Preference Shares

MONEY MANAGEMENT

Any saver will have some specific objectives or motives behind his saving. He may be providing for a future, or for a larger accumulation of wealth. His objectives may be set out as follows:

(*a*) Income at regular intervals.

(*b*) Capital appreciation or gain in wealth.

(*c*) Safety of his funds.

(*d*) Marketability and liquidity of assets.

(*e*) Hedge against inflation or fall in value of money.

All of the above objectives are fulfilled by investments in stock and capital markets. The most important objective, namely, to protect the value of his money requires planning for proper money management by the investors.

What is Money Management?

Money management refers to use of money in such a way that his investments generate an appreciation much higher than the fall in the value of money and investor's net worth will continue to grow faster than the average rate of inflation.

A saver has many alternative avenues for use of his funds and his choice among them would depend upon his own income, wealth, psychological preferences and his requirements in future. He may put his funds in physical assets like house, land, gold or in consumer durables for a better living. These are less productive than the financial assets. Nearly 50% to 55% of savings are in physical form and the rest in financial form, in the case of household sector in India. The chart 13.2 shows visually different forms of investment in the process of money management, some of which lead to the emergence of capital market.

Chart 13.2 MONEY MANAGEMENT

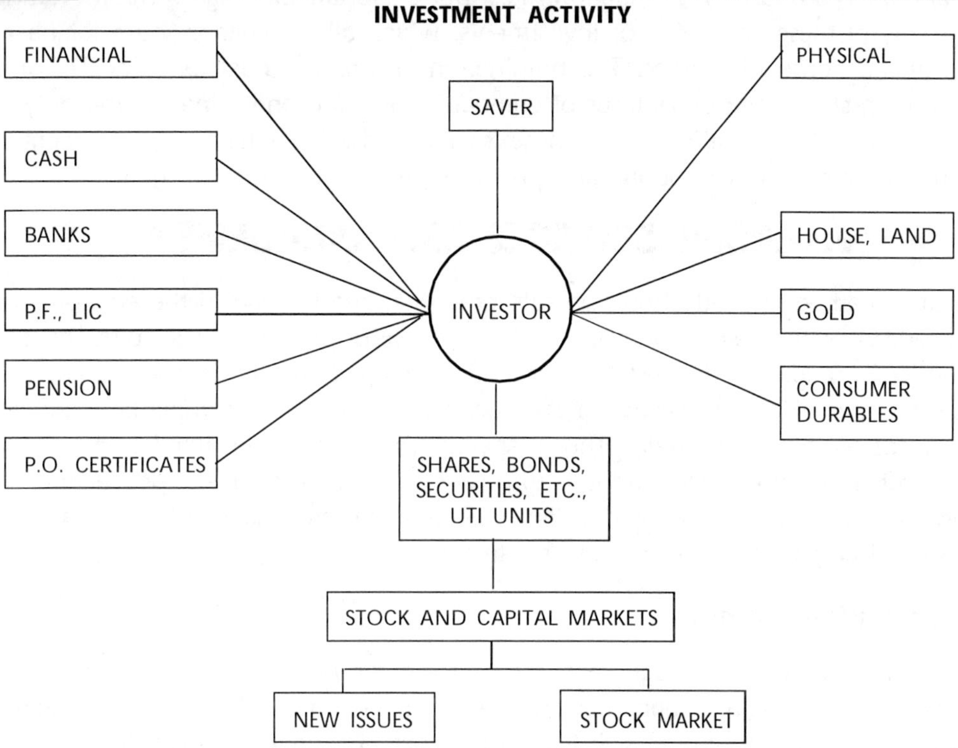

What is Investment Activity?

Investment means conversion of money into claims on money or use of funds for productive and income earning assets. Investment means many things to many persons. For a saver, investment is lending of funds for an income, capital appreciation or both. The investment may also be purchase of marketable securities or sometimes non-marketable promissory notes. These promissory notes are claims on money, payable at a future date. Sometimes, one's investment may be disinvestment of another, when the former buys the shares or debentures of the other. The total available funds to the companies have not increased by this, but this process helps the flow of investment into new issues and new securities due to increased liquidity in the economy.

Savings Allocation

Average Indian household distributes its savings in financial form in such a manner that nearly 13% is in cash and 47% is in deposits with banks.[@] The return on cash is zero in nominal terms and negative in real

@ As per the latest RBI data, 2010-11, Annual Report.

terms due to fall in value of money. The return on bank deposits may vary from 4% to 10% and can offset the fall in value of money only partially. The real returns on banks and companies' fixed deposits are negligible as inflation has been running an average rate of 8% per annum and nominal returns on them vary from 6 to 11%, which after minimum tax deduction at 20% will give a net return of only 1 to 2%. The investors are not therefore benefitting from keeping savings in cash/deposits which they do to the extent of a total of 60% of their overall savings in financial form as per the latest data. There is thus something wrong in the management of money.

The savings flowing into insurance, PF, pension funds, etc., accounted for 33% which also yields a lower rate than inflation rate, but investment in these media is necessitated for providing for contingencies such as accident, death, retirement, etc. Investment in P.O. certificates, deposits, Government securities amounted to only 6% of their financial savings. The returns on these investments are higher than inflation rate, if available tax concessions are taken into account. More recently, many tax concessions were removed with the result that their nominal returns are just above inflation rates. But a substantially higher rate of return in real terms is not possible in any of these categories of investments, which all together account for nearly 90% of the financial savings of the household sector. The holdings in UTI and mutual funds at 3% of the household financial savings and in shares and debentures of companies at 1% of the same are the only avenues which yield higher returns than the inflation rates. These savings flow have fallen more recently due to poor performance of mutual funds both in public and private sector, and markets in general.

FINANCIAL SERVICES AND MANAGEMENT

In the capitalist method of production, the role of capital and finance in the economic activity cannot be over emphasised. Over the years, countries in the communist and socialistic folds, have also shifted to capitalistic method of production and established and developed the stock and capital markets in their countries. Increasing role of private sector, market-oriented economies, competition and efficiency have become the key words of economic activity. Thus many communist countries like Poland, China, Russia, etc., have set up stock exchanges and shifted emphasis to privatisation of the means of production, distribution and capital. Even the so-called socialistic countries like U.K., France, etc., have privatised a number of public enterprises and shifted emphasis to the role of private sector.

Macro-economic Management

In any area of activity, good management is the *sine-qua-non* of success through efficiency and cost effectiveness. The objectives of management may change in detail but basically all aim at efficiency, productivity and lowering of costs and raising of profits. If it is in the area of services, the quality and cost-effectiveness would still count as important pre-requisites for its success. It is in this background that input availability and their efficient use for low cost output are necessary to promote competitive efficiency and economy. The main input resources that any economy needs are land, water, air, energy, etc., which nature endows and labour, technology, enterprise, etc., which man acquires by his efforts and applies in the productive process. Thus man and nature whose endowments vary from country to country are the two blades of the same scissors and they join in the productive process. It is the ingenuity and expertise of management to combine them in the proper proportions, so as to reduce the costs to the minimum and raise the profits or quality of service to the maximum depending on the technology used.

The activity analysis of any economy, firm or company involves the technological relationship between inputs and outputs depending upon the type of technology used. It is the management function to see that this relation of inputs and outputs is most up to date, modern and cost-effective. This activity may be in the provision of services as in the case of financial services, trading or manufacturing, etc., where efficiency and competition are the landmarks of success, management has a role which is judged by the results in terms of cost of service, quality, profits, etc.

Activity Analysis

The basis of all activity is man's desire. Thus, desire plus purchasing power leads to demand. Desire is both physical and mental and is supported by the qualities of heart, head, mind, etc. This would make supply of labour available along with management expertise, technology, etc., which are the products of man. On the other hand purchasing power comes from his command on money, claims on money, finances, wealth etc.

Thus the demand side of the activity which leads to supply may be set out as follows:

Supply of Human Resources / Labour Enterprise Management	+	Availability of Financial Resources / Money Finance and Capital	→	Land Assets Plant and Machinery, etc.	→ Production of Goods and Services

PRODUCTIVE PROCESS INVOLVES

Inputs	Technological Relation	Output
↓	↓	↓
Rent, Wages Salaries, Profits	Finance as Input	Goods and Services
↓		↓
Demand	Relation of D/S	Supply

↓

MONEY/FINANCE

Transactions Purposes	Precautionary Purposes	Asset Purposes
↓	↓	↓
Cash	Cash and Credit	Financial Assets

Management of productive activity thus involves:

A. Cash management.

B. Credit management.

C. Asset management both in micro and macro sense.

In the macro sense these elements of management are part of the financial markets and are governed by the services rendered by them. They can be depicted in the following manner.

INPUTS LEAD TO OUTPUTS AND ARE CLASSIFIED AS

PHYSICAL	**FINANCIAL**
Corresponding to physical activity	There are financial services
↓	↓
Physical inputs — land, labour, enterprise, management	Financial inputs — cash, credit and finance
CONVERTED INTO MONETARY	**FORM FOR INCOME AND EXPENDITURE**
FINANCIAL MARKETS	**FINANCIAL SERVICES**
Money and claims on money/ securities/financial investments Financial assets/trading in them	Lending and borrowing/investments, discounting, sale/ purchase of assets, hire-purchase, leasing, lease financing, housing finance, mortgage finance, etc.

FINANCIAL SYSTEM ... ORGANISED AND REGULATED

CAPITAL MARKET MANAGEMENT

ENCOMPASSES ORGANISED MONEY AND CAPITAL MARKETS INVOLVING MARKETABLE CLAIMS ON MONEY

CASH MANAGEMENT	CREDIT MANAGEMENT	ASSET MANAGEMENT
R.B.I., Banks, Financial Institutions, Government, etc., Companies and Economic Units, Users of Cash and Public	Banks, Financial Institutions, Government, Companies, Productive Units, Users of Credit, Savers and Investors, Public	Government, Business, Companies, Productive Units, Households and Public, Savers and Investors

The study on capital market management should thus encompass the totality of the financial sector services excluding the banking sector, but inclusive of money market and other financial markets. With the liberalisation of industrial and financial policies in India the integration of various segments of financial markets was accelerated and the role of private sector in the capital and money markets has increased. The dependence of the government, semi-government bodies and of the private sector on the pool of public savings and on the capital market has also grown by leaps. This was evidenced by the data for 1992-93, when the number of new issues and the amount of capital raised has jumped multifold over the past, due to reforms process. The amounts raised by PSUs in the form of equity and bonds has on the other hand risen further during 1999-2000 to 2006-07.

Chart 13.3

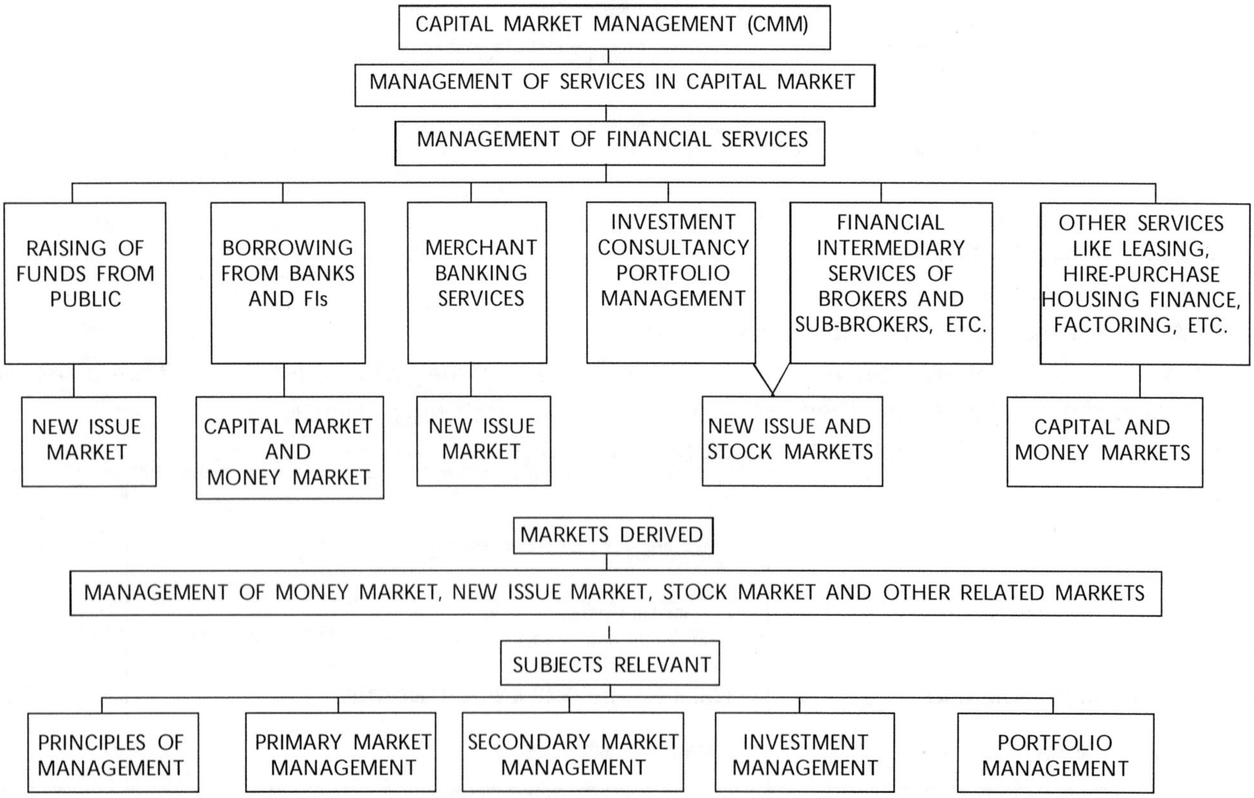

Conceptually, money flows into various markets, namely, product markets, factor markets, financial markets, etc. The macro management of money is the function of the RBI and the government. These money flows into financial markets reflect the investment and disinvestment process, conversion of money into future claims of money and *vice versa*. The need for cash and economising of cash are the basic principles of corporate finance. This leads to the use of near money like credit, master cards, bills, drafts and other instruments of credit. These result in claims on money both of short-term and long-term nature. If these instruments are of short-term nature, these relate to money market and if they are of long-term nature they belong to capital market. But in view of growing integration of markets, capital market management includes a study of both these markets.

Money market being mainly dominated by institutions, its importance is incidental to money flows *inter se* among the markets.

The emergence of various financial markets is explained in the above chart. RBI controls the generation of cash and credit and is the supervisory authority for money markets. The stock and capital markets and other related long-term markets used to be co-ordinated functionally by the IDBI in terms of the institutions in them but the markets as such are controlled and supervised by the SEBI, since May 1992.

The chart on capital market management depicts the various services rendered in the capital market and their management as a science of study.

The chart is self-explanatory in the sense that the management of financial services is the subject matter of capital market management. The chart brings out various services rendered and the intermediaries rendering these services and the emerging markets therefrom. The practices and principles involved in them are the subjects to be covered in this book.

✠ ✠ ✠

MERCHANT BANKING

14

Introduction

The success in the management of public issue of securities to a large extent, depends upon the State in which the capital market is when the public issue enters the market. Therefore, in order to appreciate the problems and prospects of the public issues and the management thereof, what needs to be seen is the state and growth of the capital market.

During the last one decade, the capital market has made tremendous progress. With the coming into force of the foreign Exchange Regulation Act 1973, on 1st January, 1974, an important step in the development of the capital market took place, as it compelled several FERA companies to enter the capital market with the issues of their shares for the purpose of diluting the non-resident holding to a lower level as required in terms of FERA and the rules framed thereunder, which offered a very good opportunity to the investors to a share in the good and attractive equity investment. From this time onwards, the capital market started showing signs of buoyancy. Simultaneously, the other phenomena were slowly but certainly emerging to the surface. The constraints on the resources of the financial institutions and banks prompted the companies with a good track record of satisfactory financial operations to their credit to enter the capital market for mobilising their long-term fund requirements either for expansion or modernisation and diversification. These developments gave a unique opportunity to investors in this country to invest in something which is worthwhile and the instruments in the form of convertible debentures which were in a dormant condition hitherto became now a very popular instrument with the investing public. During the decade 1980-90, securities in the form of partly convertible debentures became popular with the investors and through them the non-convertible debentures also became popular with the investing public, in respect of good companies with a track record. With the coming in of the tax-free public sector bonds, coupled with the reduction of the rate of interest with effect from 1st April, 1987 from 15% to 14% per annum, the non-convertible debentures have gone out of favour with the investing public in India. This is evident from the decline in the response to the issues of non-convertible debentures from 1986 onwards. All the same, it is gratifying to note that the capital market is growing, as is evidenced by the increase in the number of recognised stock exchanges in the country. In India, the investing population constitute about 1.5% of the total population or 10-15 millions in the early fifties which shows that there is a tremendous scope for further widening of the market. Already the latest estimates of investing population is placed at 50 to 100 millions including those investing in UTI and Mutual Funds. India has earned a good name as a borrower abroad, as it has always been extremely prompt in repaying its debt. There is a potential for external borrowings also. With the opening of the stock markets for foreign investments Indian companies are also permitted to go abroad. Out of total financial savings, shares and debentures account for less than 5% and hence there is large scope for switching from other avenues. The scope is bright for large and medium-sized industries to raise the contributions from the capital market. Needless to mention that the scope for the merchant banking activity is vast and there would be more and more challenges as the system evolves to greater sophistication.

What is Merchant Banking?

Merchant banks are issue houses rendering such services to industrial projects or corporate units as floatation of new ventures and new companies, preparation, planning and execution of new projects, consultancy and advice in technical, financial, managerial and organisational fields. A number of other functions such as restructuring, revaluation of assets, mergers, takeovers, acqusitions, etc., are also undertaken by them.

Chart 14.1 shows the functions of Merchant Banks.

Chart 14.1 MERCHANT BANKING FUNCTIONS

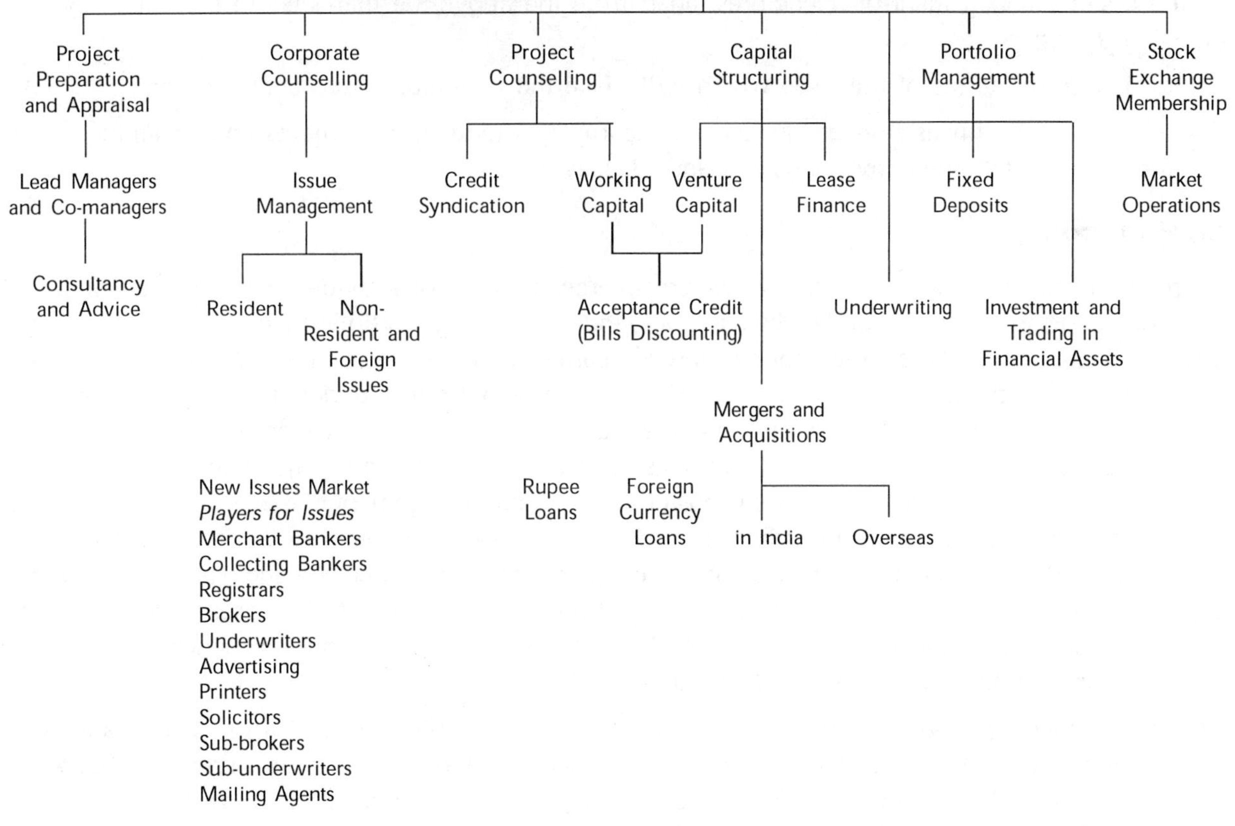

A major function of merchant banking is the issue management. The issue can be public issue through prospectus, offer of sale, or private placements, etc.

Issue Management

The issue management involves the following functions in respect of issue through prospectus:

(*a*) Obtaining approval for the issue from the SEBI and all clearances from SEBC and government..

(*b*) Arranging underwriting for the proposed issue.

(*c*) Drafting and finalising of the prospectus and obtaining its clearance from the underwriters, stock exchanges, auditors, solicitors, registrar of companies and other necessary consents required for filing the prospectus.

(*d*) Drafting and finalisation of other documents such as application forms, newspaper announcements of the prospectus material and application to the stock exchanges.

(*e*) Selection of the registrar to the issue, printing press, advertising agencies, brokers and bankers to the issue and finalisation of the fees and charges to be paid to them.

(*f*) Arranging through the advertising agency the press, brokers and investor's conferences.

(*g*) Co-ordinating the printing, publicity and advertisements relating to the issue, and work of the registrars to the issue, the receipt and processing of applications and preparation of the basis of allotment, negotiation of the same with the stock exchanges and preparation of the register of allotment.

In the case of management of debentures, apart from the above the managers to the issue have to do the following things:

(*a*) to finalise the terms of the issue which will make the debenture issue attractive; and

(*b*) to assist in the finalisation of the relative security or mortgage documents and obtaining approval thereto from the company's solicitors and trustees.

Other Functions

Merchant banks in foreign countries undertake a larger number of activities. They operate both in the money market and capital market, undertake direct and indirect lending, portfolio management for institutions, trusts, charities, etc., funds management for existing companies, underwriting for new and old companies, etc. They are also active in the money market and discount market operations in undertaking bills discounting and investing the short-term funds in treasury bills, commercial bills and other money market instruments. In India, these functions are carried on by banks themselves with the result that their merchant banking divisions confine to underwriting, consultancy, new issue business, involving management of issues and related activities. The Indian merchant banking is still in its infancy and their activities are, therefore, limited to a few selected activities of new issues market at present such as project planning, financial consultancy, advice and planning and execution of these projects, involving the preparation for the public issue, observance of necessary formalities for such issue, applications to SEBI, RBI and for listing on the stock exchange, collection and allotment of share application moneys, underwriting, etc.

Merchant bankers perform a number of functions. It has been aptly said that a merchant bank is what a merchant banker does. What it does is its own decision, its utility and willingness, expertise and experience. The functions it can perform are vast and variegated. It can set limits to its own functions. A list of functions, it can perform has been set out in this chapter. Some of the important categories of functions that it can perform and is performing is Corporate Advisory Services. A list of corporatory advisory services is given below. Of these, most merchant banks perform the functions of loan syndication, issue management, project preparation and project appraisal, valuation of assets, mergers and acquisitions, capital structuring and preparation of revival schemes, scouting for foreign collaborations and joint ventures and foreign tie-up for marketing or technology. The functions they perform depends on the staff infrastructure, expertise and experience, they have.

CORPORATE ADVISORY SERVICES

1. Formation of the Company
2. Making of Public Issue and Issue Management
3. Loan Syndication
4. Capital Structuring and Restructuring
5. Project Report Preparation and Appraisal
6. Liaison with Foreign Collaborators and making preparation for Joint Ventures
7. Making Valuation and Revaluation of Assets
8. Mergers and acquisitions
9. Help in Management Decisions
10. Expert Staff Placement and HRD Help
11. Financial Re-engineering
12. Entrepreneurial Training and Development
13. Technical Assistance
14. Raising Foreign Currency Loans, Euroissues, FCCBs, etc.
15. Quality Control and Product-mix
16. Market Survey and Research
17. Tax Planning.

Offer of Sale

Usually, when the closely-held companies, whose shares are not listed on the stock exchange, approach the financial institutions for assistance for the expansion of their existing operations or diversification, the financial institutions stipulate a condition that the company should get its shares listed. Where the capital base of the company is already large and issuing further equity capital is not justified from the servicing angle, the promoters can offer such part of their existing holding for sale through a letter of offer to the members of the public as is necessary to get the equity shares of the company listed on the stock exchange. Although the letter of offer is not governed by the provisions of the Companies Act, 1956, in practice, the letter of offer contains all the similar provisions which are to be found in the prospectus.

The offer for sale must give all material particulars relating to the company as if it were a prospectus issued under the Companies Act. In particular, it should include information regarding the shares on offer and the terms of sale, its capital structure, capitalisation of reserves, any revaluation of assets or schemes of arrangement or reorganisation, last five years' profit and loss account summarised under principal heads, contingent and tax liabilities, etc., so as to present a correct picture of the financial position of the company. The offer must be in a form approved by the stock exchange concerned and should comply with the conditions relating to public advertisement, opening of the subscription list, allotment, etc., that are applicable when a company offers its shares for public subscription through a prospectus in accordance with the presecribed listing requirements.

Any document by which the offer for sale to the public is made shall, for all purposes, be deemed to be a prospectus issued by the company and all enactments and rules of law as to the contents of prospectuses and as to the liabilities in respect of statements in or omissions from prospectuses or otherwise relating to the prospectuses, shall apply as if the shares or debentures had been offered to the public for subscription and as if the persons accepting the offer in respect of any shares or debentures were subscribers for those shares or debentures.

The said letter of offer will have to be signed by the persons offering the shares or debentures for sale in the same manner as the directors of the company sign the prospectus in terms of Section 60 of the Companies Act.

Those offering new issues collectively and individually accept full responsibility for the accuracy of the information given in this offer of sale and confirm that to the best of their knowledge and belief there are no other facts, the omission of which makes any statement in the offer for sale misleading, and they further confirm that they have made all reasonable inquiries to ascertain such facts.

The bankers have to certify that neither the stock exchange to which an application for official quotation is made nor the Central Government has any responsibility for the financial soundness of this offer, or for the price at which the offer of sale is made, or for the correctness of the statements made or opinions expressed in the offer of sale.

The initial issues should normally be at par and if further issues are made at a premium; this has to be justified by acceptable norms by the merchant bankers.

Private Placement

When the financial institutions directly subscribe to the equity/preference shares and/or debentures issued by the company, the company is said to have privately placed these securities with the financial institutions. This does not require either a prospectus or letter of offer. The terms and conditions subject to which the financial institutions agree to subscribe to the privately placed shares or debentures are usually incorporated in the debenture subscription agreement or the investment agreement entered into between the financial institutions and the company.

The company could, if it so desires, approach, in the place of financial instiutions, a well-identifiable body of persons like merchant banks for private placement. The provisions of the Act are to be interpreted strictly and therefore, if the company sends the offer to Mr. X and the offer is accepted by Mrs. X to whom the allotment is finally made, it could deem to be the public offer necessitating compliance of requirements of the prospectus. This exercise is, therefore, to be undertaken with great caution to see that the final transfer takes place only to those for whom the original offer was made. In practice, till recently the companies hardly took any recourse to this mode of private placement of their securities due to these restrictions. In the early years of this century, private placement has become more prominent, than the issues by Prospectus and Rights.

The company has to agree upon the list of persons to whom the offer is to be sent much in advance and it is thereafter necessary that the company should send offers to the same persons as per the list approved by the company with a clear-cut instruction to the offerers that the securities offered are strictly to be subscribed for by them and they alone and the those offering are not supposed to pass on the offer of the company to someone else. This would ensure that the company would receive subscription only from those persons to whom the original offers had been sent by the company and finally, the company would allot securities to the same persons.

Private placement is also being taken recourse to by the promoters for the purpose of procuring promoters' contribution. It is a moot point as to how far this is advisable and whether certain promoters are overdoing while approaching with their offer of shares to persons totally unconnected with the promoters' group and whether such a thing is, in the first place, in the interest of the promoters themselves and in the interest of the lending institutions. According to latest guidelines of SEBI, this is prohibited.

Services of Merchant Banks

Merchant banking is normally considered to be related only to the services associated with public issue management but they also offer domestic project finance syndication. Larger merchant banks in the country offer a wide range of services. Merchant banks offer generally the following services:

(*a*) *Pre-investment studies for investors:* These are in the nature of financial feasibility explorations in selected areas of interest of the client. They include such studies for foreign companies wishing to participate in joint ventures in India, and often involve a package covering advice on the nature of participation and government regulatory factors.

(*b*) *Project finance:* Once the decision to embark on a particular project/expansion/modernisation scheme has been taken, assitance in working out a comprehensive package for the project funding and pattern of financing is available from the merchant banks. They work in close liaison with the client, his technical consultants, and the funding institutions, prepare and submit complete financial dossiers, and arrange for the various sources of finance. Assistance in legal documentation for the finance arranged is also provided.

(*c*) *Working capital:* Finance for working capital, particularly for new ventures, often needs to be syndicated on behalf of the promoters, and merchant banks assist in this as well. For existing companies, non-traditional sources such as through the issue of debentures for this purpose, and others have been successfully tapped by merchant bankers.

(*d*) *Foreign currency finance:* Of late, India has become increasingly active in the international money markets, and this trend is likely to continue. For import of capital goods and services from overseas, the arrangement of various kinds of export credits from different countries is also required.

In respect of many joint enterprises and overseas ventures in the Middle-East, South-East Asia and Africa, etc., advice on the financial structuring of these projects, as well as assistance in syndication of the finance itself, is now increasingly available through the Indian merchant banks.

In addition to these wide range of services, some of the larger banks are also involved in areas such as the arrangement of lease finance, and assistance in acquisitions and mergers, etc.

Banks earlier confined most of their operations to deposit mobilisation and credit dispensation. But in India, they have diversified their activities in line with their counterparts in developed countries, and gone into merchant banking also. This innovative banking has helped many young entrepreneurs who lacked sufficient experience and had a little capital to invest to enter the field of industrial enterprise. This has led to the need for some agency which can take care of their interests from planning to execution of the projects.

With industrial organisation growing more complex day by day, there is crying need for industrial rationalisation through mergers, amalgamation and the integration of private with public companies. All this requires sophisticated planning and management which can only be provided by specialised agencies that have a flexible approach and possess a proper understanding of the problems of the corporate sector.

Merchant banks can provide counsel on capital and capital structure, the form of capital to be raised, preparing the terms and conditions of issue, underwriting, preparation of the prospectus, etc. They provide the services of financial and non-finanacial nature, and a host of related services.

The buoyancy in the country's investment climate resulted in more and more Indian and foreign banks starting their own merchant banking operations. In the wake of the equity boom witnessed after the presentation of the budget for 1985-86, merchant banking underwent a sea-change, not only in widening the scope of its specialised business but also acquiring a new dimension. The State Bank of India converted its merchant banking division into a subsidiary for exclusively carrying out merchant banking activities in 1986. Most of the nationalised banks have carved out a place for themselves in the merchant banking activities.

Corporate sector needs the services of these experts to tackle problems in technical, financial, managerial and organisational fields. A study by the Reserve Bank showed that insufficient project preparation, defective technical planning, inefficent or indifferent management and financial bottlenecks faced by promoters were primarily responsible for delay in the implementation of projects. Merchant banks have a role to play to rectify these defects.

In the post-war period, merchant banks began to diversify their activities into new directions and away from large corporations into medium and small organisations. The loan policy of financial institutions has shifted emphasis from creditworthiness of the entrepreneur to soundness of the investment proposals. Merchant banks have come to provide an integrated package of services depending on the requirements of corporate and non-corporate clients and entrepreneurs.

Basically, merchant banks are development banks but do not lend like development banks. They undertake risks of underwriting as a financial institution by lending their own name to impart confidence to the investors, advise on financial structure and arrange for financial planning, etc. Merchant bank's functions are flexible and client-oriented.

Why Merchant Banks?

The following are some of the reasons why specialist merchant banks have a crucial role to play in India:

1. Growing industrialisation and increase of technologically advanced industries.
2. Need for encouragement of small and medium industrialists, who require specialist services.
3. Growing complexity in rules and procedures of the government.
4. Need to develop backward areas and states which require different criteria.
5. Exploring the possibility of joint ventures abroad and foreign markets.
6. Promoting the role of New Issue Market in mobilising savings from public.

Functions

With increasing industrialisation of the country and the growing emphasis in the Five Year Plans on industrialisation, merchant banking in India has a very extensive role to play. The National and Grindlays Bank was the first to set up merchant banking division in India followed by the State Bank of India and other banks. Functions of the merchant banking divisions are as follows:

1. advice and liaison, obtaining consent of the Central and State Governments, for the project if necessary;
2. preparation of economic, technical and financial feasibility reports;
3. initial project preparation, pre-investment surveys, and market studies;
4. help in raising rupee resources from financial institutions and commercial banks;
5. underwriting and also for subscription, if necessary, to the new issues or syndication of loans, etc.;
6. assistance in raising foreign exchange resources so as to enable the industrial concerns to import machinery and technical know-how and secure foreign collaboration;
7. advice on setting up turnkey projects in foreign countries and locating foreign markets;
8. help in financial management and in designing proper capital structure and debt-equity ratio, etc., for the company;
9. advice on restructuring of capital, amalgamation, mergers, takeovers, etc.;
10. management of investment trusts, charitable trusts, etc.;

11. management aid and entrepreneurial aid (management audit providing designs of the complete system, operational research and management consultancy); and
12. recruitment (selection of technical and managerial personnel), etc.

Special Role of Merchant Banks

To promote the new issue market there is need for a qualitative improvement in the offer of new issues both in terms of time taken and the cost of floatation. At present the time taken for organising a new issue is between 12 to 18 months and the cost of raising new capital varies from 3% to 8% and sometimes even 20%. This can be brought down relatively by specialised merchant banking institutions by catering to the requirements of both large and small industrial units. Cost of floatation of equity and preference capital is higher for new companies than for existing companies, indicating thereby the difficulties experienced by new companies in making a new issue. Merchant banks can help saving in the cost of new companies and of small companies.

The new issue market has not succeeded fully in mobilising savings partly due to the preference of the public to company deposits and partly due to low yields on equities as compared to those on fixed interest securities. There has been a decline in the proportion of share capital in the total capital employed due to the steep rise in the cost of new issues. There are certain minimum costs to be incurred in respect of fees to brokers, promoters' expenses, underwriting commission, etc., irrespective of the size of the project. While bigger companies are able to manage this, small units find it extremely difficult to meet this minimum cost with uncertain prospects of their own internal resources in order to avoid the high cost of making public issues. Merchant banks can also help mobilising new capital for small and medium companies.

Underwriting

The main work of merchant banks relates to underwriting of new issues and raising of new capital for the corporate sector. Of the amount underwritten, some part devolves on the underwriters, which varies depending on the state of the capital market, and the intrinsic worth of the project. The SEBI has made underwriting compulsory for all issues offered to public, in 1992, but made optional since 1995. The merchant banks are now expected to underwrite to or take up a minimum of 5% of the offer to the public, as per SEBI guidelines.

Type of Expertise Required

The type of staff required for a merchant bank will depend upon its functions which are themselves flexible. The merchant bank should have an organisation large enough to deal with a number of applications at a time. The issue house which acts as the merchant banker normally pays visits to the company's plant, warehouses, and other physical assets and if a company is making its first issue, it might secure independent reports from Chartered Accountants, industrial consultants, technical experts, etc. The issue house, which is a merchant bank also, requires a report on the history of the company, details of its business, factories, plant, management, labour, competitors, profit margins, taxation, etc. They have to keep ready all the information needed in the form of dossiers with respect to the affairs of the company generally enquired into by the investing public, lending financial institutions and the government.

Secondly, a merchant bank has to suggest an appropriate time of issue and provisional terms. Once these terms are settled, the share certificates, prospectus and other documents are drafted by the merchant bank with the assistance of lawyers, accountants and others. They have to satisfy the Companies Act and other requirements of law and listing. Subsequently, the merchant bank may have to get ready the application to the SEBI for the public issues. This requires familiarity with the regulations under the Companies Act and the SEBI guidelines and the procedures to be followed and the authorities to be approached. The provisions under the MRTP Act, regulating monopoly practices and other activities of big industrial houses should also be looked into.

Thirdly, they may have to make an application to the appropriate stock exchange for quotation and satisfy the stock exchange authorities with respect to the terms of issue and prospectus. Listing requirements are to be observed and familiarity with the stock exchange rules and bye-laws as well as the provisions of the Securities Contracts (Regulations) Act would be essential. They may have to advise on the desirability or otherwise of listing on the stock exchange as well as help the company go through the process of getting their shares listed. Advertisements containing all the information legally required to be given in the prospectus must be published in all the leading newspapers. The prospectus itself should contain the number of shares, amount, time, proposed date of opening and closing, a summary of the company's business history, balance sheet, etc., to which a reference was made earlier. Once the issue is made, the work of the merchant bank relates to arranging for the allotment of shares in consultation with the company and the stock exchange authorities.

The merchant banks' work would also relate to the advice to the companies on any rights issue or bonus issue. They may advise on the documents needed, size of bonus issues or rights issue, the need for underwriting and the institutions to underwrite, the terms and other necessary actions with regard to the issue of rights and bonus shares. The issue house has to ensure that justice is done to the investing public as well as to the issuing company and that the terms are reasonable and issue price justified by the long-term prospects of the company. They have to take into account the market price of comparable shares and long-term prospects of the company and other related companies in that particular line of business. With the abolition of CCI and the repeal of Capital Issues Control Act, the free market pricing of shares offered to public is allowed. The proper pricing of shares is now the responsibility of merchant bankers.

The merchant bank may have to advise on mergers and takeovers. They may be consulted on the capital organisation, the structure of capital and terms of merger or takeover. The issue house should, therefore, have the competence of an industrial consultant as well as the expertise of a lawyer and chartered accountant among others. They should be able to appraise the balance sheet of the company to value their assets in a most impartial manner in the interest of both the company taking over and the company to be taken over.

Merchant banks should have an overall view of the type of shareholders and prospective clientele who are attracted by the type of company and industry. They have to advise the company on the type of security to be offered and nature of issue and type of placement, terms, etc., on the basis of its likely clientele for its shares. They have to keep a hold on the pulse of the market and the investment climate so as to judge rightly and advise the company accordingly.

The merchant banker should be familiar with the administrative procedures, rules and regulations governing the issue of industrial licence, import licence, capital goods import clearance, and a host of other issues with which the corporate sector is concerned. Sometimes, the companies have to secure clearance under the FEMA of 1999, particularly in the case of foreign-controlled rupee companies or subsidiaries or branches of foreign companies. Even in the case of Indian companies, foreign collaboration or joint ventures at home or abroad would require clearance from the Reserve Bank as well as from the Ministry of Finance. In addition, knowledge of the Import Trade Control Rules and Procedures and the prevailing policy in this regard for securing the import licence for import of raw material, spares, capital goods, etc., would be required.

Conclusions

The main function of merchant banks would appear to be sharing risks with the company, particularly for unquoted companies, either in terms of equity or some other basis and then help the development of the company. This role of helping the company to grow through new ideas will promote the corporate sector in a healthy fashion. A merchant bank also lends its name to the company which is an asset, particularly, for small firms to raise funds in the market. By lending the name for placing issues on the market, the merchant bank helps the company in reducing the costs of floatation and financing the project. The role of merchant banker is crucial to the growth of the new issues market.

The ability to read a balance sheet supplemented by on the spot investigations and a reasonable grasp of economic and financial environment would enable an investment expert or a banker to form an opinion on the financial soundness of the company and its business prospects. The merchant banks should have their own investment analysts to sort out the share values of the company and recommend or advise on matters of issues of shares. The main facts that they take into account are the cash flow estimates, certain financial ratios such as earnings or yield per share, high and low market price over the last few months, capital structure, book value per share, net worth per share, dividend record for the last 5-7 years' earnings, etc.

The merchant banks have come to occupy an important place on the financial scene of India. Most of the banks and some of the specialised broking firms have entered this field in more recent years. The future growth of the capital market depends, to a large extent, on the financial services rendered by the merchant banks, and the quality of their services. The SEBI had laid down some guidelines, rules, etc., relating to merchant banking

SECURITIES AND EXCHANGE BOARD OF INDIA (SEBI)

Merchant Banking — Role and Functions

(a) Authorisation

Any person or body proposing to engage in the business of Merchant Banking would need authorisation by SEBI in the prescribed format. This will apply to those presently engaged in the Merchant Banking activity, including as Manager, Consultants or Advisers to issues.

(b) Authorised Activity

(*i*) Issue Management

(*ii*) Corporate Advisory services relating to the issue

(*iii*) Underwriting

(*iv*) Portfolio Managment Services

(*v*) Managers, Consultants or Advisers to the issue

(c) Authorisation Criteria

All Merchant Bankers are expected to perform with high standards of integrity and fairness in all their dealings. A code of conduct for the Merchant Bankers is prescribed by SEBI which will take into account the following:

(*i*) Professional Competence

(*ii*) Personnel, their adequacy and quality and other infrastructure

(*iii*) Capital Adequacy

(*iv*) Past track record, experience, general reputation and fairness in all their transactions.

(d) Terms of Authorisation

(*i*) All merchant bankers shall have a minimum net worth of ₹5 crore.

(*ii*) The Authorisation will be for an initial period of 3 years.

(*iii*) All issues should be managed by at least one authorised merchant banker functioning as the Lead Manager or Sole Manager.

Issue Amount	*No. of Lead Managers*
Up to ₹50 crore	Not more than 2
Over ₹50 crores but not more than ₹100 crore	Not more than 3
Over ₹100 crore	Not more than 4

(*iv*) The Merchant Bankers shall exercise due diligence independently verifying the contents of the prospectus. The Merchant Bankers of the issue shall certify to this effect to SEBI.

(*v*) In respect of issues managed by the Merchant Bankers, they would be required to accept a minimum 5% underwriting obligation in the issue subject to a ceiling of ₹ 25 lakh.

(*vi*) Lead managers would be responsible for ensuring timely refunds and allotment of securities to the investors.

(*vii*) The Merchant Bankers involvement will continue till the completion of essential follow-up steps including listing of the securities and despatch of certificates and refund.

(*viii*) The Merchant Banker shall make available to SEBI such information returns and reports as may be called for.

(*ix*) Merchant Banker shall adhere to the code of conduct laid down and prepared by SEBI.

(*x*) Merchant Banker to ensure that Publicity/Advt. material accompanying the application form to the issue should meet the requirement of GoI/SEBI.

(*xi*) SEBI shall be informed well before the opening of the issue the *Inter se* allocation of activities/ sub-activities among lead managers to the issue.

(*xii*) Merchant Bankers performing or planning to perform portfolio management services shall furnish the details in the prescribed format.

(e) Classification of Merchant Bankers

There is only one category now, namely, *Category I: All the others were abolished.*

Category (1)	*Requirement* (2)	*Authorised to Act as* (3)
Category I	Minimum Net Worth ₹ 5 crore	Lead Manager/Co-manager/Adviser/ consultant to an issue, portfolio manager and underwriter to an issue as mandatorily required.
Category II	Minimum Net Worth ₹ 50 lakh	Co-manager/Adviser or Consultant to an issue or portfolio manager.
Category III	Minimum Net Worth of ₹ 20 lakh	Adviser/Consultant to an issue
Category IV	No net worth	Only Adviser

(f) Grading of Prospectus

Grading of Prospectus will be done by SEBI using the following parameters:

(*i*) Objective description of the project, its status and implementation.

(*ii*) Track record of the promoters and their competence.

(*iii*) Disclosure about demand-supply position, market and marketing arrangements, raw materials availability and infrastructural facility.

(*iv*) Disclosure of risk factors.

(*v*) Objective assessment of business prospects and profitability.

If highlights are provided the following deficiencies will attract negative points:

1. Absence of Risk Factor
2. Absence of Listing
3. Extraneous Contents to Prospectus

The Maximum grading points of prospectus will be 10

Points	*Category*
More than or Equal to 8	+A
More than or equal to 6 but less than 8	A
More than or equal to 4 but less than 6	B
Less than 4	C

(g) Penalty Point System

SEBI has introduced penalty point system for Merchant Bankers who fail to comply with the various provisions.The areas of non-compliance/defaults have been categorised into following four categories. The activities are classified within these four categories:

Type	*Nature*	*Penalty Points*
I	General Defaults	1
II	Minor Defaults	2
III	Major Defaults	3
IV	Serious Defaults	4

A maximum penalty of 4 points can be awarded in a single issue managed by a Merchant Banker. On reaching a cumulative penalty point of 8 they shall attract action from SEBI under clause 4 (m) of the guidelines and clause 12 of the terms of authorisation.

Reports

A statement shall be furnished at Quarterly intervals regarding the particulars of public/ & rights issues on hand with company in the capacity of Lead Manager containing the following details. The statement shall be furnished well before the beginning of the quarter.

1. Name of the company and address
2. Type and size of issue and
3. Likely dates when the issue will be opening for public/shareholders
4. Principal stock exchange where securities will be listed
5. Name of the other lead managers to the issue if any
6. Name of the co-manager and advisers to the issue, if any

The company shall also report in the required format details of the public/rights issue. As of now, the changes in SEBI Policies are as follows:

The reports to be submitted to SEBI are two only, namely, 3 day report and 18 days report (from the day of opening subscription). The SEBI has authorised the merchant bankers to have a stake up to 5% of total issue, if they want and clarified the definition of promoters, and the disclosures to be made, regarding price of shares, etc. The SEBI has authorised merchant bankers to vett the rights issue and pure debt issues themselves and Merchant Bankers Association has laid down guidelines for observing due diligence in disclosures in prospectus by themselves. The other changes in SEBI's policies are referred to at other relevant places. After 1996, many merchant bankers have closed their business due to high competition and lack of business due to subduced market conditions. According to the Association of Merchant Bankers, only 50 or so are active at present and many banks have closed their separate outfits for this work.

ANNEXURE

Initial SEBI Guidelines for Merchant Bankers

1. Authorisation

Any person or body proposing to engage in the business of merchant banking would need authorisation by the Securities and Exchange Board of India (SEBI) in their prescribed format. This will also apply to those presently engaged in merchant banking activity, including as Managers, Consultants or Advisers to issues.

2. Authorised Activities

(*a*) Issue management, which will *inter alia* consist of preparation of prospectus and other information relating to the issues, determining financing structure, tie-up of financiers and final allotment services relating to the issue.

(*b*) Corporate advisory services relating to the issue.

(*c*) Underwriting.

(*d*) Portfolio management services.

(*e*) Managers, consultants or advisers in the issue.

3. Authorisation Criteria

All merchant bankers are expected to perform with high standards of integrity and fairness in all their dealings. A code of conduct for merchant bankers will be prescribed by SEBI. Within this context, SEBI's authorisation criteria would take into account mainly the following:

(*a*) Professional competence.

(*b*) Personnel, their adequacy and quality, and other infrastructure.

(*c*) Capital adequacy.

(*d*) Past track record, experience, general reputation and fairness in all their transactions.

4. Terms of Authorisation

(*a*) All merchant bankers, including the existing ones, must obtain the authorisation from SEBI within three months from the issue of these guidelines. SEBI may extend this period at its discretion by a maximum of three more months.

(*b*) All merchant bankers must have a minimum net worth of ₹ one crore.

(*c*) The authorisation will be for an initial period of three years.

(*d*) SEBI may collect from the merchant bankers an initial authorisation fee, an annual fee and a renewal fee.

(*e*) All issues should be managed by at least one authorised merchant banker, functioning as the sole manager or the lead manager. Ordinarily, not more than two merchant bankers should be associated as lead managers, advisers and consultants to a public issue. In issues of over ₹ 100 crore, the number could go up to a maximum of four.

(*f*) The specific responsibilities of each lead manager must be submitted to SEBI prior to the issue.

(*g*) While directors, promoters and every person who authorises the issue of prospectus, shall bear full responsibility for the contents of the prospectus, merchant bankers shall exercise due diligence independently verifying the contents of the prospectus and reasonableness of the views expressed therein. The merchant bankers of the issue shall certify to this effect to SEBI.

(*h*) To ensure a direct stake of merchant banker(s) in the issue managed by them, lead managers would be required to accept a minimum 5%, underwriting obligation in the issue, subject to a ceiling. Details in this regard are prescribed by SEBI.

(*i*) Lead managers/merchant bankers would be responsible for ensuring timely refunds and allotment of securities to the investors.

(*j*) The involvement of merchant bankers in an issue should continue at least till the completion of essential follow-up steps, which must include the listing of the instrument, and despatch of certificates/refunds.

Even if many of these activities are handled by other intermediaries, merchant bankers shall be responsible for ensuring that these agencies fulfil their functions, and must enable themselves to discharge this responsibility through suitable agreements with the issuer company.

(*k*) The merchant banker shall make available to SEBI such information, documents, returns and reports as may be prescribed, and called for.

(*l*) SEBI shall prepare and prescribe a Code of Conduct for merchant bankers which they should adhere to.

(*m*) SEBI may suspend/cancel the authorisation of merchant bankers for a suitable duration in case of violations of the guidelines.

(*n*) Nothing in these guidelines shall exempt the company, its functionaries, or others from any responsibility placed on them by any existing law, regulation, guidelines or conditions imposed with any sanction.

MUTUAL FUNDS

15

Introduction

In India, the only mutual fund operating for a long time since 1964 was the UTI. It is an open-ended mutual fund, whose units can be sold and repurchased at any time. It is in the public sector, enjoying a monopoly position and some unique tax benefits such as exemption from income-tax of its entire income. Although the UTI has operated a number of schemes linked to insurance and gifts, and some tax benefits, income declared by it to unitholders is not subject to any tax deduction at source and is exempt from income tax up to a limit. UTI was alone in the field until 1987. Since 1995-96, there was a TDS, if the annual income is more than ₹ 10,000, which was removed in 2000.

Mutual funds have been set up since 1987 by the public sector banks following an Amendment to the Banking Regulation Act in 1983, which empowered the RBI to permit the banks to carry on non-banking business such as leasing, mutual funds, etc., under Section 6 of this Act. Since then, the SBI, Canara Bank, Punjab National Bank and some other nationalised banks have set up their own mutual funds. The business of mutual funds has caught the imagination of the financial community and is growing at a rapid pace in India. These funds cater mainly to individual investors and small savers. It was thrown open to private and foreign sectors since the economic reforms were started in 1992.

Definition

Mutual funds are associations or trusts of public members who wish to make investments in the financial instruments or assets of the business sector or corporate sector for the mutual benefit of its members. The fund collects the moneys of these members from their savings and invests them in a diversified portfolio of financial assets with a view to reduce risks and to maximise their income and capital appreciation for distribution to its members on a *pro rata* basis. They enjoy collectively the benefits of expertise in investment by specialists in the trust, which no single individual by himself could enjoy. Mutual fund is thus a concept of mutual help of subscribers for portfolio investment and management of these investments by experts in the field. These funds are set up under the Indian Trusts Act. UTI is governed by its own Act.

Types of Funds

These funds are of various types and set up for various purposes and objectives. Some are close-ended with contributions from members collected during a definite timeframe of a few days to a few months. Thus, the issue of Can Growth was kept open for only a few days, while the LIC Mutual Fund *(viz.,* Dhanaraksha) was kept open for a few months. The life of the fund, which is close-ended, may also be for a specific period of 5 to 7 years after which the income and profits in the form of capital appreciation, etc., are all distributed back to the members after deduction of expenses of the funds by its Trustees. Some of the mutual funds are open-ended like the UTI Scheme of 1964 under which units are purchased and sold throughout the year and a member can enter the scheme any time or walk out of it also any time. These are perpetual schemes without an end, each individual member enjoying the benefits of expert investment in the form of income and growth during the period of his stay with the UTI.

Further, the funds can be classified into three types by objectives, namely, those for income alone, for growth alone (capital appreciation) and for both. The income funds aim at the maximisation of income without pursuing the growth objectives, while the growth funds specialise in securing capital appreciation, irrespective of income. But Income and Growth Funds aim at both and in a judicious mix.

These funds can also be classified into various types based on the pattern of their investments. Some funds may invest in debentures alone or fixed interest securities like the government bonds and treasury Bills. Others may invest in variable dividend securities like equities or shares of companies. There may be a few who invest only in government and semi-government bonds. In advanced countries there are funds specialising in this manner and in fact some funds are set up only for investment in real estate. In countries like the USA and UK, where the mutual fund business has grown vastly, there are thousands of such funds, some of them being quoted and traded on the stock exchanges as well. In these countries, mutual funds are well regulated but permitted to be set up in the private sector. Besides, the funds business has just been initiated by breaking the monopoly of the UTI for the first time but even so, the permission to set up mutual funds in India was granted only to public sector agencies until 1992. The policy has been liberalised in 1992 to permit private sector also to set up mutual funds. There are at present many private mutual funds operating, and a total of about 35 mutual funds operating, including those in public and private sectors with about 755 schemes, at end-March 2011.

Unit Trust of India

The UTI was created with the aim of tapping the savings of the small man and to deploy the funds for productive purposes, offering an attractive return and growth to the investors while minimising the risk element for individual investors.

Being the first of its kind and that too in the public sector, the UTI has been vested with both management and trusteeship functions in one body which is the Board of Trustees. The Unit Trust of India Act, 1963, under which UTI was constituted, did not initially permit it to take up activities other than dealing in "units" defined under the Act, investment and dealing in securities and other business arising out of the formulation of any unit scheme. These restrictions have now been removed and the UTI has been permitted to take up such other activities as direct lending of funds, bill rediscounting, leasing, financing of housing projects, and hire-purchase financing and to set up subsidiaries for many financial services and banking.

The growth in the business of UTI, especially during the eighties, has been spectacular. The gross sales of units (under all schemes) which has amounted to ₹ 10 crore in the first year, *i.e.,* in 1964-65, recorded a rapid growth, especially since 1982-83 to ₹ 4,122 crore in 1990-91 but declined to ₹ 1,050 crore during 2003-04. During the period of 1995 to 97, there was, however, a depletion of funds due to net repurchases by the UTI, due to depressed market conditions. At end March 2000, it has investible funds of ₹ 75,000 crore which declined to ₹ 58,000 crore in 2002, due to larger repurchases, following the mismanagement of UTI-64 Scheme.

UTI Schemes for Resident Indians

The UTI offered a variety of investment schemes (funds) to the investing public, it has, in all, six open-ended investment schemes, *viz.*, Unit Scheme 1964, Unit Scheme 1971 (Unit-linked Insurance Plan), Unit Scheme for Charitable and Religious Trusts and Registered Societies 1981, Capital Gains Unit Scheme 1983, Children's Gift Growth Fund Unit Scheme 1986 and Parents' Gift and Growth Fund Unit Scheme 1987, catering to the various sections of society. A special mention needs to be made here of the more popular amongst the open-ended schemes, viz., those of 1964, 1971 and 1983.

Of the close-ended schemes, a majority are Monthly Income Schemes, specifically aimed at the retired and aged investors, giving the latter an assured level of income with a total safety of capital. Among the close-ended ones, the Monthly Income Schemes with Extra Bonus and Growth benefits seem to be more popular with the investors. There are about 41 schemes in operation at end March 2004.

For domestic investors, the UTI introduced a growth-oriented mutual fund known as "Mastershares" in September 1986. The scheme was very popular, attracting funds of ₹1.58 billion against the original target of ₹500 millions. The NAV of master-shares has moved up many times since then. Net resources mobilised by UTI in 2005-06 was only ₹3,423 crore, but before that, it was a negative figure. In 2006-07 it rose for ₹7,326 crore as net resources mobilised and further to ₹15,653 crore in 2009-10. Since 1995-96, there were seven years, when it had more repayments than receipts up to 2013-14.

Offshore Funds

The Unit Trust of India took the initiative of entering the international arena by launching the close-ended 'India Fund', in 1986, providing an opportunity for non-resident Indians and other foreign individuals and institutions to make portfolio investments in the Indian capital market. The fund was quoted on the London Stock Exchange against an issue price of £1.93, the current quotation on the London Stock Exchange is at a premium.

This was followed in July 1988 by the 'India Growth Fund', also close-ended, and quoted on the New York Exchange. The issue price for the fund is $10 and the NAV and the current quotations are substantially higher. The initial subscriptions to the two funds were limited to £128 millions and $60 millions, respectively. There are presently about sixteen offshore funds set up since 1984.

SBI Mutual Fund

The SBI Markets Limited, SBI's merchant banking and leasing arm, floated the SBI Mutual Fund (SBIMF) as manager and trustee in 1987. The SBIMF has so far developed many schemes for the benefit of the domestic investing public: Magnum Regular Income Scheme (MRIS), 1987, Magnum Tax Saving Scheme (MTSS) 1988-89, Magnum Regular Income Scheme (MRIS) 1989 and Magnum Monthly Income Scheme (MMIS) 1989 (MTSS) 1990, (MRIS) 1990, etc. The last mentioned scheme was kept open for more than a month. All the four schemes are basically income-oriented in nature, although an element of capital appreciation is built into them. As the name itself suggests, MTSS 1988-89 provided for a tax rebate of 50% of the amount invested therein under Section 80 CC of the Income Tax Act, 1961, subject to a maximum of ₹20,000, inclusive of other investments eligible under this Section. Similarly, the two MRIS conferred on investors a rebate up to ₹10,000 under Section 80L of the Income-tax Act, 1961. The first three close-ended funds launched by SBIMF in the span of a year and a quarter enabled it to mobilise funds to the tune of ₹2.47 billion and created investible resources of about ₹2.60 billion by March 1989. There are a number of other schemes floated by the SBI Cap later on.

India Magnum Fund N.V.

Although a relatively new entrant in the mutual fund industry, the SBI Mutual Fund has made remarkable strides in a short span of time. The government has approved the State Bank of India's proposal to launch an offshore Mutual Fund named "Indian Magnum Fund N.V.". This close-ended fund, constituted in Netherlands Antilles, is managed by the SBI Capital Markets Limited, in association with Morgan Stanley Asset Management, New York, a well known international investment management institution. The targeted amount of mobilisation is US$ 100 million and the duration of the fund is 25 years. It garnered $ 157 million by end-October, 1989, when it was closed.

Other Funds

Another public sector bank to enter the mutual fund field is Canara Bank who, through its subsidiary Canbank Financial Services Limited, has created the Canbank Mutual Fund (CMF). The Canbank Mutual Fund has launched many schemes so far, *viz.*, "Canshare", a growth-oriented fund with no guaranteed fixed return and "Canstock", a purely income-oriented fund on the lines of SBIMF's Magnum 1. Both these close-ended funds have fared well in the market and have declared handsome return to the investors. To cater to the demands of the corporate sector, the CMF floated two other pure money market funds — Cancigo and Cangilt — which are purely liquid funds created to attract the surplus funds of the corporate sector. Other funds called "CanGrowth" and "CanStar" were floated in 1989, for the public investors and a host of other schemes were floated later on.

Close on the heels of these mutual fund companies, the Life Insurance Corporation of India (LIC) has also constituted its own mutual fund named "LIC Mutual Fund" (LICMF). The fund was launched, on June 19, 1989, and three products have been offered for investment. The three schemes opened for investment are: (*i*) "Dhanashree" close-ended income and growth-oriented scheme, open till October 31, 1989, of units with a face value of ₹ 10 each and a minimum number of units 100, with a guaranteed rate of return of 11% p.a.; (*ii*) "Dhanaraksha" — an open-ended recurring investment scheme, the maximum amount of investment under which is ₹ 60,000 (spread over a period of 10 or 15 years), and which offers life and accident cover; (*iii*) "Dhanavriddhi" — an open-ended fixed investment scheme with investment spread over 7 years to 10 years, the starting insurance cover being equal to the amount invested, subject to a maximum of ₹ 40,000. All these schemes of the LICMF are similar to the schemes offered by other mutual funds, with the additional benefit of life and accident insurance cover in the case of "Dhanraksha" and "Dhanavriddhi".

While several mutual funds as above are already in operation, other commercial banks like the Indian Bank, Central Bank of India, Punjab National, Bank of Baroda and Bank of India and financial institutions like the General Insurance Corporation of India, have either singly or jointly, taken steps to set up their own mutual funds and their schemes are also in operation. Early in 1992, the govt. policy was changed to allow private sector mutual funds also to operate on equal terms with public sector mutual funds. Now, the private/foreign sector MFs account for about 80% of investible funds of about ₹ 6 lakh crore as in 2010-11.

Overall Progress in India

The Mutual Fund movement gained momentum in India only in the last few years, namely, since 1987, UTI being the only institution in the field till then. Its performance as well as the response received by the schemes floated SBIMF and CMF — the two initial entrants — in recent years should certainly make one optimistic about the future of this movement. GIC and LIC Mutual Funds are also reportedly evoking good response from the investing public. These developments and the entry of other commercial banks and private corporate sector have shown good potentiality for their growth in India. There are about 52 listed M.F. Schemes now in addition to a large number unlisted schemes. But the performance of majority funds being below expectations, the public enthusiasm for them has waned during 2000-04. GIC Mutual Funds ceased operating from 2004-05. Of the total 48 private MFs, set up in all these years, only 30 were operating in 2010-11. In the public sector also, many had ceased to operate except four by 2011.

Investment Policy

The investment policy of the fund would depend on the objectives of the fund, namely, income, growth or both. Normally, one-third of the funds is used for investment in the money market and government bond market where the liquidity is good. Of the rest, the bulk of the amount would be invested in fixed interest securities like debentures (CD or NCD, etc.) or fixed deposits with companies, if the objective of the fund is income. If, on the other hand, the objective is growth, the bulk of the investment would be in equities or new issues. The relative proportions would depend on the importance of the objectives of income and growth. Only a small proportion of the funds would be kept as bank deposits or treasury bills for conversion into ready cash. During 2000-04, the debt-oriented funds were more popular than equity-oriented funds.

Steps to Popularise Mutual Funds

One of the major shortcomings of the existing funds appears to be that a significant share of the funds mobilised comes from the corporate sector. Fiscal reliefs available to the corporate sector on dividends from mutual funds have been encouraging corporate investment in such funds. There is obviously a lot to be done to attract the individual investor. Commercial banks with their vast network of branches and close relationship with the household sector are, of course, very well-placed to fulfil this function. The UTI is also now geared to cater more to the individual investors.

With a view to making the mutual fund schemes more popular with the small investors, the Government of India has permitted various tax concessions to the investors. The recently announced Equity Linked Savings Scheme (ELSS) implemented by the Mutual Funds, is a further step in this direction. Investment in this scheme will have the benefit of tax concession. The LIC had additional benefits of insurance cover to a certain extent. Now, the income from investment in the UTI and other funds is treated on equal terms for tax purposes. A uniform treatment to all the mutual funds and even to venture capital funds is given so that there is a level playing field for all and performance comparisons are meaningful.

Response of NRIs

The response of non-resident Indians to the mutual fund movement in India has been so far rather lukewarm, though the offshore funds launched by the UTI has been well received by them. The sale of units to NRIs, represented less than 10% of the total sales of UTI. The outstanding amount in NRI unitholders' accounts is also relatively small.

For all MFs — Common Rules

While the RBI guidelines for mutual funds set up by banks are welcome, banks which have floated mutual funds want that the regulatory framework for operating such funds should be common for all agencies wishing to float such funds and that there should be no discrimination between the different government agencies. SEBI has also started regulating mutual funds registered with RBI. The guidelines issued by them in 1992 are set out in Annexure II, while those of RBI are in Annexure I.

The banks are given permission for their mutual funds set up by them to underwrite public issues just as the Unit Trust or insurance companies. They also are permitted to participate in the inter-bank call money market since 1990.

Since bank mutual funds are to be constituted as trusts, it was felt that these funds should be treated as trustee securities and entitled to all the tax benefits available to such securities. In such case, the income on such funds are totally tax-free as in the case of UTI.

All incomes of mutual funds who distributed 90% of their profits have now been exempt from taxation as in the case of UTI. Recently, mutual funds have been permitted to operate in the money market and the RBI has announced its willingness to permit banks to set up money market mutual funds, on a case by case basis.

Advantages of Mutual Funds

Mutual funds increase the mobilisation of investible funds of the community by pooling the resources of a large number of small savers for corporate investment. Mutual funds reduce the risk of shareholding for the holder, by evolving schemes, suitable to the preferences of the saver looking for either income or capital gains. The mutual funds develop the expertise by setting up a professionally-managed structure which would look after the needs of the investing public for gainful and low-risk investment. By pooling the savings it enjoys the economies of scale in investment management.

Some mutual funds are also area specific or purpose specific, *e.g.,* Japan Fund, India Fund, etc., which necessarily provide access to foreign investors into domestic securities of particular economies.

The mutual funds can promote the investment habit of the rural and semi-urban areas and increase the proportion of investing public and of the shareholding population in India.

Progress in Nineties

In the developing countries like India, mutual funds have a very important role to play in channelising savings into the capital market. By building up expertise to assess financial viability of projects and prospects for individual scrips, these institutions help cushion the risks for individual investor. There is considerable wisdom in encouraging commercial banks to float mutual funds in view of their very large clientele. Together with industrial liberalisation, a number of new instruments and institutions heralding a new era of financial liberalisation have come up. Mutual funds will be the wave of the future as they represent an excellent instrument for the mobilisation of savings of the rising middle class in India. There was however a setback early in the 21st century to its growth due to setback to boom conditions in the stock market and slackness in the new issues market.

Regulation of Mutual Funds

Leaving aside UTI, which has been existing since 1964, two Financial Institutions, namely, LIC and GIC has set up their Mutual Funds in 1989 and 1990 respectively. Since 1987, starting with SBI, a number of Public Sector Banks have set up Mutual Funds, which have been regulated by the RBI. The Mutual Funds of LIC and GIC were regulated by the Investment Division of Ministry of Finance.

After SEBI got legal status in 1992, all Mutual Funds have been brought under its supervision, except the Money Market Mutual Funds and Offshore Mutual Funds, which are also bound by the guidelines of RBI, and Ministry of Finance. Nearly ₹ 60,000 crore were collected by UTI and another ₹ 30,000 crore by various Mutual Funds set up since 1987, as contributions of savings from investors. The Mutual Fund movement has got a startling momentum by 1990-91 but there was a setback to this in 1992, following the securities scam in which a number of banks and Mutual Funds were involved in financial irregularities. Since then, the SEBI has tightened its regulations.

The new guidelines were laid down in respect of Mutual Funds for authorisation and licensing of all Mutual Funds and each of their individual schemes. As visualised by the govt. policy, not only public sector, but private sector and joint sector mutual funds are to be permitted and licensed henceforth by the SEBI.

The legal structure and organisation of Mutual Funds as laid down by SEBI guidelines is as follows:

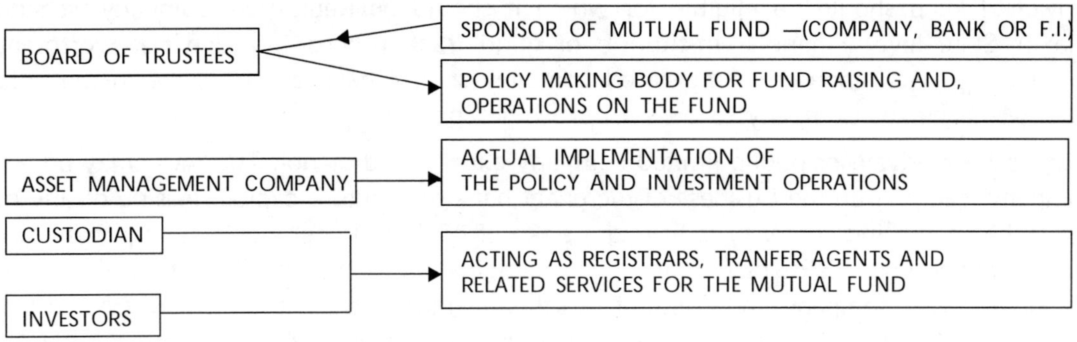

Authorisation of Existing Mutual Funds

Licensing and authorisation of existing mutual funds was initiated by the SEBI, along with the licensing of Merchant Bankers, even before the SEBI has got legal status in April 1992. As mutual funds were set up by public sector banks, they were authorised by the RBI and each of their schemes were to be approved by the latter. But gradually, SEBI tookover the responsibility of authorising and supervising them except in the case of pure Money Market Mutual Funds or the Offshore Mutual Funds which are governed by the regulations of RBI and Ministry of Finance which were also brought under the supervision of SEBI later on.

Money Market Mutual Funds (MMFs)

The MMFs can be set up by scheduled Commercial Banks and FIs, or companies as defined under Section 4A of Companies Act. The limit for these Funds set up by banks is at 2% of the sponsoring bank's fortnightly average aggregate deposits during 1991-92. They are intended to operate only in money market instruments like commercial paper and treasury bills and as they should encourage individual participation in these funds, only individuals and NRIs can subscribe to the schemes of MMFs. It was extended to companies also later. The minimum locking period is now 15 days and no minimum return should be guaranteed. The bank's reserve requirements will not apply to these funds, as per the guidelines. Later on, the RBI has also allowed the Private Sector to set up MMFs. The MMFs were allowed liquidity support from RBI to the extent of 20% of their outstanding investment in Government securities. During 2000 these funds were brought under the supervision of SEBI. RBI guidelines on MMMFs are given in Annexure III.

It has been decided to allow cheque writing facility to gilt funds and to the liquid funds' income schemes of Mutual Funds, which predominantly invest in Money Market instruments up to not less than 80% of their corpus, subject to the same safeguards, as prescribed for MMMFs. The RBI has issued operating guidelines in this regard.

The MMMFs might have been set up in the Private Sector or public sector, by banks, FIs, foreign institutional agencies or Foreign Security Firms with an Indian partner. But all of them were regulated by the RBI before October 1999. But after that, the regulation of these had come within the fold of SEBI. Besides, they have to conform to all SEBI guidelines with regard to Mutual Funds and Asset Management Companies.

The SEBI and RBI has come to an agreement in January 2000, with regard to the regulation of the Debt Market Segment in the capital market. The RBI and the government designed that the sole agency of regulation of all segments of the Capital Market should be SEBI only. In this background, the control of Money Market Funds has come to be vested in the SEBI. The corporate debt market is under the supervision of SEBI while the government debt market is under RBI.

Authorisation of New Mutual Funds

All Mutual Funds which are not exclusively dealing in Money Market instruments require authorisation from the SEBI. This authorisation is granted by the SEBI as per government guidelines since March 1992.

Sponsor of Mutual Fund should be eligible for which it should be Registered Company, scheduled Bank or all-India or State level Financial Institution of good track record, positive net worth, good management, fair dealings, etc., sponsoring registered company should have a 40% stake in the paid-up equity of the Asset Management Company to be set up by the sponsor.

The AMC should be a private or public limited company either listed or not. The AMC may be a new or an existing company, carrying on the business of merchant banking, venture capital, leasing or any other financial services. If the sponsoring company is having a stake of 40% of its net worth as required, the rest can be brought in by public issue, NRIs or foreign equity participation as permitted by the RBI. The AMC should not invest funds in any company under any of its schemes managed by it for which it has provided any financial service. The SEBI should approve the Memorandum and Articles of Association of the AMC. The AMC itself will be approved by the SEBI based on the MAA (Memorandum and Articles of Association), its business lines and subject to the restrictions on its business imposed under the guidelines.

The guidelines lay down the authorisation process subject to the following conditions:

(A) Sponsors to be eligible should be a Private or Public Limited Company, bank or F.I. The sponsoring agency should set up a Trustee.

(B) Trustee should be eligible and the Trust Deed should have the approval of SEBI. Eligibility of trustee depends on the composition of the Board of Trustees, their earlier experience and expertise, professional qualifications, etc., of each of the members of the Board, their past track record and organisation and management of Trustee Company and subject to the SEBI's approval of MAA. The Trust Board would lay down the policy.

The SEBI while granting the authorisation for the setting up of a Mutual Fund, would also approve the AMC and Custodian as part of the package. The Custodian should be different from the AMC which would manage the Fund. The Sponsor and Trustee Companies cannot act as Custodian. If the sponsor has a custodian division, it can act for other Mutual Funds not set up by the sponsor. There should be no areas of conflict between the interest of Mutual Funds, for which a custodian is rendering services and custodian. The investment criteria, expenses and income distribution, etc., are all controlled by SEBI, through their guidelines.

The approval of any agency as Custodian would depend upon its track record, experience, quality of service transparency and computerisation and other infrastructual facilities. The SEBI, may stipulate any conditions for the Custodian to act for the mutual fund in question or for one or more Mutual Funds.

Every scheme of Mutual Fund as much as the Mutual Fund should be approved by the SEBI. Every Mutual Fund should have designated a compliance officer who would deal with SEBI and is responsible for compliance with SEBI guidelines and conditions.

All applications for such approvals should be in specified forms either for authorisation of Mutual Fund or any of its schemes. It will thus be seen that the authorisation of Mutual Fund would involve approval of the sponsor, the trustee, AMC and the Custodian all together, who are responsible for the management of Public Funds.

Mutual Funds — Present Status

Many private sector mutual funds have entered the fray but the performance is far from satisfactory with the market price of many schemes quoting below the Net Asset Value which is calculated by dividing the market value of all investments + Accrued income and Receivables + other assets minus liabilities and accrued expenses except unit capital and reserves by the number of units outstanding. Valuation norms for calculation of NAV are laid down by SEBI. Mutual funds have to deduct tax at source, if they pay a dividend above ₹10,000 P.A. at a rate of 15% for individuals and 20% for companies.

Mutual funds can incur initial expenses of 6% of total funds raised and 3% every year. They have to pay 90% of their net income as dividend to unitholders.

Mutual funds are now permitted to invest up to 100% of mobilised funds in money market instruments for six months from their subscription and again revert back to 100% in these instruments six months before redemption. The details of these investment and accounting guidelines are in Annexure I and II.

There are 22 open-ended schemes, and about 30 schemes neither quoted nor repurchased at present. There are always fresh funds coming in and some funds closed due to redemption while there are some under repurchase facilities, as in the case of open-ended funds. Close-ended funds should normally be listed on stock exchanges, except when there is a repurchase provision.

The face value of mutual fund units is normally ₹ 10, but sometimes ₹ 100. For those listed and traded, there is a market price, which is different from Net Asset value. As the return for the long-term investors is more, then the total return on investment by the total funds' investment performance, since launch, the investor's annual return on such schemes may not be higher than 13-15%. But some schemes have done relatively well such as Master Share and some relatively poor such as Master Gain. Master Share was also quoted below par and U.S. 64 scheme was also in a bad shape since July 2001.

The SEBI has set up a committee on Mutual Funds late in 1995 and its recommendations were available in 1996. These relate to standardisation of NAV, calculation, exemption from listing for some schemes, management remuneration to AMCs, accounting practices, fixation of a band of 7% between purchase and repurchase prices and standardisation of such practices, etc. These aim at healthy growth of mutual fund business in India. Early in 1998, the AMCs have been asked by SEBI to double their net worth from ₹ 5 crore to ₹ 10 crore. SEBI (Mutual Fund) Regulations were amended to permit MFs to trade in derivatives and trading/ investments in Foreign Markets for portfolio balancing. The other policy changes are presented at the end of this chapter.

Taxation and MFs

So far as the MF is concerned, under Section 10 (23D) of the Act, any income received by the MF is exempt from tax. Under Section 115 R, income distributed to a unitholder or investor of the Mutual Fund shall be charged to tax at a flat rate of 10% plus surcharge if any, payable by the MF. But for funds, investing more than 50% in equity or equity related instruments the dividend distributed by MF is exempted from the above (10% plus surcharge) for three years from April 1, 1999.

The steep increase in tax rate on the income distribution by Mutual Funds from 11 to 22% in respect of debt-oriented schemes and the withdrawal of the benefits under Sections 54 EA, and EB to Mutual Funds are likely to have a negative impact on mutual fund industry from 2000-01. From 2002-03 the income distribtued by MFs is taxable in the hands of investors.

SEBI has been notifying from time to time regulations governing the Mutual Funds, their operations, their advertisement, meeting of Trustees, etc., with a view to better disclosure of investor protection and better services. For example, it is notified that any delay in repayment of moneys under schemes, which have matured by Mutual Funds is subject to penal interest rate.

So far as the unitholders are concerned, no tax is deducted at source and under Section 10 (33) of the I.T. Act, any income received by them will be exempt from income tax in their hands. Any capital gain of a long-term nature (if the same is held by investor for more than 12 months) will be subject to the following rates of tax:

Resident individuals and HUF	— 10% plus surcharge
Partnership Firms and Indian Companies	— 20% plus surcharge
Foreign Companies	— 20% plus surcharge
For FFIs/OCB/FIIs, etc.	— 10% (under Section 115 AB)

Any capital gains of a short-term nature, if the units of MF are held for less than 12 months should be added to the income of the unitholder and taxed at the following rates, which are maximum rates:

Resident Individual and HUF	— 30% plus surcharge
Partnership Firms/Indian Companies	— 30% plus surcharge
Non-resident Indians	— 30% (No surcharge)
FFIs	— 30% (No surcharge)
Foreign Companies	— 48% (No surcharge)

For residents, there is no tax deduction at source, as per the Act and the Regulations under the Act. For non-residents, the TDS on capital gains of short-term nature is 30% and of long-term nature at 20%. For Foreign Companies, the TDS on Capital gains of short-term nature is at 48% and of long-term nature at 20%. The only exemption from TDS or taxation of capital gains is in respect of tax saving equity linked schemes of MFs. These tax provisions change from year to year and have to be read as illustrations only.

Saga of Fortunes of MFs

Since 1964 and up to 1987-88 UTI strode the scene like a colossus, alone in the field as a single public sector Mutual Fund. By 1990-91, there were 5 public sector mutual funds already set up, controlling a market share of mutual fund business of 10% in the country. By 1993-94, the private and foreign sector mutual funds started their foray into this business. The international names, Morgan Stanley, Tanners, Jardine Fleming, Merrill Lynch, Prudential, etc., have appeared on the scheme of Mutual Funds.

As on March end 2011, there were 4 Public Sector Mutual Funds and about 30 Private Sector mutual funds in addition to UTI. There was a large-scale erosion in the market values of investments by UTI due to their mismanagement and scams. Net resources mobilised by UTI fell from a peak of ₹11,057 crore in 1992-93 to a net outflow of ₹6,314 crore in 1995-96. The net amount mobilised from public by UTI picked up from a low of ₹170 crore in 1998-99 to ₹322 crore in 2000-01. The Table below gives a picture of net resource mobilisation by all mutual Funds over the last two decades.

Table 15.1 NET RESOURCE MOBILISATION

(in ₹ crore)

Year	*UTI*	*Public Sector MFs*	*Private Sector MFs*	*Total*
1990-91	4553	2956	—	7,509
1993-94@	9297 (82.7)	385 (3.4)	1560 (13.9)	11,243 (100)
2000-01	322 (3.0)	1521 (13.7)	9292 (83.3)	11,135 (100)
2003-04	1050 (2.1)	3761 (7.9)	42873 (90.0)	47,684 (100)
2006-07	7326 (8.0)	7259 (8.0)	794.77 (84.0)	94,063 (100)
2009-10	15,653 (20%)	14,726 (19%)	48,166 (61%)	78,545 (100)
2010-11	–16,636	–15,684	–15,594	48,600
2013-14	4,018	7,416	48,790	54,607

@ Private Sector Mutual Funds were permitted from 1993 only.

The share of UTI fell from a high of 82.7% in 1993-94 to a low of 2% in 2003-04, while the share of private sector mutual funds rose from 13.9% in 1993-94 to 83.3% in 2000-01 and over 90% in 2003-04. There was a net outflow of funds from UTI which led to lower mobilisation of funds in 2001 to 2003.

UTI was split up into UTI-I and II and UTI-II was managed as a private fund controlled by SEBI; and UTI-I continued to be government-owned since 2001. Later UTI-II has shown better performance. The Association of Mutual Funds (AMFI) publishes data on Mutual Funds regularly.

UTI whose share was 95% of the market in 1995-96, declined to 60% in 1998-99. There were about 34 AMCs with an asset base of ₹ one lakh crore. As at end Nov. 1999, total assets of all Mutual Funds were ₹ 92,305 crore which fell to ₹ 70,200 crore by March 2001, but rose again to ₹ 1,09,299 crore at end March 2003 and ₹ 1,39,616 crore by end March 2004 and ₹ 3.26 lakh crore at end March, 2007. As per AMFI the assets under the management of MFs in India stood at ₹ 6 lakh crore, as in March 2011.

In a study by RBI in 2010-11, (Published in RBI Bulletin, May 2011) foreign liabilities of MF companies rose from ₹ 8,522 crore in 2006 to ₹ 27,446 crore in n2009. Their assets were much lower at ₹ 269 crore in 2006 which increased to ₹ 3,832 crore by March 2009. Those liabilities are the units sold to foreign residents, NRIs and other liabilities. Assets are 82,524 crores made by MF in foreign listed securities and dividends due on them.

The trend in the industry, as in general, was towards financial strengthening, mergers, takeovers, etc. The weaker ones are either closed or taken over the years 1995-2000. Equity funds started looking up and showed better performance in 1999, while debt funds were popular between 1996 to 2004. That was the worst period for equity funds as stock and primary markets were in doldrums. The years 1999 and 2000 saw again the revival of equity cult and hey days for Mutual Funds to thrive, as Stock and Capital Markets turned bullish and economy turned into a recovery phase only in 2000-01 and after a downtrend during 2001-04, the markets picked up again in 2004-05, and reached a new peak in 2006 and 2007.

The minimum paid-up capital of AMC was raised to ₹ 10 crore, but many foreign AMCs were set up more recently with 5 to 10 times the minimum required. An asset base of ₹ 500-700 crore was felt necessary for an AMC to break-even. Many public sector mutual funds like those of Bank of India, Bank of Baroda, Canbank, GIC, etc., have had difficult times. The process of mergers and restructuring helped some to revive. But the private and foreign mutual funds, barring a few exceptions like Shriram have fared better than public sector Mutual Funds. The tax sops in 1999-2000 budget have helped the mutual funds. The revival of stock markets and low interest rates and economic recovery have boosted the equity sentiment. But it was temporary and equity markets were depressed in 2001 to 2004 and so were the mutual funds from 2004 to 2008 when there was an unprecedented boom in the stock markets.

The asset base of Mutual Funds has increased by 5 times over the decade. The annual growth rate is about 30%. The trend to merger and takeover has helped the private sector mutual funds, while restructuring and financial strengthening has aided the public sector mutual funds. The competition to the public sector from the private sector was a healthy trend to boost the industry. The year 1999 saw the turning point in the mutual fund industry and the new millennium was ready for a takeoff in this industry. Investor education, change in the stock market sentiment and new distribution channels like e-banking and internet, Demat form of shareholding have all helped the industry.

Stock lending by Mutual Funds

The Mutual Funds have approached the SEBI approved intermediaries to enter into agreements to operate stock lending scheme. The Mutual Funds which showed interest in equity lending are the Canbank, Reliance, Kothari and Alliance Capital. They want to earn additional income by activising their idle core investments in their custody for badla lending of securities. This type of lending has risks associated with it, namely, reinvestment risk and potential asset-liability mismatch.

Lending increases portfolio returns on the stocks lent. But potential losses may be there due to over exposure to low credit quality clients. Lending securities to such clients is a real risk. When the M.F. lends securities, they are transferred into the name of the intermediary or the borrowing broker, while all corporate benefits continue to accrue to the M.F. Thus the MF benefits from two streams of income — one received for lending securities and another for reinvesting the cash proceeds so received. As against these benefits, the MF will have to face liquidity risk, reinvestment risk and expose the funds to the credit and interest rate risks arising out of stock lending and consequential inflow of cash. There are cases when lending institutions have lost their funds, as in the case of Harris Trust and Savings Bank, and Mellon Bank in the U.S.A.

Latest Trends

The performance of mutual funds and the investor confidence in them have received a setback since 1996, particularly due to poor performance of UTI and many scams involving UTI and banks. The nexus between banks and brokers has struck a blow to the Stock and Capital Markets and led to a negative resource mobilisation during 1995-97 by all mutual funds; mainly due to UTI. Since then the performance of all Public Sector Mutual Funds showed a marked deterioration, while the performance of Private Sector Mutual Funds revealed a relatively better performance. The main depressing factor was the poor stock market conditions, following scams and poor asset management in UTI and public sector mutual funds, particularly during 1997-2001.

The U.S.1964 of UTI, which was the pioneering scheme of UTI was in deep trouble and recorded a massive loss of market values of assets. Three Committees, namely, those of Deepak Parekh, Malegam and Tarapore have made drastic recommendations for privatisation and restructuring of UTI during 1998-2001. A scheme of protecting investor interests and of bringing the UTI under the surveillance of SEBI like other mutual funds by change of UTI Act has been announced early in 2002.

Recent policy measures relating to mutual funds are disclosure of performance of benchmarks, guidelines for valuation of unlisted equity shares, stricter adherence to their code of conduct, insider trading regulation, risk management norms and mandatory registration of intermediaries engaged in marketing of mutual fund units. The most important measure is the restructuring of UTI by repeal of UTI Act of 1963. The UTI was split into two parts in Oct. 2002 — UTI-I, comprising US-64 and all assured return schemes, taken over by the government under its own Administrator and UTI-II, later renamed as UTI Mutual Fund, taken over for private and professional management and consisting of NAV based schemes, regulated by SEBI like all other Mutual Funds. Thereafter, UTI Mutual Fund undertook serveral measures to improve its performance like organisational beef up, improved transparency, mergers of schemes, better risk management, delegation of powers and introduction of innovative schemes, etc.

The SEBI regulations of mutul funds were liberalised and streamlined from time to time. Mutual Funds were allowed to invest in mortgage backed securities of investment grade and above which would help housing finance since April 2000. Open-ended funds can now invest up to 5% of their net asset value in equity instruments of unlisted companies. Investment limit in such equities was kept unchanged at 10% for close ended schemes. The maximum limit for investment in respect of open-ended funds was raised from 5% to 10% of NAV in listed companies, in June 2000. SEBI has also banned Mutual Funds from making assurance of returns or make any claims on the basis of past performance. They were allowed to invest in listed companies abroad during 2003-04. Many other reforms were made in the new millennium.

The norms relating to code of conduct of MFs, criteria for classification of NPAs and their disclosures, treatment of income accrued on NPAs and provisions to be made, disclosures of NPAs in the half-yearly portfolio reports were streamlined. The period of initial offer of a scheme and despatch of certificates, standardisation of format, treatment of unclaimed deposits and the standards of trading by the employees were tightened. Disclosure and transparency standards relating to the Asset Management Companies (AMCs) were also made stricter.

Recent Changes in Policy

In April 2003, the SEBI had allowed the MFs to invest in equity of listed overseas company, if they have each a shareholding of at least 10% in an Indian company which is listed on Stock Exchange in India. Each MF can invest up to 10% of net assets of the fund in these securities, subject to a maximum of US$ 50 million. Later, they were allowed to trade in interest derivatives, if its disclosure, was made in the offer documents. The prior conditions for sale of or purchase of shares by the employees of MFs were liberalised to allow them to trade in securities with a gap of 30 days. The consent of the compliance officer for purchase/sale of a security would be valid for one week instead of 10 days before, effective July 2003.

In the case of bank dealings, the MFs can invest in short-term deposits with banks, but they should be reported to Trustees along with the reasons therefore. If the MF is trading in derivatives only for the purpose of hedging or portfolio balancing. Each MF could have a derivative position of 50% of the portfolio and the limit per scrip should be as approved by the Trustees of the AMCs. The SEBI issued guidelines for uniform cutoff timings for NAV for net NAV based schemes, before announcing the same on each day.

The recent measures of taxation affecting the MFA include abolition of tax on long-term capital gains in July 2003 and reduction of short-term capital gains tax from 30% to a flat rate of 10% and imposition of a tax of 12.5% on the income distributed to individuals and 20% in the case of corporate units by debt-oriented schemes and abolition of banks stripping and dividend stripping in units. Debts-oriented funds were exempted from securities transactions tax (STT), but pay capital gains tax of 10% on long-term gains and 30% on short-term gains. The above concessions were applicable only to equity-oriented schemes. The buyers of units of MF would pay a STT at 0.15% from 2004-05.

The RBI has allowed in MFs to make overseas investments up to a cap of $1 billion, if they have been approved by the SEBI. MFs can thus invest in foreign companies, listed abroad or trade in them up to a limit, as approved from time to time by RBI.

Evaluation of the Performance of the MFs

The evaluation of the performance of the MFs can be graded in two respects – one in respect of the funds mobilization from the public and second in respect of the portfolio performance of funds deployed by the MFs. More important than these two aspects is the contribution of the MFs to the growth of the economy through the deployment of funds in financial markets.

The resource mobilization as seen in the data given above in the chapter is no doubt good but if it is due to large funds contributed by the corporates and not direct from the individual savers, it is no achievement. In the absence of the data of details and breakdowns, it is difficult to arrive any worthwhile conclusion in this respect. Besides there is no consistent growth of funds mobilized by the MFs, as there are variations from year to year and in some years the resource mobilized was also poor due to depressed market conditions and poor performance of the MFs themselves. If there is good mobilization in the last few years, it was due to private sector MFs and booming market conditions. In the latest year of 2006-07, of the total net mobilization of ₹ 94,063 crore, about ₹ 79,000 crore was due to private sector MFs. The first conclusion is therefore that funds mobilization *prima facie* was poor but for the private sector MFs. In 2007-08, net mobilisation was ₹ 1,48,485 crore in total by all MFs, of which 86% was accounted by the private sector.

The MF contribution to the growth of the stock and capital markets is however very substantial, next only to the FFIs and FIIs. About ₹ 6.1 lakh crore of funds were the assets of the MFs which are deployed in the markets as assets as at end March 2010. These funds are used for the portfolio management for and on behalf of the public, which leads to the growth of the corporate sector and through them of the economy. The BSE market capitalization has grown by 17%, while the growth of the economy in 2006-07 was by 9%. The BSE SENSEX has grown by 16% in 2006-07 on top of a rise of 74% in preceding year – a total of 90% in two years. But the returns given by the MFs to the public was much less than this. This shows that the MFs in

India could not outperform the market return, as expected in theory. If some of the funds could do it, they are only the foreign controlled and managed MFs in India.

Following from the above analysis, it was also clear that the portfolio management by MFs was far from satisfactory except for a few foreign controlled and managed MFs. The reason for this state of affairs is that the expertise and experience in this line by the personnel handling in the AMCs has been far from satisfactory. This conclusion is buttressed by the fact that the weak are weeded out during the last few years. In the public sector, UTI has the distinction of mismanagement of funds under the US-64 during 1999-2001, necessitating the government interference in the UTI affairs and splitting the UTI into two units – one taken over by the govt. and other privatized to be controlled by the professionals in the FIs. Of the nine public sector MFs originally set up, five were wound up or merged with others. Of the 48 private sector MFs functioning at one time, there are only 30 functioning as in March 2011, showing the woefully high mortality rate among the MFs. The reason was the their poor performance leading to lack of viability and inadequate public support to them. The above facts clearly evidences the truth of lack of expertise among the AMCs doing the portfolio management for MFs. But the MFs have good potential.

ANNEXURE I

RBI Guidelines on Mutual Funds

Some of the commercial banks in the public sector have set up mutual funds and a few others are in the process of setting them up. On an examination of the operations of the mutual funds already functioning, it was considered necessary to issue guidelines on certain important aspects, as indicated below, with a view to their orderly functioning and in the interest of ensuring investor confidence.

Constitution and Management

(i) Every "mutual fund" shall be constituted as a Trust under the Indian Trust Act and the sponsoring bank should appoint a Board of Trustees to manage it. The Board of Trustees should have at least two outside trustees, i.e., those who are not connected with the sponsoring bank and who are persons of ability and integrity and have the proven capacity in dealing with problems relating to investment and investor protection. The overall superintendence, direction, control and management of the affairs and business of the funds should vest in the Board of Trustees.

(ii) The day-to-day management of the schemes under the fund, as may be delegated by the Board of Trustees, should be looked after by a full-time Executive Trustee who should not be concurrently discharging any other responsibility in the convened bank. If the management of the mutual fund has been assigned to the bank's subsidiary, the full-time executive trustee should not be holding any other position.

(iii) An "arm's length" relationship should be maintained between the sponsor bank and the Board of Trustees who manage the mutual fund and care should be taken that in putting through the transactions, there is no clash of interest between the sponsor bank and the beneficiaries under the schemes of its mutual fund. In case the management of mutual fund has been entrusted to a subsidiary of the bank, similar care should be exercised by the latter to avoid any clash of interest between itself and the beneficiaries under the scheme of the mutual fund.

(iv) *(a)* The sponsor bank's contribution to the corpus of the fund should be a minimum of ₹ 25 lakh or such higher amount as may be specified by the Reserve Bank. The corpus may be converted at a later date into subscription to any of the schemes of the fund with the approval of the Board of Trustees of the fund. No additional contribution should be made by the sponsor bank to the corpus without the prior approval of the Reserve Bank.

(b) In addition to the contribution to the corpus, the sponsor bank should contribute and maintain in each of the fund's schemes by way of its stake an amount equivalent to 1 per cent of the total amount outstanding. This stipulation will not however, apply to special schemes wherein the sponsor bank cannot participate.

(v) Banks should obtain the Reserve Bank's prior approval before announcing any scheme of a mutual fund, irrespective of whether it is identical or not to any of the earlier schemes approved by the Reserve Bank.

Investment Objectives and Policies

(vi) The investment objectives and policies of the mutual fund should be laid down in the trust deed and every scheme to be launched by the fund must be in accord with such broad objectives and policies and the rules and regulations framed in conditions therewith.

(vii) While inviting subscription from the public, the mutual fund should make statement of the investment objectives of the fund and its investment policies, besides the terms and conditions of the scheme.

(viii) The subscription amounts collected by mutual funds are primarily intended to be channelised into the capital market instruments like government and other trustee securities, shares/debentures of public limited companies, bonds of public sector undertakings, etc., and except for the extent indicated in (ix) below, the mutual funds should not undertake direct or indirect lending, portfolio/funds management, underwriting, bills discounting, money market operations, etc., which are essentially banking/merchant banking functions.

(ix) There is, however, no objection to the mutual funds investing the amounts initially collected for a scheme in the money market instruments, rediscounting of bills, or bank deposits for periods not exceeding six months. The mutual funds may also invest their temporary surplus fund in similar instruments up to not more than 25 per cent of their total investible funds. Such short-term/temporary investments can, however, be made only if they are permissible under the Charter of the Fund.

(x) The mutual funds should invariably take delivery of scrips purchased and, in the case of scrips sold, give delivery thereof to the purchaser. The scrips purchased should be transferred in the fund's name.

(xi) In no event should a mutual fund make short sale/purchase of securities or carry over the transactions from one settlement period to the next settlement period.

(xii) The mutual funds should not make investments in any other unit trust, mutual fund of similar collective investment schemes. The funds should not also invest in the shares, etc., of investment companies/corporations.

Prudential Exposure Ceiling Limits

(xiii) From the point of view of spreading the risk, it is necessary that the portfolio of a fund is diversified. A mutual fund should follow the following prudential guidelines in this regard:

(*a*) It should not hold, under any one scheme, more than 5 per cent of issued share capital or debenture stock of any company. In case more than one scheme is operated by a fund, such holdings in respect of all its schemes put together should not exceed 15 per cent of the paid-up capital or debenture stock of a company.

(*b*) The total amount invested by a fund from any of its schemes in the shares, debentures, etc., of any specific industry (such as cotton textiles, tea, tyres, etc.), should not exceed 15 per cent of a scheme's fund. This provision will not, however, apply to a scheme which has been floated for investment in one or more specified industries, and a declaration has been made to that effect.

Pricing Policy

(xiv) The maximum spread between the purchase and selling prices of units/shares of any scheme should not be more than 5%.

Income Distribution

(xv) The total cost of managing any scheme under a fund, including management fees and other administrative costs, should be kept within 5 per cent of the total income of the scheme.

(xvi) Income distribution by way of dividend or capitalisation of gains should not be made on the basis of revaluation of the stock holdings or unrealised capital appreciation.

(xvii) Depreciation on investments held and provision for bad or doubtful debts, if any, have to be provided for to the satisfaction of auditors before declaring any dividend. Further, a fund should also create a dividend equalisation fund for each scheme by appropriating a part of its surplus income.

Statement of Accounts and Disclosure

(xviii) A mutual fund should maintain separate accounts of each scheme launched by it, segregating the assets under each scheme. No switching of assets between the schemes should take place, except with the prior approval of the Board of Trustees and at the prevailing market rates.

(xix) The Board of Trustees of mutual funds should prepare an annual statement of accounts in respect of each of the schemes which should contain, *inter alia,* statements of assets and liabilities and income and expenditure accounts duly audited by qualified auditors. Further, an abridged version of the annual account together with the reports of auditors and the Board of Trustees, should be published for the information of subscribers to the concerned scheme.

(xx) The Board of Trustees of mutual funds should disclose the net asset value of each of the schemes and the method of valuation for the benefit of the concerned subscribers.

(xxi) Sponsor banks should furnish to the Reserve Bank duplicate, the following reports on a regular basis:

(a) A half-yearly report indicating the performance of the mutual fund as a whole as well as each scheme.

(b) Audited annul statement of accounts, together with the reports of auditors and the report of the board of trustees.

(c) Scheme-wise details of investment portfolio of the funds, value of such investments, changes in the portfolio since the previous annual report and industry-wise exposure.

ANNEXURE II

SEBI

The following are the guidelines for mutual fund:

Mutual funds have become a major vehicle for mobilisation of savings particularly from the small households sectors for investment in the stock market. In view of their growing importance in the capital market, their expanding investor base and the decision to allow mutual funds to be set up in the joint and private sectors it has become necessary to evolve a comprehensive set of prudential guidelines for the allround development and regulation of mutual funds and for ensuring investor protection. These guidelines are laid down below:

Scope

These guidelines shall be applicable to all mutual funds which invest primiarily in the capital market and also partly in money market instruments subject to the following:

(*a*) Money market mutual funds that would invest exclusively in money market instruments would be regulated by the Reserve Bank of India on the basis of specified guidelines to be laid down by the RBI. However, money market schemes of other mutual funds would be regulated by the Securities and Exchange Board of India. These regulations will be in conformity with the guidelines to be issued by the Reserve Bank for money market mutual funds investing exclusively in money market instruments.

(*b*) Offshore funds which have non-residential investors and are regulated by the provisions of the countries where these are registered shall be outside the purview of these guidelines. These funds shall continue to be governed by the rules and procedures laid down for the purpose of approving and monitoring their performance by the department of economic affairs, ministry of finance and the government's/RBI's directives on this subject.

(*c*) Mutual funds with special characteristics, *e.g.,* funds dealing with assets other than securities may be specifically exempted by the government from the purview of these guidelines.

Existing mutual funds should conform to these guidelines within a period of 6 months from the date of issue of these guidelines.

Establishment

Mutual funds shall be authorised for business by the Securities and Exchange Board of India (SEBI).

Mutual funds shall be sponsored by the registered companies with a sound track record, general reputation and fairness in all their business transactions.

Mutual funds shall be established in the form of trusts under the Indian Trusts Act. The sponsoring institution will be free to workout the details regarding the constitution of the Trust.

The Trust shall then be authorised to float one or several different schemes under which units shall be issued to the investors.

Mutual funds shall be operated only by separately established Asset Management Companies.

Asset Management Company (AMC)

Authorisation for Business

AMC shall be authorised for business by SEBI on the basis of the following criteria:

(*a*) AMCs which are already existing should have a sound track record, general reputation and fairness in all their business transactions.

(*b*) The directors of AMCs should be persons of high repute and standing having at least 10 years of professional experience in the relevant field such as portfolio management, investment analyis, financial administration, etc.

(*c*) At least 50% of the board of AMC should be independent directors not connected with the sponsoring organisation.

(*d*) The AMC should at all times have a minimum net worth of ₹ 5 crore.

SEBI shall approve the memorandum and articles of association of the AMC.

The name of the directors and any subsequent changes must be intimated to SEBI.

SEBI may lay down additional selection criteria or change them from time to time for regulating the expansion of mutual funds in the larger interest of mutual funds industry and healthy growth of capital market.

Except in the case of bank sponsored AMCs where the prior concurrence of RBI would be required, SEBI may withdraw the authorisation granted to any AMC if it is found to be not serving the best interests of investors or of mutual funds industry or of capital market. The board of trustees, of a mutual fund in such cases, should reappoint another AMC or liquidate the mutual fund as may be necessary with 3 months of withdrawal of authorisation of the existing AMC and distribute the proceeds to unit-holders.

Restrictions on Business Activities

AMC should not be allowed to act as the trustee of a Unit Trust. In other words, the AMC and the trustee should be two separate legal entities.

AMC should not be permitted to undertake any other business activity than management of mutual funds, and such other activities as financial services constantly, exchange of research and analysis on commercial basis as long as these are not in conflict with the fund management activity itself.

An AMC or its affiliate acting for a fund cannot act the AMC for any other funds. For this purpose, a company is considered as an affiliate if it is a company:

(*a*) Which directly or indirectly, and by itself, or in combination with other persons exercises a significant control over the AMC.

(*b*) Over which the AMC directly or indirectly, and by itself or in combination with other persons exercises a significant control.

(*c*) Over which significant control is exercised directly or indirectly by person or persons or the relatives of such persons whether by themselves or in combination, as are the same person or persons or the relatives of such person or persons whether by themselves or in combination who exercise significant control over the AMC.

(*d*) In which any director, officer or employee of the AMC is a director, officer or employee.

(*e*) Without prejudice to the generality of the above restriction, significant control shall be deemed to exist.

(*i*) In relation to company, where any person or combination of persons directly or indirectly own, control or hold with power to vote 3 per cent or more of the voting shares of such company.

(*ii*) In between two companies if the same person or combination of persons directly or indirectly own, control or hold with power to vote 3 per cent or more of the voting shares of each of the two companies.

No person should be a Director of more than one AMC.

No person who is a Director of an AMC should hold the position of a Trustee, or Director in a Trust company, of funds operated by the same AMC.

No person should be a Director/Trustee in more than one Trust Company/Board of Trustees.

Trustees and Trust Companies

Trusteeship functions should be carried out by separately established Trust Companies. Until such companies are formed, existing debenture-trustees, banks and financial institutions may be allowed to act as mutual fund trustees, or a separate Board of Trustees consisting of individuals of sufficient repute and experience may act as mutual fund trustees.

At least 50 per cent of the Board of Trustees shall be independent outside members. They shall not have any affiliation with the sponsoring institution or any of its subsidiaries.

The Trust Company and/or the composition of the Board of Trustees including the eligibility of each member should be intimated to SEBI.

The Trustees should have the responsibility to ensure that managers comply with the guidelines and report periodically to the investors in the fund that this is the case. This should entail, *inter alia,* the following checks:

* that investments are of the permitted kind and within set limits;
* that the fund's assets are duly protected;
* that transaction in units are properly executed by the manager which may include spot checks on;
* pricing of units;
* payments into and out of the fund;
* internal controls (*e.g.,* for capital adequacy);
* that income due to the fund is properly accounted for;
* that all expenses and charge to the fund are as permitted;
* that distributions from the fund are properly made.

In order to effect these checks the Trustees should have the right to obtain from the AMC all information concerning the operations of the Trust.

The AMC should submit a quarterly report of the functioning of the mutual funds to the Trustees. The Trustees in turn should submit a six-monthly report to the SEBI, and an annul report to the investors in the funds.

Trust Deeds

The sponsor should submit the trust deed to SEBI for prior approval.

The trust deed should include all safeguards considered to be essential for investor protection.

Custodian

The mutual funds shall use the services of a custodian registered with SEBI.

It should be ensured that the custodian should be totally delinked from the AMC.

Each authorised unit trust should be allowed to float different schemes as long as the Asset Management Company concerned meets the required capital adequacy criteria and whose authorisation has not been withdrawn by SEBI for any reason, whatsoever.

Each scheme floated by a mutual fund should have prior registration with SEBI. The asset management company should prepare a prospectus/letter of offer for each scheme and should get it vetted by SEBI before inviting public participation. SEBI shall decide each proposal within 30 days of its receipt, failing which, the scheme may be floated by the fund presuming SEBI's clearance.

Mutual funds should be allowed to start and operate both closed-end and open-end schemes.

The closed-end schemes shall be considered for approval as per the receipt, failing which, the scheme may be floated by the fund presuming SEBI's clearance.

Mutual funds should be allowed to start and operate both closed-end and open-end schemes.

The closed-end schemes shall be considered for approval as per the procedures applicable to capital issues by companies.

For each closed-end schemes shall be considered for approval as per the procedures applicable to capital issues by companies.

For each closed-end scheme, the mutual fund should be required to raise at least ₹ 20 crore and for each open-end scheme, at least ₹ 50 crore. The entire subscription should be refunded to the investors, (*a*) the minimum amount of ₹ 20 crore or 60% of the targeted amount, whichever is higher, is not raised for a closed-end scheme, or (*b*) the minimum amount of ₹ 50 crore or 60% of the targeted amount, whichever is higher, is not raised for an open-end scheme.

Mutual funds should not be permitted to keep close-end schemes open for subscription for more than 45 days. For open-end schemes, the first 45 days of the subscription period should be considered for determining the target figure or minimum size.

Mutual funds should provide continuous liquidity. Closed-end schemes should be listed on exchanges. For open-end schemes, mutual funds shall sell and repurchase units at pre-determined prices based on net asset value and such prices should be published at least once in a week.

Each scheme under the same management should have a clearly identified and responsible fund manager.

Investment Limitations

Mutual funds will be allowed to invest only in transferable securities either in the money market or in the capital market, including any privately-placed debentures or securitised debt.

(*a*) Privately place debentures, securitised debt and other unquoted debt instruments holdings shall not exceed 10% in case of growth funds, and 40% in case of income funds.

(*b*) All debt instruments must have been rated as investment grade by an approved credit rating agency; the specific approval of the board of AMC should be taken to become eligible for holding in the portfolio.

Mutual funds should not be allowed to give term loans for any purpose.

No individual scheme of the mutual fund should invest more than five per cent of its corpus in any one company's shares.

No mutual fund under all its schemes should own more than five per cent of any company's paid-up capital carrying voting rights.

No mutual fund under all its schemes taken together should invest more than 10% of its funds in the shares or debentures or other securities of a single company.

No mutual fund under all its schemes taken together should invest more than 15% of its funds in the shares and debentures of any specific industry (such as cotton textile, tea, tyres, etc). This provision will not, however, apply to a scheme which has been floated for investments in one or more specified industries and a declaration to that effect has been made in the offer letter.

No scheme should invest in or lend to another scheme under the same AMC.

Mutual funds must take delivery of scrips purchased and give delivery in the case of scrips sold and in no case shall engage in short selling or carry-forward transactions or badla finance. The scrips purchased should be transferred to the fund's name and scheme also.

Transfers from one scheme to another in the same mutual fund should be allowed only if,

(*a*) such transfers are done at the prevailing market price for quoted instruments on spot basis,

(*b*) the securities so transferred would be in accordance with the investment objective of the transferee scheme,

(*c*) transfer of unquoted instruments should be done only with specific approval of the board of trustees,

(*d*) the registration and accounting of the transaction is completed and is ratified in the next meeting of the board of trustees.

Winding up

Each closed-end scheme should have a duration fixed in a number of years, at the end of which, it should be wound up or extended with the permission of SEBI.

An open-end scheme shall be wound up if the total number of units outstanding after repurchases at a point of time falls below 50% of the originally issued number of units.

Expenses

The asset management company may charge the mutual fund with investment management and advisory fees which should have been disclosed fully in the prospectus subject to the following ceiling:

(*a*) 1.25% of the weekly average net assets outstanding in the current year for the scheme concerned as long as the net assets do not exceed ₹ 100 crore, and

(*b*) 1% of the excess amount over ₹ 100 crore, where net assets so calculated exceed ₹ 100 crore.

In addition, the asset management company may charge the mutual fund with the following expenses:

(*a*) mutual issue costs of sponsoring the fund and its schemes.

(*b*) recurring expenses including: (*i*) marketing and selling expenses including agent's commission, if any (*ii*) brokerage and transaction cost (*iii*) registrar services for transfer of shares sold or redeemed.

The asset management company, should be expected to meet all its expenses and responsible to provide the following:

(*a*) office space, supplies and personnel including analysts and portfolio managers,

(*b*) regulatory compliance and reporting services,

(*c*) preparation and distribution of the fund's prospectus, annual and periodic reports and other investor communications,

(*d*) advertising and other sales material,

(*e*) according services and preparation of tax returns,

(*f*) insurance coverage and other services.

The fees payable to the trustees shall be charged to the mutual funds.

The fees payable to the custodian for safekeeping of fund assets and related matter shall be charged to the mutual fund.

The initial issue expenses should not exceed 6% of the funds raised under each scheme.

In any case, the total of all the expenses charged to the fund except the initial issue expenses should not exceed 3% of the weekly average net assets outstanding during the current year and the same shall be disclosed through advertisements, accounts, etc.

All expenses should be clearly identified and appropriately attributed to the individual schemes.

Income Distribution

All mutual funds must distribute a minimum of 90 per cent of their profits in any given year.

Rights of the Parties

The asset management company can be changed by either the trustee company board or by 75% of investors in the fund.

If a change in the asset management company is recommended by the trustee company/board, it should be subject to scrutiny and approval of SEBI.

If the sponsor of a mutual funds recommends change of the trustee, it should be subject to the scrutiny and approval of SEBI.

SEBI should have the right to review a mutual funds's role in takeovers.

Accounting Requirements

Mutual funds should be required to segregate their earnings as current income, short-term capital gains and long-term capital gains.

Accounting for all the schemes should be required to be done for the same year ending.

For all quoted instruments, mutual funds must calculate weekly NAV at the last available closing market prices. For unquoted investments, the valuation may be done once weekly either at cost or by any other method authorised by SEBI. For investments considered doubtful, the directors' best estimate may be accepted, subject to the auditors' certificate of reasonability.

Disclosure and Reporting

SEBI will have the right to call for any information regarding the operations of the mutual funds any of its schemes from the mutual fund, asset management company, custodian, sponsor or any other person associated with the mutual fund.

SEBI will require from every mutual fund at least the following periodic reports, in addition to any other it may see fit:

(*a*) Copies of the duly audited annual statements of account including the balance sheet and the profit and loss account for the fund and for each scheme, once a year.

(*b*) Six-monthly unaudited accounts as above.

(*c*) A statement of movements in net assets for each of the schemes of the funds, every quarter.

(*d*) A portfolio statement, including changes from the previous periods, for each scheme, every quarter.

SEBI shall also lay down the accounting policies to be complied with by all mutual funds and the format and contents of the financial statements and other reports.

SEBI shall require all mutual funds to adopt a written code of ethics designed to deal with the potential conflicts of interest that may arise from transactions by the affiliated persons or companies. SEBI shall require a quarterly report from the interested persons or companies, disclosing all reportable transactions as determined by SEBI in a format prescribed by SEBI.

SEBI shall lay down a common advertising code for all mutual funds to comply with.

All mutual funds will be expected to submit to SEBI the texts of the marketing literature and advertisements issued to the investors.

The marketing and publicity brochures for each scheme shall properly disclose the investment objectives, the method and periodicity of valuation of investment, the exact method and periodicity of sales and purchases and other details considered by SEBI to be essential for investors.

SEBI can, after due investigation, impose penalties on mutual funds for violating the guidelines as may be necessary. However, for cases of penalties of suspension or de-authorisation of mutual fund entities, prior concurrence of RBI and the government shall be taken.

Appeals against decisions of SEBI lie to the Department of Economic Affairs, Ministry of Finance.

The SEBI has recently allowed the Mutual Funds to invest 100% of funds raised in Money Market up to 6 months and thereafter later 30% of funds for 6 months to one year and only 25% in Money Market and again 100% of funds in Money Market, 6 months prior to repayment to investors.

ANNEXURE III

Scheme for Money Market Mutual Funds — Guidelines (RBI)

Please refer to our circular DBOD No. 13/24.01.013/91-92 dated 29 April, 1992, wherein a scheme of Money Market Mutual Funds (MMMFs) was introduced by the Reserve Bank of India. In this connection we invite your attention to the Governor's circular No. CPC. BC.148/07.01.279/95-96 dated November 23, 1995, wherein with a view to providing greater liquidity and depth to the money market and in order to make the scheme more flexible and attractive to banks and financial institutions certain modifications to the existing scheme have been introduced. The salient features of the scheme as modified are indicated below:

1. Eligibility to set up MMMFs

MMMFs can now be set up by scheduled commercial banks and public financial institutions as defined under Section 4A of the Companies Act, 1956 or through their existing Mutual Fund/Subsidiaries engaged in Funds Management as well as mutual funds set up in the private sector. Private sector mutual funds can set up MMMFs with the prior approval of Reserve Bank of India, subject to other extent terms and conditions stipulated under the Scheme and should also get Securities and Exchange Board of India (SEBI) clearance to ensure that there is no infringement of SEBI guidelines on money market investments for amount/duration.

2. Structure of MMMFs

(*i*) MMMFs can be set up departmentally in the form of a division/department of the banks/ financial institutions/mutual funds/subsidiaries, *i.e.*, "in-house" MMMFs wherein the assets and liabilities of such MMMFs would form part of the eligible institutions' balance sheet or as separate entity, *i.e.*, as a "Trust".

(*ii*) MMMFs can be operated either as Money Market Deposit Accounts (MMDAs) or Money Market Mutual Funds (MMMFs). MMDAs schemes could be operated either by issuing deposit receipt or through issue of Passbook without cheque book facility. MMMFs could float both open-ended and close-ended schemes.

(*iii*) Where MMMFs are set up as a Trust, a Board of Trustees should be appointed by the sponsoring institution to manage it. The day-to-day management of the schemes under the Fund is set up as a Trust, should be looked after by a full-time Executive Trustee or a separate Fund Manager if set up as a Division of bank/financial institution/mutual fund/ subsidiary.

(*iv*) Banks and public financial institutions are free to formulate special schemes as per their requirements subject to the guidelines stipulated by the Reserve Bank of India. MMMFs should forward the details of the scheme together with copies of offer letter, application form, etc., to the Reserve Bank of India at least one month before announcing the launching of any scheme.

3. Size of MMMFs

The minimum size of a MMMF of ₹ 50 crore stipulated in our circular of April 29,1992 is withdrawn. Likewise, the prescription of a ceiling for raising resources under various schemes by MMMFs set up by banks/financial institutions/mutual funds/subsidiaries is also withdrawn.

4. Who can Subscribe?

As MMMFs are primarily intended to be a vehicle for individual investors to participate in the money market, the units/ shares of MMMFs can be issued only to individuals. Individual Non-Resident Indians (NRIs) may also subscribe to shares/units of MMMFs. The dividend/income on such subscriptions will be allowed to be repatriated. The principal amount of subscription will, however, not be allowed to be repatriated abroad. The corporates are also allowed to invest in them, later on.

5. Minimum Size of Investment by a Single Investor

MMFs would be free to determine the minimum size of investment by a single investor.

6. Investment Objectives and Policies

The investment objectives and policies of MMMFs should be laid down by the sponsor bank/institution or concerned mutual fund and every scheme to be launched by the MMMFs should be in accordance with such broad objectives and policies and the rules and regulations framed in this regard. While inviting the subscription from the public, MMMFs should make a clear statement of investment objectives of the MMMFs and the investment policies besides the terms and conditions of the scheme. MMMFs should not give any guarantee or indication as the rate of return on investments while announcing any scheme.

7. Investments by MMMFs

(*i*) The resources mobilised by MMMFs should be invested exclusively in the following money market instruments, namely:

(a) Treasury bills and dated Government securities having an unexpired maturity up to 1 year,

(*b*) call/notice money,

(*c*) commercial paper,

(*d*) commercial bills arising out of genuine trade/commercial transactions and accepted/co-accepted by banks and

(*e*) certificates of deposit.

It has been decided that the limits on investments in individual instruments stipulated in our circular of April 29, 1992 should be withdrawn and MMMFs are now free to determine the extent of their investments in each instrument as indicated below:

Instruments	*Limit (per cent of resources of MMMFs)*	
(*a*) Treasury Bills and dated Government securities having an unexpired maturity up to 1 year.	Minimum 25 per cent	Maximum limit withdrawn
(*b*) Call/Notice Money	Maximum 30 per cent	Maximum limit withdrawn
(*c*) Commercial Paper	Maximum 15 per cent The exposure to commercial paper issued by an individual more than 3 per cent of the resources of the MMMFs.	Maximum limit withdrawn The exposure to commercial paper issued by an individual company should, however, not be more than 3 per cent of the resources of the MMMF as a prudential requirement.
(*d*) Commercial Bills arising out of genuine trade/commercial transactions and accepted/co-accepted and accepted/co-accepted by banks.	Maximum 20 per cent.	Maximum limit withdrawn.
(*e*) Certificate of Deposit	No limit	No limit

The investments should be made in accordance with the prudential guidelines which may be issued by the Reserve Bank of India from time to time. MMMFs shall not deploy their funds in capital market instruments so that their investments are not exposed to undue risk.

(*ii*) Switching of assets between schemes should be at market rate and based on conscious investment decision; and

(*iii*) Borrowing and lending between schemes of the MMFs as also between the MMMFs and the sponsoring institutions are prohibited.

8. Delivery of Instruments

MMMFs should invariably take delivery of money market instruments purchased and give delivery of the instruments sold.

9. Reserve Requirements

In the case of MMMFs set up by banks, the resources mobilised by them would not be considered as part of their net demand and time liabilities and as such these resources would be free from any reserve requirements.

10. Minimum Lock-in period and Repurchase

The minimum lock-in period for investments in MMMFs would be 45 days (reduced to 30 days later). The MMMFs would be free to offer repurchase facilities to the investors subject to the minimum lock-in period. The details of the repurchase facility including the procedures should be made clear in the offer document.

11. Insurance cover

The funds invested in MMMFs will not have insurance cover from the Deposit Insurance and Credit Guarantee Corporation of India. This aspect must be clearly brought out in the offer documents by MMMFs.

12. Stamp Duty

The shares/units issued by MMMFs would be subject to stamp duty. Similarly, transfer of units of MMMFs after holding for a lock-in period of 46 days would be subject to stamp duty.

13. Format of certificates of MMMFs

The units of MMMFs should be issued in the form of a certificate indicating the number of units purchased by the investor.

14. Application Form

MMMFs may devise suitable application form for subscribing to their schemes.

15. Security Aspect

Since units are freely transferable, due care must be exercised by the MMMFs in the matter of printing/safe custody of the instrument. They should be signed by two or more authorised signatories.

16. Regulation of MMMFs

The setting up of MMMFs would require prior authorisation of Reserve Bank of India. Furthermore, MMMFs set up by banks, their subsidiaries and public financial institutions would be required to comply with the guidelines and directives that may be issued by the Reserve Bank of India from time to time. The private sector MMMFs would need clearance of SEBI; the approval of Reserve Bank of India would be necessary to enable them to operate in the money market.

The Reserve Bank of India shall have the powers in the interest of banking policy and public interest, to issue directions, call for any information, inspect the books and accounts of the MMMFs; any inspection of private sector MMMFs would be undertaken by SEBI.

17. Accounting

The accounts of MMMFs should be kept distinct and separate from those of the parent institutions. In the case of "In-house" MMMFs, it should be ensured that there is no conflict of interest between MMMFs and their parent organisation. The transfer of assets between MMMFs and the sponsoring institution should be at market rate and should be subject to the approval of the sponsoring institution's Board.

18. Statement of Accounts and Disclosure

MMMFs should maintain separate account of each scheme launched by it segregating the assets under each scheme. MMMFs should prepare an annual statement of accounts in respect of each of their schemes which should contain, *inter alia,* statements of assets and liabilities and income and expenditure account duly audited by qualified auditors, other than the auditors of the parent organisation. An abridged version of the annual accounts together with the reports of the auditors should be published for the information of subscribers to the concerned scheme.

19. Management of MMMFs

"In-house" MMMFs should take adequate and effective measures to ensure that management, accounting and custody of their asset should be kept distinct and separate from those relating to the bank/financial institution/subsidiary/mutual fund.

20. Net Asset Value

MMMFs should calculate Net Asset Value (NAV) of each scheme and disclose the NAVs periodically for the benefit of the investors. To start with, MMMFs may determine and disclose NAV once in a week. Thereafter, NAV may be determined twice in a week or even daily. The method to be followed for calculation of NAV should be disclosed in the offer letter of each scheme.

21. Expenses

The total expenses of the Fund including pre-issue expenses, trusteeship fees/management fees, etc., should be kept at reasonable levels and should be disclosed fully in the Fund's Annual Reports/balance sheets.

22. Furnishing Reports to Reserve Bank of India

The sponsor bank/financial institution/subsidiary/mutual fund should furnish to Reserve Bank of India, in duplicate, the following reports on a regular basis:

(*a*) quarterly report indicating the performance of the MMMFs as a whole and each scheme thereof.

(*b*) scheme-wise annual statement of accounts, together with the reports of the Auditors.

(*c*) scheme-wise details of investment portfolio of the Funds, value of such investments, changes in the portfolio since the annual report and asset-wise exposure.

(*d*) specific information on investments in certain segments of the money market as may be called for by the Reserve Bank of India.

23. Banks/Financial institutions/Mutual funds/subsidiaries desirous of setting up MMMFs may forward their applications to the Chief General Manager, Department of Banking Operations and Development, Reserve Bank of India, Central Office, Centre I, World Trade Centre, Cuffe Parade, Colaba, Mumbai 400 005 together with other supporting particulars/documents such as details of proposed constitution and organisational structure, draft Trust Deed (wherever applicable), details of scheme/s, etc.

24. Detailed operating procedures for private sector mutual funds are being worked out by the Reserve Bank and the Securities and Exchange Board of India.

VENTURE CAPITAL FUNDS

16

Venture capital is risk money, which is used in risky enterprises either as equity or debt capital. It may be in new sunshine industries or older risk enterprises. The funds which finance such risky ventures are called venture capital funds.

Venture capital was originated and popularised in the USA in the sixties. In developed countries, this capital came from pension funds, insurance companies and even large banks. Some large companies with excess funds may provide this capital to achieve diversification, market expansion and a 'window on technology' or to share in the results of R&D of others.

In India, as the majority of the above institutions are in the public sector, only the government or public financial institutions can provide the funds for venture capital.

What is Venture Capital?

Venture capital is a post-war phenomenon in the business world, mainly developed as a sideline activity of the rich in the USA. To connote the risk and adventure and some element of investment, the generic name of 'venture capital' was coined. In the late 1960s, a new breed of professional investors called venture capitalists emerged whose speciality was to combine risk capital with entrepreneurial management and to use advanced technology to launch new products and new companies in the marketplace. Undoubtedly, it was the venture capitalists' astute ability to assess and manage enormous risks and extort from them tremendous returns that changed the face of America.

Innovative, hi-tech ideas are necessarily risky. It is here that the concept of venture capital steps in. Venture capital provides long-term start up costs to high risk and return projects. Typically, these projects have high mortality rates and, therefore, are unattractive to risk-averse bankers and private sector companies.

Venture Projects

Proposals come to the venture capitalist in the form of business plans. He appraises the same, giving due regard to the credentials of the founders, the nature of the product or service to be developed, the market to be served and the financing required. If satisfied, he will invest his own money in the equity shares of the new company, known as the assisted company.

In addition to money, managerial and marketing assistance may also be provided; that is, the venture capitalist not only provides funds but also online operational advice. In short, he identified himself with the project as much as the innovator promoter and as such works hard to accomplish ambitious targets and consequent higher appreciation of his capital.

After some years, when the assisted company has reached a certain stage of profitability, the venture capitalist offloads his shares in the stock market at a hefty premium, thus earning profits, as well as releasing locked up funds for redeployment in some other venture and the cycle continues.

Indian Position

In India, most project financing schemes require at least 25 per cent of the project cost to be contributed by the promoters, while the latter can raise barely 5-10 per cent. At present, there are a few agencies such as IFCI's subsidiary company, Risk Capital and Technology Foundation of India, which provides finance to bridge the shortfall in the promoter's contribution, but they cannot fulfil the requirements of a great many budding entrepreneurs. As a result of promoters not being able to bring in those vital initial inputs of money, many of their good projects are hanging fire. Venture capital could remedy this situation as well.

A beginning was made in this direction by the setting up of venture capital divisions under the aegis of ICICI, IDBI and IFCI. Encouraged by the response to technology financing, ICICI floated a separate company — Technology Development and Information Company of India (TDICI), in collaboration with the UTI. The activity profile of TDICI includes, apart from venture capital financing, technology information, consultancy as well as entrepreneur escort services such as marketing, business management, vendor development, etc. The successful operation of this fund will hopefully spark off some interest from the private sector which will then consider entering this line of activity. Ultimately, it is only when venture capital financing becomes more broad-based and widespread that it will truly take root in the economy. In tune with its tradition of pioneering new ideas, ICICI deviated from the beaten path to usher in an unusual type of financial support. In addition to equity participation (up to a maximum of 49 per cent) undertaken by typical venture capital companies, TDICI offers the unique option of conditional loans. The entrepreneur neither pays interest on it nor does he have to repay the principal amount. If the venture succeeds, TDICI recoups its investment in the form of royalty on sales which ranges between two and eight per cent. On the other hand, if the, venture fails to take off even after five years TDICI will consider writing off the loan.

Public Financing Agencies

It is to be noted that those floating venture capital companies are either financial institutions or banks (the Andhra Pradesh Industrial Development Corporation, Canara Bank and others). This can be directly attributed to the government guidelines which restrict private sector participation in venture capital funds to a maximum of 20 per cent.

But if the concept is to make a mark in the economy it needs private sector initiative and not institutional or governmental patronage. In fact, herein lies the strategic significance of venture capital. It paves, the way for the private sector to share the burden of industrial finance, particularly risk finance with the public sector.

The activities of the venture capital fund of ANZ Grindlays Bank include making equity investments in new companies which may or may not involve any new technology or other such related risk. This activity of direct subscriptions by financial institutions and banks has been going on for decades and cannot be termed as venture capital activity. The difference in ANZ Grindlays Bank activity is one of nomenclature and not of the means of financing. Also, on the whole, venture capital is provided more in the nature of mezzanine loans than equity.

Private Agencies

One venture capital fund set up in the private sector in India is the Credit Capital Venture Fund (India) or CVF for short, the principal shareholders of which are Credit Capital Finance Corporation, Bank of India, Asian Development Bank, and Commonwealth Development Corporation. Another set up in the private sector jointly by the ICICI 20th Century Finance Corporation, Bank of Baroda, Asian Development Bank, and Asian Finance and Investment Corporation is the 20th Century Venture Capital Corporation Ltd. One reason why private capitalists are generally shy may be the high rate of capital gains tax applicable to profits of venture capital funds. Though the guidelines provide for a concessional rate of capital gains tax, the move can hardly be deemed as a 'concession' in view of the enormous risks involved in the activity.

Policy Initiatives

The idea of providing venture capital finance (VCF) to new entrepreneurs in India was mooted by the then finance minister in the long-term fiscal policy announced by him in 1985. A fresh reference to the "difficulties faced by new entrepreneurs in raising equity capital" was made by the finance minister in his 1988-89 budget speech and detailed guidelines for providing such finance or funds by registered companies were announced.

In India, the government has set up a Venture Capital Fund (VCF) with a contribution of ₹10 crore. The fund was brought into operation on 1st April, 1986, by the IDBI. For financing this fund, a levy was imposed on all payments made by Indian industries for acquisition of foreign technologies. This fund finances projects with minimum and maximum project costs of ₹5 lakh and ₹250 lakh respectively.

Grindlays Bank has set up the India Investment Fund to finance the start-up cost of entrepreneurs. This fund was subscribed mainly by non-resident Indians. The Government of India also announced in 1989 a National Equity Fund for financing small-scale entrepreneurs setting up units in rural areas and urban areas with a population of below ₹5 lakh. Institutions like ICICI, IFCI, SBI Capital Markets, Canbank Financial Services and others have also set up their own funds for providing venture capital finance.

However, in general, the experience is that the Indian financial institutions are yet to reorient their financing policies to meet the venture capital maxims. The traditional conservatism of these organisations makes their approach unacceptable. They fail to recognise that normal criteria of debt-equity ratio, existence of security etc., are not the criteria for evaluating venture capital projects. This movement failed to take off in a big way in India due to risk-shy investors and institutions and tax hurdles faced by venture capital capitalists.

Difficulties in India

Fundamentally, there are no private pools of capital to finance risk ventures in India. The public financial institutions perforce occupy a dominant position in the provision of long-term capital to Indian industry. They and the State development agencies do provide limited amounts of equity finance to assist in the development of new business but there are no private, professionally managed investment capital sources. There are no private sector insurance companies or pension funds gathering regular premium income and virtually no private banks willing to devote a small portion of their resources to the venture capital niche. It is unlikely that such enterprises will be created in the foreseeable future to mobilise private savings for investment. As answer to this situation, mutual funds and investment trusts are permitted to set up and to commit a part of their resources to the venture capital area. As part of a broader equity investment fund, given suitable standards of valuation for unquoted investments, it should be possible for fund managers to commit a portion of their portfolios to venture capital situations. The participation of the private sector in venture capital funding, as it has come to be defined in the narrow Indian context, is not possible in isolation from the opportunity to develop a broadly spread investment business. To encourage bank finance to flow into venture capital, the limit set for banks was withdrawn if the VCs are registered with the SEBI since 2000. Like Mutual Funds, the Venture Capital Funds have also to be registered with the SEBI and regulated by the SEBI.

Tax Treatment

The tax treatment of venture capital funds in India is ungenerous and falls well short of what is required. Whereas the mutual funds established by the government controlled financial institutions and nationalised commercial banks suffer no tax on either income or capital gains, a venture capital fund would suffer tax at 20 per cent on dividend income and a similar rate on long-term capital gains. Given an adequate investment spread and tax incentives, mutual funds step into the early stage financing arena, professionally assess and monitor investments and assist the launch of new medium-sized businesses. SBI Mutual Fund is already undertaking such investment work with its 'bought deals'. The creation of more funds to participate in this area of the market is now clearly seen. Early stage financings could then be syndicated between a number of professionally managed funds and a sound, competitive situation between them might also be created.

The govt. has since 1995-96, been treating the venture funds like mutual funds for tax benefits and brought them under Regulation of SEBI.

Need for Growth of Venture Capital

There is need for encouragement of risk capital in India, as this will widen the industrial base of high-tech industries and promote the growth of technology.

The initial step might be to permit the launch of mutual funds by all those banks authorised to conduct business in India, at the same time extending the investment range of such funds to embrace unquoted stocks.

Liberating the capital market would bring greater depth to the capital market as a whole, introducing more genuine investors of substance with long time horizons, provide avenues for the institutions to realise their equity portfolios more easily (freeing funds for more new investment), and generally improve market liquidity. This would improve equity cult.

So moves towards a freer and less regulated market are important in considering measures to stimulate the entry of the private sector into risk capital formation.

In December 1996, SEBI notified regulations relation to Venture Capital Funds. These regulations lay down, *inter alia,* the criteria for the establishment of VCFs, investment guidelines and restrictions, as in the case of Mutual Funds, general delegations and responsibilities of Venture Capital Funds and rights of SEBI to regulate, inspect and audit of VCFs.

In 1997-98 budget, Venture Capital Funds are allowed to invest 20% of their corpus in the equity of any single firm, as against the limit 5% earlier. These restrictions were relaxed to allow more discretion to VCFs and to permit foreign funds to flow into this business. Following the recommendations of Chandrasekhar Committee (1999) many measures were initiated to develop the Venture Capital Industry in India. These include: permitting banks to invest in VCFs and to treat this as priority sector lending, making SEBI the single point nodal agency for registration and regulation of both domestic and foreign VCFs and applying the principal of "Pass through" in tax treatment of VCFs. Both capital and technology can flow in through VCF routes more easily now as there is greater flexibility in their investment and exit. Venture Funds are now treated on similar lines as Mutual Funds for tax treatment, accounting and other practices and procedures.

The venture capital movement did not take deep roots in India so far, but the scope for further progress is enormous. During the nineties, about $ 338.5 billion is reported to have flowed into as many as 6,000 companies. Technical and technological boom facilitated this flow into India and this has broadened the contours of enterprise. This inflow continued in the early years of 21st century with an investment of $ 1.1 billion in 2004 as against $774 million in 2003. Many foreign VCFs have been permitted later on to invest in Indian markets.

Annexure at the end of this chapter sets out in some detail the guidelines, set out by the government for Venture Capital Funds to operate in India.

ANNEXURE

Venture Capital Guidelines

Venture Capital Companies/Funds which want to avail of concessional treatment of capital gains referred to in the Budget Speech of 1988-89, would be required to comply with the following guidelines:

1. Establishment

(*i*) Funds, Companies or Schemes wishing to undertake venture capital finance activities may be established using the term 'Venture Capital' if they come within, and agree to abide by, these guidelines.

(*ii*) Approvals would be given for the establishment of the Venture Capital Companies/Funds by the Department of Economic Affairs, Ministry of Finance, or such authority as may be nominated by the government, and applications for such approvals should be made with a suitable explanatory note and details of the proposal and addressed to Joint Secretary (Investments) in Department of Economic Affairs.

(*iii*) Applications for issue of capital by companies should be made as per SEBI guidelines. Composite applications for approval to establish the fund and for the issue of capital can also be made.

(*iv*) All-India public sector financial institutions, SBI and other scheduled banks, including foreign banks operating in India, and the subsidiaries of the above would be eligible to start Venture Capital Funds/Companies, subject to such approval as may be required from the Reserve Bank of India in respect of banking companies. Joint ventures as between them, or non-institutional promoters and them would be permitted, but the equity holding of such promoters shall not exceed a total of 20 per cent and must not be the largest single holding.

2. Management

(*i*) It is required that the Venture Capital Funds/Companies are managed by professional such as bankers, managers and administrators and persons with adequate experience of industry, finance, accounts, etc. If established by subsidiaries of banks/institutions, or in-house schemes, they should maintain their independence and an arm's length relationship. They would, however, be free to draw upon the professional expertise and infrastructure of the parent organisation in the interests of their shareholders and clients, and minimising costs.

(*ii*) No person would be permitted to be a full-time Chairman/President, Chief Executive, M.D. or Executive M.D. or Executive Director or a whole-time director of a VCC/VCF if he holds any of the above positions in any other company, except that he may hold such a position in an assisted company by virtue of his position in the VCC/VCF.

3. Venture Capital Assistance

(*i*) It is intended that Venture Capital assistance should go mainly to enterprises where the risk element is comparatively high due to the technology involved being relatively new, untried or very closely held, and/or the entrepreneurs being relatively new and not affluent though otherwise qualified; and the size being modest. For successful units, the possibility of high returns would exist, but the projects would initially find it difficult to raise equity from the market, especially when public issues are no longer readily available for small, greenfield companies. The assistance should mainly be for equity support, through loan support to supplement this may also be done. Venture Capital assistance, therefore, should cover those enterprises which fulfil the following parameters:

(*a*) *Size:* Total investment not to exceed ₹ 10 crore.

(*b*) *Technology:* New or relatively untried or very closely held or being taken from pilot to commercial stage, or which incorporates some significant improvement over the existing ones in India.

(*c*) *Promoters/Entrepreneurs:* Relatively new, professionally or technically qualified, with inadequate resources or backing to finance the project. Investment in enterprise engaged in trading, broking, investment or financial services, agency or liaison work, shall not be permitted. Further investment in assisted units for their expansion or strengthening, or investments for the revival of sick units, would be permitted as a part of venture capital activity, and the above parameters will not apply. The recipient venture should be established as limited company and must employ professionally qualified persons to maintain its accounts.

(*ii*) The VCP/VCC should invest at least 75 per cent of its funds into venture capital activity as explained in para 3(i).

(*iii*) During the first 12 months, any permissible investments may be made (including leasing up to 15 per cent of the funds), but a level of 30 per cent should be reached for venture capital activity by the end of the second year, and 60 per cent by the end of the third year, and 75 per cent by the end of the fifth year of operations.

The balance amounts may be invested in any new issue, by an existing or a new company, of equity, CCP, debentures, bonds or other securities approved for this purpose by CCI. A part of this may also be employed for leasing but this should not, at any stage, exceed 15 per cent of the total funds deployed, including in the first year. Activities such as money market operations, bill rediscounting, broking, portfolio, investments and fund management, financial services and consultancy, intercorporate lending would not be permitted to VCC/VCF.

4. Size

The minimum size of a VCC/VCF would be ₹ 10 crore. If it desires to raise funds from the public, the promoters' share shall not be less than 40 per cent.

5. Capital Issues

(*i*) Funds may be raised through public issues and/or private placements to finance VCC/VCFs.

(*ii*) Foreign equity up to 25 per cent by multilateral/international financial organisations, development finance institutes, reputed mutual funds, etc., would be permitted, provided these are management-neutral and are for medium to long-term investments.

(*iii*) NRI investment would be permitted up to 74 per cent on a non-repatriable basis and up to 25 per cent/40 per cent on a repatriable basis.

(*iv*) An application should be addressed to the Ministry of Finance, Investment Division, with a copy to Chairman, Securities, Exchange Board of India for foreign/NRI participation in capital issues.

6. Debt-Equity Ratio

Debt-equity ratio may be a maximum of 1:1.5.

7. Underwriting/Listing

(*i*) The VCC/VCF may be listed according to the prescribed norms. Its issue may be underwritten at the discretion of the promoters.

(*ii*) For assisted units also, listing guidelines would apply. Investments by a widely-held VCF would be treated as public participation for this purpose.

8. Exit

Pricing of shares at the time of disinvestment by a public issue of general offer of sale by the VCC/VCF, may be done by them, subject to this being calculated on objective criteria like book value, profit-earning capacity, etc., and the basis is adequately disclosed to the public.

9. Eligibility for Tax Concession

The preferential tax treatment would be available to the approved venture capital company/fund only in respect of financing of such assisted units as are eligible to be treated as venture capitalists as defined in paragraph 3. For this purpose, the unit seeking equity support from the VCC/VCF should obtain a letter of eligibility from IDBI, ICICI or any such agency that may be nominated by the government.

✠ ✠ ✠

PART IV

FINANCIAL SERVICES IN INDIA

LEASE, HIRE-PURCHASE AND HOUSING FINANCE

17

Lease, Hire-Purchase and Housing Finance come under the activities of NBFCs and are thus clubbed together. Analysis of sectoral deployment of bank credit shows that bank advances to NBFCs is only about 2.7% of total bank credit as of end 2009. Of these, Housing Finance is more important in terms of the magnitude of finance involved. Housing Finance can take any of the three forms, namely as Priority Sector Advances, regular housing and as Real Estate Loans. All these together constitutes about 24% of total non-food gross bank credit as end March 2007. This is the importance of this subject in a book on financial services in India.

What is Lease?

A lease transaction is a commercial arrangement, whereby an equipment owner or manufacturer conveys to the equipment user the right to use the equipment in return for a rental. The lease may be of different varieties and the concept has different aspects, namely, legal, accounting, fiscal, economic and marketing aspects. Of these, the legal and tax implications are the most important aspects. Broadly, there are two classes of lease, namely, long-term *finance* lease and short-term *operating* lease. These leases may pass the ownership or not, and may be an internal or international transaction. The terms of lease will also depend on the nature of the equipment, namely, consumer goods or capital goods, etc.

Finance Lease

In finance lease, lessor transfers the risk and rewards incident to the ownership of the equipment to the lessee, but the title may or may not be transferred to the lessee. Rentals are payable in instalments so as to cover the cost of the equipment plus a reasonable interest on funds invested in the purchase or manufacture of the equipment. Thus, finance lease involves financing the equipment purchase and lending it out to the lessee for use with or without the transfer of ownership immediately.

Operating Lease

In operating lease, all the risks and rewards incidental to ownership are not transferred to the lessee but involves only short-term hire of the equipment with the ownership resting with the lessor. Such short-term operating leases are prevalent in the use of motor cars, computers, aircraft, ships, etc.

The difference between the finance lease and operating lease may be set out here.

Finance Lease	*Operating Lease*
1. Ownership is transferred at the end of lease term.	No transfer of ownership.
2. Lease with purchase option.	No option of purchase.
3. Lease term is about or equal to the life of the equipment.	Lease term may be of a shorter period.
4. Lease payments cover almost all the costs of the equipment and interest on financing the purchase.	Not necessary to cover all costs of the equipment and interest on financing it.

In either case, leasing involves:

(*a*) Financing an investment in purchase of a capital asset, equipment, plant, machinery, etc.

(*b*) Taking risks of investment and lending it out for use by another party.

(*c*) Participating in the risks of enterprise indirectly through the lessee to whom the machinery/plant is lent.

Lease, Hire-purchase and Instalment Credit

Lease and hire-purchase are to be distinguished. In lease, the purchase is financed by lessor but maintenance and insurance as also risk of obsolescence are however the responsibility of the lessee. The contract may provide for the reversal of the rights back to the lessor or for the renewal of the contract. The option of purchasing the leased asset by the lessee is not incorporated in the lease contract, as it then becomes a hire-purchase agreement. In the latter case, the ownership passes to the lessee once he has paid fully capital and interest charges.

In the case of hire-purchase transaction, hire-purchaser takes the equipment on lease and lease rental is shown as a tax deductible expense but lessee cannot claim depreciation and may not show the leased asset in his balance sheet. On the other hand, the instalment credit sale is different. The asset is owned by the buyer from the beginning of the sale and payment of first instalment. The risk of ownership and use lies with the buyer and not the financier. The asset appears in the balance sheet of the buyer and the corresponding liability as the secured loan from the financier and interest paid on the loan as tax deductible item would appear in the income expenditure statement of the buyer.

Types of Finance Lease

The finance lease agreements can be further sub-divided into the following classes:

(*a*) *Leveraged Lease:* In this case, lessor which is the leasing company provides the equity capital, while the banks and financial institutions provide the loan funds in the form of term loans for the purchase of leased assets. The lessee is the beneficiary of the agreement;

(*b*) *Sale and Lease Back:* In this case, the company owning an asset sells it to a leasing company and gets it back on lease from the leasing company. In this process, the lease facilitates the freeing of funds for the company to use for other purposes;

(*c*) *Cross-border Leases:* These are international leases with the lessor supplying the equipment being placed in one country and the lessee hailing from another country. The lease agreement incorporates the terms of the use of the equipment supplied by the lessor to the lessee;

(*d*) *Foreign to Foreign Lease:* In this case, there are three parties, the manufacturer or supplier in one country, lessor in another country and the lessee who is the beneficial user in a third country.

The advantages or disadvantages of lease would depend mostly on the prevailing tax provisions and the tax status of the company.

Advantages of Leasing

1. *Financial Benefits:* The lessee does not have to pay the cost of the asset outright. If the cost of buying versus cost of lease is weighed, the company incurring losses, may prefer to have low cash outflow at present and may resort to lease finance.
2. *Flexibility of Lease:* Leasing is more convenient for assets to be used for short periods and for companies who find it difficult to get loans from banks and financial institutions. The leasing and payment of rentals can be synchronised with the cash inflows of the company.
3. *Risk of Obsolescence:* The lessee can pass on the risk of obsolescence to the lessor which is more suitable for such appliances as subject to high technological obsolescence like computers and electronic equipment.
4. *Need for Maintenance and Specialised Services:* If the lessee has to depend on the manufacturer or supplier for service and maintenance as in the case of aircraft, shipping, zerox machines, etc., it is more convenient to the lessee to lease and pass on these risks to the lessor which can provide these specialised services.

A lease will be effected if both the lessor and lessee will benefit. This can happen, if their financial position and tax paying status differ. This would depend on debt versus equity and relative costs of lease and outright purchase by debt or equity. For lease financing displaces debt and for companies with a high debt ratio, lease finance is preferred. Similarly, a sick company with a low cash accrual or a new company with a present low cash flow and a potential for larger cash inflows in future may prefer lease finance to debt or equity finance. Thus, it is the present value of all future payments on lease *vis-a-vis* the cost of outright acquisition of the asset which determines the advantages of lease finance for a company. The lessor company would also benefit by tax benefits of depreciation allowances, larger present cash flows. Such companies have low debt equity ratio and subject to high marginal tax rates. Cash rich and heavy tax paying companies would be the lessors.

Advantages to Lessor

1. Lease is an additional financial product involving ownership and risk taking for a reward in terms of rentals.
2. Lease improves profitability due to attached tax benefits to the lessor.
3. It is a marketing strategy for capital intensive goods like plant and machinery and provides a competitive edge for sale of the product by the manufacturer.
4. Lease arrangement is a simple document and less messy than the formalities to be observed for bank borrowing.
5. As a financing technique, it is more rewarding and attractive to lessor.
6. It is flexible and can be opened and closed quickly.

Advantages to Lessee

1. Leasing provides 100% finance for the cost of equipment while in the case of bank borrowing or instalment sale, it is subject to initial payment or margin requirement from the lessee.
2. Leasing preserves and improves the cash position and liquidity of the company.
3. It is flexible and can be adjusted to the cash flow forecast.
4. It neither changes the equity ownership nor dilutes the equity, nor adversely affects the debt equity ratio of the company.
5. It achieves gearing and provides a hedge against inflation and helps the tax planning.
6. It is off balance sheet method of financing, straightforward, simple and efficient.

Leasing in India

Leasing has grown by leaps and bounds in the eighties but it is estimated that hardly one per cent of the industrial investment in India is covered by the lease finance, as against 40% in USA, 30% in UK and 10% in Japan. The leasing in India covers a wide variety of industries. As per a recent report of Equipment Leasing Association of India, leasing covers both the public and private sector in respect of financing of plant, machinery, vehicles, earth moving equipment, office equipment and computers, etc.

The prospects of leasing in India are good due to growing investment needs and scarcity of funds with public financial institutions. This type of lease finance is particularly suitable in India where a large number of small companies have emerged more recently.

Sources of Funds

In the leasing field, there are both private and public sector institutions. While the public sector agencies get the support of banks and financial institutions, the private sector agencies suffer from resource crunch. The usual sources of funds for the leasing industry are equity share capital, term loans from banks and financial institutions, debentures, public deposits and inter-corporate deposits. The resources from equity and debentures is limited due to low confidence of investors in these companies and lack of free assets with these companies which can be used as security for debentures. The bank loans to this industry are also limited and are governed by the following guidelines from RBI:

(*a*) Only cash credit limits can be granted.

(*b*) Maximum bank finance will be limited to three times net owned funds and an overall ceiling of all kinds of borrowings to 10 times their net owned funds.

(*c*) For each bank finance transaction, the maximum permissible drawing is up to 75% of the asset cost at the time of acquisition. Bank finance for lease of equipment of over 5 years is not granted.

Public deposits are a major source of funds for lease finance companies. These are accepted by these companies for periods ranging from 6 months to 36 months and up to more than 5 times their net owned funds. Public deposits and inter-corporate deposits accounted for 74% of total funds mobilised in recent years.

Since April 1999, RBI restricted the leasing companies from accepting deposits of less than 24 months. The source of inter-corporate funds is not used by many companies as this is a short-term source and lease companies need mostly long-term funds. With the lack of investor confidence in these companies, and scarcity of funds with banks and financial institutions, the leasing companies in the private sector are thus faced with financial crunch. The RBI has brought them under its regulation from 1997.

Problems of Leasing Companies

The other problems of leasing companies are inadequate tax benefits and lack of concessional sales tax and absence of integrated and uniform accounting standards common to all leasing companies and lack of a common piece of legislation. The imposition of sales tax at the higher rates of multipoints led to a rise on the cost of asset acquisition under the leasing agreement. The import leasing is subject to vigorous conditions such as a minimum paid-up capital of ₹ 1 crore and the company to be listed on a recognised stock exchange. There are also problems of accounting such as treatment of these as off balance sheet items and lease rentals of accrual basis, etc. Some norms were evolved in 1989 by the Institute of Chartered Accountants of India for guidance to all dealing with leasing companies. There is another difficulty in that there is no single piece of legislation to govern leasing in India. At present, leasing is governed by Transfer of Property Act and Indian Contracts Act. There is, therefore, need for something like an Indian Leasing Act and accounting practices are to be uniform and should be incorporated in that Act.

Legal Aspects

The recent amendment to Companies Act prescribe that the companies should follow the accrual system of accounting but this causes hardship and risk of treating unrealised rentals as income for tax purposes. Besides this will not show true actual profits of the company. The treatment of rentals on accrued basis over the life term of lease would be unrealistic for the leasing company. So companies have been window dressing and different companies are following different practices. Based on legal compulsions, the companies are following different accounting practices. Besides the treatment of depreciation, allowances, etc., under the Income Tax Act and Companies Act is different which led again to varying accounting practices of companies depending on their own convenience and advantage.

Legislation of Leases

The above legal weaknesses point to the need for an integrated and co-ordinated law to govern lease. The Hire-Purchase Act, 1972 governed the lease deals but it was withdrawn in 1973. Lease is now governed under the Sections 105 to 117 Transfer of Property Act, which deals with only immovable properties and Sections 126 to 180 of the Indian Contract Act of 1872. But these are not specific to lease contracts which have their own characteristics. Hence, there is need for an Indian Leasing Act providing the legal basis for all types of lease contracts.

Finance Management

In the leasing field, there are both private and public sector institutions. While the public sector agencies get the support of banks and financial institutions, the private sector agencies suffer from resource crunch. The usual sources of funds for the leasing industry are equity share capital, term loans from banks and financial institutions, debentures, public deposits and inter-corporate deposits. The resources from equity and debentures are limited due to low confidence of investors in these companies and lack of free assets with these companies which can be used as security for debentures.

The bank loans to this industry are also limited and are governed by the following guidelines from RBI:

(*a*) Only cash credit limits can be granted.

(*b*) Maximum bank finance will be limited to three times net owned funds and an overall ceiling of all kinds of borrowings to 10 times their net owned funds.

(*c*) For each bank finance transaction, the maximum permissible drawing is up to 75% of the asset cost at the time of acquisition. Bank finance for lease of equipment of over 5 years is not granted.

Public deposits are a major source of funds for lease finance companies. These are accepted by these companies for periods ranging from 6 months to 36 months and up to more than 5 times their net owned funds. Public deposits and inter-corporate deposits accounted for 74% of total funds mobilised by them.

Since April 1989, RBI restricted the leasing companies from accepting deposits of less than 24 months. The source of inter-corporate funds is not used by many companies as this is a short-term source and lease companies need mostly long-term funds. There are thus problems of finance which management should plan properly to deal with. The public deposits are not forthcoming in large order due to failure of some NBFCs like Lloyds Finance and the non-repayment of public deposits leading to disillusionment among the public of keeping such deposits.

Tax Management

Multipoint sales tax on leasing, differential rates of tax among states, lack of concessional sales tax and absence of integrated and uniform accounting standards common to all leasing companies and lack of a common piece of legislation are some of their problems. The imposition of sales tax at the higher rates of multipoints led to a rise on the cost of asset acquisition under the leasing agreement.[@] The import leasing is subject to vigorous conditions such as a minimum paid-up capital of ₹ 1 crore and the company to be listed on a recognised stock exchange. There are also problems of accounting such as treatment of these as off balance sheet items and lease rentals on accrual basis, etc. Some norms were evolved in 1989 by the Institute of Chartered Accountants of India for guidance to all dealing with leasing companies.

The tax benefits available to leasing industry are not adequate although lease business exists to take advantage of tax provisions. The depreciation rates provided under the Income Tax Act differ from those provided in the Companies Act. The depreciation rates under the former Act are higher than the normal depreciation provided in the primary lease period. The problem arises because of the mismatch between the two legal provisions regarding the legal depreciable life of the asset. Many companies providing depreciation as per the Companies Act lose in the process and this leads to many malpractices in accounting to circumvent the law.

Tax provisions at present do not promote the growth of lease industry as tax incentives are the basis of existence of the lease facility and companies doing tax planning resort to this facility. But there are a number of ways that the government can promote this industry through changes in tax provisions, such as extension of MODVAT on capital goods to lease and hire-purchase. The introduction of VAT on a uniform basis in all states, from April 2005 might be one of such measures.

Accounting Problems

As there is no uniform law and there are discrepancies in the existing laws in relation to lease, practices also differ and no uniformity exists. For lessees, this lease is off balance sheet item. For lessors, this item appears in the balance sheet and profit and loss account but there is no apportionment of rental between principal repayment and interest payment and no separation of assets owned and leased in the balance sheet. The companies do not amortise the value of the asset during the primary lease period in which leasing companies recover 90% of the value of the asset. Most companies amortise the assets as recovered within 3 to 5 years but provide depreciation for over a 8-year period. The methods of depreciation by different companies are different and for the same company, the practice differs from asset to asset.

The Institute of Chartered Accountants of India have come out with guidelines for accounting practices and a method was suggested for accounting principles to be uniform and for equalisation of accounting method with the actual economic life of the asset.

Leasing vs. Buy Decision

For a company to decide whether to buy any equipment or take on lease two alternative computations are needed:

1. Net cost of buying, which is equal to the cost of asset less the present value of tax saving on depreciation, etc., associated with the purchase of the asset. Tax deduction under each head of lease and buy decision have to be compared. The net cost of buying is compared with the post-tax present value of the lease rental outflow.

2. Post-tax present value of the cash outflow under the buy option. All the after-tax cash flows are discounted to the present value, over the life of the asset, say 5 years.

If NPV of buying = X and

NPV of leasing = Y

and if Y is lower, leasing is the option to be chosen and if X is lower, buying is the option to be chosen.

@ Stamp duty on lease agreements in Maharashtra was brought down and made uniform irrespective of the lease period, with effect from April 1, 1994.

Leasing was offered by all-India financial institutions starting with ICICI, State level financial institutions, public sector banks and foreign banks. The banks' entry into leasing was facilitated by the passage of the Amendment to the Banking Regulation Act, 1983. Section 19 (1) of this Amended Act provided for banks to enter leasing and other non-bank financial services through subsidiaries set up by them. Even the UTI Act was amended to permit it to undertake leasing.

Banks and Leasing

Many banks and finance companies have set up their own leasing and hire-purchase subsidiaries. Leasing has grown specially in the first half of eighties both in number and in their financing of assets. Banks have adopted the method of indirect financing of fixed assets through leasing subsidiaries. This led to public sector leasing companies and private sector leasing companies and competition between them has increased although it is uneven and against the private sector. In March 1994, RBI has permitted banks to enter into leasing hire-purchase, forfeiting directly, but a limit of 10% of their advances has been kept for such business.

Marketing Management

Most of the leasing companies are doing only lease finance although a few are also doing the leveraged lease, and operating lease. Their marketing is through personal contact via the parent companies, manufacturers, lease brokers and direct letters to lessees. Sector-wise, marketing concentrated on industrial equipment up to 80-90%, while vehicles and household durables, etc., accounted for the rest. Leasing is generally clubbed with hire-purchase, finance, bill discounting and inter-corporate investments, etc. Leasing finance is concentrated in a group of companies related as associate companies and leasing is used as an instrument to rechannel funds in such cases. They have thus a captive market, in many cases, as in the case Nagarjuna Finance.

HIRE-PURCHASE

Definition

The Hire-Purchase Act 1972 defines the hire-purchase agreement as an agreement under which goods are let out on hire and under which the hirer has the option to purchase them in accordance with the terms of the agreement.

Main Contents of the Agreement

(*a*) Possession of goods delivered to hirer by the owner for use by the former.

(*b*) Ownership lies with the person lending.

(*c*) Involves a credit to the hirer by the owner on the condition that a rent is paid by the former to the latter. The rental includes both principal and interest on money invested in the goods hired.

(*d*) The ownership in property goes to the hirer on the payment of last instalment as agreed upon.

Types of Hire-purchases

(*a*) Consumer instalment credit for hire and sale of consumer durables.

(*b*) Industrial and commercial credit for hire and sale of industrial goods, plant, machinery, equipment etc.

(*c*) Hire-purchase by the dealer or producer to consumer.

(*d*) Hire-purchase by the financier or finance company, as in the case of Auto Finance.

Instalment Payments

The terms of agreement lay down the method of payment of principal and interest. Normally ownership is with the creditor and not hirer. If the ownership goes to hirer, it is lending finance for purchase of goods, and the hirer pays only interest and principal in instalments. It is an example of instalment credit.

The hire-purchase contract quotes a flat rate of interest, say 14% or 15% and for a period fixed in the beginning itself, say 3 to 5 years.

For the duration of say 3 years if the principal invested is say ₹10 lakh, at a rate of 14%, it leads to ₹1.4 lakh interest per annum and for three years, it is ₹4.2 lakh of interest which together with principal adds up to ₹14.2 lakh. This is divided say by 36 (months) to get the monthly instalment payment — roughly ₹40 thousand per month.

Advantages to Hirer

The ownership does not belong to hirer. The interest is an expense item and off balance sheet item for accounting purposes. The tax liability will be lower. No initial investment is necessary, but its use is available. No depreciation provision may be made but maintenance items may appear in his accounts. The owner's responsibility is not to maintain the goods intact for hirer to use during the hire period. It is hirer's duty to maintain it. The hirer gains in interest cost also for claiming exemption from tax liability. But unlike in the case of lease, the hirer has to deposit 25 to 30% of the asset cost as margin money. Hirer also saves on capital investment. Hire-purchase instalments are shown as term liability and depreciation will be claimed by the user of the article.

Activity Sequence

The actual sequence of events depends upon the terms of hire-purchase. There are a number of methods of doing this business. The shopowner or producer can give credit. A financier, namely, a third party can provide this hire service. Hire may be only for service and the ownership continues to be with the financier in all cases. The hirer gets the ownership at the end of stipulated period of payments of instalments. The financier may be a company, firm, shop, etc.

The customer/hirer selects the goods, machinery, equipment from the producer or shop. Then he approaches the financier or the producer to provide hire-purchase. The financier who will do the financing will do the bargaining.

Then finance company does credit appraisal of the customer and an agreement is entered into with the hirer on the terms for interest rate, instalment amount per month, terms of maintenance or repair, terms of ownership by the hirer, etc. The agreement lays down all the details regarding the legal aspects of ownership and hire, etc., and remedy in case of any lapse or failure to comply with any of the obligations by the hirer or owner as the case may be.

Instalment Payments and Ownership

After the legal agreement is entered into between the finance company and customer or client, the former pays the producer/dealer and the ownership passes to the financier. In the case of Auto Finance by banks or finance company, it is not hire-purchase but instalment. Credit and membership passes to the buyer and the financier has a lien on it.

During the period of hire, customer pays the instalments (including interest plus principal, as agreed upon) on a monthly/quarterly/half-yearly basis. These instalments are based on the amount of principal invested by the company and the rate of interest agreed upon between the financier and hirer.

On the completion of the period and after full payment of all instalments, the goods become the property of the hirer, unless the life of the goods expires along with the period of hire.

HOUSING FINANCE

Why Invest in Real Estate?

Firstly, it is a matter of policy for the government to provide shelter on the heads of all poor, disabled and backward classes.

Investment in housing is a necessity for one's own shelter and for his family. Besides in families which are breaking up from joint family system into individual unit families, a larger number of housing units is necessary. This is particularly more true in urban areas and HUDCO is trying to fill up this gap.

Investment in land is also good for a future hedge. It is not necessarily for consumption. Besides, houses leased out would give rentals, but more importantly there is some capital appreciation. Thus, investment in land in related areas and in selected residential and commercial houses would be a hedge against inflation. The rise in rentals and in land values is more than the rise in inflation rate or prices as reflected in WPI or in prices of goods and services. Thus, land values sometimes zoom up ten to twenty times, while inflation may go up by 10% only. Thus, a genuine investor keeps all these alternative uses of houses as an item of investment. Thus, investment in land and real estate would have added attraction for self-use, rentals and capital appreciation.

HOUSING INDUSTRY

Housing construction is a special category of industry, which does not come under either manufacturing or services sectors. Being a necessity, housing industry has been put under priority sector industries. Respective five year plans have been emphasising on the need for promoting Housing Finance schemes particularly for the poorer and weaker sections of the society.

National Housing Bank was set up in July 1988 with the equity support from the RBI and is intended to act as the APEX institution for co-ordinating and developing the housing finance schemes. Later, the UTI has set up in 1989, a Housing and Construction Investment Fund for direct investment in construction projects and real estate development. The entry of LIC and GIC and many banks like SBI and Canara Bank through their subsidiaries has been stated to be another landmark in the promotion of housing industry.

Banks have been directed by the R.B.I. to treat the housing financing as a priority sector activity and are permitted to allocate 1.5% of the incremental deposits for housing finance purposes. About 30% of this allocation will go by way of direct lending of which half of the amount will be earmarked for rural and semi-urban areas. About 40% of the banks' allocation will go as term loans to HFCs Housing Boards and Public Housing Agencies. The rest of the 30% will be provided in the form of subscription to guaranteed bonds and debentures of NHB, HDC, HUDCs, etc. Some banks have started housing finance directly like the Corporation Bank, while the others have done this through their subsidiaries, like SBH and ICICI.

Housing Finance Policy Aspects

Reserve Bank Controls the Commercial and Co-operative banks in respect of their Housing Finance Schemes. The existing ceiling of any bank's advances for housing purposes continues to be 1.5% of incremental deposits. In order to provide flexibility to banks in the development of their allocated funds, sub-allocations into those for direct finance, or investment in bonds of NHB/HUDCO were completely removed. Besides any investment by banks in Special bonds issued by NHB or HUDCO were to be reckoned as part of priority sector advances of banks.

NHB continued to develop the Housing Finance Sector through its regulatory and developmental role. During 1996-97, NHB has deregulated the interest rates paid on deposits accepted by HFCs, with Net worth of ₹50 lakh and above. Similarly, their lending rates for all loans above ₹50,000 are freed even for the purpose of recognition by NHB for its refinance schemes. It has also introduced a refinance scheme for the Regional Rural Banks; for their housing finance advances.

HUDCO was incorporated as a fully owned government company with the sole objective of facilitating and promoting the financing of the housing and urban development projects in the country. HUDCO's resources are raised from term loans from GIC and its subsidiaries, NHB, government loans, under various schemes linked to external agencies like OECD, government guaranteed bonds, borrowing from banks, HUDCO Bonds, interest bearing cash securities from borrowing agencies and Public Deposit Schemes, etc.

Industry Background

In India, there is a ever widening gap between the supply and demand for housing. The shortage of housing is estimated at 7.57 million in urban areas and 13.66 million in rural areas. The funds requirement of this order of housing construction is estimated at ₹1,50,000 crore. With a population growth at 2.0% per annum and increasing trend to breakdown of joint family system, the individual family units will grow and the requirements for housing will grow further.

A distinguishing feature of this industry is that here is a large component of demand for housing finance from real estate developers and speculators. Most HFCs concentrate on financing of High Income and Middle Income group housing requirements and not rural and low income group segments. The failure rate of repayments of housing finance instalments is more in the latter category. Another feature of this industry is that there are phases of boom and recession depending upon the flow of black money into this industry. NRIs are allowed to invest in housing construction, ownership and real estate development. But the flow of funds from this sector is insignificant. This industry suffers from high volumes and low margins.

Sources of Funds

In the Ninth Five Year Plan, an amount of ₹1,50,000 crore has been earmarked of which ₹52,000 crore are expected to come from the formal sector. There is a vast gap in the available resources from the formal sector.

The normal sources of supply are the following:

(1) Deposits from the Public: This is at rates ranging from 11 to 13% while their lending rate at the PLR is around 14 to 15.5%, leaving very meagre margin of profit. As these deposits are for periods up to 3-5 years and housing loans for longer periods, there is an asset-liability mismatch. The PLR and other rates have come down during 2001 to 2007 to 10-11.5%.

(2) Borrowing from Commercial and Cooperative Banks: These borrowings are very meagre for two reasons. Firstly, banks are themselves lending for housing finance either directly or through subsidiaries and as such their contribution will be in the form of their subscription to bonds floated by HFCs. Banks consider HFCs as their competitors in the field. Secondly, the lending rate of banks in the PLR which leaves very little margin for HFCD to make any worthwhile advances through bank borrowings. Banks PLR was in the range of 10.5% to 14.5% for private sector banks in 2004-05 and 11 to 12.5% in 2009-10.

(3) Refinance from NHB: The amount of funds flowing from NHB is too meagre, constituting as it is only 7% of the HFCs' advances for housing purposes.

Market for Housing Finance

The refinance from NHB is available to a selected few HFCs, who are registered with NHB and observed the rules of Income Recognition and provisioning of non-performance assets as also the capital adequacy norms. Of the HFCs numbering about 26 who are eligible to secure from NHB refinance, HDFC is a market leader with a share of 45% of the total funds disbursed in the country. The interest rates at which refinance is made available varies with the quantum of loan and the purpose for which loan is given. The maximum rate of refinance is charged to the top slab of ₹5 to 10 lakh. The individual loan limit is now ₹10 lakh and the maximum rate charged by NHB for its refinance is 15%.

The purposes for which loans are granted are for individual house construction and for co-opratives and Real Estate Developers for the construction of Housing Complexes, both for residential and commercial purposes and for repairs, expansion and modernisation. The employers and corporates are granted loans for construction of housing complexes for their staff and employees.

As between banks and HFCs, which provide Housing Finance, there is not much scope for competition. Banks have cheaper sources of funds, but HFCs have the advantage of quicker disposal of application forms and disbursement of loan instalments. Besides, as the supply shortages are enormous, both banks, FIs like LIC, UTI, GDC, etc., and HFCs have a role to supplement each other's effort in the provision of housing finance.

NHB

NHB was set up in July 1988 as a wholly-owned subsidiary of the RBI. It is expected to be an Apex body for control and regulation on the one hand and provision of refinance to banks and HFCs for the housing loans that they provided. It has started operations with a paid-up equity of ₹100 crore. The share capital was raised in stages and stood at ₹450 crore at end March 2014 and reserves of ₹3,404 crore..

It can borrow from the RBI out of its Fund, namely, National Housing Credit (Long-term operations) fund. It can borrow from the govt. from banks and from the foreign capital market. The NHB has thus augmented its resources from all these sources. The major sources of its funds are bonds/debentures and borrowings.

The institutions eligible for refinance from NHB are the following:

1. Scheduled Commercial and co-operative banks.
2. Non-banking Finance Companies, namely, HFCs, Apex Co-operative Housing Societies and State Land Development Banks.

NHB has initiated a number of new schemes for promoting housing loans.

To be eligible for refinance from NHB, the HFCs have to observe, the NHB guidelines on having a credit rating of 'A', for acceptance of deposits, maintenance of liquid assets of 12.5% of deposits, etc.

The government has started in 1992 National Housing Bank Voluntary Deposits Scheme under Voluntary Deposits Immunities and Exemption Act, 1991. Under this scheme, which was in operation for about 4 months up to end Jan. 1992 deposits made were unquestioned and could be black money, which could be used for socio-economic objectives such as slum clearance and for housing construction for the poor.

Securitisation

One of the latest methods of raising funds by HFCs is securitisation of its book debts. The major assets of HFCs are the mortgage loans with maturity up to 10-15 years. These can be converted into debt based securities which can be sold and converted into cash for the HFC. This would tantamount to recycling of funds, which were tied down in housing mortgage loans. The mechanism is expected to work as follows:

A pool of assets in the form of mortgages would be sold by HFCs to NHB, which would act as a special purpose vehicle (SPV) and would sell these pass through certificates to investors. The possible investor clients are Pension Funds, Mutual Funds, Banks, FIs, and Trusts. They are made attractive by a listing and a quotation on a Stock Exchange; in addition to a monthly fixed income and a credit rating attached to them. NHB would assist in the fixing of monthly income and extending transparency to these securities and the backing for them.

The process of securitisation would be converting the existing mortgage book debts into pass through certificates — a form of Debt Securities, for institutional investors to buy and sell, thereby developing a secondary market in them. Four major companies which are identified for this purpose are HDFC, CanFina Homes, LIC Housing Finance and Devan Housing Finance. Their total offer can be of the order of ₹100 to 120 crore, of which HDFC accounts for a share of ₹40-50 crore. The market for such securities is definitely bound to exist at least at the primary stage but the secondary market in them is yet to be developed and that may take a long time.

Policy of Housing Finance: NHB

The National Housing Bank was set up by the RBI as a fully-owned subsidiary. National Housing Credit (LTO) Fund was started to make funds available to NHB for refinance facilities that it makes available to banks, housing finance companies, co-operative housing finance societies, etc.

The government and planning commission have given a vital role to the provision of housing finance in India. The RBI has permitted banks to allot 1½% of their incremental deposits for housing finance purposes.

The institutions engaged in housing finance, require long-term funds. That is why LIC and GIC have entered this field as they have the long-term insurance funds with them. Some public sector banks have set up subsidiaries for housing finance. Thus SBI House Finance, set up in April 1988 has started lending in Eastern and North-eastern States in India. Canara Bank has set up Canfina Homes Limited and Ind Bank Housing Financial Services by Indian Bank and Andhra Bank Homes Finance Ltd., by Andhra Bank.

In May 1988, the National Housing Policy was announced for promoting expansion of housing facilities in a planned way for all classes of population, particularly the weaker and backward classes. The NHB has promoted a separate entity to guarantee the payment of principal and interest of these classes of people, namely, India Mortgage Credit Guarantee Corporation (IMCGC).

The National Housing Bank has formulated some schemes linking saving with housing loans like Home Loan Account Scheme. The amount of loan, that a saver can get is linked to the amount that he has saved in his account. This scheme is operated by banks, commercial and co-operative.

Housing Development and Finance Corporation

The Housing Development and Finance Corporation was set up in the private sector by institutions like ICICI. This organisation accepts long-term deposits and raises funds through bonds, for housing finance. The HDFC has operated two schemes:

(*a*) Home Savings Plan (H.S.P.).

(*b*) Home Loans (Individuals) Scheme.

Besides HDFC lends to companies, employers and institutions to finance their house construction for employees, staff quarters, etc.

These loans granted by LIC, GIC and housing subsidiaries of banks are for small amounts of a few thousand to few lakh. The interest rates vary from 11½ to 18% depending upon the period of maturity and amount of loan.

HDFC has pioneered a variety of housing loans, like group loans, housing complexes, societies, etc. Its sources of funds are public deposits, term loans from banks, bonds and refinance from NHB.

The HDFC provides loans for both individuals, societies and groups. It has different varieties of schemes such as step-up repayment facility, telescopic loan plan and short-term bridging loan facility.

Housing and Urban Development Corporation (HUDCO)

This corporation is financing the urban infrastructure development projects, approved by the government. It is the model agency for implementing government programmes, for eliminating the manual scavenging, for providing shelter to the poor and for low income groups. It has been giving loans through urban local boards, housing boards, slum boards, etc. HUDCO and NHB are working together in the field of housing.

HDFC supports the efforts of other agencies in this field. HDFC gets its resources from deposits of public, refinance from NHB, term loans, bonds, etc. It provides finance through loans to co-operatives, companies, institutions, for building houses. It also provides individual loans for helping low cost housing projects for the poor SC/ST/BC, etc., which has been given due attention by the HUDCO.

These agencies are co-ordinated by NHB and the government. The RBI has also a responsibility for bank finance through their directives to banks for housing purposes, particularly in areas which are underdeveloped.

BANKS AND HOUSING FINANCE

Many public sector banks have set up subsidiaries for providing services of a financial nature, such as lease finance, hire-purchase lease, consumer instalment credit, housing purchase lease, housing finance, etc., public sector banks as for example, SBI, Canfina, Ind Bank, etc., have been providing housing finance facility. Even Private sector banks like ICICI Bank provide housing finance.

For long, banks were unwilling to lend for housing, as it is of a long-term nature while bank funds are of short-term nature. But in the light of change in government policy with a view to encouraging house building, the RBI has set up the National Housing Bank in 1988 and National Housing Credit (long-term operations) Fund for providing refinance for agencies giving housing finance, namely, banks, co-operatives and Housing Finance Companies (HFCs). Besides, banks have been directed by the RBI to allocate up to 1.5% of incremental deposits for housing finance purposes, which was raised to 3% recently. The banks' direct lending for housing purchase was ₹19,71,10 crore in 2008-09, and stood at ` 3,034,20 in 2013-14.

Role of NHB

As per the RBI's data, only a few selected HFCs who are eligible for this are being provided refinance by the NHB and their deposit mobilisation business is being regulated by NHB.

Nearly all the banks are eligible to get refinance from NHB, but their efforts at housing finance are not significant. They channel their housing loans through State Housing Boards and HUDCO, and lend to their own employees and co-operative housing societies. Co-operative banks are more active in this business than commercial banks.

The long-term financial corporations like LIC, GIC, and HDFC provide the bulk of housing finance, as their funds are of long-term nature and are ideally suited for this purpose. Although their terms are most reasonable, they vary with the amount of the loan and the type of borrower. As with banks, the FIs also charge concessional rates to STs and SCs. Their normal rates ranged from 10% to 16.5% for sometime, subject to the condition that the refinance from NHB is available at 8% to 14.5% for this purpose. These rates were revised downward in the early years in the 21st century due to lowering of all rates by RBI and banks. Now the Housing Finance rates of banks are generally lower than the general advance rate.

Bank Lending Norms

Banks are permitted to lend a proportion of 3% of their deposits for housing purposes. To ensure that bank finance for housing flows to all the needy segments of the society, it has been stipulated that 30% of the total allocation for housing would be by way of direct lending to the actual parties of which at least half was to be extended as direct housing loans in rural and semi-urban areas. Another 30% of the allocation for housing is to be used for giving term loans to housing finance companies, housing boards and other housing agencies. The balance of 40% of the allocation for housing is to be utilised for subscription to guaranteed bonds and debentures of NHB and HUDCO. Banks have been permitted to exceed marginally the targets for individual housing schemes. Interest rates for housing purposes are subject to the overall guidelines on minimum rates, except in the case of finance to intermediary lending agencies which are provided at 3 percentage points below the minimum rate applicable for credit limits in the category of over ₹2 lakh. In the Monetary Policy Statement for 1999-2000, the banks have not been allowed free discretion in the grant of housing loans with respect to quantum and rates of interest. As in March 2011, banks have advanced for housing ₹3.46 crore and interest rate concessions were also given for small loans.

For loans up to ₹2 lakh, the rates may vary from 11.5% to 16.5% to the ultimate beneficiaries. For loans up to ₹5,000 to SC/ST beneficiaries, the rate applicable is 4% as is the case of loans under DRI scheme of banks.

HFC Borrowings

The financial assistance granted by NHB is growing mainly to HFCs which account for about 80-85% of the total finance provided by NHB. The HFCs are now eligible to basic refinance limit from NHB up to 5 times their Net Owned Funds (NOF is paid-up capital plus reserves). Additionally a separate refinance limit is given to HFCs depending on their effort at deposit mobilisation. Thus, for HFCs up to ₹10 crore of NOF, additional refinance up to 3 times the amount of their deposits is allowed. For HFCs above ₹10 crore of NOF, additional refinance up to 2 times the amount of deposits is allowed. Special consideration is given by NHB for finance provided to rural areas by the concerned HFCs. Taking all these factors into account, an overall ceiling is kept at 15 times the NOF for all types of refinance by NHB to HFCs.

Regulation of HFCs

Only those HFCs which are being provided with refinance (18 of them at present) are being regulated by NHB, and that too only in respect of their deposit mobilisation efforts. There are many such companies, which have cropped up over the last few years and there is no information about their credibility and financial soundness. That is one of the reasons why the Shah Committee on non-bank finance companies (1992) has suggested compulsory registration of all such companies which are accepting deposits from public and with net owned funds of ₹50 lakh, and above. They are recommended to be brought under the supervision of the High Powered Supervisory Board for the financial system, set up by the RBI and the government. All HFCs should be credit rated if they are raising deposits and public should know these ratings so that they take their own precautions before keeping their funds as deposits with such companies. These recommendations of Shah Committee were implemented during 1994 and 1999.

Some Recent Developments

1. The LIC entry into direct household mortgage loan field through LIC Housing Finance Limited in 1991.
2. The entry of GIC into home loan extension process, through a subsidiary, namely, GIC Griha Vitta Ltd., in 1990.
3. The floatation of housing and construction Investment Fund by UTI in 1989.
4. The banks have set up their own housing finance subsidiaries like SBI Home Finance Ltd., PNB Housing Finance Ltd., Canfina Homes Ltd., Ind Bank Housing Finance Ltd., etc., which accelerated the mortgage housing movement in India recently. Many private sector banks like ICICI Bank and HDFC Bank have entered the fray in a big way since 2000.
5. Permission for NRIs to enter into real estate investment in India.

Housing Schemes

The housing schemes offered by these companies, some of them in collaboration with the builders have many attractive features. The terms and conditions under which they offer loans may vary in detail but in substance they are the same. There is also keen competition among HFCs to attract the investors.

1. They sanction loans against first mortgage of the house/flat bought with the loan proceeds.
2. The minimum rate of interest on the highest slab of lending is 16.5%, and the loan amount is a maximum of ₹10 lakh and repayment period ranges from 15 to 20 years.
3. Repayment schedule is adjusted to suit the requirements of the borrower.
4. Preferential treatment is given to the individuals who save with them in the form of deposits with them.

In the private sector, HDFC, sponsored by ICICI, has done commendable work in the area of housing finance. It has schemes for societies, individuals and land development agencies.

The housing schemes offered by the HFCs fall under the following categories:

1. Straight loans against mortgage of the house either for purchase of a new house or for undertaking extensions/repairs.
2. Loans linked to savings made by the customer over a period of time.[1]
3. Preferential sanction of loans to those who have placed deposits with the company (such as at concessional rate of interest).

All the HFCs charge interest on the total principal, compounded annually for the duration of the repayment period. Only adjustments in instalment amount are allowed to suit the capacity of the borrower. In addition to interest cost, the borrowers have to bear the processing fee for applications at a rate ranging from 0.5 to 1% and an administrative fee of another 1%. Thus although the customer has a wider choice and a range of facilities for housing finance, the burden of servicing is higher and it increases particularly in the higher slabs of loan amounts.

Management Role

The management of HFC becomes a critical variable for the credibility and credit rating of HFC. Credit rating will become compulsory for their deposit mobilisation and efficiency and integrity of management will improve the credit rating and their eligibility for getting refinance from NHB.

Public members who keep deposits with HFCs have to take care to see that the management is honest and genuine. In particular, they have to think twice before putting their funds with HFCs which are not refinanced and regulated by the NHB. Besides, when any of such companies are also in real estate business or have links with builders and dealers in real estate, the public will have to be extremely careful to see that they are not fly-by-night operators. In all these aspects, management's role become critical for public image and the growth of their operations.

RBI ON LEASING AND FINANCE COMPANIES

In March 1994, RBI has announced that banks are permitted to enter directly into leasing, hire-purchase and factoring. Earlier it was only through their subsidiaries that they could do so. As per the latest guidelines, leasing can be carried out in only specified branches of bank, where the necessary infrastructure is available for evaluation but all branches can market leases.

1. Home loan accounts and savings schemes are operated by HDFC, LIC, GIC, etc. Some Cooperative credit societies also operate such housing savings schemes to give loans to the savers up to a limit linked to the amount of savings.

RBI Guidelines

The limits to such business are set out by the RBI:

1. Banks cannot exceed 10% of their total advances to leasing business.
2. Limit on exposure to any individual borrower is 25% of the bank capital and 50% to a group of borrowers.
3. Assets in leasing are subject to 100% risk weight for capital adequacy purposes.
4. Banks can credit to income account only the finance/interest charge but not both interest and capital repayment.
5. They are free to charge higher interest rates than for other advances.

Advantages to Banks

Banks have appraising skills, infrastructural advantages and larger resource base and thus post a threat of unfair competition with finance companies. On the other hand, banks have some disadvantages too. They have burnt their fingers by poor recovery when they entered into hire-purchase business.

Their overheads are high; they lack flexibility and their productivity and efficiency are poor. The finance companies stand at an advantage due to their higher technical skills, promptness and efficiency, flexibility in operations, better management skills, better recovery record etc.

Banks vs. Finance Companies

Leasing business is still in infancy in India and is bound to grow from an estimated leased assets of ₹3,000 crore at an incremental growth of ₹1,200 crore per annum. The potential growth of this business is vast and banks' entry into this business may not pose any block to the growth of private finance companies. But the management efficiency is crucial to the success in leasing business. But the margins are squeezed to smaller finance companies due to competition with bigger giants and that will be more so if banks post a strong competition. Many finance companies have already shifted to hire-purchase business due to better margins there.

Foreign banks have also gone in a big way into leases as it is a long-term exposure which is profitable. But if banks have already subsidiaries for this business, there is no point in their direct entry. Those which do not have subsidiaries may however enter into leasing through a cut in their term loans to the clients, for the reason that they can earn higher interest on leasing than on term loans. Loss-making banks may not be able to compete effectively with terms offered by finance companies.

Future of Leasing

It is possible to visualise alternative scenarios in the future of leasing business.

1. Syndication of leasing by banks with finance companies to avoid competition.
2. Bank can acquire selected portfolios of leasing companies.
3. Banks may entrust to finance companies the professional management of their portfolio of leasing for a commission.
4. As many loss-making banks cannot utilise the benefit of writing off depreciation on leased assets from taxable profits, and some are inefficient, inflexible riddled with labour problems, they may prefer to opt out of the race for leasing or set up subsidiaries for this business as well as for hire-purchase and factoring.

Thus the recent change in the guidelines for banks' direct entry into leasing will only end up as a whimper and no large-scale changes are anticipated in this business, despite the banks' low cost funds at their disposal.

The change in RBI policy in this regard is necessitated by continuing losses of many public sector banks and the need to augment their income through more lucrative non-bank financial services. Advances for housing purposes are also encouraged for the same reason by including them in priority sector advances, if they are below ₹2 lakh. Thus, leasing, hire-purchase, housing finance and factoring, etc., are all encouraged by banks in order to make them viable and profit-making in the coming years.

Credit Policy of RBI and NBFCs

As per the credit policy, effective from Oct. 1994, the limit of liquid assets to be held by the NBFCs was raised from 10% to 15% of deposits including the inter corporate deposits, bonds and debentures. Liquid assets have been defined as investments in Government, and semi-Government securities, and government guaranteed bonds and securities.

The RBI has also brought down the amount that can be borrowed by the NBFCs from banks so that the bank funds are not rechanneled through the NBFCs into the stock and capital markets. NBFCs whose main business is not leasing and hire-purchase can borrow only up to three times of their NOF, while the earlier limit was four times. For loan and investment finance companies, as well as residuary finance companies, the ceiling on maximum permissible bank finance was brought down from three times to two times of their NOF.

The RBI has asked banks to refrain from granting bridge loans against equity or debt capital to be raised from public by the NBFCs. Provision to recall loans and restrictions on fresh loans and insistence on their repayment on due dates are some of the other provisions made by the RBI in their latest credit policy. Bridge loans are also allowed now and banks have been given discretion in many matters relating to advances, as in the case of deposits.

RBI AND NBFCs

As per Shah Committee Report on Finance Companies, RBI has asked all non-bank finance companies which have owned funds of ₹50 lakh and above to register themselves with the RBI. The RBI has in mid-June 1994 asked such registered companies to abide by prudential norms as are applicable to the banks. New companies to be registered with the RBI should have rupees two crore of NOF.

These prudential norms refer to the following in particular: The NBFCs have to achieve capital adequacy of 6% of risk weighted assets by March 1995 and 8% by March 1996. On income recognition, the RBI has decreed that income due but not accrued should not be taken to the balance sheet. If payments of principal and interest are due but not received for more than six months, such loans should be classified as non-performing assets (NPAs). All accounting guidelines laid down by the Institute of Chartered Accountants in respect of leasing and depreciation, etc., are to be followed by the NBFCs.

On the classification and provisioning, the assets have been classified into four categories — standard assets, sub-standard assets, doubtful assets and loss assets. Provisioning norms for the last three classes of assets have been laid down by the RBI. The passage of the securitisation and Reconstruction of Financial Assets and Enforcement of Security Interest Act (SARFAESI) in 2002 facilitated the reduction of some sub-standard assets, as applicable to NBFCs.

The RBI has also prescribed risk weights on the on-balance sheet assets and credit conversion factors for off balance sheet items of exposures. While cash, bank balances and investments in government and approved securities have been given zero weightage, other assets have been given a weightage of 100. The off-balance sheet items carry credit conversion factors ranging from 50% to 100%.

Valuation of Investments

Investments have been classified into current and long-term investments, depending on the period of holding of one year and less or more than one year, respectively. Current investments have to be valued either on cost basis or market price whichever is lower. Long-term investments have to be valued only on cost basis.

Lending Norms — Risk Exposure Norms

As per the norms, finance companies cannot lend more than 15% of net owned funds to any single party and not more than 25% of net owned funds to any single group. Besides, finance companies cannot invest more than 25% of their owned funds in shares and debentures of another company.

Limits to Deposits

As a liberalisation, the NBFCs other than lease and hire-purchase companies, have now been permitted to raise deposits from public up to 100% of their net owned funds as against the earlier limit of 40%. This limit applies to total of deposits, bonds and debentures. Besides, they have compulsorily got credit ratings for their instruments and acceptable ratings have been laid down by the RBI. These norms apply to only registered finance companies. For non-registered finance companies, the limit on the deposits is proposed to be brought down to 25% of owned funds from public and 15% of owned funds from shareholders respectively, in a phased manner. These limits include the inter-corporate investments of such companies. The maximum interest rate payable on deposits of 3 years cannot exceed 11% with corresponding rates for lower maturities as from 2002-03.

The other policy guidelines include the following:

1. The management of Asset Liability (ALM) matching and the exposure to capital market are to be in tune with banks.
2. The simplification of the procedures for collection of interest on government securities through banks.
3. Application of nomination facility in banks to the deposits with NBFCs.
4. NBFCs are allowed to take up insurable business and to have investment in infrastructure bonds.
5. Measures of legislative process for Financial Companies Regulation Bill (FCRB) 2000.
6. Granting of registration to Asset Reconstruction Companies (ARCs). By September 2007, three such companies were registered, and three more companies have applied for registration.

Reporting to RBI

The registered finance companies have been asked to report their credit rating every half-year to the RBI. The RBI has also prescribed a format for the purpose of reporting by the finance companies, to ensure their compliance with the RBI guidelines. They have to submit their reports at the end of September and March of every year. The RBI would scrutinise the observance by companies of the prudential norms relating to capital adequacy, income recognition, asset classification and accounting standards, which have been referred to briefly above.

On the composition of capital, the RBI has stated that capital would be divided into two parts: Tier I and Tier II. Tier I would consist of paid-up equity and free reserves. From the total of the two, they have to deduct investments in and loans to subsidiaries and companies in the same group, in excess of 10% of the owned funds. This constitutes the Tier I capital of the company. Tier II capital would comprise preference capital, revaluation reserves, general provisions and loss reserves in excess of the required amounts. The RBI has also stated that applying the norms of banks, the finance companies should also have Tier I larger than Tier II.

It will thus be seen that the RBI guidelines have been issued in pursuance of the Shah Committee recommendations in regard to the regulation of the finance companies. The RBI has taken a first step in the direction of developing the non-bank financial sector in the right direction, in 1994 and followed it up in 1999, by completing registration work relating to all NBFCs, with ₹ 25 lakh of N.O.F. and above.

APPENDIX

HIRE-PURCHASE AND LEASING PROBLEMS

Finance Lease Features

Under this lease, the lessor has to show the net investment as the asset in the balance sheet and as amount receivable equivalent to net investment. All risk, and rewards relating to legal ownership are passed on to lessee. The rental incomes are shown as revenue in income expenditure statement. The tax benefits arise out of depreciation, rent, taxes, repair, maintenance, etc., which are shown as expense items. Similarly, interest on borrowed amount for buying the equipment, bad debts, expense for promoting trade and business entertainment expenses and travel, etc., up to the limits allowed are treated as expenses to reduce the taxable income.

Operating Lease Accounting

Under this lease, the ownership is with the lessor and he can provide for expenses of depreciation, maintenance, interest, etc., in its accounts. The lessor can show the rentals under expenditure in income expenditure account, but the asset does not appear in the balance sheet of lessee. Sales tax and income tax benefits do not accrue as there is no capital expenditure but only current expenditure of rental payments.

Section XIV of the Companies Act governs the provisions for depreciation as also in the Income Tax Act. Under Section 32 of the I.T. Act, the provisions related allowable depreciation, depending on its ownership as shown in the balance sheet and the type of asset class like building, machinery, equipment, etc.

The written down value (WDV) is used to provide for depreciation at 25% to 100% depending on the nature of the asset and the cost of acquisition of the asset under lease.

The table below shows the methods of presentation of the depreciation account as fixed and variable charge, for illustration.

Principal value ₹100 crore.

Year	Principal	Depreciation Charges		Rate of depreciation 20%
		Rate	Fixed	Amount Passed to P/L Account
1	100	20	20	0
2	80	16	20	4
3	64	13	20	7
4	51	10	20	10
5	41	8	20	12
		etc.	(completely written off)	etc.

The written down depreciation at 20% fixed will lead to zero value of the end of 5 years. But the written down value at 20% variable leaves value of ₹41 crore. The asset value at the end of 5 years called salvage value is the benefit accruing to the lessee but is written off liability in the balance sheet of lessor financier.

In practice, depreciation should be on the same basis as applied to similar owned assets or as approved by the accounting standard AS-6 Depreciation Accounting. The asset should be fully depreciated during the lease period or the economic life whichever is lower.

To sum up, if it is fixed amount of depreciation at 20%, every year ₹ 20 crore is deducted and the left over value of the asset will be zero. But, if the rate of 20% is on the declining amount of outstanding, at the end of 5 year lease period, it will have a salvage value of ₹ 41 crore, which is a benefit to the lessee is the case of finance lease.

Problems — Lease and Hire-purchase

1. If you require a machine costing ₹ 10,000, there are two options, namely to buy outright or take on lease. The lease rental is ₹ 1,000 per annum plus interest at a cost of 10% which comes to another ₹ 1,000 and gives a total payment of ₹ 2,000. per annum. This has to be paid over a period of 10 years. The alternative of buying it will cost you ₹ 10,000 which increases the capital expenditure with or without depreciation benefit in taxation. The maintenance of the machine is a cost item and this may lead to financing problem — the method of financing it. It becomes an item of the balance sheet, and increases the debt-equity ratio of the company.

   The present value of the payments in the case of lease is calculated as follows:

   NPV of 10 years flow at 10% is ₹ 2,000 – 10 years payment.

   The present value of this flow of funds is:

   Po = "A" multiplied by 1/(1 + r) t = 2,000 multiplied by 6.145 = ₹ 12,290

   where 6.145 is PVIFA (10% 10 years), and Po is the present value.

   If the present value of future flows are discounted to the present, it becomes ₹ 12,290.

   While in the buy decision, he has to pay only ₹ 10,000.

   It is therefore better to go for buy decision, except when he has to borrow to buy.

   This is a simplified version of the problems which the company may face in financing the projects.

2. A company needs a capital good costing ₹ 4 lakh which has a life of 5 years.

   If it buys, it has to shell down ₹ 4 lakh and if taken on lease, it has to pay for 5 years at a rate of rupees one lakh per annum. In the case of buy decision, it can defer tax payments and provide for depreciation which has a tax advantage. Assuming that the company has provided for depreciation and deferred the tax payment of ₹ 36,000 in total, which is a gain to the company finances, by accelerated depreciation, it has made this tax saving of ₹ 36,000 which means that this saving has to be spread over 4 years.

   Now the question is whether it is better to stick to buy decision or go for lease rentals at 10% interest for a period of 5 years?

   In the case of buy decision, take the present value of tax saving of ₹ 36,000 over four year-period, the PVIF (10% for 5 years),

   = 36,000 multiplied by 0.621 = 22,356. (₹ omitted)

   This gives the total cost of buy decision as 4,00,000 minus 22,356 = 3.78 lakh roughly.

   In the case of Lease decision take the present value of the principal plus the flows of lease rentals of one lakh each year — a total of 5 lakh. "A" is annuity in the form of flow of funds of 10% of 4 lakh — 40,000. Annual payments are one lakh on account of principal and interest of 40,000 a total of 1.4 lakh.

   This has to be converted into the present value.

   1.4 multiplied by PVIFA (10%, 5) that is, 3.791 = 5.311 lakh

   As the PV is lower for buy decision, of ₹ 3.78 lakh, that is preferred.

3. TVS has an option to buy a machine costing ₹150 lakhs by borrowing from bank at 14% interest or take it on hire-purchase at a flat rate of 13%. Hire-purchase instalments are spread over four years at monthly rests and equated amounts.

   It has also to pay a margin money of 25% at the beginning itself. The relevant tax rate is 30% and the depreciation is at 30% calculated on the basis of written down value (WDV). Which mode of financing is to be adopted by the company?

   Buying alternative:

   Capital investment is ₹150 lakh. To be repaid in equal instalments annually. Interest is = 150 Multiplied by 14/100 = which gives 21 lakh per annum. The PVA of interest payments is 21 multiplied by PVIFA (14, 4) which is 2.914 = 61.2. And PVA of the principal is 150 and the total of both principal and interest is 150 + 61.2 = 211.2 lakh in total.

Hire-purchase Alternative

Total charge is ₹150 lakh minus down payment of 25% or 37.50 which equals 112.50 lakh. Monthly instalment calculation at 13% for four years.

Or 48 months

Total expected annually = 112.5 multiplied by 0.13 multiplied by 4 = 58.5 lakh.

Monthly instalments of payments = 112.5 + 58.5/48 = 3.562, or 171 ÷ 48 = 3.562.

Annual payment is 3.562 multiplied by 12 that is ₹42.75 lakh, which is fixed and instalments of interest and principal are to be within this fixed amount.

Allocation of the total charge of instalment of ₹42.75 lakh.

Year	*outstanding at the beginning*	*Interest charge at 13%*	*+ Principal amount*	*= Annual payout*
1	112.50	14.62	28.13	42.75
2	84.37	10.96	31.79	42.75
3	52.58	6.84	35.91	42.75
4	16.67	2.17	40.58	42.75
Outstanding	nil	total 34.59	+ 136.41	171

Interest is estimated at 13% on the diminishing amount with the corresponding increase in the principal component, of the total annual payment which is a fixed annual Instalment. Under the fixed interest charge, however, the amount remains fixed at ₹14.62 lakh, with the corresponding changes in the principal so as to repay the total amount of principal and interest as per the agreement (*viz.*, ₹42.75).

Interest can be calculated under various methods say the effective rate, instead of the nominal rate as done in the above example, or the annual average rate, or through the method of sum of years digits, or on straight line method. In the above example for simplicity, the nominal rate is used and calculated on the declining outstanding amount each year with the fixed amount of instalment. The method adopted can be changed as per the terms of the agreement in the lease or hire-purchase contract.

The NAV of annual instalment is = 112.5 multiplied by PVIFA (13%, 4)

= 42.75 multiplied by 2.974 = 127.13 lakh.

Total NAV of annual instalment and margin money is = 127.13+37.50= 164.63.

The present value of BUY Alternative as seen above is **211.2.**

The present value of the hire-purchase alternative is **164.63**

As hire-purchase is cheaper for the company, it is preferred to the buy alternative.

Here for simplicity, the tax treatment of annual instalments and that of the depreciation charges and salvage, etc., if any, are ignored. These are introduced at a later stage. For the hirer, the ownership and depreciation privileges are not allowed and hence ignored. The ownership is passed to the hirer only after the payment of the last instalment.

Factors to be Considered from Lessee's Point of View

1. Present value of lease rentals at say 240/1000 or 440/1000.
2. Present values of tax shield on lessee points say at rates of 20% or 30% or 40%.
3. Present value of depreciation and tax shield on it — 30% or 35% rate of depreciation.
4. Present value of interest content of lease rentals and tax shield on it.
5. Present value of net salvage value.

Example: Value of the machine = ₹100 lakh.

Annual instalments – ₹24 lakh fixed on the basis of — ₹240/1000 payable annually.

Two alternatives of buy and lease:

1. Buy out right by making full payment by borrowing at a rate of 12% from a bank.
2. Lease on the basis of full payment in three (3) years to acquire the machine including the salvage value at the end of 3 years. Assume interest rate at 16%, depreciation 30% tax rate at 30%, which alternate value will you choose?

   Whose NPA is lower of the two?

A. Lease Alternative:

Investment outlay = ₹100 lakh

Annual lease rentals ₹24 lakh

1. Present value of the lease rentals = ₹24 × PVIFA (16, 3) from the Tables of PVIFA

   = 24 × 2.246 = 53.90

2. Present value of tax shield (at 30%) on rentals

   = 24 × 0.30 × PVIFA (16, 3) = 16.17, (PVIFA = 2.246)

3. Depreciation at 30%. Tax rate at 30%. Present value of tax shield on depreciation.

   Tax shield on depreciation 7.2 lakh —

   = 24 × 0.3 = 7.2 lakh — 1st year

   = 24 – 7.2 = 16.8 × 0.3 = 5.0 lakhs — 2nd year

   = 16.8 – 5.0 = 11.8 × 0.3 = 3.5 lakh — 3rd year

   7.2 × PVIF(16, 1) + 5.0 × PVIF(16, 2) + 3.5 × PVIF(16, 3)

   From the table, 7.2 × 0.862 + 5.0 × 0.743 + 3.5 × 0.641

   = (6.21 + 3.72 + 2.24) × 0.3

   For rate of tax shield, multiply by 0.3 (for the tax rate of 30%)

   = 12.2 × 0.3 = 3.6 lakh.

4. Present value of Tax shield on interest on lease rentals

   (Interest at 16%) lease rental of 24 lakh value of machine ₹100 lakh and at 16% interest on that as shown below: Lease instalment = Interest + Principal

Lease Instalment (1)	*Interest on outstanding (2)*	*Principal (3)*	*Notes for columns (2) and (3)*
24	16	8	100 × 16 = 16
24	13	11	100 −16 = 84
24	11	13	84 × 16 = 13.4
			84 − 13 = 71
			71 × 16 = 11.4 etc.

Salvage Value:

$100 - 24 \times 3 = 100 - 72 = 28$

Present value of interest component

$16 \times \text{PVIF}(16, 1) + 13 \times \text{PVIF}(16, 2) + 11 \times \text{PVIF}(16, 3)$

$= 16 \times 0.862 + 13 \times 0.743 + 11 \times 0.641$

$= 13.8 + 9.6 + 7.1 = 30.5$

5. Present value of salvage value (28)

$= 28 \times \text{PVIF}(16, 3)$

$= 28 \times 0.641 = 18$

		(Rounded up)
	1. Total present value of lease rentals from (I) above	= 54
Minus:	2. Present value of tax shield on lease rentals from (2) above	= 16
Plus:	3. Present value of tax shield on depreciation from (3) above	= 4
Plus:	4. Present value of tax shield interest payments from (4) above.	= 31
Plus:	5. Present value of salvage value, if the machine remains with lease from (5) above	= 18
	Total payouts in case of lease	= 91

B. Take the Buying option

Cost of the machine = ₹100 lakh

Cost of borrowing at a 12% rate of interest from "X" bank to be paid in three years.

Present value of outlay

$100 \times (1.12)^3 = 100 \times 1.40 = 140$

Payouts of this amount is spread or paid at the end of three years.

Present value of these payments on three years = 140

Actual outlay is ₹140 lakh while the present value of the outlay is 112.

$= 140 \times \text{PVIF}(12, 3) = (140 \times 0.712) = 99.7$

But the present value of lease payout is only ₹91 lakh, (as per the (A) above).

So leasing is cheaper than buyout by borrowing at 12%

Accounting Standards

Asset disclosure in the lessee's balance sheet is necessary. International accounting standard committee issued IAS-17, standards for lessee in (ICAI) issued accounting standard AS-19.

Accounting and reporting framework includes reporting separately the finance and operating lease, and their details. Taxation aspects again include income tax and sales tax considerations. The rentals should be allocated separately for principal account outstanding liability and interest expenditure account. In the finance lease, if the ownership passes to the lessee, it should be shown as an asset with an equal liability of repayment on the liabilities side.

Finance lease also leads to depreciation charge which should be calculated as set out in the IAS-4 — depreciation accounting. Operating lease has to be shown only in the revenue side as an expenditure on a systematic basis revealing the time period remaining for the payments. So far as lessor is concerned a finance lease should be recorded not as on asset but as a receivable amount equivalent to the net interest made in the lease. The revenue statement should include tax, interest payment and not the repayment of principal component. The revenue statement should also include profit/loss involved in the process of lease.

The lessor should disclose in the balance sheet the gross investment in leases, reported as finance leases and the related unearned income and the residual values of leased assets separately.

The finance lease terms and method of payment should be disclosed in the following form. It is a lease of 5 years, and repayments to be completed in 5 years (Figures are rounded up).

Years	*Outstanding lease liability*	*Interest charge Rounded up*	*To be lease payment*	*Allocated to Principal*
1	100	16	30.31	14.15
2	86	14	30.31	16.17
3	70	11	30.31	19.20
4	51	8	30.31	22.23
5	28	5	34.31	25.26
		54	155	101

It can be at simple interest amount equally distributed over 5 years (16%). But we adopted declining liability with each successive repayment when interest component goes on declining but the principal component goes on increasing but the total payment remains the same in each year (₹31 lakh 155÷5).

Hire-Purchase and Instalment Credit

In hire-purchase, the ownership does not pass immediately on entering the agreement. It passes at the time of his exercising the option to buy or the payment of the last instalment. In the case of the instalment credit, the contract of sale is entered into and the goods are delivered and ownership is passed on immediately. In hire-purchase, a margin of 20-25% of cost of equipment is paid by the hirer. The privileges of depreciation and tax benefits for depreciation will acrue to the hirer and not to the lessee. The cost of maintenance is borne by the hirer and he is allowed the depreciation charges and the finance charge to be claimed for tax benefits. In the case of leasing, the lessor is allowed to claim depreciation but the lessee is allowed to claim the rentals and maintenance costs against the taxable income.

The cost of hire-purchase to the hirer consists of

1. Down payment
2. Plus: Service charges
3. Plus: The present value of hire-purchase payments discounted by the cost of debt (kd).

4. Minus: Presept value of depreciation taxes shield discounted by the cost of capital (kc).
5. Minus: Present value of any net salvage value discounted by the cost of capital (kc).

Cost of Leasing

1. Lease management fee
2. Plus: Present value of lease payments discounted by cost of debt (kd)
3. Plus: Present value of interest tax shield on hire purchase discounted by kc.
4. Less: Present value of tax shield on lease payments and management fee discounted by kc, where kc is cost of capital for the company.

Cost of the machinery ₹108 lakh

I. Down payment for hire purchase at 20% = ₹108 × 0.20 = 21.6

Depreciation rate is 25%, cost of capital (kc) = 16%

Managerial cost of debt (kd) = 20%

The repayment is at a flat rate of interest of 16% and is repayable in qual instalments of 36 months or 3 years. But the life of the machine is 5 years. Salvage value is ₹33 lakh.

II. Calculation of present values – instalment payment

After down payment of 21.6, the chargeable amount is (108 – 21.6) = 86.4

The repayable monthly instalment on the basis of interest 16% on ₹86.4 lakh

$$\text{Instalment for year} = \frac{86.4 \times 16}{100} = ₹13.82$$

For three years, it is 13.82 × 3 = 41.47

For principal and interest together, monthly instalment

$$= \frac{86.4 + 41.5}{36} = \frac{127.9}{36} = 3.55 \text{ per month.}$$

and it is ₹42.6 lakh per annum. Present value of instalment: 42.6 × PVIFA (20, 3)

= 42.6 × 2.106 = 89.72

III. Present value of depreciation shield at 25% depreciation

= 27 × PVIF(16, 1) + 20.25 (PVIF) (16, 2) + 15.19PVIF(16, 3)

+ 11.39 PVIF (16, 4) + 8.54 × PVIF(16, 5)

= 27 × 0.862 + 20.25 + 0.743 + 15.19 × 0.641 + 11.39 × 0.552 + 8.54 × 0.458

= (23.27 + 15.0.5 + 9.74 + 6.3 + 4.1) × 0.35 where

0.35 is tax shield at 35% tax rate:

= (58.5) × 0.35 = 20.48.

Present value of tax shield on depreciation = 20.48

IV. Net salvage value ₹33 at the end of three years (4th year)

33 × PVIF(20, 4) = 33 × 0.150 = 15.91

Note: PVIF and PVIFA values are taken from the table at the end.

As worked, cost of hire-purchase above

I.	Down payment	21.6
II.	Plus: Present value of monthly H.P instalment	89.72
III.	Minus: Present value of tax shield of depreciation	20.48
IV.	Minus: Present value of net salvage value	15.91
	Total cost of hire-purchase	74.9

I. Total cost of buying out right

Purchase price – ₹108 lakh

Cost of maintenance at 10% = 10.8 lakh over 3 years

II. Present value of maintenance cost = 10.8 × PVIFA (20, 3)

= 10.8 × 2.106 = 22.74,

III. Value of depreciation at a rate of 25%

$$\frac{108 \times 25}{100} = 27 \text{ in 1st year}$$

= 20.25 in 2nd year

= 15.20 in 3rd year

= 11.39 in 4th year

= 8.54 in 5th year

Life of the machine is assumed to be of 5 years.

Tax shield - 27 × PVIF(I6, 1) + ... etc., (Working is shown in pre-page Item III, with the 35% tax shield)

At 35% = 20.48 as worked out above.

Total cost of buying out right is ₹108 lakh.

I.	*Total Price*	= 108
	Minus - 2 Maintenance cost tax shield of this cost	= 22.74
	Minus - 3 Depreciation cost at 25% tax shield	= 20.48
	Total cost of buying	= 64.70

Relevant hire-purchase cost is 74.9

As the cost of buying out right is cheapest under the assumption that they do not have to borrow, it is preferred to hire-purchase.

Leasing: Let us now take the alternative of leasing. The cost of the capital is 20% and the equipment cost is ₹108 lakh. Lease alternative has a lease period of 3 years. Marginal tax rate is 35%. But the life of the asset is 5 years land lease rentals are payable in advance at 30 points/1,000 = total cost of equipment ₹108 lakh.

I. Monthly payments in 36 equipment and down payment of 20%

Monthly lease is 30 for ₹1,000

Present value of monthly payments = 108 × 0.030 × 12 = 38.88 PVIFA(20, 5).

= 38.88 × 2.991 = 116.29 lakh (The multiplication by 12 is for making monthly payments, annual payments).

II. Tax shield on lease payment (to be paid in 3 years)

= 108 × 0.03(30 basis points per 1000) × 12 PVIFA (16, 3)

= (108 × 0.03 × 12 × 2.246) = 87.32

Total shield = 87.32 × 0.35 = 30.56

Present value of tax shield = 30.56

III. Tax shield for charge on credit: 108 × 0.80 × 0.16 × 3 = 41.4

Take the annual charge for 3 years at 16%

Monthly lease rentals = 108 × 0.03 = 3.24

Annual rental 3.24 × 12 = 38.88. (Here, as above, monthly payments are made annual payments).

Present value of this is = 38.88 × PVIFA (20, 5)

= 38.88 × 2.991 = 116.29

Total Present Value of Lease Alternative

I. Present value of lease payments = 116.29

II. Minus: Present value of tax shield on lease payments = 30.56

as calculated above, net........... = 85.73

III. Plus: Annual charge for three years distributed over three years as follows:

[108 × 0.80 × 0.16 × 3] = 41.47 (at 16% for 3 years).

Taking out the down payment of 20%, outstanding balance is 80%, that is 0.8 in the above equation.

Orginal cost = ₹ 108 lakh

Down payment of 20% → 108 × 0.2 = 21.6

Outstanding = 108 – 21.6 = 86.4

Subsequently from outstanding principal repayment is deducted every year, as shown below:

Assuming at 16% for 3 years

Year	*Outstanding*	*Interest*	*Principal*	*Instalment*
1	86.4	13.8	27.6	41.4
2	58.8	9.4	32.0	41.4
3	26.8	4.3	37.1	41.4

Present value of interest tax shield tax rate is 35%

= [(13.8 × 0.862) + (9.4 × 0.743) + 4.3 × 0.641)] × 0.35

= [(13.8 × PVIF(I6, 1) + 9.4 × PVIF(16, 2) + 4.3 × PVIF(16,3)] × 0.35

Marginal tax rate is 35%

= [(11.86 + 6.98 + 2.75] × 0.35

= 21.60 × 0.35 = 7.56

This is a plus factor.

For Leasing — Calculation of NPV

I. Present value of lease payments 116.29

II. Minus: Present value of tax shield on the lease payments – 30.56

III. Plus: Present value of tax shield on charge for credit	+7.56
Present value of lease alternative	93.29
I. Present value for out right buying	64.70 lakh
II. Present value for Hire-purchase	74.9
III. Present value for leasing	93.29

As the present value for buying is the lowest in the above example, this alternative is to be chosen.

Break-even Lease Rental

The break-even point is where the present marginal value of revenue is equal to marginal cost or the NPV of the project or machine is zero.

The example given below will make this clear.

Any machine purchased or leased has some outflows (costs) and inflows (returns).

If outflows minus inflows = 0, then, the NPV of the project (acquiring of machine) becomes 0, and the project becomes break-even. When the NPV becomes positive, then the project becomes profitable, otherwise it is not.

In the case of leasing the inflows or positive values includes: (from lessor's point of view)

1. Present value of Tax shield on depreciation
2. Present value of Management fee
3. Present value of Tax shield on initial direct costs
4. Present value of Salvage value
5. Present value of lease rentals

The **outflows** or negative values include:

1. Present value of lease rentals Tax shield
2. Present value of initial direct costs
3. Present value of tax on management fees

Example:

1. The initial cost of equipment is ₹300 lakh. It has a lease period of 5 years. Marginal cost of funds is 14% depreciation is at 25% on equipment. The relevant tax rate is 35%. The salvage value is zero. The other costs, include initial direct costs of 3 lakh and management fee of 5 lakh the question is how do you fix the break-even lease rental, in this case?

   Assume that the break-even level is L.

BREAK-EVEN LEASE RENTAL (BELR) CALCULATION

These rates differ for the lessor and lessee. Take the case of BELR for lessor. The value of the machine is ₹300 lakh. Depreciation is of 25% Tax rate is 35%. Let L be the BELR for this case.

I. Present value of lease rentals at 14% for 5 years

   $L \times PVIFA(14, 5) = L \times 3.433$ or $3.43L$

   where PVIFA (14, 5) is 3.433 from the tables given at the end = 3.433L

II. Present value of tax on lease rentals at 35% tax rate is $3.433L \times 0.35 = 1.201L$

III. Present value of depreciation tax shield with depreciation rate at 25% on the value of ₹ 300 lakh. The 25% depreciation is calculated on the declining outstanding, as shown below:

75 × PVIF(14, I) + 56.25 × PVIF(14, 2) + 42.18 × PVIF(14, 3) + 31.64 × PVIF(14,4) + 23.73 × PVIF(14, 5)

= [75 × 0.877 + 56.25 × 0.769 + 42.18 × 0.675 + 31.64 × 0.592 + 23.73 × 0.519] × 0.35

where 0.35 is the tax shield for the present value

= [65.7 + 43.3 + 28.47 + 18.7 + 12.3] × 0.35

= 168.5 × 0.35 = 58.99.

IV. Present value of tax shield on initial direct costs = 3 × 0.35 × PVIF(14, 1)
= 3 × 0.35 × 0.877 = 0.921

V. Present value of tax shield on management fees = 5 × 0.35 × PVIF(14, 1)
= 5 × 0.35 × 0.877 = 1.534

VI. Present value of the salvage value if any nil.

Assuming the BELR, as L, then the equipment cost = 300 lakh

+ Present value of lease rentals 3.433L

– Present value of tax shield on lease rentals 1.201L

+ Present value of tax shield on (@ 25% of cost) depreciation 58.99

– Present value of initial direct costs 3.0

+ Present value of management fee 5.0

+ Present value of tax shield on direct costs 0.921

– Present value of tax shield on management fee 1.534

The equation is as follows:

3.433L – 1.201L + 58.99 – 3 + 5 + 0.921 – 1.534 – 300 = 0

where 300 is cost of equipment

2.232L + 60.377 – 300 = 0

2.232L = 300 – 60.377 = 239.623

$$L = \frac{239.623}{2.232} = 107.35$$

BELR is 107.35 per ₹ 1,000 for the case illustrated above.

BREAK-EVEN LEASE RENTAL FOR THE LESSEE

The break-even rentals of the lessor and lessee present the range with which the actual rent falls depending on the strength of negotiation of the parties.

Example of break-even lease rental for lessee. The cost of equipment is ₹ 1,000. Depreciation @ 30%. Marginal rate of taxation 35%; useful life is 5 years

Cost of debt = 17% cost of own capital 14%

No salvage value is assumed.

1. Present value of lease rental

   = 12L × PVIFA(17, 5) = 12L × 3.199 = 38.4L

2. Present value of tax shield on lease rental

   = 12L × PVIFA (14, 5) × 0.35

   = 12L × 3.433 × 0.35 = 14.4L

3. Present value of tax shield foregone on depreciation

   = [300 × PVIF(14, 2) + 210 × PVIF(14, 2) + 147 × PVIF(14, 3) + 102 × PVIF(14, 4) + 72 × PVIF(14, 5)] × 0.35

   = [300 × 0.877 + 210 × 0.769 + 147 × 0.675 + 102 × 0.592 + 72 × 0.519] × 0.35

   = 620 × 0.35 = 217

Notes
263
161
99
60
37
620

Investment cost - ₹ 1,000 lakh

Present value of lease initials = 38.4L

Present value of tax shield = 14.4L

Present value of tax shield on depreciation = 217

Break-even lease rental is given by equation

1000 – 38.4L + 14.4L – 217 = 0

24L = 1000 – 217 = 783

$$L = \frac{783}{24} = 32.6$$

Lease rental is ₹ 33 per 1000, roughly.

NEGOTIATION

In the example 2 above, break-even level of lease for the lessee is 33 per ₹ 1,000. It was already seen in the example 1 that break-even level of lease rental was 107.35 per 1000 for the lessor.

Negotiation takes place to fix the actual level of lease rental within the range of the above two limits. The actual rental should be beneficial to both and their NPV(L) should be positive to both. Otherwise lease will not take place.

IRR BASED PRICING

IRR is internal rate of return, generated by the working of the project which may be different from the marginal cost of capital or the cost of the debt. When the IRR is equal to the expected return on investment in machine and NPV is zero; the project becomes break-even. When the NPV is positive, then only the project becomes profitable and then only lease agreement is beneficial to the lessee.

Calculation of IRR

Let us assume that the return at the positive NPV is 10% say actual NPV is 310

The return at negative NPV is say 30% and the actual NPV is = 1,880

Then IRR = Rate of Return giving positive NPV + Positive NPV ÷ NPV – (–NPV) × differential between two rates

+ NPV — ratio is 10%

– NPV — ratio is 30%

The differential is 20%.

$$IRR = 10\% + \frac{310}{310 + 1880} \times 20$$

$$IRR = 10\% + \frac{310}{2190} \times 20 = 10 + 2.83 = \mathbf{12.83}$$

Here the IRR is worked out as 12.83

As calculated above, if the IRR, giving a positive PV is say 25%, pricing of the lease rental should be below this. This is shown in the example given below.

Problem: 'X' company has a lease proposal for a machine costing ₹ 1,000 lakhs. The lease period is 3 years and the salvage value is zero. Its deprecation is planned at 40% of the cost. The company's cost of capital is 14% and its relevant tax rate is 35%. For simplicity, the ST and other taxes are ignored. What is the minimum lease rental that is acceptable to the lessee company at less than its IRR (25%)? If the cost is only ₹ 600 lakh, will it be acceptable to it?

Ans: I. Present value of lease rentals?

Assume the minimum lease rental at 'L' and NPV or NAL is zero. L is the monthly lease rental and 12L is for annum.

= 12L × PVIFA (14, 3) = 12L × 2.232 = 26.78L

II. Present value of tax shield on lease rental:

[12L × PVIFA (14, 3)] × 0.35 = 26.78L × 0.35 = 9.37L

III. Present value of tax shield on depreciation at 40% on cost.

= 400 × PVIF (14, 1) + 240 × PVIF(I4, 2) + 144 × PVIF(I4, 3)

= 400 × 0.877 + 240 × 0.769 + 144 × 0.675

= 350.8 + 184.5 + 97.2 = 632.5

NPV = 0

27.78L – 9.37L + 632.5 – 1000 = 0

18.41L = 1000 – 632.5 = 367.5

$$L = \frac{367.5}{18.4} = \mathbf{20} \text{ roughly}$$

If the cost of the machine is ₹ 1,000 lakh, then the lease rental is 20 per 1000. If the cost of the machine is shown at ₹ 600 lakh, then the lease rental will be lower at around 12-13 which will both be lower than its IRR at 25% and hence acceptable to the company.

GROSS YIELD BASED PRICING

Instead of IRR, the gross yield the per year can be used as the basis for fixing the lease rental per 1000 per year. The gross yield is the return on investment per cent for annum.

For example if the investment on a machine is ₹ 500 crore and the gross profit or return on the operation by it is ₹ 100 crore, the gross yield on the machine is calculated as follows:

= 100/500 = 20%

Like the IRR of 25%, taken earlier, one can use the gross yield of 20% in the case of gross yield based pricing for fixing the lease rental on the basis 20 or 25 points per 1000 bps (Basis points).

APPENDIX

PVIF

Table A-1 The Present Value of One Rupee

Year	1%	2%	3%	4%	5%	6%	7%	8%	9%	10%
1	.990	.980	.971	.962	.952	.943	.935	926	.917	.909
2	.980	.961	.943	.925	.907	.800	.873	.857	.842	.826
3	.971	.942	.915	.889	.864	.840	.816	.794	.772	.751
4	.961	.924	.888	.855	.823	.792	.763	.735	.708	.683
5	.951	.906	.863	.822	.784	.747	.713	.681	.650	.621
6	.942	.888	.837	.790	.746	.705	.666	.630	.596	.564
7	.933	.871	.813	.760	.711	.665	.623	.583	.547	.513
8	.923	.853	.789	.731	.677	.627	.582	.540	.502	.467
9	.914	.837	.766	.703	.645	.592	.544	.500	.460	.424
10	.905	.820	.744	.676	.614	.558	.508	.463	.422	.386
11	.896	.804	.722	.650	.585	.527	.475	.429	.388	.350
12	.887	.789	.701	.625	.557	.497	.444	.397	.356	.319
13	.879	.773	.681	.601	.530	.469	.415	.368	.326	.290
14	.870	.758	.661	.577	.505	.442	.388	.340	.299	.263
15	.861	.743	.642	.555	.481	.417	.362	.315	.275	.239
16	.853	.728	.623	.534	.458	.394	.339	.292	.252	.218
17	.844	.714	.605	.513	.436	.371	.317	.270	.231	.198
18	.836	.700	.587	.494	.416	.350	.296	.250	.212	.180
19	.828	.686	.570	.475	.396	.331	.227	.232	.194	.164
20	.820	.673	.554	.456	.377	.312	.258	.215	.178	.149
21	.811	.660	.538	.439	.359	.294	.242	.199	.164	.135
22	.803	.647	.522	.422	.342	.278	.226	.184	.150	.123
23	.795	.634	.507	.406	.326	.262	.211	.170	.138	.112
24	.788	.622	.492	.390	.310	.247	.197	.158	.126	.102
25	.780	.610	.478	.375	.295	.233	.184	.146	.116	.092
30	.742	.552	.412	.308	.231	.174	.131	.099	.075	.057
35	.706	.500	.355	.253	.181	.130	.094	.068	.049	.036
40	.672	.453	.307	.208	.142	.097	.067	.046	.032	.022
45	.639	.410	.264	.171	.111	.073	.048	.031	.021	.014
50	.608	.372	.228	.141	.087	.054	.034	.021	.013	.009

PVIF

Table A-1 The Present Value of One Rupee (*Contd.*)

Year	*11%*	*12%*	*13%*	*14%*	*15%*	*16%*	*17%*	*18%*	*19%*	*20%*
1	.901	.893	.885	.877	.870	.862	.855	.847	.840	.833
2	.812	.797	.783	.769	.756	.743	.731	.718	.706	.694
3	.731	.712	.693	.675	.658	.641	.624	.609	.593	.579
4	.659	.636	.613	.592	.572	.552	.534	.516	.499	.482
5	.593	.567	.543	.519	.497	.476	.456	.437	.419	.402
6	.535	.507	.480	.456	.432	.410	.390	.370	.352	.335
7	.482	.452	.425	.400	.376	.354	.333	.314	.296	.279
8	.434	.404	.376	.351	.327	.305	.285	.266	.249	.233
9	.391	.361	.333	.308	.284	.263	.243	.225	.209	.194
10	.352	.322	.295	.270	.247	.227	.208	.191	.176	.162
11	.317	.287	.261	.237	.215	.195	.178	162	.148	.135
12	.286	.257	.231	.208	.187	168	.152	.137	.124	.112
13	.258	.229	.204	.182	163	.145	130	.116	.104	093
14	.232	.205	.181	.160	.141	.125	.111	.099	.088	.078
15	.209	.183	.160	.140	.123	.108	.095	.084	.074	.065
16	.188	.163	.141	.123	.107	.093	.081	.071	.062	.054
17	.170	.146	.125	.108	.093	.080	.069	.060	.052	.045
18	.153	.130	.111	.095	.081	.069	.059	.051	.044	.038
19	.138	.116	.098	.083	.070	.060	.051	.043	.037	.031
20	.124	.104	.087	.073	.061	.051	.043	.037	.031	.026
21	.112	.093	.077	.064	.053	.044	.037	.031	.026	.022
22	.101	.083	.068	.056	.046	.038	.032	.026	.022	.018
23	.091	.074	.060	.049	.040	.033	.027	.022	.018	.015
24	.082	.066	.053	.043	.035	.028	.023	.019	.015	.013
25	.074	.059	.047	.038	.030	.024	.020	.016	.013	.010
30	.044	.033	.026	.020	.015	.012	.009	.007	.005	.004
35	.026	.019	.014	.010	.008	.006	.004	.003	.002	.002
40	.015	.011	.008	.005	.004	.003	.002	.001	.001	.001
45	.009	.006	.004	.003	.002	.001	.001	.001	.000	.000
50	.005	.003	.002	.001	.001	.001	.000	.000	.000	.000

PVIF

Table A-1 The Present Value of One Rupee (*Contd.*)

Year	*21%*	*22%*	*23%*	*24%*	*25%*	*26%*	*27%*	*28%*	*29%*	*30%*
1	.826	.820	.813	.806	.800	.794	.787	.781	.775	.769
2	.683	.672	.661	.650	.640	.630	.620	.610	.601	.592
3	.564	.551	.537	.524	.512	.500	.488	.477	.466	.455
4	.467	.451	.437	.423	.410	.397	.384	.373	.361	.350
5	.386	.370	.355	.341	.328	.315	.303	.291	.280	.269
6	.319	.303	.289	.275	.262	.250	.238	.227	.217	.207
7	.263	.249	.235	.222	.210	.198	.188	.178	.168	.159
8	.218	.204	.191	.179	.168	.157	.148	.139	.130	.123
9	.180	.167	.155	.144	.134	.125	.116	.108	.101	.094
10	.149	.137	.126	.116	.107	.099	.092	.085	.078	.073
11	.123	.112	.103	.094	.086	.079	.072	.066	.061	.056
12	.102	.092	.083	.076	.069	.062	.057	.052	.047	.043
13	.084	.075	.068	.061	.055	.050	.045	.040	.037	.033
14	.069	.062	.055	.049	.044	.039	.035	.032	.028	.025
15	.057	.051	.045	.040	.035	.031	.028	.025	.022	.020
16	.047	.042	.036	.032	.028	.025	.022	.019	.017	.015
17	.039	.034	.030	.026	.023	.020	.017	.015	.013	.012
18	.032	.028	.024	.021	.018	.016	.014	.012	.010	.009
19	.027	.023	.020	.017	.014	.012	.011	.009	.008	.007
20	.022	.019	.016	.014	.012	.010	.008	.007	.006	.005
21	.018	.015	.013	.011	.009	.008	.007	.006	.005	.004
22	.015	.013	.011	.009	.007	.006	.005	.004	.004	.003
23	.012	.010	.009	.007	.006	.005	.004	.003	.003	.002
24	.010	.008	.007	.006	.005	.004	.003	.003	.002	.002
25	.009	.007	.006	.005	.004	.003	.003	.002	.002	.001
30	.003	.003	.002	.002	.001	.001	.001	.001	.000	.000
35	.001	.001	.001	.001	.000	.000	.000	.000	.000	.000
40	.000	.000	.000	.000	.000	.000	.000	.000	.000	.000
45	.000	.000	.000	.000	.000	.000	.000	.000	.000	.000
50	.000	.000	.000	.000	.000	.000	.000	.000	.000	.000

PVIFA

Table A-2 The Present Value of an Annuity of One Rupee

Year	*1%*	*2%*	*3%*	*4%*	*5%*	*6%*	*7%*	*8%*	*9%*	*10%*
1	.990	.980	.971	.962	.952	.943	.935	.926	.917	.909
2	1.970	1.942	1.913	1.886	1.859	1.833	1.808	1.783	1.759	1.736
3	2.941	2.884	2.829	2.775	2.723	2.673	2.624	2.577	2.531	2.487
4	3.902	3.808	3.717	3.630	3.546	3.465	3.387	3.312	3.240	3.170
5	4.853	4.713	4.580	4.452	4.329	4.212	4.100	3.993	3.890	3.791
6	5.795	5.601	5.417	5.242	5.076	4.917	4.767	4.623	4.486	4.355
7	6.728	6.472	6.230	6.002	5.786	5.582	5.389	5.206	5.033	4.868
8	7.652	7.326	7.020	6.733	6.463	6.210	5.971	5.747	5.535	5.335
9	8.566	8.162	7.786	7.435	7.108	6.802	6.515	6.247	5.995	5.759
10	9471	8.983	8.530	8.111	7.722	7.360	7.024	6.710	6.418	6.145
11	10.368	9.787	9.253	8.760	8.306	7.887	7.499	7.139	6.805	6.495
12	11.255	10.575	9.954	9.385	8.863	8.384	7.943	7.536	7.161	6.814
13	12.134	11.348	10.635	9.986	9.394	8.853	8.358	7.904	7.487	7.105
14	13.004	12.106	11.296	10.553	9.899	9.295	8.746	8.244	7.786	*7.367*
15	13.865	12.849	11.938	11.118	10.380	9.712	9.108	*8.560*	8.061	7.606
16	14.718	13.578	12.561	11.652	10.838	10.106	9.447	8.851	8.313	7.824
17	15.562	14.292	13.166	12.166	11.274	10.477	9.763	9.122	8.544	8.022
18	16.398	14.992	13.754	12.659	11.690	10.828	10.059	9.372	8.756	8.201
19	17.226	15.679	14.324	13.134	12.085	11.158	10.336	9.604	8.950	8.365
20	18.046	16.352	14.878	13.590	12.462	11.470	10.594	9.818	9.129	8.514
21	18.857	17.011	15.415	14.029	12.821	11.764	10.836	10.017	9.292	8.649
22	19.661	17.658	15.937	14.451	13.163	12.042	11.061	10.201	9.442	8.772
23	20.456	18.292	16.444	14.857	13.489	12.303	11.272	10.371	9580	8.883
24	21.244	18.914	16.936	15.247	13.799	12.550	11.469	10.529	9.707	8.985
25	22.023	19.524	17.413	15.622	14.094	12.783	11.654	10.675	9.823	9.077
30	25.808	22.397	19.601	17.292	15.373	13.765	12.400	11.256	10.274	9.427
35	29.409	24.999	21.487	18.665	16.374	14.498	12.948	11.655	10.567	9.644
40	32.835	27.356	23.115	19.793	17.159	15.040	12.332	11.925	10.757	9.779
45	36.095	29.490	24.519	20.720	17.774	15.456	13.606	12.108	10.881	9.863
50	39.197	31.424	25.730	21.482	18.256	15.767	13.801	12.234	10.962	9.915

PVIFA

Table A-2 The Present Value of an Annuity of One Rupee (*Contd.*)

Year	*11%*	*12%*	*13%*	*14%*	*15%*	*16%*	*17%*	*18%*	*19%*	*20%*
1	.901	.893	.885	.877	.870	.862	.855	.847	.850	.833
2	1.713	1.690	1.668	1.647	1.626	1.605	1.585	1.566	1.547	1.528
3	2.444	2.402	2.361	2.322	2.283	2.246	2.210	2.174	2.140	2.106
4	3.102	3.037	2.974	2.914	2.855	2.798	2.743	2.690	2.639	2.589
5	3.696	3.605	3.517	3.433	3.352	3.274	3.199	3.127	3.058	2.991
6	4.231	4.111	3.998	3.889	3.784	3.685	3.589	3.498	3.410	3.326
7	4.712	4.564	4.423	4.288	4.160	4.039	3.922	3.812	3.706	3.605
8	5.146	4.968	4.799	4.639	4.487	4.344	4.207	4.078	3.954	3.837
9	5.537	5.328	5.132	4.946	4.772	4.607	4.451	4.303	4.163	4.031
10	5.889	5.650	5.426	5.216	5.019	4.833	4.659	4.494	4.339	4.192
11	6.207	5.938	5.687	5.453	5.234	5.029	4.836	4.656	4.487	4.327
12	6.492	6.194	5.918	5.660	5.421	5.197	4.988	4.793	4.611	4.439
13	6.750	6.424	6.122	5.842	5.583	5.342	5.118	4.910	4.715	4.533
14	6.982	6.628	5.303	6.002	5.724	5.468	5.229	5.008	4.802	4.611
15	7.191	6.811	6.462	6.142	5.847	5.575	5.324	5.092	4.876	4.675
16	7.379	6.974	6.604	6.265	5.954	5.669	5.405	5.162	4.938	4.730
17	7.549	7.120	6.729	6.373	6.047	5.749	5.475	5.222	4.990	4.775
18	7.702	7.250	6.840	6.467	6.128	5.818	5.534	5.273	5.033	4.812
19	7.839	7.366	6.938	6.550	6.198	5.877	5.585	5.316	5.070	4.843
20	7.963	7.469	7.024	6.623	6.259	5.929	5.628	5.353	5.101	4.870
21	8.075	7.562	7.102	6.687	6.312	5.973	5.665	5.384	5.127	4.891
22	8.176	7.645	7.170	6.743	6.359	6.011	5.696	5.410	5.149	4.909
23	8.266	7.718	7.230	6.792	6.399	6.044	6.723	5.432	5.167	4.925
24	8.348	7.784	7.283	6.835	6.434	6.073	5.747	5.451	5.182	4.937
25	8.422	7.843	7.330	6.873	6.464	6.097	5.766	5.467	5.195	4.948
30	8.694	8.055	7.496	7.003	6.566	6.177	5.829	5.517	5.235	4.979
35	8.855	8.176	7.586	7.070	6.617	6.215	5.858	5.539	5.251	4.992
40	8.951	8.244	7.634	7.105	6.642	6.233	5.871	5.548	5.258	4.997
45	9.008	8.283	7.661	7.123	6.654	6.242	5.877	5.552	5.261	4.999
50	9.042	8.305	7.675	7.133	6.661	6.246	5.880	5.554	5.262	4.999

PVIFA

Table A-2 The Present Value of an Annuity of One Rupee (*Contd.*)

Year	*21%*	*22%*	*23%*	*24%*	*25%*	*26%*	*27%*	*28%*	*29%*	*30%*
1	8.26	.820	.813	.806	.800	.794	.787	.781	.775	.769
2	1.509	1.492	1.474	1.457	1.440	1.424	1.407	1.392	1.376	1.361
3	2.074	2.042	2.011	1.981	1.952	1.923	1.896	1.868	1.842	1.816
4	2.540	2.494	2.448	2.404	2.362	2.320	2.280	2.241	2.203	2.166
5	2.926	2.864	2.803	2.745	2.689	2.635	2.583	2.532	2.483	2.436
6	3.245	3.167	3.092	3.020	2.951	2.885	2.821	2.759	2.700	2.643
7	3.508	3.416	3.327	3.242	3.161	3.083	3.009	2.937	2.868	2.802
8	3.726	3.619	3.518	3.421	3.329	3.241	3.156	3.076	2.999	2.925
9	3.905	3.786	3.673	3.566	3.463	3.366	3.273	3.184	3.100	3.019
10	4.054	3.923	3.799	3.682	3.570	3.465	3.364	3.269	3.178	3.092
11	4,177	4.035	4.902	3.776	3.656	3.544	3.437	3.335	3.239	3.147
12	4.278	4.127	3.985	3.851	3.752	3.606	3.493	3.387	3.286	3.190
13	4.362	4.203	4.053	3.912	3.780	3656	3.538	3.427	3.322	3.223
14	4.432	4.265	4.108	3.962	3.824	3.695	3.573	3.459	3.351	3.249
15	4.489	4.315	4.153	4.001	3.859	3.726	3.601	3.483	3.373	3.268
16	4.536	4.357	4.189	4.033	3.887	3.751	3.623	3.503	3.390	3.283
17	4.576	4.391	4.219	4.059	3.910	3.771	3.640	3.518	3.403	3.295
18	4.608	4.419	4.243	4.080	3.928	3.786	3.654	3.529	3.413	3.304
19	4.635	4.442	4.263	4.097	3.942	3.799	3.664	3.539	3.421	3.311
20	4.657	4.460	4.279	4.110	3.954	3.808	3.673	3.546	3.427	3.316
21	4.675	4.476	4.292	4.121	3.963	3.816	3.679	3.551	3.432	3.320
22	4.690	4.488	4.302	4.130	3.970	3.822	3.684	3.556	3.436	3.323
23	4.703	4.499	4.311	4.137	3.976	3.827	3.689	3.559	3.438	3.325
24	4.713	4.507	4.318	4.143	3.981	3.831	3.692	3.562	3.441	3.327
25	4.721	4.514	4.323	4.147	3.985	3.834	3.694	3.564	3.442	3.329
30	4.746	4.534	4.339	4.160	3.995	3.842	3.701	3.69	3.447	3.332
35	4.756	4.541	4.345	4.164	3.998	3.845	3.703	3.571	3.448	3.333
40	4.760	4.544	4.347	4.166	3.999	3.846	3.703	3.571	3.448	3.333
45	4.761	4.545	4.347	4.166	4.000	3.846	3.704	3.571	3.448	3.333
50	4.762	4.545	4.348	4.167	4.000	3.846	3.704	3.571	3.448	3.333

CREDIT RATING SERVICES

18

Why Credit Rating?

There was an enormous increase in the demand for capital by companies and investors had no way to know the credit quality of the companies whether they were strong financially, or weak in some respects, but more importantly whether they were frauds. Generally, equities are not rated, as their risk is not measurable and they being the owners of the companies have to take the residual risk. But when companies issue bonds or debentures or any debt instruments, they can be rated. Here again, the company is not rated but the instrument, issued by the company is rated, for its capacity to service that instrument.

Rating in USA

In USA, John Moody has issued his first rating in 1909, when he published a Manual of information on US Railroad Companies. Slowly, his ratings became popular with investors. He gave Triple A for the least risk and C for higher risk. He began to rate all companies issuing bonds and even bonds of foreign governments, issued in the USA. During 1920s, Standard and Poor ratings became equally popular and they began to rate the companies and govt. and semi Govt. bonds, issuing to the public. After the depression of thirties as, rating became more important and "Investment" grade companies, as defined by rating agencies were being made eligible for trading. In USA, bulk of the bond issues are rated either by Moody's or Standard and Poor and investors are used to these ratings. Subsequently, these agencies have become global rating agencies, in the eighties and nineties.

What is Credit Rating?

Credit rating is essentially giving an expert opinion by a rating agency on the relative willingness and ability of the issuer of a debt instrument to meet the debt servicing obligation in time and in full.

How to Understand Ratings and Rating System?

These rating grades are quite common with Triple *AAA*, as least risky. *AA* less risky, *A* more risky, *B* just adequate to service and *C,* inadequate to service and highly risky and *D* is default prone. The agency rating will add their own prefix or suffix to those grades to indicate their stamp of rating. Thus in India, at present there are six rating agencies, and it is now made compulsory that companies issuing debt instruments not convertible within 18 months to get the ratings and publish them. If a company is not satisfied with a rating of an agency, it can go to another agency.

What Instruments are Rated?

Among debt instruments in capital markets bonds, debentures not converted into equity within 18 months, preference shares and different categories of debt instruments are to be rated. Besides, among the money market instruments, commercial paper and short-term instruments of less than one year and fixed deposits of one to three years are also rated. When rating is done analysis of the company's financial and operational aspects is carried out on the basis of the data available at that time. Presently, all bonds and debentures are to be rated even if they are convertible into equity within 18 months.

Limitations to Ratings

These ratings are no doubt important to the investment activity in the capital market. But they have their own limitations.

1. They do not give ratings of equity, as equityholders are supposed to take risk. More recently, equity has also become rateable.
2. Ratings of bonds, debentures and other types of instruments of debt are rated, only as indicators of risk.
3. Ratings are only matters of opinion but coming from bodies which are experts in the field, they have some weight.
4. Ratings become out of date soon and hence they are to be updated, at least every six months and any fresh information or developments may change the grade of rating.
5. Ratings play a useful role to investors when the regulatory authority takes no responsibility for those who raise funds, and investors are left to fend themselves.
6. Credit ratings become necessary when many default prone companies are entering the market, for which there is no regulatory provision.
7. Credit rating agencies should maintain expert professional staff with qualifications and competence of lawyers, CAs, CS, MBA, finance and marketing and bankers, etc. Besides their staff should be permanent and not too frequently changing. If these conditions are not satisfied ratings become undependable.

Key Factors Considered

Rating process involves detailed exercises involving analysis of financial statements, visits to the factory and offices of the company holding of discussions with auditors, bankers or creditors, etc. Detailed desk work, outdoor work and work of specialists like those of bankers, CAs, etc., are to be dovetailed and various factors are to be examined. The types of analysis attempted in this process are the following:

(*i*) *Business Analysis:* Under this head, the risks involved in operations of the companies are examined, namely, *industry risk,* with competition from others, market factors, demand and supply position, govt. policies, etc. *Marketing risk* with competitive advantages or disadvantages, market share, selling and distribution network. Quality of customer service, *operating efficiency* involved in locational advantages, labour co-operation, cost efficiency and operating margins and lastly *legal* position, as reflected in security offered, Trust Deed and Trustee's reputation, etc.

(*ii*) *Financial Analysis:* Under this head, the rating agency examines the *accounting* quality under methods of depreciation, income recognition, treatment of bad debts, contingent liabilities, etc. *Earnings protection,* under projection of future earnings, EPS, profitability ratios, proportion of interest to G.P. and N.P., etc., *Adequacy of cash flows,* reflected in working capital management, current ratio, inventory to sales, etc., and *financial flexibility,* examined in terms of capital financing plans, flexibility in financing through alternative methods, planning methods and their flexibility.

(*iii*) *Management Evaluation:* This is examined in relation to track record of promoters, managers and top executives, their qualifications and experience, planning and control systems, capacity to adjust with flexibility, foresight to meet adverse situations, goal setting, monitoring and evaluation with a view to achieve goals.

(iv) Regulatory and Competitive Environment: This is assessed in terms of the structure and regulatory framework of the financial system, the efficiency of operations of the regulatory authorities, trends in regulation or deregulation and the reactions of the competitors to regulations, etc.

(*v*) *Fundamental Analysis:* Under this head, the rating agency considers the company's *liquidity management*, capital, structure, debt leverage, long-term solvency, short-term solvency, matching of cash inflows to outflows and ratio analysis of the company. It will also consider assets quality, in terms credit risk management, receivables to current assets, systems of monitoring the sector credit, individual customer risk and management of problem credits. The company's *profitability* and financial position is also analysed, through study of historic profits, spread on funds deployment, revenues on non-fund based services, accretion to reserves, profit margins, etc. Besides, the impact of *interest and tax rate* changes on company's net profits is analysed. The interest as a proportion of cash inflows or of gross profits is also used to examine the interest burden and potential for future earnings and the impact of debt burden on them is analysed. These and many more of such fundamental factors of the company are also analysed.

Risk and Credit Rating

All investments are risky and debt instruments carry a risk less than that of equity. Besides risk on debt instruments is easier to assess, but the residual risk of equityholders is unlimited. The debt instruments only are thus credit rated. The risk on these instruments can be known to investors before investing in these instruments.

Confidentiality of Information

The information supplied to the credit trading agency is confidential and many times during discussions, they come to know a lot more information than the public know. Under these conditions, rating agency is under an oath of secrecy. The agency only gives the grading to the company and does not publicise it without the permission of the company, while the company itself is free to use it or not. If not satisfied with one rating agency, it may go to another.

Subjective factors in Assessment: The agency rating has no fixed formula and it has to encounter a number of subjective elements like management quality, asset quality, auditor's quality, accounting accuracy, etc. Despite the highly competent and experienced staff, the credit rating agency can give only an indication and cannot claim any foolproof and 100% reliability of its assessment.

Rating in India

The rating work in India is in its infancy and it has drawn heavily on the experience of USA and UK. With the setting up of CARE in the private sector, it has now opened up competition among rating agencies and efficiency and cost-effectiveness will be taken into account. The govt. policy is to make rating compulsory in future for all debt instruments including deposits and other instruments of raising both short-term and long-term debt. These ratings have to be updated on a quarterly basis.

Credit rating agencies are brought under the regulaion of SEBI in recent years and SEBI has isued a set of guidelines to them. Now all registered NBFCs have to be compulsorily rated, if they accept deposits, from the public.

CRISIL (Credit Rating and Information Services of India Ltd.)

The CRISIL was set up in 1988 jointly by the ICICI, UTI, LIC, GIC, SBI and ADB along with a number of other financial institutions. The objective of this institution is to rate the debt obligations of Indian companies on a voluntary basis with a view to providing the investors a guide as to the risk of timely payment of interest and principal by the company. The rating is at present confined only to fixed deposits, debentures, preference shares and short-term instruments like commercial paper. The CRISIL does not rate equity shares or the performance of the company as a whole. The ratings are specifically meant for the instruments referred to above.

CRISIL Rating and Investor Protection

Investors should also be familiar with the ratings given by the Credit Rating and Information Services of India Ltd. (CRISIL) for protecting their interests. The CRISIL ratings are given only for debt instruments of companies, namely, Commercial Papers (CP), debentures, bonds and fixed deposits. Since early 1992, the ratings of Investment Information and Credit Rating Agency (ICRA) are also used by companies. These are given on a voluntary basis and may be publicised or not, depending upon the company's own perception of the impact of these on the investors. The ratings in use by the companies are published by the CRISIL in their "CRISIL Rating Scan". The companies use them only when the ratings are favourable to them and when they are making any public offer for deposits or debentures, etc. The investors should examine these symbols with regard to their benefits and their implication. Since a rating given can be revised upwards or downwards, the investors should keep a watch on any such revisions. Unfortunately, the CRISIL itself would not publicise them for the benefit of the investors as it is a private and autonomous organisation and is under no obligation to do so. The SEBI guidelines now insist that all companies should get these ratings and publicise them compulsorily, if they are borrowing through issue of debentures. Many companies accepting fixed deposits are also using these CRISIL ratings. Rating of company deposits is made compulsory under the new companies Bill 1993. RBI has made rating compulsory for all registered NBFCs which raise deposits from public.

The implications of the rating used are as follows:

For Debentures, simple 'A' and 'B' are used; for preference shares, 'Pf' is prefixed. For fixed deposits and short-term instruments, 'F' and 'P' are prefixed.

Debenture Ratings		*Implication*
Triple A — (AAA)	—	Highest Safety
Double A — (AA)	—	High Safety
Single A — (A)	—	Adequate Safety
Triple B — (BBB)	—	Moderate Safety
Double B — (BB)	—	Inadequate Safety
B, C and D	—	High risk and default-prone
Fixed Deposits Ratings		
F Triple A — (FAAA)	—	Highest Safety
F Double A — (FAA)	—	High Safety
F Single A — (FA)	—	Adequate Safety

FB, FC and FD are inadequate, high-risk and default-prone instruments.

ICRA

Another Credit Rating Agency was set up later, namely, The Investment Information and Credit Rating Agency of India Limited, registered in 1991, sponsored by the IFCI and a number of other financial institutions. It has its headquarters at Delhi, while the CRISIL has its headquarters in Mumbai.

Credit rating is now mandatory for all debt instruments issued by the companies both short-term and long-term. The debentures of both convertible and non-convertible nature require credit rating, whether they are convertible within 18 months, or not.

As investments have a risk, investor should know the extent of the risk he is taking. For this, risk rating is necessary, particularly now when interest rates on debentures are freed. Debentures, bonds, preference shares and fixed deposits are eligible to be rated. The rating is instrument-wise but not for the whole company. The ratings given by the credit rating agency like ICRA are indicators of the correct opinion of the relative capability of timely servicing of debts and obligations by the company.

The ratings given are AAA, AA or A for safety, BBB, BB or B for less safe investments C and D indicate no safety and default respectively. But as equities are essentially risky and investor is willingly entering the risky investment of equity, credit rating for equity is neither possible nor necessary. Only in respect of debt instruments, investor wants to avoid risk and so he should know the extent of the risk, he is taking. Equity-holder is the owner and takes risk voluntarily while the debentureholder is creditor and he does not want to take risk in respect of interest or in payment of the principal. But more recently, even equity is being rated by some agencies.

Factors Considered

In evaluating the instruments in question, any credit rating agency takes into account the various risks involved in servicing of instruments. They undertake business analysis, financial analysis, management evaluation and fundamental analysis. They also take into account the regulatory and competitive environment faced by the company and other relevant factors.

In business analysis, the agency takes into account the legal position in terms of prospectus, memorandum, articles of association, etc., industry risk, demand and supply position for the company's products, market share of the company and its operational efficiency. In financial analysis, the agency evaluates the accounting quality of the company, its inventory norms, depreciation policy and its accounting and audit methods. The financial flexibility is shown in the capital structure, methods of raising funds, adequacy of working capital funds, cash flows and earnings protection, etc.

The CRISIL also evaluates the management risk as judged by the track record of the management, planning and control system, managerial expertise, tax planning and expansion plans of the company. In general, the goals and objectives of the company, its sales and assets growth, capacity to overcome adverse economic and market conditions, etc., will be assessed by the CRISIL.

Under fundamental analysis, evaluation is carried out for the equity earnings per share, book value, capital and sales turnover, management, debt-equity ratio, current assets to liabilities ratio, contingent liabilities, etc. Besides, the asset quality will be judged by the risk element of various assets and interest and tax sensitivity of the company and its profitability position in general.

Ratings

All the above types of analysis will be done by experts after discussions with the company executives, its suppliers, customers and market competitors. The information is gathered on a confidential basis and assessed with a view to examine the capacity of the company to service the instruments issued to the public.

Broadly, there are three categories of ratings:

(*a*) Long-term Instruments (Debentures and Preference Shares)	Triple A to triple B
(*b*) Medium-term Instruments (Fixed Deposits)	FAAA to FA
(*c*) Short-term Instruments (C.P., etc.)	P_1 + to P_3

The rating indicates the degree of risk and the highest safety possible is under the rating of AAA or FAAA or P_1. The creditworthiness is indicated in the ratings and reflects the capacity of the company to service them adequately with a view to ensure the timely payment of interest and principal.

Advantages

For the company a good rating from CRISIL will help raise funds in the capital market. Although many companies have got their instruments evaluated by CRISIL to get an independent view of their credit standing, a few only have publicised them. For the investors these ratings help them in making a decision of their investment in various instruments. Besides such ratings have a demonstration effect and improve competitiveness of the companies to outperform each other. The services of CRISIL are charged to the company and the use of the rating is left to the choice of the company. If it chooses not to use it, it is free do so. This rating is also updated from time to time by the CRISIL whenever additional information is available and compulsorily every year. The lay public and the investors would benefit from such information about the performance of the company and their servicing capacity. This will in turn help to improve the climate of investment and the tone of the capital market. Under the latest guidelines rating is compulsory for all issues of debentures, either convertible or non-convertible even if their maturity period is less than 18 months. It is made compulsory for deposits raised from the public by NBFCs. Rating agencies charge their fees for doing this work to the company.

CARE

A new credit rating agency was set up in April 1993 in the private sector and many more have come up later, when credit rating became compulsory for all debt instruments. The new institution is called the Credit Analysis and Research Limited for its activity of credit analysis and rating. The objects and functions of CARE are the same as those of CRISIL and ICRA. Companies will now have a better choice in entrusting the work of rating of their debt instruments issued to the public. The choice will be based on the efficiency and cost-effective service given by the various credit rating agencies. CARE has started operations in November 1993 and their operations increased faster than that of ICRA.

Duff and Phelps

This is a recently set up credit rating agency in the private sector with foreign collaboration. It has started rating the companies' debt instruments since 1996. It has provided effective competition to the existing agencies.

All agencies are expected to publicise the ratings and also update the ratings on a quarterly basis. SEBI has given guidelines for rating function and brought them under its regulatory framework.

CRAs are required to attain a minimum net worth of ₹5 crore. They are prohibited from rating the instruments floated by their promoters and also borrowers of promoters' institutions.

Fitch Ratings (India) Ltd.

Fitch Ratings India Ltd., is also a rating agency, which is a 100% owned subsidiary of a foreign company. It is recognised by the SEBI for its operations in India.

SME Rating Agency (India) Ltd., is the sixth rating agency to be recognised by the SEBI for its operations in India. It also rating the instruments of corporates issued to public for their credit rating. The six rating agencies are CRISIL, ICRA, CARE, Duff and Phelps, and FITCH Ratings.

✠ ✠ ✠

ROLE OF REGISTRARS

19

Who are Registrars?

Registrars are a class of intermediaries in the capital market, who are important for investor services of various kinds, such as collection of data on applications for new issues, tabulation, their classification and allotment of shares to applicants and despatch of allotment letters and/or refund orders, etc. They are expected to arrange for payments to underwriters, brokers and other agents involved in the marketing of new issues and undertake all activities connected with new issue management until the shares are listed on the stock exchange. If they also act as transfer agents for the securities of the company, then they keep the registers of shareholders, effect endorsements, arrange for splits, consolidation of shares, transfer of shares, give notices for calls, arrange for receipt of call money, endorsements of moneys paid and do all incidental and consequential acts in both the primary and secondary markets.

Categories of Registrars

As per the SEBI guidelines, Registrars to Issues (RI) and Securities Transfer Agents (STA) are the two categories of issue house managers in the capital market. The RI is responsible for all activities ranging from designing of application forms to processing and despatch of refunds or allotment letters. The STA on the other hand undertakes all investor services in the secondary market, such as transfers, splits, consolidation of shares, etc. The SEBI has laid down a code of conduct for them and practices and procedures to be followed.

Appointment of Registrars to Issue

Registrars to be eligible to be appointed by the company, should have been registered with the SEBI. To be registered with the SEBI, the criteria adopted are the competency and expertise, adequacy and quality of manpower, their track record, adequate infrastructure such as computers, data storage space, etc., and capital adequacy for the work. The tenure of authorisation and terms, etc., are laid down by the SEBI. A code of conduct is also laid down for their observance.

The company appoints the merchant bankers and in consultation with them the registrars and other agencies for new issue management. Although all these agencies have to work together, the Registrars have a major role, next to merchant bankers, particularly in respect of servicing of investors. The company has to keep a deposit of 1% of the issue with the Stock Exchange.[@]

Pre-issue Role

1. They help identifying the collection centres and attend all the meetings of the company with merchant bankers for arrangements. The minimum number of collection centres was first reduced to 30 instead of 57 as earlier, which has been further reduced to 4 in 1995.
2. Suggest draft application form to the merchant bankers.
3. Assist in opening collection accounts with banks.
4. Send detailed instructions to collecting branches, for collecting of applications along with cheques, drafts, stock invest, etc., and remittance of funds.
5. Make arrangements for controlling banks' meeting and workout the modalities of receiving the collection figures on a regular basis until the subscription list is closed.

Role during the Currency of Issue

1. Receive the collection figures in the evening of everyday.
2. Tabulate and classify the collection data on the basis of the standard pro forma of slabs of shares applied for.
3. Keep the merchant bankers and the company informed of the data on progressive totals of subscriptions.
4. When the company closes the issue, stock exchange (regional) has to be kept informed of the closure. From then onwards, registrar's work of allotment will start under tight time schedule. They have to keep the regional stock exchange informed of the progress of the work.

Pre-allotment Work

1. Procure all application forms from the collecting bankers and segregate invalid application forms, like those of minors, odd lots, multiple applications, no signatures, etc.
2. Of the valid applications, segregate cash, cheque and stock invest applications and group them into category-wise lists. Stock Invest Method of payment of application money was discontinued in mid-nineties, due to change in practices.
3. During the tabulation for reclassification, record the in-house control number and capture all relevant data under new numbers.
4. Prepare the lists with inverted numbers and then approach the regional stock exchange for finalising the basis of allotment, in the event of oversubscription.
5. Finalise the allotment as per the basis approved by the exchange.

Post-allotment Work[@@]

1. Letters of allotment and refund orders are kept ready after getting them printed. They have to be mailed on or before 30 days from the closing date of subscription. For any delay beyond that they have to seek the permission of the Registrar of Companies and the relevant regional stock exchange. With the introduction of Demat form of share allotment, allotment letters are expected to be posted within a few days as per the SEBI guidelines (a fortnight to one month).

[@] As a refundable amount, if the terms of listing of the issue are satisfied by the company.

[@@] The company has to arrange for payments to all intermediaries in the market such as merchant bankers, collecting bankers, registrars, etc.

2. Submit all statements to the company for their final approval before posting.
3. Arrange to pay the brokerage to brokers and underwriting commission to underwriters and submit their relevant statements to the Stock Exchange before listing.
4. Observe the rules under the Companies Act, Listing Agreement and govt. policy guidelines and assist the company in getting these allotted shares listed on the stock exchange.

Registrars and I.P.O.s

The role of Registrars in the primary market has declined significantly from the boom period of 1992-97 in the primary market. The number of new issues and the amounts raised by the non-Government Public Limited Companies have declined during the post-1997-98 period due to sluggish secondary market, recourse to external commercial borrowing and private placements by the corporates. During the last decade since 1997, the resource mobilisation through private placement has grown by two or three times, mainly due to the banks and financial institutions both in the private and public sector. There were very few public offerings by manufacturing and service sectors and they were made through *"Book Building"* process with a request for bids in wholesale and retail within a range of share prices of ceiling and floor. The interest of retail investors has considerably dwindled during these years due to market volatility and investor disenchantment with stock and capital markets.

Complaints against Registrars

Despite the fact that they are licensed by the SEBI, on the basis of their competence and expertise in the field, quality of staff and their reputation, complaints have been increasing. As referred to earlier, rules and regulations to be followed and the code of conduct to be observed by them are all set out by the SEBI. Besides, they have to submit to the SEBI, periodical reports on the following particulars and any others as may be specified by the SEBI:

—"The issues in respect to which they are acting as Registrars and the agreements they entered into with the companies, the number and nature of investor complaints and time taken to redress the grievances, statistical analysis of the time taken for various activities before allotment and after allotment."

The Registrars have an onerous responsibility in tabulating and classifying the applications, weeding out the duplicate and multiple applications, segregating the invalid applications and reclassifying the valid applications eligible for allotments in the event of oversubscription, prepare the final list of allottees, to get the approval of the stock exchange for the actual allotment and despatch of allotment letters and/or refund orders within the time period allowed by the stock exchange. Many malpractices have been reported, due to some unscrupulous Registrars and investor complaints have been increasing. The SEBI has been nominating a public representative to oversee the allotment procedure and practice by the registrars. Proportional allotment has been prescribed to reduce discretion, and possible malpractices by Registrars in the event of oversubscription. The SEBI control on Registrars and Merchant Bankers has become stricter.

Delay in Despatch of Allotment Letters or Refund Orders

Investors in the New Issues Market fill in application forms along with pay order or cheque for the amount to be paid with application form. They have to be sent letters of allotment or refund orders. They may sometimes get allotment advice which is not transferable if a share certificate is to be sent and not a letter of allotment. This has to be done within 30 days from the last day of subscription.

Some Registrars do not observe the time limits set for them by the government and the Stock Exchanges.

Under Section 73 of the Companies Act, the company which has been permitted to be listed on any Stock Exchange has an obligation to repay the excess money within a time limit to the applicants in the event of oversubscription to the issue. Besides the manner of allotment in such cases has to be approved by the Stock Exchange, where the company's shares will be listed. After the company has followed those guidelines of the Exchange, the compliance certificate and the distribution schedule of applications have to be submitted to the Exchange.

The Registrars should despatch the allotment letters or refund orders within a time limit of 30 days from the date of the closure of subscription list. The amount of more than ₹1,500 have to be sent by warrants under registered post. If any excess monies are not refunded within this time limit after giving an allowance of 8 days as grace period, the company becomes liable to pay interest on everyday of default at the rate varying from 4% for a delay of less than 15 days to 15% for delay more than 60 days. The company has to file with the regional Stock Exchange a statement signed by the chief executive within 5 working days that the allotment letters and refund orders are despatched within the prescribed time limit. Non-compliance with these conditions will be punishable by the stock exchange and by other competent authorities. The Stock Exchanges have been given powers to monitor compliance of these conditions.

As early as in 1986, the government has issued an order to the companies to send by registered post only, the Refund Orders, Allotment Letters and Certificates. Besides, refund orders should be marked 'Account Payee' and encashable at par in the place of the applicant.*

As per the listing agreement of the Stock Exchange, the company would have agreed that the letters of allotment and letters of regret should be issued simultaneously. If the company finds it difficult to do this, it should issue a Press statement to the effect that letters of allotment are being posted and they will be followed later by Refund Orders.

In case, Refund Orders do not come within the time limit referred to above, including the grace period, investor can claim interest for the delayed period under Section 73 (2A) of the Companies Act. Any default of action under Section 73 (2A) attracts a penalty of ₹5,000 on the officers of the company under Section 73(2B). In case, refund order does not come even after 6 months, punishment to the company officers extends to imprisonment for a term up to one year. Under 621 of the Companies Act, the Investor can also proceed against the company for criminal breach of Section 73 (2A).

The investors are advised to contact first the Regional Stock Exchange concerned regarding the delay in getting letters of allotment or Refund Orders. It is possible, the company has been granted permission by the Stock Exchange and Registrar of the Companies to exceed the time limits for genuine reasons of a large number of investors, troubles of the collecting bank or large volume of the workload involved. If such extension of time is not granted by the authorities and the delay is not explained by the Company through a press release and through the competent authorities like Stock Exchange, then the Investor has a right to make a complaint to the Department of Company Affairs and to the Registrar of the Companies. The same complaint could also be made to SEBI which will take action against the erring companies under Section 27 of the SEBI Act. All these complaints should be addressed to the SEBI, Mittal Court, B Wing, Nariman Point, Mumbai 400 021. The SEBI has powers to regulate the working of Registrars to the issue, bankers to the issue and merchant bankers etc., under Section 11 of the SEBI Act. This power read with Section 27 of that Act, empowers the SEBI to take penal action against the issue managers for any investor complaints regarding the delay or non-despatch of refund orders/or allotment letters.

The Stock Exchange can also take action under the listing agreement, but these powers are limited to pursuasion and a threat of delisting or suspension of trading in that company's securities. But the latter measures are not in the interest of investors due to loss of liquidity for their investments. These complaints to SEBI should not debar the investor from making complaints under the Companies Act Section 73 (2B) or Section 621, to file criminal proceedings before the court or to make complaints to the Registrar of the Companies/Department of Company Affairs.

* Under the amended guidelines, they can be sent under certificate of posting also to save in rising costs of new issues.

The same process of complaints and the letters of grievances can be adopted for delayed return of Debenture Certificates, Debenture Allotment Letters or Refund Orders for Debenture Applications. Lastly mention may also be made of investors' right to approach the District Forum or State Forum, *viz.,* State Consumer Redressal Commission or District Consumer Forum in the respective States. When the complaint is made to the Stock Exchange, it should be addressed to the regional Stock exchange of the company and to the officer-incharge of the Investors Grievances Cell. Most important of all, the timely submission of the complaints to the respective authorities soon after the time has expired is necessary.

District and State Consumer Redressal forums may not take up cases of public who are not actual but potential investors, as they have to come under the definition of consumers. Secondly, a money claim or loss should be involved in such cases for consumer forum to take up the case.

Delay in Listing of New Issues

Investors put their money in shares and debentures for some definite advantages that they have over other investments, namely, marketability, safety, income and appreciation. Of these the marketability is most important, as when they want funds back, they can disinvest these shares and debentures, which is possible only when these are listed on a Stock Exchange. Thus, the time of listing is important for investors. Investors wait for nearly 1 to 3 months, to get letters of allotment and share certificates during which period their money is tied up. If there is any delay in listing, this facility of disinvestment will be denied for a further period. So delay in listing is a major complaint of investors in the stock market.

Legal Provisions

A public limited company which intends to offer shares or debentures to the public for subscription by the issue of prospectus shall have to get these securities listed on one or more Stock Exchanges, under Section 73 of the Companies Act. Before such issue is made, the company is required to apply to the Stock Exchange for permission to be traded. If such permission is considered, the allotment and shares certificates are all subject to the permission and approval of the Stock Exchange, under the Listing Agreement to be entered into between the company and the Stock Exchange.

The listing is to be done on a recognised Stock Exchange. The prospectus should state in which Stock Exchange or Exchanges the application for listing has been made.

Of these Stock Exchanges, the Principal Stock Exchange for the company is the one in whose area the registered office of the company is located.

Under Section 21 of the SC (R) Act the government has the power, which is now exercised by the SEBI, to compel any public company to get its shares listed on the Stock Exchange. The government has exercised this power many times and with the result the schemes of UTI like Master Shares and of many Mutual Funds have been listed on the Stock Exchanges. This has helped the provision of liquidity to these schemes so listed much more than what it would have been.

Allotment of New Issues of Listed Companies

Section 69 of the Companies Act has laid down the conditions for making the allotment. Allotment refers to the division of share capital into definite shares of a particular value, in terms of equity or debenture and assignment of such shares to different persons. This section laid down the allotment of shares designed to be listed and allotment should be done in consultation with the Stock Exchange. Allotment should not be done unless a minimum amount of 90% of the issue offered has been subscribed for. As per the present guidelines, all issues offered to the public need not be fully underwritten. Despite this, if only 90% of the subscribed amount has been collected by the company, the application moneys received from the public are to be returned within 120 days from the last date of subscription.

If a company received oversubscription, it cannot retain any amount in excess of the amount notified for subscription, as per the latest guidelines of the SEBI.

In such cases of over subscription, there should be a minimum allotment of 100 shares of ₹10/- each per applicant. The pattern of allotment is also laid down under the guidelines. This power of laying down guidelines and approving the allotment is given to the Stock Exchanges, where its shares are being listed.

Listing Formalities

The listing application has to be submitted to the exchange where it is proposed to be listed. This should comprise of:

(*i*) Letter of Application

(*ii*) Form of Application

(*iii*) Supporting Documents

(*iv*) Distribution Schedules

(*v*) Listing Agreement.

All listed companies are expected to have allotment letters and share certificates of a standard form and size, as approved by the Exchange. They are also expected to observe the following rules:

(*i*) Allotment should be done in marketable lots.

(*ii*) Minimum allotment is 100 shares of ₹10/- each.

(*iii*) Preparation of certificates to be mechanised, with separate serial numbers for each series.

(*iv*) The allotment should be completed within 30 days, from the date of closure of subscription list.

(*v*) Allotment letters and certificates should be sent by registered post before the expiry of the time limit.

(*vi*) Refund orders should be sent at the same time by cheque a/c payee, payable at par at the place of the applicant.

(*vii*) If these refund orders are not sent within 30 days, as indicated above, then the companies will have to pay interest on the amount to be refunded.

If the company is in default in refunding within the time limit and even after a grace period of 8 days, the company and its directors are liable to repay the money with interest which may vary from 4% for delays of less than 15 days to 15% for delays of more than 60 days.

The letter of application to the Stock Exchange for listing should be forwarded to the Exchange before filing the prospectus with the Registrar of Companies.

Listing of the shares of a company will be done only after the company has despatched the letters of allotment and a certificate to that effect is produced from the company secretary and/or the auditors. After all the other formalities are observed permission to trade and to get a quotation will be given by the Stock Exchanges within 7 days after that. If for any reason these formalities could not be completed within the time limit, the Stock Exchange can grant extension of time if it is satisfied of the reasons therefor.

Listing Complaints

If there is a complaint of investor in respect of delay of listing, such investor should contact the regional Stock Exchange for that company asking for the reasons for the delay in listing. Failing to get a satisfactory reply within a reasonable time, the investor should complain to the Investors' grievance cell of the SEBI — Mittal Court, 'B' Wing, Nariman Point, Mumbai-400 021.

Delay and Non-delivery of Shares after Transfer by the Company

The object of all transactions in securities is delivery of shares which will entitle the holder to the privileges as the owner or creditor of the company to dividends, interest, rights, bonus, etc. The law relating to transfer of shares is laid down under Sections 108 to 113 of Companies Act and Section 22 A of S C(R) Act.

The Transfer Deed (Form 7B) under Section 108 should be properly filled in and stamped and signed before presenting to the company for effecting the transfer. Here the transferee or buyer has a responsibility for filling up the T.D. properly before presentation. A few examples of care to be taken by him are as follows:

(1) Avoiding overwriting or mistakes of omission and commission.

(2) The name of the company should be spelt as given in the Share Certificate.

(3) The value of stamps affixed should be as per the Stamp Act say Paise 50 per ₹100 of the Purchase Price of the Shares and they have to be cancelled.

(4) The value of the shares should be as per listed official quotations on the day of the execution of order.

(5) Signature of the Transferor should tally with that in the company's register.

(6) The signatures of Transferors in the case of joint holders should be in the order in which the names appear.

There are a number of other conditions for a valid transfer deed to bind the company for effecting the transfer. Most importantly, the Transfer Deed should not be time barred and should be within 12 months of the date of stamping by a competent authority like Registrar of Company or Book closure of the Company whichever is later. The Transfer Deed is valid for 12 months in the case of listed companies and 2 months for non-listed companies.

Companies Act enjoins on the company to register the shares and deliver within 2 months from the date of presentation and refusal to transfer for any valid reason such as listed below should be intimated to the transferor and transferee giving reasons for refusal to transfer. As per the listing agreement between the company and the Stock Exchange (Clause 3 (C)), only one month time is given to effect transfer. Any delay beyond this period, has to be permitted by the Stock Exchange.

Section 22(A) of the SCR Act has made it obligatory to register transfer of shares except for four valid reasons. The responsibility for proving the reasons for non-transfer is laid on the company and that has to be done within 2 months of the lodgement of shares. The reasons for refusal to transfer are as follows:

(1) Technical defects in the Transfer Deed or Share Certificate in which case the company has powers to refuse the transfer without referring to Company Law Board.

(2) The transfer of a security is in contravention of any law as MRTP Act or FERA.

(3) The transfer is prohibited under any Court Order or a Tribunal.

(4) The transfer may result in a change in the composition of Board and destabilise the management.

In the case of last three reasons, the refusal to transfer can be decided by the Company Law Board whose decision is final. A decision to refuse has to be made by the company within two months for the transfer and the decision has to be intimated to the transferor and transferee and the final decision is to be left to the Company Law Board.

For non-transfer and refusal to intimate the transferor and transferee by the company of the non-transfer or delay in effecting the transfer, the investor has the following remedies:

The preventive remedies are to ensure that the law and rules relating to transfer are observed by the transferee and transferor. The buyer should have sent the documents to the Transfer agents or share Transfer

Department and not to the Registered Office of the company, unless the Transfer Department is also located in the Registered Office. The details with regard to this and the addresses of these are available with the Stock Exchanges. Thus, in the case of Tata Timken, the Registered Office is Tata Centre, 43, Chouringhee Road, Kolkata but the address of Registrars and Transfer agents is ABC Computers Pvt. Ltd., 43.3, Hazra Road, Kolkata. If the investor sends it to the Registered Office it is likely to be delayed and even misplaced if it is not sent by Registered Post with Acknowledgement Due. The time taken by the company will be longer in this case.**

Secondly, the investors should check-up with the Stock Exchange — or Registrar of Companies whether the company is given extension of time beyond the limits permitted as per the rules for effecting the transfer. This is the case sometimes at the time of book closure. All the correspondence with the company should be done through Registered Post with Acknowledgement Due. If the company refuses to reply even after the lapse of two months permitted for effecting transfer and despite repeated reminders, then under the Companies Act, the investor can apply to the Company Law Board within two months of intimation of refusal, or 4 months from the lodgement of shares for transfer if the company fails to respond to the investor. The investor in Andhra Pradesh under the jurisdiction of Hyderabad Stock Exchange can apply to the Company Law Board of Southern Region, namely, Bench Officer, Company Law Board, Southern Region Bench, Block 1, 5th Floor, Shastri Bhavan, 26, Hoddows Road, Chennai-35. He can also apply to the Grievances Cell of the Hyderabad Stock Exchange, Himayat Nagar, Hyderabad- 29 if it is a regional Stock Exchange for that company. Alternatively or in addition to the above, he can file a complaint to SEBI, Mittal Court, 'B' Wing, First Floor, Nariman Point, Mumbai-400 021.

Any delay beyond the permitted period by the company is punishable as per the Government Press Note dated 11.1.91. Sections 111 and 113 of the Companies Act deal with the subject. Section 111 enjoins on the company the obligation to intimate the transferor and transferee the refusal to transfer and the reasons therefor. Under Section 113, the company has to register the shares in their books within two months from the date of receipt of the concerned share certificates along with a valid Transfer Deed properly executed. The Company's power of refusal on any ground was taken away from the company; the only ground on which they can refuse is the improper execution of transfer deed or signatures not tallying or not properly stamped, etc. The power to refuse transfer formally lies with the Board of Directors. If the decision to refuse is made, it has to be referred to Company Law Board under SC (R) Act, by the company.

Sometimes, the delay by the companies may be due to internal difficulties of the company such as pressure of work or time for closure of accounts or for the coming new issues or rights, etc. The delay may also be *malafide* to reduce the floating stock in the market to jack up their prices.

In all these cases, complaints have to be made to the Registrar of Companies, the Stock Exchange and the SEBI. The investor can himself sue the company under Section 621 or request the Registrar to do so, if needed.

The Consumer Protection Forums can also take up such cases of investor grievances. In Andhra Pradesh, the State Consumer Disputes Redressal Forum, located in Secunderated can take up the complaints of investors in respect of their rights such as refund of allotment money, etc. In each State, the District and State level forums of this type exist to take up the complaints of the above nature. The State Forums take up cases above ₹1 lakh and District Forums for cases below ₹1 lakh.

Many Investors have also complained that the Registrars of Companies do not take any action and they also do not respond to the investors promptly. The reason for the indifference on the part of companies and the Registrar of Companies may be attributed to some defects or lapses on the part of the investors themselves due to ignorance of the law and procedures and practices relating to transfer of shares. Many investors commit mistakes, and errors of omission and commission are taking place in respect of the Transfer Deed and signatures and stamps paid.

** In the case of All Season Foods the Registered office is at Nasik, but the Share Department is at Nariman Point in Mumbai.

Some Investors also commit frauds and counterfeit signatures; they also produce false certificates or sell certificates which are not transferable or there was no proper verification and witnessing of the signatures. Some certificates may be under prohibitory orders of a court because of a dispute between the two parties, regarding the ownership of the shares.

Sometimes shares in the name of minors, or in benami names are introduced in the markets and sent for transfers. Some Investors also sell third party certificates, without producing a proper power of attorney.

A number of malpractices are being effected by investors themselves and the victims of these frauds are other investors and buyers, whose shares when sent for transfer to the company are kept in abeyance. These shares will get blocked up subsequently, when any suspicion arises regarding bonafides of signatures or of the transfer deed, the company will be forced to keep such application in suspense.

Although as per law, they have to inform both the transferor and transferee within two months of the receipt of the application for the transfer, the companies do not comply in such cases due to the unconfirmed doubts of the company, laziness and inefficiency of the staff etc.

Sometimes the Companies might have sent letters through certificate of posting to the transferor and the transferee and they are found missing. It is also possible that investors do not take proper care to inform the company of any change in their addresses or to correct any mistakes in their addresses. Investors also take this matter in a casual manner and do not take prompt action. All this will not justify the actions of the companies and their duties to send letters of refusal, to the transferee within two months.

The Companies are also bound to send all the correspondence by Registered Post which they do not observe. Thus non-receipt of transfer advice or share certificate duly transferred within two months as required as per law is not complained. Thereafter, immediate reminders to the Company and complaints to stock exchange and registrar of companies are not made by the investors.

Investors are also ignorant of the rules of how to make and when to make and to whom to make complaints. Thus, if the company does not respond and does not effect transfer within 2 months and not intimate the reason for refusal to transfer, the Investor should complain within 4 months from the date of the lodgement of the Share Certificates for transfer with the Company. He should make a written complaint to the CLB and also follow the rules of making a complaint with the CLB on an approved format.

It will thus be seen that the complaints of investors will arise partly due to their own lapses and ignorance and partly due to the fault of the company including malpractices, such as reducing the available supply of shares in the market and deliberate delay to protect the interest of some interested parties among the investors. Many companies also commit mistakes due to their own ignorance of staff problems and mistakes of their own staff. It is therefore necessary, that each of the complaints of the Investors should be examined in detail to find out the reasons for delay in transfers and the return of the share Certificates.

Non-Receipts of "Rights" Offers

Legal Provisions

Section 81 of the Companies Act has provided for further issues of capital, in the form of Rights under certain conditions, *viz.*,

(1) After two years of the formation of the company.

(2) After the expiry of one year from the date of allotment of shares made for the first time after its formation.

(3) Either of the above and whichever is earlier.

(4) During that period if the company has proposed to increase capital by allotment of further shares, they have to issue compulsorily rights to the existing shareholders in proportion to their holdings.

Under Section 81 (I-A), a special resolution can be passed in the general meeting of the company that such rights offers should be made not only to the persons who are on the registers of the company but any public member can accept such rights.

Such offer should be accepted within 15 days of the offer failing which, the offer will lapse.* Such Rights offers to public under Section 81 (I-A) should be by a special resolution in the general meeting. But if a simple majority of voting procedure has been used for passing the resolution, then it has to be accepted by the Central Government, before such issue can be made to the public.

This further issue of shares by the company to its members with rights to renounce them in favour of third party does not require the issue of a prospectus. If within 15 days of the offer of such rights, they are not accepted or renounced in favour of the third party, the Board of Directors may dispose of such shares as they think appropriate.

If such further issue of shares is not made to the existing shareholders, the company and every officer in default shall be punishable under Section 629(A) with a fine of ₹ 500/-. If such rights offers are to be allotted to outsiders, the company has to pass a special resolution authorising the Board to allot such right shares to the public under Section 81 (I-A).

This increase in the capital through rights issue should not increase the paid-up capital beyond the authorised capital. If it increases beyond the authorised capital, the capital clause of the memorandum and articles of the company is to be altered permitting the increase of the authorised capital.

Pre-issue Formalities

The Board has to get the approval of the draft offer of the Rights Application Form from SEBI. The time of issue and the dates for opening and closing of the register for determining the list of shareholders who are eligible for such Rights offer are to be informed to the Registrar of Companies, Stock Exchange where its shares are listed and to SEBI. The issue letter of offer can only be sent to the investors after the SEBI's approval.

A copy of the special resolution authorising such rights issue along with a draft letter of offer and other terms of offer, Application Form, etc., should be submitted within 30 days to Registrar of the Companies under Section 192 of Companies Act. Thereafter, offers are to be sent to the shareholders for their acceptance or rejection. In respect of such Rights not accepted, and for which no applications have been received, the company has to make allotment of them in consultation with the Stock Exchange. The allotment date and the letter of allotment, etc., are to be approved by the Stock Exchange. Right issue has to be kept open for a minimum of 30 days and a maximum of 60 days. The letter of allotment and regret letters if any are to be sent to the members along with the refund orders, within 30 days as in the case of public issues. From the date of allotment within one month, a return on the allotment of shares has to be filed with the Registrar of Companies in Form No. 2. Share Certificates are to be issued to shareholders within 3 months of the date of allotment.

Complaints Regarding Rights

Many complaints are made by the investors of the non-receipt or delayed receipt of the rights offer by the company. Such complaints will arise out of company's negligence to post in time and secondly due to the postal delays. Thirdly change of address of the investor or wrong recording of the address may also lead to non-receipt or delayed receipt of rights offer. It is also possible that company's officers may purposely delay the posting of these offers or post them with an old date so that unsubscribed portion can be allotted to the friends and relatives of the directors.

Under the law, the unsubscribed portion can be allotted by the directors in consultation with the Stock Exchange.

* In case of a listed company, the shareholders will have four weeks' time to accept or reject.

Investors to be on Guard

Many companies announce the Rights well in advance to jack up the share price quotation in the Stock Market. Some investors are attracted by the uptrend in prices at the time of the offer of Right at concessional price and buy them at the high price, in the market, but find to their dismay that prices have fallen after the allotment of rights. The investors are advised to be wary of such companies resorting to malpractices and study the behaviour of prices of such companies and their past track record. Some companies announce the rights but will not issue for months together.

Transfer Agents or Registrars are also negligent due to the staff inefficiency. The change in the address is not recorded for months. The investors should therefore try to get the confirmation that change of address has been effected before the rights are offered.

Under Section 206(A) of the Companies Act, if any transfer application is received by the company but registration is not done, the company is within its right to keep in abeyance such rights offers pending the claim by the transferor or seller. If the transferor advises that the rights be given to the transferee, then the company is bound to send the rights to the buyer.

If any of the above complaints are to be made, the investors are well advised:

(*i*) to keep a track of the dates when the offer is made and the last date for acceptance and renunciation.

(*ii*) to note when is the record date for rights.

(*iii*) to write to the company well before the last date of acceptance asking for the rights quoting his ledger folio and certificate numbers, and non-receipt of the rights offer.

(*iv*) to complain to the proper authorities mentioned above soon after the last date is over but the rights offer has not been received by the investor, from the company despite the notice to the company of such non-receipt.

In all cases, of complaints they have to be made promptly along with the evidence of postal stamping and a copy of the delayed letter of offer which denied him the opportunity to acquire such shares. If no satisfactory reply comes from the company, complaint may be made to the Stock Exchange where it is listed. The same complaint can also be sent to the SEBI for restitution of their right to the offer. Many times, the companies do not reply, if the mistake is on their side. In such cases, the investors are advised to take action without delay, even before the last date of acceptance is over.

Some investors buy such shares in the market as they are likely to issue rights. Since they purchase cum-rights, they expect the rights to come to them. But the seller might get these rights, if the name of the buyer is not registered with the company well before the record date. Any delay or technical defect on the part of the transferee is enough of an excuse for the company to keep such shares in suspense, without registration, thereby disallowing the investor his rights although he has purchased cum-rights.

Annual General Meetings or Special Meetings of Companies

Legal Provisions

The general meeting of the company may be called by giving a notice to the members of not less than 21 days in writing. Shorter notice is permitted only if it is consented to all the members in the case of Annual General Meeting and 95% of the members' consent in the case of any other meeting. Sometimes the articles of the Company may provide for a longer notice of more than 21 days. If the company has advertised the notice of the annual general meeting in daily papers and also sent individual notices to the shareholders, allegation of any investor that he did not receive notice of 21 days in writing will not hold good. Courts will not issue interim injection stopping the meeting. It is possible that the company might have secured the consent letters in Form No. 22A of the companies (Central Government's), general rules and forms of 1956 from members approving delay.

Members controlling 95% of the paid-up share capital having voting rights consent for a shorter notice any objection from dissenting members will not be taken into account. Notice of the meeting of the members of the company can be served by posting letters by Registered Post, or Certificate of Posting. In the case of notice of the meeting, it is deemed to have been served on the member at the expiration of 48 hours after the letter containing the notice is posted. The mode of servicing documents on the members including notice of any meeting of the members of the company is governed by Section 53 of the Companies Act. If the general meeting is called and the conditions of Section 171 are not followed and the notice of less than 21 days is given, then the company and the officer under default are all liable for punishment under Section 629(A).

A notice should mention the place, the date and hour of the meeting and the agenda of business to be transacted. The persons entitled to the notice are the members of the company, holders of shares and persons entitled to the shares as a consequence of the death or insolvency of the member.

Members' Rights

The right of the shareholders to receive the notice of the meeting is a statutory right of the member. So all members of the company whose names appear in the Register of the Company have a right to receive the notice of the meeting. Notice of the meeting addressed in the newspapers, circulating in the neighbourhood of the Registered Office of the company is enough evidence of serving the notice on the member whose address is not with the company. In cases of annual general meetings, ordinary business to be conducted should include consideration of the annual accounts, balance sheet, declaration of dividends, appointment of Directors and Auditors. All other business is deemed to be special business.

Under Section 182 any member cannot be prohibited from attending the meeting and voting on the grounds that he has not held share for any specified period preceding the date of the meeting. A shareholder has no right to claim dividends unless the Board of Directors have recommended a dividend. Besides, a shareholder cannot ask for raising of the dividend recommended by the Board. He could however, ask for a cut in the dividend.

Under Section 206(A) right to dividend can be kept in abeyance if an instrument of transfer has been received by the company for registration, but such transfer could not be affected by the company for any reason. Unclaimed dividends and unpaid dividends have to be transferred to unpaid dividend account maintained by the company. Under Section 219, all the members of the company are entitled to receive copies of balance sheet and other documents within 21 days before the day of meeting.

Non-Receipt of Debenture Interest or Debenture Repayment

The Company Law has provided for issue of equity shares, preference shares, warrants and debentures, among others, by the companies. In recent years, the attractiveness of debentures has increased due to the issue of convertible debentures, with the facility of conversion into equities within a specified period. The government is also keen to develop the debenture market in India in terms of the recommendations of Pherwani Committee and the earlier committees on market reforms. The Mumbai and Delhi Stock Exchanges in addition to NSE have already started special trading sessions for bonds and debentures on trading days.

The problems with regards to debentures are:

(*i*) Non-receipt or delayed receipt of debenture certificate or allotment letters.

(*ii*) Non-receipt or delayed receipt of interest on debentures.

(*iii*) Delay in registering transfers of debenture certificates and

(*iv*) Delay and non-repayment of debenture amount on maturity.

The Company Law has provided that debentures can be issued on the same lines as in the case equity shares by the companies. Section 2 of Companies Act had defined debentures as including debenture stocks, bonds and any other securities of a company whether subject to charge on the assets of the company or not. While shares cannot be issued at discount, debentures stocks can be issued at discount. It is a debt instrument and acknowledges the debt of the company to the investor. It can be convertible or non-convertible, registered or non-registered, secured or unsecured, etc.

At present, debentures should be redeemable compulsorily after a period of say 7 years. Under Section 117, debentures with the voting right cannot be issued.

The Government has issued guidelines for the issue of debentures by Public Limited Companies and also for issue of rights debentures for working capital purposes. Under Section 118, the investors in debentures have a right to secure a copy of the debenture trust deed. The company is bound to supply the same within 7 days of such request even at a price. In terms of the government guidelines (SEBI) any debenture which is not convertible within 18 months is treated as a debt instrument. It has to be issued subject to the appointment of the debenture trustee (financial institution) and the debenture trust deed to be executed within 6 months of the issue of debenture certificates and building of debenture redemption reserve fund from out of the profits with the objective of redeeming debentures. The debenture trustee is responsible to the debentureholders and the latter have a recourse to the debenture trustees in case of any failure on the part of the company in respect of the rights of debentureholders.

Under the existing SEBI guidelines, all convertible debentures, if the conversion is after 18 months and all non-convertible debentures have to be compulsorily rated by a credit rating agency[@@] for the credit standing of these issues, as regards payment of interest and repayment of principal.

For Public Sector Companies, and for debentures which are convertible within 18 months and debentures which are privately placed with financial institutions, credit rating is not compulsory but is optional.

The interest rate offered on the debentures can be decided by the company with the help, if necessary, of merchant bankers, depending on their credit rating. From August, 1991 debenture interest rate ceiling was removed and these interest rates are freed from government controls.

For the issue of debentures, the general guidelines are that these can be issued only after commercial production has started and the debt equity ratio should not exceed 2:1 and any issue of debenture for working capital purposes should not exceed 20% of the gross current assets.

The debenture certificate should have a face value of ₹ 100. These should be listed on a Stock Exchange, if they are issued to the public. A premium of 5% of the face value is allowed to be paid to investors at maturity in the case of non-convertible debentures.

The Trust Deed and the appointment of the Trustee has to be accepted by the SEBI. Any clause in the Trust Deed to indemnify the Trustee is void. The debenture trustee can attend the annual general body meetings of the company and represent the interests of debentureholders. The Trustee is liable for any breach of the terms of the Trust as also the company. Under Section 121, the matured debentures can be reissued but the option of conversion into new debentures has to be given to the debentureholder. The companies are prohibited from issuing debentures which are irredeemable.

The debentures issued to the public are to be secured against the mortgage of assets of the company and the provisions in respect of these are laid down in the Trust Deed. The debenture Trustee can enforce on the company, as per the Trust Deed payment of interest and principal or any other complaints from the investors such as delay in issue of debenture certificates or delay in transfer of debenturs on an application for such transfer. The Trustee has the powers to enforce the provisions of Trust Deed and receive a court degree on

[@@] Investors should note that credit ratings should be AAA (for highest safety) AA (for good safety) or A or A+ for adequate safety. If the ratings are BBB, BB, B they represent moderate and inadequate safety and risky investments.

the company. The latest SEBI guidelines insist on the registration of debenture trustee with the SEBI before a company can appoint them as Trustee.

Under Section 113, every company issuing debentures shall deliver debenture certificates within 3 months of the allotment and in case of application for transfer within 2 months of such application. Time limits prescribed under Section 113 can only be exempted by the Company Law Board. The decision of the Company Law Board has to be implemented by the company within 10 days.

Debentureholder is entitled to copies of balance sheet and annual report under Section 219. The company has to furnish free of cost these reports on demand to the debentureholders. For any complaint with regard to non-delivery of debenture certificates, delay in such delivery or non-payment of interest and principal in time, etc., the debentureholder has to appeal to the debenture trustee as per the Trust Deed. The Debenture Trustee has the power to take up the matter with the company and enforce the rights of investors. The investor in debenturs has no voting right and cannot attend the annual general body meetings, but the Debenture Trustee can do these things on behalf of investors.

All complaints should be addressed to the Debenture Trustee or to SEBI and the Companies Act is silent on the rights of debentureholders. However, he has a right to ask for a copy of the Trust Deed under Section 118 of the Act and if a Debenture Trustee is not appointed, the investor has to write to the company secretary regarding the non-receipt of debenture allotment or certificates and if no satisfactory reply comes the investor should write to the grievance cell of the SEBI, regarding the complaint. The investor can also send a notice under Section 434 asking why the company has not paid interest or the principal amount on maturity, and failing to get any satisfactory reply, investor can also file the winding up petition under Section 433. The investor in debentures can also appeal to the State or National Commission of the consumer protection or district consumer forums for enforcement of his rights. Although legal opinion is divided on the powers of these forums, some of the State and District Forums have taken the case of investors, interpreting them as consumers. For non-receipt of interest and debentures, investors can complain under Section 12 of COPRA before the District Forums or State or National Commissions.

Rules on Fixed Deposits of Companies

The deposits of companies are a form of unsecured loans from the public or promoters and investors of the company. The power to borrow in the form of deposits by companies is vested in the Board of Directors. In terms of the Companies Act, Section 370 Inter-corporate Deposits are also a form of loans but as per Companies (Acceptance of Deposits) Rules, inter-corporate deposits are not considered for the purpose of the limits to total borrowing of the companies. The companies can accept deposits after the resolution passed by the Board of Directors and after giving advertisement in the daily newspapers. Such offer of acceptance of deposits has to be made in terms of the Companies Acceptance of Deposits Rules issued by the Department of Company Affairs. Such advertisement should also contain the statement on the financial position of the company.

These deposits are unsecured and most risky. The assessment of the risk by the credit rating agency is not compulsory in the case of fixed deposits. As such, the investor has no way of knowing the degree of risk that he is exposed to in contributing to the fixed deposits of the companies. Rating was made compulsory for NBFCs registered with RBI in 1997.

Terms of Offer of Fixed Deposits

Invitation to deposits from public for various schemes of deposits are invariably published in newspapers in the form of a statutory advertisement giving the following details:

(*i*) Terms of acceptance of deposits, rate of interest on different maturities, minimum amount of deposits, cumulative or non-cumulative nature of the deposits, etc.

(*ii*) Brief details of the name of the company, date of its incorporation, business carried on by it, places where the company has offices and names and address of directors.

(*iii*) Details of profits and dividends for the last three years.

(*iv*) Summarised financial position of the company (i.e., assets and liabilities) as appearing in the two latest audited balance sheets, along with details of contingent liabilities not provided for.

(*v*) Details regarding maximum amount of deposits which that company can accept.

(*vi*) A specific declaration that deposits accepted are unsecured and would rank *pari passu* with other unsecured liabilities.

(*vii*) A statement of deposits remaining unpaid.

Acceptance of Fixed Deposits

A company cannot accept deposits in excess of 35% of its paid-up capital and free reserves. Of this, 25% deposits can be accepted from the public and the rest 10% from the shareholders of the company. The minimum period of acceptance of deposits is six months and the maximum period is limited to 3 years in the case of non-bank and non-financial companies. The maximum rate of interest that can be offered on deposits cannot exceed 15% per annum which now stands at 11% in 2008 and is now freed from control. A ceiling on brokerage payable on deposits has been fixed at 2%. The interest earned on fixed deposits of companies does not enjoy any exemption from income tax. Neither does the amount of deposit qualify for any exemption under wealth tax. Under the existing provisions of the Income Tax Act, tax on interst paid/ payable is deducted at source if the interest payment exceeds ₹ 2,500 in a financial year unless suitable declaration is furnished by the depositor in regard to the total income of the depositor not exceeding the minimum liable to tax in a financial year.

The acceptance of deposits by non-bank, non-financial companies is governed by the Companies (Acceptance of Deposits) Rules 1975 as amended from time to time. Along with the prescribed application form, the terms of conditions of acceptance of deposits are required to be furnished by companies, to the C.L.B./or Registrar of Companies.

A careful study of either the financial data in the advertisement or the prescribed particulars as available within the application form would generally reveal the working results and financial position of the company.

Regulation of Terms of Acceptance

In order to reduce the misuse of powers given to companies to borrow unsecured deposits, the precautions taken by the government are as follows:

(*i*) Under Rule 3 of the Acceptance of Deposits Rules, the maximum period (3 years) and a minimum period (6 months) are laid down.

(*ii*) Maximum interest rate payable is fixed at 11% for a period of three years but these rates can be varied depending on the credit rating, and interest rate policy of the government and the RBI.

(*iii*) Limits are set on the brokerage to be paid to brokers for securing deposits from the public and would vary from 1 to 2% depending on the period of maturity.

(*iv*) Limits are set on the total quantum of deposits which can be mobilised from the public: (*a*) 10% of the aggregate share capital and free reserves as deposits up to six months from directors, shareholders, etc., (*b*) 25% of the paid-up capital and free reserves from others, namely, public as deposits above six months.

Complaints Regarding Fixed Deposits

These complaints are mainly non-repayment of principal amounts or non-payment of interest or delays in these respects. Section 58 (A) of Companies Act deals with the acceptance of the deposits by the companies. Section 58A (9) has provided for compulsory repayment of maturing deposits. Only the Company Law Board has been empowered to take cognisance of the non-repayment of the deposits or non-payment of interest on fixed deposits, and action can be taken by the C.L.B. for any complaints of investors.

The following types of deposits do not come in the purview of Company Law Board:

(*i*) Deposits made for booking purchases of scooter, car, etc.

(*ii*) Deposits accepted by financial companies like hire-purchase finance company, a housing finance company, an investment company, a loan/mutual benefit financial company, a chit fund company, which are governed by the rules made by the RBI.

(*iii*) Deposits accepted by companies which have been notified as 'relief undertakings' under special laws enacted by various State Governments. Court rulings point to the fact that the monetary liabilities of relief undertakings during the notified period stands suspended and any proceedings including the proceedings for compulsory repayment of deposits under Section 58(A)(9) shall accordingly remain stayed.

(*iv*) Deposits accepted by a sick industrial company covered by the Sick Industrial Companies (Special Provisions) Act, 1985 in respect of which, the Board for Industrial and Financial Reconstruction has specifically, by order, suspended the operations of any contract, agreement, settlement, etc., under Section 22(3) of the Act.

Besides, the complaints with regard to fixed deposits of even listed companies cannot be made to the Stock Exchanges as they have no jurisdiction on them under the Listing Agreement.

Repayment of Deposits

An additional contingent provision is the obligation of the company to keep 15% of the deposits maturing during the year as current or other deposit accounts with a Scheduled Bank or in Government securities to be used only for repayment of deposits to public. This again ensures some safety to investors with regard to repayment, provided for under Rule 3(A) of Acceptance of Deposits Rules.

Besides under sub-Section (3A) of Section 58(A), the company is under an obligation to repay deposits on maturity, unless it is renewed for a further period, a breach of which is an offence punishable under the Act.

Premature Repayment

Rule 8 of Acceptance of Deposits Rules provide for premature repayment of deposits at the request of depositors, even after a cut in interest rate payable as a penalty.

Issue of Duplicate Certificates

Rules also provide for issue of duplicate receipts after securing indemnity bond from the depositor in the event of loss of the certificate. The depositor has to apply to the company in the event of the loss of the certificate and go through the legal formalities for issue of duplicate by the company.

Transmission of Deposits

If a joint holder dies, the amount is payable to survivor. If the investor is a single holder, the transmission of deposit will be as per the will of the deceased or to the legal heirs, in the event of his death *intestate*.

A succession certificate or probate or letters of administration is called for in these cases. The heirs will have to go to the court having jurisdiction for this. The company may insist on production of an affidavit and an indemnity by the legal heirs or representatives. As the formalities for legal compliance in this respect are cumbersome and time-consuming, the investors are advised to put these in joint names.

Procedure for Making Application to Company Law Board

The person holding a matured fixed deposit which he has not renewed and which the company has failed to repay, has to make an application in triplicate in Form No. 11. The application has to be accompanied by a fee of ₹50 payable by way of bank draft in favour of the Pay and Account Officer, Dept. of Company Affairs, New Delhi/Mumbai/Kolkata/Chennai.

The Company Law Board has four Regional Benches. The aggrieved depositors may make an application to the Bench of the Company Law Board having jurisdiction according to the Registered Office of the Company. The Andhra Pradesh companies come under the jurisdiction of the Chennai Bench.[@@] The Company Law Board would, after giving a reasonable opportunity of hearing to the company and other persons interested in the matter, make suitable orders for repayment of such deposits. Non-compliance of the order of the Company Law Board is punishable offence attracting penalty by way of imprisonment up to 3 years and fine of not less than ₹50 for everyday till such non-compliance continues.

Where the deposit which has fallen due for payment remains unpaid, the depositor can seek remedy in a civil court, or can file an application for winding up of the company to the court after serving on the company written demand requiring the company to repay the deposit. (Sections 433, 434 and 439 of the Companies Act, may be referred to for the purpose).

Problems of Odd Lots

Many investors get in possession of odd lots, which are saleable only at a discount. They lack in marketability and liquidity.

What are Odd Lots?

Share Certificates which contain a number of shares which are not marketable in the Stock Exchanges as per their trading rules are called Odd Lots. The marketable lots vary from 5 shares in the case of ACC, 50 shares in the case of Apollo Tyres to 100 shares in the case of a majority of companies. These are fixed by the Stock Exchange for trading purposes, in the case of listed companies.

Any Share Certificates falling in between these marketable lots like 2, 4 or 28 or even 60, etc., are all called Odd Lots. As these are not marketable in the regular trading time, they are quoted at a heavy discount of 15 to 20% over the market prices. The investors holding odd lots suffer to that extent. After demat form of share holdings, the question of odd lots did not arise, in the new millennium.

How Odd Lots Arise?

At the time of first allotment of new issues, all companies are obliged by listing Rules of Stock Exchanges to allot shares only in marketable lots. The Share Certificates as originally issued by companies are thus, either in marketable lots or in multiples of it. But, subsequently odd lots will emerge due to the following reasons:

(i) Issue of Rights Shares: When rights shares are issued by companies in the ratio of 1:4, to existing shareholders, for every holding of 4 shares, the investor is entitled to one share. Thus a shareholder having 100 shares (which is marketable) would now get 25 shares which are an odd lot. The ratio in which the "rights" are declared would decide the extent of odd lots distributed to the shareholder, in the form of rights.

[@@] The address of this office is C.L.B. Bench Officer, Southern Regional Bench, Block 1, 5th Floor, Shastri Bhavan, 26, Haddows Road, Chennai - 600 035.

(ii) Bonus Issues: The issue of bonus shares would also lead to emergence of odd lots, depending upon the ratio in which these bonus shares are issued. Thus the bonus is in the ratio of 3:1 indicating that one bonus share is issued for every holder of 3 shares. Then a shareholder having 100 shares in the company will have to get 33 shares as bonus shares and a 1/3rd fraction of a share which might be paid in cash at the market price.

(iii) Convertible Debentures: Debentures issued with a right of conversion into equity at a premium or at par may lead to issue of shares in smaller lots than in marketable lots. These may be partly or fully convertible debentures. Thus a fully convertible debentureholder of 10 debentures of ₹100 each might be entitled to only 4 shares, each equity share of ₹10 is issued at a premium of ₹15. Here an odd lot of 4 shares will emerge due to conversion.

Problem of Odd Lots

The liquidity of odd lots is poor. It is difficult to get a buyer of odd lots but there may be more sellers due to the difficulty of consolidating the shares into marketable lots. The holders of odd lots therefore lose in realised price to the extent of 15-20% over the market price.

Remedies

The practices of the companies which lead to odd lots could not be changed all of a sudden. But the government has advised listed companies to effect consolidation on their own and issue certificates in marketable lots to the extent possible.

The companies are also advised to collect odd lots from the members in favour of a nominee of the company who will consolidate and sell them in the market and distribute the proceeds after deduction of expenses to the odd lot holders *pro rata*. But these guidelines were not followed by companies.

Some Stock Exchanges have introduced schemes for special odd lot trading sessions, and listed some brokers for this purpose of odd lot trading. These tradings are as between the members on behalf of their clients. These are expected to help consolidation of holdings into marketable lots. The Stock Exchanges which have special sessions for this purpose are Mumbai, Ahmedabad, Delhi and Kolkata.

Other Measures

The financial institutions like UTI, LIC, and GIC, Canbank Financial Services, etc., have also taken some steps for relieving the troubles of odd lot holders. They started purchasing odd lots during specified timings on specified days. Some of them purchase but not sell. UTI does not give cash but only its own units in exchange for odd lots. The UTI had also launched a scheme in 1990 to arrange for the purchases of odd lots in special counters in Mumbai, Delhi, Kolkata, Ahmedabad and Chennai. These schemes as also of LIC, GIC, etc., are only confined to purchases and not sales and in only selected scrips. Even so, the discount over the market price ranges from 2% to 5% as administrative costs. Payment will be made to odd lot holders only after verification of signatures on Transfer Deeds by the company which may take about a month or so.

The service charges, administrative costs and discounts charged by brokers will all cost the investors to the extent of about 20% of the market price. Even the schemes of financial institutions will put the investors at a financial loss for no fault of theirs although they give liquidity to their investments. They do not sell odd lots but only buy them, so that investors on their own cannot consolidate their shareholdings. Thus the prevailing schemes of odd lots are only palliatives and not remedies.

Self-protection by Investors

(1) The best help is self-help of investors. In the case of rights, they should apply for additional rights so as to consolidate the odd lots into marketable lots on their own. If the companies are good enough, they may allot out of rejections and renunciations of "rights" by others.

(2) In the case of convertible debentures, they may buy debentures in such number that they do not lead to odd lots on conversion. This requires precautionary planning on the part of investors.

(3) Investors should advertise in the financial press or weeklies, etc., which deal with shares and securities for offers of odd lots in the shares in which they want to consolidate. They should thus buy odd lots from other investors and consolidate the shares with the help of such advertisements or contacts with sub-brokers who have clients with odd lots to sell. They should thus buy rather than sell to consolidate shares. If they sell, after consolidation they will stand to gain rather than lose.

The best remedy is however for the government to ban the issue of odd lots by the companies in the public interest which is a matter for the SEBI to take up under investor protection. Under demat form of trading, odd lots do not arise and trading in old lots has no relevance then. This is one of the advanatages of demat form of trading.

✠ ✠ ✠

UNDERWRITING SERVICES

20

Underwriting is a financial service covering the risk of non-subscription to new issues in the capital market. It is a contract between the issuer of securities and the underwriter to the effect that the latter assures the subscription from the public to the extent of the amount agreed upon. In the event of under subscription, the underwriter subscribes the short falls not exceeding the commitment, agreed upon. This service is like a guarantee for a certain amount of subscription from the public or persons to whom the offer is made. The risk of non-subscription or undersubscription is covered in this contract. In a sense, it is an insurance for the company or issuer that the amount offered is subscribed. This will enable the company to successfully implement its project or secure the objectives of issue, like completion of a project, to meet the cost over-runs or execute the expansion plan, etc.

The coverage of risk is rewarded with a reward in the form of a commission at a rate of 1 to 5% of the underwritten amount. This is the advantage of backup support, and ensures the success or full subscription to the issue. The underwriting commission is payable in both the cases of full subscription or oversubscription and in the event of devolvement due to under subscription, if the underwriters have met the devolvement.

Before 1994 SEBI insisted that there should be compulsory underwriting of all public issues whether of equity or debt. At that time exemption was given to issues of Rights, issues made to reserved categories or preferential allotment and the issues made by Development Financial Institutions (DFIs). Underwriting of all issues is now made optional.

Who are RUWs?

Merchant banks who act as lead managers or co-managers also used to underwrite a certain amount, say 5% of the offer as it is in their interest to get full subscription and make the issue a success. Otherwise the efficiency and payments to merchant bankers will be in jeopardy. The company enters into an agreement with the merchant bank for leading the issue to success. Similar agreements are entered into with underwriters ensuring full subscription to the amounts underwritten. A minimum amount of 5% of the total is to be underwritten by merchant banker to confirm their commitment as per SEBI guidelines, or to be subscribed by them.

The registered underwriters are those who are licensed and registered with the SEBI, as it is a prior requirement for all RUWs to do underwriting business. The RUWs are merchant banks, Stock broker, banks, FIs and other companies and firms, who are authorised by the SEBI. As per the SEBI Act and the Rules made thereunder, all intermediaries in the capital market require registration and licence from the SEBI.

Eligibility for RUW

The eligibility for underwriters to be registered with the SEBI is as follows:

(*a*) Minimum net worth of ₹ 20 lakh

(*b*) Past experience in this business

(*c*) Outstanding underwriter commitments

(*d*) Record of defaults or failures, if any

(*e*) Integrity and overall reputation.

Agreement is to be entered into between the issuer (company) and the underwriter and a model underwriting agreement was put down by the SEBI laying down the obligations and rights of both the issuer and the underwriter. The agreement ensures the transparency, disclosures and conditions for devolvement on RUW. It prevents malpractices by both the issuer and the underwriter.

SEBI Regulations

A code of conduct is laid down for RUWs. The regulations for underwriters are laid down by SEBI, as in the case of Merchant Banks and Portfolio Managers. These regulations stipulate obligations and responsibilities of underwriters and procedure for inspection and audit by SEBI officials. The code of conduct lays down what underwriters should do and should not do. They can underwrite a total commitment to the extent of 20 times their net worth. Any underwriter has to keep the confidentiality of the information on the company or project and cannot take advantage of any inside information of the company. The underwriters are debarred from resorting to manipulation of prices, price rigging or cornering of shares. The penalties and suspension of RUWs, in such cases are all provided for in the regulations.

Obligations of Issuer

(*a*) Time is the essence of the agreement between RUW and the company — within 30 days of signing the agreement with RUW; the company has to send the final prospectus for Registration with ROC.

(*b*) Full and fair disclosures to be ensured and underwriter should be kept informed of all facts and changes made if any, in the prospectus or in the project implementation.

(*c*) Issue to be kept open for 10 days (maximum) in the event of undersubscription.

(*d*) The issue should be open to the public within 3 months from the date of agreement with RUWs.

(*e*) No lapses on the part of the issuer as per the agreement.

Right of the RUWs

(*a*) Right to abrogate the agreement, if the issuer fails in any of his obligations.

(*b*) Right to information, full disclosures and timely action by issuer.

(*c*) Right to market the issue and sell the issue through any acceptable methods of marketing strategies.

(*d*) To appoint sub-underwriters, sub-brokers, etc., who are responsible to the underwriter and to the company.

(*e*) Adequate application forms as per the agreement and copies of prospectus are to be made available to the RUW within 21 days, prior to the opening of the issue to the public.

Obligation of the RUWs

(1) When undersubscription takes place RUW has to meet the devolvement on a *pro rata* basis as per the agreement.

(2) For devolvement to be effective, RUWs have to be informed of the state of subscription and the extent of undersubscription within 30 days since the closure of the issue.

(3) After notice of devolvement, the RUW has to check-up the facts and pay-up along with the application the devolved amount by cheque within another 30 days from the date of notice of devolvement to the RUW.

SEBI (Underwriter) Rules and Regulations

These are issued under Section 11 of SEBI Act for compliance by underwriters.

No person can carry on the activity of the underwriter, unless he is registered with the SEBI, under Section 12 of the Act. Besides, every registered stock broker and merchant bankers of calegory I, holding a valid Certificate of Registration under Section 12 of the Act shall be entitled to act as underwriter.

The rules and regulations provide for registration of underwriters, inspection and audit of their business, penalties and suspension etc., for violation of rules and defaults. In terms of Regulation 1, the RUWs are required to enter into a legally binding agreement, a draft of which is made available by SEBI for adoption by companies and underwriter. The agreement provides for all contingencies, obligations and rights of underwriters and of the issuers.

Marketing of issue by underwriters, use of the services of sub-underwriters and sub-brokers for marketing of the issue, enforcement of the contract, when devolvement is not enforceable and when it is enforceable, etc., are all laid down in the agreement.

Underwriting Commission

This is the compensation for risk taking by the underwriters, viz., the risk of non-subscription or under-subscription. This commission is payable whether the persons intended to subscribe have subscribed or not. In the event of non-subscription, the course of action is to ask for subscription to be made good by underwriters, but payment of commission is necessary in either case, namely, devolvement or no devolvement.

Devolvement Rules

The RUW is discharged from his commitment, if the issue is fully subscribed or if the company has received valid applications from him or others bearing his seal and code for the amount committed by him. In case of undersubscription the surplus applications procured by any one underwriter would be apportioned to all other underwriters in the ratio of their gross underwriting obligations.

SEBI guidelines of disclosure and investor protection provide that if the company does not receive a minimum of 90% of the issue, including the accepted and paid as devolvement on the underwriters, within 120 days from the date of opening of the issue, the company shall refund the application money and in the case of disputed devolvement the company has to refund the money, if the above conditions are not met. The SEBI guidelines thus give 120 days to the company much more than in the Companies Act and underwriters can be called upon to discharge their liabilities, if there are no lapses on the part of the issuer, but within time limit of 120 days from the date of opening the issue.

Merchant bankers are held responsible for appointing the underwriters and scrutiny of their integrity, net worth and credentials and ensuring the collection of moneys from them in the event of devolvement. The merchant bankiing has to report to the SEBI issue-wise on all public issues, the amounts underwritten, the amounts devolved and acceptance and non-acceptance of devolvement and the reasons therefore.

The action of SEBI on the underwriters is based on these reports of the merchant bankers. Underwriting activity is thus strictly supervised by SEBI and penalties of suspension, cancellation and revocation of the licences are all enforced on them for violation of the rules and regulations.

Consequences of Defaults

The company has recourse to the law for enforcement of the contract and sue the underwriters for breach of contract under Section 73 of the Contract Act. Unless otherwise, it is proved that there are lapses on the part of the issuer or the conditions of the agreement are violated by the issuer, the law suit is sustainable against the underwriter, as per the contractual agreement. The underwriters are absolved of their liabilities, if there are lapses on the part of the issuer and his part of the obligations were not performed satisfactorily. The SEBI evaluates the underwriters continuously and monitors through the reports of the various merchant bankers.

Underwriting Commission

The rates of commission as approved by Companies Act are 5% of the issue or price of shares of equity and 2.5% of the issue in the case of debentures. Section 76 of Companies Act provides for payment of commission but this should have been authorised by the Articles of the Company and underwriting agreements are delivered in time to ROC and the payment of commission is provided for in the agreement.

But contrary to the Act, the government through the Ministry of Finance circular of the May 1985, provided for the lower rates of commission as shown below:

Commission on	*On the amounts subscribed by public*	*On the Amounts devolved on underwriters*
(a) Equity issue	2.50%	2.50%
(b) Preference shares and debenture		
— For Issue of less than and upto ₹ 5 lakh	1.50%	2.50%
For issues of more than ₹ 5 lakh	1.00%	2.00%

The above are the ceiling rates permissible and actual commission payable will be subject to bargaining and are to be incorporated in the agreement, entered into between the issuer and the underwriter. The underwriting commission can be varied from underwriter to underwriter depending on the quantum of underwriting, their credit rating and other terms of the agreement. But no underwriting commission is payable on the portion allotted to promoters, directors, collaborators and employees.

The companies are not permitted to offer discounts or incentives for subscribing to the issues. Similarly, no payments above the ceiling rates of commission are permissible as per the SEBI guidelines.

Legal Provisions

The Companies Act 1956 makes provision for employing the services of underwriters and payment of commission for this purpose. Section 76 of the Act makes the following provisions:

1. A company can pay commission to any person in consideration of his subscribing or arranging for subscriptions to any shares and debentures of the company offered to public and shareholders.
2. Such payment of commission should be authorised by the Articles of the Association of the company.
3. The Act has provided a ceiling on such commission at 5% of the price of the shares or debentures or at the rate authorised by the Articles, whichever is lower.
4. Prospectus should disclose the Rate of Commission and the underwriters and sub-underwriters, if any.

5. A copy of the contract or agreement with the underwriters and the commission agreed upon in it will be delivered to the ROC for registration.
6. Under Article 5(b) of the Schedule I of the Stamp Act, Stamp duty is payable on the underwriting agreement at 6 paise for ₹10,000 or part thereof the value of the securities underwritten, subject to a maximum of ₹10.

Underwriting is now optional in India, as per SEBI guidelines. The rates of commission are also fixed lower by the government, namely, 1 to 2½% of the amount underwritten in supercession of the legal provisions.

In case of merchant bankers or lead managers, a minimum of 5% of the public offer is expected to be taken up for subscription and/or underwriting with a view to ensuring their stake in the issue. In the case of stock brokers doing the underwriting business their stake is to be limited to 5% of the total issue and relative to their net worth and they have to take prior permission of the Stock Exchange authorities.

Types of Underwriting Agreements

1. *Agreement to sell* through Boughtout Deals. In OTCEI, the sponsors or merchant bankers buy in wholesale and sell in retail to the public.
2. *Part Underwriting:* A part of the issue can be sold through a selling agreement which the underwriters agree to for a commission.
3. *Firm Subscription vs. Underwriting:* In the case of LIC, UTI, GIC, they prefer to make full subscription in their own name to the extent of the amount underwritten.

Agencies Underwriting in India

The major institutional agencies doing underwriting work in India are — All-India Development Institutions and State level FIs, banks, stock broker firms, etc. These institutions are LIC, IFCI, ICICI, GIC, SIDCs, SIFCs, etc., and banks to a limited extent. At the present juncture, the bulk of underwriting is done by the IDBI, ICICI, LIC, UTI, etc., followed by broker firms and banks in that order. The banks can underwrite within the permitted limits of 10% of their incremental deposits earmarked for advances against shares and debentures. There are similar limits for development financial institutions and investment financial institutions. No institution can subscribe to more than 30% of the paid-up capital of a company and the SEBI has fixed an overall limit of 24% for FFIs and another 24% for Indian FIs.

Brokers are paid a brokerage as well as commission depending on the activities, which they undertake, namely, marketing and underwriting. If they only undertake marketing through their sub-broker and investor network, they get a brokerage of ½% to 1% depending upon the amount of sales. Similarly, for underwriting they get a commission varying from 1 to 2½%, depending upon the terms of agreement.

✠ ✠ ✠

MARKETING OF ISSUES

21

With the increasing number of new issues flooding the market, some of them bunching at the same time, keen competition has emerged in the new issues market. This has led to larger fish swallowing the smaller fish and smaller companies facing rising costs, devolvement and undersubscription. Bigger and well established companies having reputed promoters with a track record and professional management could secure easily oversubscription multifold. Medium and small sized projects and relatively new and first generation promoters face stiff competition. Adequate pre-issue planning and proper marketing strategy have become absolutely necessary. Investors have become extremely choosy and shy of the majority of new issues.

Need for Aggressive Salesmanship

There is absolute need for aggressive sales strategy in addition to complying with all statutory regulations. The bigger companies can spend large amounts on TV, Cable channels, and Radio advertisements, which are more expensive, but the medium and smaller companies have to adopt cost-effective strategies with a longer mileage. Newspapers, brochures and direct mailing are adopted by all the companies in addition to investor and broker conferences. There is need for innovative approach for effective sales at least cost. For this, market research is necessary.

Innovative Ideas

Market research should yield centres with large investor base. Direct approach to big investors for block selling and investor conferences at selected centres for medium and small investors are also necessary as also the selection of proper media and a right mix of video-audio and printing media. First, a budget for sales promotion has to be drawn up and the media has to be chosen to suit the budget. Second, to be effective and get the best results out of the media adopted, the media should get at the targeted groups and there should be a time schedule for these advertisements.

Normally, companies give the contract to an advertising agency for planning and executing the advertisement in consultation with merchant bankers. These have become stereotyped under the following heads:

(1) TV and Radio: These are most expensive but yet give wide coverage in the country and abroad. The most popular time for the public to see and listen is sought after by companies which can afford it.

(2) Newspapers, Journals, Magazines, etc.: The advertisement should be in the dailies which are most widely circulated and should cover major centres and major States which are leading in investment collections.

(3) Hoardings and Banners, etc.: These have more telling effect, if kept in critical traffic centres. As they can be retained in those places for a few days prior to the opening of issue, they will have a better effect on investors.

(4) Brokers' and Investors' Conferences: These are held at centres which have the maximum investment potential.

SEBI's Code of Advertisement

1. Any advertisement should be truthful, fair and clear.
2. It should be factually correct and not an exaggerated or misleading statement.
3. It should not contain any promise or guarantee of income or appreciation or any other gains.
4. It should not contain any information not given in the prospectus.
5. Corporate advertisement should not be given during the period, that subscription is kept open. Product advertisement if given should not refer to corporate performance.
6. During the period subscription is open, no statement should be given to the press about the state of subscription or oversubscription.
7. No slogans or non-factual titles or glorifications should appear in the advertisement.
8. No models, celebrities, or fictional characters should be displayed in the offer documents.
9. Financial data to be given, should be for the past three years relating to sales, profit, dividends, etc.
10. No incentives should be given to brokers, underwriters, investors and other connected parties.

Lead managers have the responsibility of overseeing the observance of the above code of conduct. The practices should be fair and disclosures full and correct. They should recommend cost-effective but fruitful means of advertisement, suitable to the company in terms of the size of the issue, location of the company and of the potential investors and the means of correct tapping of that potential.

Advertisement Campaign

Publicity campaign can start after the prospectus is filed with the Registrar of Companies. Pre-issue campaign should include the corporate advertisement relating to the public issue and is to be released to the various newspapers both regional and national. The text of the advertisement should not violate any guidelines of SEBI on advertisement and should be approved by the company and lead manager.

The lead manager in consultation with the company select an Advertising Agency with prior experience in this. The Budget for Advertisement for the issue should be decided by the company in consultation with lead manager. In tune with the Budget, the media for making advertisements are chosen. The content of the Banner, Hoardings, Press Release or Advertisement in daily papers and investor or broker conferences should be worded carefully. Sometimes companies choose to have press conferences, separately at various centres depending upon the size of the issue. At such conferences, some advertisement materials or brief writeups on the project/company, etc., are given. These materials should not contain any new information not contained in the prospectus. If the well drafted materials containing highlights and risk factors are given at these conferences, they will be useful to the press reporters also to write about the company and the project, for which news is being made.

Collection Centres and Rising Costs

Leaving aside the mandatory costs, non-mandatory costs include the above advertisement and mailing expenses, among others. To reduce these costs the SEBI has reduced the collection centres, as required by regulations to 30 in 1994 and further to 4 in 1995, excluding the centres where the stock exchanges are located which should have collection centres compulsorily and dispensed with the registration requirement for letters of refund orders and other amounts not exceeding ₹ 1,500. The SEBI code of advertisement also aims at reducing the cost as also to ensure fair practices by the companies in the new issue process.

Advertisement Expenses

Advertisement and propaganda, one of the important items of expense among non-mandatory costs is dependent upon the size of issue, reputation and track record of the promoters and management objects of issue and timing, etc. Relative to total issue amount, such items of expense constitute a heavy proportion in case of a small company, and if issue amount is small and promoters have no track record and less known to the investing public. The position becomes much worse if the time of issue is unfavourable due to depressed conditions in the primary market or secondary market. Such companies face severe competition from the bigger companies and those existing companies with a good track record. The bigger the size of issue, for an existing company with a track record, the lower is the relative cost on advertisement and propaganda.

The cost of advertisement becomes critical for many new companies without track record, irrespective of the size of issue. Such companies should plan properly with an advertisement budget and entrust the job to highly cost efficient agencies. The media should be chosen in a manner as to produce best results at least cost. Thus, the expenses should be optimal for such companies to produce best results. This requires a lot of market research and makes it necessary to keep a pulse on the various segments of the investing public. Advertising agencies chosen for the purpose should therefore be highly efficient with a competent research staff.

In an environment of competition, companies go out all the way to lure the investing public to make the issue a success. Luxury, exuberant discounts, presents, etc., bordering on profligacy have been indulged in by many companies. At the other extreme, insufficient advertisement and custs in the use of stationery may lead to undersubscription. Both the extremes are to be avoided. In the process of competition and undercutting, many companies have been found to resort to unethical practices. As noted earlier SEBI has therefore laid down a code of advertisement to be followed by companies during and before the new issue to the public.

Mailing Agents

Another important clog in the new issue machinery is the role of mailing agents. The mailing work can be entrusted to private agency or to postal authorities. Preliminary spadework has to be done by having discussions on the volume of work and time schedules involved in each item of mailing work. The Registrars are mainly responsible for the arrangements to be made for the mailing work and complaints of investors with regard to non-receipt and delay in receipt of letters of refund orders and letters of allotment, etc., are all addressed to the Registrars. Registrars incur expenses in regard of correspondence but they are reimbursed by the company.

In the issue work involved, postal or mailing expenses are incurred under the following main heads: (1) For sending reject applications for not filling the application form properly, lack of signature, unsigned cheques, mistakes in cheques, etc., (2) For despatch of refund orders for non-allotment or partial allotment, (3) For posting letters of allotment, and (4) For despatch of share certificates to successful allottees.

Pre-issue Mailing

Before issue is opened or closed, postal services are used to send stationery — application forms, letters of offer or copies of prospectus. Direct mailing to investors is also done by some registrars and companies. Correspondence with brokers, sub-brokers and underwriters and despatch of stationery to them are all the responsibility of the registrars. If mailing work is too large and private couriers charge heavily, the only way left with the registrars is to post them from different postal centres or cities and spread the postal work for a number of days. In this process, if the correspondence is not well planned, delays occur leading to delay in listing and investor complaints.

Mailing Work after the Issue is Closed

After the issue is closed, and during the period when issue is open, collection bankers have to use courier services to advise the controlling banks and the registrars on the list of applications, accompanying cheques, DD, stock invest etc. As per the arrangement made for crediting the cheques and DD and storing the stock invest until the allotment is also made, the collecting banks do the needful under advise to the Registrars and the company. During the pendency of the issue, such statements and correspondence is done through a special messenger, fax or telex and electronic network in some cases. Sometimes, speedpost and private couriers are used when the matter has to come from far off centres or cities. Collecting and controlling banks are responsible for telexing or mailing the list of applications, their names and addresses, cheque or DD numbers and stock invest numbers separately on a daily basis during the currency of subscriptions and finally at the closing of the subscriptions.

Investors go on corresponding with the registrars for non-receipt of letters of allotment or refund orders. They inform the change of address or give other instructions pending the allotment. Thousands of letters of such nature are to be acknowledged by the registrars and investor complaints are to be attended to if SEBI guidelines are to be followed. Besides, the registrars have to correspond with brokers to the issue and underwriters, collecting and controlling bankers among others. All this involves huge correspondence and mailing expenses.

Some registrars do not enter into any correspondence with the investors, until the allotment process is completed, that is 70 days from the closure of subscription.[@] This leads to more investor complaints. Some cost-effective methods of sending printed aknowledgement card or standard reply can be kept ready for some cases. More importantly, these expenses can be reduced, if the collecting bankers themselves scrutinise the applications at the time of receipt, along with the DDs, cheques, etc. That will reduce the errors and lapses on the part of the investors which will eliminate some correspondence.

As per the SEBI guidelines at present, all correspondence of a value of ₹ 1,500 or more have to be sent by registered post, while those with lower value can be sent by certificate of posting. This will no doubt lower the costs to some extent. Despite all this, the advertisement and mailing costs normally touch 4 to 5% of the total issue amount, if the issue amount is of small size. In sum, there is need for proper planning to reduce the costs of issue, by controlling mailing and advertisement expenses and by adopting cost-effective methods.

✠ ✠ ✠

@ This period is reduced to 30 days since May 1, 1996.

CUSTODIAN AND CUSTODIAL SERVICES

22

Who is a Custodian?

In the generic sense, custodian is one who keeps the safe custody of the valuables of somebody else, a customer or client or an investor. In the case of investor, the valuables are his investments and securities. The safe custody of valuables, in olden days used to be done by merchants, traders, indigenous bankers, shroffs, etc. In the modern days, the safe custody and custodial functions are performed by the commercial and cooperative banks. Gold, silver, jewellery, ornaments and a host of other valuables are safely preserved in Lockers by the banks for its customers.

Safe custody is also provided by employers to their employees in respect of some personal effects. Thus Stock Exchange authorities provide safe custody lockers for keeping the valuable shares, securities, bonds, etc. of their member brokers and of their clients. The clubs and social organisations also provide safe lockers, on a temporary basis for its members. Railways and airways provide safe custody of passengers' personal luggage and effects in the clockrooms.

The principle of safe custody is thus an old traditional function and refers to many related services, such as preservation from theft, fire, accident, loss, etc., risk avoidance or risk reduction, and insurance for preserving the valuables intact in physical form. In modern parlance, safe custody or custodial services are used in the sense of intermediary services or financial services of non-banking nature. The dictionary definition of the term custodian refers to the agent or broker or banker who keeps the safe custody of the client's valuables or investments of the public in securities, which are financial claims.

Custodial Services in Capital Market

The custodial services refer to the safe custody of share certificates and securities or keeping deposits of them for physical handling of receipts and deliveries or for keeping accounts and after-sales services in the form of collection of dividend, rights, bonus, etc., and sending for and receiving after transfer in the books of accounts of the company before bookclosure or record dates, etc.

In the capital market, custodial services are used in the OTC Exchange of India, NSE and B.S.E.; SHCI provides custodial services to FIs and Mutual funds and banks. Mutual funds require custodial services for each of its schemes. The sponsor banks provide these services or the Mutual funds have set up their own in-house custodials.

SEBI Guidelines

In mutual fund industry, custodian is an important constituent of the structure, to be approved by the RBI and the SEBI. As per the SEBI norms, custodian has to be an independent organisation, delinked from the sponsors, the trustee and AMC. The approval of the AMC, sponsors, Trust Board and custodians by the SEBI is a composite exercise and composite authorisation. Although some public sector Mutual funds have set up their own Custodian Division, SEBI now insists that they can provide their service to other Mutual funds, not set up by their sponsor. This will ensure that sponsor is kept at arms length from the AMC custodian. Besides, there should be no areas of conflict of interest between the various organs of the Mutual funds, namely, sponsors, trustees, AMC and custodians. The custodian track record, the volume of business handled by it before, its organisational strength, its infrastructural facilities, like office staff, computer and telex, fax, communications facilities, etc., are taken into account before licensing them.

Approval of SEBI

For approval of SEBI, the sponsor has to furnish the details of the custodians, in format IV of the SEBI. The following particulars are required to be provided:

(*a*) Name of the institution, address, Fax No., etc.

(*b*) Name of contact person, address, Fax No., etc.

(*c*) Background information, experience, volume of business handled, etc.

(*d*) Organisational infrastructure and other details on the No. of Companies, Trusts for which it has provided the custodian services.

The SEBI has to examine the suitability of each of the constituents of the Mutual fund and give a composite approval for all of the constituents with or without any changes.

SHCI and banks have been providing custodial services for more than one agency. Many foreign banks like ANZ Grindlays, American Express as also the Citibank extend the custodial services to more than one agency. Thus, many FFIs and FIIs and foreign security firms are using the services of these India based foreign banks as custodians. As the Indian Securities cannot be taken out of India under the FEMA, these foreign organisations and institutions have to depend upon the Indian banks and foreign banks in India to keep safe custody of its securities purchased under ADR/GDR/IDR issues, made in foreign markets, deliver these securities as and when disposed of to the counterparties, provide the ancillary and consequential acts such as follow up support of getting securities transferred into client's name before the book closure or record date, collect dividends, rights bonus entitlements and other incidental services.

Custodians for Mutual Funds

Mutual funds run by the subsidiaries of nationalised banks have as their custodian their respective sponsor banks. Banks have the expertise and facilities for acting as custodians. They provide lockers and custodian facilities for the clients and their own Mutual funds.

The institutions which are acting as professional custodians are Stock Holding Corporation of India (SHCI), Citibank and some other foreign banks, B.O.I. holdings for B.S.E. Brokers and Industrial Investment Trust Ltd. The SHCI has been providing the custodial services to its sponsors, like UTI, IDBI, ICICI, LIC, GIC, etc. But later on, it extended its services to many MFs, banks, etc.

The responsibilities of the custodian are as follows:

(1) Receipt and delivery of securities.

(2) Holding in Trust the securities or safekeeping.

(3) Keeping account of all receipts and deliveries.

(4) Collecting income/dividend and follow-up support like rights, and bonus collection, getting transfers effected before book closure or record dates.

(5) Corporate actions and services of dividend declaration, fees collection, etc., and to act as transfer agents.

The functions of custodians are as follows:

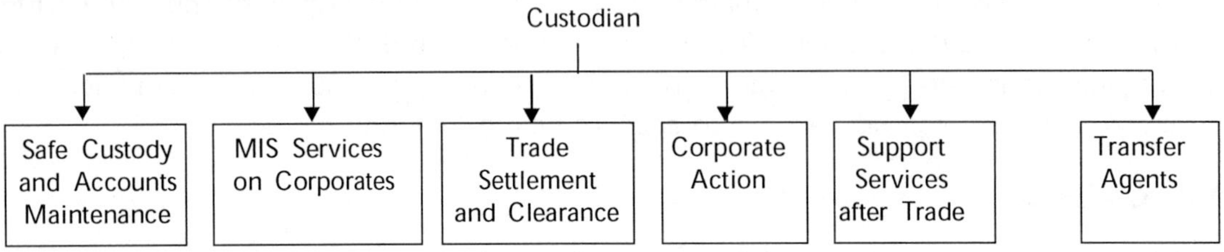

SHCI

Leaving aside the Citibank and other foreign banks who provide custodial services to more than one agency or customer, the institutional agency set up by the Indian FIs in 1988 for the specific purpose of providing the custodial and depository services in the capital market is the SHCI.

It was set up under the Companies Act with a paid up capital of ₹10.5 crore in 1988, by seven All India financial institutions, namely, IDBI, IFCI, ICICI, UTI, LIC, GIC and IRBI. It provided these services to the sponsors to start with and extended them for a fee to others like some Private Mutual Funds, banks and other institutions, who are active in the capital market. Its services are being priced on a no profit/no loss basis both to the sponsors and other customers. For the first time, in 1990-91 it has made breakthrough by covering its expenses by its income and earned subsequently incidental profits.

SHCI has its headquarters in Mumbai, and regional centres in New Delhi, Kolkata and Chennai. It has membership of the Stock Exchanges in these centres so that it can participate in clearing and settlement on behalf of its sponsors and clients.

SHCI is a board managed company with a whole-time Managing Director. It has professionalised expert staff and its operations are all computerised. It runs on commercial lines and levies fees for its services based on the guidelines given by its Tariff Advisory Committee. It has a number of functions, the more important of which are set out below:

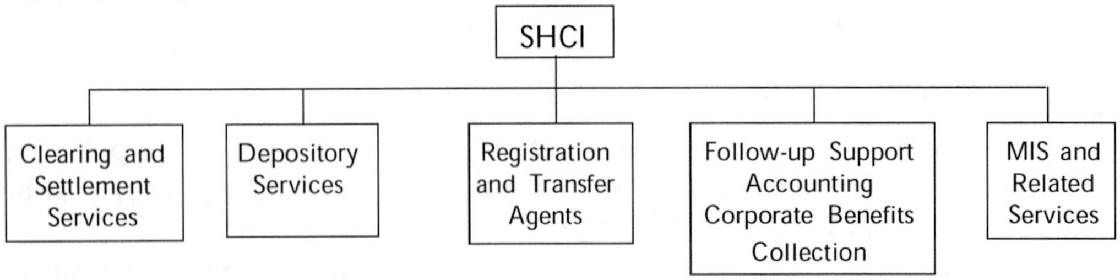

OTC Exchange Custodian

The OTCEI, set up in 1990 became operational in 1992 and has provided for custodial services for its members. It is an important constituent of the exchange, as the shares traded on OTCEI need not be physically handled and simple counter receipts can be used as transferable property in lieu of share certificates.

The chart shows the Constituents of the OTCEI

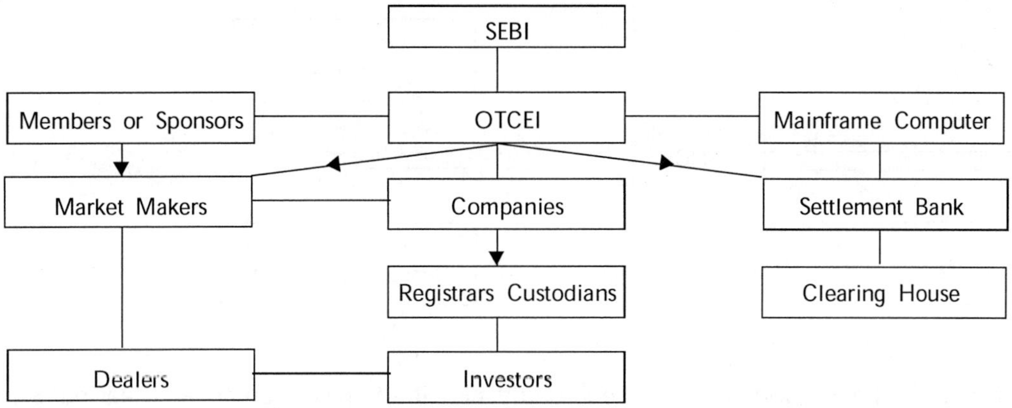

Custodian/settler keeps the physical custody of certificates while Registrars will pass entries in the register of the company for transfers from one party to another. The settler receives for record keeping all the documents (CRs) and Transfer deeds duly filled in, etc. C.R.s are Counter Receipts.

The settler keeps the signatures of the investor and counter signatories for all scrips and passes them on to the Registrar for effecting the transfers, after verifying the signature. The Registrar and custodian makes the allotment of shares, effect transfers of shares, not exceeding 0.5% of the capital of the company. They maintain the register of members and keep the custody of certificates to be exchanged with CRs, on the request of the investor. Otherwise, physical certificates are kept in safe custody and deposit with the custodian and CRs would reflect the possession of certificates and evidence of the ownership for buying and selling, there is no need for physical certificates as CRs are validly acceptable by all the parties in the OTCEI including the investors. There is no need for physical certificates and they are immobilised by Demat form of share holdings with the custodian in the trading system carried out electronically by the OTCEI. It is because of the facility of trading through counter receipts which are substitutes for the share certificates with distinctive numbers indicating evidencing the ownership.

STOCK HOLDING CORPORATION OF INDIA LIMITED (SHCIL)

Corporate Profile

SHCIL is a company incorporated under the Companies Act with an authorized share capital of ₹ 250 million and a paid-up capital of ₹ 105 million fully subscribed by the 7 all-India financial institutions, *viz.*, Industrial Development Bank of India, Industrial Finance Corporation of India, Industrial Credit and Investment Corporation of India, Unit Trust of India, Life Insurance Corporation of India, General Insurance Corporation of India (including its subsidiaries), and the Industrial Reconstruction Bank of India, now IIBI. SHCIL will be the agency to set up support facilities for NSE including the custodial services.

Organisational Structure

SHCIL is a Board-managed company and has a whole-time Managing Director in charge of the day-to-day management. SHCIL's operations are now streamlined and are computer aided. SHCIL has compact organisational structure and employs professionals, qualified and trained in the relevant areas. SHCIL operates on commercial lines and levies fees/charges for its various services as determined by the Tariff Advisory Committee. Besides the Mumbai Operations, SHCIL has created facilities in the major market centres in India with the opening of regional centres in New Delhi, Kolkata, Chennai, etc.

FUNCTIONS

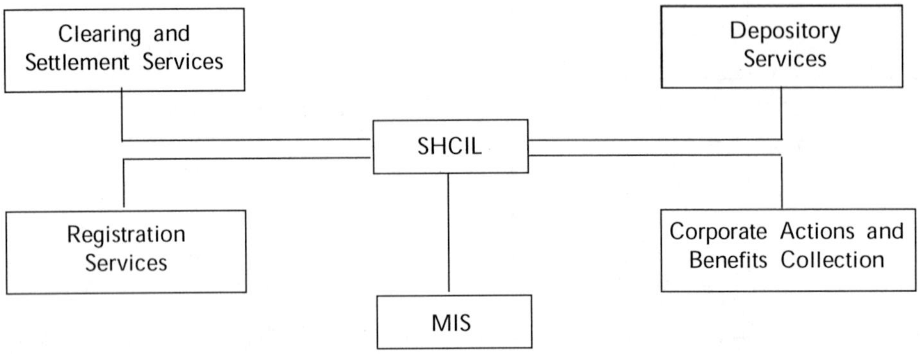

The services offered by the corporation can be broadly classified into 5 areas — Clearing Services, Registration/Transfer Processing, Depository Services, Corporate Action and Benefits Collection and MIS. All these services form part of the line functions.

As these services are relevant to the National Market System it is entrusted with the task of setting of supporting agencies, as recommended by the Pherwani Committee.

1. National clearing and settlement system for making settlement on a national basis.
2. The Central Depository Trust to keep physical custody of shares and to usher in scripless trading system.
3. The Securities Facilities support corporation for providing supporting infrastructural facilities.

Functions

In the first instance, SHCIL is offering its services to its own seven promoter institutions. It acts on the basis of Letter of Authority/Power of Attorney issued by the financial institutions and render the following services:

(*a*) Clearing services.

(*b*) Depository services.

(*c*) Support services.

(*d*) Management/information services.

(*e*) Development services.

The SHCIL is eliminating paperwork which clogs the post-trading activities. It does so by replacing the physical transfer of shares by passing the necessary receipts and keeping the shares with itself as a depository for the sponsoring financial institutions. In other words, SHCIL has ultimately emerged as a bank for securities. The book entry transfer system will eliminate needless paperwork and speed up the transfer of securities and the related payments and receipts. Unlike under the earlier system which generally involved considerable delays in the actual transfer of shares to the buyer after he has paid for them and hand over the scrips to his broker, under the computerised book entry transfer system, the transfers and the related payments can be affected within a couple of days. The inefficiency of the then prevalent share transfer system, where speculative transactions played a dominant role can be reduced by this system of paperless transfers, if this can be extended also to all investors. It is already extended to the members of the BSE by the setting up of BOI Holdings. In the form of dematerilisation of physical certificates, there is only paperless transfers.

Clearing Services

SHCIL is a member of the Clearing House of the major Stock Exchanges. It provides the post-trading agency work for the FIs. It receives and/or delivers the securities on behalf of the institutions after each settlement of the Stock Exchange. The SHCIL monitors the execution of the purchase/sale orders of the institutions by the brokers. It lodges securities and transfer deeds for Share Departments. The SHCIL ensures that the securities are duly and in time transferred to the names of the institutions.

Depository Services

SHCIL has provided a custodial service for securities and related services to the institutions while the securities are in its custody. Those services related to the collection of dividend warrants, and interest cheques; it attends to the necessary consolidation or splitting of shares, redemption and collection of bonus and rights and other privileges attached to shares, debentures and other instruments.

Support Services

The SHCIL arranges to monitor interest/dividend payments due to the institutions and ensures that the warrants are received from the companies and deposited in the banks to the credit of the institutions without delay.

Central Depository System

The govt. has accepted the system of multiple depositories and SEBI was asked to frame guidelines for their operations. These depositories kept physical custody of share certificates leading to immobilisation of shares to be followed later by dematerialisation and complete book entry system of trading as at present.

This means that the statement given by the depository is evidence of the ownership of the shares. This method was operated for the FIs and FFIs and banks and mutual funds, in the beginning and was extended to corporates and individuals. Later on, the depository will transfer the securities between the participants through electronic book entry, while the settling bank will effect the transfer of funds.

Listing of Securities NSE

All medium and large sized companies eligible to be listed on regular Stock Exchange can be listed on NSE. Some of them may be listed and traded on regular Stock Exchanges also. The same formalities of listing are observed by NSE and a listing agreement is entered into with the company, as on a regular exchange and as approved by the SEBI/govt.

Settlement System

Trading period will vary for the debt segment from that of equity segment. For capital market operations the trading is done in equities, convertible and non-convertible debentures. Trading network can be spread all over the country, depending on the electronic link through the satellite. A rolling settlement system operated in NSE with settlement period of T + 7. Thus, a rolling T + 7 period means that transactions on a given day (T) will be settled seven days later T + 7. On that day, funds and securities are exchanged by passing electronically proper debit and credit entries. This settlement system was changed later to T + I system due to electronic trading and clearing facilities offered in some exchanges for selected securities.

Services of SHCI

(A) Clearing Services

As member of major Stock Exchanges, the amounts due are paid on pay-in day and share certificates due to deliver are delivered, unless the transactions are as between sponsor members who are all having accounts with the SHCI. On the pay-out day cheques are received and certificates due for purchases are delivered to the corporation. The accounts on behalf of its sponsors are maintained and the net position is duly informed to the client members.

(B) Registration and Transfer Process

The corporation have developed a system of exclusive courier system of deliveries to the companies for effecting transfers. It has a computer system of tracing out the stage of processing and for the identification of the scrips in the process.

(C) Safe Custody

The SHCI has facility for depository services. It can store millions of scrips. It has a state-of-the-art custody vault at a large plot in Vashi (Navi Mumbai) and computerised system of tracing them out. The corporation has a system of inspection and audit of all certificates received from members sent for transfers, received from the company and deposited in safe custody in its vaults.

(D) Corporate Actions and Benefits of Collection

The SHCI provides the services after trade, in the form of sending them for collection of warrants, dividends, rights and bonus, etc. It has tie-up with an all-India financial services company for courier network for this personalized service from the company in respect of collection of interest and dividends, etc. It has also a system of computerised accounting after deposit of its warrants, dividends, interest, etc., and sending reconciliation statements to all its members and clients.

(E) MIS

The management information system on the corporate activity, their book closures, record dates, dividend dates, etc., are all collected and there is online sharing of this information to all its clients. It has a shift communication system for informing offshore clients as also those from across long distances to share information and eliminate unnecessary movement of paper.

Automation

The corporation has extended its services to all public sector banks, subsidiaries and mutual funds, at the request of the govt., in view of its efficient infrastructure and professionalised services. The corporation has fully computerised system located at all its headquarters and regional offices, inter-linked through an efficient networking system. It has linked itself to the major stock exchanges and to all members and customers.

Citibank

The range of custodial services offered by Citibank are a wide spectrum of activities. Some of them are briefly set out below:

(1) Settlement and registration

(2) Safekeeping and depository function

(3) Corporate and follow-up support services

(4) Tracking and follow-up support services

(5) Management of cash account

(6) M.I.S. (Management Information System)

(7) Other functions:— Reconciliation
- — Internal audit controls
- — Insurance
- — Secrecy, etc.

Custodian Services and Depository

The govt. has accepted in principle the use of Depositories as early as September 1995, for the purpose of promoting the paperless trade in securities, by immobilisation of physical certificates in the depositories. The enabling Act, namely, Depositories Act was passed in 1995 and the country's first depository went on stream on Nov. 7, 1996, namely, National Securities Depository Ltd., set up by N.S.E. and UTI and Physical certificates are immobilised by them and statements given by the Depository participants are good enough as evidence for trading.

NSDL (National Securities Depository Ltd.)

N.S.E. has promoted along with IDBI and UTI the NSDL, which became operational in November, 1996. The depository is a bank for securities and share certificates. It provides an alternative to the manual system of settling shares.

An investor can open an account with a Depository Participant (DP, say a bank) with a nil balance or some securities. He has to mark on the share certificate, "submitted for Dematerialisation" and punch the share certificate, before giving the same to the D.P.; the D.P. would then send it to the Registrars who would see the genuineness of the shares. Once the Registrars give their approval, the certificates would be entered into the Depository.

Trading on the NSE was separate for physical delivery and Depository Delivery. The DP, once advised by the Central Depository, will pass the entries in the passbook of the investor.

Advantages of Depository

It eliminates the problems and risks in trading in physical certificate. Risks of bad delivery, undue time lag for effecting transfers, loss in transit, theft or fake certificates, etc., are avoided by transfers through Depository. The cost of transfer are also lower, due to absence of stamp duty and postal charges. The transaction costs of DP may be around 7 basic points and an additional custody charges may be levied by the DP to the investor. Even so, the total costs will be lower for Depository than for physical transfers. Transfers will take place within 7 to 15 days, if the shares are dematerialised for the first time. In case the shares are already immobilised, the transfers will be effected within a day or two. Besides the quality of shares is ensured as these are affected through book entries.

Large handling of physical shares was a thing of the past. It will bring in large-scale trade through domestic and foreign institutions, Mutual funds, etc.

Besides boosting liquidity, it will ensure transparency in deals and the deliveries will be clean and quicker. Institutional trade and large orders are facilitated by the Depository transactions eliminating the need for physical transfers.

Transfer deed, stamp duty and laborious process of time-consuming filling up of transfer deeds and sending them to the company, etc., are dispensed with under the Depository system. The trade by institutions and Mutual funds will increase due to reduced costs of transactions and quicker delivery.

The entire process of clearing and settlement for Depository deals is smoother and quicker. The National Securities Clearing Corporation (NSCC) will coordinate the Exchange clearing members and custodians with the clearing bank and NSDL. NSCC will act for quicker and safer settlements as netting of the deals and book entry transfers from clearing bank and NSDL to the clearing corporation is easier. The buy and sell brokers in the NSE will advise their deals to NSE and NSCC. The pay in and pay out will now be on the same day under the Depository system. Every clearing member of the Exchange must also maintain an account with the Depository Participant (DP). The trading members use the services of DPs and as they keep a clearing account with a bank, say the Canara Bank they keep a security account with the DP, say SBI.

To start with there were 14 NSDL's participants. These DPs are for example SHCIL, GTB, HDFC Bank, Citibank, SBI, etc. These participants are advised by the traders of their sales and purchases and they make necessary pay-in and pay-out orders to the NSCC. The settlement of all deals are effected immediately and simultaneous pay-in and pay-out will take place on the same day. (T+1)

The accompanying chart will show the operations in the DP (Bank for securities). It is as easy as operating a bank account for securities. Suppose, the investor has a bank C.A. with SBI and also securities account with them. The securities are deposited in the vaults of the NSDL. The investor sells the securities from his account with the DP, say SBI. His securities account is debited and securities are credited to the NSDL and his C.A. with SBI credited with cash received from the sale proceeds. The reverse is the case when he purchases the securities. His securities A/C is credited with DP and CA with them is debited.

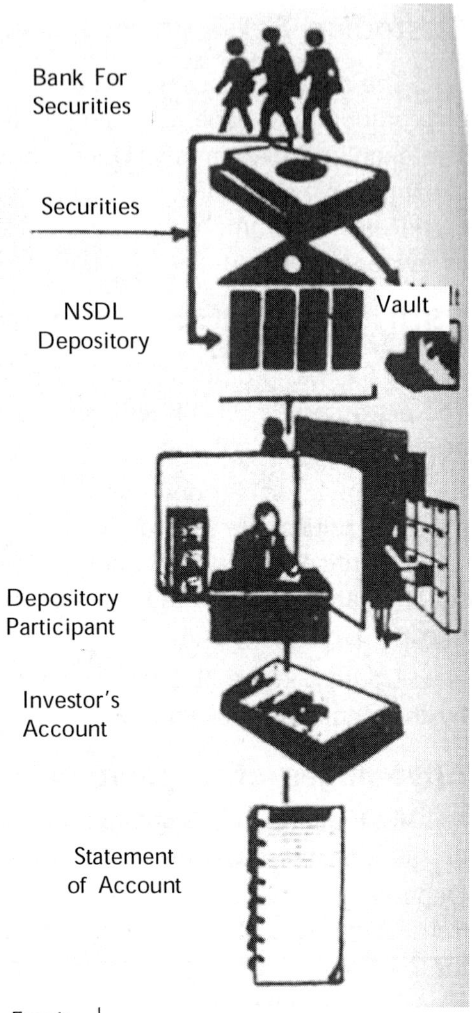

The new order of settlement is shown in the following chart. Depository is in the picture both at the paying and receiving end so far as securities are concerned. Similarly, clearing bank deals with the funds for pay-in and pay-out. Buyer gets the shares and seller the money on the same day or the next day. The chart below shows the dealings in securities (pay-in and pay-out) on left side while the dealings in funds between the buyer and seller through the clearing bank are shown on the right side of the chart. Both sides of the deal take place simultaneously and transaction is mostly completed on the same day.

SETTLEMENTS: THE NEW ORDER

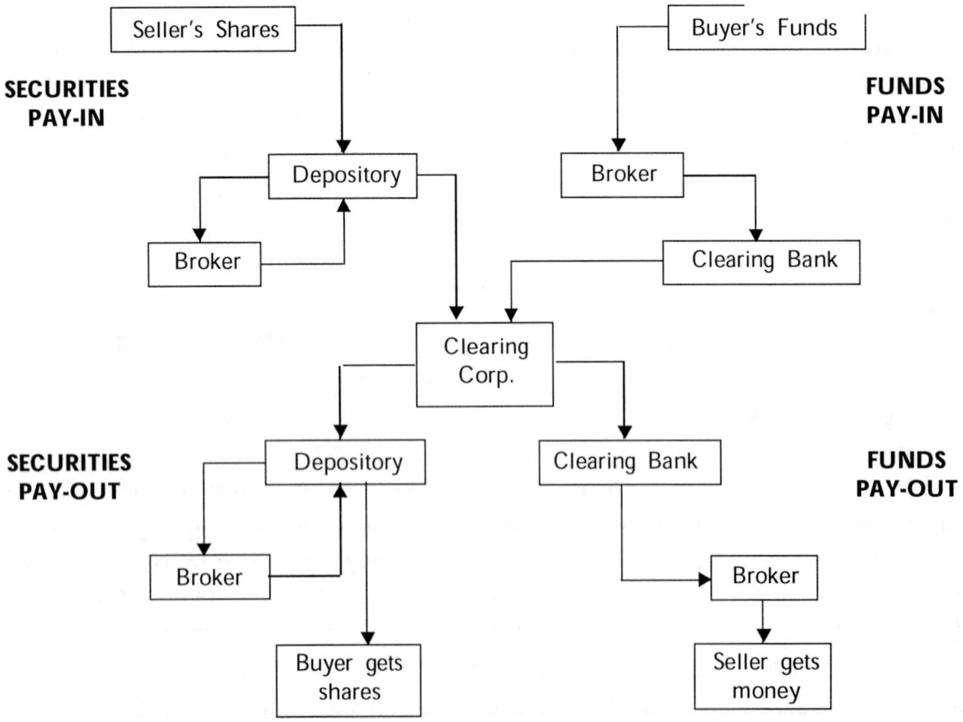

✠ ✠ ✠

FACTORING AND FORFAITING

23

Definition

Factoring is a service of financial nature involving the conversion of credit bills into cash. Accounts receivables, bills recoverable and other credit dues resulting from credit sales appear in the books of accounts as book credits. Here the risk of credit, risk of creditworthiness of the debtor and a number of incidental and consequential risks are involved. These risks are taken by the factor which purchases these credit receivables without recourse and collects them when due. These balance sheet items are replaced by cash received from the factoring agent.

Factoring is also called "Invoice Discounting" or purchase and discount of all "Receivables". Although these can be with recourse or without recourse, normally the risk is taken by the factoring agent. The discount rate includes the loss of interest, risk of credit and risk of loss of both principal and interest on the amount involved.

Many banks have set up subsidiaries for undertaking the factoring service. The factor buys the bills receivables or other book accounts, only if they are considered good for credit and are acceptable to him for the risk he takes. This service of buying the Credit Instruments may be a continuous or an adhoc service varying from Bill discounting to total take over of administration of sales ledger and collection of credit sales ledger and collection of credit sales. Credit functions involving granting of limits for cash in conversion of credit receivables include administration of sales ledger, credit control, credit approval, collection of credit bills, credit insurance etc.

TYPES OF FACTORING

The factoring services are of varying categories some of which are listed below:

(1) Limited Factoring

In this case, the factor discounts only certain invoices on a selective basis and converts credit bills into cash in respect of those bills only.

(2) Selected Buyer Based Factoring

In this case, the approved buyers of a company, based on their reputation and creditworthiness approach the factor for discounting their purchases or bills to the company in question. The claims on such buyers are paid by discounting the bills without recourse to seller and seller gets the cash.

(3) Selected Seller Based Factoring

Here, the seller sells all his accounts receivables to the factor, after invoicing the customers (who are normally approved by the factor). The seller passes on all the documents like the invoice delivery challan, contracts, etc., to the factor who takes over the remaining functions as reminders to the buyers maintaining the accounts, collecting the funds and do all consequential and incidental functions for the seller.

(4) Factoring with Recourse

Here the factor acts as an agent for collection of bills and does not cover the risk of customer's failure to pay debt or interest on it. The factor has a right to recover the funds from the seller client in case of such defaults as the seller takes the risk of credit and creditworthiness of buyer.

(5) Maturity Factoring

This factoring service provides no advance credit or financing to the client. The maturity date-wise the bills collection work is entrusted to the factor who in turn for a charge arranges to collect the funds due. This can be with recourse or without recourse. If it is without recourse payment is made to the client on a discounted basis which includes the coverage of risk and the factor proceeds against the debtor as per the contractual forms and law.

(6) Full Factoring

Under this system, the factor renders all services of collection of receivables, maintenance of sales ledger, credit collection, credit control and credit insurance. The factor also provides a drawing limit based on the bills outstanding maturity-wise and takes the corresponding risk of default or credit risk and the factor will have claims on the debtor as also the client creditor.

There are a number of other variants of this service, in terms of maturity-wise bills collection, maintenance of accounts, complete take over of all bills in the ledger, with or without recourse, etc., advance granting of limits to a limited discounting of invoices on a selective basis. These methods are all prevalent in most advanced countries, but in India only a beginning has been made. There is no insurance against risk of the debtor failure and as such many factoring agencies like SBI Factors are doing factoring for good companies with recourse.

Potentiality for Factoring in India

Banks provide generally bill collection and bill discounting and with recourse. They provide working capital finance based on these bills classified by amounts maturity-wise. Such bills if accumulated in large quantities will burden the liquidity and solvency position of the company and reduces the credit limits from the banks. It is therefore felt necessary that company assigns these book debts to a factor for taking them off from the balance sheet. This reduces the workload, increases the solvency and improves the liquidity position of the company.

In 1988, a study group under the Chairmanship of C.S. Kalyana Sundaram was constituted to examine the feasibility of factoring services in India, their constitution, organisational set up and scope of activities. The group recommended the setting up of specialised agencies or subsidiaries for providing the factoring services in India with a professional by expertise in credit assessment, debt collection and management of sales ledger, and other related services. Defaults or delays in collection and in repayment can still remain which is the risk to be taken by the factor for a fee. The group has estimated a good potential for this service to the tune of about ₹ 4,000 crore mainly emerging from the S.S.I. sector and medium and large companies which experience in collection problems, and delays in collection and consequential liquidity problems.

Later, the Vaghul Committee Report on Money Market Reforms has confirmed the need for factoring services to be developed in India as part of the money market instruments. Many new instruments were already introduced like participation certificates, commercial paper, certificates of deposits, etc., but the factoring service has not developed to any significant extent in India.

The Reserve Bank allowed some banks to set up subsidiaries on a zonal basis to take care of the requirements of companies in need of such service. Thus Canara Bank, SBI, PNB and a few other banks have been permitted to set up jointly some factors for Eastern Zone, Western Zone, Northern and Southern Zones. The progress of the activity did not show any worthwhile dimension, so far.

Modus of Operations

If a company wants to factor its receivables it submits a list of customers, their credit rating, amount involved, maturity and other terms. If the factor scrutinises the list of buyers and they are in the approved list, the factor gives its decision of the clients and the amounts they will discount and acts as factor for those receivables. In some cases, the factor may take all receivables on wholesale discounting basis. The factor then takes all the documents in respect of approved list and pays up to 80% to 90% of the amount due, less commission to the company which in turn removes these instruments, from its books of accounts and shows cash inflow as against bills receivables written off.

FACTORING AND FORFAITING

Banks have been given more freedom of borrowing and lending both internally and externally and the recent measures of financial deregulation have freed the controls on the interest rates to a large extent and facilitated the freer functioning of the banks in lending and investment operations. Besides since 1994 banks are also permitted to enter directly into leasing, hire-purchase and factoring services, instead of through their subsidiaries, as before. Banks are now free to enter or exit into any fields depending on their profitability and commercial considerations. Of course these activities are subject to certain guidelines from the RBI.

Factoring and forfaiting have not taken off in the Indian soil due to lack of expertise and experience in this line. The risks involved in this context in India are high and banks are conservative. Even after setting up the subsidiaries for the purpose in 1991, the actual business was started only in April 1994.

Factoring Services Rendered are the following

1. Purchase of book debts and receivables.
2. Administration of sales ledger of the clients.
3. Prepayment of debts partially or fully.
4. Collection of book debts or receivables with or without documents.
5. Covering the credit risk of the suppliers.
6. Dealing in book debts of customers without recourse.

Mechanics of Operation of Factoring

1. Assess the credit standing of the client.
2. Set a credit risk limit and open a line of credit.
3. Factor fixes the limits to credit exposure and time periods.

4. Client sells the goods to the customer and invoices the bills assigning them to be paid to the factor.
5. Copies of invoice and receipted delivery challans are handed over to the factor for further action.
6. Factor provides the payment up to 80% of value of invoice after scrutiny of the documents.
7. Customer who purchased has to provide the rest of 20% of the value.
8. Factor sends statements for the bills purchased and collections made and charges debited to the client.

What is Forfaiting?

Forfaiting is the conversion of foreign credit bills into cash by discounting them. Only foreign bills are involved in the transactions.

Bills for the supply of raw materials include:

— of inputs

— of capital goods.

Earlier consortium lending and government to government lending is replaced now by the forfaiting. It is discounting at fixed rate for bills of trade and involves providing finance for any type of and duration of international trade flow.

Factoring vs. Forfaiting

1. Forfaiting applies to international trade only, while factoring refers to domestic bills — purchase and discount.
2. Risks taken are risks of debtor, debtor country, currency risk, goods at sea, etc., — these are specific to forfaiting.
3. Forfaiting through EXIM Bank or in collaboration with Foreign Forfaiting agency, in foreign country.
4. Forfaiting involves accepting the above risks and discounting the bills/promissory notes and other documents in international trade thereby making a credit sale by exporter only a cash sale in practice.
5. Forfaiting is either with Recourse or without Recourse. Mostly, the preference of exporter is for forfaiting without recourse, in which risk is borne by the forfaiting agency.
6. Conversion of credit bills to cash — only foreign bills are used through foreign agencies, or importers in the importing country or in a third country.
7. R.B.I. permission was granted to EXIM Bank for forfaiting, along with other services, it renders to exporters.

Problem Areas in Forfaiting

1. There is no legal framework to protect the banker or forfaitor except for the existing covers for the risks involved in any foreign trade transaction.
2. The forfaitors suffer from lack of reliable data on credit rating of foreign agencies or importer or foreign country. As such, even EXIM Bank may not cover some countries like Nigeria which are high risk countries.
3. High risk country and political risks dissuade the services of factoring and banking to many clients.
4. High costs are involved due to high risks in this area.
5. There is need for some changes in law for developing a secondary market in them.

6. Forfaiting can be separately provided for any single shipment or a series of shipments for a deal involving many shipments, but the rates will vary depending on the risks involved. These risks vary very widely depending on the time period, distance, nature of the trade and contractual terms etc. The commodities and countries involved determine the degree of risk that the factor has to bear in the transaction and whether it should be made with recourse or without recourse.

Factoring and Forfaiting

Banks do provide non-bank financial services in the form of leasing, hire-purchase, housing finance, factoring and forfaiting. By an amendment to the Banking Regulation Act in 1983, banks have been permitted to provide these services either through their own departments or divisions or through their subsidiaries, set up for the purpose. Banks have set up merchant banking and mutual fund subsidiaries and have been undertaking direct and indirect lending for housing purposes. Other services such as leasing and hire-purchase were undertaken on a limited scale and more so through their subsidiaries. In fact the services of factoring and forfaiting were only a recent development following the recommendations of the Kalyana Sundaram Committee, set up by the RBI in 1988. Since then, considerable work has been done preparatory for the successful operation of these services by banks.

Vaghul Committee Report on money Market reforms has also suggested the development of new instruments of factoring and forfaiting services for trading in the money market, in 1989. Later, the first factoring company was started by the SBI in 1991, followed by Canara Bank and PNB, setting the subsidiaries for the purpose. While the SBI would provide such services in the Western region, the RBI has permitted the Canara Bank and PNB to concentrate on the Southern and Northern regions of the country respectively for providing such services for the customers.

The distinction between factoring and forfaiting has to be borne in mind at this juncture. Both are similar in that they relate to the purchase of book debts; while the factoring refers to purchase of domestic book debts and receivables, etc., and forfaiting refer to the foreign bills, book debts and receivables, etc., and both refer to the conversion of credit to cash transactions of clients. Credit risk and collection troubles are the responsibilities of the factoring agency. In the case of forfaiting there are country and currency risks also in addition to the credit risk of the party. On the basis of the statement of the bank, providing the factoring services, the client can draw funds up to the limits, which in turn depend on: New book debts factored, old book debts factored and collected and amounts realised and charges debited to the client.

Other Services

The factoring agency, being generally the banker or its subsidiary knows the client and his creditworthiness. The other services provided depend upon the banker-customer relationship, his requirements and receivables and this position is reviewed periodically. The factor provides his client with a periodical statement on sanctioned limit, utilised credit and balance outstanding, etc. The data on the list of book debts taken over, realised, age-wise classification of them, collected and due for collection and those with recourse and without recourse, etc.

Impact of Forfaiting

Both factoring and forfaiting are alike so far as the bank's services are concerned. Both purchase bills for cash or accept for collection. The attendant risks and returns are different in these cases and the method of credit assessment and risk and examination of documents will all be different.

Another aspect of these services is the effect of them on the balance sheet of the factor and the client respectively. So far as the factor is concerned, it is an off balance sheet item in the case of bills with recourse. But if the bills are taken without recourse, they will appear as contingent liability in the footnotes. The reverse is the case of the client, whose balance sheet will now be devoid of such burden on the debts or receivables and give a better and healthy picture. So far as the client is concerned, the changes in the balance sheet due to factoring and forfaiting are brought out in the example given below:

Factoring and Balance Sheet

Impact of factoring on the balance sheet entries is shown below:

In (₹ crore)

Current Liabilities		*Current Assets*		
Bank Borrowing against		Inventory	100	
Inventory	70	Receivables	80	180
Against Receivables	40	Other Current Assets		20
Total	110			
Other Current Liabilities	40			
Net Working Capital	50			
	200			200

Original Current Ratio 1.33:1 — (200 : 150)

Assets of receivables of 80 are purchased by the factoring agency. Factor pays 80% of this (64) to the client. Due from factor remains 16. The new balance sheet will appear as follows:

Current Liabilities		*Current Assets*	
Bank Borrowings against Inventory	70	Inventory	100
Other Current Liabilities	16	Receivable (Due from Factor)	16
New Working Capital	50	Other Current Assets	20
	136		136

New Current Ratio is 1.58:1 — (136:86)

The new current ratio is better for the client and his credit rating goes up before public eye.

Bills purchased by the factor will be off balance sheet item for the factor.

If it is with recourse, it appears as a contingent liability.

Effects

This leads to reduction in debts and less collection problems. It is an off balance sheet item. Reduction in bank finance, improvement in current ratio of the client, higher credit standing, reduction in costs, time saved and more efficiency for production and distribution and better planning, etc., are the major effects.

Resources for forfaiting or factors: The factoring agencies are set up by banks with a paid-up capital as subsidiaries of banks. They are permitted to borrow or have resources through deposits, bonds, etc., from the public or financial institutions and companies. Normally the RBI permitted them to borrow up to one time their net owned funds. In January 1997, the factors were permitted to raise resources up to three times their net owned funds to help augment their resources and expand their activities, if they are registered with RBI and credit rated along with the observance of RBI regulations.

Advantages of Factoring/Forfaiting

In India, credit information is not freely and fully available and banks do not provide the services of collection of book debts of clients. The banks do finance the receivables but with recourse and for limited periods as shown in their cash flow and funds flow statements. But many times, funds are not received in time and many assets become non-performing assets of banks. As the borrower cannot realise his funds from his debtors, due to defaults or delays, etc., the companies find themselves in a straight jacket. They have to adopt all kinds of dubious methods of borrowing from one bank to pay another bank, sell off some assets to repay the bank loans or show a fresh limit with the same bank as if the old loan has been repaid. The RBI inspection teams have traced out many such irregularities in banks' dealings with clients. To avoid such irregularities, proper credit appraisal and credit rating are necessary. Besides, prompt follow-up action to avoid the increase of non-performing assets, is necessary both from the point of view of the banks and the company.

Factoring is a method whereby risk of debtors, buyers and company customers are passed on to a specialised agency. The work of collection of bills and wholesale trade in bills is not developed in India and factoring is the only way this can be introduced and developed in India.

Factoring is useful to SSI units, who do not have organisational set up and small and medium units who cannot afford specialised staff for it. Such units can show improved liquidity and solvency by using the factoring services and take off the book debts from the balance sheet.

✠ ✠ ✠

INSURANCE SERVICES

24

(1) What is Insurance?

Insurance is a financial service for collecting the savings of the public and providing them with a risk coverage. The risk may be certain events like death, retirement, pension, education, marriage, etc., or uncertain events, like theft, accident, fire, ill-health, etc. Marine insurance is one category which covers risk of sea voyage, of shipping, cargo, etc. Motor car, scooter and two-wheeler and three-wheelers are also provided with insurance, called vehicle insurance. Building insurance,theft insurance, etc., and crop insurance are the other categories of risk coverage, introduced by GIC.

(2) Why Insurance?

They help provide protection to investors from some certain or uncertain risks. These are contractual savings, which the investors are forced to provide for. This will constitute voluntary involvement in savings, but turn into compulsory or forced savings through contractual obligation. These are generally medium and long-term savings and the investments of this type provide a low return but needed for risk coverage of life, accident, fire, etc.

(3) Categories of Insurance

The following major categories are important:

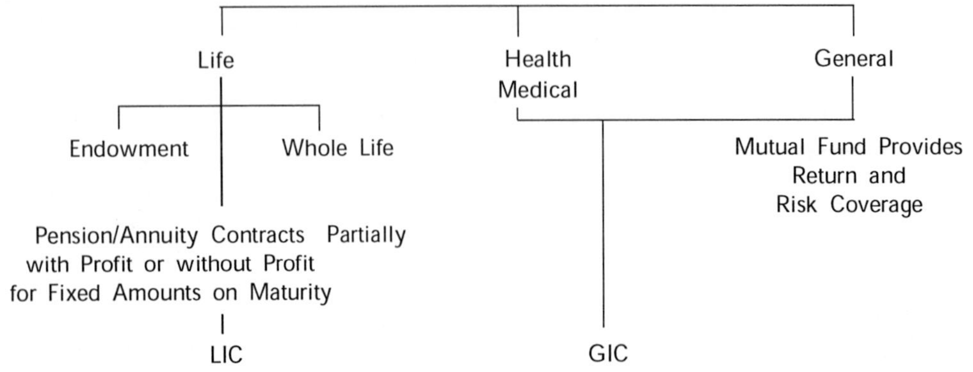

LIC has for long a monopoly of life insurance. Life insurance was there in India since 1818 carried by private and foreign insurers. In 1956, life insurance was nationalised and LIC was set up by taking over the business of about 245 large and medium companies doing business of life insurance. The P&T Dept. conducts some business of life insurance for its own employees, and UTI provides ULIP Scheme with life insurance coverage from the LIC.

What is an Insurable Risk?

To be an insurable risk, it should have the following features:

1. The theory of insurable risk is based on large numbers. There should be a large number of homogeneous risks or exposures to risk, so as to be amenable to calculation of reasonable losses. The probability such an event occurring is logically predictable such as motor accidents, deaths, etc. They should also be amenable to estimates of monetary equivalents of such losses.
2. They should be defined and measurable. The specific loss to be insured should be capable of definition and predictable and measurable. Mental tension or loss and peace of mind are not measurable and cannot be indemnified.
3. Determinable probability distribution of such adverse events, happening should be present.
4. There should be randomness in the happening of such a risk of loss.
5. Such risk or loss should not be catastrophic or completely wiped out such as through floods or acts of god or nature.
6. The premium should be ascertainable and economically feasible to both insured and insurer.

Insurance vs. Gambling

Gambling creates risk, while insurance covers and transfers the possible risk. Gambling deals with speculative risk but insurance deals with pure risk which is existing or likely to occur. The probability of its occurring can be reasonably estimated or anticipated for risk to be insured.

Principles of Insurance

1. **Indemnity:** Indemnity means that the insured person is placed financially in the same position as he was before the event occurred.
2. **Utmost good faith:** The basic principle underlying the insurance is to act under good faith. Both the insurer and the insured should disclose the facts, conditions and materials known to them before the other party to the contract.
3. **Subrogation:** The principle of subrogation should be observed. This means that the indemnifier or insurer gets all the rights and remedies of the insured after indemnification and steps into his shoes for all his legal rights and normal remedies.
4. **Contribution:** The insured should have paid all the premiums due up to the point and there is only one contributor or one insurer for the same property or risk or valuation. In other words, the subject matter of the insurance should be covered by one agency only and the insured should not get the benefit from several agencies for the same indemnified object.
5. **Insurable interest:** The insured must have the sole and legal right to the insurable object and should not be co-owner or a partner or part-owner. The subject matter of insurance must not be subjudice or under litigation.

Legal Basis of Insurance

Insurance Act 1938 is the primary Act that governs the insuranced business in India. It provides for the registration of the insurers, payment of premiums, powers of the governments, accounts and audits, etc., and settlement of claims.

Life Insurance Corporation Act 1956: This Act along with regulations, thereunder deals with the setting up of the LIC, its functions, powers, capital, conduct of business and its defined activities and investments, etc.

General Insurance Business Act 1972: This has provided for the nationalisation of general insurance by the formation of GIC to takeover of all the four existing general insurance companies. The GIC is the holding company of the four nationalised general insurance companies namely, National Insurance, New India Assurance, Oriental Fire and United Insurance companies.

There are a number of other legislations which impinge on the insurance business, like the Motor Vehicles Act 1988, Marine Insurance Act 1963, the carriage of goods by Sea Act 1925, the Merchant Shipping Act 1958, the Indian' Ports Act 1963, the Indian Railways Act 1890, the Indian Post Office Act 1898 and the Carriage by Air Act 1972, etc.

More important than all these Acts is the Act for setting up of a Regulatory Authority for the Insurance Business namely, Insurance Regulatory and Development Authority Act, 1999. This Act provides for the establishment of an Authority to protect the interests of holders of insurance policies to regulate, promote and ensure orderly growth of the insurance industry and for matters connected and incidental to the main business. This Act has also amended the Insurance Act 1938, LIC Act 1956 and General Insurance Business (Nationalisation) Act, 1972, on certain matters of their regulation. All private sector and public sector insurance agencies are brought under one umbrella of Regulatory Authority. The recent economic reforms had thrown open the insurance business to the private and foreign sectors. As these are subject to some conditions and guidelines of the government, an overall Regulatory Authority was considered necessary to enforce these conditionalities.

Milestones in Insurance Development

In 1912, the Indian Life Assurance Act was enacted as the first statute to regulate the life insurance business in India.

In 1928, the Indian Insurance Companies Act was enacted to enable the government to collect the statistical information on both Life and non-life insurance business in India.

In 1938, the Insurance Act consolidated and amended all the earlier Acts on the subject for protecting the interests of the public.

In 1956 nearly 245 Indian and foreign insurers, provident societies were taken over by the government and nationalised. In the same year, the LIC of India Act was enacted to enable the LIC of India to have a monopoly of life insurance business in India.

Similarly, the General Insurance was also regulated by the General Insurance Council, a wing of the Insurance Association of India, and it framed a code of conduct for ensuring sound business practices.

In 1972, the General Insurance was nationalised by the General Insurance Business Act of 1972. Then 107 insurers were amalgamated into four companies, viz., the National Insurance Company Ltd., the New India Assurance Company Ltd., Oriental Insurance Company Ltd., and United India Insurance Company Ltd. The GIC was incorporated to oversee all these companies, and act as a holding company for the General Insurance Business.

Costs and Benefits of Insurance

The cost of insurance is the risk taken by the insurer and his possible liability for indemnification of the insured. Only insurable risks are covered and calculated risk is taken over by the insurer which he can cover by reinsurance with another agency. The costs also include the administrative and managerial costs, frauds, cheating and mistakes, etc.

The benefits of insurance are many and varied; with the risk being covered, production can increase and starting from crops to manufacturing, all economic activities can be protected by insurance. This helps the growth of economy and raise the standards of living of the people. Internal and international trade can expand to higher levels. By coverage of life and man's possessions like houses, vehicles and other properties, the public can live in peace and with safety. Social security is provided to all citizens in developed countries; pensions and provident funds are helping the poor and needy to lead a comfortable life, in the oldage. This security to man can be extended to cattle, crops, animal husbandry, forestry and fisheries as well. In some countries, insurance covers the lawyers, and doctors' fees, and hospitalisation charges, etc. The child's future of education is protected by insurance, as well as the marriage expenses. There are innumerable examples of such insurance benefits, making life easier for the common man.

How Life Policies are Valued?

The life fund is built out of the excess premiums and investment income over the payments due to maturing claims and expenses on revenue and capital accounts. The method of valuation is discounting future income and expenditure back to the present. The rate of discount used in this respect is the same as the rate of interest, which the assets of the fund are expected to earn on an average.

The life fund so calculated is to be compared to the present value of future liabilities. The surplus is the value of life fund minus the present value of future liabilities due to maturing claims of endowment, life pension, etc. This surplus is available for distribution to policy holders and for ploughing back into reserves of LIC. Policy holders with profits only are eligible for bonus or sharing of surplus.

This surplus may be on Revenue Account, namely, excess of future income over future outgoings and/ or on the Capital Account which arises when the value of the fund is balanced by the values of the various assets of the Life Fund as reflected in the balance sheet.

Rates of bonus declared on whole life which is more risky is higher than on the endowment policies. The surpluses generated and bonus declared has been increasing over years, which shows how profitable is the insurance business. The cry for privatisation is firstly due to inefficiency of the LIC and GIC who operate in a monopoly fashion this business and the poor rewards for the investors. Secondly, the huge margin of profits between the premiums paid and outflows on account of endowment life is an eyesore for the private sector to enter into this business over the last four decades from 1950 to 1990, the Life Fund has jumped by nearly 100 times and so is the investment business of the LIC.

It is clear that with the increase in business, its investments also increased and the funds at its disposal mostly of long-term nature are meant to be used for the government infrastructure and social sectors of the economy. Over the years due to the socio-political objectives of the government, LIC has spread its coverage to urban, semi-urban and rural population. The percentage share of new business from the rural areas is around 40% of the total number of policies, but in terms of the sums assured, it may workout to around 30-35%.

Term insurance, whole life insurance, endowment policies, annuity contracts, individual insurance, group insurance, pension plans are a few types of insurance policies marketed by the LIC. Presently, LIC offers about thirty plans of insurance of which a handful say 5-6 of them account for 95% of the total new business.

Investment Pattern of LIC

Insurance Act of 1938 governs the pattern of investment of insurance funds. It has to invest at least 50% of the controlled funds in government and approved securities, 15% in other investments which include loans for social welfare purposes to State Governments, for housing and water supply, Municipal securities, co-operatives, etc. About 35% of its investments can be in the approved categories, which include shares and debentures of co-operative societies, immovable property loans for housing to individuals and co-operatives, etc. The government has also laid down that bulk of the funds are to fund the public sector and for priority sectors and socially desirable activities such as infrastructure, water supply, housing, etc. The LIC's investment in industrial sector is around 35%, but it is expected to spread its risk in a number of companies. The maximum equity capital of any one company, which LIC can hold is 30% which is still on the high scale compared to the limit of 24% for all FIs set by the SEBI. The above guidelines under Section 27 (A) of Insurance Act was amended in April 1975. The general pattern of investment of LIC and GIC is as depicted below:

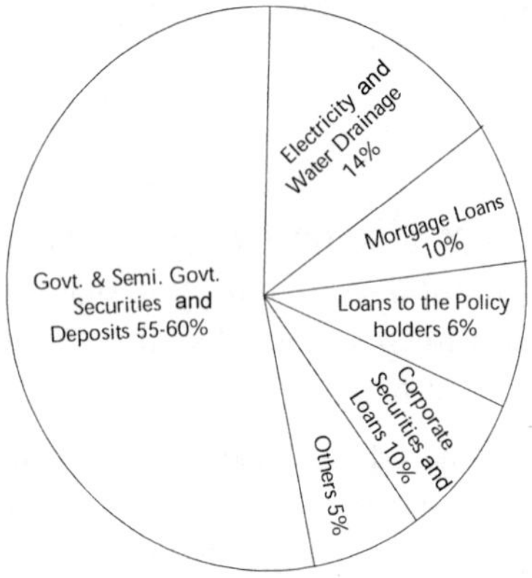

LIC Pattern of Investment

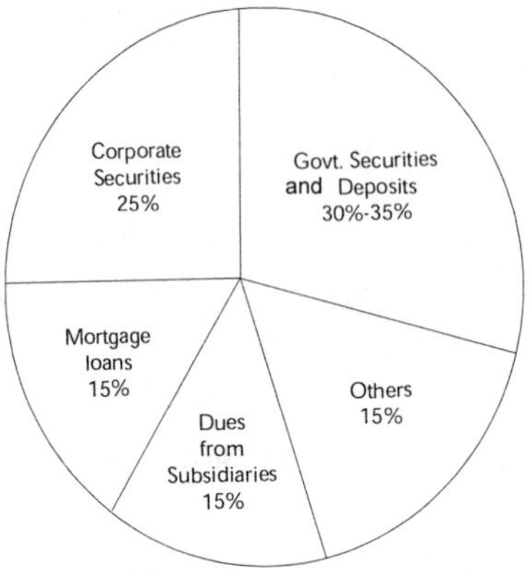

GIC Pattern of Investment

Social Priorities Concerned

Housing purposes	10-15%
Water Supply Electricity	15%
Road Transport	2%
LIC Policy holders (some of which are for Housing)	6-7%

The Amended Section laid down more detailed guidelines for investment by LIC as under:

All funds of the LIC life business and capital redemption insurance business, shall be invested as given below:

The total investments of LIC was ₹1.39 lakh crore in 2000 which rose to ₹9.17 lakh crore in 2010 and ₹10,70,180 crore in 2012 and ₹15,111.33 crore in 2014. Of these investments, about 70-75% is in the public sector.

(*a*) In Central Government Marketable securities — not less than 25%.

(*b*) In Central Government, State Government securities and Government guaranteed marketable securities (including (a) above) — not less than 50%.

(*c*) In socially-oriented sectors, public sector co-operative sector, housing, policy holders, etc., including (*a*) and (*b*) above — not less than 75%.

In investment of the balance 25%, the government guidelines are as follows:

(*a*) 8% or about that, should be earmarked for loans to policy holders within the surrender values.

(*b*) 2% or about that to be invested in immovable properties.

(*c*) The rest of the amount can be spread over a number of corporate units.

The tenets of investment are to protect the interests of policy holders on the one hand and of the economy of country on the other. The corporate investments would come as a last priority for promoting the industrial growth consistent with taking minimum risk and not exposing the public funds to speculation or trading on the stock market. The LIC funds flow to industries in the form of firm underwriting, investment in senior securities, secured bonds and fixed income securities. In brief, the LIC investments in corporate sector should be to act as a catalytic agent to provide public subscription and encourage industrialisation.

LIC is the largest single mobiliser of savings in the public sector, and now the insurance sector has been kept open to private and foreign sectors. The objective of nationalisation of insurance sector was to keep the use of these large funds for promotion of the economy and economic growth under the planned system of development and to channel these public funds for socially desirable activities for promoting social and economic welfare.

As per the more recent data premium income worked out to 20% of investible funds of LIC and grew at an annual rate of 30 to 40%. Life insurance as percentage of total investment of financial sector as 24% in 2010-11.

These objectives are seen in the sector-wise distribution of LIC investments.

As of the latest period, (2011), investments in public sector account for 74%, joint and co-operative sector for 1% and the rest say 25% in private sector. Even so, LIC invests only in public limited companies and not private limited companies. The mode of investment is to grant loans/advances underwriting and firm commitments or subscriptions for new issues of equity and bonds or secured debentures, etc. Even so, LIC has emerged as one of the major sources of funds to the industry, accounting for about 63% of the total financial assistance from FIs. LIC's share fell to 44% of the total disbursements of all FIs in 2010-11. LIC investment funds stood at ₹7,62,892 crore at end 2009. Its financial assistance to corporate sector as disbursements were ₹27,017 crore during 2006-07 and ₹38,994 crores in 2010-11.

LIC		2006-07	2011-12
		₹	₹
Paid-up share capital	–	500 crore	10,000 crore
Reserves	–	287 crore	42,722 crore
Insurance Reserves	–	2806 crore	6,28,238 crore
New Business Premium Income	–	30,888 crore	20,288 billion
Investment Pattern (Broad Categories)			in 2011
(*a*) In capital market –		22%	5%
(*b*) In govt. and approved securities –		66%	
(*c*) In Infrastructure projects –		6%	95%
(*d*) Others		– 6%	
Average Return on the Investment of Insurance Funds 8.2% and 12% in 2011.			

Source: LIC Annual Report 2006-07.

The actual employment of funds by LIC shows its strict adherence to the investment objectives and guidelines of the government. As per the latest data nearly 53-54% of the total LIC funds are invested in government and other approved securities, 23-24% in Housing infrastructure development, etc., and 17-18% in Corporate Sector while the rest are channeled into water works, co-operatives, industrial estates and miscellaneous activities (Based on LIC Annual Reports) and these accounted for about 7%. LIC covers up to two-thirds of the total life insurance coverage in a year.

Organisation and Management of LIC/GIC

LIC was set up by taking over by the government, the existing insurance companies, provident societies and other insurers doing the life insurance business. The LIC Act was passed in 1956, by which a large number of insurance companies (245 plus 97 provident societies) were nationalised. These companies became units and divisions of the Monolithic organisation, called the LIC. It has regional and zonal offices, in addition to District and Taluka units. In all districts, rural and semi-urban areas are covered by the LIC offices. LIC has a monopoly of life business; endowment, pension group insurance gratuity, superannuation, non-medical insurance, salary savings scheme, and annuities, etc., are some of the important schemes that LIC has got. It has set up the LIC Mutual Fund for mobilising savings of the public, particularly from rural and semi-urban areas and provide a good return to investors.

Like the LIC, GIC was set up by nationalising the non-life business of insurance sector in 1972. The GIC operates as the holding company of its four subsidiaries, namely, National Insurance, New India Assurance, Oriental Fire and United India Insurance Companies. GIC has both direct and indirect business. Its direct business is the aviation insurance. Its indirect business is re-insurance premium from its subsidiaries. Direct insurance is mostly in the hands of the four subsidiaries. All the 68 Indian insurers and 45 Non-Indian insurers who did business before nationalisation got merged and taken over by the four subsidiaries of GIC. These four subsidiaries have branches all over the country and concentrate on non-life insurance business like marine, fire, accident, medical expenses, car and vehicle, insurance, etc. GIC has launched a number of innovative schemes; like crop insurance, cattle and live stock insurance, insurance for visitors in bank premises, Mediclaim, Householders comprehensive policy, insurance to professionals and stock brokers, etc.

Investment Policy

As compared to LIC, GIC collects savings of public in the form of specific policies and premiums for covering some risks, like fire, accident, motor car and vehicle insurance, house burglary, etc. These are also contractual savings but the events are uncertain unlike life, retirement, pension, etc., in the case of LIC.

The yearly premium increase of GIC, by combining the business of all subsidiaries of it, may come almost near to the premium incomes of LIC. Both LIC and GIC have introduced innovative schemes and entered the areas of Mutual funds, housing finance, venture capital, insurance cum savings schemes, etc.

Unlike the LIC, GIC's investment pattern is more diversified into other than Government securities. Government and semi-Government securities invested by the GIC along with the deposits with the government constituted only 30%, while corporate securities and fixed deposits with companies worked out to 35% of the total funds of GIC. Housing and mortgage loans took away 15 to 20% and 10% of this funds are due from subsidiaries. Thus, while LIC investment portfolio is weighted in favour of Government and semi-Government securities, the GIC investments are tilted more in favour of corporate securities, with Government securities coming next in importance, followed by housing and mortgage loans. GIC can invest up to 50% in private corporate and non-government sector. Loans and other financial assistance disbursed by LIC was ₹ 38,994 crore in 2010-11 and that by GIC was ₹ 1,237 crore in 2010-11.

The investment in Government and Semi-Government securities at 50% and social priority sector investments at 15% for LIC funds are minimum levels, while the 35% for corporate securities is the maximum level permitted by the Government.

LIC policy of investment is criticised even so for diversion of public funds to family concerns in the corporate sector and neglect of the socially desirable channels for water, drainage, electricity and other infrastructural facilities. LIC can invest not more than 25% in private corporate securities. PF and trusts are not allowed to invest in stock market, while banks have recently been permitted to invest up to 10% of their incremental deposits in stock market.

Role of LIC in Capital Market

LIC enters the money market as a large supplier of funds. The RBI has permitted the operations of LIC and GIC in the call money market as the lender of funds to the banks in need. LIC is the largest single mobiliser of funds in the form of savings of the public for investment accounting for about 20-25% of the total financial savings of the household sector. LIC is also one of the large supplier of funds to the corporate sector in the form of subscription to new issues underwriting and firm commitments, loans and advances to industrial units, etc. Loans against policies are also given for investment in housing, industrial estates, etc. The LIC having control of a large chunk of funds is a large operator in the capital market, both for Government securities and corporate securities. Only it does not use its funds for speculation or trading on the stock markets, but 75% of its funds are invested in Government and semi-Government securities. LIC support to the capital market and the industrial sector is also an important factor to reckon with in the Indian economy.

Following the reforms in the capital market and in the financial sector, reforms in the insurance sector were also contemplated. The performance of LIC and GIC in investor services has been deteriorating. Despite its operation in huge funds, the margin of profits and profitability is poor. High premiums and poor after-sales-service and inefficient marketing have been the major weaknesses of the insurance sector. The LIC being in the public sector, accountability is poor, and management efficiency is low due to lack of initiative and bureaucratic and political interference into their working.

Need for Reforms

With the monopoly of the government in this sector, it has led to:

(1) The monolithic structures, with centralisation of decision and bureaucratisation of the administration.

(2) Inefficiency of manpower and low productivity due to rising costs and wage bills, due to lack of competition and poor management.

(3) Interference of political and bureaucratic forces on the working of these companies.

(4) The use of the public funds was found to be uneconomical and wasteful and the purpose of nationalisation of insurance was defeated while the objective of directing these funds for socially useful projects, national welfare measures and infrastructure projects, etc., was only partially achieved.

There is no regulatory authority, independent of the government departments, and as such the Malhotra Committee recommended the setting up a Regulatory Authority for insurance separately. It has also become necessary to introduce efficiency, competition and market-oriented forces into this sector, to improve customer service and to reduce costs and thereby reduce the premiums payable by the public to those services.

The recommendations of the committee for reform in insurance sector under the chairmanship of R.N. Malhotra (1994) are now being implemented by the government and a Bill was introduced in the Parliament in the later half of the year 1996. This Bill was passed in 1999 and insurance sector is privatised with entry of foreigners upto 26% holding. Insurance Regulatory and Development Authority was also set up in 1999 and some proposals of private and foreign companies to enter into insurance business were already approved. This agency called IRDA has already laid down guidelines as to ownership, management commission charges, etc., for both life and non-life companies.

Malhotra Committee

The major recommendations of Malhotra Committee on the reforms in the insurance sector are as follows:

1. A strong and effective Insurance Regulatory Authority is to be set up on the lines of SEBI for the capital market, which is already done.
2. LIC should be registered as a company under the Companies Act and its paid-up capital raised from ₹5 crore to ₹200 crore with government holding only 50% and the rest by the public at large. Its paid-up capital in 2012 stood at ₹100 crore.
3. LIC zonal offices should have more powers and there should be greater decentralisation of decisions and authority along with a reorganisation of both the central office and zonal offices and branches.
4. GIC should function independently as the Indian Re-insurer and all the four subsidiaries of GIC should be more independent companies.
5. GIC paid-up should be raised to ₹200 crore of which 50% should be held by the government and the rest is privatised.
6. The mandatory investment of insurance funds in government sector should be reduced in stages from 75% at present to 35% only.
7. Entry of private and foreign enterprises may be allowed into insurance business, subject to certain guidelines.
8. Cooperative Sector and Postal Departments may be permitted to undertake life insurance business.
9. All insurance companies have to transact a minimum business from the rural areas.
10. Tariff Advisory Committee should be delinked from GIC and should function independently to advice on tariff matters and there should be no monopoly rates for all insurance companies.
11. Computerisation of LIC and GIC offices and development of an MIS in both the offices.
12. Insurance companies should be free to assign the right job to right surveyors, who are to be trained for the jobs.
13. Pension schemes should be linked to savings with some tax reliefs to the pensioners.
14. The institution of Ombudsman should be set up to settle disputes on personal claims up to ₹5 lakh more quickly and reduce litigations.

Objectives of Insurances

1. Family of insured is protected.
2. Provision of retirement and oldage.
3. To provide funds for education, marriage and donations to charitable institutions like hospitals and schools.
4. To get tax relief from income tax, wealth tax and gift tax, the premiums paid as well as the sum assured.
5. To insure own life or those of any other members of the family.
6. Instalment payments in quarterly or monthly basis in addition or as alternative to yearly payments.

LIC has accumulated large sums of savings of the public, in the form of premiums. They are the basis for their investible funds. The pattern of investment is as laid down under the Insurance Act and as per government guidelines. As at end March 2011, investments by LIC were at ₹10,70,276 crore of which investments in Central and State Government securities (Public Sector) were ₹7,99,009 crores (75%).

LIC has to invest atleast 50% of controlled funds in Government and approved securities. Another 15% will be in priority sector investments like housing, water supply, Municipal securities and Co-operative Sugar factories. The rest of the 35% is allowed to be invested in permitted categories of approved investments which included shares, debentures of private and public limited companies and of Co-operative Societies. Actually LIC invests only in listed public limited companies and not private limited companies.

As insurance funds are the public funds, their investments are controlled by government guidelines. They are not expected to use the funds for speculation or trading. The investments are to be safe and mostly liquid with marketability. The housing loans to State Governments, Co-operative Housing Societies, HUDCO, Housing Boards, Housing Finance Societies and individual policy holders are granted, as part of the priority sector commitments.

INSURANCE SECTOR REFORMS

Reference was already made to the opening up of the insurance sector to foreign and private enterprise for breaking the monopoly of the public sector in this business. The insurance business can now be undertaken by corporates with foreign participation of 26% of total equity and another 26% to be left to private enterprise leaving the rest for public participation. The main objective of these reforms is to widen the base of public participation in this sector, as recommended by Malhotra Committee.

The IRDA Act was passed in 1999, and immediately thereafter, the Insurance Regulatory and Development Authority of India was set up to oversee the insurance sector so as to promote and regulate it in the public interests. The Banks' and NBFCs' entry into the insurance sector is regulated by the RBI guidelines of January and June 2000 and further amendments effected to them from time to time, in the policy announcements of the RBI.

RBI and Insurance Reforms

With the passage of IRDA Act in 1999, and the setting up of Insurance Regulatory and Development Authority of India in 1999, there began a foray into this sector by banks and NBFCs. RBI has laid down guidelines for FIs and banks to enter into insurance sector in Janaury 2000.

These guidelines are broadly set out below:

1. FIs and banks are barred to run insurance business due to high risks involved, either departmentally or through subsidiaries. They could however stake up to 50% in these ventures, along with the Indian partners and foreign investors.
2. Such entrants need to have a net worth of ₹500 crore or more and a reasonable level of NPAs, below the industry average.
3. Their CRAR should not be less than 10% of assets.
4. Their subsidiaries should have a satisfactory track record and continuous profitability over the last 3 years.
5. Their share in equity participation in joint ventures of insurance business should not exceed 10% of their net worth or ₹50 crore whichever is less.
6. Their participation in Joint Ventures should not exceed 30% of the paid-up capital of the insurance company, with an important provision, that the total amount invested in all subsidiaries and joint ventures should not exceed 20% of the banks' or FIs' net worth.
7. Banking business should be kept separate and not contaminated by inducting insurance business into the former due to high risk nature of insurance business.
8. RBI being controller of foreign exchange has along with the government fixed ceiling of 26% of FDI in insurance sector. More recently in 2005, the government proposed to raise it to 49%.

The above guidelines apply only to main insurance business and not to insurance broking, agency or surveying, etc. The guidelines for them as also reinsurance business are the responsibility of IRDA.

IRDA

The IRDA Act 1999 provided for three categories of insurer to carry on the business in India. These are the following:

(1) A public company which has two categories in operation, namely, public limited and public unlimited companies. Of these, the public unlimited companies, set up mostly in the U.S.A. are not eligible to do insurance business. Similarly, private limited companies as such are also not allowed. Only public limited companies registered in India are eligible.

(2) A society incorporated under the Co-operative Societies Act, 1912 in India or under any other law relating to co-operative societies, is eligible.

(3) A body corporate, incorporated abroad under the law of that country, not being in the nature of a private company, is also entitled to carry on insurance business.

As per the Act, an Insurance Regulatory and Development Authority (IRDA) was set up to regulate the pricing, organisation and servicing of the insurance agencies.

Since IRDA Act provides for divestment by the domestic promoter after 10 years, one of the ways of allowing the U.S. majors who are public unlimited companies to invest in Indian insurance sector is to allow a fourth category, namely, deemed public companies. The government was committed to divestment by domestic promoters in favour of public after 10 years. After the divestment, domestic and foreign promoters would hold equity shares of 26% each, while the rest of the stake would be dispersed in favour of the public. The Malhotra Committee which laid down the broad framework for the insurance sector to be opened up recommended a wide dispersal of shareholding of the proposed insurance companies.

NBFCs and Insurance

The RBI guidelines for NBFCs' entry into insurance business were released in June 9, 2000. The following are the major highlights of these guidelines:

1. NBFCs need a minimum net worth of ₹500 crore for entry into insurance joint venture.
2. The maximum stake in insurance Joint Venture is 50% of the paid-up capital of Joint Venture.
3. NBFCs with net owned funds of ₹2 crore and above can only act as agents.
4. The minimum CAR is pegged at 15%, if the NBFCs are in loan and investment business with public deposits. Others should have at least 12% CAR, irrespective of whether they accept public deposits or not.
5. Ineligible NBFCs can make investments up to 10% of the owned fund or ₹50 crore, whichever is lower, in the insurance company.
6. Those NBFCs qualifying for entry into insurance business will have to apply to RBI for permission.

The RBI guidelines for banks were already referred to earlier.

Internet and Insurance

Professionally qualified intermediaries will emerge in insurance as competition is forced upon them. The role played by agents is likely to be partly replaced by internet and e-commerce. Insurance being opened up will use all the tools of new technology in its activities. Information and database is necessary for decision making on pricing and reinsurance. This can be achieved only by total computerisation and connectivity of operations. The necessity of cost savings and the prevalence of competition force the need for proper pricing of all insurance products and efficient and prompt servicing of customers. This can be secured by use of latest information technology in insurance business. Computerisation is necessary for database, sales and advertisement and even for its investment operations, including portfolio management. After-sales service of customers also requires the total computerisation of all operations in insurance. The LIC has already computerised and premium can be paid through the internet.

Foreign Equity for Insurance Broking

IRDA is reported to have decided to allow 76% of foreign equity in insurance broking, although only 49% foreign equity was the standard level for foreign participation. However, 100% of foreign equity in the case of foreign owned subsidiaries is permitted in some sectors. In NBFC sector foreign equity was capped at 49%, as in the case of many sectors of the economy.

The CII has recommended a minimum capital of ₹ 50 lakh for reinsurance brokers and ₹ 10 lakh for ordinary brokers. The reinsurance brokers provide reinsurance to insurance companies. In many markets, brokers provide non-life business, as well as group life and mortgage insurance. In U.K., the brokers are required to ensure that the assets exceed the liability by the amount of capital requirement. Solvency margins would have to be presented in case brokers who are permitted to collect premium and are thus handling the money of the insured. In Japan, solvency margins and minimum capital requirements are not needed as they are not empowered to conclude contracts, accept representations or to receive insurance premiums. In India, the requirements would depend on the emerging market condition and practices.

Surveyors as Intermediaries

Insurance brokers, agents, surveyors, etc., are the different types of intermediaries in the insurance sector. The surveyors are like auditors, who render the service to the consumer in the form of hasslefree settlement of claims in the shortest time possible. Once the claims arise, they are to be scrutinised, assessed and settled for the benefit of insured.

Insurance Broking

An insurance broker would provide the following services *inter alia*:

1. Presale and after-sale service to customers.
2. Provision of relevant information to underwriters to assess risks and decide premium.
3. Design covers that meet client requirements.
4. Recommend risk improvement and loss minimization measures.
5. Provide risk management and insurance education.
6. Collection of premiums.

IRDA is permitting up to 76% of foreign equity in insurance broking. The minimum capital requirements for reinsurance brokers is expected to be ₹ 25 lakh and for ordinary insurance brokers ₹ 10 lakh.

The preamble to the IRDA Act, states as follows:

"To provide for establishment of an authority, to protect the interests of holders of insurance policies to regulate, promote and ensure orderly growth of insurance industry and for matters connected thereto or incidental thereto and further to amend the Insurance Act, 1938, LIC Act, 1956 and General Insurance Business (Nationalisation) Act, 1972."

This industry has grown tremendously since the nationalisation in 1970, when there were 108 insurance companies, both Indian and foreign, with a total premium contribution of ₹ 105 crore. In 2000, there were four nationalised insurance companies with a premium income of more then ₹ 10,000 crore, which represents an increase of 100 times over a period of 30 years. The industry has more than 4,000 offices throughout India and a formidable pool of skilled manpower, both in technical and marketing fields and a big network of agents and field workers.

Disposal of Claims

The existing insurers are saddled with six lakh outstanding third party claims, involving total provisions for outstanding liabilities at ₹ 4,000 crores. There are large number of third party claims arising out of road accidents and motor vehicle insurance. The disposal of these claims through the established judicial system of Motor Accident Claims Tribunal is very slow. Similarly, only a small number of claims is disposed of through the forum of Lok Adalats. The insurance companies have not been able to settle the claims quickly, as a result of these problems. The arrears of disposal attract interest burden on the liabilities, in addition to their administrative problems and costs. The investment income was inadequate to cover these rising costs of outstanding claims.

The banks proposed to enter the insurance business, through a subsidiary promoted by them or through fund based agency business, undertaken departmentally. The banker will be enabled to leverage their existing network of branches for selling the insurance products for additional non-fund income. The banks can utilize their surplus manpower and infrastructure for better productive uses of insurance business.

The banks foray into insurance business led to some failures due to high risks involved even in some developed countries. RBI has come out with some guidelines for banks' entry into insurance business in the year 2000, as already referred to.

There are three areas of general insurance business into which banks can enter:

1. Marketing of General Insurance Products.
2. Management of Assets/Investments.
3. Management of liabilities.

However, in the case of marketing of the insurance products and management of assets, banks may be suitable but not in the management of liabilities.

Non-life Business

The market penetration in non-life business was very low at 0.55% of the GDP, as against 4.5% in developed economies of USA, Japan, etc. It is expected that there is large potential to be tapped and the current level of premium of $2 billion non-life sector alone can grow up to $20 billion in the next ten years. This can easily be achieved by opening up the insurance market to competition and entry of foreign and private enterprise into it. With the influx of foreign players and capital into the arena, the technical, managerial and financial expertise available in the world's leading insurance markets is now available to India.

The benefits to the economy by the opening up of the insurance sector are expected to be very large. The resource mobilisation and investments will increase and consumers and public will benefit by improved efficiency, better service, lower premiums and better quality products. The vast middle and lower income groups and rural population are to be brought into the fold of insurance protection. The new products like crop insurance, cattle and animal insurance, house burglary, theft insurance, etc., will go in number and volumes. These developments will strengthen the insurers and bring in advanced insurance practices of the west, and the state-of-the-art and work class technology transfer, socio-economic uplift and increased industrial and commercial activity through massive investment options would flow thereby.

The growth of general insurance business up to 1999 when the IRDA Act was passed and the insurance sector was opened up to private and foreign sectors was shown in the following Table.

INDICATORS OF GENERAL INSURANCE INDUSTRY

(₹ in crore)

	1973	1999	Growth Times
1. Capital	37	375	10 times
2. Free Reserves	62	6758	109 times
3. Net worth (1 + 2)	99	7133	72 times
4. Technical Reserves	268	14,190	55 times
5. Investments	355	19,168	54 times

Source: E.T. Dec. 29, 1999.

Pricing of Insurance Products

Under the deregulated regime of insurance, the growth of insurance business will depend on the fair pricing of the products on sale. The insuring public will demand both competitive price and better service under the new competitive environment. This requires a transparent pricing regime which is equitable to both insurers and insuring public.

Today, the major part of insurance business is governed by Tariff structure formulated by Tariff Advisory Committee, which also revises the rates of premiums based on experience of claims from different categories of risks insured. Now the market moves towards detariffing of pricing. The shift from tariffed structure to detariffed structure is difficult and time-consuming, but is necessary for the new environment of open and free market for insurance.

Meanwhile, the Tariff Advisory Committee must apply its mind to existing gross imbalances and econometrics in Tariff Structure and Costs. The establishment and servicing costs have to be kept to the minimum. At present, in India, statute enjoins a permissible limit of costs to the insurance companies at about 19.5% of their gross direct premiums. This includes the cost of intermediaries agents. The existing set up is such that some units are exceeding the given cost limit. The current high cost ratio of insurers has to be brought down by realistic rationalisation of manpower, as the fixed costs are high at present. There are imbalances between the fixed management expenses and cost of processing business. If the industry has to attract professionals and further investment, there is need for existing companies to cut their costs, reduce the manpower expenses per ₹ 1,000 of insured amount or premium income and move to a detariffed price regime.

✠ ✠ ✠

MERGERS AND ACQUISITIONS

25

Introduction

In the Indian Law, Companies Act, FERA, MRTP Act and Listing Agreement contain measures to deal with mergers, acquisitions and takeovers. There are three type of takeovers — friendly and arranged marriages, hostile takeovers through acquisition of controlling share and bailout acquisitions of non-viable undertaking and sick companies.

Most of these legal provisions appear very effective on paper but in substance, they have little inherent strength and can be easily circumvented.

Existing Law: Transfer Provisions

Transfer of shares: In any takeover operation, the person or group acquires shares of a certain percentages from the open market in order to gain control of the target company. These shares may be picked up in recognised stock exchange.

Refusal to register transfer: Under Sec. 111, the refusal to register the transfer of shares to the transferee has to be within two months and reasons for such refusal should be given. The refusal to transfer shares gives the target company substantial amount of time and is often the start of a prolonged litigation.

As per Section 22 A of SC (R) Act, the board of directors can refuse to register the transfer on only one or more of four grounds, namely:

(*a*) that the instrument of transfer is not proper or has not been duly stamped and executed or the certificate relating to the security has not been delivered to the company or that any other requirement of law relating to such transfer has not been complied with;

(*b*) that the transfer is in contravention of any law; like FERA, MRTP Act, etc.

(*c*) that the transfer is likely to result in such change in the composition of the board of directors as would be prejudicial to the interest of the company or to the public interest; and

(*d*) that the transfer is prohibited by any order of any court or tribunal or other authority under any law for the time-being in force.

Prima facie clause (c) will most likely be invoked by the target company on the ground that the transfer is likely to be prejudicial to the interest of the company or even to public interest. This involves investigations into facts and will finally depend upon the subjective satisfaction of the Company Law Board (CLB) as to whether or not the transfer is likely to result in prejudice or otherwise.

Inter-corporate Investments

(*a*) The aggregate of the entire corporate investments in all other bodies corporate taken together should not exceed 30% of the subscribed capital of the investing company.

(*b*) Apart from the above restrictions, investments in the shares of any body corporate should not exceed 10% of the subscribed capital of the other company.

(*c*) In addition to the aggregate ceiling of 30% and subject to the 10% ceiling limit, the aggregate of investments in all other bodies corporate in the same group should not exceed 20% of the subscribed capital for the investing company. The specific ceiling limits of 10%, 20% and 30% are to be replaced by "such ceiling limits as may be prescribed", in public interest.

Merger Provisions under Compromise

Under Sec. 391 to 394, of Companies Act, any competent court can enforce a compromise or arrangement between the creditors and members, whereby the company can be reconstructed and two or more companies may be amalgamated under the proposed scheme of compromise. Information on the compromise has to be supplied to all creditors and members under Sec. 393.

Where an application is made to the court under Sec. 391 for the sanctioning of a compromise, which involves a merger or acquisition, the court has powers to sanction the scheme, under Sec. 394.

Under the scheme of compromise given under Sec. 394 the whole or any part of the undertaking, property or liabilities of one company may be transferred to another company. The allotment of shares of transferee company to the shareholders of transferor's company and the terms and conditions of the same, as have been laid down under the scheme of compromise or arrangement are to be approved by the High Court. If approved within 30 days after the order is passed, every company involved in the order shall cause a certified copy of the court order to be filed with ROC.

The court shall give notice of every application made under Secs. 391-394 to the Central Government and shall take into account the representations made to the government by any interested parties in this regard.

Under Sec. 395, the scheme of transfer of one company's assets to another, if approved by holders of 9/10th in value of total paid-up capital is binding on the minority but the power and duty to acquire shares of shareholders dissenting from the scheme is to be given by the court order. A notice of four months is to be given to all the members to approve the scheme. After the expiry of four months, within two months after that date the company gives to the minority shareholders a chance to offer their shares for sale. After that time period, the court may pass an order to effect the arrangement of merger or acquisition and acquire the shares of dissenting shareholders on the terms approved by the court.

Under Section 396, the Central Government has powers to order for the amalgamation of any two or more companies in the national interest.

When any such companies are amalgamated under Sections 391 to 396, the company has to preserve the books of account and cannot dispose them without government consent.

Acquisition from Dissenting Minority

This Section enables the purchaser (s), to compel the minority to sell the shares to them provided the stipulated requirements are satisfied, *viz.:*

(*a*) the purchaser company makes an offer to the shareholders of the company in which it proposes to acquire shares;

(*b*) the offer should be accepted, within four months, by holders of not less than 9/10th of the total value of shares;

(*c*) the remaining shareholders who do not accept the offer are to be treated as dissenting shareholders;

(*d*) the transferor company can give notice within two months after the expiry of the said four months to the dissenting shareholders and dissenting shareholders have then to transfer the shares to the transferor company;

(*e*) the minority can, however, apply to the court on the ground that the scheme of purchase is illegal or unfair. The case law on this subject shows that the offer must be "fair". However, when 9/10th of the shareholders have accepted the offer, it is indeed difficult for the minority to establish in court that the offer is unfair.

FERA: Deals with NRI Mergers

Secs. 19, 26 and 29 of FERA relate to transfer of shares. These provisions are invoked only when one of the parties is a Non-Resident Indian (NRI) because the Act prohibits persons from entering into contracts with NRIs for purchase of shares without the general or special permission of the RBI. However, the general impression is that the NRIs can sell their shares to other NRIs, and there is nothing that can be done by the RBI. Thus, if the shareholders of a company in England sell their shares of a company having business interests in India to other NRIs or companies in England itself or in other countries, the Act will not apply. But, in fact the RBI does have wide powers in these cases as well.

Under Sec. 19 (5) of FERA, the shares of a company registered in India cannot be transferred by a person resident outside India to another person whether resident in India or outside India. Such a transfer will not be valid unless the transfer is confirmed on an application made to the RBI.

MERGERS AND ACQUISITIONS

Theoretical Aspects

In India, the role of acquisitions and mergers has increased in recent years due to prevailing trends of privatization and globalization in the economy. The influence of foreign forces has increased enormously on the financial and commodity markets in India. This led to the greater forces of competition operating on the industry. In this context the survival of the fittest is the only option open to the industrial units. The economic units are thus facing with the alternatives of strengthening themselves or going to the wall. The week ones are weeded out. The viable units are being strengthened by mergers or acquisitions or expansion and diversification. It is in this context the importance of mergers and acquisitions has to be viewed.

First, theoretical aspects backing this activity have to be set out. The theoretical basis of mergers and acquisitions is firstly the economies of scale. Mergers and demergers are the offshoot of the adjusting the units to the optimum size in terms of the economies of scale. Mergers are needed when the units want to expand and demergers are wanted when the excess fat has to be shed and diseconomies are to be met by dropping the lines of activity or divisions not viable and have to be given up. Acquisitions are needed when the unit is cash rich and finds that the easiest and cost-effective method of expansion is acquisition rather than setting up a new unit or expansion through setting up any fresh lines of activity all by itself. Acquisitions are possible through own funds or borrowed funds, if they are worthwhile by all criteria and economic value added is higher than the costs incurred for the additional project. Mergers and acquisitions are also needed for diversification.

Another economic factor influencing this activity is the competency and efficiency in certain lines of activity much more than other lines of activity. This factor of competency is in terms of the human resources, technology used and management experience. In the lines of activity where it has efficiency, it can expand through mergers and acquisitions and contract in the lines where it has no competency. In this context also, mergers and acquisitions play an important role on the industrial scene.

Yet another factor affecting the mergers and acquisitions is the environmental forces and the factor endowments unique to the unit or units. Thus, some units in India are specializing in the BPO activity and developed Western countries like U.S. and U.K. use these services from the Indian firms. Similarly, in IT industry, there are many knowledge based activities which are developed in India, such as telecommunications , media, computer software, etc., developed on the basis of the human resource endowments of the intelligentia of the country. Added to it, the time gap between Western developed countries and India is an additional advantage for transmission of the data and the results of the R&D efforts.

Theoretically, the least cost combination of the product-mix may be got by mergers, demergers and acquisitions. Any economic unit is in constant endeavour to maximize profits which encompasses the lowering of the costs, changes in the compositions of the product-mix, and input-mix, etc. Here the cost benefit analysis holds good for the micro unit namely the firm in question. Whether to go for mergers or acquisitions in India or abroad, the finance manager has to take into account the added costs and consequent benefits flowing from this activity. Here as elsewhere, both financial analysis and economic analysis has to be applied. And it is the top management's decision that finally prevails. Both foreign and domestic companies can be the target of acquisition.

Yet another factor that governs the decision for or against mergers is the conflict between the owners and creditors of the company and when they go to the courts, the decision may be compromise formula of merger of two companies. This involves the economic conflicts resolved by the court order. The Law and Rules of the governments make the final decision based on the economic and financial data placed before it. Here, the provisions of Companies ACT, SEBI Regulations and govt. guidelines play a part.

Mergers can be friendly affairs and on mutually agreed terms and conditions or forced on them by the court or the government. The theoretical logic of it is that the creditor company has every right to take care of the debtor company for its own interest of recovery of its dues and if necessary takeover the company by acquisition. Such mergers and acquisitions are arranged by mutual consent in a friendly manner or by the court order.

Another way mergers take place is by the application of the rules and regulations of the Listing Agreement of the stock exchange if it is a listed company. Section 49 A and B of Listing Agreement provide for the disclosures by the listed company of the price and quantum of acquisition of the other listed or non-listed company being acquired. The reason for the acquisition may be bail over of the company or strengthening of the competency of the company taking over or the prevention of the mismanagement of the company, to be taken over.

There is another way such mergers take place namely through the intervention of the BIFR in respect of the non-viable and sick companies referred to it or taken up by them *suo motto* for rehabilitation. In this case, the rationale is economic basis of making the poorly run company become viable and to make the weak ones strong and strong ones stronger, as the principle of the survival of the fittest is the rule in the modern competitive world of privatization and globalization. Survival of the fittest and weeding out the weaker ones is the rule of the day.

While on the subject of globalization, it is apt to mention the side effects of this trend are far too serious and need to be countered effectively. One is to withstand the cost competency and high level of productivity comparable to the world trends. Second, the rupee appreciation is standing counter to the interests of the exporters and imports are growing faster than exports, which is leading to the balance of payments problems of the country. Thridly, the imports are priced higher, particularly for crude oil and commodities, which leads to fear of imported inflation and expectation of further inflation. This has direct and indirect effects on the investment climate in the economy which may lead to the slow down of the growth rate of the GDP.

In view of the above and other repercussions of the globalization and privatization trend globally and their effects on inflation on the domestic economies it is relevant to know well the theoretical myths and realities of the inflation as a economic parameter to be reckoned within the economies of mergers and acquisitions and in the discussion of the theoretical and ideological aspects of this subject.

Importance of Valuations in Mergers and Acquisitions

Foreign forces are more prominent on the financial markets due to large inflows of foreign funds by FIIs and FFIs and their operations in the stock and capital markets in India and other emerging economies where the phenomena of mergers and acquisitions is more relevant. Besides, imports and services to be paid abroad are all influencing the inflation and inflationary expectations. Corporates and their investment activity are vitally effected by inflationary expectations. Mergers and acquisitions are to be valued for their net asset value which are again a function of the inflation, as many of these operations are involving the foreign companies or MNCs who are supposed to be accounting as per prevailing international standards and that involves the inflation adjusted figures. Much of the inflation in the developing countries is imported due to prevailing high prices of crude oil and gold and other internationally traded capital goods which are necessary for their investment and growth. Besides in more recent years the world economies are more inter-linked through aid, trade and operations of the MNCs.

If mergers are ordered by the courts or by the BIFR, valuations of net assets are compulsory. If the acquisitions are made through the stock exchanges, Listing agreement imposed certain conditions of which the dissenting minority have to be compensated at prices and their fair valuation and disclosures of values and prices, etc., are all strictly enforced by the SEBI. International mergers are all valued at the inflation adjusted values of assets, namely at constant dollars. If thus an Indian MNC say Ranbaxy is buying out a foreign company or Mittals are acquiring ARCELOR company, there were lots of pinpricks on pricing and satisfying the shareholders of the acquired company. In this context, many issues arise on pricing the shares of merged companies' shares and their fair valuations. In the case of foreign companies being acquired or merged, valuation is a critical component of the merged companies or bought out companies and there are internationally accepted valuers like ***Price Waterson and other International Merchant Bankers.***

In valuation of the companies for their true worth, there are many interested parties in addition to the acquired and acquiring companies namely the share holders of both companies, the regulators of the country or countries, the stock exchanges where they are listed, the concerned governments and investors in general. In the case of compromises between creditor and debtor companies or takeover of the sick companies the court's and the BIFR's or the governments consents are necessary which all look into the valuation aspects also.

Valuations have to take into account the inflation adjusted figures of the asset values. Many internationally listed companies are already presenting figures of their accounts in constant dollars or constant rupees where adjustment is made for the inflation in the respective countries. In the case of banks, the net assets are taken after the non-performing assets are excluded or adjusted for their realizable values as testified by their approved auditors. The audited financial figures are taken and adjust them for the currently realizable values in the valuation of the assets under mergers and acquisitions. Such is the importance of valuation and the role of inflation in this process.

Conceptual Part of M&A

This chapter highlighted so far the need for proper valuation of assets of the acquiring and acquired companies and their market valuations before and after merger — both at current and constant prices, which needs the consideration of the lameduck measure of inflation. It's myths and realities are to be studied to emphasise its weaknesses. This often neglected part of the M&A activity, requires further research.

Types

Acquisitions and Mergers are of Two Types, Namely Friendly and Hostile. In either case the basis for this activity is mutual benefit or forced by the circumstances of the case namely imposition by the courts, BIFR or the govt. The causation is the differences in valuations of the market of the shares of the companies, the state of the market and differences in P/E multiples, ratios of book values to the market values, technological differences and inter-corporate affiliations and relations of subsidiaries to the parent companies, etc. In a booming market the M&A activity is larger than in a depression. Weaker ones, under valued ones, the start ups, and non-viable units are the usual targets of takeover.

Mergers can be of the domestic companies or foreign companies which are also called cross-border mergers. The latter involve more problems due to differences in technological changes, H&R attitudes, R&D efforts, Tax differences, govt. hurdles, exchange controls, legal barriers, stock valuation difficulties, comparison of RONW, ROI, PAT or P/E ratios, etc. Inflationary pressures, rates of growth of GDP market practices and procedures, regulatory measures of the govts. may be different leading to the complexities in merger process or acquisition process.

Causation

Competition, free market forces, privatization and globalization force the weaker ones to consolidate or die. Survival of the fittest and strongest is the order of the day. It is in this context, that the strong tries to become stronger and weak to become strong as the alternative is to wither away in competition. Better corporate governance, higher technology, better managerial efficiency give the strength to a company to raid other weaker ones with similar systems and practices or related area operations, etc., complementary to its operations or related through the R&D efforts. The expected economies of scale, help of better technology, larger market access, costs and benefit analysis showing positive benefits, better corporate governance, higher productivity and larger investor wealth are the expected gains from this M&A activity. Stock performance after merger, market valuations of the stock are the immediate measures of benefits. The final measures of the benefits are the RONW, ROI, PAT and P/E ratios.

Benefits

Firm's objectives are to maximize the investor wealth, improve the share valuation and grow through the diversification, expansion and modernization. The alternatives to original setting up of the plants or projects, are the acquisitions of the start ups or the weaker ones or mergers of the competitive and complementary companies. It is cheaper many times to go for the M&A activity, or takeover of the sick and viable units and develop them to profitable stage. This activity is hostile if it is opposed by a few share holders or the promoters in which case the shares of the company have to be acquired through the stock market operations. Such acquisitions are subject to the provisions of the Section 40A and B ***of the Listing Agreement of the Stock Exchange***. The benefits also depend on the method of financing the M&A activity, either in cash or equity or a combination of them. Whether the acquisition is of subsidiaries or related firms, or foreign firms in the same line or related lines or it leads to vertical integration, or horizontal integration or geographical spread are the factors to be considered.

Merger and acquisition activity is generally guided by the goals of expansion, diversification, growth of investor wealth, market discipline, changes expected or real of govt. policy, deregulation, better competition or more regulation, etc. Market expectations of the company, its reputation, its management goals and growth prospects are the general guidelines for any activity in this line. The merger has to be beneficial for both to be a friendly takeover. Otherwise it becomes hostile takeover when the regulations of the SEBI will apply and the acquiring company has to clearly state its intention and acquire the shares in the market at the current prices.

The M&A activity can be classified as per the number of mergers or acquisitions and the amounts involved, industry-wise, sector-wise, and geographical coverage-wise. In India more recently during the years of booming markets 2004 to 2008, M&A activity was as its height. During the years 2003 to 2007, the amount involved in acquisitions rose from ₹23,787 crore in 2003 to ₹60,282 crore in 2005 and fetched to ₹2.04 lakh crore in 2007. As between mergers and acquisitions, the latter outnumber the former in India during the last few years in the new millennium. During all the years in the new millennium acquisitions are more than the number of mergers. Thus in the year 2006-07, acquisitions numbered about 924 as against the mergers of 358 only. Actually the M&A activity was growing only in the new millennium due to the ongoing economic and financial reforms and the opening of the economy, privatization, globalization of the markets and banking and financial reforms in the process.

Industry-wise, the major activity was seen in acquisitions in the I.T. sector, chemicals, pharmaceuticals, metals, oil, BPO, and related activities of R&D efforts. Product-specific and brand-specific companies have been raiding the wave of this activity by foreign acquisitions of similar products and brands competing in the respective markets. Computer software and knowledge based industries and service-oriented industries have seen this wave more visibly in recent years.

The objective of this chapter is to emphasise the neglected part of M&As, namely valuations of stocks of the companies before and after merger, and valuation of the assets of the firms in question in real terms and the pitfalls of the use of **Inflation Index**. This overview of the mergers and acquisitions shows the conceptual parts of the activity and tries to convince on the vagaries of fortunes of this activity and uncertain outcomes but a certain trend towards the greater role of this activity in the years to come. The causation, benefits expected and the trends are clear but more research is needed on the measurements of the costs and benefits, final outcomes and its impact on the globalization process through proper valuations of assets and stocks of the companies concerned.

Clause 40 of the Listing Agreement

This clause (now applicable to all Indian Stock Exchanges) stipulates certain rules that must be followed in the acquisition of shares of another company (the target company) or in the "Securing of effective control" of the management of the target company. If the prescribed rules are not followed, the stock exchange will delist the shares of the target company.

1. A public announcement must be made through newspapers (English and vernacular) in the 'prescribed manner'. The stock exchanges where the shares are listed must be notified immediately.

2. After the negotiation is completed, both the purchaser and seller must inform the concerned stock exchanges about the conclusion of the deal.

3. Thereafter, an offer should be made to the remaining members in the form of a circular containing details regarding the identity of the purchaser, source of funds, reasons of the purchase, future proposals, etc. The circular has to be approved by the Regional Stock Exchange where the registered office of the company is situated.

4. Such an offer must be made within two weeks from the date of approval and has to be kept open for at least six weeks from the date of the offer. The offer, if amended, will have to be kept open for a further period of six weeks.

5. If as a result of purchase of shares, there is a change in the management of the company, this must be intimated to the government.

Provisions of Listing Agreement

Clause 40A: When any person acquires or agrees to acquire any shares in the company and when the total nominal value of such shares so acquired or agreed to be acquired together with the total nominal value of the shares already held by such person, exceeds or shall exceed in the aggregate 5% of the voting capital of the company, the Stock Exchange shall be notified within 2 days of such acquisition or such agreement for acquisition, by the company, by the authorised intermediary and also by the acquirer.

Clause 40B: A public announcement of a takeover offer shall be made both by the offeror company and the offeree company when —

(*a*) Any person in his own name or in the name of any other person acquires, whether by a series of transactions over a period of time or otherwise, shares which, when aggregated with shares already held or acquired by such person, shall carry 10% or more of the total voting rights of the offeree company, or

(*b*) Secure the control of management of a company, by acquiring or agreeing to acquire, irrespective of the percentage of the voting capital, the shares of the directors or other members, who by virtue of their shareholdings together with the shareholdings of their relatives, nominees, family interest, and group, control or manage the company, or

(*c*) If the offer is made by a person other than the ultimate offeror the identity of such other person shall be disclosed at the outset in the public announcement as also in the notification to the Stock Exchange.

SEBI Guidelines

SEBI has formulated regulations in this regard with an outline for a transparent and orderly framework for substantial acquisition of shares of companies listed on the Stock Exchanges by any person, a corporate entity or otherwise, whether or not it is covered by the listing agreement. It has therefore a wider scope than the present clause 40 A and B of the Stock Exchanges Listing Agreement which is restricted to listed companies only and is effective only when either of the parties of an acquisition is a listed company.

TAKEOVERS AND MERGERS

With the increasing competition from giant companies, multinationals and even foreign companies, smaller and inefficient companies have no chance of survival in India. Friendly takeovers and mergers will be more common than before and will be encouraged by the government and shareholders alike. But takeovers may become hostile and aggressive, in the absence of any code of conduct for companies. Thus, government has come out with a code of conduct for such hostile takeovers, early in Nov. 1995. Friendly takeovers will voluntarily follow the SEBI guidelines or listing guidelines.

Mergers can take place in the case of subsidiaries of a parent company or through inter-corporate investments up to 30% of the investing company, or up to 10% of investee company or 20% of equity of the same group company.

Mergers have some advantages in the following cases:

1. They are related companies or foreign subsidiaries, in which case the provisions of FEMA and RBI approval are complied.
2. They belong to different tax groups and the merger gives the tax advantages as in the case of OBC merger with G.T.B. The losses of one can be offset by the profits of the other with the result that the joint company will gain in tax burden.

3. Economies of scale can be got by merging competing and complementary units of manufacture.
4. The advantages of offshore units can be reaped by their merger with one of the domestic units if they are related.
5. Capital gains and losses are offset by government measures as in the case of dematerialisation of non-profit making units like some stock exchanges (BSE).
6. Inputs of the one unit can be output of another, in which case merger of the two is useful to both. The manufactures of ancilliaries or parts can be merged with the manufacture of final product, on the presumption that both units will gain thereby.
7. For some reasons of complementarity or competitive nature, two or more units can be merged in respect of some divisions or in whole.
8. Demerger and divestment can also take place for similar reasons, as stated above.

Main Highlights

1. Acquisition of shareholdings beyond 5% of a company's paid-up capital has to be disclosed within 4 days.
2. Acquirer holdings more than 10% shares in a company is required to make half-yearly disclosures to the Stock Exchanges where they are listed about the extent of their shareholding.
3. SEBI is empowered to investigate and scrutinise the acquisition and sale of securities by raiders, for any violations under Sec. 30 of SEBI Act, 1992.
4. The norms have divided the takeovers into three types — negotiated open market and bailout.
5. In the case of bailout takeovers, public offer to purchase shares is not mandatory for the acquiring company. Bailout takeovers of sick companies are exempt from these provisions.
6. In negotiated takeovers, acquirer cannot acquire more than 10% shares of a company, unless he also made a public offer for another 20% shares at the acquisition price or the average price quoting over the last six months.
7. In open market takeover, acquirer cannot acquire more than 10% shares unless he makes a public offer at a price not lower than the highest open market price paid by acquirer or average price in the last six months.
8. The SEBI has powers to issue directives or initiate criminal proceedings against the concerned parties for any violations of the code, and the provisions thereof, in the interest of investors. By an ordinance of January 1995, the SEBI was given powers to take penal actions against those violating Takeover Code and the Rules of the govt. in this regard. The acquirer in hostile takeover bids will be stalled by the company and the SEBI.

TAKEOVER BIDS AND ACQUISITIONS

A takeover bid is generally understood to mean an offer made to the holders of securities carrying voting rights, to acquire their securities for a consideration, the purpose of the offer usually being to acquire control of the company or consolidate control by the existing management. This being so, any substantial acquisition of shares in a company may be made with different objectives in view. It may primarily be for the purpose of seeking management control of the company or its consolidation by the existing management.

Different sets of circumstances can also be envisaged under which substantial acquisition of shares may take place. Often, this takes place with the approval and agreement of the existing management, resulting in a friendly takeover of the company, in such cases shares are acquired through negotiations. There may also be cases, where a person, a corporate entity or otherwise, or a group of persons acting in concert, acquire shares from the open market or by negotiations without the knowledge of the existing management, to obtain management control of the company; these will be cases of unfriendly or hostile takeovers. There may also be some potentially sick companies in which large amount of institutional funds are locked up and public interest is involved and in which a change in management can help bring about the revival of the unit; these are cases of bailout takeovers and would need to be treated on a different footing from other takeovers. Substantial acquisition of shares can also result from a situation when an Indian promoter may buyout the shares of a foreign partner who may like to disinvest for a variety of reasons, or a foreign partner may like to take advantage of the present liaberalisation policies and increase his stake in the business; there could also be an *inter se* transfer of shareholdings among various persons or entities belonging to the same management group. In all the latter cases, no change in management is contemplated.

It is therefore important that the process of substantial acquisition of shares is fair, transparent and equitable to all parties concerned in the process, and above all, the rights of shareholders are protected in such events.

SEBI's objective and approach and underlying principles are furnished below:

If industry has to thrive in a deregulated market, it should be prepared to accept the discipline and the competition of the marketplace without relying on the dead hand of protective bureaucratic governance. Regulation, where necessary, has to be kept to the minimum.

Keeping in view these new tenets, and in the spirit of the recent changes in policy giving greater freedom for the inter-play of market forces with minimum bureaucratic intervention, the Regulation for Substantial Acquisition of shares in listed companies has been devised to provide an orderly framework within which such transactions can take place and for the protection of the interest of shareholders.

Guiding Principles

The regulation is based on the following principles:

1. Equity of treatment and opportunity to all shareholders.
2. Transparency in acquisition of shares.
3. Fair and truthful disclosure through public announcement.
4. Availability of sufficient time for shareholders to make properly informed decision.
5. Avoidance of undesirable practices in substantial acquisition of shares and clandestine transactions.
6. Protection of rights for small and minority shareholders.
7. Avoidance of use of price sensitive information concerning a public offer by all persons, privy to confidential information for their own profits.

B.I.F.R. AND MERGERS

Under Sick Industrial Companies Special Provisions Act, 1985, BIFR has powers to decide on the package of reviving the sick units, including mergers and amalgamations of sick units with healthy units interested in the sick unit or in the same line of activity as the sick unit.

Thus, recently BIFR proposed the merger of the sick chemical unit, namely, Rama Krishi Rasayan Ltd., with the other group company, namely, Rama Phosphates Ltd. The latter company is a healthy unit interested in and connected with the sick unit by group affinity. The government policy is now towards closure of sick units and privatisation of public sector units, if they are sick. The role of BIFR is now relegated to the background. The BIFR Act was repealed recently by the passage of the Sick Industrial Companies (Special Provisions) Act in 2004. The sick enterprises are allowed to merge with strong ones or closedown.

Voluntary Inter-group Mergers

Sometimes the mergers take place on a voluntary basis without going to BIFR. Thus, Reliance Petroleum was taken over and merged with Reliance Industries a few years back. Hindustan Lever Ltd., has effected a number of group mergers. Thus Stephen Chemicals Ltd., which was a subsidiary and erstwhile sick company was taken over by HLL to boost manufacturing capacity of the Wheel brand of detergent soaps.

As an example of takeover, McCann-Erickson of the U.S. has taken over 51% stake in the Indian associate, Tara Sinha McCann-Erickson (TSME). Thus, TSME will henceforth be known as McCann-Erickson India Ltd.

Similarly, in March 1995, the four companies of Williamson Magor Group, namely, McLead Russel India Ltd., Namdang Tea Co. India Ltd., Williamson Financial Services Ltd., and Salasar Industrial Services Ltd., have made an open offer to the minority shareholders of UCIL for buying up not more than 20% of its shares from minority shareholders who are interested. This offer is made under the relevant SEBI guidelines and Clauses 40A and 40B of the Listing Agreement. The offer price was ₹175 and for maximum shares of 100 from each respondent. This price is the same as the one at which the UCIL's shares for 51% stake were acquired by the Williamson Magor Group. As of mid-March 1995, when the offer was made, the UCIL's share was in the range of ₹140 to ₹170.

The price of ₹175 was the negotiated price which happened to be higher than the average of the weekly, high and low of the closing prices of UCIL's shares quoted on the Stock Exchanges during the twenty-six weeks prior to Nov. 23, 1994, when acquisition was first officially announced. Such acquisitions have taken place later on also.

These acquisitions and mergers are carried out as per the prevailing SEBI guidelines.

Benefits

Mergers should benefit both the companies — the giver and taker. This is possible, if the products and markets are complementary and strengthen each other. They can be suppliers or end-users which can provide backward or forward integration. Mergers can also lead to elimination or reduction of competition, if the transferee and transferor companies are in the same line of production. The merger can save in taxes and in depreciation or in writing off the losses, if the loss making company is acquired by the profit making company.

Takeovers are a different story in that the company taken over can be both competitive and complementary. Takeover can be both friendly and unfriendly. In friendly takeovers — these are arranged, as between the companies through a bargain table. Thus, the holding company can takeover a loss making subsidiary. A foreign multinational company can acquire a larger stake in Indian subsidiary or collaborator.

Hostile takeovers are unfriendly acquisitions of shares, in a way as to hold a controlling interest in the company. But the takeover code of SEBI will apply to such takeover bids. The Clauses 40 A and 40 B of Listing Agreement and Takeover code of conduct to be observed by the companies under the SEBI Guidelines will govern such takeovers. The Ordinance of January 1995 amending the SEBI Act has given penal powers to SEBI to punish the companies violating the code of conduct provisions.

✠ ✠ ✠

SAMPLE CASE STUDIES ON COMPANIES (GOING PUBLIC OR MAKING NEW ISSUES)

26

The number of issues and the amounts raised in the new issue market have grown multifold during 1992-1993 and 1993-1994 and again during 1996-98. During 1994-1995, a number of cases of devolvement were also reported, despite the near boom conditions in the new issue market. Some of such cases are briefly set out in this chapter. The boom conditions were sought to be exploited by some companies through charging high premiums, rigging up prices before issue or adoption of other malpractices like false statements by omissions or commissions.

Booming New Issue Market

During 1994-95, there was a rise in number of new issues by 74% — to 1,343 from 770 in the preceding year, but the amount raised rose by only 6% from ₹ 12,544 crore to ₹ 13,312 crore in 1994-95. If the firm allotments and the rights issues are also considered, there were 1,658 issues involving an amount of ₹ 27,404 crore in 1994-95, as compared to 1,143 issues involving an amount of ₹ 24,342 crore, in 1993-94 — a rise of 12.5% in amount.

In the light of booming new issue market, the malpractices of companies have increased in those years. Many of the cases of cheating and duping the investors are in the form of omissions of previous bad record of promoters or making exaggerated statements of future prospects or dropping some vital facts having a bearing on risk of investors.

There were some cases where the stock invest was misused by companies for getting allotment in collusion with the issuing company. Later, in 1994 RBI has prohibited the use of Stock Invest by companies and institutions and confined them only to individuals and Mutual Funds. Despite this some companies are reported to have used the cancelled stock invests to make allotments to show the minimum subscription of 90%.

Some Corporate Malpractices in New Issue Market

Many promoters were using the stock lending method of banks to have the bank funds instead of bringing in part or full the promoter's quota. Assume that promoter fell short of his contribution; he uses his existing shares or those to be allotted; which is something like short selling without having shares and then borrow or buy shares to cover up. Some promoters are also using non-transferable promoters' quota shares for borrowing from banks and financial institutions. As banks are not permitted to sell and buy shares in the stock market, they are accepting the non-transferable shares for lending. As a further step of cheating, some promoters are creating fake share certificates to borrow from banks for temporary periods. The MD of MS Shoes fell short of funds for contribution to his part of rights issue and he asked for 30 days' time to bring in funds. Some promoters have got funds on the basis of this method of borrowing or from companies under inter-corporate lending, or get the bridge finance from banks and divert them to show their share in the paid-up capital, either in rights issue or public issue.

Some companies are making private sale of Director's quota which is not transferable. A few companies are resorting to private sale of shares before public issue but constituting a part of public issue with the connivance of registrars. Director's quota is sometimes raised by private sale of shares to friends and relatives which will be subsequently shown in Director's quota. Directors holding more than the required 20% or 25% transfer them to relatives and friends or put them in employee's quota to make them transferable. Many more of such practices were noticed in the market to get over the regulations of the SEBI. All these malpractices took place before the ken of the SEBI itself as it was just set up.

MS Shoes Case

MS Shoes has raised capital in the month of February 1995. It has been allowed to raise ₹699 crores from the public. The issue was opened on Feb. 14 for fully convertible debentures, convertible into equity at a premium of ₹189 for a share price of ₹10. But the market price was ₹509 at that time which was in fact a Cum-Rights Quotation. The company failed to disclose to the public that market price was quoting Cum-Rights. When it came to the notice of SEBI, it has directed the company to make a public statement in the press that its share quotation in the Market is on Cum-Rights basis. The company issued the correction on Feb. 13, just a day before the issue was opened. However, the TV advertisement continued to compare the issue prices of ₹199 to the market price of ₹505. In view of this lapse, the Securities and Exchange Board of India asked the company to give the option to the investors to the effect that any allottee who wishes to get the money refunded, can make the application within 20 days from the date of receipt of allotment letter.

It was soon realised that the MS Shoes was undersubscribed and thus led to devolvement on underwriters, but the latter refused to put in their money in view of the company's statement of the closure of issue on the earliest closing date giving the impression that it was fully subscribed. This development meant that merchant bankers have failed and underwriters have to shell down nearly ₹500 crore to make the issue fully subscribed.

Meanwhile the SEBI has sent a show-cause notice to the company's Managing Director Shri Sachdev and handed over the case to CBI. It is understood by CBI that the lapses are also found in the hierarchy of SEBI. The SEBI has chosen to take action against all the intermediaries concerned, SBI Caps as the lead manager, and others like TFCI, Lloyds Finance, Bank of Baroda and Indbank for their lapses.

CBI investigations showed that the MD of MS Shoes Ltd., namely, Pawan Sachdeva can be charged with criminal breach of trust, complicity with SEBI officials, dishonest intentions and concealment of facts in his rights cum public issue, made in Feb 1995. The complicity of SBI officials came in when they gave Sachdeva 30 days of time waiver to bring in ₹130 crore towards his share or rights.

The rights cum public issue has devolved and the merchant bankers and underwriters were held responsible for this flop. But equally responsible is the SEBI for their lapse to enquire into all omissions and commissions in the prospectus and to investigate the promoters' track record for personal honesty, integrity and dependability. Otherwise, investor protection cannot be ensured by SEBI, the watchdog of the Capital Market.

Case of Vinay Chem Pharma

This company's Managing Director Mr. Vinay Kumar Reddy was projected as a man of good stature without disclosing any of his past antecedents in the prospectus. The company raised ₹2.36 crore on March

4, 1995 and in fact it was oversubscribed as investors had no idea of his background. Mr. Vinay Kumar Reddy cheated the public without disclosing that, earlier his properties were attached for selling away some 203 metric tonnes of groundnuts sent to him for crushing by APSOSGF. At that time, he was a partner of the Saptagiri Industries at Naidupet, in Nellore district A.P. The interesting case of Saptagiri Industries was not known very widely and not mentioned in the prospectus.

Vinay cheated the public with another Company, namely, Greenwealth Plantation Pvt. Ltd., claiming to raise plantations on 400 acres of land, with teakwood. There was neither wood nor Teak and land. The land is supposed to be in Vandodu in Nellore dt. and investors paid huge sums for trading in teakwood. This is a case of unscrupulous promoters who can cheat the public by many methods.

He raised successfully ₹2.36 crore on the name of the company recently promoted by him, namely, Vinay Chem Pharma. This company had its registered office in Hyderabad replacing that of Greenwealth Plantations. As the amounts are likely to be used partly or fully to repay his past debts or diversion of funds, this is yet another case of companies cheating the gullible investors even before the very ken of SEBI.

Case of Malvika Steel

Investors charged the Malvika Steel with cheating and duping the innocent public. The information given about the availability of natural gas was misleading and incorrect. The prospectus stated that it is "the only integrated steel plant in the country to have the benefits of natural gas". Although Usha India Ltd., which sponsored the Malvika Steel, entered into an agreement with Gas Authority of India Ltd., for supply of natural gas from HPJ pipeline, it cannot be taken for granted that they will supply the natural gas to this project. Legally, the GAIL has to investigate and approve the project, which requires natural gas, namely, the Malvika Steel. It is in this context that the statements made in the prospectus are misleading to investors. It is also reported that the issue has devolved on the underwriters.

The Malvika Steel raised through public issue ₹288 crore on April 25, 1995. SEBI was investigating the complaints against the company regarding the misstatements in the prospectus. Usha India whose earlier name was Usha Rectifier has a notoreity of having cheated the public at one time earlier (with a public issue of ₹700 crore in 1989). The amount raised for the project at Gowriganj in U.P. was being diverted to Malvika Steel. The amount of ₹270 crore has already been transferred to Malvika Steel. Diversion of funds, delay and abandonment of projects, raising of resources in excess of requirements and misstatements or incorrect and incomplete statements in the prospectus are some of the malpractices of companies, injuring the public interest and duping the investors.

Windowdressing for Full Subscription

If any issue has received poor response, such companies have to keep open the subscription list till the last closing date. Examples of such issues are Stan Organics, Carnation Industries, Ahura Welding, Sterling Tools, etc. Some issues have been undersubscribed like Malvika Steel and Bhushan Steel, in the past. These issues have devolved on underwriters. Another category of companies have, in an attempt to windowdress, closed the list on the earliest closing date, to give the impression that its rating is high and it is fully subscribed, but this is achieved by some finance company or by lead financial institution putting in funds in the last minute by application. There are many such companies who have misled the investors in the past. Essar Oils was involved in some irregularities in listing, as reported in the press, by the B.S.E. in May 1995.

Fake Certificates and Lost Warrants

Among the malpractices of companies, registrars and other intermediaries, mention may be made of forged certificates, fake shares and lost warrants. The creation of fake certificate involves the complicity of some directors or insiders in the company and the registrars. Forged documents have been recently found in large numbers particularly after the Harshad Mehta's scam was unfolded. Many companies have also reported surfacing of fake certificates, in the process of scrutinising for the transfer of certificates.

The knowledge of printing and screen processing and the expertise in art work are all necessary for creating the duplicates and fake certificates of a company's shares. Forgery of share warrants and dividends was also reported. These go with loss of certificates and dividend warrants in transit and in postal custody. Unfortunately, the gullible public and investors become a prey to these malpractices as they cannot detect the fake from the genuine; only the company and the registrars and transfer agents will be able to detect on the basis of company's record of signatures and other evidence.

Misuse of Stock Invest

The big stock invest holders like financiers, brokers and underwriters are asked to send their stock invests to the company's Registrars and the obliging Registrars provide allotments to these applicants on the basis of Duplicate stock invest. In fact, such financiers keep the original stock invest with them but send the copies to the Registrars. The stock invest holder takes a letter from the promoter asking him to the safe-custody of the stock invest, as a legal precaution.

Once allotment is made and the allotment letter issued, it is subsequently transferred to the promoter who exchanges the stock invest for a cheque from the company. It is a type of financial accommodation of the stock invest holder or cash surplus individuals and financiers to the promoter for an agreed term and a rate of interest. It is understood that the rate varied from 3% to 5% per month and the accommodation was for three to four months. Thus an investment of ₹1 crore for three months tides over the difficulty of undersubscription with a temporary financial accommodation at a rate of interest of 30% to 60% per annum.

Rigging up of Share Price

Another area where companies are found to indulge in malpractices is in rigging up of prices in the share market. This is particularly indulged by companies just before they make rights or public issue, and is going by the term of insider trading. Although insider trading regulations and penal provisions are there to punish the culprits, it is found to be difficult to get evidence to book the culprits.

Some unscrupulous promoters or directors may connive with the stock brokers to operate in the market in such a way to boost the prices of the company's share. By manipulation of the demand pressure in the market, and rigging up of the prices, the share price of the company may be kept at higher levels, as to make the terms of public issue or rights issue attractive to shareholders and investors.

As referred to, M. S. Shoes came out with a public-cum-rights issue in February 1995 with a heavy premium of ₹189 on the face value of ₹10 per share. Before the issue was opened on Feb. 13, the market price was artificially kept high at around ₹500 to 600. This quotation was however on cum-rights basis which was not revealed in the advertisements made by the company in banners, paper advertisements and T.V.

M.S. Shoes was also blamed for the rigging up of the prices by SEBI. Mr. Sachdeva, the M. D. of M. S. Shoes was reported by the press to have operated through a Delhi broker who in turn dealt with a Mumbai broker in the rigging up operations in the stock market before the issue opened. The Delhi broker as also the Mumbai broker were found in financial difficulties due to non-payment of some dues by Mr. Sachdeva in this respect.

The practice of such rigging operations before the issue is opened is quite common among companies. The same complaint is made in respect of very good companies like Reliance and Essar. Even Pennar Paterson was alleged to have resorted to rigging operations, as the market price was below offer price of ₹10 plus ₹35 premium in May-June 1995. SEBI was reported to have started investigations into same reported price rigging operations, afterwards.

Such rigging operations are based on INSIDER information subject to INSIDER TRADING REGULATIONS. The SEBI has the powers to catch the culprit, namely, the insider indulging in such operations and impose penalties. But lack of enough evidence is generally the cause for not booking the culprits. This is so even on the advanced stock markets like New York and Tokyo. In a poorly organised market like India, this is more so and it is difficult to produce evidence due to lack of transparency.

Scam of 2001

A more recent example of rigging and short selling based on insider information was noticed in the case of proposed merger of UTI Bank and GTB, which did not take place due to intervention of SEBI and RBI. This was master minded by a broker Ketan Parekh in March-April 2001. The mass short-selling during the same period was attributed to elected board members of BSE, including their President, Anand Rathi. These activities were investigated by SEBI and some brokerage houses including CSFB, Nirmal Bang, and First Global were debarred from undertaking brokerage business. Action was also taken by removing Anand Rathi and others involved in BSE from their positions and barred their brokerage houses from doing any further business in this line. Madhavapura Mercantile Co-operative Bank was also involved in lending to these brokerage houses and for activities in the capital market. Bank funds in the capital market was thus a major accelerator of the scam in March 2001. Global Trust Bank Chairman was reported to be involved in stock market scam for lending to stock brokers who could not payback the funds. This led to the financial difficulties of GTB and a run on the bank led is to its merger with OBC.

UTI Scam (2002-03)

The Unit Scheme of 1964 was in deep trouble due to managerial lapses in the Investment Dept. of UTI and alleged political interferences during 2001-02. The investors in this scheme lost lakh and crore due to fall in the market values of the investments of UTI in this scheme. The government has rescued them to some extent by splitting the UTI into UTI-I, taken over by the government in full and UTI-II privatised and brought under the SEBI Regulations. This was another case of scam involving corruption and mismanagement of the public funds.

CDR Hospital (2003-05)

CDR has sought deposits from public, whether they are patients or not luring them with concessions in charges if they use the services of the hospital. After the expiry of the due date, they could not repay due to losses, suffered by the hospital (C.D. Reddy) and the matter went to CLB, and even court for justice to the depositors. This is a case of mismanagement and cheating the public.

✠ ✠ ✠

PART V

SEBI AND ITS REFORMS

SEBI AND INVESTOR PROTECTION

27

Introduction

The term "Investor Protection" is a wide term encompassing various measures designed to protect the investors from malpractices of companies, brokers, merchant bankers, issue managers, Registrars of new issues, etc. "Investors Beware" should be the watchword of all programmes for mobilisation of savings for investment. As all investments have some risk element, this risk factor should be borne in mind by the investors and they should take all precautions to protect their interests in the first place. If caution is thrown to the winds and they invest in any venture without a proper assessment of the risk, they have only to blame themselves. But if there are malpractices by companies, brokers, etc., they have every reason to complain. Such grievances have been increasing in number in more recent years.

The complaints of investors come from two major sources:

(*i*) against member broker of Stock Exchanges;

(*ii*) against companies listed for trading on the Stock Exchanges.

Besides, there can be complaints against sub-brokers, agents, merchant bankers, Registrars, issue managers, etc., which cannot be entertained by the stock exchanges as per their rules.

Complaints against Members

Investors have complaints against brokers regarding the price, quantity, etc., at which transactions are put through, defective delivery or delayed delivery, delayed payment or non-payment, etc., non-settlement of vyaj badla dues, non-payment of agreed brokerage to authorised assistants, etc. In the event of default of a member broker, the dues of clients are also to be looked into.

There is a grievance cell in many Stock Exchanges which attends to investor complaints. Of the total, nearly 95% are against companies and they are more difficult to settle, as many companies do not attend to the complaints promptly despite reminders and warnings by the Stock Exchange, in view of the fact that penal powers of the Exchange are limited.

The grievance procedure in respect of complaints against members is as follows:

(*a*) Joint meeting of members *vis-a-vis* the clients for an amicable settlement.

(*b*) Arbitration proceedings by the committee under the byelaws.

(*c*) Special committee appointed by the Executive Director for settlement.

(*d*) Disciplinary proceedings including warnings, fines, penalties, etc., particularly in cases of fraud, cheating, etc., by the members.

Grievances Cell

Complaints against members were in the nature of non-payment of sale proceeds, non-settlement of accounts, etc. Of the total complaints against members, about 85% are settled during the year, itself.

Complaints against Companies

The complaints against companies are in the nature of non-receipt of allotment letters, refund orders, non-receipt of dividends, interest, etc., delay in transfer of shares and in splitting and consolidation. The clearance of these complaints is also attended to by the Cell by writing to the companies, follow-up telexes, etc., and finally by warning to delist the companies concerned. But the clearance of these complaints is slow due to the non-compliance or slow compliance by the companies to the references made by the Cell. The powers of the Stock Exchange are limited to warnings and delisting of shares and as such compliance by the companies was poor.

Customers' Protection Fund

The Customers' Profession Fund is constituted by many Stock Exchanges to safeguard the interests of the investor clients from defaults of the stock brokers. The Fund is financed by way of a levy on the turnover of members and from out of the listing fees paid by company, earmarked by the Exchanges.

The Fund is being administered by the Stock Exchange for the benefit of the clients of the member brokers, in case of a default of a member. The compensation of any single client is, however, limited to ₹2 lakh on BSE. When a member is declared a defaulter, the net assets in the hands of the Defaulter's Committee after defraying costs, charges, expenses, etc., relating to the realisation of the assets will be used to meet the claims of the Exchange, clearing house and then the admitted claims of the members of the Exchange against the defaulter. After meeting all these claims, if anything is left over, the claims of the clients of the defaulting member will be satisfied. If nothing is left over, the genuine claims of clients can be met from the Customer's Protection Fund. This is the same procedure adopted by other Exchanges also where this Fund was set up.

Under the New Companies Bill 2008, providition wa made for an Investor Education and Protection Fund with the Dept. of Corporate Affairs for promoting investor education directly or indirectly and for general investor protection.

As per the SEBI guidelines, Stock Exchanges have also set up Trade Guarantee Fund to meet any unforeseen payment difficulties and delays in clearance.

Investors Beware

Investors in stock and capital markets need a word of caution. Firstly, these investments are more risky, returns are uncertain and share values are subject to wide fluctuations. Secondly, such investments require an art and expertise to pick up the right stocks, failing which the investors would burn their fingers. Thirdly, the players in the market, namely, brokers and issuers of securities, namely, companies, are not rated high for their honesty with the result that investor complaints against stock brokers and companies have been increasing over the years. It would, therefore, be necessary for investors to prepare themselves well before entering this market.

Specific Goals

The investor should be clear in his objectives of income, capital appreciation, short-term gains or long-term gains, etc. He should have made already enough investment in housing and for a regular income to meet his minimum needs and comforts of life. Even if all the stock market investments are wiped out due to a market crash, the investor should not be a pauper on the streets. Besides, if the investor spends sleepless nights on the fall of share prices, he cannot be a good stock market investor. Nor can he gloat over a sporadic success and be a spendthrift.

Pre-requisites of Investor

The investor should have abundant common sense and a strong heart to withstand the vicissitudes of fortune. He need not be a holder of high academic degrees like an MBA from Harvard or a finance graduation from the Wharton School. Nor does he need to have hereditary characteristics or family tradition of investment. The only requirement he should have is abundant logic and common sense and strong nerves and develop the art of investment on a scientific basis.

Although Peter Lynch[1] calls it an art and is skeptical of the application of academic scientific theories, the fact remains that he attributes the success of investors to personal preparation, hard work involved in the collection of relevant information, knowledge and research and analysis. This shows that it is expertise combined with intuition that plays a vital role in this game on the Dalal Street. Unlike a chess game which requires intelligence or a football game which needs physical prowess, the stock market game requires both an art and a scientific technique.

Preparing to Invest

Investors desiring to invest in stocks require a lot of preparation. The weak-hearted and risk-averter should first make an entry by buying only debentures, particularly convertible debentures of good companies, or subscribe to new issues of promising and well-established companies. After sufficient study and preparation, the investor should act like rag-pickers in the market, picking up scrips on a selective basis. That means selected companies from promising and growing industries should be picked up after collection of all relevant information and data on the companies and a scientific analysis of their fundamentals. The undervalued scrips should be purchased at the right time with the help of technical analysis. Rumours and advice of so-called consultants have to be carefully scrutinized. As the market investment is both a science and an art, it requires both expertise and intuition. There is need for prior preparation and a lot of homework before investments are undertaken. A high degree of caution and planning is necessary but the scientific basis and knowledge are to be acquired by a proper study.

Balance Sheet Study

Investors entering the stock market should also get into the habit of detailed and careful study of the balance sheets of companies in which they wish to invest. Similarly, they should examine carefully the detailed prospectus before subscribing to the new issues of companies. The habit of relying on rumours, or advice of brokers or friends should be replaced by the habit of self-study of balance sheets and prospectuses of companies. The factors which should be looked into and ratios that should be analysed and the aspects that should be examined are set out under fundamental analysis.

Choice of a Broker

Investors should as far as possible deal only with registered members of recognised Stock Exchanges. In places where there are no Stock Exchanges, they may deal with those sub-brokers who have connections with

1. Peter Lynch: *One Up on Wall Street,* Penguin Books (1990), p. 27.

registered brokers. An honest and dependable broker is to be chosen through proper introduction and orders should be placed with him in a proper manner with limits on prices at which sales or purchases can be made. As and when a transaction is completed, he should insist on a contract note in due time.

Protection in the New Issues Market

The main source of information on which investors depend in the new issues market is the prospectus, which should contain correct statements of facts. Any false statements, fraud, etc., are punishable under the Companies Act. Under Section 56 of the Companies Act, the Directors are subject to civil liability for any misstatement of facts or untrue statements.

Under Sections 63 and 68 of the Companies Act, the Directors are also liable criminally for any fraud of false statements in the prospectus. Companies' liability for misstatements arises from untrue statements and statements which are material for investors and particulars on which investors depend to make investments. The directors or promoters of the company are thus subject to both criminal and civil liability under the Act for any misstatements in the prospectus. Even so, the small investors cannot afford to go to court and, should therefore, carefully read and examine the prospectus for viability of the project and marketability of the product and for the integrity and dependability of the promoters. The investors have also a responsibility to assess the prospects and the risk involved in the project before making any investment.

Protection for Fixed Deposits

Section 58A of the Companies Act deals with the subject of Fixed Deposits. There are some rules which apply to non-banking companies, private and public limited companies, who wish to raise deposits from the public.

No deposits can be invited from investors or the public unless the companies follow the rules and guidelines made by the Department of Company Affairs in consultation with the RBI. Interest rates, maturity period of deposits, and the amount permissible to be raised by the companies are all given in the form of guidelines by the Department of Company Affairs. The companies have to follow these guidelines while accepting deposits from the public. Renewal and repayment are also regulated by the Companies Act and the rules framed by the Department of Company Affairs. When a company fails to repay the deposit, the depositor can complain to the Company Law Board (CLB) in the specified form duly filled in, together with the fees for non-payment of interest or non-repayment of deposit. The order of the CLB is final and binding on the company and the company has to comply with it. Any non-compliance with the order of the CLB or violation of the provisions of the company law would invite penalty of imprisonment and fine. This provision however, does not apply to sick companies.

Guidelines to Investors

1. Deal with a registered member of the stock exchange. If you are dealing with a sub-broker, make sure that all bills and contracts are made in the name of a registered broker.
2. Insist that all your deals are done in the trading ring.
3. Give specific orders to buy or sell within the fixed price limits and/or time periods within which orders have to be executed.
4. Insist on contract notes to be passed on to you on the dates, when the orders are executed.
5. Make sure that your deal is registered with the stock exchange in the computer. In the case of a dispute, this will help trace the details of the deal easily.
6. Collect a settlement table from the Stock Exchange mentioning the pay-in and pay-out days. Each Stock Exchange has its own trading periods which are called settlements. All transactions done within this period are settled at the end of it. All payments for shares bought and their deliveries take place

on the pay-in day. An awareness of pay-in and pay-out days is useful when a broker tries to make excuses.

7. Keep separate records of dealings in specified shares (Group A) and non-specified shares (Group B). The settlement for each is on different days.
8. Execute periodic settlements of dues and delivery of shares to avoid accumulation of transactions.
9. Insist on delivery. If the company returns your papers and shares with objections, contact your broker immediately.
10. Ensure that shares bought are transferred in your name before the company's book closure date. This is necessary to make sure that you receive benefits like dividend, interest and bonus shares. All companies have a book closure date on which the list of shareholders in the company is finalised.
11. Complain if the broker does not deliver the shares bought in your name. Proceed to contact another broker with the bill/contract given to you by the earlier broker, and the Exchange authorities and the latter will purchase the shares on your behalf. In such an event, the first broker will have to pay the difference in price.
12. Do not sell shares that are not transferred in your name after the book closure as these are not valid in the market.
13. Do not sell/deal in shares where any one of the holders has passed away. In cases where the holder has died, a succession certificate is necessary. In cases where one of the joint shareholders passes away, the surviving holder should send the shares along with the death certificate to the company. Only after the name of the deceased has been deleted from the shares, can they be transferred.
14. Do not expect the money for shares to come immediately. It will take at least a week from the date of transaction.
15. Unless you have a special arrangement with the broker, do not expect the adjustment of purchases and sales against one another. One pays first and receives later.
16. Do not take delays or harassment lying down. You have to complain to the Grievance Cell of the stock exchange or the Securities and Exchange Board of India (SEBI) in case of delay or harassment.

Legislative Protection to Investors

The Companies Act and the Listing Agreement of the Stock Exchanges provide certain safeguards to investors. The normal complaints against companies and the protection available are listed below:

Complaints	*Legislative Provision*	*Relief Provided*
1. Delay in refund of excess application money or allotment letters	Section 73 of the Companies Act as amended by Amendment Act of 1988	Payment of interest for the delayed period beyond 30 days from the closure of subscription list at the rate of 15%.
2. Delay in transfer of shares	Section 111 of the Companies Act	A time limit of two months provided in the Act for effecting transfer. As per the Listing Agreement, the time limit is only one month from the lodgment of shares.
3. Refusal to transfer shares	Section 22(A) of SC(R) Act. This section lists the reasons for which transfer of shares can be refused	Transfer can be refused only for specific and valid reasons given in the Act and not otherwise.
4. Problem of odd lots	Listing Agreement provides for issue of certificates in marketable lots and avoidance of odd lots. The problem of odd lots does not exist under demat form of trading.	Need for consolidation of odd lots and ensuring the issue of shares only in marketable lots through conversion of debentures or rights issue, provision of an odd lot trading session and listing out brokers willing to trade in odd lots.

5. Takeover bids	New clauses of 40(A) and 40(B) of Listing Agreement SEBI Rules on take over Bids	Purchases or acquisition of shares beyond 5% to be notified to the stock exchange. Acquisition beyond 10% puts an obligation on the transferor and transferee and intermediary to notify the Stock Exchange and the public and offer to the other shareholders of the company to buy at their price or the highest market price during the preceding six months.
6. Insider trading, rigging and other malpractices	SEBI (Insider Trading) Regulation 1992	The investors have to guard themselves regarding the price and their investment.
7. Delay and non-payment of interest/ fixed deposits by companies	Section 58 (A) of the Companies Act	Complain to the Company Law Board.
8. Delay and non-payment of dues or non-delivery of shares, etc. by brokers	Rules, Bylaws, etc. of the Stock Exchange	Complain to the Grievance Cell of the concerned Stock Exchange and to SEBI.

Note: The SEBI has also been receiving investor complaints and besides taking up the matters with companies, merchant bankers, etc., they are publicising such complaints in the newspapers for the public to know and isolate the concerned companies. The Dept. of company affairs is also receiving complaints against companies and the matter is also pursued by them.

Credit Rating and Investor Protection

Investor should also be familiar with the ratings given by the Credit Rating Agencies for protecting their interests. The CRISIL ratings are given only for debt instruments of companies, namely, Commercial Papers (CP), debentures, bonds and fixed deposits. Since early 1992, the ratings of Investment Information and Credit Rating Agency (ICRA) are also used by companies. CARE is another agency in the credit rating business, operating since 1993. Duff & Phelps is another private agency set up in 1996 for rating purposes. Another foreign subsidiary Fitch Ratings India Ltd., has also been rating the companies for their issues in addition to SME Ratings India Ltd., These are given on a voluntary basis and may be publicised or not, depending upon the company's own perception of the impact of these on the investors. The ratings in use by the companies are published by the CRISIL in their "CRISIL Rating Scan." The companies use them only when the ratings are favourable to them and when they are making only public offer for deposits or debentures, etc. The investors should examine these symbols with regard to their benefits and their implication. Since a rating given can be revised upwards or downwards, the investors should keep a watch on any such revisions. Unfortunately, the CRISIL itself would not publicise them for the benefit of the investors as it is a private and autonomous organisation and is under no obligation to do so. The SEBI guidelines now insist that all companies should get these ratings and publicise them compulsorily, if they are borrowing through issue of debentures. Many companies accepting fixed deposits are also using these CRISIL ratings. Rating of company deposits is made compulsory under the New Companies Bill 1993 and by RBI in the case of NBFCs. The SEBI has brought these agencies under its control and gave Directives and a Code of Conduct. These matters relating to rating were already discussed in a separate chapter.

✠ ✠ ✠

28

FUNCTIONS OF SEBI

Introduction

The government has set up the Securities and Exchange Board of India (SEBI) in April, 1988. For more than three years, it has no statutary powers. Its interim functions during the period were *(i)* To collect information and advice the government on matters relating to Stock and Capital Markets *(ii)* Licensing and regulation of merchant banks, mutual funds, etc. *(iii)* To prepare the legal drafts for regulatory and development role of SEBI and *(iv)* To perform any other functions as may be entrusted to it by the government.

The need for setting up independent govt. agency to regulate and develop the Stock and Capital Market in India as in many developed countries was recognised since the Sixth Five Year Plan was launched (1985) when some major industrial policy changes like opening up of the economy to outside world and greater role to the Private Sector were initiated. The rampant malpractices noticed in the Stock and Capital Market stood in the way of infusing confidence of investors which is necessary for mobilisation of larger quantity of funds from the public and help the growth of the industry.

The malpractices were noticed in the case of companies, merchant bankers and brokers who are all operating in the Capital Market. The need to curb these malpractices and to promote healthy Capital Market in India was felt. The security industry in India has to develop on the right lines for which a competent govt. agency as in U.K. (SIB) or in U.S.A. (SEC) is needed.

As referred to earlier, malpractices have been reported in both the primary market and secondary market. A few examples of malpractices in the primary market are as follows:

(*a*) Too many self-styled Investment Advisers and Consultants.

(*b*) Grey Market or unofficial premiums on the new issues.

(*c*) Manipulation of market prices before new issues are floated.

(*d*) Delay in allotment letters or refund orders or in despatch of share certificates.

(*e*) Delay in listing and commencement of trading in shares.

A few examples of malpractices in the Secondary Market are as follows:

(*a*) Lack of transparency in the trading operations and prices charged to clients.

(*b*) Poor services due to delay in passing contract notes or not passing contract notes by brokers/sub-brokers.

(*c*) Delay in making payments to clients or in giving delivery of shares.

(*d*) Persistence of odd lots and refusal of companies to stop this practice of allotting shares in odd lots, which does not exist now.

(*e*) Insider trading by agents of companies or brokers rigging and manipulating prices.

(*f*) Takeover bids to destabilise management.

Objectives

The SEBI has been entrusted with both the regulatory and developmental functions. The objectives of SEBI are as follows:

(*a*) Investor protection, so that there is a steady flow of savings into the Capital Market.

(*b*) Ensuring the fair practices by the issuers of securities, namely, companies so that they can raise resources at least cost.

(*c*) Promotion of efficient services by brokers, merchant bankers and other intermediaries so that they become competitive and professional.

Pending the legislative sanction to SEBI it carried out the functions of supervisory and advisory body of the govt. It has initiated the basis for control and regulation of the market, arranged for the licensing of merchant banks, mutual funds, etc., and performed the advisory functions to the govt.

The legislation giving powers to SEBI was passed on 4th April, 1992 in the form of the Securities and Exchange Board of India Act, to protect the interests of investors in securities and to promote the development of and to regulate the securities market and for matters connected therewith or incidental thereto.

Leaving aside Chapter I dealing with preliminaries and definitions, Chapter II deals with establishment, incorporation, administration and management of the Boards of Directors, etc. Chapter III provides for the transfer of assets and liabilities of the existing Boards to the new Board, under the Act.

Investor protection is the major responsibility of the SEBI. For this purpose, the draft prospectus of the companies is scrutinised for full and fair disclosures and guidelines have been given in the form of a code of conduct for all the players in the capital market. Merchant bankers are held responsible for fair disclosures of the companies in the new issues market. Prospectus is graded and penal points are awarded for any lapses of the merchant banks. Similarly, licensing and registration of all intermediaries in the capital market including underwriters, registrars, portfolio managers, etc., was also completed. In particular registration and regulation of all brokers and sub-brokers of stock market, control of insider trading, inspection and audit of stock exchanges and their members were taken up in full swing. The SEBI had spread out its powers of regulation to all corners of the primary and secondary markets. Its powers and functions have expanded from time to time.

The substantive part of the powers and functions of the Board is however, incorporated in Chapter IV. Thus, Section 11 of the Act specifies the functions as follows:

Regulatory	*Developmental*
(*a*) Registration of brokers and sub-brokers and other players in the market.	(*a*) Investor education.
(*b*) Registration of collective Investment Schemes and Mutual Funds.	(*b*) Training of Intermediaries.
(*c*) Regulation of stock exchanges and other S.R.O.s, merchant banks, Portfolio Managers, etc.	(*c*) Promotion of fair practices and a code of conduct for all S.R.O.s.
(*d*) Prohibition of all fraudulent and unfair trade practices.	(*d*) Conducting Research and Publishing information useful to all market participants.
(*e*) Controlling Insider Trading and takeover bids and imposing penalties for such practices.	

Chapter V deals with registration of Stock brokers, sub-brokers, Transfer agents, etc., on which action was already taken by the SEBI, since May 1992. The members of recognised Stock Exchanges and their authorised sub-brokers operating as on 21st Feb., 1992 were already registered with the SEBI. The SEBI has got powers under the Act to collect information, call for special audit and impose fines, penalties, etc. The activities of SEBI are financed by grants from the govt. in addition of fees, charges, etc., made by SEBI. The fund called the SEBI General Fund, is set up to which all grants, fees, charges, etc., are credited. This fund is used to meet the expenses of the Board and to pay salaries of staff and remuneration to officers, members of the Board, etc.

In Chapter VII of the Act, the Central Govt. has taken powers to issue directions to the SEBI Board, to supercede the Board if necessary and to call for returns and reports etc., as and when necessary. The final powers over SEBI rests with the govt., as can be seen from Sections 20 and 28. An appeal lies with the Central Govt. from any decision of the SEBI by the aggrieved party under Section 20. The Section 28 gives the power to the Central Government to exempt any person or class of persons from the operation of sub-Section (1) of Section 12, dealing with the registration of intermediaries. The Central Government has also powers to give any guidelines or to make regulations and rules for SEBI and its operations. An Appelate Authority was set up by the government to attend to any complaints on the decisions of SEBI.

SEBI has spread its network of control to all intermediaries in the market. Many more powers under SC(R) Act were delegated by the govt. to the SEBI. Legislation on Amendments to SEBI Act and on Insider Trading was effected. In September 1994, SEBI has been delegated concurrent powers with the government under many provisions of SC(R) Act such as recognition and derecognition of Stock Exchanges. By an ordinance passed in January 1995, SEBI got more powers on companies, intermediaries and Stock Exchanges and their members. SEBI can now impose penalties and file suits for insider trading, violation of listing agreement and failure to redress the investor grievances and takeover bids and violations of its guidelines. By an Amendment to SEBI Act, 2002, SEBI got penal powers of search and seizure by the Board of SEBI and the powers of Securities Appellate Board, were also set out.

SEBI Guidelines

SEBI has issued guidelines from time to time which run into volumes and have been published as handouts separately. Such guidelines are issued separately for New Issues market, Stock market, Mutual Funds, Merchant banks, Registrars and transfer agents, Underwriters, Brokers, sub-brokers, Portfolio Managers, etc. Thus the SEBI guidelines encompass all the intermediaries in the Capital Market, and a code of conduct is also laid down for each category separately. The guidelines and the code of conduct are to be observed under the ken of SEBI and lapses are subject to penal points. In fact all the intermediaries have to seek first the licence and registration for operating in the capital market. The criteria and eligibility requirements for each category are separately set out by the SEBI. During 1994 even FFIs and Foreign Broker firms were licensed by SEBI to operate in Indian capital market. Under FEMA, the RBI has also to grant permission to operate in the Indian Market by FFIs, FIIs and OCBs, NRIs, etc. In view of the voluminous material involved in these regulations of SEBI, a brief outline is attempted in respect of major reforms involved.

Reforms in the New Issues Market

1. Free entry and free pricing of new issues in the capital market subject to observance of some guidelines.
2. Minimum public offer of 25% of paid up capital later reduced to 20% to be eligible for listing on stock exchanges out of which half is reserved for investors applying for ₹ 10,000 and less. Some companies falling short of this requirement as in 2008 were asked to rectify this short fall.
3. Minimum subscription by Promoters and Directors at 25% for issues less than ₹ 100 crore and 20% for paid-up capital of more than ₹ 100 crore.
4. Preferential allotment to OCBs and FFIs is subject to a ceiling of 30%, later reduced to 20% and a lock-in period of 5 years which was removed in 1996.
5. FFIs and foreign security firms are allowed to operate both in the new issue market and stock market but through Indian brokers.
6. Reservation of quotas under public subscription can be had up to 20% for FIs and Mutual Funds, 24% for FFIs and OCBs which were withdrawn in 1996 and 10% for employees.
7. Stock Invest was introduced as a mode of making payments replacing cash and cheque for applying for shares and debentures. This will save loss of interest for investors from the time of applications to the time of allotment. This was withdrawn by the RBI later on due to malpractices in them by corporates.
8. Private placement of non-transferable shares of promoters and directors was prohibited as also the sale of shares under discount to institutions and mutual funds, etc.
9. Minimum number of shares to be applied for was raised to 500 from 100 shares earlier, so as to reduce the workload of the companies with large number of applications for smaller lots, although this would hit the small investors with a few hundreds, for investment. This minimum was lowered to 200 shares in 1996 as against 500 shares earlier.
10. Allotment on a proportional basis was introduced in the event of oversubscription so as to reduce the evil of multiple applications. No amount of oversubscription can be retained by the companies. The SEBI representative will be present at the time allotment to prevent any malpractices by companies. In the event of undersubscription of less than 90% of the public issue, the full application amounts have to be returned within 120 days from the opening date of subscription.

Details of SEBI Guidelines — for Capital Market

(1) SEBI guidelines were issued after the repeal of the Controller of Capital Issues Act whereby the CCI guidelines became out of date. New guidelines by SEBI were issued starting from the month of June, 1992. Some CCI guidelines were still retained, as in the case of those for premium fixation.

(2) *Guidelines for new issues made by new companies:* They have to be issued at par. Free pricing is permitted only if the new company is promoted by the existing company with not less than 50% of equity.

(3) New issues made by Private Limited Companies and closely held companies can be made by free pricing, for listing purposes if such companies have had three years of track record of consistent profitability out of last 5 years. Not less than 20% of equity is to be offered to the public, in such cases.

(4) Public issues by existing listed companies can be made through free pricing, if they are further issues and if they are disclosed in the prospectus. The NAV and the market price have to be considered for the last 3 years. The companies with foreign holding wishing to enhance the limit up to 51% will have to get the

prices approved in the general body meeting by a special resolution under Sec. 81(A) of the Companies Act, and subject to RBI approval.

(5) *Listing of shares on the O.T.C.:* If the new issues are made through OTC, normal guidelines will apply if the sponsor is not taking any share. If the shares are taken by the sponsor, subsequent offer to the public may be made at such a price as the sponsor may deem fit. The promoters should retain 25% quota with a lock-in period of 5 years, the sponsor should act as market maker for a period of at least 3 years and also find another market maker for compulsory market making. These conditions were relaxed later on to encourage OTC Listing.

(6) Underwriting is optional if the issue is made to the public and should not include reserved or preferential quota or employees' quota. If the subscription is not up to 90% of the total issue from the public including contribution of underwriters, the public should be refunded of their subscription within 120 days from the date of opening the issue. The compulsory underwriting provision was also waived for smaller issues and was made optional later on.

(7) *Composite issues:* Issues to the public by existing company can be priced differently as compared to the rights issued to shareholders.

(8) *F.C.D. and P.C.D.:* The issues of F.C.D.s with a conversion period of more than 36 months will not be permissible unless conversion is optional. In case F.C.D.s are convertible after 18 months, credit rating is compulsory; the D.R.R. has to be created in such issues with a maturity of more than 18 months. In case, the non-convertible portion of the P.C.D. is to be rolled over, non-maturing debenture holders should have option to withdraw from the scheme.

(9) *New Financial Instruments:* The terms and conditions of the new instruments such as Deep Discount Bonds, debentures with warrants and secured premium notes, etc., should be disclosed clearly so that the investor can assess the risk and return scenario of the instrument.

(10) *Reservation in issues:* The unreserved portion offered to public should not be less than the minimum required for listing purposes. Preferential allotment can be made to promoters, companies, shareholders of those companies, NRIs, Employees and Associate Companies of the same group. The allotment shall be subject to a lock-in period of three years, if it is made on firm basis, outside public issue.

(11) *Deployment of issue proceeds:* Where the total proceeds exceed ₹250 crore, the company will voluntarily disclose the arrangements made to utilise proceeds. When the total issue proceeds exceed ₹500 crore, there is need for making compulsory disclosure and for the financial institutions to monitor the deployment of funds, to the stock exchanges.

(12) *Minimum interval between two issues:* 12 months should elapse between the public or rights issue and bonus issue. The promoters should bring in their share of the capital before the public issue.

(13) *Employees' Stock Option Scheme:* The reservation for employees should not be more than 10% at present and this quota is non-transferable for 3 years and subject to a maximum allotment of 200 shares per employee, and the lock in was removed later on.

(14) *Lock-in Period:* The lock-in period for promoters' quota is 5 years and the lock-in period for preferential allotment for associates and friends is 3 years. The lock-in period for promoters was later reduced to 3 years.

(15) *Bonus Shares:* Bonus issues are to be made out of free reserves, the share premium collected in cash, Development Rebate Reserves and Investment Allowance Reserve. Contingent liabilities disclosed in the audited accounts should be deducted from net profits for calculation of residual reserves. Residual reserves after the bonus issue should be at least 40% of the increased paid-up capital. 30% of the average profits before tax for the previous 3 years should yield a rate of dividend of 10% on the expanded capital base. Reserves out of revaluation should not be used for bonus payment. Bonus issue cannot be made in lieu dividends and if there are partly paid-up shares, no bonus issue is permitted. Expanded paid-up capital after bonus issue

should not exceed authorised share capital. When a company has P.C.D. or F.C.D., Pending Conversion, no bonus issue can be made unless this right is kept open to the holders of F.C.D. and P.C.D. falling due for conversion within 12 months.

(16) *Debenture issues:* All debentures which have a life of more than 18 months should have a D.R.R. created by company out of profits. D.R.R. should be created only for non-convertible portion of the debentures. Contribution to D.R.R. should commence from the date of commercial production and when there are profits after tax, interest and depreciation. The D.R.R. will be considered as a part of the general reserves for payment of the bonus issues. D.R.R. should be created and maintained at 50% of the amount of the debentures before repayment starts. Some liability has already been redeemed by the company. D.R.R. and the creation of Debenture Trust are necessary only if the debentures have a maturity period exceeding 18 months. The Lead Institution for each issue should monitor the use of debenture funds either for the working capital or for the project finance. The SEBI now insists on prior licensing of Debenture Trustees.

(17) By a recent amendment to Listing Agreement, the companies have been asked to provide half-yearly and quarterly unabridged balance sheet to shareholders. The companies have to give the disposition of the funds raised in public issues and compare the actuals with targets every six months, when they present balance sheet to investors.

SEBI Reforms on Stock Exchanges

The SEBI regulation of stock exchanges and their members had started as early as February 1992 and the reforms later introduced have been on a continuous basis. It was started with the licensing and registration of brokers and sub-brokers in the recognised capital exchanges. This was later extended to underwriters, portfolio managers and other categories of players in the stock market including foreign securities firms, FFIs, Debenture Trustees, Collecting bankers, etc. The SEBI guidelines and regulations are changing quite frequently that one has to update them through Daily Press only.

The other reforms are briefly summarised below:

1. Compulsory audit and inspection of stock exchanges and their member brokers and their accounts.
2. Transparency in the prices and brokerage charged by brokers by showing them in their contract notes.
3. Broker accounts and client accounts are to be kept separate and clients' money are to be separately maintained in bank's accounts and the same to be reported to the stock exchanges.
4. Board of Directors of stock exchanges has to be reconstituted so as to include non-brokers, public representatives, and govt. respresentatives to the extent of 50% of the total number of members.
5. Capital adequacy norms have been laid down for members of various stock exchanges separately and depending on their turnover of trade and other factors.
6. Guidelines have been laid down for dealings of FFIs and foreign broker firms in the Indian stock exchanges through Indian brokers.
7. Badla and carry forward business which was banned on major exchanges early in 1995 was reintroduced in October 1996 and renewal business was also subject to close scrutiny, for cash shares.
8. New guidelines for corporate members have been laid down with limited liability of directors and opening up of their membership to more than one stock exchange without the limiting requirement of experience of five years in one exchange, as imposed earlier.
9. Demat form of trading was made compulsory in all scrips.

10. Rolling settlement was made compulsory in some scrips on a T + 1 basis.
11. By the Securities Amendment Act in 1999 trading in derivatives was allowed and derivatives were made securities eligible for trading. Mutual funds and FIs were allowed trading in derivatives for hedging purposes.
12. Collective Investment Schemes or Nidhis were brought under the ambit of control of SEBI.
13. Daily and weekly settlement system with maturities of 1 to 5 days were allowed and continuous net settlement system (CNS) was also permitted.
14. Automatic Lending and Borrowing Mechanism (ALBM) was introduced by NSE on similar lines as the carry forward system on BSE and was provided with guidelines by SEBI.
15. Disclosure norms for listed companies were tightened through quarterly and half-yearly results to be provided and by introduction of corporate governance rules and guidelines.

SEBI's Recent Reforms

The stock exchanges have been directed to follow a uniform procedure for maintenance of Arbitration Record and Listing Records. A uniform policy is made applicable with regard to listing by establishment of a Central Listing Authority in 2003. But the stock exchange are free to charge Listing fees, as they deem necessary.

During 2003-04, the SEBI in Consultation with the RBI and the government has allowed the electronic trading in interest rate derivatives on the notional Government security and 91 days Treasury Bills. Banks have since been allowed to trade in interest rate derivatives in addition to FII, NRIs, etc. Currency derivative trading was also started on NSE in 2008.

The SEBI has also streamlined the guidelines under Disclosure and Investor Protection (DIP) for IPOs through Book building process by unlisted companies, and those disclosure norms for bulk deals. The Clause 49 of the Listing Agreement was amended to improve corporate governance. The stock exchanges were directed to inspect every year, at least 20% of active brokers, instead of 10%, as used to be earlier.

The RBI has directed that only FIIs and NRIs can trade in derivatives and not OCBs. The securities brokers are allowed to participate in commodity markets as also the selected banks as per the guidelines of the FMC but security brokers have to setup separate units for this purpose.

The SEBI insisted on the demutualisation of all stock exchanges on a uniform basis, failing which they would be derecognised. This means that trading and ownership of stock exchanges should be in different hands or persons or agencies.

✠ ✠ ✠

INSTITUTIONAL STRUCTURE IN CAPITAL MARKET

29

Development and Investment Institutions

Functionally, there are two types of financial institutions in the Indian capital market, namely, developmental institutions and investment institutions. In the former category, there are institutions of all-India stature, namely, IDBI, IFCI, ICICI and IIBI, and at State-level stature, namely, State Finance and Development Corporations. In the category of investment institutions, there are all-India bodies like UTI, LIC, GIC, etc., and State-level bodies like the State Industrial Development Corpns. (SIDCs) and State Industrial Investment Corpns. (SIICs) and State Infrastructural Development Corpns. The all-India bodies provide finance, entrepreneurial guidance, training and technical guidance, etc., to the all-India projects and regional projects of medium and large size. They lend at concessional terms for the development of no-industry districts and backward regions. Among the all-India bodies, IDBI is the leader of financial institutions. But in 1988, the SEBI was set up as the developmental and regulatory body of the securities industry in India.

The state-level bodies provide finance and entrepreneurial guidance to State-level small and medium entrepreneurs and undertake developmental and investment activities to promote infrastructure and industrial growth in the respective States. Some of them have set up industrial estates and undertook joint ventures with the private sector to promote industries in their respective states.

These are the main players in the market, either in the primary market or in the secondary market. Besides giving loans and advances to industrial units, they invest in their debentures and equity shares, provide the seed capital for new and small entrepreneurs, underwrite stock, shares, debentures and various other instruments in the capital market or subscribe to new issues or buy or sell these instruments in the secondary market, etc. A number of mutual funds have also become players in the market since 1987.

The SEBI as the regulatory authority deserves our first attention as this book is concerned with the security markets. This was discussed in a separate chapter.

Of the major players in the market, namely, the financial institutions like LIC, GIC and UTI, the bulk of the activity is generated by the UTI by its mobilisation of savings from the public through its various schemes, referred to below. It has today investible funds to the tune of about ₹60,000 crore and it actively participates in trading in the market and in subscribing to new issues of shares, debentures, etc. A detailed write-up of the activities and functions of UTI was already discussed in the chapter on Mutual Funds.

UTI and its Objectives

The Unit Trust of India (UTI) was set up in 1964 with a major contribution from the RBI under the Unit Trust of India Act, 1964. Subsequently, with the passing of ownership of UTI to government in 1976, the IDBI became its shareholder along with the LIC, SBI and other financial institutions. Its activities, namely, the schemes it operates to mobilise saving and its investments, are all governed by the Act. It had originally a paid-up capital of ₹5 crore and it was the only Unit Trust or Mutual Fund in the public sector allowed to operate in India. It was accorded special treatment for tax assessment and tax deductions. Not only is its investment income-tax free but its dividend payments are also tax-exempt up to certain limits in the hands of the investors.

Its main objectives are to mobilise savings, particularly from the low and middle income groups, to channelise these savings into productive investment and to provide an assured income to savers. It provides the savers with expert investment service, portfolio management and assured income. The risk-averting savers would not normally invest in stock and capital market. They are afraid to do so due to lack of expertise and easy access. The UTI provides expert management of their funds, steady income and liquidity for their investment through repurchase facility. The UTI mobilises the savings through the sale of its units and operates a number of schemes with varied characteristics to suit the requirements of savers and investors. These characteristics include income, capital appreciation, liquidity through repurchase, an element of insurance, etc.

Activities of UTI

The activities of UTI include a wide variety of services to the corporate world as well as investors. It can underwrite new issues, make direct subscription to public issues or private placements, keep deposits with banks and companies and operate in the money market by subscribing to Treasury bills, commercial bills, etc. It can also partake in the inter-bank market as a lender or borrower of short-term funds. It can borrow from the RBI or the government in case of need.

The units of UTI are in denominations of ₹10 or 100, through which it mobilises funds from the household and business sectors. It can also sell units to foreign individuals and institutions. For example, NRIs are eligible to invest in the units without prior permission of the RBI on a non-repatriation basis. The UTI has a network of agents all over India to sell units and service the unitholders. It has arrangements with some banks to operate its schemes. Its investor base is around 5 crores of the population.

Investment Pattern

The normal pattern of investment of its funds is broadly as follows although it may vary from year to year. After 2002, UTI was reorganised and there are no comparable data for later years.

(at end June 2013)

	% of total investment
Equity	55.9
Debentures and preference shares	30.1
Advance deposits for underwritten shares/debentures	—
Term loans	0.8
Government Securities	8.6
Money Market Instruments	4.3
Deposits with companies } Deposits with banks }	0.3
Total	100.0

It will be seen from the above that the bulk of its funds flow into the corporate sector in the form of loans, deposits, debentures, equity, etc. Barring about 12% with banks and in Government securities, and Money Market Instruments, the rest is invested in high-yielding corporate instruments.

Two unit schemes, *viz.,* India Fund and India Growth Fund, were floated in foreign countries to mobilise foreign funds for investment in India. These two offshore funds were operated since 1986. The first one was India Fund floated in July 1986 in association with the Merrill Lynch and collected $75 million. These shares were quoted in London. The second fund, namely, India Growth Fund, was launched in July 1988 and mobilised $60 million. These shares were quoted in New York. These two funds have been doing well in their performance with the result that a number of other offshore funds were floated by UTI itself and the Grindlays Bank, SBI Caps, Canbank and others.

Besides, the UTI has also launched two Venture Capital Funds in 1989 and 1990 respectively for the promotion of greenfield companies and new ventures having a high-risk component.

Schemes Offered by the UTI

UTI had more than 40 schemes in operation in 2004:

1. *Unit Scheme 1964:* It was perpetual scheme, each unit with a face value of ₹10, transferable and repurchased by the UTI. Dividend income from the UTI qualifies for deduction of income tax under Section 80L of the Income Tax Act and eligible for Wealth Tax exemption up to ₹5 lakh. Reinvestment facility as an alternative to dividend distribution is available. This was closed in 2002, due to mismanagement of investments early in 21st century and UTI was restructured, as referred to in an earlier chapter.

2. *Unit-linked Insurance Plan (ULIP) 1971:* Schemes of 10-year and 15-year periods are available both with life insurance and accident insurance. The target amount is a maximum of ₹60,000 and the age limit is 55 years. The life coverage is secured from the LIC by the contributions of UTI. The contributions of the insured are payable yearly or half-yearly.

3. *Capital Gains Unit Scheme (CGUS):* Investment in part or in full of the capital gains due to sale of any long-term capital assets in the Capital Gains Units Scheme would qualify for exemption from capital gains tax under Section 54A of the Income Tax Act. This investment is to be made within six months of the date of the sale of capital assets and there is no maximum limit. This is to be held for a minimum period of three years. Dividend income along with others is exempt under Section 80L of Income-tax Act up to ₹12,000 and from the wealth tax up to ₹5 lakh.

4. *Children's Gift Growth Plan:* Units with a face value of ₹10 are gifted to a minor child under this scheme, maturing at the age of 21 by the child. Gifts up to ₹20,000 were exempt from gift tax, at that time but gift tax was abolished in recent years.

5. *Various Close-ended Schemes:* Such schemes as monthly income unit scheme, growing income unit scheme, etc., were started in various years since 1982 for meeting the varying needs of investors.

6. *Master Shares floated for Indian investors and India Fund and India Growth Fund, etc., for foreign investors:* The Mutual Fund Subsidiary Unit Scheme (Master Shares) 1986 are quoted on the stock exchanges and are treated as shares. A third offshore fund was initiated in 1989-90 with the help of a Japanese securities firm and ADB, in addition to the two, referred to above.

UTI has set up its own Bank (UTI Bank) and some subsidiaries to serve its investors, during the nineties.

The first three schemes are the most popular of all and account for 70 per cent of the total investible funds of the UTI. The second venture capital fund which is managed by the Technology Development and Information Company of India Ltd., was set up in March 1990 with a contribution of ₹35 crore from the UTI and contributions from other financial institutions. This fund like the earlier one helps the financing of greenfield ventures from new entrepreneurs to promote industrial growth.

IDBI

The Industrial Development Bank of India (IDBI) is the leader in the Indian capital market. It has both regulatory and developmental functions. The IDBI was established in July 1964 as a wholly-owned subsidiary of the Reserve Bank but was transferred to the ownership of Central Government, under the Public Financial Institutions Laws (Amendment) Act, 1975.

The role of IDBI in the market is to promote and develop industries as per the planned projections of the government, to provide technical and consultancy assistance for the expansion and modernisation of industry and for rediscount and refinance facilities to financial institutions. The IDBI operates a number of schemes for the benefit of promoting enterprises and concessional finance facilities are also provided for industries in backward areas.

The IDBI, as the leader in the market, co-ordinates, guides and monitors the credit facilities by all-India and State-level financial institutions and development corporations. The IDBI also undertook the responsibility for promoting and financing the small and cottage industries and also the import-export trade of the country until separate bodies were set up for them. Thus, the EXIM Bank was set up in 1981 for assisting the export-import trade sector and in particular for promoting exports. The Small Industries Development Bank of India (SIDBI) was set up in 1989 to help small and cottage industries.

The paid-up capital of the IDBI was ₹100 crores up to 1980 and raised to ₹659 crores by March 1997 and stood at ₹653 crore in 2004. The main sources of funds for the IDBI are borrowing from government, RBI and from the market by issue of bonds and debentures, both internal and external.

Schemes of IDBI Assistance

The major schemes, performance-wise, are as follows:

(*i*) Textile Modernisation Fund Scheme for the purpose of promoting modernisation of jute and cotton textile industries;

(*ii*) Venture Capital Fund Scheme for the purpose of developing new ventures and promoting risky ventures by new technicians and new entrepreneurs;

(*iii*) Technology Upgradation Scheme for the purpose of upgrading technology in selected capital goods industries;

(*iv*) Energy Conservation Scheme for the purpose of financing of energy-saving proposals of industries; and

(*v*) Seed Capital Scheme for the purpose of providing initial seed capital in the form of promoters' contribution to new ventures.

The IDBI operates direct assistance schemes whereby project appraisal and financing for medium and large-scale projects is undertaken. It co-ordinates its activities with all-India institutions like IFCI, ICICI, etc. It is the leader and provides guidance and co-ordination of services for long-term financial institutions.

It provides refinancing under the Industrial Loans Scheme for the loans extended by commercial and co-operative banks and SFCs. This refinance is for assisting SSIs, transport operators and units in the backward areas, etc.

The IDBI undertakes a number of promotional activities like provision of finance out of the Technical Assistance Fund for techno-economic surveys, preparation of project report, undertaking industrial potential survey, promoting market research, training and conducting entrepreneurial development programmes, etc. It has set up or contributed to setting up a number of Venture funds.

The IDBI has also sponsored a number of technical consultancy organisations in different parts of the country to help the new entrepreneurs with identification of projects, preparation of project reports, market studies, setting up of science and technology parks and promoting research and development in the areas of capital market. The promotional role is also noticed in its operation of the Seed Capital Assistance Scheme referred to earlier. Under this scheme, SFCs provide special seed capital to SSIs out of the funds provided by the IDBI for this purpose. The IDBI has also its own scheme to help middle-sized projects up to ₹ 1 crore with Seed Capital through the SIDCs and SIICs. Besides, the IDBI also contributes to the share capital and bonds of SFCs and other financial institutions. It has set up a Development Assistance Fund for the purpose of providing assistance to projects approved by the Central Government, which may not be financed by banks and FIs. It operates a Bills Rediscounting Scheme under which banks and financial institutions can get rediscount of bills and promissory notes arising out of the sale of machinery and capital goods on a deferred payment basis.

Sources of Funds

The IDBI also borrows from abroad and secures funds under arrangements with foreign financial institutions, foreign banks and foreign governments and operates foreign lines of credit, secured by the government. The foreign funds are used for financing of the foreign currency component of the project finance, for providing foreign currency loans and financing of imports and to make payments to foreign suppliers of capital goods, plant and machinery in foreign countries. It can borrow from the govt. and the RBI, but it has been borrowing from the capital market since 1994, through issue of different varieties of bonds and debentures. It has set up a Mutual Fund and a number of subsidiaries for provision of various financial services. The IDBI is converted into a Universal Bank and merged with its subsidiaries, including the IDBI Bank in 2004-05.

ICICI

The Industrial Credit and Investment Corporation of India (ICICI) was set up in 1955 in the Private Sector to meet the private sector financial needs and to channel the World Bank assistance to the private corporate units. The objectives of this corporation were to encourage industrial investment in the private sector and to promote participation of private capital, both internal and external, with a view to widening the base of industrial development and of capital market in India. It has been providing full merchant banking services, Venture capital financing and allied financial services.

The ICICI has been assisting both private and joint-sector enterprises with rupee and foreign currency loans and advances, underwriting, guaranteeing of loans from other agencies, equity participation and other forms of assistance particularly to the new enterprises.

The sources of funds of ICICI are its paid-up capital, borrowing from the government, IDBI, RBI, etc. It can also raise funds from the capital market by issue of bonds or equity and borrow from abroad with the permission of the government.

It has contributed to the development of backward areas through industrial growth, promotion of investment priorities of the government and for the growth of private corporate sector.

It has set up Venture Capital Funds for the promotion of greenfield companies and risk capital investment and joined the other financial institutions in setting up SHCI, CRISIL and OTC Exchange of India Ltd. It has recently set up its own bank and a mutual fund, like the UTI. ICICI has now become a full-fledged universal bank by merger with the ICICI Bank.

IFCI

The Industrial Finance Corporation of India was set up in 1948 by the IFC Act, 1948 for the purpose of assisting the medium and long-term projects for capital expenditure on projects, expansion, modernisation and technological upgradation, etc. It has also a promotional and developmental role, particularly in relation to the small and medium-scale entrepreneurs.

It has now a paid-up capital of ₹ 4,002 crore of which 50% is held by the IDBI and the rest by the scheduled commercial and co-operative banks and other financial institutions. The IFCI has borrowed heavily in more recent years from the market by the issue of bonds. Its reserves stood at ₹ 5,057 crore whereas same amount of the paid-up capital was ` 1,926 crore.

Functions

Its operations extend to both rupee loans and foreign currency loans. The foreign loans are through foreign credit lines from foreign banks and foreign governments, etc. It can also provide underwriting and guaranteeing facilities to the industrial concerns. It can provide term loans or contribute to the debentures or equity.

Under the IFC Act, it can provide financial assistance to limited companies either in the private, public or joint sectors and co-operative societies engaged in the following activities: (1) Manufacturing, preservation and processing of goods; (2) Shipping; (3) Mining; (4) Hotel Industry; (5) Electricity generation and distribution, etc.

The IFCI collaborates with other FIs in financing all big projects of ₹ 10 crore and above. It concentrates mostly on medium and large-scale projects, as in the case of ICICI and IDBI. By an agreement with other FIs and IDBI, the IFC specialises in financing of certain industries like jute, cement, sugar, etc. Due to its continuing financial problems and losses it is proposed to be merged with IDBI.

IRBI

The Industrial Reconstruction Bank of India was set up in 1985 by reorganising the earlier IRCI to provide assistance to sick but potentially viable units and extend finance for their modernisation, expansion or diversification.

Its paid-up capital at present is around ₹ 200 crore and other sources of funds are the borrowings from the government and the RBI, IDBI and others. It can also raise funds by the issue of bonds to the public and market borrowings. These are used for term loans, hire-purchase, leasing finance, etc., for industrial reconstruction and rehabilitation.

Functions

The IRBI has its Head Office at Kolkata, while the rest of the institutions of all-India nature referred to above have their head offices either in Mumbai or Delhi. The IRBI mainly assists the sick jute and cotton textile industries and the sick units in other industries. The potential viability of these units at a future date and their national importance in terms of employment and output are also taken into account by the IRBI.

Its sources of funds are the government, borrowing from the IDBI, RBI, etc. It can also issue debentures or bonds to the public or raise deposits from the public. These funds are advanced to the assisted units in the form of term loans, working capital term loans, investments and other forms of assistance.

IIBI

In 1997, IRBI has been completely restructured, when it had become sick by itself, due to financing of sick industries. The N.P.A.s of sick industries were wiped off and paid-up equity of ₹ 199 crore as at end March 1996 was brought down to ₹ 73 crore at end March 1997. It is converted itself into a limited company with a new name of Industrial Investment Bank of India with a share capital of ₹ 446 crore. It has shed off its outfit of financing sick industries into one of financing industrial investment for growth, expansion, diversification, etc. It has now become a development financial institution with a five year tax holiday in addition to completely restructured capital structure.

The specialised institutions for foreign trade and small industries are EXIM Bank and SIDBI respectively. The National Housing Bank is the apex bank for Housing Finance to provide finance and refinance to HFCs like HDFC. There is also shipping credit and investment corporation of India to help with finance and refinance to shipping companies. This list is illustrative but not exhaustive of the finance institutions in the capital market.

INSURANCE COMPANIES

Life Insurance Corporation (LIC)

The provision of life insurance in India is the monopoly of the Life Insurance Corporation of India (LIC). It provides cover of risk of life, retirement, disability, etc. Since 1956, when it was set up as a nationalised public body, it was acting as a major financial institution in the capital market for mobilising savings through premiums for life and endowment insurance and using these funds for investment in government and corporate securities for economic growth. The LIC operates in both the money and capital markets although it is a long-term financial institution. It was referred to already.

Its sources of funds are the paid-up capital (₹ 100 crore), premium collections, borrowing from government and the RBI and presently, the mobilisation of savings by insurance companies accounts for about 24% of the financial savings of the household sector in 2012.

Under the Insurance Act, as applied to the LIC, the pattern of investment is laid down. The proportion of funds to be deployed at their discretion was hardly 25% of the total investible funds, while the rest are earmarked for specified Government and semi-Government securities (50%) and for lending for socially-desirable projects like housing finance loans, mortgage loans, loans to approved bodies for electricity, housing, water, etc., (25%).

The LIC invests in shares/debentures of companies, provides rupee loans to companies, makes initial subscription and underwriting of new issues of shares and debentures, etc. It has control over a huge volume of funds and has an important role in the stock market and capital market operations. Investments by the LIC are of gigantic proportion as in the case of U.T.I.

It has set up in 1989, a Mutual Fund for operating various schemes for mobilisation of savings from the public, particularly from the rural and urban areas and channel these funds to the stock and capital market. The LIC has considerable expertise in investment management by virtue of its earlier operations of funds.

In addition to all these activities the LIC makes direct lending to industry, subscription to initial and further issues of shares and debentures of companies, financial institutions of the Centre and States, etc. Out of the total disbursements of all financial institutions to the industry, LIC's contribution comes to around 50%.

General Insurance Corporation (GIC)

The General Insurance Corporation (GIC) was set up by the government in 1971 by taking over the then existing GIC and merged all the then existing insurance companies into four subsidiaries in 1974 (National, New India, Oriental and United India). The details are set out in another chapter.

The objectives of the GIC are to carry on the general insurance business other than life, such as auto, accident, fire, etc., to aid and advise the subsidiaries to conduct the insurance business and to help the conduct of investment strategy of the subsidiaries in an efficient and productive manner.

Its sources of funds are paid-up capital, reserves, profits and premium income. It can also like the LIC, operate in the money and capital markets, earn on underwriting and making of long-term loans and investments. Its investment policy is governed by the Insurance Act like the LIC and its investments are accordingly spread in specified proportions in Central and State Government securities, semi-government bonds, debentures, preference shares and equity shares of companies, deposits with companies and other loans and advances.

LIC and GIC together make financial assistance to the industry to the extent of about 60% of the total financial assistance of the all-India financial institutions in recent years. Insurance is discussed in a separate chapter.

Mutual Funds

As referred to earlier, the UTI had the monopoly of Mutual Fund movement until 1986, when for the first time public sector banks were allowed to set up mutual funds with the prior approval of the RBI and the government. This was made possible under the government's scheme of financial liberalisation and the passage of the Banking Laws Amendement Act 1983. The SBI Caps and CanBank Financial Services were the first to set up mutual funds to mobilise savings for investment. Subsequently, the Indian Bank, Bank of India, Punjab National Bank, Bank of Baroda, etc., have set up their own Mutual Funds. The schemes floated by them have varying characteristics as regards income, growth, maturity, etc. To give examples, SBI Magnums, Canara Bank's CanStock, CanShare, CanGrowth and CanGilt, etc., are a few such schemes. The LIC and GIC have also set up Mutual Funds on the same lines as the banks in 1989-90. Since 1992, private sector was also allowed to set up mutual funds and there are as many as 22 private sector mutual funds operating in 2008. There are at present 26 Mutual funds other than UTI of which four are in the public sector, at present.

The schemes of LIC Mutual Fund have some special characteristics, in that they include an insurance element also. Examples are Dhanaraksha and Dhanavriddhi. Both these schemes have an insurance cover and a proportion of investment is set apart for this. Proof of age and certificate of good health are necessary for insurance cover.

SFCs/SIDCs

The State Financial Corporations have been set up after the passage of the State Financial Corporations Act in 1951 by the Government of India. These are development finance bodies designed to provide the short and medium-size enterprises with term finance and promote the growth of industrialisation in the states. There are 18 SFCs at present, including the Tamilnadu Industrial Investment Corpn., set up by various State Governments. Their total paid-up capital as in 2012 was around ₹ 3,043 crore and their outstanding loans and advances are about five times the paid-up capital. Its loans and advances are about ₹ 9,349.

Their sources of funds are issue of bonds and debentures in the market, fixed deposits from the public, borrowings from RBI, IDBI, State Governments, etc. These funds are deployed mostly as loans and advances to the various medium and small enterprises, investments in Government securities, corporate shares, debentures, etc. These bodies are to assist in particular small-scale industries, units in backward areas, new entrepreneurs, etc. Some State Governments have set up Industrial Development Corporations, Industrial Investment Corporations and state-level Infrastructural Development Corporations for the promotion of industrial enterprises in the States through equity participation and through loans and advances, including entrepreneurial assistance, seed capital to new enterprises, etc.

These are set up by the State Governments for promotional activity, infrastructural development, financial, managerial and entrepreneurial guidance to the industrialists, provision of industrial sheds/plots for setting up of small units, etc. They help in backward area development and promotion of industrialisation in the states in particular.

Besides, there is the National Small Industries Corporation (NSIC) and National Industrial Development Corporation (NIDC) in the country. The former helps the SSIs with the promotional and extension services, hire-purchase finance, supply of marketing network, raw materials, etc., while the latter provides the consultancy services, designing project planning and project preparation, etc. Thus many of these institutions in the capital market are developmental and promotional in nature.

SHCIL (Stock Holding Corporation of India Ltd.)

One of the important institutions set up more recently for toning up of the stock and capital markets in India is the Stock Holding Corporation of India Ltd. (SHCIL). It was intended to facilitate quicker share transfer among financial institutions, *inter se*, and their transfers with other investors, members of Stock Exchanges, etc. It provides infrastructural facilities for post-trading services, such as clearing, depository and other support services. Its services were later extended to banks, mutual funds etc.

Organisational Structure

The SHCIL was set up in 1988 by seven all-India financial institutions, *viz.*, IDBI, IFCI, ICICI, LIC, GIC, UTI and IRBI. It has a paid-up capital of ₹ 10.5 crore subscribed by the sponsoring FIs. SHCIL is Board-managed and has a whole-time President in charge of day-to-day management. Besides its office at Mumbai, SHCIL has branches at other important cities where stock exchanges are functioning. SHCIL is operating on commercial lines and will levy fees/charges for its various services so as to cover its costs and earn a sufficient surplus for expanding its activities and for giving a reasonable return on its equity.

Functions

In the first instance, SHCIL is offering its services to its own seven promoter institutions. It acts on the basis of Letter of Authority/Power of Attorney issued by the financial institutions and render the following services:

(*a*) Clearing services.

(*b*) Depository services.

(*c*) Support services.

(*d*) Management/information services.

(*e*) Registration and Transfer agents.

The SHCIL is eliminating paperwork which clogs the post-trading activities. It does so by replacing the physical transfer of shares by passing the necessary receipts and keeping the shares with itself as a depository for the sponsoring financial institutions. In other words, SHCIL will ultimately emerge as a bank for securities. The book entry transfer system will eliminate needless paperwork and speed up the transfer of securities and the related payments and receipts. Unlike under the present system which generally involves considerable delays in the actual transfer of shares to the buyer after he has paid for them and the actual receipt of the price consideration by seller after he has handed over the scrips to his broker, under the computerised book entry transfer system, the transfers and the related payments can be effected within a couple of days. The inefficiency of the present share transfer system, where speculative transactions play a dominant role can be reduced by this system of paperless transfers, if this can be extended also to all investors. It is already extended to the members of the BSE by the setting up of BOI Holdings. A Central Depository was set up by NSE in collaboration with IDBI and UTI to take care of depository function to investors trading on the NSE and other Exchanges.

Further details can be seen in Chapter 22 on the functions and working of SHCI.

Some of the other institutions are covered in another chapter.

✠ ✠ ✠

REFORMS AND STATE OF CAPITAL MARKET

30

Introduction

As referred to earlier the tone of the capital market depends on the available savings and investment in the economy, on the one hand, and the performance of the industry and the economy in general, on the other. Among others, in India the monsoon and agriculture, industrial growth and performance of the corporate sector in particular, reflecting the fundamentals in the economy would influence the tone of capital and stock markets. In particular, the government policy, the psychological expectations and a host of other factors play a role in influencing the capital market.

New Capital Issues

The main indicator of the state of the capital market is the quantum of new capital issues floated or raised. There has been a quantum jump in the amount of new issues raised in the market over the last decade. From hardly ₹ 100 crore per annum in the seventies, the amount of capital issues increased to ₹ 5,651 crore in 1988-89 and it further rose to ₹ 9,665 crore, including PSU Bonds in 1990-91 and further to ₹ 30,824 crore in 1994-95 but fell to ₹ 15,746 crore in 2003-04 before rising to ₹ 31,600 crore by 2006-07 and to ₹ 3,740 crore in the form of debt. Over the decade of eighties, capital issues rose by nearly 10 times. Similarly, the total financial assistance disbursed to industries by all-India and State level financial institutions has also gone up substantially from ₹ 38,650 crore in 1995-96 to ₹ 75,364 crore in 2000-01 but fell thereafter to ₹ 29,526 crore by 2003-04 as those granted to private sector have fallen. This has gone up again to ₹ 60,396 crore by 2006-07 and ₹ 78,438 crore in 2010-11 — an all time high — due mainly to the larger issues of bonds by PSUs in that year. The quantum of new issues varied from year to year depending upon the market conditions, costs of issue, need for funds and a host of other factors.

The capital market which remained subdued in 1987-88 improved in 1988-89 and there was in fact a boom in the market since 1989-90. The volume of resources raised from the capital market as new issues to public, right issues, etc., has increased substantially. In recent years, the issues of public sector bonds have also increased. In 1988-89, the public sector bonds raised was for an aggregate amount of ₹ 2,566 crore, and they rose to ₹ 5,586 crore in 1993-94 and stood at ₹ 3,070 crore in 1994-95 and ₹ 12,536 crore in 2003-04 and ₹ 14,265 crore in 2006-07. The issue of bonds by PSUs is a new feature of the eighties and nineties. The amounts raised by UTI and mutual funds stood at ₹11,342 crore in 1994-95 but the net figure for 1996-97 was minus ₹2,039 crore. The fall is explained by net outflow of funds from UTI. The funds raised fell in the second half of nineties due to depressed market conditions. The funds raised increased in the early years of 21st century and stood at ₹47,684 crore, in 2003-04 and ₹93,985 crore in 2006-07.

Factors Affecting Markets

The liberalisation of industrial policy since the initiation of the Seventh Five Year Plan (1985) and the introduction of a number of new instruments like convertible debentures and cumulative convertible preference shares have facilitated the expansion of the capital market of the order referred to above. Resources raised through debentures rose sharply in recent years. Of the total debenture issues, convertible issues constituted 70-80%. The eighties have seen a quantum jump in the new issues and the cult of equity has begun to grow aided by many tax benefits and the operations of mutual funds in the economy. A number of venture capital funds were set up by financial institutions to help new and risky ventures. Many public sector banks and LIC and GIC have come out with their mutual funds recently, which have helped the new issues market as well as the secondary market. In addition to the UTI, these mutual funds started mobilising funds for investment in the capital market since 1987.

The tax benefits include the exemption of dividend income up to a limit from income tax ₹15,000 P.A. raising of the exemption limit for deduction of income at source from ₹1,000 to ₹2,500 per annum as interest on debentures and tax exemption for investment in new equity issues of new companies up to a limit and fiscal concessions for venture capital funds, etc. Reduction of holding period for shares from 3 years to 1 year for computation of long-term capital gains is another tax concession. Besides, financial restructuring and deregulation have also helped the sentiment. In 1997-98, dividend income in the hands of investors is made tax free.

Some of the policy measures have in particular aided the capital market boom. Firstly, the ceiling on inter-corporate investment and loans was raised to 30% of the net worth of investing companies as against the earlier 10% ceiling. Secondly, the norms relating to foreign investment were relaxed recently to allow foreign equity participation not only in new companies but also in existing companies up to a limit of 51% as on 1991. Thirdly, three new instruments for raising resources have been launched, namely, partly convertible debentures of 5 years with buyback facility, non-repatriable NRI bonds issued by SBI and Offshore Funds by UTI and SBI. Besides Zero Coupon bonds, warrants, secured premium notes, etc., are being issued. The Offshore Funds are Indian Growth Fund and Indian Fund launched by the UTI, and India Magnum Fund launched by the SBI Caps which garnered large amounts of Offshore Funds for investment in the Indian capital market. The Canbank Mutual Fund has also floated an Offshore fund called "IS Himalayan Fund" in collaboration with Indo-Suez-Asia Investment Services Ltd. These funds are partly invested in Indian markets (up to 20%). Later, a number of public sector banks, foreign banks and FIs have raised Offshore Funds.

Corporate Scenario

There were nearly 2 lakh companies registered in India and the trend of registration is showing a strong upswing. Of these the largest number of companies are registered in the Northern region, followed by the Western region, which accounted for about 6,679 companies.

More than 6,000 companies are listed on all exchanges in India. Their market capitalisation at end March 2011 was ₹68 lakh, for companies listed on the BSE. As the latest Annual Report of BSE has put it, nearly 85% of the paid-up capital listed on all-India basis was on the BSE. The market capitalisation of listed companies on the BSE accounts for nearly 50% of the market value of listed equity on an all-India basis. The turnover of trade on the BSE is estimated at around two-thirds of the total all-India turnover on all Stock Exchanges. These data would bring out clearly the importance of the BSE in terms of listing and trading of securities markets for the corporate sector. But since 1995-96, NSE emerged with a larger trade turnover than the B.S.E.

The Domestic Savings rate is around 34-35% of GDP in recent years. Of this nearly 94% is accounted by the household sector. The contribution of public sector continued to be negative, or negligible. So is the contribution of private corporate sector.

The rate of gross domestic investment was at about 36% and the shortfall in domestic savings was made good by foreign savings. Private corporate sector recorded a gross capital formation of 8% of GDP, during the quinquennium of 2002-2007 which was higher than public investment at about 3% of GDP during the same period.

Of the total household sector savings, nearly 55% was invested in financial assets (2011-12), of which investments in share, and debentures, including Mutual Fund Schemes amounted only to 2 to 4% during the decade of 2002-12.

The above data show the importance of the capital market in the investment pattern of the households and the role of corporate sector in this scenario at the macro level.

Secondary Market

In tune with the growth of the new issues market, the secondary market also expanded fast during this period. In the secondary market, the number of recognised stock exchanges has risen from 8 in 1980-81 to a total of 23 in 2004, excluding OTCEI and NSE. The membership of the Stock Exchanges has also increased substantially to around 6,000 by end 2007 from about 1,200 a decade ago. The listed companies of all stock exchanges stood at more than 6,000 in 2007. Market capitalisation has also shown a substantial increase in the eighties and nineties. The value of turnover of trade has also increased nearly ten-fold over the decade to around ₹11 lakh crore on the B.S.E. and ₹36 lakh crore on the NSE, in 2010-11.

Measures Influencing Stock Market

A number of regulatory and developmental measures have been adopted to improve the secondary market operations as well. The amount of capital listed on the BSE has risen sharply in the last few years, as referred to earlier. This has led to larger problems of regulation.

With a view to reducing delays in the listing arising out of conversion, the Stock Exchanges were asked to monitor the issue process and keep at least 1% of total issue as deposit with the Exchange to ensure that all formalities of listing are observed. The government has amended the SCR rules in December 1988 to permit multiple membership of Stock Exchanges and measures for granting of membership to institutions have also been taken up. In October 1988, the Bhansali Committee's recommendation on share transfer procedures was implemented, whereby the newly-allotted shares have to be treated on par with the old shares for delivery purposes, subject to the adjustment of the dividend depending on the time of allotment. The minimum capital for listing has been raised to ₹3 crore of which of ₹1.8 crore should have been issued to the public effective in February 1989. This was raised to ₹5 crores and above in October, 1995 of which atleast 25% should be issued to public and ₹10 crore and above since early 1996 on the major national exchanges. The guidelines for listing have also been amended particularly with regard to book closure and record date and to give more powers to the Stock Exchanges to monitor the allotment of new issues and to curb insider trading and takeover bids. Banks have been permitted to lend up to 90% of the value of shares to be acquired by the employees out of their quota of new issues subject to a ceiling of ₹20,000. Banks were asked to finance market makers and brokers against securities more liberally. In 2001, there was Ketan Parekh Scam on the BSE involving the use of insider information by Board members, and misuse of bank funds leading to bank enquiry and removal of all elected Board members. This has necessitated better vigilance by RBI on use of bank funds in the stock market limit up to only 5% of their net advances and by SEBI on the manipulation and rigging up of prices.

Measures to Promote Capital Market

Many important policy measures were announced by the government recently to promote the capital market which may be briefly set out below:

1. The utilisation of the proceeds of the Mega issues of more than ₹ 50 crore will be monitored by the concerned financial institutions. A provision is also made for a minimum subscription of 90% for a public issue before allotment can be made.
2. The government has approved the creation of Over the Counter Exchange of India (OTC) sponsored by leading financial institutions which would help the introduction of a multi-tiered market for securities.
3. The Employee's Option Scheme was partially modified restricting the allotment of the unavailed portion of the public/rights issues earmarked for employees only to financial or investment institutions or mutual funds.
4. In January 1990, the government modified the guidelines for bonus shares. According to the new guidelines, a company may make a further application for issue of bonus shares after 12 months instead of 24 months previously, from the date of sanction of the earlier issue. Besides, it was announced in January 1991 that no prior sanction of govt. is necessary for the issue of bonus shares up to ₹ 1 crore, provided the companies follow the normal guidelines.
5. Introduction of trading in derivatives, which has surpassed trading in cash market.

New Industrial Policy

Industrial policy measures announced in May 1990, also helped the process of liberalisation giving an impetus to the growth of the market. The emphasis was laid on the growth of export industries, free entry to MRTP companies into many categories of industries, move to privatisation, etc.

Industrial licensing policy was liberalised to exempt all ventures up to ₹ 25 crore of investment in fixed assets in non-backward areas and up to ₹ 75 crore in notified backward areas and for export-oriented units. The ceilings of investment for SSIs and ancillary units were raised and imports of capital goods and raw materials have been liberalised. Licensing was completely dispensed with except for 18 categories of industries in July, 1991. The economic and financial reforms were started in July 1991.

The Eighth Plan starting in 1992 has shifted emphasis to the promotion of agriculture, employment and infrastructure industries. The government has announced more liberal steel and cement policies to make entry into them easier and to pursue more realistic pricing policies. Electricity generation has been kept open to the private sector and privatisation has been the new theme of the government along with efforts to make public sector units more viable and accountable financially and to force them to depend on own resources and the capital market rather than on the government budget.

Many policy measures were initiated before the finalisation of the Eighth Five Year Plan. In August 1989, the government have issued guidelines to the mutual funds, financial institutions and banks for the disposal of their investments made under various equity support schemes, so that these funds can be recycled for other purposes. Boughtout deals, private placements, etc., need no longer have lower or upper limits for the amounts invested under these schemes. The conditions for minimum public offer for such companies are also waived. These institutions are permitted to make private placements or offer of sale to the public at fair prices, as fixed by certain criteria, acceptable to the government.

In January 1990, the Stock Exchanges have been authorised to set up a monitoring system for issues of over ₹ 10 crore, arising out of conversion. The Stock Exchanges should enquire into any delays beyond the permitted 10 days after finalisation of terms and report the matter to the government and SEBI.

In April 1990, the government have imposed guidelines for stricter control on public issues, rights, etc. If a public issue is not subscribed up to a minimum of 90%, the entire amount should be refunded to the applicants within 120 days of the opening of the issue. Rights issues are not to be permitted to be kept open for more than 60 days. The promoters have to make their subscription in advance before the issue opens for public. If the devolvement fell on the underwriters, they would have to make good the shortfall. If including the contribution of underwriters, the minimum subscription of 90% of offer is not secured, a provision is also made to pay interest at 15% on delayed period beyond the period normally permitted from the closure of issue, if the refunds are not made before that date.

The government has also given guidelines for operations of financial institutions in the secondary market. Any purchases or sales above 1% of the paid-up capital of a company have to be publicised and the Stock Exchanges have to be informed.

With a view to encouraging the closely-held companies to go public and seek through the issue of bonus shares, the restrictions on their issue have been relaxed. The time gap between any two issues of bonus has been reduced from 24 to 12 months in the case of all companies, early in 1990.

The government has through the SEBI initiated action to control and regulate the activities of Mutual Funds and merchant bankers. Conditions have been laid down for their licensing and their regulation with the SEBI was necessary for starting of their operations. Many merchant banks have since been licensed by the SEBI.

The listing guidelines have also been modified to impose stricter discipline on companies. Under Clause 16 of the Listing Agreement, the companies have now to give a notice of 42 days for book closure or record date, as against the earlier limit of 21 days. Clause 40 of the Listing Agreement has also been amended to regulate the purchase of shares over 5% of paid-up capital of a company for destabilising the management or for takeover bids. Amendments to Clause 40 of the Listing Agreement include the insertion of Clauses 40A and 40B. As per Clause 40A, when any person acquires 5% or more of the voting capital of the company in aggregate, the acquirer, the company and the intermediaries have to notify the Stock Exchange of such acquisition within two days. As per Clause 40B, if a person or body corporate acquires 10% or more of the voting rights of the offeree company or secures the control of the management of the company by acquiring the shares of Directors of the company, the offerer company shall notify to the members of the offeree company to purchase their shares at the negotiated price.

The government has given powers to the Stock Exchanges to shift from specified group to non-specified group, the shares of a company issuing rights. The Stock Exchanges have already powers to list and delist the shares of a company. But wider enforcing powers and penal provisions are necessary to deter the companies from indulging in malpractices. The recent changes under listing agreement are to ask all listed companies to provide unabridged balance sheets and to give data on the sources and uses of funds. The power of penalising the companies for violation of listing agreement is now bestowed on SEBI.

Potential for the Capital Market

The potential for raising resources from the capital market is infinite. At present only 1 to 4% of household savings in financial form is mobilised as units of UTI and shares and debentures of the corporate sector, as against similar proportions of around 25%-20% in the USA and Japan. The shareholding population in India constitutes only 4-5% of the total population (around 50 million) against 25% of the population in the USA and other western developed countries. The growth of institutional funds and the setting up of mutual funds have recently imparted buoyancy to the markets which may help them to expand, and increase investor base. The operation of FIIs and FFI etc., have added depth to the markets.

The financial deregulation, development of new instruments of money market and the setting up of new subsidiaries of banks for undertaking financial services have all aided the deepening and widening of the capital market in India.

Special Features of the Indian Capital Market

The capital market in India has exhibited some special features in the recent past which are worthnoting here:

1. Greater reliance on debt instruments as against equity and in particular, borrowing from financial institutions.
2. Issue of debentures, particularly convertible debentures with automatic or compulsory conversion into equity without the normal option given to investors.
3. Floatation of Mega issues for the purpose of takeover, amalgamation, etc., and avoidance of borrowing from financial institutions for the fear of their discipline and conversion clause by the bigger companies, which has now become optional.
4. Avoidance of underwriting by some companies to reduce the costs and avoid scrutiny by the FIs. This has become optional now.
5. Fast growth of mutual funds and subsidiaries of banks for financial services leading to larger mobilisation of savings from the capital market.

There are a number of other features of the capital market which are relatively more unhealthy and are brought out in the authors' study on "Ownership and Distribution Pattern of Shareholdings of Companies", published in the Stock Exchanges Review of March 1990 (BSE). The share of small shareholders up to ₹ 10,000 has declined proportionately as compared to five years ago, while the relative share of large shareholders increased. This pattern of allotment is, therefore, regressive in nature. The results of the study also showed that the share of the corporate units increased while that of individuals declined which is again unhealthy due to the fact the real net savings emanate in India only from individuals and households and not from companies. The proportional system of allotment accelerated these unhealthy features. The so-called boom in the capital market during 1990-92 and 2006 to 2008 was thus only a bubble built on the excess liquidity in the economy, caused by the RBI's creation of currency and expansion of money supply beyond the normal requirements of productive activity. The flow of funds from banks, mutual funds, etc., and misuse and frauds committed by some brokers has led to the bubble of speculation which has burst in April 1992 following the CBI enquiries into these practices. The fact that the contribution of NRIs has declined is another disquieting feature in the capital market. Following the securities scandal of some Mumbai brokers, the market crashed in May 1992. The later upswing proved the strength and resilience of the Indian Capital Market, and larger inflows of funds through FFIs and FIIs.

The capital market reforms were initiated in 1991, as part of the Structural Reforms comprising industrial deregulation, privatisation, globalisation, and financial reforms through liberalisation of domestic economic policies and foreign exchange policies. Foreign direct investment is permitted up to 51% of equity in 34 select areas and automatic approvals are granted up to the permitted levels and in selected industrial sectors for foreign technology and foreign investments by the Secretariat for Industrial Approvals and the Foreign Investment Promotion Board. A new Foreign Investment Promotion Council was set up in 1996 to monitor and promote foreign direct investment.

Trade policy was also liberalised to allow freely exports and imports subject to a small negative list. All quantitative restrictions were abolished and discretionary controls and most of the licensing requirements were dispensed with in the EXIM policy for the Eighth Plan period of 1992-97 and Ninth Plan (1997-2002). This trend continued during 10th plan 2002-07.

Rupee was made convertible on trade account in March 1993 and on current account in March 1994. There was a further liberalisation of the FERA regulations since 1992 with the result that free inflow of funds by FIIs and FFIs, etc., was allowed for investment in the capital market and Rupee was allowed to float with the RBI fixing the reference rate for its deals in Dollar vs. Rupee.

Narasimham Committee

A high level committee on the financial system with Shri M. Narasimham as the Chairman was set up in 1991, which made far-reaching recommendations for banking sector and non-banking financial sector to improve the flexibility and operational efficiency of the markets and the institutions, namely, banks and financial institutions. The major recommendations are being implemented in the direction of deregulation, and liberalisation of policies.

In the area of capital market reforms, the Narasimham Committee emphasised the need for strengthening the SEBI powers, vesting of CCI powers in the SEBI and freeing of operations in the capital market with the SEBI as the Supervisory and Regulatory authority.

As per the recommendations, the SEBI Act was passed in March 1992 vesting legal powers on SEBI to act as regulatory authority on the stock and capital markets in India and also for all the intermediaries such as Merchant bankers, Registrars, brokers, underwriters, etc. Mutual funds are brought under the control of the SEBI first in 1992 and venture capital funds later in 1995. All these funds are kept open to the foreign sector and the private sector since 1992 and not necessarily to the public financial institutions, as before. Later SEBI regulation was extended to all intermediaries in capital market including rating agencies.

Free Entry to Capital Market

In May 1992, the Capital Issues Control Act was abolished and the functions of Capital Issues Controller were entrusted to SEBI. But with freedom to enter capital market to raise any amount they want from the public by the corporates and free pricing of securities issued to the public, a new era of free capital market was ushered in. Now, any company is free to enter the capital market anytime to raise any amount they want and at any price that they can justify to the SEBI and investors. The SEBI powers in this regard are to oversee and vet the draft prospectus, with a view to ensuring investor protection. Slowly these powers of vetting and ensuring the transparency and full disclosures in the prospectus came to be delegated to the Merchant bankers, in respect of right issues and debt issues and since 1996 all public issues and rights issues. Only statements and copies of prospectus are lodged with the SEBI in respect of these issues. Even in respect of equity issues, the SEBI has delegated responsibility to the merchant bankers later in 1996. But the final powers of control and penalisation by SEBI would deter the companies and the Merchant bankers for any lapses. The grading of draft prospectus and penalty points awarded for any lapses to the Merchant bankers were the methods of control by the latter, which were thus rationalised and merged to strengthen them but it reduced their number.

Liberalisation Measures

Interest rates on debentures and on P.S.U. bonds were freed in August 1991 with the result that they can now offer any rate to the public depending on their credit rating. All debt instruments are to be compulsorily credit rated by a credit rating agency. There are at present six credit rating agencies, which are awarding credit rating to the money market instruments, and debt instruments of debentures, deposits, etc., in the capital market which was recently extended to equity issues also. These agencies are:

CRISIL: Credit Rating Information Services of India Limited, *IICRA:* Investment Information and Credit Rating Agency and *CARE:* Credit Analysis and Research Ltd., Duff & Phelps Credit Rating Agency, Fitch India Ltd., and SME Rating Agency.

As referred to earlier, the business of mutual funds, venture capital funds and credit rating and even banking have been kept open to the private sector and foreign enterprise. Accordingly, many private and joint sector mutual funds, venture funds, and private banks have started operating since 1993-94. Nearly, 100 venture funds were cleared by the RBI until 2008, to operate in India.

The interest rates on deposits of NBFCs were freed from control by the RBI since 1996.

The ceiling rate of interest on lending by financial institutions was replaced by a minimum lending rate of 15%. Since August 1991, companies with good standing and credit rating were permitted to borrow through commercial paper in India and through GDR and FCCBs abroad. The FFIs and FIIs are permitted to operate in the Indian capital market and some foreign security firms were also registered with SEBI for acting as intermediaries. In the stock and capital market banks and PSUs are permitted to borrow directly from the public in the capital market. Even public financial institutions including IDBI have been allowed to access funds directly from the public.

Quantum of Funds: The result of these reforms is that the quantum of funds raised from the capital market rose phenomenally in the middle of nineties. The amount of equity raised rose faster. Many new companies have become public to raise funds in the capital market and many public companies have sought listing on the stock exchanges. New capital issues raised were already referred to in an earlier chapter. These amounts relate to those raised by non-govt. public limited companies, in the form of equity and preference shares plus debentures, convertible or non-convertible either as rights or public issues.

During the 12 months of 1995-96 (April 1995 to March 1996) there were 1,421 public issues, through prospects aggregating ₹ 10,529 crore, as compared to 1,332 issues for ₹ 19,699 crore in the preceding year. The quality of the issues is poorer and the public response was reported to be lukewarm and discretionary during late 1994-95 and 1995-96. The number of issues and the amount of issue fell further due to depressed primary market after 1997. In 2003-04, only 27 issues were made for ₹ 3,210 crore by non-government public limited companies. In 2007-08, the amount was ₹ 1,63,637 crore. Afterwards the amount fell due to depressed markets following global recession.

New Instruments

Qualitative changes include a larger number of equity issues relative to debt, in the early years of 21st century as against the opposite trend in the latter half of nineties. Among debt instruments, convertible debentures either partly or fully convertible have become popular. A number of new financial instruments have come into vogue after 1992. Innovative financial instruments are introduced like convertible preference shares, secured premium notes, warrants, zero coupon bonds, deep discount bonds, discount bonds, flexibonds, loyalty coupons, etc.

In the foreign capital markets, the Indian companies have issued global depository receipts, listed and traded abroad, foreign currency bonds, convertible bonds, foreign currency notes, eurocurrency bonds, etc. Both private sector companies and public sector undertakings raised funds abroad for varying periods of time, say 5 to 9 years.

The depth and width of the capital market in India has expanded, as judged by the following factors:

(*a*) Quantum of funds raised in general.

(*b*) Quantum of funds raised by PSUs and public financial institutions.

(*c*) Premium at which they raised these funds.

(*d*) The variety of instruments, through which these funds were raised.

(*e*) The number of issuers of securities, the intermediaries and the final investors which have all gone up phenomenally during the nineties.

(*f*) The number of investors are estimated to have risen to 40-50 million from hardly 10-15 million before the reforms were started in 1991.

(*g*) The FFIs, FIIs, NRIs, OCBs, etc., have all been permitted to operate in the Indian capital market, both under direct investment and portfolio investment.

SEBI Guidelines

The SEBI set up originally in April 1988, became a legal entity in March 1992 and has since acquired larger and sweeping powers early in 1995. The SEBI has first started with issuing guidelines for merchant bankers, mutual funds, portfolio managers and then extended its regulations to all intermediaries in the market, like brokers, sub-brokers, underwriters, registrars, custodians, collecting bankers, debenture trustees, etc.

SEBI has issued regulations for controlling insider trading, frauds and malpractices, for takeovers and acquisitions, central depositories and practices of brokers in particular of all Stock Exchanges. A code of conduct to be followed by all registered intermediaries in the market has been laid down by the SEBI, separately for each.

The SEBI guidelines have also provided for market makers who will specialise in buying and selling of securities by offering two-way quotes. To ensure that market makers would be in a position to impart liquidity to scrips and reduce volatile movements in share prices, bank finance is made available to them as per the RBI guidelines of August 1993. Banks have been permitted to grant limits to market makers on commercial considerations and working capital requirements for them may be met by banks. The existing minimum margin of 50% of loans to individuals against shares/debentures/bonds would not be applicable to bank advances to market makers as also the prudential limits of ₹5 lakh for each against shares.

Regulations of underwriters of capital issues and capital adequacy norms for the stock brokers in the recognised Stock Exchanges were announced in October 1993. At the same time, the SEBI issued guidelines for disclosures in prospectus for investor protection. Allotment of new issues was made on a proportionate basis and minimum application amount was made for ₹5,000/- which was reduced to ₹2,000 in Oct. 1996. Reservations for various categories like Indian FIs (20%), Indian Mutual Funds (20%), FFIs (24%) and Associate Companies (10%) and employees (10%) were allowed subject to a maximum reservations of 75% (including the promoters' contributions of 20% in the case of paid-up capital of more than ₹100 crores and 25% in the case of paid-up capital of less than ₹100 crore). In all cases of public issue with a view to securing listing on recognised Stock Exchange, the minimum public issue was fixed at 25%, reduced to 20% in some cases in 1993 instead of 60% minimum prevailing earlier. These reservations were all scrapped in October 1995, except those of minimum public issue, promotors' quota of 20% or 25% and employees' quota of 10%. Merchant bankers are allowed a quota of 5% of post-issue equity since October 1995.

SEBI issued separate guidelines for Development Financial Institutions, Debenture Trustees and Asset Management Companies and for the various instruments of issue like FCD, PCD, NCD and bonus issues.

Underwriting, which was compulsory earlier was made optional in October 1994. Preferential allotments have to be made at market related prices for listed companies or at the net asset value basis in the case of unlisted companies.

Strengthening of SEBI Powers

By a gradual process, the powers of the govt. under the Securities Contracts (Regulation) Act 1956, to control the Stock Exchanges and their members were delegated to the SEBI; with final appellate power however resting with the Ministry of Finance. Besides, by an amendment to the SEBI Act in 1995, the SEBI has been entrusted with more extensive penal powers and more extensive coverage of their jurisdiction. Options and futures which were earlier illegal are permitted to be introduced subject to the SEBI's approval. Control on listing provisions of listing agreement with the companies and penal powers for violations of the listing agreement now rest with the SEBI. Even companies, banks, FFIs, FIIs and NRIs, etc., are brought under the SEBI powers in respect of their capital market operations. Powers to grant recognition to Stock Exchanges, inspection and audit of Stock Exchanges and Stock brokers' membership and other matters relating to Stock Exchanges, including the recognition to Attached Trading Floors have been given to the SEBI.

Venture capital funds are brought under the control of SEBI and similar to guidelines given by SEBI for Mutual funds, guidelines are also given for venture capital funds in February 1996. Under the Amendment to SEBI Act, 1995, many more powers on controlling the intermediaries, investors and all players in the stock and capital markets including penal powers — both civil and criminal are now vested in SEBI. In 2000, SEBI was declared by the government as the single and role controlling agency for the capital market. Venture Capital Funds, Nidhis, Credit-rating agencies, MMMFs etc., were all brought under SEBI regulation after 1999-2000. However, an Appellate Authority was set up later to take up cases of complaints against SEBI's rulings, namely Securities Appellate Authority.

Stock Invest

The stock invest is a method of making applications for new issues in lieu of cash or DD or cheque. This instrument provides protection for investors against loss of interest and delay in allotments. In March 1992, the SEBI in consultation with RBI has designed this instrument to be issued by banks like the pay order or DD but with a difference that the money kept is now on lien with the bank until the allotment or non-allotment but earning interest for the investor during this period. The money will be credited to the company only on allotment and not before. The instrument is valid for 4 months before which the company has to make allotment, or advise refund of the instrument due to non-allotment. At the end of 4 months, the investor has to get back the funds in the event of non-allotment or partial allotment. On giving the indemnity to the bank the investor can make the bank vacate the lien on the deposit and thereafter use the funds for himself in the event of non-allotment or default of giving advice by the company after 4 months from the issue date. As the instrument is issued against a deposit of money in savings or fixed deposit with the bank, the money is kept on lien with the banks during the period of 4 months earning interest on savings account or fixed deposit at the current interest rates.

In September 1994, the RBI has directed that the use of stock invest should not be misused and that it should be confined to mutual funds and individual investors. The RBI has also removed the lock-in period of one year for NRIs and OCBs for transfer under the portfolio investment scheme. Lock-in periods were also removed for all categories except for promoters. Stock invest has lost its relevance due to reduction of alloement time to 30 days and dematerialisation of Physical Certificates, and it was banned by the RBI afterwards.

Changes in Listing Guidelines

The listing agreement has been amended in many directions since the reforms were started. Firstly, the unabridged balance sheets have to be given to the shareholders. Secondly, the company has to submit statement on an yearly basis to the Stock Exchange showing the variations between utilisation of funds and projections given in the prospectus or letter of offer and sources and uses of funds. Thirdly, the minimum paid-up capital has to be ₹10 crore for getting itself listed on the B.S.E. as in the case of N.S.E. In the case of other Stock Exchange the minimum paid-up capital for listing was raised from ₹3 crore to ₹5 crore only. Besides, the companies should have a track record of two years of commercial production before listing. Since April 1996, the company to be eligible for listing should have a record of dividend payment in three out of the preceding 5 years or it has been appraised by public FI which has taken a stake in the issue. Since May 1996 the Exchange can reject listing for violation of the requirements. The listed companies have to effect transfers and splits and consolidation, etc., within one month of the receipt of request. In the event of signature differences, the company has to send to the seller to get his signature authenticated by a registered stock broker and that should be taken as final for effecting transfers. This measure announced by the B.S.E. should help the process of quickening the transfers and reduction of delays in bad deliveries. Another directive was issued to the effect that companies should ensure in allotment of public issue that there are 5 shareholders for every ₹1 lakh issued capital and atleast 10 shareholders for every ₹1 lakh in case of offer of sale.

Guidelines for Takeovers

The SEBI has issued guidelines for takeovers and substantial acquisitions to supplement the provisions of the listing agreement in this regard — Clause 40 A and 40 B. In November 1994, the SEBI issued the regulations for "substantial acquisition of shares and takeovers". These regulations provide for disclosures within 4 days. When acquirer's shareholding exceeds 5% of the paid up capital of the listed company that requires half-yearly disclosures; if the holding exceeds beyond 10% the Stock Exchange requires the acquirer to offer to other shareholders shares under takeovers. It contains separate provisions for bailout takeovers and negotiated acquisition of shares. SEBI has power to investigate any violations of these regulations.

In March 1995, SEBI permitted listing of investment and finance companies, leasing and hire-purchase companies and amusement parks on the OTCEI. Those were prohibited earlier to be listed on the OTCEI. Even in the case of regular Stock Exchanges, the listing requirements for finance and Investment Companies are more vigorous and need a three year track record of profitability, before getting listed, in addition to a paid-up capital of more than ₹5 crore and the company should have been registered with the RBI as the NBFC.

Relaxation of Some Restrictions

During the year 1995, many of the provisions were relaxed as in the case of removal of reservations, exemption from vetting by SEBI in respect of rights issues and debt issues and from October 1996 of equity issues also. The proportional allotment system is continued with an amendment in May 1995 giving a minimum of 50% quota of the total offer made to the public out of the public issue reserved for the individuals applying for less than 1,000 shares in each case. For listing requirements the minimum public offer continues to be 25% and out of that, 50% of that is reserved for small investors applying for shares not exceeding 1,000 in each case. The 25% norm of public offer was reduced to 10% in 1999 for I.T. and other related companies seeking listing provided they have been profit making over the preceding three years.

Details for Investor Protection

The prospectuses and abridged prospectuses would have to contain some additional details on accounts as per the requirements of the Institute of Chartered Accountants of India. Following the acceptance of the Malegam Committee Report in October 1995 the SEBI has further clarified the required disclosure guidelines in March 1996, which were made applicable from May 1996. The offer documents should contain more details as shown below:

The accounts should show the adjusted data if footnotes or auditors statement contain any qualifications, such as, incorrect accounting practices, or changes made in such practices; changes in the activities of the company such as change in suppliers, distribution agency or loss of market share; significant accounting policies, accounting ratios and financial statements properly audited; other ventures or companies promoted by the same promoters and information on them; the details of the public or rights issues made in the preceding three years and a comparison of the actuals with the projection made in those offer documents; details of tax implications say the book depreciation and tax depreciation and their profits; accounting ratios to be given are EPS, RONW and NAV, and a profit forecast for the year immediately before and as on issue date and capitalisation details of equity and debt equity ratio, etc.

Policy Changes in New Issue Market

In January 1996, the SEBI has dispensed with the requirement of a minimum promoters' contribution and lock-in for listed companies with a three year dividend track record in the past five years. The lock-in period for employees in their stock option schemes was also withdrawn, preferential issue guidelines, published by SEBI will continue to operate and lock-in will still apply to any preferential allotment made to promoters, but pricing of such issue would be based on the market prices. The lock-in for promoters and directors has since the beginning of the scheme been exempt for *inter se* transfers among the directors and promoters. Some changes were already referred to under listing.

Since July 1995, the letters of offer for pure rights issue, unaccompanied by public issue are required to be filed with the SEBI but no vetting of the same is done by the SEBI and no acknowledgement card is necessary for rights issues. In January 1996, the SEBI announced that it has stopped vetting all pure debt issues also, if unaccompanied by conversion facility into equity and if such issues are credit rated for adequate safety. Since October 1996, SEBI stopped vetting fresh applications of equity issues also. Such issues would be vetted and finalised by the merchant bankers themselves.

The regulations for custodians were finalised by the SEBI in January 1996 containing all the details about registration, annual fees, code of conduct, segregation of activities of each client, annual systems audit books of accounts, records, etc., to be kept for inspection, etc. The custodians would not be allowed to delegate work except to other registered custodians. The reports to be submitted to SEBI by the custodians have all been incorporated in these regulations. Book Building Process was encouraged and initial public offer through book building has been picking up.

Institutional Strengthening

The reforms, included the setting up of OTCEI in August 1989, which started operations in October 1992. The National Stock Exchange (NSE) was recognised by the govt. in 1993 and it started operations in 1994. Both the Exchanges, namely, the over the Counter Exchange of India and the National Stock Exchange have computerised structure trading systems and have unique features like shorter settlement periods (T + 5) and quicker payments and deliveries within a period of 7 to 14 days. While the OTCEI is for smaller companies and venturesome and risky companies, the NSE is for bigger companies with a wide network of shareholders.

NSE has two major components, namely, debt market, which started operations early in July 1994 and equity market which was launched in November 1994. In the debt segment, Money Market instruments, PSU bonds, and Govt. securities are traded, while in the equity segment there are presently 909 companies with a trading value of ₹ 4,000-6,000 crore or more per day on an average. These are all big companies already listed on other Stock Exchanges. Trading on the NSE is over the counter, through the Telex, Telephone and through electronic media. The RBI has given directive to all operators in Money Market and Govt. securities market to channel this trade through NSE which has considerably strengthened its trading. Similarly, the govt. patronage and encouragement is also there for the NSE to grow rapidly.

Electronic Trading

The OTCEI has started a new tier in the stock trading operations, through the electronic media. It is meant for smaller companies of ₹ 30 lakh to ₹ 25 crore of paid-up capital and companies, which are venturesome and risky, due to new entrepreneurs, new products, long gestation projects, etc., are eligible to be listed here. It has listed companies, with paid-up capital above ₹ 25 crores also. It has more than 100 companies, and average value of transactions *per month* is only ₹ 25 to 30 crore. It has about 100 members and 250 dealers and about 3 lakh investors with it. Although it has many advantages like transparency, quick delivery, market making with no speculative fervour, it is not popular and has very low volumes.

NSE on the other hand, has become popular with larger trading volumes with more than ₹ 6-11 lakh crore per annum in recent years. Only those with a paid-up of ₹ 10 crore and above and market capitalisation of above ₹ 50 crore are listed on this exchange. Its growth was faster both in the number of listed companies and volume of trading due to its growing network centres all over the country.

With the introduction of BOLT, and its becoming operational in May 1995, by the BSE, and subsequent expansion to other centres with terminals, a new era of electronic trading started, with NSE and BSE competing to set up online trading terminals throughout the country. In October 1996 the BSE was permitted to expand its BOLT to centres where there is no Stock Exchange and in centres where there is an exchange it has entered into a MoU with them. Other stock exchanges are also in the process of changing over to online trading and inter-exchange trading also takes place leading to a national market system and an intermarket trading system. These are already operating in many developed countries like the USA and UK. The internet websites of selected brokers are permitted to be used for trading by the clients through these brokers. Giving of orders and payment orders are now routed through brokers electronically.

Stock Exchange Reforms

Starting with the licensing and registration of stock brokers and sub-brokers, many far reaching reforms were effected in the operations of the stock markets, since May 1992. It has made regular inspections of Stock Exchanges and their member brokers as and when necessary. Their accounts and books are subject to special inspection and audits. Capital adequacy norms were laid down for brokers depending on the Stock Exchange and its activity and the members' turnover. The books of accounts are to be kept in a manner that the clients' accounts are separated from those of broker's own accounts, starting with a separate bank account for clients. Contract notes are to show transparency in deals with price, brokerage and service tax shown separately. The contract notes and bills are to be passed duly on time, failing which brokers are liable to penalties, depending on the days of default.

The composition of the Board of Directors is to be changed to comprise of 50% of the total directors to be from elected members and the other 50% from non-elected public members including three from the SEBI nominated persons and/or of the govt. The surveillance departments of the exchanges are to be strengthened and rigorous application of margins and other regulations on trade are expected from the Stock Exchange authorities.

The SEBI has issued regulations on unfair trade practices, frauds, etc., in November 1995 with penal powers for punishing any party including investors for indulging in malpractices in the market.

All the brokers and sub-brokers and other players will be liable for action for any price manipulation, or misstatements, misleading information and any other fraudulent practices. Listing agreement has provided for quarterly and half-yearly balance sheets to be published for some companies with a larger paid-up capital. Provisions are also made in the listing agreement for better corporate governance.

Market Makers

The SEBI has notified norms for market makers, in October 1995. The companies seeking listing, with paid up capital ranging between ₹3 crore and ₹5 crore and without a track record of commercial production of at least two years, shall have to appoint market makers compulsorily. They have to be appointed on the exchanges, where the shares of such companies are to be listed. Each such market maker has to undertake an obligation to offer two-way quotes for a minimum period of 18 months. Besides, there should be an additional market maker for each such company to undertake the obligation for at least 12 months from the date of allotment of shares. Such quotes offered by them shall be for 3 marketable lots, and the spread between the bid and offer rates should not exceed 10% at any time. For availing them to do this, the market maker should have an inventory of a minimum of 5% of the post-issue capital of the company, allotted to him by the company at the time of issue. The bank finance for such inventory holding and RBI guidelines in this regard were already referred to. The same guidelines will apply whether the company is listed on OTCEI or on regular Stock Exchanges.

Listing of companies with paid-up capital of not less than ₹5 crore was not allowed on the regular Stock Exchanges, as per the SEBI guidelines, given in October 1995, following the recommendations of Malegam Committee for raising the threshold limit for listing to ₹10 crore of paid-up capital.

BOLT System

BSE went over to online electronic trading system in January 1995, called BOLT, similar to that of NSE and this became fully operational in May 1995. Besides BSE moved to a weekly settlement system in specified shares and in another B1 category of cash scrips with about 200 of them, during Feb. 1996. The BSE has also raised the minimum paid-up capital for listing of companies to ₹10 crore at the same time. If a company is already listed on a Stock Exchange and requires listing on BSE, it should have a paid-up equity of at least ₹5 crore and net worth of ₹10 crore and minimum market capitalisation of 15 crore. For all companies which have got acknowledgement card on or before February 26th, 1996 the limit of paid-up capital of ₹5 crore will apply and for those securing SEBI approval after February 26, the limit of 10 crores will apply. The trading and settlement cycles are also brought on par with NSE. The trading cycle on BSE was from Monday to Friday while that on NSE was from Wednesday to Tuesday. Besides, carry forward is allowed on BSE, but not on the NSE. Settlement is through the clearing house for both BSE and NSE. The payout will be after 15 days on BSE and 10 days on NSE. The auctions will also be quicker on BSE, for each settlement, as in the case of NSE, at present. BSE is quickly following whatever NSE is doing to achieve quicker settlement and delivery and to attract more volumes. With this objective, BSE raised the threshold limit for listing to ₹10 crore, moved on to a weekly settlement system and quicker auctions for each settlement. The BSE has also allowed expansion of online trading system (BOLT) to members of other Stock Exchanges and have terminals in other cities since August 1995, to counter the move of the countrywise network of terminals by the NSE. The neck to neck competition between NSE and BSE has almost drowned the operations of smaller exchanges and their volumes have shrunk. Some Regional Stock Exchanges have started an Inter-connected Stock Exchange to be operational from October, 1998.

Badla Trading

Badla was banned in March 1994 and has reintroduced again, following the G.S. Patel Committee recommendations in March 1995. After five months of prolonged deliberations, the SEBI came out in July 1995 with a modified badla proposal which was not the same as recommended by the G.S. Patel Committee. This proposal of July 1995 was turned down by the stock exchanges and brokers. Later again a compromise proposal was put up in October 1995 which was adopted finally by the BSE in Jan. 1996. Even this modified badla was accepted only by 50% of the brokers and confined to a few scrips in 'A' Group shares which have come to have a weekly settlement since March 1996. This modified badla will have stiffer margins, transparency and daily reporting with a maximum period of 90 days by which, the position has to be squared up or delivery given or taken. In July 1997, Verma Committee went into the issue of modifications in the badla, presently operating on a two track system (one for carry forward and the other for delivery) and recommended many changes so as to bring it to the system prevailing before 1995. Later, the NSE adopted Automatic Lending and Borrowing mechanism (ALBM), to help short selling and lending securities, similar to badla trading and carry forward facilities on the BSE.

SEBI's Insider Trading Regulations

The SEBI has got legal powers in January 1995 to enforce these regulations and penalise the culprits. As per these Insider Regulations, an insider means any person who is or was connected with the company or is deemed to be so connected and who is reasonably expected to have access, by virtue of such connection to unpublished price sensitive information, in respect of securities of such company. A person is deemed to be a connected person, if such person is a group company, or any subsidiary, an official of the Stock Exchange or stock brokers, merchant banker or any intermediary in the market, or a director or an official of any of these companies or agencies or of the financial institutions financing that company or banker of the company or any related person or relative to any of the above categories of persons. If such persons have access to the unpublished price sensitive information and is proved to have used it for personal gain or profits or price manipulation, they are liable to be penalised under these regulations. Such price sensitive information should be unpublished and confidential and if published, it should materially affect the price of security of the concerned company. Such information relates to dividends, bonus, rights, financial results, likely issue of shares, expansion plans, amalgamations, mergers and takeovers contemplated, disposal of any of its assets, acquisition of another company or its subsidiaries, and any other information bearing on financial policies, financial results or earnings, etc.

Central Depository System

In Sept. 1995, the govt. have accepted in principle the proposed law for settling up of depositories and of a central depository for immobilisation of physical certificates. The central depository is to be set up as a Trust to hold the physical custody of shares and effect transfers by book entries without the need to deal and transfer the physical certificates between parties. This is to be sponsored by public financial institutions and banks and will have a minimum net worth of ₹50-100 crore, as proposed by the SEBI. This central depository can be connected to a number of share depositories for effecting transfers in book entries. The foreign financial institutions, foreign institutional agencies, NRIs and OCBs have for long required the depository of this type for facilitating their trade in the Indian stock markets. The foreign security firms who were licensed by the SEBI, are operating in India, but physical custody of the Indian securities has to be handled by Indian custodian such as a bank which can now be converted into the depositaries to be licensed by the SEBI. Above all these depositories there will be a central depository which will co-ordinate these depositories and the *modus operandi* of these operations were worked out by the SEBI. The guidelines and regulations in respect of the operations of depositories will help smooth *inter se* operations among depositories and their operations with the central depository. A National Securities Depository Corporation was set up in November 1996, and the system of Demat Trading is now operative in respect of almost all scrips, including CPs, gilted securities, etc.

Corporate Membership

The applicant company must be a company registered and satisfy the requirements of Section 12 of the Companies Act and meet with the financial net worth criteria as laid down by SEBI from time to time. There should be two experienced directors who are eligible to be members of a Stock Exchange as per SC(R) Rules and Rules and Bye-laws of the Stock Exchange. For NSE requirements the minimum net worth should be ₹ one crore and minimum paid-up capital ₹30 lakh and an undertaking that they would have an arrangement or office in Mumbai. Two experienced directors should be whole-time persons and hold at least 5% each of the paid-up capital of the company and the identified dominant shareholders of the applicant company should hold at least 51% of the paid-up capital, along with other family members. In Nov. 1994 the rules were amended by the govt. for non-Indians and NRIs to become directors of stock broking companies.

The net worth requirements for the corporate members change from Stock Exchange to Stock Exchange. Two directors in the firm should possess at least two years of experience in dealing in securities, portfolio managers, investment consultants, etc. The company can have any number of shareholders. The liability of members is limited and they can acquire membership of more than one exchange provided they satisfy the financial requirements of each separately. The company should only confine to stock broking and related financial services like underwriting, market making, portfolio management, investment consultancy, merchant banking and related services.

Exchange Reforms

SEBI desired that all the stock exchanges should go for online electronic trading latest by June 1996. Already BSE, DSE and VSE have gone for electronic trading and it is followed by Kolkata and Ahmedabad

Stock Exchanges. The smaller exchanges being shrouded into sideline, by the enlarging network of N.S.E. and B.S.E. online trading into various cities, are hastening to strengthen themselves by trying for inter-exchange trading or joint trading for a group of smaller exchanges or regional groupings.

Among the reforms which have recently taken effect are immobilisation of physical transfer of shares, the launching of Depository system, online electronic trading for all exchanges, registration of all sub-brokers throughout the country to be eligible for client order booking and enforcement of capital adequacy norms and change in the composition of the Board of Directors of all Exchanges. Book Build process is yet to take off as the equity limit of ₹100 crore for this, fixed in 1995 is too high for many companies. Book building helps the private placement of big premium issues by inviting a syndicate of big merchant bankers and underwriters to give their quantities and prices at which they are prepared to subscribe. The lead manager will be the book-runner, who then fixes the premium on the basis of these bids. The limit of ₹100 crores referred to above was removed in 1996. Rolling settlement and continuous net settlement systems were introduced. Monitoring system was strengthened in the Stock Exchanges.

Takeover Code

The SEBI has finalised the code for takeovers, based on the Report of Justice P.N. Bhagwati (August 1996). Takeovers will not be free for all any more. Only genuine takeovers will have to use the mechanism of SEBI Code.

Takeover is the acquisition by any interested party, individuals, corporate bodies, etc., of the shares of an existing company. It is mandatory to make a public offer to buy shares of the company, if the acquirer is acquiring more than 10% of the shares of the target company. SEBI has got powers to control the acquisition of shares for any change in control of management. Preferential allotments are exempt from the requirement of a public offer. In public offer, the minimum offer price is to be the highest of either the negotiated price, the six months average of highs and lows, or the price paid by the acquirer for buying of shares in the target company in the last one year.

The acquirer, making a public offer, has to deposit 10% of the total offer amount in an escrow account, which can be forfeited in the event of default. As against the earlier limit of 14 days, competitive bids have to be kept open for 21 days. Directors of the target company have a right to make their own recommendations on the offer to shareholders. Competitive bids have to be made within 21 days of public offer announcement and the original bidder has to revise the offer within 14 days of the competitive bid or withdraw from the offer.

Public offer can be revised upwards in the price and quantity also, within the time limits. The grounds for withdrawal from the offer are clearly specified by the SEBI.

The SEBI has permitted vetting these offers by the merchant bankers and not by SEBI itself. The merchant banker has to file the offer documents with the SEBI within 14 days of the public announcement. The acquisitions of the existing managements which do not attract public offer norms are as follows:

Acquirer holding 10 to 25% of the equity can acquire additional shares at the rate of 2% per year. Those holding 25 to 50% of the equity can acquire shares at the rate of 5% per year, without triggering the takeover code. Takeover code does not apply to unlisted companies.

Healthy takeovers are now more easy with the result that the earlier family run concerns can be targeted to be acquired by other managements also. If mergers are promoted by such takeovers and acquisitions, the capital market can become healthier.

The takeover code provides for orderly takeovers, transparency of terms, fairness to existing shareholders. If the acquirer wants to acquire by an agreement with the existing management, he has to make a public offer to buy from existing shareholders another 20% of the target company and keep 10% of this offer amount in an escrow account with a bank.

The code has also defined takeover and the word control. Control shall include right or power to appoint or remove a majority of directors or M.D. or change or formulate policy decisions exercisable by a person or persons, directly or indirectly.

There are however clear guidelines to follow for the hostile takeovers. The role of financial institutions and the Foreign Investment Promotion Board is also being defined in the new code. Both the Foreign and Indian Collaborator would be asked to make a public offer for such number of shares as it has agreed to take up, at the price at which the preferential allotment would be made to him. If they could not get from the public (the required number of shares), then the course of preferential allotment to them could be adopted by the company. Justice Bhagwati was also in favour of applying the code to preferential allottees and to allotment of primary issues in the new issue market as that route can also be used for secret takeovers. But primary market purchases are kept out of this takeover code.

The existing promoters and directors will no longer be able to manipulate to make a company sick and avoid takeovers. The buyback arrangement allowed in the new Companies Bill will also wardoff takeover of healthy companies. The code is designed to facilitate healthy takeovers, even if they are hostile to the existing management. But these regulations apply to listed companies. An unlisted company can takeover a listed company to get its shares listed on the Stock Exchanges. The takeover code applies to all acquirers and raiders whether they are Indians, NRIs, OCBs or FFIs, etc.

Critique of Bhagwati Committee's Report

1. Exempting acquisition of shares through the preferential offer route is not fair. If a public offer is made, and he is not able to acquire the entire quantity required from the public, then only preferential allotment may be justified at the minimum price as governed by SEBI guidelines.
2. It is not fair to the non-management shareholders to limit the offer to 20% of their holdings. It should be 100% of their holdings, as they may like to get out of the company, if the management is changing.
3. Managements with a 51% stake can consolidate their holdings without also attracting the provisions of the guidelines, as the code has made some provisions for them.
4. Regulation (3) says that nothing contained in regulations 10, 11 and 12 shall apply to requisition of shares in companies, whose shares are not listed on any stock exchange.
5. Persons acting in concert, have excluded developmental institutions (FIs) which might lead to some loopholes.
6. Regulation (12) states that even if there is a change in control without acquisition of shares or voting rights a public offer has to be made. The code has provided for such change in control without acquisition of shares.
7. Major loopholes are in terms of encouraging the takeovers by cash rich companies and by NRIs and foreigners.
8. Acquisitions in small quantities and through rights and new issue route would still be possible.

These are some of the limitations of takeover code.

Ongoing Reforms

There are a number of ongoing reforms to be noted. The finance minister had indicated his policy of continuing reform process in October 2000. Some reforms are in the form of change in laws, as in the case of Labour Policy and Exit Policy in industry. Fiscal Responsibility Act was passed in 2000-01, ensuring limits to budgetary expenditures and fiscal deficit. The government is determined to bring down the equity of government in banks to 33% and below. The government has allowed the foreign investment in private banks upto 74% in 2005. Banking reforms aimed to bring down the NPAs, based of new guidelines of RBI.

Besides the introduction of new Bankruptcy Law has merged the Sick Industries Companies Act and the Insolvency Laws.

The other reforms include propping up the industry for raising production and investment, further relaxation of Foreign Direct Investment, particularly for cellular operations and the introduction of new Competition Law. There was a revenue package for the Special Economic Zones as announced in the EXIM Policy during the year 2001. FII investment in equity issues in their portfolio management was larger than in debt issues in recent years. FDI in equity was also encouraged by the government, rather than in debt form. The corporate debt market is yet to be developed in the stock markets, although trading in government debt is growing at a worthwhile rate in recent years. The SEBI allowed brokers to extend margin trading facility to their clients in April 2004. The RBI has also allowed banks to extend finance to brokers for margin trading earlier in 2001. In 2004-05 budget, the government imposed a Securities Transactions Tax to be borne by both buyers and sellers on the Stock Exchanges. Simultaneously, the budget also abolished long-term capital gains tax and reduced the short-term capital gains tax from 30% to 10% for Stock Exchange transactions. The FDI limits were raised for telecommunications, civil aviation and insurance sectors in 2004-05, in addition to raising the ceiling for FII investment in debt funds. These had a favourable impact on the market. The later budgets were also favourable to accelerate reforms in fiscal, tax fields and investment and growth.

There may be many repetitions in this Section and in relation to other Sections of this book, due to the fact that the subject matters are all related or connected in some form or other.

✠ ✠ ✠

PART VI

FINANCIAL MARKETS IN INDIA

NEW ISSUES MARKET AND PROBLEMS

31

Definition

The new issue market deals with the raising of fresh capital either for cash or for consideration other than cash by companies, govt. and semi-govt. bodies, PSUs, etc., and encompasses all institutions dealing in the issue of fresh claims. The forms in which these claims are incurred are equity shares, preference shares, debentures, rights, bonus, deposits, miscellaneous loans, etc. All the financial institutions in the capital market which contribute, underwrite or directly subscribe are part of the new issues market. Thus, development corporations or banks like IDBI, IFCI, ICICI and investment corporations like LIC, GIC, UTI and other financial institutions contribute to the bulk of the underwriting activity and direct investment. Banks and brokers have also been participating in underwriting of capital issues in a larger measure. Some of the banks have already started merchant banking divisions to help floatation of issues by companies. Brokers have been underwriting limited amounts of new issues on the strength of their own or borrowed funds. These brokers may be individuals, partnership firms or private limited companies formed as investment and consultancy firms. They also undertake management of the share issue, act as lead managers, advisers and consultants, etc., or do liaison work for getting loans from banks, after getting clearance from the SEBI.

Normally, the whole amount of public issue is underwritten by one institution or by a group of institutions jointly. The underwriting institutions including banks would consult among themselves before they accept joint underwriting. Sub-underwritting is common in India among brokers and consultancy firms. Some brokers do sub-underwriting along with banks or other financial institutions. Many of these agencies are primarily intermediaries and provide financial services of various kinds. Sub-underwriters sometimes include institutional investors, investment trusts, provident funds, etc. Underwriting is now optional for smaller issues, as per the latest SEBI guidelines. The underwriting commission is about 2½% and brokerage 1 to 1½% for the issue of shares and debentures.

In case the issue is fully subscribed, the underwriters will get their commission or brokerage but if the issue is undersubscribed, the underwriters have to shoulder the responsibility of direct subscription *pro rata* on the basis of their commitments and to the extent of their underwriting responsibility.

Functions

The government and the corporate sector are the main borrowers from the capital market and are the issuers of securities. The methods of raising funds in the case of corporate sector are retained earnings out of profits and external borrowings. These external borrowings may take any of the following forms, which are in addition to the original issue of share capital in the form of equity and preferences shares (including CCPs). These can be from the domestic markets or foreign markets.

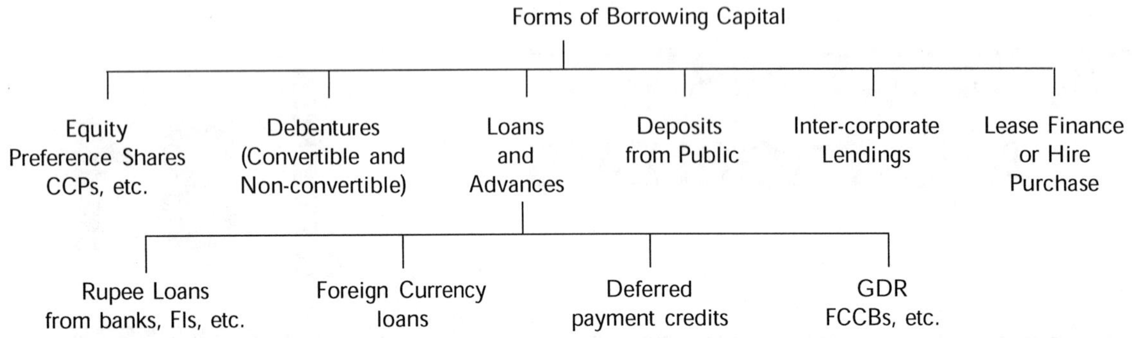

Fig. 31.1

The objectives for which funds are raised may be for setting up new projects, expansion, diversification, modernisation of existing projects, mergers and takeovers, etc. The proportion in which funds are raised in various forms as own capital (equity) and debt capital (borrowings and debentures, etc.), indicate the capital structure of the company and measures the leverage in the form of ratio of borrowed funds to owned capital and the servicing commitments of the company on borrowed funds.

Methods of Floatation

Initial issues are those floated by new companies for the first time, while further issues are subsequent issues floated by the existing companies. Issues can also be classified as those given for cash, for exchange of technical know-how, exchange of shares of another company or exchange for any other services rendered by the agencies or promoters.

The placement of the issues may be through (*i*) prospectus, (*ii*) offer of sale, (*iii*) private placement, and (*iv*) rights issue.

(a) Offer Through Prospectus

Public issue with prospectus is the most popular method of raising funds by the public limited companies. This involves inviting subscription from the public through issue of prospectus. This method of raising funds accounts for the bulk of capital raised and is necessary for listing of shares on the exchanges. The price at which the securities are offered for sale is at the face value of the share in the case of new companies and may be at a premium or discount in the case of old companies. The prospectus is a document which is a notice or circular or advertisement inviting offers for subscription or purchase of any shares or debentures from the public. The prospectus should contain authentic data and should be delivered to the Registrar of Companies for registration. The prospectus would contain details with regard to the name of the company, address, activities, board of directors, location of industry, authorised, subscribed and paid-up capital, dates of opening and closing of the subscription list, names of brokers and underwriters, etc. The draft of the prospectus should be approved by the Board, solicitors, lending financial institutions, and the stock exchanges in which they are to be listed.

(b) Offer of Sale

The method of "offer of sale" consists of outright sale by the company instead of offering shares to the public or through intermediaries such as issuing houses or sharebrokers. In this case, the company sells shares *en bloc* at an agreed price to brokers or merchant bankers who in turn resell them to the investing public. The issuing houses may act as agents of the company in such cases. Offer of sale of shares takes place in the case of existing shareholders purchasing *en bloc* and then reselling them to the public. Similarly, foreign collaborators or promoters may sell their shares to the Indian public through offer of sale which may be either through brokers or through prospectus.

(c) Private Placement

The third method of issue of shares is private placement which is defined as sale by the issuing house or broker to his own clients of securities previously purchased by him. Under this method the issuing houses or financial intermediaries buy them outright with the intention of placing them with their clients afterwards. Here the brokers act as almost wholesalers selling them in retail to the public. These brokers would make their profit in the process of reselling to the public. This method of private placement is used to a limited extent in India but is very popular abroad. Before the issues are placed in the market by the promoters, they sell to their own friends and well-wishers as the Govt. guidelines require a minimum contribution from the promoters and their friends. Private placement is also made by bargaining with the financial institutions for their share of contribution. The newly-established OTCEI (Over the Counter Exchange of India) has adopted this method for the companies to be listed on it.

(d) Rights Issue

Another important method of placing shares to the public is, the right issue which is next in importance to the placing of shares through prospectus. The rights issue is an offer with a preemption right to the shareholder of existing companies to contribute to the share capital or its debt capital in the form of debentures. An existing company can issue rights to augment its equity base, if necessary. These are offered to the existing shareholders in a particular proportion to their existing shareownership. The ratio in which the new shares or debentures are offered to the existing shareholders of the company would depend on their requirements of capital. The rights are themselves transferable and saleable in the market. No new company can issue rights shares. Under the Companies Act, where a company increases its subscribed capital by the issue of new shares either after two years of its formation or after one year of the first issue of shares whichever is earlier, these have to be first offered to the existing shareholders with the right to reserve them in favour of a nominee.

A company issuing rights is required to send a circular to all existing shareholders. This circular letter should provide information on how the additional funds would be used and their effect on the earning capacity of the capital. The company should normally give a time limit of at least one month to two months to shareholders to exercise their right before it is offered to the public. Rights may also be offered through underwriters. If a company is doing well, rights will be received well by the shareholders and the need for underwriting may not be felt.

One of the conditions for issue of rights is that the shareholders be given an opportunity to apply for additional shares. Besides, if the rights are not fully taken up, the balance is to be equitably distributed among the applicants for additional shares. Any balance still left over after making such allotment is required to be disposed of by the company in the market at the ruling price or the issue price.

Debt versus Equity

The capital structure of a company depends on its requirements of fixed assets and a proportion of working capital. Equity and preference capital being in the nature of permanent capital, owned funds should cover the bulk of the fixed assets and would also be the basis on which long-term debt capital can be raised by the company. These requirements vary from company to company, as some industries and units are more capital-intensive than others.

Equity by itself may not be adequate or economical as debt capital is cheaper than equity and provides a leverage for raising the level of profits to equityholders. On the other hand, availability of debt itself depends on the existing equity base as that would determine the state of the company as servicing of debt depends on the equity base and the net earnings of the company through efficient use of capital. These twin considerations are kept in mind to assess the requirements of both equity and debt in the capital structure.

Debt may be short-term or long-term and includes bonds, debentures, loans and advances. The considerations influencing the two are different. While short-term finance influences the liquidity of the company, long-term finance affects the capital structure, and is an alternative to equity. The reliance on debt has increased in India due to tax treatment of interest on debt as expenditure of the company. Debt includes all fixed interest-bearing securities, loans, deferred payments and preference shares with a redemption period of less than 12 years. Debt may be from government, other companies or financial institutions. Debt from government is confined to mostly public sector enterprises and a few private sector enterprises of public importance. Loans from other companies are governed by Section 370 of the Indian Companies Act designed to limit the inter-corporate lending, particularly those under the same management. The ceiling on such lending is now fixed at 30 per cent of the share capital of the investing companies.

Short-term debt is mainly provided by trade credits and borrowing from banks. Companies are generally opposed to too much short-term debt due to the adverse effect of it on the subjective valuation of shares by outsiders. Too much of short-term debt *vis-a-vis* equity implies that the company has not even adequate capital base to support operations and in periods of financial stress, such a firm might be forced into liquidation.

The Indian Companies Act and the govt. guidelines place some limits on borrowed funds. The upper limit is an amount equal to the paid-up capital and reserves without prior approval of the shareholders in a general meeting. Guidelines would not normally allow debt more than twice the paid-up capital and free reserves.

Rights of Conversion of Debt into Equity

As per the policy of the government since June 1971, the public financial institutions retain the right of conversion of a part of rupee loans granted by them to any firm into equity, if the assistance exceeds a limit of ₹0 lakh. Such a right is left optional to the financial institution if the loan is between ₹25 lakh and ₹50 lakh. The exercise of this right implies a larger role to the joint sector and the participation of the financial institutions in the future prosperity of companies. This right is now exercised by all-India financial institutions after a period of 5 years from the date of issue of loan. The extent and terms of conversion depend upon the agreement, negotiated between the company and the financial institutions. The conversion in the case of new companies is at par and for old companies, it may be at a premium or discount. This right of conversion of loan into equity was withdrawn by govt. in the latest financial reforms except when the repayment instalments are in arrears.

Advantages of the debt are as follows:

1. It provides for larger increase in profits due to larger trading made possible by debt finance, without a need for additional equity.
2. It improves the earnings of equityholders due to larger earnings at a lower cost of debt than of equity finance.
3. There is no interference in management matters which takes place by the issue of new equity capital.
4. There are tax advantages for debt which are not available for equity. Debt carrying capacity would, however, depend upon the level of gross profits and equity base.

As against these, there are a number of advantages of equity:

1. Debt is to be repaid while equity would remain with the company.
2. Equity increases the interest of the promoters and their stake in the company.
3. It improves the credit standing of the company for future borrowing and acts as a buffer for future fluctuations in the fortunes of the company.
4. It provides greater leeway for the company to adjust to the changing economic climate and investment conditions.

Debentures are issued by the old companies normally while new companies depend on loans from financial institutions. A special category of debentures which have become popular in the eighties was convertible debentures. Debentureholders of this category are permitted to exercise the option of conversion into equity of the company after a period of time. Some companies have provided for compulsory conversion, instead of giving option. Such debentures are very attractive to the investing public if the company is doing well, as they give a future right to participate in the profits and prosperity of the company. The company in turn would benefit by not only attracting funds as debenture capital at present but also by widening the equity capital base in future. This type of issue is particularly suitable for expanding and diversifying companies.

Share capital includes equity shares and preference shares with a period of redemption of 12 years or more. A share is a form of transferable right representing the interest of the owner in the company, either of equity or preference capital. For a new company, some minimum equity base is necessary to prove the stake of promoters and the willingness of risk-taking. What is the extent of the minimum would depend upon the project cost, the state of the capital market, national importance of such a project, the financial institutions' interest in it and the general level of interest rates, the background of company, the cost of capital for the company from various sources, etc.

Preference Shares

Preference shares are a category of shares having a preferential right in respect of payment of dividend and repayment of principal. The Companies Act authorises the issue of preference shares and the fact that various companies have issued preference shares indicates that they have a role to play in the capital structure of the companies. Preference shares are of various categories, namely, redeemable preference shares, cumulative and non-cumulative preference shares and participating preference shares.

Redeemable preference shares are to be redeemed out of profits or capital specially raised for the purpose. Under the Companies Act as recently amended, redemption of the preference shares is now compulsory after 9 to12 years. No such shares will be redeemed except when they are fully paid-up and provision is made for a special reserve fund called capital redemption account created for the purpose of redemption.

Cumulative preference shares have a right to be paid dividends in arrears in a cumulative manner, once the company makes profits. In 1985, the government has introduced a new instrument of cumulative convertible preference shares (CCP) issued at 10% fixed dividend. These are convertible into equity after 3 to 5 years. Non-cumulative shares have no right of accumulation of arrears. Participating preference shares have a right to participate in residual profits after all the claims of creditors and owners are met along with equityholders.

Preference shares stand in between debentureholders and equityholders in the matter of rights. While a debentureholder is a creditor who is to be paid irrespective of the profits made, the equityholder gets the residual as owner of the company. Preference shares are a hybrid category standing in between these — neither a complete creditor nor owner of the company. Preference shareholders have priority of repayment of principal over equity shareholders in the event of winding up of the company. They have also the right to participate in the left-over assets or capital after the equityholders are paid in full.

Voting rights of the preference shareholders are exercised in the event of arrears of dividends for more than two years and in matters relating to the interests of the preference sharesholders. In practice, these voting rights are highly circumscribed by the overwhelming power of the equityholders who are a majority. In almost all companies, preference shareholding constitute roughly one-third or less of the total equity holdings. A norm of preference to equity ratio of 1:3 is generally insisted by the govt.

So long as the company is doing well, the preference shareholders have nothing to grumble and they are paid their due dividends. They are treated as good as creditors in such circumstances, but in times of adverse conditions, profits are not adequate to pay dividends to the preference shareholders and they are not treated as creditors but as owners, though their interests may not be identical with the equityholders. They are, however, bound by the decisions of the majority equityholders. The creditors of the company, *viz.*, financial institutions, banks, etc., have a greater say so far as their dues are concerned than that of preference shareholders. If institutions are preference shareholders themselves, then the situation is somewhat better as they can bargain for better terms. Whatever is the category of holders, these shareholders would suffer from capital depreciation once the shares are quoted and traded on the exchanges, due to a rise in interest rates in the market.

Preference shareholders are generally at the mercy of the equityholders particularly in adverse years. They would neither be able to get away from the company nor improve the lot of the company by management changes and active interference. It is in this sense that preference shareholders are in perpetual bondage to the company.

Preference shares are in demand despite such disadvantages, particularly with the financial institutions. The investors' preference for these can be explained by the following features of preference shares: (*i*) less risk, (*ii*) fixed income and *(iii)* special attractions like cumulative dividends or redeemable shares.

From the point of view of the company, preference shares are chosen for the following reasons: (*i*) it would be cheaper to issue preference shares than equity although costlier than the issue of debentures; (*ii*) equity shareholders gain by the gearing ratio provided by the preference capital in the capital structure of the company as it is a fixed interest security; (*iii*) the companies can cater to the needs of investment trusts, UTI, LIC, etc., who require fixed interest securities in their portfolios and preference share capital neither dilutes the equity nor interferes with management by equityholders.

From the point of view of the company, it is costlier to issue preference shares than debentures as the company would have to earn more to maintain a given return on preference capital than that of debentures. Thus, to earn ₹ 14 to pay a dividend of 14 per cent to preference shareholders, the company would have to make profits of almost double that, whereas to pay ₹ 14 to debentureholders, the company needs to earn only ₹ 14. For the purpose of taxation, the interest paid on debt or debentures is treated as part of the expenses and commitment on gross profits, whereas the dividend paid on preference shares is taxable. The grossed-up rate is the rate which the company has to earn in order to pay a dividend to the preference shareholders and would depend upon the rate of taxation on the company and the coupon rate on the preference share. The higher the tax rate the higher should be the gross profits of the company in order to maintain a given rate of distribution to preference shareholders.

Bonus Shares

There are certain regulations regarding the issues of bonus shares enforced by the govt. The Companies Act, however, takes no notice of bonus shares except for a passing reference that share premium may be applied by a company for issuing fully-paid bonus shares to the members. The issue of bonus shares is a normal practice adopted by the companies to bring the paid-up capital in line with the market value of the shares. Companies, are not required to get the consent of the govt. under the latest guidelines. Bonus issues are permitted subject to the following conditions:

1. They are made out of free reserves (free and unencumbered from any commitments or charges).
2. They may be issued out of general reserves or capital profits or reserves not including reserves out of revaluation of assets and not based upon cash accruals, or out of development rebate reserves or development allowances reserves, capital redemption reserve and share premium received in cash.
3. Total amount permitted to be capitalised for bonus share issue should not exceed the total paid-up equity of the company (except in certain cases such as dilution of foreign companies).
4. Residual reserves after issue of bonus shares should be at least 40% of the increased paid-up capital.
5. After the declaration of bonus shares, one-third of the pre-tax profits of the company should be able to meet the requirements of at least 10% dividend on the increased capital of the company.
6. Bonus shares are permitted only if all the existing shares are fully paid-up and are not in lieu of a dividend.
7. The time lag between two such bonus issues should be at least 12 months.
8. A resolution for the proposed capitalisation should be approved by the general body of the shareholders provided the Memorandum and Articles of Association permit such an issue of bonus shares. After the issue of the bonus shares, the paid-up capital should not exceed the authorised capital of the company.

The issue of bonus shares would not require any govt. clearance under the latest guidelines.

Bonus issue is permitted before conversion of a private limited company into a public limited company provided the interests of the participating public are protected to the extent of the equity interest of the existing shareholders. The issue of preference shares as bonus shares is generally not favoured except when the proposed preference shares are redeemable and the ratio between the equity and the preference capital does not exceed 3:1.

Free reserves out of which bonus shares are to be issued are accumulated retained earnings, capital and current reserves and general reserves not specifically earmarked for any purpose, and sinking fund reserve for debentures (after the debentures are redeemed), development rebate reserve or investment allowance reserve, capital redemption reserve and share premium account received in cash.

Cost of Floatation

The cost of raising equity is generally lower than the cost of raising preference shares and debentures. The fixed cost of floatation include underwriting commission, brokerage, etc., and are generally expressed as a percentage of the capital floated. The variable cost relates to those expenses such as administration fees, etc. Expenses vary from issue to issue depending upon the nature of the company, the amount of issue, structure of the capital (equity, preference, etc.). Although brokerage and underwriting commission are generally fixed at 1½% and 2½% respectively giving a total of about 4% of the total floatation, the other expenses vary between 3 and 5% of the total amount floated. The managing merchant bankers to the issue who do the secretarial work and co-ordination are given commission of 1/2% for managing the issue. The variable cost element varies with the nature and size of the company, the amount of issue, and is different for new and old companies. Besides, the cost of floatation of new companies is generally higher than for existing companies, in view of the economies of scale under "other" expenses for the latter companies as they do not have to undergo all the formalities of bringing out the issue.

As per the study on "Capital Issues and Public Response" published in the RBI Bulletin of October 1989, the cost of new issues as a percentage of the amount floated has risen from 8-9% in 1981-83 to 11.5% in 1984 and fell to 9.3% in 1985. In respect of a few companies, the variable costs are as high as 20% while the average variable costs are about 5% of the new capital issued. These costs should have risen substantially at present; the rates paid to Registrars and merchant bankers are, however, variable and amenable to bargaining.

Registrars are paid at a rate of ₹ 3 to 5 handling charges in respect of each successful application and merchant bankers at 0.5% or less of the issue offered.

The amount of funds, raised in the new issues market is referred to in another chapter. There is another indicator of the magnitude of funds channeled into the corporate sector in the capital market, namely, the assistance sanctioned and disbursed by the development corporations of all India and State-level nature and investment corporations like UTI, LIC and GIC, etc. The disbursement made by them in total had almost doubled over the last few years and increasing at a rapid rate. Similarly, the capital issues and capital raised have also increased substantially. The bulk of the rise was on account of debentures. More recently the right issues and private placement have increased due to their lower costs of issue. During the early 21st century, the capital issues have come down in the non-government private corporate sector, particularly for the debt issues in the form of debentures and preference capital.

Underwriting Activity

In the new issues market, the major activity relates to underwriting and marketing of new issues. In India all financial institutions and brokers undertake this business. Banks have entered this market in a big way by starting their own divisions of merchant banking or their subsidiaries. Insurance and investment companies are also an important category of underwriters. While banks and financial institutions account for the bulk of underwriting, UTI, insurance and consultancy companies and brokers account for the rest.

Underwriters and financial institutions subscribed more for preference shares and debentures than for equity shares as the latter are more attractive to the investing public and thus devolve less on the underwriters. The amount subscribed by them is higher in debentures as part of their policy of investment in corporate sector in high yielding and fixed income securities.

Brokers help in the floatation of new issues not only through underwriting or as managing brokers but also as financial consultants, advising on the proper capital structure, methods of raising capital and requirements of the Companies Act and the Securities Contracts (Regulation) Act, and listing requirements, etc.

Abuses in the New Issue Market

Government has been attempting to regulate the abuses in the new Issue market in collaboration with the stock exchange authorities. The SEBI has taken over this responsibility of regulating and developing the new issues market since 1992. These abuses relate to the following categories. Firstly, the companies were publishing projected figures of turnover, profits, dividend, etc., of future years which are not warranted. Secondly, companies have been making exaggerated claims about prospects to the public in press conferences and privately circulated brochures.

Thirdly, advertisements about oversubscription were used to be made falsely, which the government prohibited if not accompanied by documentary evidence. Fourthly, trading in new issues prior to the formal listing of such issues is also prevalent. Besides rigging up of prices before floating of new issues, arranging and manipulation of high premiums on new issues are also rampant. Lastly, delays in refunding the application money, issuing of allotment letters, posting of share certificates, etc., are quite common.

Problems of the New Issue Market

It will be pertinent to summarise briefly the main problems of the new issue market here. Firstly, the new issue market could not mobilise adequate savings from the public as less than 1 to 4% of financial savings of the household sector are mobilised for investment in shares and debentures. A large portion of the capital requirements of companies is placed on the market privately or with financial institutions.

Secondly, the new issues market suffers from functional and institutional gaps, particularly in terms of the new instruments to appeal to the investing public. Thus, a wholesale market for new issues is yet to develop in India and merchant banking is in its infancy. The merchant banks are presently not playing a developmental role. In technical, managerial and entrepreneurial aspects, particulars in project preparation and technical aspects, adequate attention has not been given so far. This would be the responsibility of merchant banks and is not at present performed by them with the result that small investors are duped by the companies. Merchant bankers are now asked by the SEBI to do this. Thirdly, with a risk aversion in the new issue market, funds are diverted from the risk market to less risky debentures as well as deposits with the companies. Companies have themselves shifted away in the eighties from equity financing to debt financing and to larger reliance on debentures of convertible nature in more recent years. The costs of floatation have also been found to be abnormally high, particularly for new and small-sized companies. There is much scope for rationalising and economising the administrative costs of floatation of new issues in which banks can play an important role through merchant banking divisions.

In semi-urban and rural areas if the investor has to send application forms to centres where banks are authorised to accept them, he has to spend on securing a bank draft, postal charges for sending, and suffer loss of interest and collection charges for refund orders. There are inordinate delays in allotment of shares, refunding of application money, posting of share certificates and effecting transfer of shares, etc. These are to be despatched by registered post, or by certificate of posting in some cases, which is not done by many companies at present and they do not pay any interest for the delayed period as required by law.

All these problems would amount to considerable hardship to the small investors in the countryside. Similarly, dividend warrants, refund orders, interest payment not being encashable at par in all centres; the investors again lose. As the time taken for allotment is often two to three months or even more, there is considerable loss of interest on money to investors. The time limit for allotment was reduced to 30 days in 1996. These hardships are more in rural and semi-urban areas and do great injustice to them *vis-a-vis* those in metropolitan centres.

Another feature of the market is that existing companies with a good track record received good response for new issues as compared with new companies. The underwriting support and devolution on underwriters was more in the case of new companies due to the cautious response of investors to these companies. There was also evidence to show that investors do prefer debentures to equities and more so, if they are convertible debentures. Recently, new regulations are imposed by SEBI on merchant banks, which may improve the climate of investment in the new issue market. The merchant banks have to give due diligence certificate: they have to certify the bonafides of the information contained in the prospectus, justify the price fixed for the share and take the full responsibility for vetting and scrutiny in the case of rights issues. Their code of conduct is enforced by their own association (AMB).

Primary Market

The experiment in free pricing, being new in India created some problems of undue over pricing initially by some companies. Soon within a few months, investors became more discrete in making investments in new issues with hefty premiums. Many new issues have become flops in raising subscriptions, if their premiums are unreasonably high. It is now obvious that the experiment of free pricing will survive the criticism of the public particularly due to stricter norms by SEBI for better disclosures and more rational justification of the premium fixed by merchant bankers.

Accompanying the demand for control on premium is the pressure of the public to regulate the timing of the entry of companies in the new issues market and on the quantum of their issue. These steps being retrograde steps for the ongoing reforms, it is left to merchant bankers and the companies to decide on the basis of their experience and expertise. The demand for such controls emerged due to unrestricted entry of companies and the bunching of new issues at the same time and high premiums confusing the investors as to what to contribute with their limited funds.

The Problem of timing and bunching of new issues will also lead to investor problems in the form of scramble for limited resources and inadequate appraisal of the projects. This may result in poor response to some new issues.

Public Response

As against the oversubscription of more than 10 times in respect of 51% of the issues in 1991-92, the public response to new issues in 1992-93 was poor. As per the 'PRIME' Data, 86 companies (16%) have to extend the subscription date till the last closing date, and 67 companies (13%) have to extend the closing date by 1 to 6 days and even so the undersubscription was many times covered up by institutional backup and discount sales to Mutual Funds and Financial Institutions.

One thing seems certain that the absolute amount of premium collected was by far the highest in 1992-93 and secondly the proportion of funds raised in the form of equity went up, while the same in the form of debt has come down as seen from the following table. More importantly the funds raised in the form of rights were only ₹3,851/- crore in 1991-92 while the same were ₹12,792/- crore in 1992-93. The emerging trends are clear and striking and amount of rights came down to ₹6,741 crore in 1994-95, and further to ₹2,663 crore in 1996-97. Premium issues have come down since 1996-97, but rose again after 1999-2000 due to many I.T. companies which went public, particularly in 2006 and 2007.

SHARES OF EQUITY/PREMIUM IN PERCENTAGES

(in percentages)

	1988-89 1990-91	*1991-92*	*1992-93*	*1994-95*	*1995-96*	*1996-97*	*1999-2000*	*2003-04*	*2006-07*
Equity	63.8	47.4	27	34	44	45	11.3	22.4	32.0
Premium	—	25.0	24	32	31	14	42.1	38.6	65.2
Debt	36.2	27.6	49	34	25	41	46.6	39.0	2.8

Source: B.S.E./Prime and RBI Reports.

Note: As per B.S.E. Data barring about 35 issues, which are more than fully subscribed, others have faced some difficulty or other in getting full subscription 1994-95. In 1993-94, the total funds raised including the public issues and rights amounted to around ₹19,355 crore and in 1994-95, they were ₹30,824 crore and in 1995-96 ₹22,919 crore. During 1993 and 1994 the Premiums barring a few stray cases have also come down. During 1995, and 1996 the new issue market was mostly subdued following malpractices by companies. The proportion of debt raised rose steeply after 1995-96 due to depression in the market for equities. During the early years of 21st century equity markets picked up again and debt markets have taken a second place. This was particularly evidenced by the data in 2006-07.

TABLE ON EQUITY-DEBT SCENARIO

New Capital Issues *(₹ crore)*

	Equity raised	*Debt*	*Total*
2000-01	2,607	3,210	5,818
2001-02	860	4,832	5,692
2002-03	460	1,417	1,878
2003-04	2,471	1,251	3.721
2004-05	11,452	1,627	13,079
2005-06	20,899	245	21,154
2006-07	29,756	847	30,603
2007-08	56,848	6,788	63,636
2008-09	14,671	Nil	14,671
2009-10	25,298	180	25,478
2010-11	24,830	Nil	24,830
1913-14	5,812	5,869	11,681

Souce: RBI, Handbook of Statistics

It will be seen from the above table that debt component predominated over equity due to cost considerations of the corporate sector. But after 2004-05, equity become more favoured due to policy of the government of reducing the debt servicing burden of the total amounts raised, the bulk is through prospectus and loss by rights and private placement. The existing companies raised most of the funds for expansion, diversification and fresh investments, but very few new companies entered the markets.

NEW ISSUES MADE IN 2013-14

(1)	Equity	₹ 5,812
(2)	Debt (Fixed interest securities)	₹ 5,869
	Total new issues	₹ 11,681
	of which	
	(i) Through prospectus	₹ 7,105
	(ii) Rights	₹ 4,756
		₹ 11,861

Timing of New Issues

Crowding of new issues, sometimes as many as 6 to 10 new issues opening in one week, would be hazardous to both the companies and investors. It would be impossible for investors to come to any right conclusion of issues which are good in their view. This also leads to their subscription for only 100 to 200 shares and spreading their funds in as many issues as possible. Here again the investors have to learn to cope with the alternative avenues of investment and proper education of investors is necessary to enlighten them to be selective in investments by use of tools of research and analysis and for deciding for themselves the extent of risk taking and whether to invest in new issues or mutual funds schemes and to what extent they invest in alternative avenues.

Added to the above complaints the SEBI's raising of the limit of minimum subscription to 500 shares or shares worth ₹ 5,000 recently from the existing level of 100 shares has been criticised as retrograde for the growth of investment cult. But it is justifiable both from the point of companies and for better services for the investors. Those who apply for 100 shares have been putting in multiple applications and have been found to be applying to as many new issues as possible as if it is lottery unaware of what issues will be allotted to them and how much. Such gambling should not be encouraged on the part of investors. As per our sample survey of investors, nearly 52% of respondents are applicants for only 100 shares, who apply for about 5 issues at the same time, to take a chance for allotment, as if it is lottery and such practices are to be discouraged. Now such category is eliminated by SEBI. In October 1996, this limit is again reduced to 200 shares to attract investors back to the market.

Cost of Capital Issues

One of the burning problems in capital structuring of companies is the cost of capital used by the company. Broadly capital can be owner capital and debt capital. The normal understanding is that debt capital is cheaper due to tax advantage it enjoys and leverage extended by it to equity capital. The equity capital is considered cheap but if alternative use of capital and opportunity cost is taken into account it is not the cheap source.

The concept of cost of capital is relative to the stage of the growth of the company, the nature of its product, its available alternative sources of funds, etc. Thus, a brand new company has to perforce depend on the share capital and particularly from promoters, FIs and the public issue of equity. If it is an old company and is also a capital-intensive company, it has to depend heavily on debt capital relative to equity capital on term loans, debentures, public deposits, etc. If it is an existing profit making company, besides share capital and cash accruals, it has to depend on the public issues and rights issues of equity and debentures.

The approximate cost of borrowed funds to the company, is shown below. But these estimates are rough and ready proximate numbers and will vary from company to company and from time to time. The cost of raising funds from each of the methods will depend on the rate of interest/return and the accompanying costs of raising the funds.

TABLE ON FUNDING METHODS (2007)

	Margins	*Rate Per Annum (including costs of raising)*
(*a*) Bank Term Loans (or FI Term Loans)	20-25%	12 -14.5%
(*b*) Bank Working Capital	25%	12.75 - 13.25%
(*c*) Public Debentures/Bonds		
(*i*) Convertible	—	10 - 12%
(*ii*) Non-convertible	—	12% and 14%
(*d*) Public Deposits	—	11% - 14%
(*e*) Deferred Credits Supplier's Credits	25-40%	14 - 16%
(*f*) Hire-Purchase/Lease, etc.	25%	20%

It will be seen from the above that the minimum rate is 10-14% while the maximum rate is around 20% if it is from organised sector and this includes the cost of raising funds.

Corporate studies have shown that nearly one-fourth to one-third of the fund requirements are met from internal accruals or retained earnings. The rest are raised from the capital market through new issues or from borrowings from financial institutions and public through loans, advances and deposits.

Whether a company goes for public issue, right issue, or for borrowing from institutions will depend on a number of factors, such as cost and available limits with Banks, FIs and for raising public deposits, as they are all related to equity share capital and free reserves and earning potential to service these forms of raising funds to the company. The reliance on new issues market is thus one of the alternatives available to the companies and if new issue is the method chosen, it can be internal or domestic markets or foreign markets or it can be either for equity or rights, debt, etc. The costs on all these types of raising funds vary and the cheapest method is borrowing abroad but it is open to very high rated and creditworthy companies only.

Wasteful Procedures on Public Issue

As referred to earlier, the investors in New Issues Market had some difficulties in that a vast majority of them read the Form 2-A (Memorandum of Prospectus) but complain of the difficulty of reading due to small print. Many depend upon the opinion of Brokers/Sub-brokers, due to difficulty of reading the prospectus or due to lack of time or lack of expertise in reading the prospectus intelligently. As per our sample study, the majority of investors depend on what daily newspapers write on the new issues (34%) and on journals (17%) and on friends/brokers/relatives, etc. (47%). It will be thus seen that only a small proportion of investors seem to be educated enough in the capital market analysis. So education is the prime need of the hour.

Many application forms are not used at all or misused as wastepaper and the selected investors receive the same forms from more than one source. There is thus wasteful expenditure on application forms. Another wasteful expenditure is on too many intermediaries — two or more co-managers in addition to lead manager, too many brokers/banks and too many collection centres. Compulsory underwriting also adds to the cost, as underwriting is a matter of investor protection and forced on company as per SEBI guidelines and presently it is optional.

Although nearly 90% of the small investors applied for less than 500 shares and about 52% applied only for 100 shares, the SEBI has raised the minimum subscription as ₹ 5,000 or 500 shares. Innumerable applications mainly from small investors applying for 100 shares sometimes in multiple applications and in fictitious names may lead to larger workload and wasteful expenditure to the company. The same may lead to larger investor complaints. So the minimum subscription limit was already raised. This was again brought down to 200 shares to boost the market and the investment interest of small investors in 1996.

On the same lines of argument, for smaller issues of ₹50 crore or less, it may be left to the company to reduce the number of managers to the issue, brokers and underwriters and the number of collection centres. Some regional issues may prefer concentrating on selected centres, if they are confident of raising their subscription. Underwriting may raise costs but may be necessary for confidence of investors, provided stricter enforcement is made of their underwriting obligations, which hopefully SEBI's new code for underwriters would achieve. Underwriting is dispensed with now in many cases. The vetting of draft prospectus for all issues has been dispensed with and merchant bankers are given the responsibility. The minimum connection centres were reduced first from 57 to 30 in 1993 and then to 4 in Sept. 1995.

Another problem of investors which our survey has highlighted is the limited use of "stock invest", despite its many advantages.

The reasons are as follows:

1. Procedural formalities in the bank branch for issue of stock invest, which are now simplified.
2. The charges made by banks for issuing the stock invest, while a cheque or cash involves no cost, but the practice of charging is now dispensed with.
3. The fear of discrimination by the company in the allotment for those who apply through stock invest. The SEBI has allayed these fears to a large extent.
4. The inefficiency in service in many banks leading to waste of time and the torture of extended formalities.

With the reduction of allotment period to 30 days from the closure of subscription from the erstwhile period of 70 days, the relevance of stock invest was made insignificant in the new scenario since 1996 due to introduction of Demat form of trade and after that this facility was withdrawn. The SEBI was reported to have approved blocking of bank funds without companies making IPOs taking them until the allotment is completed. The time period for the rights issue to be kept open was reduced from 109 to 43 days.

The investors are not obviously convinced of the superior advantage of stock invest over the cheque/draft which inhibits the use of stock invest. Firstly, it is a matter of education and secondly, it is a matter of improved services by bank branches, which is not under the control of SEBI. It is in this context advantageous to encourage big companies to have their own collection centres, superceding the banking system. The quality of services may be better in the private sector banks which are coming up, or the companies can have their own arrangements.

Another wasteful expenditure is in the hands of the company. With the prime objective of making the issue a success, the companies compete among themselves to throw Dinners/Lunches at Press Conferences, Brokers' Conferences and Investors' Conferences, etc. The SEBI guidelines have come out prohibiting such Five Star Lunches/Dinners as it may tantamount to bribing/or discounting/or extending incentives.

Need for Analytical Data

Another complaint of investors is that information contained in the Form-2A (Memorandum on Prospectus) is too formal and trivial. Many companies do not provide analytical data and results of research and qualitative information on a true and factual basis which are truly educative and informative to investors. In this context, the Investor Service Fund which the companies are asked to set up under the new companies Bill 1993 may be used for investor education on new issues through voluntary non-profit associations, such as Rotary Clubs, Investor Associations, etc. Investment Analysis should be paid through them to get all issues analysed and qualitative information is provided to the investors through such forums. At present some Investor Associations are active in such education. But no Stock Exchange barring B.S.E. is doing this work of educating the investors on a regular basis, although they have been asked to set apart some funds out of listing fees for investor services cell and some for customer protection fund. The SEBI can enforce on the Stock Exchanges to use such funds for spread of investor education and information by themselves or through accredited agencies or through non-profit making bodies in the local areas.

At present, majority of Stock Exchanges have not reorganised their Boards to bring in 50% for public representation on their boards. Very few have their Training Centres and Investor Education Programmes. It is hoped that SEBI will insist immediately on the Stock Exchanges to change their Bye-laws, in this regard.

✠ ✠ ✠

MONEY MARKETS AND ITS INSTRUMENTS

32

Introduction

In this chapter, discussion is centred on the money market and its components in India. Although short-term Government securities, UTI units, PSU bonds, etc., are also a part of the money market these are not discussed in this Chapter.

Money market has no geographical constraints and relates to all dealings in money or monetary assets. J.S.G. Wilson[@] defined the money market as a "centre in which financial institutions congregate for the purpose of dealing impersonally in monetary assets". This is giving too literal an interpretation of money market. In fact, 'money market' is a wide term and encompasses a variety of transactions, instruments and institutions. Money market is a centre where borrowers and lenders of money and near money assets are put together. It may comprise a group of such markets for various types of money assets characterised by relative liquidity or nearness to money. Such assets may be called call money, treasury bills or bills of exchange, etc. Secondly, although there are various centres of money market such as Mumbai, Kolkata, Chennai, etc., they are not separate independent markets but are inter-linked and related. Thirdly, in a true sense of free and perfect competition, there should be only one price for each category of money assets, which would result from dealing of purchase and sale made on a purely impersonal basis and through blind economic forces. The financial institutions dealing in these assets may be spread over so wide a geographical area that it would be impossible to specify the geographical limits of the market. The fact that there are some geographical centres does not limit the operations to these centres.

Developed and Underdeveloped Markets[@@]

Indian money market is not well developed. Following the Vaghul Committee recommendations (1989), a number of new instruments have been introduced to develop the market. The essential characteristics of a developed money market such as the ones in London or New York are integrated structures between sub-markets, free flow of funds as between sub-markets or segments of the same sub-market, a high degree of

---

[@] J.S.G.Wilson: *Monetary Policy and Development of Money Market.*

[@@] E. Nevin: *Capital Funds in Underdeveloped Countries.*

specialisation with regard to dealings in instruments by various institutions and a single price for each of the instruments traded.

An important aspect of the Indian money market is the seasonality in the demand for funds following the agricultural operations. The busy season for funds extends from November to April and the slack season from May to October.

Besides, the Indian money market is also characterised by imperfect flows from the foreign money markets due to the operation of exchange controls in the economy despite some liberalisation recently and freeing of the rupee. Another important aspect of the money market is the dichotomy between the organised and unorganised markets which was referred to already. Unlike a developed money market, the Indian market is not characterised by a high degree of integration and cohesion.

The essential pre-requisites for integration are that there must be links between the several sub-markets and their relative prices for each of the assets traded and continuous contacts and relationship of borrowings and lending are maintained through the spillover flow of funds from one sub-market to another. Although the degree of risk and uncertainty varies from segment to segment and there are various frictions and hurdles to shiftability of funds such as costs of brokerage, commission, taxes, etc., which might explain to some degree the difference in prices between the sub-markets, there should be an essential unity of purpose in securing the highest return for funds and a general free flow of funds and information in the market. The integration may not be possible if there are special groups of institutions with separate standing and methods of operation and customers are attached to these institutions, each such group tending to be isolated from the others. This is the case particularly with the indigenous banking system in India and moneylenders and landlords.

Integration of this market with other sub-markets helps the siphoning off of the excess or shortfall in this market to others such as Treasury bills or Government securities market. Integration also aids the more economical use of cash by banks who are the major institutions in the market.

Integration and Specialisation

A well developed market would satisfy both the criteria of integration and specialisation. If the market is well integrated, the flow of funds between sub-markets will be free and quicker, increasing thereby the value of transactions. Specialisation is a natural result of the growth of the market, as the specialist is bound to emerge as soon as a sufficient demand develops for his services. In India, the market is not specialised to the degree present in Western developed countries, as we do not have discount houses, acceptance houses or underwriting houses. The need for such institutions has not been felt and the volume of business did not warrant the emergence of such specialist houses.

Modern discount houses have developed on the basis of the growth of bill business as in U.K. The merchants who were acting as intermediaries for those who wished to invest in bills began to evolve as dealers in bills themselves acting as wholesalers for the banks to buy and sell in retail.

Another example of the specialist institution is the acceptance banker who developed into acceptance houses doing the business of accepting a bill of exchange by lending its name for a client known or recommended to them, thereby facilitating negotiations. Acceptance business is very prominent in the London market by virtue of its acting as a financial centre for various parts of the world.

The trend towards specialisation is seen in the USA also in the development of firms for Government securities dealings, houses specialising in placement of private commercial bills and those concentrating on handling bankers' acceptances and federal funds, etc.

Advantages of Mature Money Market

The advantages of a mature money market are multifold. The gaps between the separate sub-markets can be bridged by operators through arbitrage which lead to a single price for each category of assets. Secondly, it facilitates the profitable deployment of surplus funds of banking institutions. Thirdly, where money market is compact and integrated the control by the central bank would be easier. The central bank action would percolate quickly from one segment to another of the market and be more effective. The central money market may be developed alright but not properly linked with the periphery markets in the unorganised sector as in India. Alternatively, as in Thailand and a few other less developed countries, even the central money market is not well developed and the central bank's action may have to be direct and the traditional indirect instruments may not work. Fourthly, a developed money market helps promote certain attitudes and practices by bankers regarding the maintenance of minimum reserves and cash. Healthier practices by banks in this regard help control by the central bank. In addition, the central bank may exert its influence by consultation directly with the respective groups of interests in the market such as Discount Houses Association, Accepting Houses Association or Foreign Exchange Dealers Association and this also facilitates operation of the instrument of moral suasion by the central bank. In 1994 Securities Trading Corporation was set up to deal in Govt. securities on behalf of the RBI, to promote gilt-edged market. Earlier in 1988, Discount and Finance House of India was set up to develop the money market in India.

Sub-markets[@]

The call money market in India and Pakistan and federal funds market in the U.S.A. are examples of a sub-market dealing with near cash or overnight money. The demand comes from banks who fall short of reserves overnight or a few days and the supply comes from those who have got excess reserves with them. In India, this is called the inter-bank call market, wherein funds are borrowed overnight for book adjustments by banks who fall short of the statutory cash reserves requirements. Brokers put through these transactions between banks or the banks may choose to deal directly among themselves. In London and Paris, the discount houses who deal with bills wholesale require such funds for holding the bills. In New York, such funds may emanate from Government security dealers. Both in U.K. and U.S.A. as in India, the dealers in the market act as intermediaries for these dealings in inter-bank funds. Not infrequently the banks put through their transactions by themselves. In U.S. banking, the need for such market is more than in India and U.K., where branch banking predominates and branch adjustments for excess funds can always take place. The federal funds market in the U.S. provides a mechanism for meeting shortage of funds. In some countries, where exchange control does not restrict their dealings abroad, the banks may depend more upon correspondents abroad for excess or shortfall of funds than in India.

In the inter-bank market in India, in addition to all banks, foreign and Indian, GIC, UTI and LIC which are non-bank institutions also operate, mostly as lenders. RBI is the apex body for these institutions and acts as the lender of last resort to the market. In the inter-bank market, foreign banks are the main borrowers because by the nature of their operations they finance trade and operate in the market mostly with a narrow cash base. This sub-market is the most sensitive to changes in liquidity, as the stringency or surfeit of funds with the banks and the impact of the credit control operations of the RBI are felt here. After 1994 Mutual Funds, other institutions and companies are allowed to operate in this market.

In the ultimate analysis, it is the readiness of the central bank to act as a lender of last resort to the market that sets standards of liquidity to be kept by banks and their readiness to lend in turn. The integration of sub-markets also depends on the central bank acting as a lender of last resort. In a country like India with a seasonal ebb and flow of demand for bank funds either the banks keep excess reserves (which was true upto sixties in India) or have a ready recourse to the central bank. In the latter event, the central bank may impose discipline on the banks' operations. Generally, banks loathe the hegemony of central bank and hence prefer to keep excess reserves as far as possible particularly in India. When some banks keep excess reserves, others can always borrow from them and thus the inter-bank market began to develop and thrive. The rate depends on the excess funds of the banking system as a whole and is regulated by the inter-bank agreement through

[@] V.A. Avadhani: *Studies in Indian Financial System,* JAICO (1978).

the Indian Banks Association. The rate varies from day-to-day and transaction to transaction. The inter-bank agreement specified the maximum rate of 10 per cent in this sub-market, which was withdrawn in May 1989. Now, the rate may fluctuate freely depending on the market forces. For example, the call rate averaged 19.84 per cent during the second half of March 2007 and reached an intra year high of 54.32 per cent as on 30th March 2007. This shows the width of fluctuations of the call rates.

In India there is a good bill market in which all banks, and particularly the big banks, discount approved inland and foreign bills. There is, however, no true market in bills as there are no further dealings in them, except when they are rediscounted with the Reserve Bank or IDBI or EXIM Bank.

Treasury bills constitute a separate segment of the market. These are of *three months* duration (91 days), issued on tap by RBI on behalf of the government for financing government investment and other expenditure. In addition, there are Treasury bills of six, and twelve months duration. Mostly banks, UTI, LIC, etc., contribute to these bills in addition to government departments or agencies with surplus funds. These bills are now sold on auction basis, and interest rates are freed.

In the structure of money market in India, mention may be made of the role of stock brokers. They are a part of the money market as they borrow finance for carrying out stock market transactions and carry-over business. Some of the badla financiers borrow from commercial and co-operative banks for supplementing their own resources for stock market operations. Limits are sanctioned to these operators and brokers by the commercial banks.

Bill Market in India

A bill of exchange is an instrument in writing containing an unconditional order by the maker directing a specified person to pay a sum of money to the order or to the bearer of the bill. Such bills augment the instruments of financial transaction, supplementing the available resources in times of seasonal stringencies for the purpose of refinance from the Reserve Bank.

The Reserve Bank of India Act has provided for refinance to commercial banks through buying or rediscounting of bills of exchange or other commercial paper eligible for rediscount under the Act. This provision under Section 17 of the RBI Act was meant to relieve the seasonal stringency in the absence of a properly organised bill market. The factors which affected adversely the growth of a bill market in India are the lack of uniformity in drawing bills, varying borrowing practices in different parts of the country with respect to bills, absence of distinction between trade bill and finance bill, high stamp duty, and popularity of cash credit and overdraft and arrangements as a means of borrowing from commercial banks. In India there is a traditional attachment to cash transaction and neglect of credit transactions, which has also hindered the growth of a bill market.

Institutional Structure

At the head of the structure of the Money Market is the RBI which controls and regulates this market through DFHI. The control extends to all those operating in the Call Money Market mostly Financial Institutions, Banks and Mutual Funds. More recently all companies and individual units have been operating in the Money Market.

The commercial paper (CP) issued by companies for raising short-term working capital is being developed in India. The participation certificates (PC) issued by banks and financial institutions, certificates of deposits (CD) issued by banks and factorisation bills are the other instruments that are being developed in this market. The institutions operating in these markets are banks, development finance institutions like IFC, ICICI and IDBI, investment finance companies like the LIC, UTI, GIC, etc., and other financial institutions. In the inter-bank money market, however, only the LIC and UTI have been permitted to operate in addition to banks. In 1990, the GIC, IDBI, NABARD, Mutual Funds and other financial institutions have also been permitted to operate. In April 1991, the RBI allowed the entry of any entity with bulk lendable resources of ₹ 20 crore and above as also the Money Market Mutual Funds to enter the Call Money Market. This market is being developed in India by the establishment of Discount and Finance House by the Reserve Bank in April 1988, in collaboration with the financial institutions. In April 2001, the RBI started some reforms in the Call Money Market for making it a truly inter-bank market and restricting the non-banks from their use of this market.

The money market is underdeveloped but developing at present. The qualities of a developed money market such as cohesion, integration of sub-markets, specialisation in various categories of business and openness to foreign forces are absent in India. There is no secondary market for many instruments like Treasury bills, Commercial bills, CPs and CDs, etc. Recently, schemes for the development of secondary market in commercial paper and for trading in certificates of deposits and participation certificates have been initiated by the RBI.

Characteristics

The money market establishes the link between the RBI and banks and the policy of RBI is felt in this market first before it percolates to other markets. The inter-bank market matches the deficits and surplus of banks; SBI and foreign banks are the major players in this market. This market provides an important area or venue for central bank intervention in the economy. It is also a venue to secure the short-term requirements of banks and FIs. This provides a link between the cash and near-money assets and to various sub-markets in the money market and to long-term wing of the capital market. Operations in this market extend to dealings in UTI units, PSU Bonds, short-term bonds of semi-government and government sector, etc.

DISCOUNT AND FINANCE HOUSE OF INDIA (DFHI)

The RBI is the leader and controller of Money Market and to perform these functions on her behalf, the DFHI was designed and set up by the RBI in April 1988 with a paid-up capital of ₹100 crore. This was supposed to oversee and supervise the Money Market operations. It can operate and intervene through the bid and offer rates in the inter-bank market, treasury bill market, rediscount or discount treasury bills, short-term commercial bills, commercial paper and other money market instruments. Of the paid-up capital, ₹51 crore was contributed by the RBI, ₹33 crore by Public Sector Banks and ₹16 crore by Public Financial Institutions. Thus, DFHI is a public sector institution for the purpose of stabilising the money market through purchase and sale operations in the instruments of trading.

Its sources of funds are the following:

(a) Paid-up capital of ₹100 crore.

(b) Credit limits of ₹200 crore with Public Sector Banks.

(c) Backup refinance lines with the RBI.

Its functions at present are as follows:

1. Operations in inter-bank call money market.
2. Purchases and sales (through bid and offer rates) of Treasury bills of 91 days, 182 days and 364 days respectively.
3. Discount and Rediscount of Commercial Bills, Certificates of Deposit and Commercial Paper, etc.
4. Buying and selling of government securities with banks and Financial Institutions.

For the Treasury bills, Commercial bills, etc., it gives bid and offer discount rates, say 364 days, T.B.s 9.90% (Bid) and 9.50% (Offer) and for commercial paper it gives only one discount rate, say 10.75%. For Government securities it quotes both buying and selling prices, at which it does business on a daily basis. The work of Govt. securities trading was entrusted to the Securities Trading Corporation set up in May 1994.

TABLE 32.1 RELATIVE RATES OF RETURN AT YEAR END MARCH

(%ages)

	1991	1995	1996	1997	2000	2004	2008	2012	2014
Call Money Rate Average	21.5	15.63	16.28	3.66	9.09	4.37	4.95	4.51	8.1
91 days Treasury Bills (Auction)	—	11.99	12.97	7.96	9.16	4.38	6.48	8.09	8.2
182/364 days Treasury Bills (Auction)	10.08	11.94	13.20	10.10	9.93	4.45	6.58	8.29	8.4
Certificate of Deposits	12.44	12.50	17.13	11.38	10.00	5.16	7.0	9.62	9.2
Commercial Paper	15.10	14.50	20.15	11.88	10.62	5.19	7.35	8.35	8.10
Bank Maximum Deposit Rate	10.00	12.00	12.00	10.00	10.00	8.00	9.60	9.75	10.0
Bank Minimum Lending Rate	16.00	15 to 17%	16.50	15.00	12.00	13.00	13.50	10.75	10.3

Source: RBI Annual Reports (Rates fell after October 1996.)

DFHI Rates

It was only in 1992, that the DFHI has started operation in the Government securities market in addition to its operations in the money market. While the discount or rediscount rates are given in the case of money market instruments, actual purchase and sale prices as offered by the DFHI in the Government securities market are published by the Press, as released by the DFHI. Since June 1994, STCI has begun its operation in Govt securities.

It should also be noted that DFHI is operating in crore of rupees in a variety of instruments both in money market and the Govt. securities market. Bulk of these operations are in response to the market conditions and to absorb the excesses of supply and demand.

New Money Market Instruments

The excess cash balances of corporate units, banks and financial institutions flow into money market. But the money market has for long remained underdeveloped, confined to inter-bank call market and 91 days Treasury bills. It was only since the publication of Chakravarthy Committee Report on the Monetary System (1985) that reforms started. Beginning with freeing of some interest rates and raising the coupon rates on govt. securities, a new institution of DFHI was set up and new instruments of trading were introduced as referred to earlier. Thus Treasury bills on auction basis were initiated for 14 days, 91 days, 182 days and 364 days, respectively.[@] The rates on them are determined by free market forces. These come under government sector instruments.

For encouragement of bill finance by banks and to promote a Secondary Market in bills, the RBI has permitted the issue of negotiable usance promissory notes against trade bills discounted by banks. The govt. has waived the stamp duty payable on trade bills so as to encourage the Secondary Market in them.

The following new instruments are introduced in the Banking Sector and in the Private Corporate Sector:

(*a*) 91 days participation certificates, involving non-transfer of underlying asset risk to the borrower but subject to a ceiling rate of 12% (ceiling rate removed in 1993).

(*b*) 91 to 180 days p.cs., bearing the full risk of underlying asset but subject to a floor rate of 14% (ceiling since removed).

(*c*) *Commercial paper:* The companies with good credit rating say P_2 are allowed to borrow through issue of commercial paper of 91 to 182 days with market determined rate of interest.

(*d*) Certificates of deposit of 6 months to 12 months, representing the deposits of the other sectors in the banking system which are negotiable and tradeable.

@ 14 days and 182 days Treasury bills were discontinued as per the April 2001 monetary measures announced by the RBI.

(e) *Factorisation Bills*: Involving the bills receivable and supply bills payable to companies and banks converted into factorisation bills with or without recourse. These factoring and allied services are being provided by subsidiaries set up by banks, namely, SBI, Canara Bank, PNB, etc. These bills are purchased by the subsidiaries mentioned above from the creditors and the funds are collected in due course from the debtors. These bills can be either with risk or without risk, involved in all debt collection.

Classification of Money Market Instruments

The instruments of Money Market fall under the broad heads shown below:

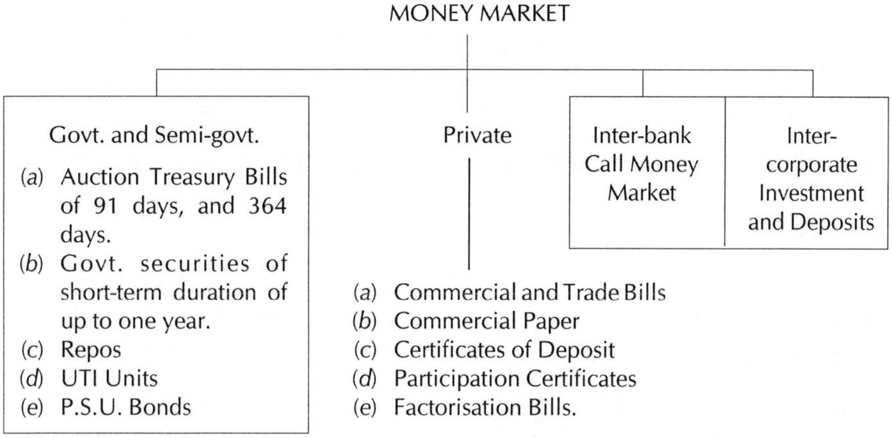

Among the instruments more recently initiated, no progress worth the name was made in respect of participation certificates and factorisation bills. Although some headway was made in respect of commercial paper and certificates of deposit, there is no Secondary Market in these instruments, as visualised by the R.B.I. The reason for this is that the holders of these bills keep them in their portfolio until maturity for two reasons. Firstly, many banks and financial institutions lack the technical expertise of proper portfolio management and secondly there was no well developed market for many segments of the money market. Till recently, there were no worthwhile avenues of investment open to the operators in the money market. Only over last three or four years, new instruments were brought into the money market and a secondary market is being developed in them along with financial deregulation and liberalisation of procedures in the market. The market is now open for a larger number of players and the volume of funds flowing into the market has since increased enormously. These developments were the result of recommendations of Vaghul Committee on Money Market Reforms and recommendations of Narasimham Committee on Financial Reforms.

Money Market Rates

The most liquid of the money market instruments, namely, call money has a rate which fluctuates widely from 1% onwards, as it depends upon the liquidity position of banks. The highest rate is probably on the L.C. Bills of 90 days and Non-L.C. Bills which may go up to 19 to 22%. The Tables below give various instruments of money market and their rates of return, yields to maturity and other details of duration, etc. The main instruments traded in this market which can be seen from the accompanying tables are Treasury bills, Clean and L.C.Bills, commercial paper and certificates of deposits, etc. The expertise of management lies in selecting the right mix of assets consistent with his fund position and market conditions, to suit his liabilities mix.

TABLE 32.2 MONEY MARKET RATES

(in percentages)

Category of Instruments Rate of Interest	Approximate 1996	Oct. 1998	Sept. 4-10 2000	March 2004	March Oct. 1995	March 2007	March 2013	March 2014
1. Call Money	10 -16%	2 to 6%	7 - 9.5%	8.4 - 9.5	4.5 - 4.8	7.22	7.17	8.28
2. Bill Discounting								
Commercial Bills	9%-10%	13.5%	12-15%	10 - 10.6	4.70 - 6.50	8.75	8.5	8.51
Treasury Bills	10 -15%	7 to 12%	7-10%	9 - 10	4.30 - 4.45	7.75	8.0	8.71
3. Deposits (Inter-corporate)								
30 days	14.5%	18%	10%	10	10	free	free	
90 days	15.5%	20%	10-12%	11	11	free	free	9.5
4. Certificates of Deposits	7-12%	12-19%	10-12%	10	5.16-6.00	7.0 -10.75	0-10	8.5
5. Commercial Paper								
90 days	12.75%	13.0%	11%	10.62	6.00	8.59	8.7	8.45
180-364 days	14%-16%	20.15%	14%	—	7.00	11.33	15.0	9.18

Note: Rates fell after October 1996, due to changes in RBI Credit Policy and lowering of CRR of banks in October 1996.

Commercial Paper (CP)

CP is a short-term instrument of raising funds by a company. Originally CP is carved out of the bank cash credit limits and there was surety that on maturity, it would be repaid out of bank credit limit. This link was cut off in Oct. 1994, with the result that the CP stands on creditworthiness of the company.

The commercial paper is a new money market instrument introduced by the RBI. A company with a net worth of more than ₹10 crores (later reduced to ₹4 crores) can issue a commercial paper. Its maximum permissible bank finance (MPBF) for working capital requirements should not be less than ₹25 crores (later reduced to ₹4 crore). It should have a current ratio of 1.33: 1 and a credit rating of excellent (PI) (plus) should be secured from the CRISIL (later relaxed to P_2 only). A company should be listed on one or more of the stock exchanges and can be a FERA company or Indian company.[@] The maturity period should be 3-6 months and the issue should be for a minimum of ₹1 crore (later reduced to ₹25 lakh) and in multiples of ₹25 lakh (later reduced to ₹5 lakh).

The secondary market transactions may be for an amount of ₹5 lakh and multiples. The RBI's prior permission is required for each issue and the general permission is required for each company to enter this market which was later delegated to the banks. The CP should be raised only for working capital purposes and should be less than 75% of the cash credit limit of bank's finance to the company. This was made 100% in cases the bank finance limits are more than ₹20 crore. In 1996, it was completely delinked from cash credit limits of banks. The banks are authorised to decide on the terms and amount of the CP issued by the company. The company will have to bear the expenses of issue, commitment charges, stamp duty, etc. These are not permitted to be underwritten. The NRIs are permitted to invest on a non-repatriation basis. A company may enter into stand by facilities with the bankers to ensure the meeting of the CP liabilities of the company. The brokers can enter only in the secondary market trading as the issue is not permitted to be underwritten.

Certificate of Deposits (CD)

Only banks can issue the CDs. It is a document of title to a time deposit. It is a bearer certificate and is negotiable in the market. The minimum CD should be for ₹1 crore, later lowered to ₹50 lakh and in multiples of ₹25 lakh, later lowered to ₹10 lakh.

It is issued by banks against deposits kept by individuals, companies and institutions and is marketable after 45 days. It can have a tenure of 91 days to 1 year. Banks are to observe CRR and SLR rules. These are

@ Since withdrawn during the financial reforms in 1992.

permitted up to 1% of average aggregate deposits, later raised to 10% of average aggregate deposits. They are issued on discounting basis. No loans and no buybacks are permitted and no duplicates are to be issued by banks. Banks cannot discount them or negotiate them.

Certificates of deposits are permitted to be issued during 1991-92 by the All-India Financial Institutions like IDBI, ICICI, IFC, etc. The maturity period for them may range from 1 year to 3 years and the RBI may fix an aggregate limit for them. There is no ceiling interest rate on them.

Participation Certificates

As in the case of certificates of deposit, participation certificates are also issued by banks for periods ranging from 3 months to 6 months or up to a maximum period of one year. All these instruments are as per the recommendations of Vaghul Committee Report on Money Market for the development of Money Market instruments for participating in the advances by a bank in need of funds by other lender banks and FIs. Two types of such certificates are being developed.

1. 91 days p.cs involving no transfer of the underlying asset risk to the borrower but subject to a ceiling rate of 12.5%.
2. 91 to 180 days p.cs bearing full risk on the underlying asset but not requiring statutory reserves unlike in the above case and subject to a floor rate of 14% (ceiling rates on all were removed in 1994).

The first one is unsecured debt, but securitised for the purpose of negotiation and development of Secondary Market. The second one which may extend up to one year is more risky and carry a higher return.

Repos Transactions

A major development in the Govt. securities market is the introduction of a repurchase facility. This instrument of repurchase Agreement (Repos) is between the RBI and the commercial banks, started since December 1992. Its rate varies from day-to-day.

This is an asset for short-term liquidity management of banks. The period of Repos has stabilised at 14 days since August 1993. The rates on Repos depend on the market conditions and varied from 5% to 11.5% in 1993-94 and from 5.5% to 7% in 1994-95 and from 14 to 25% in 1995-96 and from 4.75 to 6% in Nov. 2004. These rates include both Repo and Reverse Repo rates and maturity varies from one to 14 days. The RBI reference rates are announced on a daily basis.

The Repos can also be effected between banks and financial institutions and among banks themselves. The instrument has since become popular with banks. The RBI stipulated that it should be for a minimum period of 3 days since September 1995 and reduced later to one day. It is now used to set limits to call money rates.

A new line to Reverse Repo facility was opened to the DFHI and STCI (Securities Trading Corporation of India) by way of liquidity support from the RBI. This enabled RBI to intervene in the market to arrest the excesses. This was started in 1994-95. Now Repo market is used to control liquidity in the system.

Management in Money Market

Conversion of cash into short-term instruments of Money Market, utilise the surpluses of cash for earning positive return and conversion back into cash to meet liquidity needs is the main objective of Money Market operations. The management of such activities of investment has to balance between the opposing objectives of liquidity needs on the one hand and income earnings on the other. This requires expertise and experience. Besides the selection of proper instruments among Treasury bills, Commercial bills, Intercorporate Investments, commercial paper, etc., involves a critical choice, as that should enable the manager to maximise returns without sacrificing the needs of liquidity. Should he use his funds in bill discounting, investment in commercial paper or other avenues of Money Market and in what proportion? In this selection process, he should have a clear direction of the period for which he can spare the funds, risk he can take and the return he can expect or aim at.

In the process of management of funds, the finance manager thus has to have a perspective of

1. Return aimed at
2. Risk prepared to take and
3. Time duration of investment.

Money Market provides a buffer between cash or liquidity and long-term high return investments in the stock and Capital Market. The cash inflows due to maturing Money Market instruments are to be adjusted to synchronise with outflows, as projected by the funds manager.

SECURITIES TRADING CORPORATION OF INDIA LTD. (STCI)

The RBI has set up the STCI in May 1994, with an authorised capital of ₹500 crore. Its objective is to promote a secondary market in Govt. securities. So far this work was partially attended to by DFHI, but to give full push up to Govt. securities market, the STCI was set up, while the DFHI would continue to operate in Money Market.

Government securities market depends on their gross borrowings from the public. The gross borrowigs by the Central Govt. stood at ₹5,580 billion in 2012-13 and that of the State Governments stood at ₹1,773 billion in 2012-13.

The STCI started operations in June 1994 with a paid-up capital of ₹125 crore. During 1994-95, the first year of its operations, its operation extended to Govt. dated securities (an amount of ₹39,631 crore), in Treasury bills (₹310 crore), in borrowing and lending in Call and Notice Money (₹26,418 crore). DFHI also operates in call funds, Treasury bills, in addition to commercial paper, Commercial bills, CDs, and term deposits, etc.

In Portfolio Management also, the manager has to keep a proportion of his funds in Money Market instruments. This proportion depends on the objectives of the fund, growth versus regular income or various combinations of these objectives. Once the proportion allotted to money Market instruments is chosen, next, the major task is the allocation of the allotted funds into various instruments within Money Market depending upon their risk-return characteristics.

The basic principles of management would apply in respect of investment in Money Market also. Cost effectiveness and maximisation of returns are the objectives that the management aims at. These objectives can be achieved by a proper choice of the instruments bearing in mind their characteristics.

The Money Market instruments are classified under the category of government instruments, inter-bank call money, corporate instruments, PSU bonds and UTI Units, etc. The risk on govt. and semi-govt. instruments is lower, but their return is also low compared with the investments in the corporate sector. Thus, investment managers aiming at higher returns concentrate on bill discounting, commercial paper, certificate of deposits and inter-corporate investment. But a judicious combination of investment in call money for higher returns and in the Treasury bills for quick liquidity would be necessary for a balanced investment. Besides, he has to balance the maturities of asset instruments with the liabilities falling due and secure a proper asset liability mix for the company.

SECURITIES TRADING REGULATIONS

33

The Securities Contracts (Regulation) Act, 1956 (the SCR Act) is the basis for regulation of Securities Contracts and the Stock Exchanges in India. It was enacted in 1956 and came into force on February 20, 1957. It regulates the business of trading on the stock exchanges and options trading and provides for recognition of stock exchanges and related matters like listing of securities, transfer of securities, etc. The regulation of trading is also governed by the Rules and Bye-laws of the stock exchange.

Objectives

The Preamble to the Act says: "An Act to prevent undesirable transactions in securities by regulating the business of dealing therein, by prohibiting options and by providing for certain other matters connected therewith".

The Act defines what is a security. The Act also lays down what transactions in securities are legal and what are void and illegal.

A reading of the preamble itself indicates that the key word is "securities" which has been defined in Section 2(h) of the SCR Act. The definition is inclusive in nature and includes shares, scrips, stocks, bonds, debentures, debenture-stock or other marketable securities of a like nature in or of any incorporated company or other body corporate. It also covers government securities and rights or interests in securities. But it does not include securities of private companies as they are not capable of being dealt in on a stock exchange and are not marketable securities due to the possible restrictions on transfer. The shares of public limited companies which are closely held and which are not dealt in on a stock exchange are also outside the purview of the said Act, as their transferability may also be limited.

Coverage

Section 28 of the SCR Act also empowers the Central Government in the interest of trade and commerce or the economic development of the country to issue a notification in the *Official Gazette* and specify any class of contracts as contracts to which the SCR Act will not apply. In pursuance of this power, the Central Government has issued a Notification dated 27th June, 1961 specifying contracts for pre-emption or similar rights contained in the promotion or collaboration agreements or in the Articles of Association of limited companies as contracts to which the SCR Act shall not apply. By another notification dated 13th May 1966, the Central Government has declared that contracts pertaining to sale or purchase of shares of government companies (as defined in Section 617 of the Companies Act 1956), which are not listed on any recognised stock exchanges, shall not be subject to the constraints of the SCR Act. The Central Govt. by an ordinance in 1995 permitted trading in options contracts and by several notifications trading in UTI and other MF schemes were also allowed.

Recognised Stock Exchanges

Besides the Act, the Securities Contracts (Regulation) Rules were made in 1957 to regulate certain matters relating to the stock exchanges. Section 3 of the SCR Act lays down that a stock exchange is required to apply to the Central Government for recognition. In terms of Rule 3 of the Securities Contracts (Regulation) Rules, 1957 (the SCR Rules), this application has to be made in the prescribed Form A. The application for recognition in Form A has to be accompanied by a copy of the bye-laws of the stock exchange and also a copy of the rules of the stock exchange.

On receiving such application, the Central Government, in terms of Section 4 of the SCR Act read with Rule 5A of the SCR Rules, makes an inquiry as to whether the rules and bye-laws are in conformity with the prescribed conditions and whether it would be in the interest of the trade and public to grant recognition to the applicant stock exchange.

After making such an enquiry and if the Central Government is satisfied that the prescribed conditions have been met, it grants recognition to the stock exchange. Such recognition is granted in Form B as prescribed under Rule 6 of the SCR Rules, and it may be for a temporary period or on a permanent basis. The Bombay Stock Exchange was the only exchange which was recognised on a permanent basis from the beginning of the operation of the Act.

Mention may be made here to the provisions under Rule 9 of the SCR Rules which lays down that all contracts between the members of a recognised stock exchange have to be confirmed in writing and are to be enforced in accordance with the rules and byelaws of the stock exchange.

Options in Contracts

The word "contract" has been defined in Section 2 (a) of the SCR Act to mean a contract for or relating to the purchase of securities, or sale of Securities.

The expression "option in securities" means a contract for the purchase or sale of *a right to buy or sell* securities in future and a contract for the purchase or sale of *a right to buy and sell* securities in future.

The expression "spot delivery contract" means a contract which provides for the actual delivery of securities and the payment of a price thereof either on the same day as the date of the contract or on the next day.

The difference between a "spot delivery contract" and an "option in securities" is that the latter is a contract in future of an intangible right to buy or sell the securities, while the former provides for the actual purchase and delivery of securities.

Section 13 of the SCR Act empowers the Central Government having regard to the nature or volume of transactions in securities, to issue a Notification in the Official Gazette declaring that a "contract" entered into in a notified state or area otherwise than: (*i*) between members of a recognised stock exchange in such state or area; or (*ii*) through or with such member shall be illegal.

Under the SCR Act and the Rules, Bye-laws of the Stock Exchange monopoly to stock exchanges recognised by the government is given thereby barring the unrecognised stock exchanges to operate in such areas.

Section 20 of the SCR Act prohibits "option in securities". By this section, options in securities are not only made illegal but are also void. Options, derivatives future contracts have been brought under the definition of tradeable contracts on the exchanges in the mid-nineties. The more important effects of this Act are that:

(*i*) options in securities are illegal and void but made legal by an ordinance of Jan. 1995.

(*ii*) only spot delivery contracts or contracts for cash or hand delivery can be entered into with those other than members of the stock exchanges.

(*iii*) contracts other than spot delivery contracts (such as contracts for cash or hand delivery) can be entered only between members of the stock exchange or through or with such members, in places where a recognised stock exchange exists.

Regulation of Trading

Securities are claims on money and trading in them involves passing of contracts or entering into agreements. The contracts of general nature are regulated by the Indian Contracts Act but contracts in securities are governed by the special Act, namely, Securities Contracts (Regulation) Act. This special Act supersedes the general Act but where there is no provision in the special Act as in the case of principal and agent relationship or bailer to bailee relationship, the Indian Contracts Act will apply. The SC(R) Act is supplemented by the rules framed thereunder and the Rules and Bye-laws of the Stock Exchange which are approved by the government and adopted by the stock exchanges.

Under the Rules and Bye-laws of the Exchange, all trading activities and post trading issues are governed by a set of rules. The Bye-laws provide for business days, hours of trading, trading floor and authorised clerks and remisiers who can put through the deals, etc.

The trading floor is supervised by the exchange authorities; only brokers and their authorised clerks can enter the floor and make deals. The rules provide for quotations for bid/offer rates for all listed securities and permitted securities for deals and trading lots, etc. The rules of the game involve the records of the purchase and sales transactions in the Souda block books, comparison of Soudas, taking delivery are all important aspects of regulation of trading. In case of disputes in the trading floor or in their recording of deals, etc., the Rules and Bye-laws have provided for arbitration and settlement of disputes and dispensation of justice in various tiers of judicature as in the case of courts of law.

Trading is regulated by the stock exchange authorities as per the Rules and Bye-laws of the exchange supervised by the SEBI and the government. As per the rules, the admission to trading, the method of recording of deals, the price quotations, types of bargains to be struck, rules governing each category, margins to control trade, restriction on prices and quantity of trade, etc., are all regulated by the exchange. Provisions for inspecting the accounts of brokers, control on their cornering of shares, closing out and buying-in are provided for. The exchange regulates trade through

1. Fixation of daily margins on purchases and sales.
2. Fixation of *ad hoc* margins on total turnover on excessive speculation.
3. Carry forward margins on outstanding purchases and sales at the settlement.
4. Fixation of ceiling and floor prices for any volatile scrip and forcing trading of a scrip to spot basis.
5. Penalties on violation of rules.
6. Fees and charges for any services rendered by the exchange.
7. Arbitration and settlement of disputes between members and between members and their clients.
8. Stopage of trade in any scrip temporarily through circuit breaker if it is raising or falling in price beyond 5-10% spread on any trading day.

As part of the regulation of trading, arrangements are also made by each stock exchange for settlement and clearance with the help of a bank. The giving and taking delivery of shares, settlement through net payment or receipt by each member through a clearing bank, arrangement of auction for effecting deliveries in case of failure to deliver by any member are arranged by the exchange. Where there are securities for clearing with facility for carry forward from one settlement to another, the exchange provides facility for badla financing and carry forward of net outstanding position.

Restrictions on Transferability

Section 22A was introduced in the SCR Act by an amendment and has come into force effective from 17th January, 1986. The net effect of this section is that a public limited company whose securities are listed on a recognised stock exchange cannot refuse to transfer shares lodged with it for transfer, unless the case for refusal falls under the specific provisions laid down in Section 22A. This section has been introduced to ensure that public companies whose shares are listed on a recognised stock exchange do not act in an arbitrary or capricious manner in dealing with a transfer application lodged with it. Thus, a public limited company whose shares are listed on a recognised stock exchange can refuse an application for transfer only for the first of following grounds. For the rest of the grounds *(ii)* to *(iv)* the company has to make a reference to CLB.

(*i*) that the instrument of transfer is not proper or has not been duly stamped and executed or that the certificate relating to the security has not been delivered to the company, or that any other requirement under the law relating to registration of such transfer has not been complied with;

(*ii*) that the transfer is in contravention of any law;

(*iii*) that the transfer is likely to result in such change in the composition of the board of directors as would be prejudicial to the interests of the company or to the public interest; and

(*iv*) that the transfer is prohibited by any order of any court, tribunal or other authority under any law for the time-being in force.

The above Section 22A is a very welcome change made in the SCR Act and ensures that transferability of listed securities is not denied on frivolous grounds by the company. If a transfer is refused, it has to be done within the specified period of two months and the reasons for refusal have to be intimated to the transferor and transferee.

Section 22A applies only to listed companies. This right to refuse registration of shares without adequate reason has been taken away only for listed companies.

The transfer of shares fall within the purview of the Companies Act. Section 82 describes the nature of shares and declares them as movable property. Since shares are a movable property, ordinarily a simple delivery should be enough to complete the transfer. Section 82, however, leaves it to the companies to lay down in the Articles of Association the manner in which the transfer should be effected. It is a general practice in India that the Articles of a Company invariably empower the Board of Directors to refuse the registration to transfer of its securities.

It is Section 111 which recognises the right of companies to refuse registration of transfer of shares and has been substituted by a new one by the Companies (Amendment) Act, 1988. The recasting of Section 111 has been made in pursuance of the recommendations of the Sachar Committee. The Committee considered that, while it might be necessary to retain and recognise the right of directors to refuse registration of transfer of shares if so authorised by the Articles of the Company, this right should be hedged in with adequate safeguards. Specially, under Section 111, as it stood prior to the amendment in 1988, the company was not required to give reasons for refusal to register transfers and it was the right of the adjudicating body only to require the company to disclose reasons at the appellate stage. It has now been made a compulsory requirement for companies to disclose the reasons for refusal to register any transfer at the initial stage itself, that is, at the time of refusal and convey the same to the transferor and the transferee.

Under Section 22A of SCR Act as presently under Section 111 of the Companies Act, corporate managements can easily stall the takeover bids. The assumed contravention of some or the other law, *viz.*, MRTP, Industrial licensing, FERA, Benami law to mention some, would come handy to counter the takeover bid.

In terms of this provision, the Board of Directors gets two months period reckoned from the day the instrument of transfer along with the share certificates is lodged with the company within which to form an opinion and in case it proposes to refuse registration, to make a reference to the CLB and forward the copies of such reference to that transferor and transferee. Thus Section 22A, as at present, promotes the interest of the company as also of the transferor and transferee.

Securities Laws (Amendment) Act of 1999 has brought about many changes in the securities regulation. More importantly it has broadened the definition of securities so as to bring within its ambit and instruments issued by Collective Investment Schemes. It was already noted that Collective Investment Schemes or mutual funds were brought under the control and regulation of SEBI. The govt. and semi-government companies, even with a public holding of 10%, securitised debt instruments, Government securities and a host of new instruments are now permitted to be listed and traded on stock exchanges.

✠ ✠ ✠

INSTRUMENTS OF ISSUE AND TRADING

34

The major instruments of trading on the stock market are equity shares of companies followed in that order by debentures, public sector bonds and Government securities. Trading in Government securities is over the counter as between brokers, banks, financial institutions, etc. The system of auction trading with bid and offer rates to arrive at a competitive price is mainly with respect to the equity shares. There is no worthwhile trade in preference shares.

Issues of Securities

There are various alternative issuers of primary securities, which all compete for the savings of the public. Classified by the sectors of the economy and the nature of their activities, these issuers may be set out as follows:

(*a*) Central and State Governments.

(*b*) Quasi-government Bodies and PSUs.

(*c*) Finance and Investment Corporations.

(*d*) Private Corporate Sector.

(*e*) Commercial Banks including Public Sector Bodies and FIs.

Government Securities

The government is the major borrower in India. The instruments issued are stock certificates, promissory notes, bonds, etc. Besides, the government also raises funds through National Savings Certificates and other instruments of savings sold by the post offices.

On a gross basis, the centre borrowed ₹ 5,580 billion and the states borrowed ₹ 1773 billion in 2012-13. The Central Government borrowed on a net basis ₹ 4,694 lakh crores and the governments ₹ 1,64,585 crores in 2013-14 on net basis.

The Central Government borrowed from the market in recent years nearly ₹ 3.58 lakh crore and State Governments another ₹ 88,000 crore per annum on a net basis. The public sector undertakings borrowed a securities of major chunk of about ₹5,600 crore on Central and State Government guarantees in 1993-94 which rose to ₹10,325 crore in 2006-07 and ₹53,608 crore in 2010-11 and ₹50,865 crores in 2013-14 as referred to earlier. As the financial institutions are mostly in the public sector, the borrowing by the government and the public sector constitute the major component of the total issue of securities. But the secondary market in these securities is limited. But trading in government securities and PSU bonds takes place and is confined to a few institutions and banks as they are the major holders.

Although the P.O. savings instruments are held by the non-bank public and households, there is no secondary market in them as they are not marketable. The bonds and securities issued by the financial institutions and co-operatives are not attractive to the public to hold as their returns are low and they are not marketable. Thus, the secondary market trading is mainly confined to the securities of the private corporate sector.

Corporate Securities

The reason for wider public interest and trading in corporate securities is the attractive returns on them, free transferability, and marketability. Although the interest rates on various financial instruments are fixed by the government, namely, those on preference shares at 14% and fixed deposits with companies are freed in 1996 the returns or yields on *equities* are attractive and freer transferability of these securities attracts wider trading in them. The ceiling rate on debentures was removed in 1991 with the result that the companies can offer any rate that their creditworthiness permits. It is to be admitted that some tax saving instruments of government and post offices carry a higher net return after tax as in the case of NSS, NSCs, CTD and annuity deposits but they are not transferable and not tradable. The private corporate sector borrowed more than ₹26,440 crore in 1994-95 and ₹16,371 crore in 1995-96 and ₹10,457 crore in 1996-97 from the capital market, most of which will be available for trading, as they are quoted on the stock exchanges. Ths issues made by corporates declined later and stood at ₹3,675 crore in 2003-04, but rose to ₹31,600 crore in 2006-07 and rose further to ₹3,61,500 crore in 2012-13. .

Corporate Debentures

Debentures are securities of creditor nature and represent the loans taken by a company from the public. Debentures are mostly secured either by a fixed charge or a floating charge on the assets of the company. Sometime back unsecured debentures, called naked debentures, were issued but are not permitted by the government now.

There are various types of debentures, namely, registered and unregistered debentures, convertible and non-convertible debentures, redeemable and non-redeemable debentures, etc.

Registered holders of debentures are those whose names appear in the registers of companies. These debentures are transferable like equity shares by the execution of transfer deeds and registration of transfer in the books of the company. These transfer deeds may not be date-stamped as in the case of equities and there is no special form for these securities. The rates of stamp duty payable on debentures vary from State to State and are different from those paid on equity shares (which is 50 paise per ₹100 of value of the contract).

The unregistered debentures are bearer bonds, which can be freely transferred by endorsement and physical delivery, without registration with the company. Besides, there is no need for execution of a transfer deed. These securities are like bearer bonds issued by the government or public sector undertakings, government or semi-government bodies. Presently, these are not popular and are not issued by the companies due to the difficulties of establishment of ownership at the time of repayment of principal and the fear of loss of certificates, etc. Interest is paid to the holder on the production of the attached warrants in their case.

Redeemable debentures are those which are repaid after a fixed period of time, normally 7 years, as per the terms of issue. The principal amount is repaid in one or more instalments as the case may be. Irredeemable debentures are those which are not repayable at any fixed date, but can be redeemed at the will of the company or may be perpetual debentures to be repaid on liquidation of the company only. Such irredeemable debentures are not permitted by the govt.

More recently, convertible debentures have become attractive to the public and are issued by many companies. These are convertible into equity in part or full or in instalments spread over a number of years. Partly convertible debentures have two components: of ownership capital (convertible portion) and creditor capital (non-convertible part). These enjoy the benefits of both riskless return on the non-convertible portion and variable risky return of equity along with capital appreciation at a future date. The conversion is sometimes optional and sometimes compulsory. Those which are not convertible are also tradable and transferable like other debentures. They may also be redeemable at a specified fixed date of 7 to 9 years.

The private corporate sector is not permitted to issue non-redeemable debentures and bearer bonds. These are not attractive to the investing public. The companies find it easy to attract the public with convertible debentures, which are either partly or fully convertible into equity and convertible in one or more instalments depending on the company's own cash flow and profitability projections for the years ahead. During recent years, a good chunk of the capital raised was in the form of convertible debentures. The proportion of convertible debentures to total debentures is 60 to 80% in the latter half of nineties.

Other Securities

Leaving aside Government securities and private corporate securities referred to earlier, the broker firms also deal in UTI units, Master Shares, investments in Mutual Funds, CPs, Inter-corporate investments, etc. The more important category of intermediation done by the brokers is in the mobilisation of public deposits with companies and arranging inter-corporate deposits, inter-corporate investments, etc. They also deal in P.S.U. bonds and shares of P.S.U. who have recently started disinvesting in favour of the public.

As per the norms laid down in the Companies Act, corporate units can lend their surplus or borrow the deficits to meet their short-term requirements for periods of one to six months. The limit on such investments is 25% of their total assets. These deposits being unsecured are high-risk instruments.

The role of brokers here is to act as intermediaries between the lenders and the borrowers and bring them together. For this brokers need to have contacts with the top executives of companies and know in advance their requirements and surplus and deficit positions. This activity of brokers goes in conjunction with their deposit mobilisation for companies.

Company Deposits

Another investment avenue for savers and additional source of funds to the corporate sector is the fixed deposits of various maturities. Companies of non-financial nature are also allowed to accept deposits from the public for one to three years and the rates of interest allowed to be offered are freely decided by the company depending upon the maturity and size of the company along with its credit rating. Here the brokers act as middlemen on a brokerage varying from 0.5 to 2% of the funds mobilised.

The regulations governing the mobilisation of deposits by non-government public limited companies are different from those of finance companies and chit funds. The latter are regulated by the RBI and the former by the Department of Company Affairs and Registrar of Companies. The finance and leasing companies are permitted to accept deposits of 2 to 5 years and interest rates on them are free from any control.

There are two types of deposits, namely, cumulative and non-cumulative. In the case of the former, interest is reinvested and paid in a cumulative manner at the time of maturity. In the case of the latter, interest is paid monthly, quarterly or half-yearly.

Commercial Paper

Another instrument for raising finance by companies is the commercial paper. The issue of commercial paper by established companies has been permitted by the RBI since January 1990. These are unsecured promissory notes issued by companies, with a net worth equivalent to ₹4 crore and a maximum permissible bank finance of ₹10 crore. The company should have a credit rating of P_2 from the CRISIL and a status Health Code No. 1 from bankers. The company should have a current ratio of 1.33 : 1 and should have been listed on a stock exchange.

The tenor of these instruments should be 3 to 6 months issued with a minimum size of ₹25 lakh in denominations of ₹5 lakh each. The ceiling amount of such issue is now 100% of the cash credit limit with banks. The trading unit should be of ₹5 lakh. Further details of this instrument are given in the chapter on Money Market.

The issue which should be in the form of usance promissory notes should not be underwritten but should be privately placed. In this process, brokers have a role for placement and sale of this issue. The initial investor would pay the discounted value of the CP with a given tenor of 3 to 12 months and this determines the discount rate. The investor could be individuals, banks, companies or unincorporated bodies.

The stamp duty and other charges like issue expenses, commitment charges, credit rating charges, etc., are all payable by the company. The interest rate on these instruments is determined by its discounted value. Thus, if the paper of 6 months' tenor for ₹100 is discounted for ₹93, this gives an interest rate of 14% per annum, *viz.*, $\frac{(100-93)\times 12}{6} = 14$.

The CP is an instrument which is unsecured and hence the interest rate would be higher than that on the inter-bank rate or the bill discounting rate. This rate should be comparable to the rate on inter-corporate investments.

As the brokers are already operating in the inter-corporate market as also in company deposits, it is expected that they also play a role in the marketing of commercial paper. A time may come when the secondary market can also be developed in them. Although these instruments fall more aptly in the short-term money market, the brokers are eligible and are operating in this market as much as in the new issues market or the long-term capital market.

Legal Provisions

Under the Companies Act, 1956, the public limited company may raise resources from the public through issue of equity shares, preference shares, bonds or debentures or warrants coupons, etc. The govt. and semi govt. bodies or PSUs may issue securities, bonds, etc.

Allotment to applicants has to be made within 70 days from the last date of subscription, as per the listing agreement and reduced to 30 days in 1996. In the case of oversubscription, allotment is to be made in consultation with the stock exchange, in the case of public limited companies.

Allotment letters are themselves transferable but delay in allotment often takes place beyond permitted 30 days. If the allotment letters or refund orders are not posted within 8 days after the time limit, the company is liable to pay penalty at a rate of 4 to 15% depending on the total delay period, under Section 73 of the Act.

The allotment letters are expected to be sent by registered post. Any complaints in this regard have to sent to the Registrar of Companies, in addition to the Stock Exchange in respect of listed companies.

Despatch of Share Certificates

As per the Section 113 of the Act, the investor is entitled to receive the share certificate within three months after allotment. This section also provides relief to the investor in case of default; the investor must first serve notice on the company. If ten days after receipt of this notice, the company fails to deliver the share certificates, then the investor can make a reference to the Company Law Board (CLB). The officers of the company responsible for the default are punishable with fine as per the Act.

Debenture Certificates

There is no provision in the Companies Act in case of any default in respect of debentures, either in respect of payment of interest or repayment of principal. However, in respect of non-receipt or delay in receipt of debenture certificate, the investor can proceed against the company under Section 113 of the Act as in the case of equity or preference share certificates.

Under Section 118 of the Act, the investor can ask for a copy of the Trust deed and avail of the rights as provided in it. He can ask the Trustees for redressal of his grievance under Section 119. If he fails to get the redressal, he can even send a notice under Section 434, after which he can also file a suit for winding up of the company under Section 433. Under the latest law, all debentures should have a time span of not more than 7 to 9 years and they should be compulsorily redeemed after that and in the case of preference shares after a period of 12 years.

Fixed Deposits

Companies raise funds through deposits from public upto a limit. But these are not securities and not transferable. The acceptance of fixed deposits by companies is governed by Section 58(A) of the Companies Act and the Companies (Acceptance of Deposits) Rules, 1975, issued by the dept. of the company affairs. The periods of maturity, interest rates, the limits to the amounts to be accepted are all set out in these rules, which are formulated by the dept. of company affairs. The Act has made it compulsory for companies to repay these deposits on maturity. If there are any grievances of non-receipt of interest or principal in this regard, the investor can apply to the Company Law Board for redressal of grievance, on a specified pro forma along with a fee for it. The ruling of the CLB is binding on all the parties.

Law Regarding Dividends

Under Section 207 of the Act, the company declaring dividend is obliged to pay it to the investor within 42 days from the date of declaration. For non-payment or default in this regard, Section 207 has provided for the imposition of penalties on the concerned officers. The investor can also take recourse to Section 621 and file criminal proceedings against the officers for default. In case of wrong payments of dividends also, such as payment to transferor when the transferee is entitled to it under the rules, the company is liable for default.

New Companies Bill 1993

The new bill has provided for the simplification of procedures, reduction in the number of returns to be submitted and a number of other far-reaching reforms. This has sought to empower the C.L.B. to take up cases of companies defaulting in payment of principal or interest in respect of debentures, prohibits companies from accepting deposits in the event of a default on principal or interest on earlier deposits and provide for the nomination facility for the depositor, shareholder, debentureholder, etc. It has exempted the requirement of endorsement on the share transfer deed for transactions of nominal value, and arranged for the setting up of an Investors' Protection Fund for the benefit of the investors.

Among the important provisions in the new Bill mention may be made of the following:

1. Compulsory rating for creditworthiness of all debt instruments, including fixed deposits.
2. Issue of new instruments like non-voting equity shares.
3. Provision for buyback of shares, if necessary.

SEBI Guidelines

Under the latest SEBI guidelines, companies, including PSUs, and Development Financial Institutions are allowed to issue any type of new instruments. They are also free to price them or fix any interest rates or coupon rates, depending on their credit rating. But the terms and conditions of the new instruments should be clearly stated in the beginning itself so that investors can have a chance to decide whether to invest in them or not.

Equity Shares

Equity shares constitute the ownership capital of a company and the equityholder has the right of voting and sharing in profits and assets in proportion to his holding in the total net assets of the company. He is entitled to all rights and obligations of the owners and to residual profits and assets of the company after all the claims of creditors are met. As he is entitled to residual profits, the dividend distributed to him may be uncertain, variable and fluctuating. The equityholder gets his return in the form of dividends distributed plus capital appreciation on his shares.

The dividends distributed depend upon the net earnings of the company after meeting the interest on loans and debentures, depreciation, taxation and any dividends declared on preference shares. The earnings of a company vary from year to year depending upon the profits of the company as return on capital employed. Earnings per share are calculated by dividing net earnings of the company (after all the commitments are met such as interest, depreciation and taxation) by the number of equity shares. Thus, assume that the net earnings of the company are ₹ 2 crore and there are equity shares of one crore for ₹ 10 each, then the earnings per share can be worked out as ₹ 2. This would influence the share prices in the market which will lead to fluctuations in prices and capital appreciation or depreciation.

The earnings per share of a company depends on a host of factors like the amount of debt per equity share, the ratio of current assets to current liabilities and gross profit to net worth. The price of a share is expressed as a multiple of the earnings per share, if the ratio of price (P) to earnings per share (EPS) is taken. For example, the earnings per share of the Tisco is ₹ 6.5 and the Tisco's share is quoted at, say, ₹ 190. The multiple is 29 times. This multiple depends on many factors such as the outlook for profits, the quality of the management, dividend and bonus policy of the company and investors' expectations regarding the performance of the company.

The companies follow different practices regarding distribution of profits and retention for expansion and diversification. The future earnings depend on the retention policy and expansion plans. The market price in turn depends on the dividend distribution, earnings capacity, expansion and diversification programme and growth prospects. Generally, companies with growth prospects will have a large capital appreciation and share prices show a substantial rise from the value. They have a good dividend record and are called blue chips. Thus, Tisco share price is around ₹ 190 with a face value of ₹ 10. Although the dividend distributed is as high as 30%, still the yield is around one per cent. The average yield on equities in the market is around 3-5% which is relatively low compared to the yields on other securities, but if capital appreciation is also considered, then the return on equity may be much higher than other securities such as debentures or preference shares.

Non-voting Shares

In July 1996, the government have announced their clearance for issue of non-voting shares by companies up to 25% of the paid-up equity of the company. This measure was intended to shore up the investment climate in the sagging capital market in India. The government has not however come out with detailed guidelines for issue of these non-voting shares.

The issue of non-voting shares will no doubt attract, a class of investors, who are not interested in corporate governance as such but in their dividend income. If such investors are given shares at a discount over the price offered to voting shareholders it will probably attract a large number of individual small investors into the market. But the problems of their market trading, and whether these should be kept separate from the voting shares in respect of price quotations in the market and the exchangeability of voting with non-voting shares, etc., will have to be settled before such shares can be issued.

In such scenario and with divided opinions on the subject no company has come out with the offer of non-voting shares. The government had not decided as how to make such issues and the detailed guidelines on non-voting shares were not issued. There are both advantages and disadvantages of such shares, from the point of view of the companies and the investors. The matter deserves a detailed scrutiny before the issue of such shares materialises.

Dividend Distribution

The dividend payments are regulated by the Central Government under Section 205 and 205A of the Companies Act. According to the Company Transfer of Profits to Reserves Rules framed under the above sections in 1975, an amount representing at least 2.5%, 5%, 7.5% and 10% respectively of the current profits have to be transferred to reserves if the dividend declared in any year is between 10-12.5%, 12.5-15%, 15-20% and above 20% respectively of the paid-up capital. A company can transfer a higher percentage of profits to reserves, provided the shareholders are given dividends at a rate of not less than the average of the last three years with an adjustment for the bonus issues. According to the company's Declaration of Dividends out of Reserves Rules framed under the above sections in 1975, a company can draw on the reserves to pay the dividend subject to the following conditions:

1. The rate of dividend paid is the same as for the last 5 years or 10% whichever is lower.
2. The total amount withdrawn from the reserves should not exceed 1/10th of the net worth (Equity Capital + Reserves).
3. The balance in the reserves after withdrawal should not fall below 15% of the paid-up capital.

Dividend Policy

Dividend policies of companies are the offshoot of a number of factors such as the expansion programmes of the company, choice of capital financing methods, cost of external capital and the government policy, etc. Some companies distribute all the earnings as dividends and they have no expansion or modernisation plans. At the other extreme, some companies retain a large proportion of their earnings for future growth. Some maintain a consistent dividend of, say, 12% or 15% and plough back the rest into reserves. Different companies distribute different proportions of their net earnings. The interests of the shareholders are kept in mind as dividend income is the main income of some investors. If, however, larger earnings are retained, these reserves could be used later for the issue of bonus shares, while using these funds for expansion and diversification. Thus, whether profits are distributed or not, these are shareholders' funds. They are given either as dividends or as bonus shares at a future date.

The dividend distribution is sometimes manipulated to the advantage of the promoters. This is particularly true in closely-held companies and private limited companies. If the personal tax liabilities of promoters dictate lower distribution of dividends for the purpose of tax planning, the company itself decides to declare lower dividends and increase the retentions. Then the policy is of lower dividend distribution. In the case of companies having fluctuating profits, a prudent management may also declare lower dividends and retain larger profits. Besides, some unscrupulous promoters may desire to disinvest in a company when they may choose not to retain any profits but to declare all as dividends. Sometimes, dividend distribution is also dictated by the promoters' concern to manipulate the share prices. Since the distribution policy of a company affects its prices, such manipulations will be in the interests of a few and to the detriment of the majority of shareholders.

The Companies Act provided against such contingencies and to foster financial discipline among the companies and to protect the interest of investors. With these objectives, the government have announced some guidelines in 1975 for controlling the transfer of profits to reserves and the use of reserves to declare dividends.

If the minimum average of the dividend rates in the last 3 years is maintained, then it is possible for a company to transfer more than 10% of the company profits to reserves. If the distributable profits are about 20% lower than the average distributable profits of the last 2 years, then the above rules regarding minimum distribution of dividends do not apply. The rules formulated by the government have the objective of securing a compromise between excessive distribution and excessive retention so that the interests of both the company and the investors are protected.

Sections 104 and 105 of the IT Act require that the statutory percentage of distributable income will be distributed as dividend, which varies from 45% in the case of consultancy companies to 90% for an investment company. When dividend distribution is less than the statutory percentage, then the company is liable to pay income tax at higher rates. But these provisions are changed from time to time to suit to the emerging fiscal policy.

Other Instruments

Among the other categories of ownership capital, mention may be made of preferred ordinary shares and deferred ordinary shares. Preferred ordinary shares carry dividend and capital repayment rights ahead of the ordinary shareholders but only after the claims of the preference shareholders are met. The deferred shareholders are a category whose claims on dividends and assets of a company are ranked after the demands of ordinary shareholders are met. These deferred shares are also called founder shares enjoying the voting rights in more than proportionate terms as compared to ordinary shares. But these are no longer existing as the voting powers have been equated among all ordinary shareholders, including promoters and founders. Those categories of shareholders falling under ownership capital now enjoy equal rights in respect of equity shares whose dividends are variable and hence called variable dividend industrial securities.

Bonus Shares

Retained earnings of a company are kept as reserves in various reserve accounts. These are shareholders' funds and are used for purposes of capital expenditure or current expenditure of the company. When they reach a level of accumulation, they are distributed as bonus shares to the present equityholders in a certain ratio to their existing holdings.

Bonus shares can be issued without the consent of the govt. or SEBI subject to their guidelines on bonus Issues:

1. Bonus shares can be issued out of free reserves comprising general reserves, development rebate reserve, share premium received in cash, capital redemption reserve and balances held in the debentures redemption, sinking fund and in profit and loss account. Under free reserves, all reserves except reserves built on revaluation of assets involving no cash accruals are included.

2. The issue of bonus shares cannot be in lieu of dividend.
3. The residual reserves after the proposed capitalisation should be at least 40% of the increased paid-up capital.
4. 30% of the average amount of profits before tax of the company in the last three years should yield at least 10% of the increased capital of the company. This ensures that profitability of the company is adequate to service the increased capital base.

But a company which has defaulted in respect of statutory dues to the employees such as PF, Gratuity, etc., is not permitted to issue bonus shares. Similarly, a company which has defaulted in its liabilities on fixed deposits or debentures cannot issue bonus shares. The other details are given under the heading of SEBI guidelines. Bonus shares are now valued at zero for taxation purposes and for calculation of capital gain.

Rights Shares

Companies can also issue rights shares which are a right to buy the equity shares of the company given at par or a premium to the existing shareholders in a particular proportion to their holdings. Under Section 81 of Companies Act, companies issuing further capital after two years of the formation of the company or after one year of the first allotment of the shares have to offer the same as rights to the existing shareholders.

The premium used to be fixed on the basis of the average book value of the company and post-tax earning capacity of the shares normally capitalised at 15% and even at 10% if the market price is substantially higher than the fair price. The average of the two prices worked out on the basis of book value and the earning capitalisation model is accepted. If earnings per share is ₹3 and capitalisation rate is 15%, then the fair price is $3/15 \times 100 = 20$ according to the earnings capitalisation formula. The price on the basis of book value is, say, ₹30.[1] Then the average of these two prices ₹20 and ₹30, namely, ₹25 is taken as the fair price for fixing the premium (namely, ₹15 on a share with the face value of ₹10).[2]

The rights are quoted in the market. The price of the rights will depend on the ratio in which they are issued. If the ratio is 1:3 and the market price is ₹50, then valuation of rights is done as follows:

Let the premium be ₹15, then,

$$\frac{50 \times 3 + 25}{4} = \frac{175}{4} = 44$$

The value of one right is ₹44 – 25 = 19 which is got for three shares (₹6.33 for one existing share).

Rights can be issued only if authorised by a special resolution of the company. The company making the rights has to inform the existing shareholders as to the use to which the additional funds are put, the future earning capacity of the company and other financial indicators such as sales, estimated gross profit or loss, etc. This information would enable the shareholders to decide to opt for the rights or not.

Preference Shares

Preference shares are of a hybrid category having ownership rights like equity and also a fixed income like creditor capital. They have preferred rights for payment of dividend, along with arrears, if any, if such provision is made in the Articles of Association. They are paid their fixed dividend before any dividend is declared to the equityholders. Besides they have also similar preferential right over equity to payment of capital and their share of assets in the event of winding up of the company. This right is, however, subject to the claims of creditors.

This instrument is suitable to some investors who would like to take some risk but not as much as equityholders but more than debentureowners. They get an income which may, however, fluctuate depending

1. Book value is net worth of the company divided by the number of equity shares.
2. The method of premium fraction adapted by the erstwhile CCI is given in a later chapter.

upon the profits of the company but fixed, if profits are adequate to service all preference and equityholders. They may also get back their capital after a fixed period like debentures as per the present law.

The return on preference shares is fixed by the govt. at 14% since April 1987 which is not applied now. The preference shareholders do not enjoy any voting rights except in respect of resolution affecting their rights or when their dividends due are in arrears for the past two financial years.

There are various types of preference shares like redeemable and non-redeemable, cumulative and non-cumulative, participating and non-participating and convertible and non-convertible.

Preference shares are redeemable generally after 12 years and for this purpose, the company is required to provide for transfer out of profits a sum to the reserves called Capital Redemption Reserve. If there is no provision to redeem these shares, they are non-redeemable. As these non-redeemable shares were not popular, they were abolished by the Companies Amendment Act of 1988.

Preference shares which have a right to receive dividends in a cumulative fashion are called cumulative preference shares. These enjoy the right to receive dividends in all the years in which the dividends are skipped, as profits were inadequate in those years. The fixed dividend on preference shares should be paid later in a cumulative way when profits are adequate before any dividends are declared for equityholders. Those which have no such right are called non-cumulative preference shares.

Preference shares are convertible, if there is a provision for their conversion into equity after a specified period in a particular ratio to the existing equity shares. Preference shares may not be convertible if no such provision is made. Preference shares are participating, if they can share in profits in excess of a guaranteed fixed return, if such a provision is made in the Articles of the company and specify the level of profitability such as an equity dividend of 20%. If these are not so participative, they are called non-participating.

CCP

A new instrument called Cumulative Convertible Preference Shares was introduced by the government in 1985, the features of which are as follows:

1. The CCPs can be issued by any public limited company to raise finance for new projects, expansion and diversification, etc.
2. The amount of issue of CCP will be to the extent of the equity issue to the public for subscription.
3. The dividend payable is fixed at 10%.
4. The entire issue of CCP would be convertible into equity shares between three and five years.

These issues have not proved popular with the companies as the dividend on their shares is not a tax deductible item as in the case of interest on debentures. Besides, the dividend of 10% for the first 3 to 5 years has not proved attractive to investors.

But preference shares as a class are attractive to institutions and individuals in the high income brackets as the dividend income on them is tax exempt under Section 80L unlike interest income on debentures and company deposits. But companies themselves do not find these preference shares as an attractive alternative to raise funds, except in the special conditions when the company is unable to raise funds from fresh equities from the public or in the form of rights.

The existing instruments of issue and their features are set out in the chart attached. These are presently traded and other new instruments are set out at the end. The chart 1 gives the marketable instruments which are traded by type of issuer, ownership rights, yield, return, extent of trading, tax status, etc.

Government and Semi-government Bonds

In the Capital Market the major issuers of securities are companies, Government, P.S.U. and U.T.I. and Mutual Funds. The Government securities are no doubt less risky and more creditworthy due to government's credibility, but the public interest in these securities is poor due to lower rates of interest on these securities and lack of capital appreciation. The instruments issued by government are the Stock Certificates, Promissory notes, Bonds etc. Besides the gvernment raises funds through issue of Treasury bills of 91 days to 364 days for short-term requirements of funds for their expenditure. There are also instruments of Post Offices, which are another source of raising funds for the government. These instruments are NSC, NSS deposits, Time deposits, Indira and Kisan Vikas Patras, etc. But these postal savings instruments are not transferable and marketable. The government — Central and State securities and the bonds issued by the semi-government undertakings are popular with banks, FIs, companies, etc. The public sector undertakings also issue bonds, shares and borrow through deposits from public. These bonds and shares are however transferable and marketable. Bonds are either taxable or tax free and interest rates vary accordingly. Bearer bonds are not allowed to be issued at present.

Equity Shares — Public Issue

SEBI guidelines cover the public issue through prospectus, rights, private placement or offer of sale. In these cases the draft prospectus is to be approved by the SEBI which is now delegated to merchant bankers.

Debt equity norm is 1:2, which is relaxable for capital intensive projects. Equity preference ratio should be 3:1; current ratio should be again 1:2 for issues to finance working capital. Underwriting is normally mandatory but is left optional to companies more recently. Cost of public issue is governed by the guidelines as follows:

Cost of Issue Guidelines

Equity and Convertible debentures up to ₹5 crores should have a mandatory cost plus 5%. For issues above ₹5 crore, the mandatory costs plus 2% is permitted. For NCDs, and debt instruments the corresponding limits are the mandatory costs plus 2% and mandatory costs + 1% respectively. The mandatory costs include expenditure on bankers, underwriters, listing fees and other payments to solicitors, auditors, etc. The non-mandatory costs include all the others like those of stationery, advertisement, etc.

New Instruments

1. *Secured Premium Notes*: These are the instruments, issued by companies for raising debt which can be converted into equity or redeemed at a premium after 3 to 5 years. No coupon rate is fixed.
2. *Discount Bonds and Deep Discount Bonds*: These are sold at a discount today to secure a face value of ₹100 or ₹1,000 after 5 to 30 years. The discount rate depends on the amount of discount and the number of years to maturity.
3. *Warrants*: These are entitlements to buy an equity at a concessional price after a period of 2 to 3 years. These are debt at present, but can be converted into equity.
4. *Loyalty Coupons*: These are entitlements to the holder of debt for 2 to 3 years to exchange into equity shares at discount prices. These are to be held by the original subscriber for a period for the entitlement.
5. *Zero Coupon Bonds*: These are debt instruments with a Zero rate of interest and redeemed at a premium securing capital gains to the holder. This has no fixed coupon rate.
6. *Non-voting Equity Shares*: Somewhat equal to preference shares for which terms have not been finalised and companies have not yet issued to public.

Instruments of Foreign Borrowing

GDRs — equity shares of Indian companies, converted from rupees into foreign currencies for investment by foreigners — Eurocurrency bonds or Foreign currency convertible bonds, or Floating Rate Notes.

Chart 1 **THE EXISTING INSTRUMENTS ISSUED IN THE CAPITAL MARKET**

Marketable Instruments	*Type by Issuer*	*Ownership Rights*	*Yield/Return*	*Trading or Marketbility*	*Tax status (varies from year to year)*	*Redemption if any and Remarks*
Equity Shares (Rights and Bonus)	Companies	Ownership Capital	Average 3 to 4% (variable return) Expected return Risk free return (12%) plus risk premium (15 to 20%)	Group A Group B good trading	Income up to a limit tax exempt, among others Investment in new issues exempt up to limits under Section 88A	Nil
Preference Shares Convertible Non-convertible Redeemable Non-redeemable Participating Cumulative Non-cumulative	Companies	Both Ownership & Debt	14%	No trading	Exempt from Income tax under Section 80L	Redeemable in 7 to 10 years
Cumulative Convertible Preference Shares (C.C.P.)	Companies	Both Ownership & Debt	10%	No trading	Taxable	Convertible into equity in 3 to 5 years
Debentures Convertible Non-convertible Registered Non-registered Secured Non-secured Redeemable Non-redeemable	Companies	Debt capital	Rates Freed	Limited trading	Taxable	Redeemable in 5 to 7 years Non-redeemable debentures are not allowed now
P.S.U. Bonds	Public Sector units	Debt capital	9% to 10.5% tax free	Limited trading	Both taxable and tax free	Redeemable in 5 to 7 years
P.S.U. Shares	Public Sector units	Equity capital	13% to 14% taxable	Good trading in bank shares	Taxable	Nil

Bonds — debt instruments in foreign currencies issued by Indian companies. Offshore Funds — Funds raised in dollars or sterling by public FIs for investment abroad up to 80% and for investment in India up to 20% of the Fund. These instruments are traded and quoted in foreign markets.

Warrants are either detachable or not. The warrantholder at the time of conversion is entitled to that right. Warrants are tradeable like the rights entitlements, but the loyalty coupons are not tradeable.

Some more instruments which have been recently issued for raising funds by financial instutitons are the following:

1. *Floating Rate Bonds:* SBI has issued Floating Rate Bonds in 1993. Although no coupon rate is fixed, the rate of interest payable half-yearly is adjusted at two percentage points above the bank's deposit rate of say, 12%. If the bank deposit rate is changed, the interest rate payable on these bonds will also change. In the case of borrowing abroad in foreign currencies, the floating rate notes are issued with a clause that interest rate is above 1 per cent or 2 per cent above the LIBOR (London Inter-bank Offer Rate). These are loans or debt instruments of short duration of 6 months to one year, but renewable on the same terms or different terms, for longer periods.

2. *Zero Coupon Convertible Bonds:* These were issued at one time by L & T and they do not carry any interest until conversion. When conversion is given into equity, at the end of one year to three years, the terms are favourable and the equity shares will be at par, when the market price is much above. The loss of interest

for one to three years is compensated by the favourable conversion of debt into equity. There are alternatives to those belonging to high income tax brackets, who can postpone payment of tax for a period.

3. *Capital Indexed Banks:* These are issued by companies, government and PSUs with a face value fixed but redeemable at a value based on Inflation Index. They carry a fixed coupon rate, payable half-yearly or yearly.

4. *Gold Indexed Bonds:* These are expected to be issued by the government for mobilisation of public funds for the government to meet their expenditure mostly of a capital nature. The private gold hoards are supposed to be dehoarded and made useful to government for their expenditure on infrastructure and projects thereof. Gold can be valued at the prevailing international prices, both while receiving and repaying back at a maturity time.

New Capital Issues

The new capital issues made by non-government public limited companies in any year represent extent of new capital to be listed on the Stock Exchange and the quantum of liquidity aailable in the market. Time series of data for a period available in the extent of new issues by such companies are presented below for illustration. These show that for the majority of years, debt issues predominate over the equity issues.

The dominance of debt over equity reflects the risk aversion of the public and the market.

(Amount in crore)

There are many years, in which debt Predominated.

Year	*Equity*	*Fixed interest Societies (Debt)*	*Total New Issues*
2000-01	2608	3210	5810
2001-02	860	4832	5692
2002-03	460	1418	1878
2003-04	2471	1251	3722
2004-05	11452	1627	13079
2009-10	25299	2680	27879
2010-11	24830	2626	27456
2011-12	8152	7528	15680
2012-13	1388	2217	16101
2013-14	5812	5869	11681

Source: Handbook of statistics, RBI

✠ ✠ ✠

STOCK MARKETS IN INDIA

35

Stock exchanges are the most perfect type of market for securities whether of government and semi-government bodies or other public bodies as also for shares and debentures issued by the joint-stock companies. In the stock market, purchases and sales of shares are effected in conditions of free competition. Government securities are traded outside the trading ring in the form of over-the-counter sales or purchases. The bargains that are struck in the trading ring by the members of the stock exchanges are at the fairest prices determined by the basic laws of supply and demand.

History of Stock Exchanges

The only stock exchanges operating in the 19th century were those of Mumbai set up in 1875 and Ahmedabad set up in 1894. These were organised as voluntary non-profit-making associations of brokers to regulate and protect their interests. Before the control on securities trading became a central subject under the Constitution in 1950, it was a State subject and the Bombay Securities Contracts (Control) Act of 1925 used to regulate trading in securities. Under this Act, the Mumbai Stock Exchange was recognised in 1927 and Ahmedabad in 1937. During the war boom, a number of stock exchanges were organised even in Mumbai, Ahmedabad and other centres, but they were not recognised. Soon after it became a Central subject, Central legislation was proposed and a Committee headed by A.D. Gorwala went into the Bill for securities regulation. On the basis of the committee's recommendations and public discussion, the Securities Contracts (Regulation) Act became law in 1956.

What is a Stock Exchange?

"Stock exchange means any body or individuals whether incorporated or not, constituted for the purpose of assisting, regulating or controlling the business of buying, selling or dealing in securities." It is an association of member brokers for the purpose of self-regulation and protecting the interests of its members.

It can operate only if it is recognised by the government under the Securities Contracts (Regulation) Act, 1956. The recognition is granted under Section 3 of the Act by the Central Government, Ministry of Finance, Stock Exchange Division.

The powers of the Central Government under the Act are far-reaching and include the following in particular:

1. Grant and withdrawal of recognition, approval or change of bye-laws.
2. Call for periodical returns from the Stock Exchange.
3. Direct enquiries on the members or on the Stock Exchange.
4. Liability of the Exchange to submit annual reports.
5. Directing the Stock Exchange to make certain rules.
6. Supersede the Governing Board of the Exchange, if necessary.
7. Suspend the Governing Board of the Exchange, under alnormal conditions in the Exchange.
8. Impose any other conditions or regulations for trading.

Bye-laws

Besides the above Act, the Securities Contracts (Regulation) Rules were also made in 1957 to regulate certain matters of trading on the stock exchanges. There are also bye-laws of the exchanges, which are concerned with the following subjects:

Opening/closing of the stock exchanges, timing of trading, regulation of blank transfers, regulation of badla or carryover business, control of the settlement and other activities of the stock exchange, fixation of margins, fixation of market prices or making up prices (Havala rates), regulation of taravani business (jobbing), etc., regulation of brokers' trading, brokerage charges, trading rules on the exchange, arbitration and settlement of disputes, settlement and clearing of the trading, etc.

Regulation of Stock Exchanges

The Securities Contracts (Regulation) Act is the basis for operations of the stock exchanges in India. No exchange can operate legally without the government permission or recognition. Stock exchanges are given monopoly in certain areas under Section 19 of the above Act to ensure that the control and regulation are facilitated. Recognition can be granted to a stock exchange provided certain conditions are satisfied and the necessary information is supplied to the government. Recognition can also be withdrawn, if necessary. Where there are no stock exchanges, the government can license some of the brokers (licensed dealers) to perform the functions of a stock exchange in its absence.

Recognition by Government

As referred to earlier, a stock exchange is recognised only after the government is satisfied that its Rules and Bye-laws conform to the conditions prescribed for ensuring fair dealings and protection to investors. Government has also to be satisfied that it would be in the interest of the trade and public interest to grant such recognition. Mumbai, Kolkata, Delhi, Chennai, Ahmedabad, Hyderabad, Bangalore, Indore, etc., have so far been granted permanent recognition. Others are granted temporary recognition from time to time.

The rules of a recognised stock exchange relating in general to the constitution of the exchange, the powers of management of its governing body and its constitution (including the appointment thereon of not more than three government nominees), the admission of members, the qualifications for membership, the expulsion, suspension and readmission of members, the registration of partnerships and the appointment of authorised representatives and clerks must be duly approved by government. These rules can be amended, varied or rescinded only with the previous approval of government. Likewise, the bye-laws of the recognised exchanges providing in detail for the regulation and control of contracts in securities and for every aspect of the trading activities of members must also be sanctioned by government and any amendments or modifications must be similarly approved. Government's authority extends much further to make or amend *suo motto* any rules or bye-laws of a recognised stock exchange, if it so considers desirable in the interest of trade and in public interest.

The Act empowered the government with even more drastic powers — the power to make enquiries into the affairs of a recognised stock exchange and its members, to supersede the governing body and takeover the property of a recognised exchange, to suspend its business, and lastly, to withdraw the recognition granted to an exchange should such steps be deemed indispensable in the interest of trade and in public interest. Government has thus complete control over the recognised stock exchanges.

Licensed Dealers

The recognised stock exchanges are the media through which government regulation of the stock market is made effective. Where there are no stock exchanges, the Securities Contracts (Regulation) Act, 1956 empowers government to license dealers in securities and prescribe the conditions subject to which they can carry on the business of dealing in securities. These licensed dealers are now operating for OTCEI and NSE.

Securities Contracts (Regulation) Rules, 1957

Under the Act, government has promulgated the Securities Contracts (Regulation) Rules, 1957 for carrying into effect the objects of the legislation. These rules provide, among other things, for the procedure to be followed for recognition of stock exchanges; submission of periodical returns and annual reports by recognised stock exchanges; inquiry into the affairs of recognised stock exchanges and their members; and requirements for listing of securities. The rules are statutory and they constitute a code of standardised regulations uniformly applicable to all the recognised stock exchanges.

Present Recognised Stock Exchanges

At present, there are 23 stock exchanges recognised under the Securities Contracts (Regulation) Act, 1956. They are located at Mumbai, Kolkata, Chennai, Delhi, Ahmedabad, Hyderabad, Indore, Bhuwaneshwar, Mangalore, Patna, Bangalore, Rajkot, Guwahati, Jaipur, Kanpur, Ludhiana, Baroda, Cochin and Pune. The recently recognised stock exchanges are at Coimbatore and Meerut. The NSE and OTCEI have been given recognition during 1989 to 1992 and they were fully functional. A stock exchange has also been set up at Gangtok, Sikkim early in 1986. No recognition has been sought for this body as the jurisdiction of the Securities Contracts (Regulation) Act, 1956 has not so far been extended to the areas covered by the State. In 1996, the stock exchange at Visakhapatnam was given recognition for electronic trading. A decade ago, there were hardly 8 stock exchanges in the country. And in principle recognition is granted to Vijayawada exchange in 1998, which was not tunctional if it is organised on electronic system and with a clearing house to be set up within six months. A new Inter-connected Stock Exchange (ICSE) connecting 14 regional exchanges is also granted recognition. The ICSE started trading before end 1998 with uniform settlement cycle and a separate clearing corporation to develop an inter-connected market system at national level. Out of total 23 stock exchanges, there is no worthwhile trading on 19 exchanges in India at present in constituting a wastage of resources.

The stock exchanges operate under the rules, bye-laws and regulations duly approved by government and constitute an organised market for securities. They offer the most perfect type of market for various reasons. There is an active bidding and in the case of shares and debentures a two-way auction trading, so that purchases and sales are made in conditions of free and perfect competition. The bargains that are struck by members of the exchanges are the fairest price determined by the basic laws of supply and demand. In consequence, though gilt-edged securities represent ownership of government public debt and shares and debentures of joint-stock companies represent interest in industrial property — mills and factories, plant, machinery and equipment — they become the most liquid of assets and capable of being easily negotiated.

Qualifications for Membership

The members of recognised stock exchanges should have the following qualifications:

These are modified by SEBI as and when needed, as they are to be registered by the SEBI also.

— Age 21, Indian Citizen, not bankrupt.

— Not compounded with the creditors.

— Not convicted for fraud or dishonesty.

— Not engaged in any other business except as agent or broker.

— Educational qualifications should be 10+ 2.

— Not connected with a company or corporation.

— Not a defaulter of any other stock exchange.

Companies and financial institutions are not members as per the earlier rules. But the government has permitted change in the bye-laws of the exchanges to permit corporate and institutional members and also grant permission for a member of any stock exchange to be a member of another stock exchange during 1993-1994 reforms.

Members are prohibited from entering into contracts with persons other than members or from dealing with clients as principals. Spot delivery transactions are exempt from the provisions of the Act. Contracts can be passed only by the members in the notified areas where the stock exchange exists. The sub-brokers can also pass valid contract notes or confirmation notes, if they are registered with SEBI.

Organisation

The recognised stock exchanges at Mumbai, Ahmedabad, Indore are voluntary non-profit-making associations, while the Kolkata, Delhi, Bangalore, Cochin, Kanpur, Ludhiana, Guwahati and Kanara stock exchanges are joint-stock companies limited by shares and the, Hyderabad and Pune stock exchanges are companies limited by guarantee. Since the Rules or Articles of Association defining the constitution of the recognised stock exchanges are approved by the Central Government, there is a broad uniformity in their organisation. In fact, the Chennai stock exchange was reconstituted and the Kolkata stock exchange had to undergo a major reorganisation as a condition precedent to their recognition by the Government of India. The latest trend for the stock exchanges is demutalisation, which means that the ownership will be dissociated from the traders and dealers. Bombay stock exchange has made the ownership public by issue of shares, which was done in August, 2005. In the case of NSE and OTCEI, the ownership and control are dissociated, from the beginning itself.

Governing Body

The governing body of a recognised stock exchange has wide governmental and administrative powers and is the decision making body. It has the power, subject to governmental approval, to make, amend and suspend the operation of the rules, bye-laws and regulations of the exchanges. It also has complete jurisdiction overall members and in practice, its power of management and control are almost absolute.

Under the constitution, the governing body has the power to admit and expel members, to warn, censure, fine and suspend members and their partners, attorneys, remisiers, authorised clerks and employees, to approve the formation and dissolution of partnerships and appointment of attorneys, remisiers and authorised clerks, to enforce attendance and information, adjudicate disputes and impose penalties, to determine the mode and conditions of stock exchange business and regulate stock exchange trading in all its aspects and generally to supervise, direct and control all matters and activities affecting the stock exchange. The organisation of Mumbai Stock Exchange is typical. The members on roll elect 16 members to be Directors on the Governing Board, who in turn elect a President, Vice-president and Treasurer. The Executive Director is appointed by the government on the recommendation of the Governing Board to be the Chief Administrator of the exchange. There are also three representatives from the government, three from the public and one from the RBI on the Board to represent their interests. As per the SEBI guidelines, the exchanges have agreed to have 50% representation to non-members on the Governing Board.

Functions of Stock Exchanges

Stock exchanges provide liquidity to the listed companies. By giving quotations to the listed companies, they help trading and raise funds from the market. Savings of investors flow into public loans and to joint-stock enterprises because of this ready marketability and unequalled facility for transfer of ownership of stocks, shares and securities provided by the recognised stock exchanges. As a result, over the hundred and fifty years during which the stock exchanges have existed in this country and through their medium, the Central and State Government have raised crores of rupees by floating public loans; Municipal Corporations, Improvement Trusts, Local Bodies and State Finance Corporations have obtained from the public their financial requirements, and industry, trade and commerce — the backbone of the country's economy — have secured capital of crore of rupees through the issue of stocks, shares and debentures for financing their day-to-day activities, organising new ventures and completing projects of expansion, diversification and modernisation. By obtaining the listing and trading facilities, public investment is increased and companies were able to raise more funds. The quoted companies with wide public interest have enjoyed some benefits and asset valuation has become easier for tax and other purposes.

In tune with the growth in the new issues market during the eighties, the secondary market also expanded fast during this period. The number of stock exchanges has increased from 8 in 1980 to a total 24 in 1996 including Visakhapatnam stock exchange recognized in 1996. The membership of the stock exchanges has also increased substantially to around 8,000 from about 1,200 a decade ago. The listed companies of all stock exchanges stood at about 6,000 in 2007, of which about 90% are listed on B.S.E. The market capitalisation has also shown a substantial increase in the eighties and nineties. The volume of daily turnover of trade has also increased more than ten-fold over the decade. The share dealings per day put through were as high as ₹8,000 to 10,000 crore, on some days in 2012.

Listed Paid-up Capital and Market Capital

The paid-up share capital of listed companies in 1946 was ₹270 crore while in 1997, the figure was more than ₹1.1 lakh crore. The market value of the capital of these listed companies stood at around ₹5.5 lakh crore in 1995 which rose to ₹9,12,842 crores by March 2000, and further to ₹16,98,428 crore by March 2005, and ₹68,36,878 crore by March 2011. This worked out to about 94% of GDP as at end March 2011.

Who Owns the Securities?

The gilt-edged securities are officially listed on the recognised stock exchanges as soon as they are issued to the public by the authorities concerned. These securities constitute the largest amount of debt traded on the stock exchanges as the government sector is the major borrower in the economy.

Almost the entire outstanding rupee debt is owned by the commercial banks, the Life Insurance Corpn., Provident Funds and charitable trusts less than one per cent is owned directly by individuals. But anyone who has a bank account or is a policyholder or a beneficiary of a public or private trust is basically involved in the ownership of gilt-edged securities. Therefore, an increasingly large number of persons is being interested indirectly in Government securities. Their number will grow as savings increase and development under the Five-Year Plans is financed by public borrowing on a more extensive scale. This evidences the influence of the gilt-edged market and its vital significance in the economic life of the country.

The growth and present position of stocks and shares of joint stock companies listed on the recognised stock exchanges indicate a substantial increase in the public stake in listed stocks over the past. A study of the ownership pattern of the companies listed on the BSE in 1989 by the author showed that individuals continue to be the major category of holders although their share declined from 56.4% in 1984 to 45.9% in 1989. The shares of corporate bodies and financial institutions have stood at around 28.4% and 11.2% respectively in 1989. The share of corporate bodies has increased from 17.8% in 1984 to 28.4% in 1989. This trend got accentuated due to proportional allotment system imposed by SEBI, in 1993. The share of individuals might have gone down later due to growth of mutual funds and prolonged depressed new issue market since 1995.

Mumbai: The Premier Exchange

The Mumbai stock exchange was the premier stock exchange in India at one time. It was the first to be recognised on a permanent basis in 1957. The capital listed in Mumbai accounted for about 40% of the overall capital listed on all the stock exchanges, whereas its share of the market capitalisation amounted to around 90%. In terms of the total number of companies and total number of stock issues listed also, Mumbai ranked first.

The B.S.E. and N.S.E. regularly publish statistics on market turnover of securities though similar figures for the other exchanges are not available on regular basis. It is, however, roughly estimated that the turnover of Mumbai stock exchange was about 60%-70% of the overall turnover of all the stock exchanges in the country, but with NSE leading in the trade turnover on a daily basis, the share of BSE came down to less than 40%.

The number of companies quoted on the stock exchanges was more than 6,000 of which those listed in Mumbai are about 5,000. The number of deals put through in the session on the Mumbai stock exchange, namely, 10 a.m. to 4.00 p.m., is around ₹ 2,700 crores. The daily turnover however stood higher at around ₹ 6,163 crore on the NSE.

Patel Committee

A high-powered committee under the chairmanship of Shri G.S. Patel, former Chairman of the Unit Trust of India, was set up by the Union Government in May 1984 to make a comprehensive review of the functioning of the stock exchanges and make recommendations.

The terms of reference of the Committee included *inter alia,* the following:

- to examine the general functioning of the stock exchanges as an integral part of the financial system;
- to suggest measures to improve the overall service to investors by the members of stock exchanges and to encourage small investors particularly in semi-urban and rural areas to invest in industrial securities;
- to look into the existing system of organisation and management of stock exchanges with a view to broadbase it so as to make it representative of all concerned interests and to suggest a uniform model of organisation, etc.

After deliberations which lasted more than a year, the Committee submitted its Report to the Union Finance Ministry in December 1985. In the light of the recommendations made by the Committee in their interim Report, the government issued several guidelines and directives to the stock exchanges relating to matters of securities on the stock exchange, creation of a Customers' Protection Fund and insurance cover for members of stock exchanges, etc.

Regulations on Trading

As regards the regulations on trading in the ring of the exchange, the stock exchange authorities used to operate a variety of regulations in the following ways:

Firstly, only authorised clerks of the members were permitted to enter the trading ring with their badges. Souda Block Books or confirmation memos were provided by the stock exchange. Entry into the trading ring is restricted to members and their authorised clerks.

Secondly, the Monitoring Deptt. of the exchange keeps a watch on the price movements and the trading volume of the members and take such action as is necessary to control excessive trading and speculative fervour. It may impose *ad hoc* margins, suspend trading and enquire into any special developments.

Thirdly, in the case of any disputes on the trading floor as between members or their authorised assistants, the floor committee appointed by the Board can officially intervene and give their judgement on the dispute, whether relating to the price or quantity or the scrip or there can be administrative intervention by inspectors. In the case of post-patavat (settlement) objections, an administrative committee will go into the matter. In the case of other disputes, the lower bench and the full bench or the Governing Board may examine and give their decisions which are binding on the members. These disputes may relate to Soudas in the trading ring regarding the rate and rights, frauds, etc. Certain matters of dispute are referred to a special committee appointed by the Executive Director.

Fourthly, the Operations Department of the stock exchange will supervise the operations, make any announcements at the time of trading, suspension of trading or collection of quotations, giving of company information, etc. The fixation of different types of margins, making up prices (Havala rates) and supervision of trading, etc., are the responsibility of the Executive Director and Inspection Dept. The auctions of shares and related matters connected with settlement are looked into by the Operations Department.

The types of margins imposed are as follows:

1. Daily margins on purchases or sales of members at varying rates or on the total outstanding position in each scrip.
2. Carryover margins at the time of settlement on each of the scrips at varying rates up to 50% or more depending upon whether they are purchases or sales.
3. Limits imposed on total trade by each of the members in all scrips together to keep a control on overtrading by members.
4. *Ad hoc* margins, imposed specially on any scrip or scrips subject to high speculative attacks.
5. Suspension of trading in any scrip for any period of time, shifting of a scrip from group A to group B and *vice versa,* etc., depending on conditions of trading in the scrip, through circuit breakers.[@]
6. Fixation of minimum or maximum prices for any of the scrips.
7. Change or reduce the trading hours.

To give examples of how margins operate on trading, let us take the following cases:

Member A has purchased 500 and sold 200 with a net purchase position of 300 scrips. The price of the Tisco scrip is ₹115. The margin on purchase is at a rate of ₹5 per scrip. Then the purchase price becomes ₹115 - 5 = 110. An amount of 300 × ₹5 = ₹1,500 is deposited with the stock exchange to the credit of the member.

Member B has purchased 800, sold 1,000 with a net sale position of 200 scrips. The price of the Century scrip is ₹3,400. The imposed margin is ₹400 per scrip. Then the sale price becomes ₹3,400 + 400 = ₹3,800. An amount of 200 × ₹400 = ₹80,000 is kept with the stock exchange to the credit of the member.

These margins will apply in the same manner whether it is a daily gross or net position or carryover

@ Circuit breakers give orders for stoppage of trade in any scrip, if its price rises or falls beyond say 5 to 10%.

net position. Margins are also imposed on gross purchases and sales scrip-wise. But they vary depending on the scrip, its price and speculative position in the market. These rates are different for purchases and sales. The net price after adjustment of margins is used for the purpose of carryover.

Investor Protection

Certain measures of investor protection adopted by the exchanges deserve special mention here. Firstly, the exchanges have set up a Customer Protection Fund, in tune with guidelines issued by the Ministry of Finance. The objective of the fund is to compensate the investor clients of member brokers who have defaulted. In all geniue cases of claims, the clients are compensated up to a maximum which varies from exchange to exchange. This Fund is financed by a levy on the turnover of members collected at the rate of one rupee for every ₹10 lakhs of turnover and by contributions from the listing fees, at the rate of 2% collected from the companies. The stock exchanges were exempted from income tax on contributions for setting up of Investor Protection Fund from April 2000. Capital gains exemption from taxation was also granted to stock exchanges after demutualisation of stock exchanges into corporate bodies.

Another service provided was through Investor Complaints Cell set up a decade ago, but rechristened as Investor Service Cell in some exchanges. The service was strengthened to render expeditious service to the investors and to attend to their grievances. As many as thousands of complaints are received per month, of which 90-95% are against the companies and the rest against the brokers. The nature of complaints is non-receipt of refund order, allotment letters, dividends, brokerage, underwriting commission, etc. of the complaints received, about 50% are attended satisfactorily.

Another service provided by major exchanges is to arrange an insurance policy to broker-members through the New India Assurance Co. This policy covers the perils of forgery, fabrication of securities and transfer deeds and receipts, identity of the transferor, loss of securities in transit, etc., which the brokers are subject to during their transactions with clients for delivery of shares for transfer. In view of this protection, the brokers can attest the signatures of transferors which will help quicken the process of share transfer.

To expedite the process of delivery of shares in the settlement and clearing procedure of the stock exchange, the BOI Shareholdings Ltd., was set up jointly by the Bank of India and the stock exchange, Mumbai in November 1989. This new organisation takes over the clearing and delivery of shares for both 'A' and 'B' Group shares on the stock exchange. The actual delivery of shares as between the member brokers is now replaced by Delivery Slips, passed or credited and debited with BOI holdings. No physical transfer of shares takes place and hence it saves a lot of time involved in delivery after clearing. This function is taken over by the NSDLs and clearing corporation after the introduction of Demat form of transfer and stoppage of physical form of share holding after 1996.

Many stock exchanges have also provided a service to investors in the form of fixing up an odd lot trading session for half hour everyday or on every alternate Saturday and shortlisting a group of brokers who agreed to deal in odd lots for the benefit of purchase/sale/consolidation, etc., of odd lots. The investors can get quotations for odd lots in major scrips and deal in them more freely than before. The service of purchase from investors of odd lots was later extended by the UTI, GIC and Canbank and others as an over-the-counter facility. But this was dispensed with after dematerialisation of shares, when the odd lot problem itself disappeared.

Measures to Promote Healthy Stock Markets

With a view to reduce delays in listing arising out of conversion, the government has issued a circular authorising the stock exchanges to take action and monitor the issues of over ₹10 crore and if the delay is deliberate without adequate reasons, the exchange should report the matter to the Registrar of Companies, SEBI, etc., and also take suitable action. The government has amended the SCR rules in December 1988 to permit multiple membership of stock exchanges and to enable the granting of membership to financial and corporate institutions.

In October 1988, the Bhansali Committee's recommendation on share transfer procedures was implemented whereby the newly allotted shares have to be treated on par with the old shares for delivery purpose, subject to the adjustment of the dividend depending on the time of allotment. The minimum capital for listing has been raised to ₹3 crore of which ₹1.8 crore should have been issued to the public effective February 1989. This was further raised to ₹5 crore from October 1995.[@] The guidelines for listing have also been amended, particularly with regard to book closure and record dates and to give more powers to the stock exchanges to monitor the allotment of new issues and to curb insider trading or takeover bids. Banks have been permitted to lend up to 90% of the value of shares to be acquired by the employees out of their quota of new issue subject to a ceiling of ₹20,000. Individual Bank are allowed to lend up to 5% of their incremental deposits against shares and debentures, this limit was removed later for sometime, but reimposed in 1997.

The government has approved the creation of over-the-counter Exchange of India (OTC) which would help the introduction of a multi-tiered market for securities. Stock exchanges have been directed to transfer the scrip of company from the specified section to the spot section if the company intends to come out with the rights issues. The Employees' Option Scheme was partially modified restricting the allotment of the unavailed portion of the public/rights issues earmarked for employees only to financial or investment institutions or mutual funds.

As it has been found that the various stock exchanges are following different methods of calculating the amount of dividend to be deducted while trading in the new shares, which are on a *pari passu* basis, the government has clarified in June 1990 that all stock exchanges should follow the same practice and the new shares should be traded and delivered along with old shares provided the new shares are traded and delivered at least one day in the relevant settlement period. The dividend can be deducted from the price for the new shares at not more than the amount of dividend for one year.

Clause 40 of the listing agreement has been replaced by 40A and 40B. Under clause 40A, when any person acquires 5% or more of the shares of a company in terms of its nominal value, the stock exchange should be notified within four days of such acquisition or agreement to purchase by the company, by the intermediary or by the acquirer. Under clause 40B, if there is a takeover offer, a public announcement of the offer should be made both by the offeree and offerer. This requirement is necessary when any person acquires shares carrying 10% or more of the total voting rights of the company through their shareholdings or to secure control over the management of the company. The offer should be made public and by a public announcement and notification to the stock exchange and SEBI with regard to the terms of offer, identity of offeror and other terms and conditions and such information should be made available to all the shareholders of the offeree and offeror companies. Clause 41 was added recently to the listing agreement to enforce half-yearly publication of results of the working of the company as well as quarterly results in some cases.

The government has also notified certain guidelines for institutional transactions in shares. For any sale of over 1% of paid-up capital of the company, the information regarding such transactions should be reported to the SEBI and the concerned stock exchanges and to the public within a day of the transaction through a press release. The Board of each financial institution should lay down the criteria for such transactions. The guidelines also state that all purchases or sales should be for delivery and they should be made through approved brokers at market prices. Besides no sale should be made at a negotiated price to non-institutional buyers. If, in the case of a sick company, the management changes, and such negotiated sale takes place, that should be disclosed to the public through a press release and also to the SEBI and the concerned stock exchange.

Clause 16 of the listing agreement has also been amended to require companies to fix the date of book closure and record dates either on the 1st or the 16th of any month and to give a notice to the exchange

---

@ It is ₹10 crore and above on NSE, BSE, DSE, etc.

of at least 42 days in advance. The company should also ensure that the time gap between the book closures and record dates should be 90 days. The company is also required to undertake that the securities delivered for transfer will be transferred even if there are signature differences, if it is attested by a member of the stock exchange.

As regards the capital issues, undersubscribed in the rights or public issues, the companies have been instructed to refund all the application monies within 120 days of the opening of issue if a minimum of 90% subscription is not secured. If the refund orders are not passed even on the expiry of 10 days after a period of 120 days, interest at the rate of 15% is payable. This has been amended in 1996, referred to later. The subscription amount would be kept in a specific bank account and companies will have no access to the funds unless the concerned stock exchange has permitted the allotment. This allotment will not be permitted until the 90% limit of subscription is achieved. It is also essential for the promoters to make their subscriptions in advance before the public issue opens and give a certificate to this effect to the concerned exchange. If the level of 90% is not reached by the public subscription, the underwriters will have to make the subscriptions up to their limits of underwriting to achieve the minimum level of 90% subscription. The stock exchanges and in particular the regional stock exchanges are thus given a crucial role in the allotment and listing of new issues.

These matters relating to reforms in stock exchange are dealt with in many places in the book under capital market, stock market and SEBI measures on new issues market, listing and Stock Exchange Trading and Regulations. It is bound to lead to some repetition which became unavoidable due to the need to make each chapter self-explanatory.

Latest Reforms of the Stock and Capital Market

Reforms being a continuous process, starting from May 1992, there have been some new measures, or modifications and amendments to existing Rules and Regulations, announced by the SEBI, RBI or the Government of India. The following are some of the reforms and the rest were mentioned at other appropriate places in the book.

During the last quarter of 1995, the SEBI initiated measures to prohibit unfair trade practices, manipulation of prices, misleading statements and other fraudulent practices to induce sales or purchases of securities with a view to influence the prices and make undue profits or gains out of such practices. On October 25, 1995, the SEBI notified the regulations on "Prohibition of fraudulent and unfair trade practices" relating to securities markets.

On December 21, 1995, the SEBI announced a series of measures to check the other malpractices in the securities markets, namely, provision for imposition of penal margins on net undelivered portion at the end of each settlement, special margin on buyers in the case of rise in prices and suspension of trading by one or more stock exchanges in respect of scrip, subject to undue price gyrations and manipulations.

The SEBI clarified on March 1, 1996 that vetting of all non-convertible debt issues is delegated to merchant bankers, and that lock-in period for preferential allotment was removed for all categories except for the promoters. The disclosure norms and responsibilities of merchant bankers were tightened and revised guidelines were issued for the employees stock option scheme.

Early in 1996, the entry norms for companies were tightened and measures were initiated to promote a healthy growth of both the primary and secondary wings of the capital market.

A company should have a track record of dividend payment for a minimum of 3 years out of immediately preceding 5 years, to be eligible for its shares to be listed on a recognised stock exchange. However, a manufacturing company, whose issue and project have been appraised by a public financial institutions or a bank, which has also participated in its funding, may make a public issue to get its shares listed on a stock exchange.

On May 15, 1996 it was announced that the allotment process of a listed company or of the one proposing listing, should be completed within 30 days, instead of the earlier period of 70 days. Thereafter, the company will be required to pay interest at a rate of 15% per annum for the delayed allotment or refund of application money beyond the permitted period. Besides public issue made for listing by a company should have at least 5 shareholders from the public for every ₹ 1 lakh net capital offered to public through prospectus and 10 shareholders for every ₹ 1 lakh offered through offer of sale.

Custodians were brought under the SEBI net of regulations in mid-May 1996, when the SEBI notified "Custodians of Securities Regulations" on May 16, 1996. These provide for registration of custodians, and specify the prior requirements for registration in terms of net worth, experience and expertise. Besides, they set out the responsibilities and obligations of the custodians and procedures to be followed for audit and inspection of their accounts and the procedure to be followed in case of default.

The SEBI notified "Depositors and Participants Regulations" (1996) on June 19, 1996, containing the regulations for prudential norms for setting up depositories and formalities to be adhered to by the participant. The Depositories Act was passed by the Parliament and received the President's assent in August, 1996, and it embodied matters relating to regulation of Depositories, the Central Depository and the matters, connected therewith or incidental thereto. Consequent on the passing of the Depository Act and the Rules framed thereunder by the SEBI, UTI and NSE have provided for dematerialisation of physical certificates and electronic transfer of funds.

In August 1996, exemptions were granted by SEBI for Bought out Deals or offers of Sale by Companies listed on OTCEI, from the requirement of 3 years dividend paying track record, in order to make a public issue. Subsequently, following Dave Committee Report and its recommendations many concessions and liberalisations were accorded to OTCEI, for making it a vibrant and active trading centre. These in brief relate to the relaxations of requirements for listing on the OTCEI, and of market making, capital requirements, trade and settlement on T + 7 basis in respect of permitted securities, etc. The OTCEI also took a number of measures to give incentives to sponsors and dealers in the market, to help them activate the dormant trading on this exchange, for the last few years.

In July 1996, the govt. permitted the FIIs to invest in any company up to 10% of its equity as against 5% permitted earlier. Besides FIIs are allowed to invest to any extent in Unlisted companies. The SEBI has widened the definition of FII to include any university Funds, Endowments, Foundations, charitable Trusts/ Societies of Foreign Origin. FIIs were permitted to invest up to 100% of debt of Indian companies.

In August 1996, SEBI notified that all stock exchanges to introduce weekly settlements to conduct auctions within 8 days of the settlement in case members fail to deliver shares and to ban the system of renewal of contracts in the cash groups. It was decided in October 1996 to allow any stock exchange to expand their online trading to other centres outside their jurisdiction, if it is through terminals for on-line screen based trading system (such as BOLT).

Companies whose equity is not listed are allowed to get their debt instruments listed on stock exchanges for imparting liquidity to them. The minimum application size of subscription to a public was lowered from ₹ 5,000 to ₹ 2,000 in October 1996, to encourage small investors to come back to the capital market. The SEBI has decided to grant any stock exchange recognition, if it is trading online-screen based system and establish clearing house within six months from the start of electronic trading. Under this principle, Vijayawada stock exchange was granted recognition in 1998 subject to the above conditions. The need for these regional exchanges was lost due to introduction of BOLT system.Vijayawada and Visakhapatnam stock exchanges have become non-starters.

SEBI issued guidelines for securities lending scheme on Feb. 1997, in terms of which the intermediaries related to securities lending need to be registered with the Regulator. The guidelines laid down the methods of securities lending and stipulated obligations and responsibilities of the approved intermediaries. This scheme is introduced to quicken deliveries of securities and facilitate short selling and at the same time, investors can earn additional return by lending securities.

To eliminate some of the possible malpractices SEBI announced that all negotiated deals on the stock exchanges should result in compulsory delivery of securities. All stock exchanges are advised to set up clearing houses and settlement Guarantee Funds, if they have not already set up.

To help growth of investor confidence disclosure and investor protection guidelines were codified and a compendium was prepared. In the norms of entry into the capital market, the stipulation of dividend payment in at least three out of the preceding five years was changed to immediate preceding three years. Further, the promoters' contribution for public issues has been made uniform at 20% of the total offer, irrespective of the size of the issue, with effect from August 1997.

The limit for aggregate investment of FIIs, NRIs, OCBs, etc., was raised to 30% from the erstwhile 24%, with effect from April 1997. The Reserve Bank also revised the guidelines for disinvestment by foreign investors in respect of valuation of unlisted or thinly traded scrips.

Restrictions on the sale of securities and their remittance of funds were allowed without reference to RBI, in the case of these FFIs, NRIs and OCBs, provided they pay the required taxes through the authorised dealer, who is keeping their accounts.

The Reserve Bank permitted the banks to invest in the scrips in the stock market up to 5% of their incremental deposits. This ceiling of 5% includes also any loans to stock brokers against shares and debentures and advances to individuals against such securities approved by banks. Banks are encouraged to lend liberally to market depending on the assessment of their creditworthiness. An additional limit of 5% of the bank's incremental deposits was given to them to enable them to make investments directly in corporate bonds and securities including those of PSUs. Any loans given to a company in anticipation of its raising resources through public issue and to meet the promoters' contribution will be covered under the above 5% investment ceiling granted to banks in April 1997. All these measures of both RBI and SEBI were aimed at boosting the sagging market sentiment particularly in the primary segment of capital market, during 1995 to 2001.

The I.P.O. through book building is being encouraged. The minimum public offer of 25% of the total offer was reduced to 10% in the case od I.T., Telecommunications, Multi-media, etc., for purposes of listing, provided they are profit earning over the last three years. For the measures of reform in further detail, reference may be made to chapter 28 also, on SEBI guidelines. These reforms, guidelines and modifications are on a continuing basis and one has to keep update only through daily financial press.

✠ ✠ ✠

OTCEI AND NSE

36

Securities Exchanges

A well-developed securities market ensures easy and quick marketability to the securities which imparts liquidity to them. If this objective of liquidity is to be ensured, all the securities, good or bad, have to have a market for trading and dealings. This market can be fostered and developed by proper marketing strategies and provision of infrastructure for the purpose. One such strategy is to have a multi-tier market to suit the various types of securities.

The companies may be in various stages of growth, young and newborn, growing, mature and decaying, etc. All cannot have equal status in terms of liquidity, safety, marketability, etc. Similarly, all cannot satisfy the same standards of performance in terms of return, risk, service to investors, etc. So, in order to meet the objectives of the market, and to meet the varying types of companies, there is a method of differentiation of the market segments by creating some tiers of exchanges with varying requirements of standards. These meet the different characteristics of the companies and at the same time, ensure product differentiation for investors to have more than one method of trading and investment. It is with these motives that a multi-tier structure of exchanges is established and promoted by many countries.

Structured Markets

In many developed countries as in the USA, there is a well-structured market for securities. There, the secondary market trading in securities can be classified as under:

First Market: Trading on the floor of the exchange of the listed companies.

Second Market: Trading over the counter for OTC issues.

Third Market: Trading outside the Exchange floor of listed securities of the exchange with the aid of brokers.

Fourth Market: Trading of the listed securities of the exchange off the floor without the aid of brokers as between buyers and sellers.

The OTC market as seen above is one such tier of the structure and generally comprises:

(1) Inactive issues and less liquid shares, not eligible for listing in the regular exchange.

(2) Thinner issues with limited public holding but command some national trading interests.

(3) Actively-traded issues listed on the OTC.

OTC Defined

Over-the-counter Market is a market where buyers seek out sellers and *vice versa* and then attempt to arrange terms and conditions for purchase/sale acceptable to both parties. It is a negotiated marketplace that exists anywhere as opposed to the auction marketplace, represented by activity on the Securities Exchanges.

Thus, in the OTC, trading takes place by putting buy and sell orders by telephone, telex, letter, oral message, etc. There is no particular marketplace in the geographical sense.

The OTC relates to a type of security trading in which the market caters to some basic objectives, like:

(*a*) quicker liquidity;

(*b*) fixed and fair price;

(*c*) liquidity for a less traded security or that of smaller company;

(*d*) simplified process of buying and selling;

(*e*) creation of public interest in risky but viable ventures; and

(*f*) easy and cheaper means of making public sale of new issues.

Investor Interests

As companies differ in their size and performance, there is need for different tiers for their listing. Besides, there is another reason why a well-structured market is necessary for future growth of the capital market in India. The uninitiated individual investors are at present left to the mercy of the professional traders and big bulls and bears on the regular exchanges. These individual investors have different investment profiles of risk-return combinations and other perceptions of income, safety and liquidity which are completely different from the professional investors, institutional investors, mutual funds, financial institutions, etc. For such category, a different and simpler type of market is needed, which the OTC provides. The rules of fair practice, charging fair and reasonable prices in relation to market conditions, a maximum mark-up policy of, say, 5% as in the NASDAQ are some examples of standardisation of rules and regulations, which will protect the uninitiated investors from being cheated by brokers, players, etc., in the market. Such rules are also adopted in India. In the USA, for example, the bye-laws and rules imposed by SEC on their OTC, namely, NASDAQ, will protect the investors and they have also a right to complain about any unethical practices of members with respect to prices or margins, etc. These rules are of four distinct categories in the USA:

(*a*) Uniform practice code in their dealings among the member firms.

(*b*) Code of procedure for violations of these rules and dealing with complaints.

(*c*) Rules of fair practice, specifying the rules governing the members *vis-a-vis* the investing public.

(*d*) Code of Arbitration laid down the procedure for arbitration of disputes between brokers and investing members of the public.

Practices Abroad

In OTC, the broker can act as an agent or principal. He acts as agent when he puts through the transaction with a market-maker or some other broker. He then charges a commission. But if he acts as a principal, he is a market maker himself, quotes both bid and offer rates and executes the order at his quoted price but does not charge commission as his profit lies in the spread between bid and ask prices. Dealing with the market-makers helps the investors save on the commission paid to the agent broker and to be assured that he is charged a fair price as the market maker is supposed to know the position of the company and its performance to fix a fair price.

Although there is no trading place and no apparent visibility of the bargaining process as in the trading ring of the exchanges, the OTC rules would impose strict norms of fair margins and competitive bidding by the market makers. As trading is computer based there is transparency of all deals and prices. Besides, to check on the brokers' quotations, the investor can enquire with the market makers for the bid and offer rates for any scrip.

OTC and New Issues Market

As per the practices in the USA, OTC dealers can operate both in the primary and secondary markets, while on the stock exchange, market-makers or specialists can only operate in the secondary market. Besides, the OTC market keeps its doors open to all types of new issues, namely, those that are not eligible to be listed on the regular stock exchanges, and those that are eligible. The advantage of being on the OTC is the lower cost of raising new issues, the lower expenses of servicing and maintaining the existing investors in its registers, etc.

The cost of raising fresh issues has to be kept low, so that new entrepreneurs and fresh entrants into the market can raise funds at lower rates than the existing ones as well as the bigger companies. The loading to share prices that the speculative elements will lead to may overburden the regular and the smaller investors. Correct pricing of shares, keeping the cost of trading and of raising of new issues to the minimum are some of the objectives of the OTC.

OTC and Stock Exchange

Besides introducing structural changes, the OTC can correct some of the drawbacks of the existing market mechanism on the stock exchanges like illiquidity of a number of scrips, speculative manoeuvring, rigged-up prices, delays in the realisation of the proceeds of sale or delivery of scrips and high volatility of prices, etc., referred to below. The major problem so far as the public is concerned is that this should help new and small investors to come into the corporate folders and, for the companies to raise the necessary capital at the lowest possible cost. Besides, the share valuation defy any laws or reasons. In the case of new issues of new companies, there is no acceptable method of valuation. There are also innumerable difficulties in the valuation of even the existing shares. Only highly qualified experts among the merchant bankers can provide a guide for correct valuation. Regular stock exchanges may or may not reflect the correct values.

Advantages of OTC

Briefly, specific advantages of OTC as it operates abroad can be set out as follows:

(1) Advantages to smaller companies and less liquid companies to be listed as they are not eligible for listing on the regular exchange.

(2) Lower costs of new issues and lower expenses of servicing the investors.

(3) Family concerns and companies closely held can go public through OTC.

(4) Competition as between the dealers exists better than on the regular stock exchange and the larger the number of dealers, the better is the market.

(5) Dealers can operate both in new issues and secondary markets at their option.

(6) Greater freedom to choose stocks by dealers for market making in both the primary and secondary markets.

(7) Information flows are freer and more direct from market makers to customers due to close contacts between firms and market makers.

(8) Regulatory measures are adopted and a strict code of conduct exists for members.

Structural Weaknesses in India

In India, there are many structural weaknesses in the securities market. To start with, there is a mushroom growth of companies without proper assessment of their viability, with the result that the number of listed companies grew to more than 9,000 at one time, of which hardly 300 to 600 companies are well-traded. In nearly 90% of the companies, there is no liquidity as the market is not developed in them. In a study made by Shri Paul Joseph on thinly-traded shares, it was shown that leaving aside a large number of shares in which there is either no trading or there is no information on their trading, nearly two-thirds of the companies for which information is available are not traded well in the sense that they are traded only for less than 50% of trading days. Nearly, one-half of these companies are traded only in less than 10% of the trading days. This clearly brings out the woeful lack of liquidity, despite the common belief that the stock exchanges provide liquidity to investors. (Thesis of Shri Paul Joseph submitted to the University of Hull, U.K., 1990).

Secondly, there are large number of small companies which are closely held and in which public holding is small and hence no market exists for them. The study of Shri Paul Joseph has also shown that nearly 75% of the inadequately traded companies have a paid-up capital less than ₹3 core and their public holding is poor. Nearly 80% of the thinly-traded companies have public holding of less than 60% of the paid-up equity. In the bulk of these companies, there are less than 10,000 shareholders on their registers which can hardly lead to any public interest. In most of such companies, the holding of promoters and financial institutions is so heavy that no public interest exists and trading cannot take place. Thus the main factors which explain the lack of proper trading are the size of equity paid-up and the share of public holdings. For such companies, OTC can be expected to provide a market through an open sale to public. In 1996, there are 1,204 companies, which have paid-up capital of less than ₹3 crore on the B.S.E.

Thirdly, there is inadequate supply of good scrips leading to supply and demand imbalances in them for many reasons. This is mainly due to the fact that financial institutions are holding large chunks of these scrips which they do not part with. They have become major investors rather than mere financiers which may really be objectionable from the point of view of making the issues widely held by the public. Besides, managements in India are jealously guarding themselves against possible takeovers, outside interference and threat to their family interests. They generally do not part with their shares due to the fear of possible management interference or takeover which can be mitigated only by the OTC.

Fourthly, the existing market mechanism does not permit the public to know the correct share values both in the primary and secondary markets due to manipulation of premium in the new issues market and rigging and speculation in the secondary market. The free market forces do not operate and the control of SEBI and the stock exchanges is inadequate. The correct share pricing can be ensured by market makers in the OTC if they are guided and regulated properly.

Fifthly, there is a major complaint of neglect of genuine investors, small and less educated investors and rural and semi-urban public. These categories do not have enough knowledge of the market operations and are cheated by the so-called sub-brokers. To begin with, the prices they pay may not be fair prices as they are manipulated by speculative forces and the knowledge of fair prices is not spread and understood by the investors. Besides, they are overcharged due to brokerages and commissions, etc. They are misguided by the investment magazines, companies, brokers and sub-brokers about the prospects of the companies. The problems of these investors are manifold and they are growing both in the new issues market and secondary market. These problems can be reduced to some extent if the OTC can operate in a way that fair prices are fixed and advertised by the market makers and the cult of investment through OTC is spread to rural and semi-urban areas and to less educated investors. Of course, the small investors can also be served better if mutual funds become popular with them.

Sixthly, delivery of shares to buyers and payment of money to sellers is at present taking an unduly long time on the major stock exchanges. Many investors have suffered due to the funds being tied up in application money in new issues and in the sale of shares on the stock exchanges. Sometimes, funds could not be realised for more than three to six months. Similarly, companies do not send the shares or allotment letters for long periods of time with the result that shares could not be sold and money realised. There are innumerable such complaints by the public against companies and brokers. Many of these problems can be reduced if trading is shifted to OTC, where the methods of operations are such that the scope for manipulation, speculation and malpractices is less. The time gap in many of these operations would also be less and liquidity requirements can be met quickly and easily. There are also infrastructural deficiencies, lack of transparency, and market discipline and inadequate institutional structure, architectural gaps and imperfections in free flow of informations, etc.

Yet another problem is price volatility of shares on the regular stock exchanges. The daily fluctuations of prices are sometimes so wide that genuine investors suffer, if they are not wary. The speculative pressures are responsible for these wide fluctuations and it is reported that jobbers' spread is also wide in many scrips. These problems lead to some complaints from genuine investors who are not interested in speculative gains. Their calculations may go wrong and price changes as between the placing of order and its execution may lead to an adverse position to the parties. Such problems may not exist in the OTC, where buying and selling of shares is like shopping in a departmental store with fixed fair price tags.

Role of OTC

In the above context of prevailing structural weaknesses in the securities markets in India and the malpractices rampant in both the primary and secondary markets, drastic reforms are long overdue. Firstly, there is urgent need for legislative reforms by amendments to existing laws, and consolidating into one Act, whereby the legal loopholes can be plugged and corporate behaviour can be improved. Many malpractices and defaults of companies can be corrected by penal powers given to the SEBI.

Secondly, control and supervision of the activities of the merchant bankers, advisers, investment consultants, etc., are necessary to reduce the malpractices and improve the climate of new issues market. The SEBI has initiated steps in this direction and laid down guidelines for merchant bankers, and other intermediaries.

Thirdly, certain malpractices adopted by the Registrars to new issues, banks, companies, etc., involved in allotment of new issues to the public, despatch of refund orders, share allotment letters, etc., have all been brought under the net of penal provisions for protecting the interests of investors and public.

Fourthly, as the major culprits in primary and secondary markets are the companies themselves, the provisions relating to the new issues, transfer of shares, issue of dividend warrants and services to investors in all forms should be brought into the ambit of heavy penalties imposed on companies for all investor complaints. The motto that the investor is the king has to be enshrined in the legislative framework of the Companies Act, Securities Contracts (Regulation) Act and the SEBI Act. Some of the measures of SEBI aimed at controlling the above malpractices.

So far as the secondary market is concerned, a multi-tier exchange system for trading as in New York and London, has to be developed in India. A beginning in this direction is made through the OTC Exchange of India. Secondly, a large number of companies in which there was no trading and which were only listed on the stock exchanges for the purpose of quotation and for the tax benefits should be delisted if there is no public interest in such companies. Another exchange can thus be permitted for trading in the delisted companies and if the companies are really interested in promoting public interest, trading will take place in such an exchange for those companies which are viable.

Companies with a capital base of not less than ₹5 crore of paid-up equity and a public issue of ₹1.25 crore can be listed on the regular stock exchanges since October 1995. Such companies should have a track record of two years after commercial production was started which has since been amended in 1996. The type of companies not eligible to be listed on the regular exchange now enter the OTC Exchange.

There are two other categories of companies which deserve special attention in India, namely, sick companies and the public sector companies, which the government would like to privatise. In respect of these two categories, acquisition and takeovers can be encouraged and/or a slow process of public participation in their issues can be promoted. The public sector companies, which require revitalisation to improve efficiency, may be shifted to the joint sector with a gradual increase in participation by the private sector. The shares allotted to the public in this respect can also be traded in the stock exchange whereby their performance can be assessed from time to time.

In India, more recently public sector financial institutions have set up venture capital funds for promoting risky enterprises by the new entrepreneurs. The promotion of these companies and their popularisation with the public should be their responsibility. The OTC can take care of them, so that these venture capital greenfield companies can have a better future in the Indian markets. The financial institutions which have set up the OTC Exchange may also think of a separate counter for sale of shares of existing companies, which are good in their track record and whose shares are in demand with the public. Normally, institutions do not sell their holdings to individuals as they deal in large volumes but only acquire from the public and individuals. Thus, there is a great imbalance in supply and demand for the blue chip companies and debentures of good companies with triple "A" rating are not easily available. This institutional counter should buy and sell at fair prices rather than at the market prices, as the latter include a large component of speculative burden loaded to the fair price to the great disadvantage of the small investors, retired persons, widows, etc.

There are many such potential reforms possible in the Indian capital market. The OTC Exchange of India is perhaps the most important reform which can take over trading in a number of companies under the above categories but it should be admitted that OTC is only a beginning of the reforms in the direction of multi-tier structure of exchanges in India. The advantages of the OTC referred to above can be realised depending upon the role that it assumes in future.

Over-the-counter Exchange of India (OTCEI)

Although the Indian stock exchanges had a hoary antiquity and history of more than 100 years, they are still in their adolescent stage. The markets suffer from many weaknesses, despite diverse regulatory and reformatory measures taken by the government. This is because these measures were half-hearted and *ad hoc,* and in response to emerging situations and conditions.

Despite a large number of companies of more than 9,000 listed on these markets, hardly 20-30% of these enjoy any worthwhile liquidity and marketability. In fact, deliveries are hardly 20-25% of the total trade turnover.

Secondly, the stock exchanges have no effective powers to control the malpractices of companies listed despite the enabling provisions laid down in the Listing Agreements as these cannot be enforced by them in the absence of penal powers.

Thirdly, the supply of shares of good companies is limited due to a large component of them being concentrated with the financial institutions and mutual funds. The public holding of many of these companies is limited to 20-30% of their total paid-up capital on an average.

Fourthly, even when there is liquidity and marketability of shares, the time taken to realise cash from sales is unduly long, ranging from two to three months, due to settlement and clearance procedures of the exchanges. Lastly, the cost of raising funds through new issues has increased sharply and many small companies find it difficult to raise funds under these conditions. Besides, there are many malpractices both in the new issues market and the secondary market, in the form of delay of refund and allotment orders, rigging up of prices before listing, delay in effecting transfer of shares of more than 2 to 3 months and insider trading, overcharging and other malpractices in the secondary market. Besides, excessive speculative activity has marred the prospects of correct valuation of shares with the result that the real investors suffer and some are duped by manipulators in both new issues and secondary markets. The market being single tier, there is no effective competition.

In this type of monolithic structure of the securities market, there is a great need for reforms. A properly-tiered structure with companies of various sizes of paid-up capital and liquidity is to be developed in India. A market of multi-tier structure exists in many developed countries, as over-the-counter market, cash counter, 24-hour trading, options, futures trading and trading in index derivatives, etc.

In India, an attempt has just been made in the direction of developing a multi-tier market with the opening of the OTC Exchange of India.

Objectives of OTCEI

The formal approval of the government for the setting up of the over-the-counter Exchange of India was granted in August 1989 under the Securities Contracts (Regulation) Act, 1956, but the actual operations started only in October 1992. It was an event of far-reaching consequence for the Indian capital market as it introduced another tier to the structure of the securities market. It provides a less expensive method of getting shares listed for trading and for raising capital from the market. The OTC market will initially prove a boon to the small investors as it provides easier liquidity and quicker transactions and ultimately help in the formation of "national market".

Shares could be bought and sold over the counters with licensed dealers and across the country. Initially, the OTC market will permit trading in the shares of "greenfield companies" nurtured by the mutual funds and venture capital funds. But eventually, the OTC market will create a market place for all tradeable securities listed as well as convertible and non-convertible debentures. The objective is to impart liquidity to every existing instrument and more particularly to those for which small investors are unable to get a fair price. The OTC market has covered many places where there are stock exchanges initially after experimenting in Mumbai and later on extend its ambit to the remote areas as well. The investor is protected against manipulation by brokers and companies and has a better chance of security as no speculative effect or rigging is possible in the market.

The small investors invariably complain of lack of reliable advice due to manipulated market information and too much delay in transaction and harassment. They have no easy method of finding out fair prices. These investors are taken for a ride by unscrupulous promoters of new companies who present a rosy picture of their non-starting projects, obtain huge subscriptions from gullible investors and then vanish from the scene or divert the funds to other purposes. The OTC market will protect small investors from the malpractices of brokers as well as promoters by quoting reasonable prices as judged by the fundamentals and at competitive spread. Investment and disinvestment are made easier and quicker and better liquidity is provided.

Establishment of OTC

The OTC Exchange was promoted jointly by the Industrial Credit and Investment Corpn. of India (ICICI), the Unit Trust of India (UTI), IFCI, IDBI, SBI Capital Markets Ltd., Canbank Financial Services Ltd., the General Insurance Corpn. (GIC) and the Life Insurance Corpn. (LIC). To start with, it was set up with a paid-up capital of ₹5 crore in Oct. 1990. The above institutions are the sponsor members of the OTC Exchange, and their main responsibility is to sponsor the assisted companies' shares in the market. In other words, any company which wants to list its shares on the OTC Exchange will have to be sponsored by an OTC member. The sponsors will have also to perform the market making function, apart from appointing a second market-maker and licensed dealers.

Market makers are like jobbers, who offer over the telephone two-way quotes everyday for the securities of these companies. The bid and offer prices depend on the value that the market places on the scrip and may even be below par. The appointment of market makers and dealers, supervision of their work and disciplinary action, if needed, are the responsibilities of the OTC Exchange Board.

Listing on OTCEI

Any company, new or existing, intending to sell its securities through the OTC market, must offer at least ₹20 lakh to the public and have a paid-up capital of atleast ₹30 lakh. Even in the case of a new company, the sponsors offer securities to the public which are privately placed with them by the company. The companies save in issue expenses as the OTC will negotiate the issue price and make placement of these shares. It provides a method of raising funds in the market and does not interfere with the management stability. The companies which would list in this exchange are small companies with a paid-up capital of less than ₹3 crore, but with ₹30 lakh or more, closely-held companies going public and venture capital funds. Companies listed already on a stock exchange have also been listed on the OTC. Companies with paid-up capital of more than ₹3 crore, but less than ₹25 crore can get listed on OTC if they are not listed on regular stock exchange.

Investors Benefitted

Although the basic framework of the OTC Exchange is that of a national market, yet there is no physical location, no counters, no trading ring, no stock exchange building and no hustle and bustle scenes as at the conventional stock exchanges. The buyers and sellers living apart from each other trade in corporate securities over the telephone and the computer network. The system cuts across urban and rural areas, extending the frontiers of the stock market to the entire country. The market maker who may be the sponsor initiates trading by quoting two-way prices (bid and offer rates) for the security for which he wants to create a market. The other important person involved is the "licensed dealer" who has been licensed to trade in securities by the OTC Exchange Board. The deals in securities are negotiated through telephone or in person at convenient locations. The licensed dealers can buy and sell at prices exhibited by market makers through the electronic network or telephones. They in turn quote their prices to the public for investment and disinvestment.

The role of the OTC market envisaged in India is similar to that in the US, UK and Japan. These OTC markets are fully automated exchanges where transactions are completed through a network of telephones/tellers/computers right from the first centre to the last centre. In addition, only professional people are authorised to render financial services. In India too, these infrastructural facilities and professional services are being used for the success of the OTC market. It is necessary to ensure a dependable and efficient telecommunication system and information network to provide accurate online data and prices for this type of trading. Greenfield companies and venture capital activities will get a boost by the OTC. Besides, the private limited companies and closely-held companies can be helped to go public and raise capital from the capital market.

Market Players

These market players are set out in the accompanying chart 36.1. The members are sponsors who buy wholesale and make the market through a network of licensed dealers. The final buyers and sellers are investors dealing in retail. The other players are the companies whose shares are listed, custodians and registrars for the company's shares. The OTC provides facilities for purchase on the spot by payment of cash/cheque or selling with an arrangement for payment within, say, six days or less. The transfer of shares from one name to another can be done by the OTC members without reference to the company up to a limit. In fact, shares can be replaced by counter receipts issued by the market makers/sponsors. Ringless trading and transactions at any place are possible in this system.

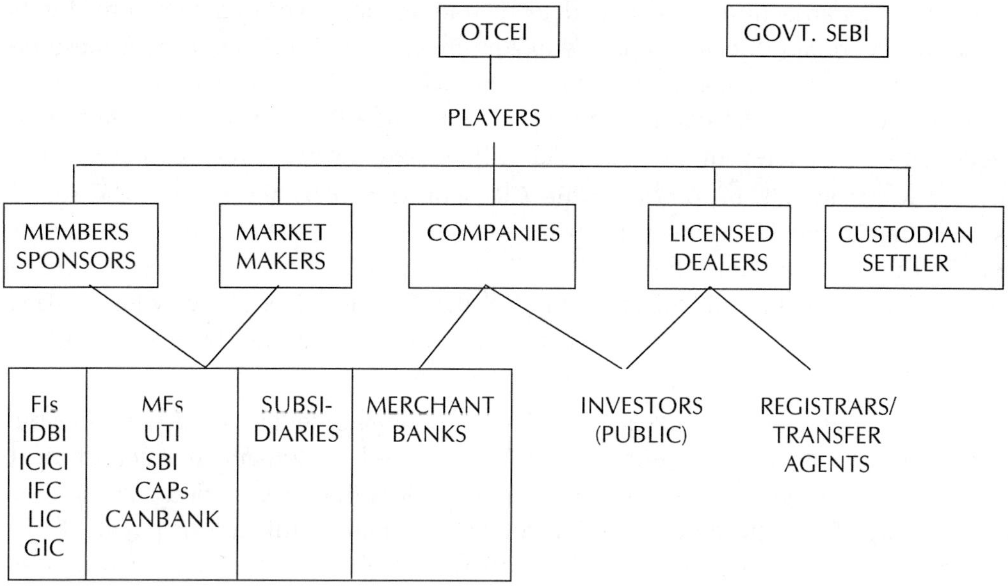

Chart 36.1

Listing Procedure

The company to be listed should appoint a member of OTCEI as its sponsor, who appraises the project as to its viability and underwrites and arranges for the public issue after fixing its price.

The proposals have to be approved by the SEBI before public issues, in addition to the other formalities to be observed by the company under the Companies Act. The sponsor would certify to OTCEI as to the fairness of price, full and fair allotment of all shares to the public and guarantee to its full subscription and make market until it is listed and cannot withdraw during the first three years of market making. An additional market maker may be arranged by the sponsor, if necessary or required by the company. These requirements of compulsory market making were relaxed during 1996.

The sponsor has to arrange for appointment to transfer agents and to effect share transfers within 15-18 days. The actual counter receipts would serve as share certificates which along with the transfer deed will be presented to the transfer agents for transfer. These counter receipts will be issued by dealers on the basis of the deal that they had reported to OTCEI. The standard share price is ₹10/- and traded in minimum lots of 100 or its multiples. The investor has also to register with OTCEI before he does any business with the dealer.

The OTCEI will have to approve the draft prospectus and other agreements of the company in addition to the SEBI's approval. The letter of offer and listing formalities are to be observed before a listing agreement is actually entered into with the company.

There are about 108 companies listed on OTCEI in 1997, as against 49 at end March 1995. The growth of OTCEI after 1997 was inhibitied due to fall of interest of investors in this exchange for lack of speculative gains. There are also permitted securities traded on OTCEI. The listing has undergone further changes after Dave Committee Report referred to later.

Trading on the OTCEI

All other rules and regulations of the OTCEI will apply and requirements of the Companies Act and SEBI Act have to be fulfilled, before listing and trading. After initial public offer (IPO), OTC counter receipts (CR) are issued to the investor. This CR will have 3 copies — one for investor, one for the counter and one for the custodian and settler. The CR will give the details of the company, name of the settler, price and brokerage, total value of transaction, time and date of transaction, investor's signature, his bank A/c No., and unique transaction code and dealer's code, etc. Any investor in OTC has to give these details in a pro forma to the dealer. In case of transfer, Application Acknowledgement Slip (AAS) is also generated in three copies and investor also gives to the counter the stamped and attested transfer deed. At the end of the day, all transfer deeds along with relevant CR and AAS will be sent to the settler or custodian.

If the investor wants to sell, he produces the CR, sent to him by the settler. The seller signs on the TD and hands over the CR and TD to the counter for sale. After the sale, the counter gives sale confirmation slip (SCS) to the investor. Three copies of the SCS will be prepared — one for investor, one for the counter and one for the custodian. At the end of each day, all the CRs and SCs along with the TDs will be sent to the custodian. Each counter will report by telex all CRs and SCs, issued by it to the OTCEI along with a consolidated statement showing company-wise transactions.

The counter will send to the Registrar the TDs filled by the seller along with the buyer's CR and signature of the transferee, if the share transfer is to be effected. Automatic transfer to the buyer's name will take place within seven days, if the transactions involve less than a specified size of holding say 0.5% of the company's equity. Thus, the time taken for delivery of share certificate or payment of sale proceeds will not take more than 10-15 days. There will be no speculative manipulation of prices and investor is protected from these malpractices on the OTCEI. There are about 46 centres all over the country where this exchange operates.

It will be seen from the above that the setting up of the OTC in India is the first step in the right direction. It will be the beginning of a multi-tiered structure for the securities market in India. It will mitigate some of the evils and malpractices of both the primary and secondary markets. It can reduce if not eliminate some of the investor complaints. It can hopefully promote a wider base of investor interest in the countryside and a healthier capital market in future. The raising of resources from the capital market, particularly by small entrepreneurs and venture enterprises, will be made easier and cheaper. The OTC has thus an important role to play in India for the future of the capital market.

Dave Committee

During the last few years, since 1995 however, both the listed companies and the volume of trade did not show the expected growth. In fact, daily volumes declined significantly to less than ₹5 crore sometimes during the depressed phase of the market namely, 1995 and 1996. This led to the appointment of a committee headed by S. A. Dave which reported in October 1996. The terms of the committee include suggestion of measures to revive the OTCEI and make it viable and lively. The report made wide ranging recommendations, the more important of which were set out below.

The Dave Committee (1996) recommended enlargement of the settlement cycle from T + 3 to T + 5, weekly settlement of trade in permitted securities as on regular exchange and removal of ceiling on companies' paid up capital for listing on OTCEI and relaxation of norms of listing, so as to allow all companies not eligible to be listed on regular exchanges to seek listing on the OTCEI. The promoter FIs should be permitted to build up inventory over a period of the sponsored company's stock. The floor of 5% or paid-up capital to be held by market maker should be reduced on a graded basis of 1 to 5% depending on the paid-up capital of the company. Trading in the unlisted companies like NASDAQ in the U.S.A. are recommended to be permitted. Futures, options and forward contracts should also be allowed on OTCEI, as on regular exchanges. These recommendations are being implemented.

A Critique of Listing as a Service

The law and the guidelines of government regarding listing were set out here. The more recent changes and a critique of these reforms are set out in the following paras:

The minimum paid-up capital for listing on the National Stock Exchange was fixed at ₹10 crore and above. Following this the bigger stock exchanges like BSE and DSE have also raised the limit to ₹10 crore from the existing limit of ₹5 crore. Companies with paid-up capital of ₹3 crore to ₹5 crore are now listed on the regional stock exchanges like Cochin, Chennai, Bangalore, Coimbatore, Hyderabad, etc., whereas companies with paid-up capital of less than ₹3 crore and more than ₹30 lakh can now be listed on the OTCEI. At present, OTCEI is listing companies with paid-up capital up to ₹25 crore provided it is satisfied about the other requirements of OTCEI, namely, the sponsoring by a member and their compulsory market making by at least two market makers with a stake of 5% of equity issued by the company.

OTCEI and Dave Committee

As referred to earlier, the Committee headed by Dr. S.A. Dave went into all aspects of the working of OTCEI and has made certain recommendations relating to listing, among others. As per the present SEBI guidelines, public offers can be made for purposes of listing on stock exchanges by companies above a minimum of two years of commercial production for new companies, and with a dividend record of 3 years out of the last preceding five years or which have been appraised and funded by the financial institutions up to 10% of the project cost. Dave Committee has recommended that those that do satisfy the above requirements and whose post-issue paid-up capital is less than ₹10 crore and hence not to eligible for listing on the major stock exchanges should be reserved for listing on the OTCEI, provided they satisfy the other listing requirements of this exchange. It appears SEBI and the government have not accepted this as it will affect the interests of smaller stock exchanges. The Committee also recommended that the SEBI should remove the upper limit of ₹25 crore for listing on OTCEI and allow all companies irrespective of the size of the paid-up capital of the company. Besides, all companies which did not satisfy the minimum shareholding criteria for being eligible for listing on the regular stock exchange are recommended to be listed on the OTCEI. The companies making an offer of sale and not a public offer, and offering a Boughtout Deal (BOD) without fulfilling the 3-year dividend paying record or the criteria of appraisal and funding by the financial institutions, should be allowed to be listed on the OTCEI, as made out by this Committee. Besides, trading in unlisted companies and listing of companies delisted from the regular stock exchanges being ineligible for trading there, have also been commended for OTCEI trading.

The provisions for market making which is precondition for listing on OTCEI are also recommended to be modified by the Dave Committee. The companies with a paid-up capital upto ₹10 crore only should attract market making of a mandatory type but on a graded basis as shown below:

- With capitalisation up to ₹5 crore — an initial market-making inventory of 5% is compulsory.
- With capitalisation between ₹5 to 10 crore — an initial market making inventory of 2% only is compulsory.
- Companies with capitalisation above ₹0 crore — only 1% of paid-up capital as initial market making inventory to be compulsorily held.

Broadly, Dave Committee recommended many methods of broad-basing the trade on OTCEI by relaxation in listing requirements, namely, removal of upper limit norms for market makers and trading in unlisted securities like that on NASDAQ in USA, etc. The companies delisted on regular stock exchanges for reasons of not satisfying the recent SEBI guidelines for continuing listing, such as a minimum of 5 shareholders for ₹1 lakh of paid-up equity should also be eligible for listing on the OTCEI, as recommended by the Committee.

Route of Permitted Securities

Securities which are not listed on any one exchange can be permitted by that exchange authorities to be traded on that exchange, if they are listed on any other stock exchange in India. This provision is great facility to investors and is being used by many exchanges. In fact, trading volumes in permitted securities is larger on smaller exchanges, than on listed securities. The Dave Committee has recommended that SEBI should allow the OTCEI a free hand to increase the number of companies under the permitted list category to include both equities and debentures, as they think proper. Besides, in respect of these permitted securities, there should be a uniform settlement period and weekly netting of trades, on the OTCEI as in other exchanges. In fact, inter-market trades can be settled better, if all the markets have a uniform settlement period of T+5 or T+3 and a national clearing system for inter-market deals including those on OTCEI.

Defeating the Objectives of Listing

The basic objective of listing is to provide continuous liquidity for buyers/sellers, greater transparency to deals and ensure a fair method of trading with free and unfettered competitive forces. Are the stock exchanges able to safeguard the interests of genuine investors with the above objectives? Instead of giving a direct answer to it, one can give a host of examples. Of 5,700 listed companies on BSE, 600 companies are having a paid-up capital of less than ₹1 crore and nearly half of them are not traded at all (58% in the case of BSE as admitted by its president). The companies which are regularly traded on a daily basis are estimated at less than 2000 companies, which is less than 50% of the total listed companies. The system of continuous liquidity for all listed companies is not provided by the stock exchanges. Besides, transparency in deals are only ensured in OTCEI and NSE electronic trading and in BSE Online Trading, but these are confined mostly to institutional investors, foreign financial institutions and corporates. The fair auction type of trading without manipulation and rigging of prices is also of limited application. With only 20% or 25% of shares in the hands of the public, wide shareholding pattern is not possible and promoters and institutions holding the majority stake are able to manipulate the prices as they want. This has defeated the very purpose of listing to serve investor interest. The SEBI guidelines of minimum number of shareholders and minimum paid-up capital for listing are also many times violated by the mergers and acquisitions. The Malegam Committee has recognised the possible misuse of merger route for listing of an unlisted company, which is not otherwise eligible for listing. The merged companies have not ensured that 25% of the enlarged paid-up capital is held by the public and that there are a minimum number of 5 shareholders for every ₹1 lakh of paid-up equity. Besides, even this 25% of the issue to the public is inadequate in the case of good companies. The government has also become a party to defeat the very purposes of listing. The government has allowed big PSU shares to be listed, even if the public do not hold 25% of the shareholding. Even their offer to the public is not direct, but through bids from the Mutual Funds and financial institutions. Many investors have burnt their fingers by buying these divested shares at exorbitantly overvalued prices and hefty premiums. This problem of fixing high premiums, based on the criteria approved by SEBI itself, has resulted in considerable hardship and losses to investors after listing in the market. It is understood that, out of 2,601 new issued listed between January 1, 1994 and July 12, 1996, 2,505 issues have suffered erosion in values after listing. The objective of ensuring fairplay to investors has again failed in this present system of listing with any prices fixed by merchant bankers and companies jointly although they were apparently justified as per SEBI's existing criteria. Investor protection in this regard can be ensured only by provision of buyback arrangement of a safety net, if the market price falls below the issue price by 10%. Another area of investor concern is the increasing proportion of finance and investment companies offering new issues, sometimes at heavy premiums. Many of these companies, registered with RBI as the NBFCs, satisfy the listing criteria with the paid-up capital of more than ₹5 crore. They were found to manipulate the subscriptions for securing listing and raising public funds. They have failed to satisfy the investors due to lack of capital appreciation, because of fluctuating fortunes of the stock and money markets on which their profits depended, although at the time of listing, they have shown a track record of profitability and three years of dividend-record. Even Dave Committee had admitted that SEBI was unable to scrutinise each individual case separately about the companies violating the shareholding distribution pattern and criteria for continuing the listing on the stock exchanges.

The amendments recently introduced in listing agreements have also failed to be enforced in many cases. Thus, the requirement of supply of unabridged balance sheets to investors was observed more in breach by many companies. Similarly, the requirement of quick disposal of transfers through attestation of the signature by registered member brokers to avoid bad delivery has failed to be effective, and in many cases, they are not implemented at all by the registrars and companies. Many such defaults have led to increasing investor complaints and disillusion.

Weaknesses of OTCEI

Despite the reforms of the OTCEI, it has not attracted trading investors, due to lack of speculative element and capital appreciation. It is found that majority of investors want capital to be appreciated if invested in listed securities. Besides the method of listing and trading involving market making did not attract many brokers and sub-brokers into this market. Although some of the recommendations of Dave Committee were implemented and the permitted securities to be traded on the OTC were expanded, the OTCEI did not attract investors and the companies to any significant extent. The NSE has emerged as the leading Stock Exchange in India in the new millennium, both in the daily volume of trade and in the development of the wholesale debt segment traded.

The Annexure sets out the guidelines of the government and the SEBI on the OTCEI as originally issued.

ANNEXURE

Government Guidelines on OTCEI

It has been decided by the government that the issue of securities by companies and their listing on the OTCEI will be governed by the following guidelines:

(*i*) the minimum issued equity share capital of a company for eligibility for listing on the OTCEI will be ₹ 30 lakhs, subject to a minimum public offer of equity shares worth ₹ 20 lakh in face value;

(*ii*) for companies with an issued equity capital of more than ₹ 300 lakh, the minimum public offer should be 40% of the issued capital or ₹ 20 lakh worth of shares in face value, whichever is higher, in relaxation of Rule 19(2) (b) of the Securities Contracts (Regulation) Rules, 1957;

(*iii*) companies with an issued equity capital of more than ₹ 300 lakh seeking listing on the OTCEI will have to comply with the listing requirements and guidelines as are applicable to such companies for enlistment on other recognised stock exchanges;

(*iv*) companies covered under the MRTP Act/FERA may be listed on the OTCEI only if they satisfy the guidelines for listing on other recognised stock exchange, such as minimum issued equity capital of ₹ 500 lakh or such other limit as may be prescribed from time to time;

(*v*) a company with an issued equity share capital of more than ₹ 25 crore will not be eligible for listing on the OTCEI;

(*vi*) companies which are engaged in investments, leasing, finance, hire-purchase, amusement parks, etc., shall not be eligible for listing on the OTCEI; these are now permitted to be listed on OTCEI since March 1995;

(*vii*) a company which is listed on any other recognised stock exchange in India would not simultaneously be eligible for listing on the OTCEI; they are now allowed as permitted securities.

(*viii*) the minimum number of centres for collection of application forms in respect of issue of securities by companies under the OTCEI shall be four, one each from the Northern, Western, Southern and Eastern regions of the country. However, OTCEI shall have power to increase the number for the issue of securities made by a company;

(*ix*) whenever securities are issued to the public, the price will be determined by the merchant banker in consultation with the company;

(*x*) company shall not issue securities at par in case the securities are eligible to be issued at a premium.

The OTCEI shall make it clear to the companies, their shareholders and investors that tax concessions, if any, in respect of companies listed on it and investments in their shares will be as per the tax laws and/or the decisions of the Department of Revenue, Ministry of Finance. It is also clarified that the functioning and operations of the OTCEI shall be subject to the provisions of the Securities Contracts (Regulation) Act, 1956, the Companies Act, 1956 and other relevant laws which are applicable to the corporate sector and the investors.

Issue of Shares through OTC — SEBI Guidelines

Where a direct public issue is made through OTC without the sponsor taking any shares, the normal guidelines for disclosure and investor protection shall apply.

Where the shares of a company has been taken by the sponsor, such shares may be offered to the public at a later date at such price as the sponsor may deem fit in accordance with the regulations of OTC subject to the following conditions:

(*i*) the promoters after such offer retain at least 25% of the total issued capital with lock-in period of five years later reduced to 3 years from the date of the sponsor taking up the shares;

(*ii*) the sponsor agrees to act as market maker for the shares atleast for a period of three years on a compulsory basis and also finds an additional market maker for such compulsory market making; and

(*iii*) the sponsor compulsorily gives two-way quotes based on minimum or maximum trading prices as may be stipulated by OTC in respect of the scrip.

NATIONAL STOCK EXCHANGE

The National Stock Exchange was set up by IDBI and other all-India Financial Institutions in Mumbai in November 1992 with a paid-up equity of ₹25 crore. It was recognised by the govt. in the same year and the exchange started operations in wholesale debt market in June 1994 and in equity trading in Nov. 1994. The wholesale debt market or the money market segments would cater to banks, FIs, etc., to encourage high value transactions in PSU bonds, UTI Units, Treasury Bills, Govt. securities and call money. There will be no trading floor of the exchange. Trading is in large volumes and over the telephone, telex, etc. Trading is done on computer with the help for PC Terminals in broker offices. The capital market segment is also similarly on computer based trading. The settlement will be on T + 7 basis for equity trading. For listing, the companies should have a minimum paid up capital of ₹10 crore.

Benefits accrue to both issuers of securities and investors. As this is screen based trading with a national network, transparency and cost-effectiveness is ensured. Besides, the investment counters can be spread wide in the country under the NSE electronic network.

Around 1,300 companies are already listed on NSE including permitted securities. Trading in them is continuing simultaneously with those in the principal and regional stock exchanges. As the National Securities Depository limited is set up, in Nov. 1996 book entry of deals and immobilisation of physical certificates has taken place. At present, the volume of daily trade is around ₹8,000 crore, and it tops all exchanges with about 50% of the total turnover of all exchanges.

National Market System

A high powered study Group on the Establishment of New Stock Exchanges under the Chairmanship of Shri M. J. Pherwani has submitted its Report in June 1991. This Study Group has recommended some criteria for setting up of new stock exchanges and favoured the licensing of additional trading floors (ATF) instead of multiplying the number of stock exchanges in the country.

The Study Group has also recommended the setting up of a model National Stock Exchange at New Bombay (NSE) which will develop the National Market System in the country. The infrastructure in terms of space, Telecommunications, Computerisation, online processing system, Library, Research facilities, Publicity Dept, etc., are all recommended for the "National Market" to be set up by NSE.

The market will have two types of members, *viz.,* participating trading members, who can only trade on their behalf and intermediary trading members (dealers) who can deal on behalf of their clients. Trading members will have computer terminals connecting to the *other* trading members (PTM) and to the central computer system at the NSE. Trading orders to buy and sell securities or to borrow and lend are entered into the computer system and stacked in its memory in an order book. Trading being order driven, it will be matched with a matching counter order. If matched, both the buyer and seller are informed by the NSE computer system. By the end of the trading day, the exchange system will give out rates and a list of completed transactions for each trading member.

Characteristics — NMS

The characteristics of National Market System are as follows:

1. Completely automated system in terms of both trading and settlement procedures to be provided through the Securities Facilities Support Corporation.
2. Compulsory market makers/jobbers to provide liquidity and ready market.
3. The members would be as large as 1,000 and Corporate and Institutional members would also be there drawn from various parts of the country and to represent the professionals on an all India basis.

4. Only large and medium sized companies and PSUs are to be listed on this exchange and it will complement the existing exchanges.
5. The NSE would have a separate trading time allotted for debt instruments in order to have the beneficial effect of creating an active secondary market in debt instruments.

Objectives

The objectives of this NMS are as follows:

1. To help the privatisation of Public Sector Units through listing of their shares on this exchange.
2. To spread the investment habit and cult to savers in the rural and semi-urban areas as well.
3. To professionalise the members with a view to improve the investor services and make it comparable to international markets abroad.
4. To create more employment opportunities in the service sector within the orbit of the Capital Market.
5. To promote the market for debt instruments.

Study Group Recommendations

As per the recommendation of the Study Group, the present system of stock exchanges has failed to cater to the needs of the genuine investors. The debt market or debenture and bond trading was neglected and speculation and manipulation of the markets became the order of the day. The Study Group has therefore recommended the setting up of a new National Stock Exchange at New Mumbai and National Market System, based on the New Mumbai stock exchange transactions (NSE).

The NMS was to be developed on a three tier basis for uniform and high quality trading, settlement, clearing and depository services for the nation as a whole. The three tier Stock Market structure is as follows:

1. Principal stock exchanges comprising the five major exchanges at Mumbai, Delhi, Kolkata, Chennai and Ahmedabad.
2. Regional stock exchanges comprising other exchanges in the country.
3. Additional Trading Floors, sponsored and managed by the principal or a Regional stock exchange, as the case may be.

Experience in Foreign Countries

In the U.S., the Securities Act Amendments of 1975 directed to SEC to work towards setting up of a NMS. The SEC has left the initiative to the security industry. In 1977, the New York stock exchange has linked itself to Philadelphia stock exchange to create an Inter-market Trading System (ITS). By 1981 almost all the stock exchanges were linked to New York exchange. The ITS arranges for concurrent display electronically of the current quotes of eligible shares. The broker has a choice to put his deal either in the exchange where he is physically present or in any other exchange. If he decides to deal in another exchange he has put his order or commitment to trade in the electronic system. This is valid for a fixed period at that specified price. If it is accepted by anybody in that exchange, the deal is put through. Otherwise it is rejected.

The companies under NASDAQ (National Association of Security Dealers Automated Quoted system), have also joined the NMS as a next stage in 1982. Such companies satisfying some financial criteria were designated as Tier I companies and are designated as part of NMS. Some other companies have also been permitted to be on NMS on Tier II on a voluntary basis. More than 1,000 companies of NASDAQ are traded on the NMS and constitute an important component of the NMS in the U.S.

In U.K., London is the market around which all other markets revolve and before the London market the other stock exchanges fade away into insignificance. The NMS in U.K. is developed on the basis on London quotes and other markets are more or less trading floors only.

The Inter-market Trading System in U.K. connects all stock markets in U.K. to London and the trading pattern revolves around the London Quotes although the other stock markets have maintained their individualities. The electronic display on the Quotes around the whole of U.K. of all scrips quoted in London facilitates the Inter-market Trading System.

The eight national stock exchanges in FDR of Germany were linked in 1989 into a single screen based trading system, wherein Frankfurt became the centre piece of the trading and others were trading on the basis of Frankfurt Quotes. But in none of the other developed or developing countries, a new stock exchange was set up to develop the NMS, as proposed by Pherwani Committee. The reason is to present competition effectively to the Semi-monopoly position of B.S.E.

The Mumbai stock exchange which accounts for 2/3rds of total trading in India has claimed that it could act as the Centre piece of NMS as New York in USA and London in UK and that there is no need for setting up a separate New Mumbai stock exchange (NSE), as suggested by Pherwani Committee. But the govt. has accepted the Committee's recommendations and entrusted to the Stock Holding Corporation of India (SHCI), the task of setting up the Central Depository System to immobilise the Paper Certificates, a National Clearing and Settlement Corporation to administer a National Settlement System as between the stock exchanges and a Securities Facilities Support Corporation to establish and maintain an electronic network for this purpose. It is thus that N.M.S. had come into existence.

NATIONAL CLEARANCE AND DEPOSITORY SYSTEM

The new system which the Stock Holding Corporation of India is assigned to set up by the Ministry of Finance for clearance and depository functions of the stock exchanges at the national level is called the National Clearance Settlement and Depository System. It comprises of (a) National Depository System (b) National Trade Comparison and Reporting System and (c) National Clearance System.

From the worldwide experience, there does not appear to be any single system which can be transplanted on Indian soil as it is. There is a complexity of legal hurdles, procedural and habit problems to face in India for a change of this type.

Present Settlement and Clearance System

The growth of equity cult in India in eighties has put the present system of settlement and clearance to serious strain. Besides the workload on the Clearing Agencies and Share Transfer Agencies has increased multifold. These led to many problems to investors arising out of systematic risks like counter party risk, credit risk, bad deliveries, long delayed deliveries, counterfeit scrips, forged scrips, etc. These have increased to alarming levels in more recent years. The Indian investors may not themselves tolerate these developments not to speak of International investment Groups or Funds, interested in Indian markets.

Our present system had outlived its usefulness and since it is not possible to have a revolutionary change in the system, it is better to evolve a system of settlement based on dematerialisation of physical certificates and transfer of shares on the basis of book entries in a phased manner.

The new system will have to be based on a change in legal system, changes in banking practices, settlement and clearance system. To start with, a book entry system for transfers as between broker members can be arranged as is done by the Bombay stock exchange with the Bank of India holdings, set up separately for this purpose. At the national level, the National Depository was set up in Nov. 1996 along with many other depositories. The Central Depository System was accepted by the govt. and SEBI guidelines are issued for setting up of the depositories and the Central Depository.

National Trade Comparison and Reporting System

Its function is to establish the forms and conditions of contracts after trade execution in the securities markets. First the trade execution and then reporting of these for matching of the terms of the contracts and trade comparison will lead to the output of National Trade Reporting Systems as matched transactions. This will be the input for the National Clearing System.

National Central System ensures that clearing as between brokers of different stock exchanges should be through book entries. This would mean that clearing can take place nationally on a standard basis to prepare the matched transactions for a depository settlement.

The Central Depository System aims at immobilisation of physical certificates. This is done by means of book entries with Central Depository who keeps custody of all physical certificates as a first step. As a next step, new issues will be made as book entries only and not as physical certificates. Book entry transfers will lead to quicker transfers and at lower costs. It can meet the increasing workload of investment activity and dealings leading to increasing volume of transfer work.

To put into practice the above system, a number of hurdles have to be overcome and changes have to be effected in the legal system, inheritance rights, pledges and hypothecation and practices of banks in this regard, practices of companies with regard to share transfers etc. The legal system should recognise the transfer of ownership by the necessary book entries. The rights of beneficial ownership are to be vested on the basis of the records with the depository. The practices of banks and other financial institutions have to be changed also to permit pledge and release of pledge on the basis of hypothecation of National Depository System holding on behalf of the investors and not by physical scrips, as before. Companies and transfer agents have to recognise the book entry transfer system. Similarly, the need for transfer deed and collection of stamp tax for transfers have to be modified to suit the book entry system of transfers. Some of these changes are being implemented in the transfer mechanism adopted for the National Securities Depository Ltd., set up in Nov. 1996 by N.S.E. with 14 participants. NSDL is sponsored by IDBI, UTI along with NSE.

EMERGING ROLE OF STOCK EXCHANGES

1. As per the existing law, the stock exchange is an association of member brokers for the purpose of facilitating and regulating trading in securities. It is thus a self-regulatory organisation (SRO). The traditional emphasis was on regulation by the SRO in the interests of members.

2. The worldwide trend is now towards greater self-regulation by the SROs along with the co-ordinating and supervisory role of the government. At the same time, the role of SROs including those of merchant bankers and mutual funds has increased in the direction of stricter enforcement of a code of conduct and the rules of the game in the conduct of their business. The SEBI is however moving in the direction of more regulation, as the market is in initial stage of development.

3. In the evolution of the role of the stock exchanges, the trend is moving more in the direction of the public interest. The investor population has increased and are demanding and their interests have become paramount both in the eyes of the government and the SROs for reasons of promoting the capital market. This has led to a greater emphasis on the developmental role of stock exchanges. The representation of public on the Board of Directors and the facilities provided to redress their grievances through the Grievances Cell of the stock exchanges have all proved to be in this direction. The stock exchanges are moving in the direction of inter-linkages, national market system and nation wide electronic trading system.

4. The stock exchanges have been growing as Public Service Institutions by providing a variety of services to the investors. To give examples of such services, mention may be made of the following:

(a) Provision of Directory of Corporate information useful for a scientific assessment of the fundamentals of the companies before making investment.

(*b*) Publication of share prices at which trade took place daily in various scrips traded — open, high, low and closing along with the volume.

(*c*) Publication and supply to public of useful handouts/handbooks/pamphlets giving out information on the stock exchanges — the operations and developments in the capital market, etc.

(*d*) Investor education and training programmes for investors.

(*e*) Settlement of disputes between member brokers and their clients and investors.

(*f*) Attending to the investor complaints against registered members and listed companies.

5. The future role of stock exchanges will be radically different from the present, as their developmental role will be increasing much faster than their regulatory role. Along with increasing self-regulation and a stricter enforcement of a code of conduct on the members, the stock exchange will emerge as Public Service Institutions catering to increasing demands of investors in the country. Of the developmental activities, education, training and research will dominate in the years to come bringing the stock exchanges and the public nearer and together. This is conspicuous by its absence now.

6. With the increasing emphasis on the National Market System and the growth of automation, the new trend would be integration and inter-linking of stock exchanges at the regional and national level. This trend would be beneficial to investors, in that they would enjoy a better market and fair play. Quicker services and better price realization at lower costs could be achieved by the new system. The stock exchanges would thus move in the direction of a National Market system through mutual co-operation and co-ordination and electronic linkages of the trading floors through the satellite telecommunication system and quicker display of information. The BSE has introduced the BOLT online electronic trading. The BOLT of BSE is now kept open to members of other stock exchanges, which may open up a National Market System in India. SEBI has permitted them to expand BOLT into other centres also in October 1996.

7. Where there are no stock exchanges, trading floors would be provided and electronic display of the prices of shares in the National Market would help trade in the local trading floors. In the computer-aided trading system, there will be no need even for the trading floor, but until the complete automation takes place, the trading floor system may continue, as it is more economical than setting up of separate stock exchanges at innumerable centres. Even so, recognition was granted to Visakhapatnam stock exchange to trade on Electronic trading system, in September 1996, which did not materialise.

8. With the setting up of the Central Depository System and the National clearing and settlement system, there is dematerialisation and immobilisation of physical paper certificates and the trading and settlement would take place on the book entry system. The method of passbook entries in the banks would be the order of the day for the stock exchanges.

NSE Operations

The recommendations of Pherwani Committee were accepted by the govt. and accordingly NSE was set up and recognised by the govt. As reported earlier, it has first started trading in money market instruments, Govt. securities and other debt instruments on OTC basis. In the capital market segment, corporate equity shares are traded on a weekly settlement basis since November 1994. It has no trading floor. Each trading member will have a computer in his office, anywhere in India which will be connected to the Central Computer System of NSE through leased lines or VSATs (Very Small Aparture Terminals) for an interim period, to be followed by a satellite link. The members for debt market will be different from the equity market and the same members cannot operate for both markets, as originally visualised.

The NSE will operate two segments, namely, debt market (Money market) and equity market (Capital market) and operations in both are separately maintained. Post-trade services are also automated. For confirmed traders, the settling bank will arrange for payment and clearance and depository for effecting transfers by electronic book entry system. The clearance and settlement facility is provided by Canara Bank for the BSE and many banks are providing the depository facility for NSE. The RBI has permitted NSE and OTCEI brokers to deal in Government securities and in the money market.

Central Depository System

The govt. has accepted the system of multiple depositories and SEBI was asked to frame guidelines for their operations. These depositories will keep physical custody of share certificates leading to immobilisation of shares to be followed later by dematerialisation and complete book entry system of trading in future.

This means that the statement given by the depository is evidence of the ownership of the shares. This method is to be operated for the FIs and FFIs and banks and mutual funds, in the beginning and will be extended to corporates and individuals. Later on, the depository will transfer the securities between the participants through electronic book entry, while the settling bank will effect the transfer of funds.

Listing of Securities

All medium and large sized companies above ₹10 crore of paid capital eligible to be listed on regular stock exchanges can be listed on NSE. Some of them may be listed and traded on regular stock exchanges also. Thus, as at end March 2012 there were 1,228 listed companies on the NSE. The same formalities of listing are observed by NSE and a listing agreement is entered into with the company, as on a regular exchange and as approved by the SEBI, and govt.

Settlement System

Trading period on anyday will vary for the debt segment and equity segment. For capital market operations the trading is done in equities, convertible and non-convertible debentures. Trading network can be spread all over the country, depending on the electronic link through the satellite. There are more than 1,100 terminals spread over about 100 cities at present. A rolling settlement system operates in NSE with settlement period of T + 7. Thus a rolling T + 7 period means that transactions on a given day (T) will be settled seven days later (T + 7). On that day, funds and securities are exchanged by passing electronically proper debit and credit entries. Later by stages, the settlement system was brought down to T + 3 and T + 1, and Rolling Settlement System on both NSE and BSE.

The National Securities Depository Limited (NSDL)

This is an organisation promoted by the Industrial Development Bank of India, the Unit Trust of India and the National Stock Exchange of India Limited to provide electronic depository facilities for stock traded in the equity and the debt market.

The National Securities Depository Limited has been registered with the Securities Exchange Board of India and launched on Nov. 7, 1996 as India's first depository to facilitate trading and settlement of securities in dematerialised form. Settlement of securities in dematerialised form will eliminate problems that are normally associated with settlement through physical certificates, like tearing/mutilation of share certificates due to careless handling, loss of certificates by postal authorities or delays with registrars, problems of bad delivery of shares, etc. Cases of forgery of certificates will be eliminated in an electronic environment. Settlement of trades will be faster and hassle-free leading to shorter settlement cycles.

What is a Depository?

A depository is an organisation where the securities of a shareholder are held in the electronic form at the request of the shareholder through the medium of a depository participant.

A depository can be compared to a bank for securities. If an investor wants to utilise the services offered by a depository, the investor has to open an account with the depository through a depository participant

— this is very similar to the opening of an account with any of the branches of a bank in order to utilise the services of that bank, as a Depository Participant (D.P.). Many banks are also offering this service.

The depository can legally transfer beneficial ownership which a custodian cannot. The main objective of a depository is to minimise the paperwork involved with the ownership, trading and transfer of securities.

Facilities offered by NSDL:

1. Enable surrender and withdrawal of securities to and from the depository (*i.e.,* dematerialisation and rematerialisation).
2. Maintain investor holdings in the electronic form.
3. Effect settlement of securities traded on the exchanges.
4. Carry-out settlement of trades not done on the stock exchanges (i.e., off-market trades).

Rematerialisation

If anybody wishes to get back his securities in the physical form all he has to do is to request his depository participant for the rematerialisation of the same.

Advantages of the Depository

There are a number of reasons why investor should opt for the electronic form of holding securities. Depositing investor's securities with NSDL will give freedom from the worries of loss of share certificates through theft, mutilation, fire, etc.

The process of opening an account with a depository participant is similar to the opening of a bank account. The investor can get a list of depository participants from NSDL. The depository participants may also advertise the services offered by them once they are registered. The investor can approach any DP of his choice and fill up an account opening form.

The depository participant will give a passbook or a statement of holdings. The statement of holdings will be despatched to the holder periodically by the depository participant; however, the statement of holdings can be sent to holders, as and when requested for a fee.

The depository has not prescribed any minimum balance. In fact, the holder can even have zero balance in his account. However, the depository participants may fix some minimum limits and charges for any shortfalls.

About the Depository Participants

Similar to the brokers who trade on behalf of the customers in and outside the stock exchanges, a depository participant is the representative (agent) in the depository system. The depository participant will maintain the securities account balances and intimate to the holder about their holdings from time to time. According to SEBI guidelines, financial institutions, banks, custodians, stock brokers, etc., can become participants in the depository.

There are absolutely no restrictions to the number of DPs that the investor can open accounts with. Opening an account with a depository participant is very similar to opening a bank account. Just as a person can have savings or current accounts with more than one bank, the person can open depository accounts with more than one depository participants.

The person can exercise the option such as a rights issue or optional conversion of debentures to shares. The holders do have a choice of either physical or electronic mode of holdings. However, corporate entitlements such as bonus will be made in the same form as the original holdings.

The depository will also establish a help desk which will direct the holder to the approprite agency. When the depository is ready to start functioning, it will advertise the helpdesk telephone lines.

NSDL'S FIRST PARTICIPANTS

SHCIL
ILFS
IIT TRUST CORP. SERVICES
GLOBAL TRUST BANK, Replaced by OBC
HDFC BANK
CITIBANK CUSTODIAL SERVICES
MORGAN STANLEY CUSTODIAL SERVICES
RELIANCE SHARE AND STOCK BROKING
JANTA SAHAKARI BANK
INDUSTRIAL DEV. BANK OF INDIA
STATE BANK OF INDIA
STANDARD CHARTERED
NATIONAL SEC. CLEARING CORP.
DEUTSCHE BANK

Legal Aspects

NSDL was set up by passing the Depositories Act, 1996 but with retrospective effect from Sept. 1995. Companies Act and SCR Act and Stamp Act were amended to the extent necessary. Section 22A of SCR Act dealing with restrictions on transfer of shares was deleted. Sections 108 and 111 of the Companies Act were amended to dispense with transfer form and other formalities relating to the physical transfer of shares. The depository's statement is a valid documents of title, under law and transfers are effected by book entries in the passbooks of DPs.

✠ ✠ ✠

STOCK MARKET OPERATIONS AND FUNCTIONS

37

Introduction

On any Stock Exchange, there are members who deal with client orders, institutional orders and online business (arbitrage operations). Some brokers specialise in the new issues market and some in badla financing. Some act as jobbers, making two-way offers to buy and sell in selected shares. All members are permitted to trade in the Trading Ring. Each member is permitted to have authorised assistants up to a maximum number as fixed by the Stock Exchange. The members do trading on their own behalf or on behalf of their clients. If the member acts as a broker, he is doing retail business or purchase and sale transactions for the customers. If a member is doing wholesale business, offering both purchase and sale prices (bid and offer) to the other member brokers then he is called a jobber. Both brokers and jobbers are an essential part of the stock market operations.

The purchase and sale transactions in the market relate to dealings in securities listed on the Stock Exchange, namely, Equity Shares, Preference Shares, Debentures (both convertible and non-convertible), Gilt-edged Securities and semi-government bonds. Listing of securities of the corporate sector is done in accordance with the regulations embodied in the Securities Contracts (Regulation) Act, 1956 and the Securities Contracts (Regulation) Rules, 1957 and the Bye-laws of the Stock Exchange. The securities of the Centre, State and semi-government bodies are listed for trading automatically after they are issued to the public without any listing fees, and listing formalities.

Specified and Non-specified Groups

The listed securities of the companies are classified into a specified group and non-specified group (cash list) on the basis of certain criteria. Those included in the specified list should be fully paid-up equity shares listed already on the Exchange for at least three years on the cash list and the company's paid-up equity capital should be at least ₹5 crore. The shares should have been actively traded while on the cash list. The equity shares should be widely disbursed and a large volume of shares is available with the public for trading. The company should have a record of good earnings and dividends over the past few years before inclusion in the specified list. Speculation is permitted only in the specified list. Trading is genuine, if delivery is taken or given and speculative if no delivery is involved. Those which are first listed will be kept in non-specified or cash group. In addition to specified (A group) and non-specified groups (B group), there is a category of permitted securities. These are not listed on that exchange but listed on some other exchange, but permitted to be traded here. On the BSE, however, there is no permitted category.

Customers' Orders

The investor can place an order by telegram, telephone, letter or in person. The order may be for the purchase or sale of a specified number of shares of a company at a specified rate or range of prices. The member broker is a custodian for the shares/securities of his client till they are sold or delivered. The order to buy or sell may be given for a fixed price or at a maximum or minimum price range which is also called a limit order. Some orders are 'At Best' or 'At the Market price'. The member broker has to execute the order at the best obtainable price in the market on a specified date. Some orders may be 'Immediate' or 'Cancelled', which signifies that the broker has to buy or sell at the specified price immediately such as sell 100 Colgate at ₹430 and if the price in the market is unfavourable, the order is cancelled. Some orders are open orders, which can be executed at any time within a range of prices while others are discretionary leaving the discretion to the broker.

After receiving the orders, the member enters these orders in his books and then purchase and sale orders are distributed among his authorised assistants to handle them separately in the specified list, non-specified list and others. The member would have three alternatives in executing the orders. He may go to the trading ring to buy or sell the required shares. Alternatively, the member can set off matching orders of purchase and sale of different clients of his own or purchase or sell from out of his own stock of portfolio held by him. But all these orders have to be executed at the prevailing market prices on that day.

Trading Ring

There are three types of trading systems in India:

1. Physical outcry system as in a Trading Ring.
2. Jobber Driven auction system which can be both in physical contact or through the computers.
3. Purely computerised electronic system as in NSE and Bombay Stock Exchange online trading.

Trading on the Stock Exchange is officially done in the trading ring for a few hours from 10 a.m. to 4.00 p.m. Trading before or after official hours is called kerb trading. In the trading ring, space is provided separately for specified and non-specified sections. The members or their authorised assistants have to wear a badge or carry with them identity cards given by the Exchange to enter the trading ring. They carry a souda block book, or confirmation memos, duly authorised by the Exchange and carry a pen with them. On the trading ring, there are jobbers in some Exchanges who do wholesale business of purchase and sale, giving two-way quotations of bid and offer for each share. The jobber may specialise in some scrips and stand at a specified place in the ring indicating the share or shares that he is trading in. The authorised assistant approaches one or more jobbers specialising in the scrips that he wishes to buy or sell and make the best possible bargain with the jobbers. When the deal is struck, both jobber and broker make a note in their souda block books of the transaction, or enter into confirmation memos.

Some members are both jobbers and brokers. Each jobber tries to purchase and sell those shares he is specialising in such quantities that he can match as far as possible the purchases and sales in each share by the end of the day. According to the supply and demand position of the shares, the prices of purchase and sale would vary in the market and the jobber would do his best to match his purchases and sales and the margin between the purchase and sale prices would be his profit.

Block Book (or the Souda Book)

After each order is executed, suitable entries are made in the concerned member's block book (or pass confirmation memos). This is a book of transactions executed on the floor and appropriate entries are made after every deal to record the number of shares traded, the prices of the purchase/sale, and the name or code number of the other member through whom the deal was finalised. Each page of the souda book or the block book taken to the floor of the Stock Exchange should be duly authorised by the Stock Exchange authorities.

It is mandatory to submit a copy of the Souda Sheets (separate for specified and non-specified) by 4.00 p.m. every evening to the Stock Exchange. If the Stock Exchange authorities find untallied transactions (*i.e.,* if some details do not match with what the counter-member has recorded), they will issue a memo and the member is required to attend to it immediately and clear the objections raised therein and return the memo.

Contract Note

From the souda block book (where the transactions are sketchily written up), the details are transferred to the souda book (which gives complete details). From the souda book the contract notes are drawn up. It is important to ensure that the contract note is written up on the day of the deal and posted to the client. This is a proof that the contract was executed on that day and not on any other day since prices fluctuate everyday. Besides, under Article 43 (b) or (bb) of Schedule 1 of the Indian Stamp Act, the broker must affix a revenue stamp (based on the value of the contracted transaction or face value whichever is higher). As all these transactions are computerised, only computer generated memos and notes, etc., are given to the Stock Exchange authorities and clients, as the case may be.

Drawing Up of Bills

For A Group Both sale and purchase bills are prepared along with the contract note and it is posted on the same day or the next day.

For B Group Bills are prepared only after receipt of delivery order/payment order.

Thus in a purchase transaction, once the shares are delivered to the client and the client effects payment for the purchase and pays the stamp fees for transfer, a bill is made out giving the total cost of purchase, including other expenses incurred by the broker in the price itself. Now all these have to be shown separately from brokerage and price.

Cum- and Ex-dividend

Sometimes, shares are purchased cum-dividend (or sold cum-dividend) but delivery is made/given ex-dividend. This means that though the buyer is entitled to the dividend, he gets the shares only after book closure for dividend payment. The dividend thus goes to the seller while it rightly belongs to the buyer. The price paid to the seller is adjusted for full dividend. Thus when the bill is made out, the broker has to credit the buyer for the dividend and debit him only with charges for stamp fees and other expenses net of dividend. Similar situations arise in the case of shares bought cum-bonus/cum-rights, but where the delivery is effected ex-bonus/ ex-rights. Further, for tax purposes, the document that the ITO relies on is not the contract note but the bill which gives the total consideration of the transaction.

Settlement in Specified List

Settlement for scrips purchased and sold in the specified list is different from those of the non-specified list because in the case of the former, speculative transactions are allowed to be carried forward to the next period. Stock Exchanges allow speculative trading in shares listed in the forward list, permitting thereby for short-selling and long-buying of shares.

All transactions on the specified list are taken stock on the badla day, once a week, being every Friday. The mechanics of these badla transactions are quite intricate, though pretty logical. In any settlement period — a week — (effectively 5 trading days), there would have been a certain amount of genuine buying/selling as well as speculative buying/selling. The day on which such transactions are posted for settlement or carry forward is called the "Badla Day".

All those contracts which are not to be carried over are settled between the members by effecting deliveries and payment before the next badla day.

Two things may happen on the badla day as far as speculative transactions are concerned:

1. They are carried forward from one settlement period to the next by drawing up a fresh set of contract notes to give effect to the carry forward.
2. Either an interest called Seedha Badla is paid by the buyer to the seller or charges Undha Badla is paid by the seller to the buyer depending on the net overbought or oversold position in any scrip.

To effect steps (1) and (2) stated above, the Stock Exchange authorities fix the HAVALA RATE and, the CARRY FORWARD MARGIN and the BADLA CHARGES are determined by the market forces. Havala Rate is the price at which each scrip in the specified list can be carried forward, also called the Standard Rate or the Making-up price. The rate is normally based on the closing price of the scrip on the day prior to the badla day, *i.e.,* based on the closing prices on the last trading day. If the Stock Exchange authorities wish to impound a part of the profit by bulls or bears (*i.e.,* the price difference between the contracted rate and the havala rate) as a result of excessive speculative activity in the scrip between the two settlement periods, they can decide to fix a havala rate which in their opinion is the most representative.

The Carry Forward Margin: This margin is fixed by the Stock Exchange authorities on all scrips, with a right to levy heavy margins on those which are subject to heavy speculative activity. Different charges are payable by the buyers and the sellers. The Havala Sheet, which is published by the Stock Exchange, lists the MARGIN requirements to be paid by the bulls/bears on each scrip, as also the carry forward rates for both (after adjusting the margin with the havala rate).

The Badla Charges (also known as Vyaj Badla): The carry forward charges or interest is to be paid by the buyer or seller in each scrip depending on whether the net position in that scrip is overbrought or oversold.

Badla Charges

Undha Badla charges are payable when there is more "speculative selling" than "speculative buying" in any scrip, *i.e.,* when the scrip is oversold. In effect, this means that there are more buyers willing to take delivery than there are shares available for delivery.

It is generally found that there is always more "speculative buying" than "speculative selling" in the Stock Exchanges based on human psychology. Two possible reasons could be given for this situation. First, it is more difficult for a person to comprehend that he can first sell what he does not own and buy it back at a lower rate later and make a profit than to comprehend that he can buy something today and sell it later at a profit. Short sales are more speculative and are controlled strictly by the Stock Exchange and SEBI.

The second reason is that if the floating stock in a scrip is limited and there is excessive short selling, then the bull operators can capitalise on this technical position and demand delivery or demand extortionate interest charges at the settlement. The bear operator is then caught as there is no floating stock to deliver and he then has to purchase scrips from the market or borrow them from a financier to deliver. He may then have to pay a heavy price for these scrips. This proves a deterrent to excessive short-selling. In this case, it is possible that shares due for delivery can be auctioned in the market and delivery secured and the amount involved is debited to the member due to deliver but failed to do so.

On the other hand, a bull operator who is long or overbought can always borrow money or take delivery of scrips if he finds that the badla financier is charging exorbitant interest rates. Money is easier to obtain than shares. Badla paid for purchases carried forward is called Seedha Badla.

Though the badla rates are fixed by the market forces of demand and supply of funds and scrips, the Stock Exchange has the authority to intervene if they think that the rates are unreasonable, and could as a result destabilise the market.

Factors Influencing Badla Rates

The badla charges or the amount of interest charges (also called Vyaj Badla) that are contracted to be paid as a result of carrying forward a transaction are based on several factors, namely:

(*a*) The total amount of badla finance available in the market.

(*b*) The technical position of the market, i.e., the extent to which it is overheated in terms of speculative buying, and hence the total volume and value of shares overall which have to be financed.

(*c*) The total amount of badla finance available for a particular scrip — some scrips are not favoured by the financiers due to their poor liquidity — and for several other reasons.

(*d*) The overall money market interest rates.

(e) The psychological state of the market, whether bullish or bearish.

Carry Forward Facilities

If the buyers/sellers wish to carry forward their transactions from one settlement period to the next settlement period, they draw up a fresh set of contract notes to give effect to the carry forward of the purchase/ sale at rates which reflect the havala rate, the margin and the badla charges. Havala rate is the standard rate applicable to a share for carry forward purchases, fixed by the Exchange.

Example 1

Assume that a broker has transacted a sale order at the rate of ₹700 per share and that the standard rate for the share is fixed at ₹730, the carry forward margin payable is ₹40 per share for the seller, and that the badla charge is fixed at ₹4 per share.

So, a contract note would already have been drawn up, stating — Sold N number of shares at ₹700 (minus brokerage) per share.

The seller then has a choice of either giving delivery or carrying the transaction forward to the next settlement period.

(*i*) If he wants to give delivery, then the settlement will be made at the rate agreed upon, being ₹700 (less brokerage) per share.

(*ii*) If he carries it forward:

(*a*) A new contract will be drawn up as having purchased shares at ₹770 (Havala Rate ₹730 + Margin ₹40 + brokerage) per share.

(*b*) A new contract will then be made on the same day as having sold N shares at ₹774 (the rate on the purchase contract ₹770 + badla charges receivable ₹4) per share.

Note: If the Havala Rate is less than the selling rate of ₹700, say, ₹680, then the rate on the contract in (a) will be ₹720 (₹680 + ₹40) and the rate on the contract in (b) will be ₹724.

Example 2

Suppose a broker has executed a purchase order of N number of shares at ₹700 and the carry forward margin on the buyer is also ₹40 and all others are as in the above example. Therefore, a contract note effecting this purchase would have already been drawn up as having bought at ₹700 (plus brokerage). The buyer then has a choice of either taking delivery or carrying it forward:

(*i*) If he wants to take delivery, then the settlement will be made at ₹700 (plus brokerage) per share.

(*ii*) If he wants to carry it forward:

(*a*) A new contract is drawn up as having sold N shares at ₹690 (Standard rate ₹30 – Margin payable ₹40 – Brokerage) per share.

(*b*) A new contract will then be made on the first day of the next settlement period as having bought N shares at ₹694 (the rate of the sale above ₹690 + badla payable ₹4).

Note: As in the above note, if the Standard Rate is (say) ₹680, then the rates in the above contracts will be ₹640 and ₹644 respectively.

Therefore, for carrying forward a contract to the next settlement, the following steps have to be taken on the Badla day:

1. Draw up a contract squaring up the position. The price in this contract note will be the respective carryforward rates specified in the Havala Sheet.
2. Draw up a fresh contract maintaining the position which was to be carried forward, the rate being the one indicated in (1) above + the badla charges.

Book Closure Badla Financing (BCBF)

Such financing differs from the normal fortnightly financing, as financiers take interest for a month as against for a fortnight in the normal badla financing.

BCBF is for a one-month period (unless otherwise stated), because it takes 14 days to get delivery of scrips purchased from the clearing house and the buyer is given a further 14 days to lodge the shares for transfer.

The share becomes ex-right or ex-dividend one month before the book closure day, *i.e.,* on the book closure badla day. When the company announces the book closure date, the Stock Exchange accordingly fixes a suitable badla day, which is about a month prior to this date, as the book closure badla day.

BCBF occurs at the time of book closure for dividends, bonus issues, right issues, etc.

BCBF money costs more due to the following reasons:

1. The longer holding period (and hence the greater the risk) and the fact that the shares have to be lodged for transfer. Besides, financiers also charge for stamp fees on transfer and the cost of materials and registered post charges.
2. The financier who takes delivery of the shares on behalf of the buyer has to lodge the shares for transfer to his name, and hence the identity of the new owner becomes known. This creates a psychological fear in the mind of the financier, and thus such financing can be done with only the "tax paid" money.

Settlement in Non-specified Shares

All business transacted in any week, between a Monday and Friday of the week, is settled on the next Saturday (not the one immediately following). The price at which they are actually bought or sold is considered for the settlement. Delivery is made on the following Monday.

If for some reason the settlement is not made within three settlement periods, then the difference in the price can be claimed by the buyer. Here the buyer has an advantage in that, if the price were to go up within this stipulated time and settlement has not been made (*i.e.,* he has not received delivery), then he can claim the excess amount, or he can demand delivery of the shares.

Settlement and delivery in respect of specified shares take place as between the members and through the clearing house. Both delivery of shares and payment or receipt of money would be through the clearing.

But in the case of non-specified shares, delivery of shares is done directly as between the members while payments and receipts are effected through the clearing bank.

After the Badla Day

All deliveries of shares/payments arising out of the badla day adjustments have to be settled with respective deliveries and payments before the next badla day.

The transactions contracted by the member in respect of specified shares are entered into the "Settlement Register". The transactions executed during the settlement period with the clients/other members are balanced in this register and the outstanding transactions are adjusted at the "Carry Forward" or the "Havala" rates on the badla day.

Thereafter, the balances in the client's accounts are posted to the clients' ledger. In the case of non-specified shares, transactions are directly entered in the clients' ledger from the Souda Book.

Kinds of Delivery

A contract which has been executed on behalf of a client or on the member's own account, culminates in the delivery/receipt of payment for shares.

Deliveries of securities can be effected in four ways:

1. Hand Delivery
2. Spot Delivery
3. Special Delivery
4. Delivery for clearing

Hand Delivery

Delivery and payment should be completed on the date stipulated when entering into the bargain, which shall not be more than 14 days following the date of the contract.

Spot Delivery

These transactions are to be settled by delivery and payment on the date of the contract or on the next day. For completion of the contract, the actual period for the despatch of the securities or remittance of money through post is excluded in the computation when the parties to the contract reside at different places.

Special Delivery

Delivery and payment made anytime exceeding 14 days, but not exceeding 2 months, following the date of the contract as may be stipulated when entering into the bargain and permitted by the Governing Board or the President.

The three types of transactions described above, namely, spot delivery, hand delivery and special delivery, are called "spot" or "ready transactions". They must be settled by delivery and payment and cannot be carried forward.

Delivery for Clearing

All transactions in securities in the specified list are effected only through the clearing house. The securities for delivery will be delivered to the buyer within a week and the seller receives his member dues within the same time from the clearing house on the respective "pay-in" and "pay-out" days. This trading is called forward trading or badla.

The function of the clearing house is confined to the receipt and delivery of securities and receiving payments from members for their sales. In the event of a member defaulting on his liability to the clearing house, the responsibility for recovering the amount due from the member, on account of his purchases, devolves on the other member with whom the transaction was entered into. The clearing house does not come into the picture. This custom forces each member to examine the financial soundness and integrity of the other member before concluding a transaction.

Present Position of Badla

The badla trade was banned in March 1994. Subsequently, trade volumes declined and liquidity was impaired. The govt. had second thoughts and a Committee on Review of Badla System was appointed in Feb. 1995, under the Chairmanship of G.S. Patel.

After the G.S. Patel Committee submitted its report in March 1995, there was a long delay in the acceptance of their recommendations. The SEBI gave some proposals and the Stock Exchanges gave counter proposals but finally on October 5, 1995, the SEBI has announced the acceptance of the Committee's recommendations in full.

The recommendations accepted are as follows:

(*i*) Carry forward of deals are permitted subject to more rigorous scrutiny and transparency.

(*ii*) A flat margin of 15% will be recovered from brokers for carry forward deals and on a marked to market basis every week. Margins will depend on the market prices from time to time, adjusted on a weekly basis.

(*iii*) A capital adequancy norm of 3% for individual brokers and 6% for corporates has been stipulated. Brokers are allowed self-certification, in place of audit, regarding their deals carried forward. The Stock Exchange or SEBI would however check on those self-certified statements.

(*iv*) Mandatory squaring up is imposed for all transactions carried forward within 90 days.

(*v*) The Stock Exchanges will strengthen their monitoring system and review the position of capital adequacy norms of brokers in badla deals, so as to protect the investors interests. The stipulation of publishing the carry forward position broker-wise, scrip-wise, before the start of each badla session was retracted. This leads to total acceptance of G. S. Patel Committee recommendation and the system was thus implemented, until it was replaced by Compulsory Rolling Settlement System.

J.S. Varma Committee (July 1997)

This committee recommended the Modified Carry Forward System (HCFS), which consists of the following features:

1. Elimination of the limit of 90 days for carry forward system.
2. Elimination of settlement only by delivery after 75 days.
3. Removal of the limit of ₹10 crore on the financier funding.
4. The clearing house should have an insurance policy, covering the aggregate value of shares lying with them.
5. Abolition of the twin track system of seggregating carry forward trades and delivery trades.
6. A uniform margin of 10% of the gross position (instead of 15% as before) with a daily marking to market prices.
7. In case of Vyaj Badla, the financier should be allowed to take custody of the shares with safeguards.

The shares lent by badla financiers will continue to be deposited with the clearing House.

8. Capital adequacy and other prudential safeguards should be strictly enforced.
9. Scrips chosen for carry forward should have sufficient floating stock.
10. Exchanges should strengthen the maintaining and surveillance system to enforce the rules on the carry forward trading.

The above recommendations are kept in abeyance. Meanwhile, B.S.E. has carried forward some reforms to improve liquidity and better investor protection. A separate 'F' Group of securities was created for trading in odd lot instruments. Corporate membership was increased to 96 by August 1997. BSE introduced in 1997 uniform weekly trading and settlement for all scrips and screen based trading in odd lots through Bolt terminals. BSE has got the SEBI approval for introduction of Trade Guarantee Fund (TGA) to protect the investor interests better, in the event of any failure of brokers.

Trends in Primary and Secondary Markets

The primary market, which turned sluggish in 1995-96, continued to rule bearish in 1996-98 as well. Total fund mobilisation from the capital market declined from ₹26,419 crore in 1994-95 to ₹3,138 crore in 1997-98 — and further to ₹1,878 crore by 2002-03. The investment activity in general continued to be sluggish. The number of issues dropped as well as the quantum. There was no single issue under Book Building Process and there was no single P.S.U. disinvestment offer in 1997-98.

The private placement has of course recorded a faster rise in respect of debt instruments. The private placement market was active growth 13 to 15 issues a month in 1997-98. A total amount of ₹30,983 crore was raised mainly in the form of debt in 1997-98 both by public and private agencies and corporations, including financial institutions, which rose to ₹59,216 crore by 2003-04.

During 1998, the major stock market reforms relate to control on short sales, heavy margins on some speculative scrips, and stricter measures of control on broker operations. For the first time, continuous roll over settlement system is recommended for adoption by NSE and BSE, uniform settlement system for all stock exchanges and dematerialisation of all Govt. securities traded by institutions and banks.

Merchant bankers are now of only one category with a minimum net worth of ₹5 crore. The Asset Management Companies are directed to double their net worth from ₹5 crore to ₹10 crore.

The Inter-connected Stock Exchanges connected many regional Stock Exchanges including Chennai has finalised the criteria for membership, trading practices, settlement and clearing procedures. This was recognised by the govt. in 1998.

The Sensex reached a bottom of 2,795 on January 25, 1998 — the lowest level over for last three years, barring 2713 reached in December 1996. The B.S.E. National Index also touched a low of 1,239 in January 1998. This is in tune with the lowest levels reached by FII purchases and sales during January-February 1998. The FII net purchases were the highest during July-August 1997, when the BSE sensex also reached a three year highest point of 4,605 on August 7, 1997. The FII investments also witnessed similar gyrations. The influence of FIIs operations and the trading sentiment on Wall Street and Nasdaq in the U.S.A. and other foreign markets is seen on the Indian market during early 2000 and 2001. Partly, the openness of the markets and the listing of some Indian I.T. companies and their ADRs in these foreign markets are the reasons for these inter-linkages. There was another market crash in March 2001, mostly due to manipulation and scams. There was recovery in the market since 2004 and the Sensex crossed the level of 13,072 at end March 2007 and even touched 20,000, at one time early in 2008, before reaching to a high of 21,005 in 2010-11 and 27,500 by end Dec. 2014. The BSE Sensex gave an average of 17,282 in April 2012. The volume of corporate debt trade is not much on the BSE but the volume on NSE was at ₹50,150 crore in 2011-12, after reaching a high of ₹54,480 crore in 2009-10 and reached 56,826 in 2013-14 (Averages).

✠ ✠ ✠

TRADING IN THE EQUITY MARKET

38

The bulk of trading in the stock market is in equity. This chapter is devoted mainly to equity market to be followed by debt trading in the next chapter.

Pattern of Trading

Trading in the stock market takes place under three sections:

(*i*) Group (A) — Specified shares.

(*ii*) Group (B) — Non-specified shares. (Now split into B_1 and B_2 on@ the BSE).

(*iii*) Group (C) — "Others".

Under Group (A), only those actively traded (about 150 on the BSE) are included. The criteria for listing in specified group has been dealt with in an earlier chapter. The rest of the listed securities are placed in Group (B). There are about 6,000 scrips in total and 2,000 companies regularly quoted on the BSE in recent years of which 90% are equities. Out of these equity shares, only about 2,000 companies are traded on a daily basis. The trading in the rest is nil or negligible. Under Group (C), only odd lots (tradable lots being 5, 50 or 100, depending upon the face value) are traded to provide liquidity to them through BOLT terminals. "Others" include those which have poor fundamentals and deplorable investor services and which might be delisted any time. The permitted securities are those that are not listed on the exchange, but are permitted to be traded on this exchange, also called foreign securities as they are listed on other stock exchanges in India. B.S.E. has no permitted list. The BSE had created two other sections during 2000-04, namely, 'T' Section for delivery on cash basis, and 'Z' category which included scrips of companies not having good track record of profitability and investor services.

The securities traded may be corporate securities, semi-government securities or public sector bonds. The latter are not traded on the trading floor but over the counter through telephone, telex, etc., as between brokers, RBI, etc.

@ B_1 are well traded scrips among the B Group and have weekly settlement while B_2 are not well traded but have normal weekly settlement.

The instruments of trading are equity shares, preference shares, debentures, CCPs, PSU bonds and Government securities.

The two main stock market indicators are price and quantity of shares traded. The market indicators are the velocity of price changes or spread of market prices (volatility) and the intensity of trading per hour, Advances to Declines ratio, Market capitalisation, Trade turnover, etc., which are discussed in a later chapter.

Barring the equity which have a variable dividend, the other securities have a return fixed and trading in them is restricted. In fact, there is no trading in preference shares and less in PSU bonds. Only in respect of equity shares and that too of major companies, there is trading of any worthwhile magnitude. The equity shares are ownership capital enjoying tax exemption for dividend income along with some others and have a good marketability. There is also an exemption up to a limit in respect of investment in new issues of specified companies. Investment in shares, securities, etc., is also exempt from wealth tax. The market, therefore, provides good liquidity to only equity shares and that too of a limited number of companies. Trading in debt instruments is being promoted on NSE and BSE.

One indicator of the market trading is the turnover of shares in volume and value. At present, the monthly market turnover is around ₹75,000 to one lakh crore with average daily turnover of around ₹8,000 to 10,000 crore on the BSE. Nearly, 60-70% of trading is confined to the specified group (A Group). The delivery ratio is low at about 39% of the total trading and the volatility, as measured by coefficient of variation was high at 23%.

Another indicator of the market trading is the price in terms of individual scrips and for groups of securities in the form of indices. The BSE publishes two types of series — Sensitive series of 30 most actively traded scrips and secondly, National series of 100 actively traded scrips on the major stock exchanges of Mumbai, Ahmedabad, Delhi, Kolkata and Chennai. These showed a good degree of appreciation. The appreciation reflects the corporate performance, on the one hand, and increase in liquidity in the economy, on the other.[1] The rise in prices of shares has provided a hedge against inflation, if these prices are considered for a longer period of 5 to 10 years. Thus, the market is providing liquidity in major shares and also acting as a hedge against inflation. Another important function provided by the market is the increase in the capital raised from the public in terms of new issues and the volume of securities to be traded in the market. But the number of stocks well traded are limited to top 200 companies. Of the 7,353 listed companies in 2005, only 36% or 2,610 companies are traded, of which only 1,960 companies are traded for more than 100 days in a year. The fresh capital listed on the stock exchanges has also increased accordingly. In the year 2008, the listed companies on BSE were around 5,000 and on the NSE at around 1,300.

Latest Developments

Dematerialisation of physical share certificates and compulsory Demat form of trading in increasing number of shares has increased the volumes of trading. Introduction of Rolling Settlement in most of the scrips has however reduced the volumes due to reduced role of Badla. Internet website trading facility by selected broker firms has helped investors in upper classes. e-broking has links with e-banking and both are growing. The linkages with foreign stock exchanges have become firm with a number of Indian listed companies being listed on Nasdaq New York and London exchanges. Besides, derivative trading was introduced in Index futures on NSE and BSE. The ALBM[@] on NSE is rated as equal to forward trading and badla on BSE.

The controls on Mutual Funds, Venture Capital Funds, India Funds, Initial public offers, etc., were modified to promote investor protection and better transparency and disclosures. SEBI is made the single nodal agency for control on VCFs, MMMFs and FFIs, etc.

The growth of I.T. companies and those of multi-media, telecommunications, etc. on the stock exchanges has increased the trade volumes on the one hand and volatility of the market on the other hand.

---

1. V.A. Avadhani, "Monetarist Approach to Share Prices in India", *Stock Exchange Review*, May 1991.

@ ALBM is Automatic Lending and Borrowing Mechanism.

TRADING AND SETTLEMENT

Speculative Traders vs. Genuine Investors

The investors in the stock market can be classified as genuine investors and speculative investors. The former take delivery of shares and give delivery with no intention to deal in carry forward business. The latter, however, do not give or take delivery of shares but only deal in differences in purchase and sale prices. Even if they take delivery, their intention is to make gain on differences between purchase and sale prices. Long-term gains are the motive of the genuine investors. Any genuine investor can have short-term gains of a few months when he buys and sells along with delivery. The essential difference between these two classes lies in the intention to take and give delivery of shares or to just carry forward and to gain in differences.

Types of Speculators

On the stock markets, there are various classes of brokers, depending on their actions and specialisation. Essentially, a broker is an intermediary between buyers and sellers of securities. His clients may be individuals, institutions like companies, trusts, charities, etc., banks and financial institutions (including mutual funds). Some of these clients may be speculators also doing business to carry forward and dealing in differences in prices. Secondly, there are jobbers or *Taravaniwallas* who are wholesalers doing both buying and selling in selected scrips. They give both bid and offer prices for the scrips they trade in. They are like market makers in foreign markets. Thirdly, there are *badliwallas* financing the carry-forward transactions and lending securities when necessary. Such carry forward or *badli* transactions are facilitated by blank transfer of TDs with shares. These blank transfers are transfers without any insertion on them, the names of the transferees and without any need for payment of stamp duty, etc.

On the stock exchange, there are two main categories of speculators, namely, bulls and bears. Bulls are *Tejiwallas* who buy shares in expectation of selling at higher prices. Bears are known as *Mandiwallas* who sell securities in expectation of a fall in prices and buying at a later date. Stags are those members who neither buy nor sell but apply for subscription to new issues expecting to sell them at a higher price later when these issues are quoted on the stock exchange.

Activities of Brokers

In addition to the above classes of brokers who are members of the stock exchange, there are a few who act as arbitrageurs as between two or more stock exchanges. Thus these members buy in one market and sell in another market to take advantage of the price differences in the same scrip as between different markets.

Some brokers specialise in dealing in the specified Group (A) which are speculative scrips and some have carry forward facility (badla). There are others who only deal in non-specified Group (B) where delivery of shares is given and taken. There are a few dealers who also specialise in odd lots which are not in the marketable lots so as to facilitate buying and selling in them for investors. Some stock exchanges hold separate trading sessions for odd lots and debentures where the brokers put through their transactions. Marketable lots are shares of 100 or 50, when the share's face value is ₹ 10; and 5 when the shares are of face value of ₹ 100 and ₹ 50. Trading in odd lots is no longer necessary, as the problem of odd lots does not exist now.

There is a separate category of brokers dealing only in new issues, underwriting, marketing, lead management and even merchant banking, etc. Besides, many brokers also undertake the business of mobilising fixed deposits for companies. Some activities akin to money market operations are undertaken by brokers like arranging inter-corporate investments, discounting of commercial bills of exchange or trading in UTI units or PSU Bonds, etc. Some brokers specialise in Government securities market, which is a part of the stock market operations. The Government and semi-Government securities and government guaranteed bonds are quoted on the stock exchanges. Their trading does not take place in the trading ring but over the counter of the brokers *vis-a-vis* the investing banks, financial institutions or other brokers.

As referred to earlier, many brokers undertake activities in the primary market in addition to the secondary market. These two markets are complementary and brokers having activities in both the markets are at an advantage in that they can secure contacts with companies, lead banks, financial institutions, etc. They can secure shares of these companies underwritten or marketed by them for keeping as their inventories. In this market, the brokers act mainly as marketing agents sometimes as underwriters, issue managers, lead managers, merchant bankers, consultants and even as registrars. The most common activity undertaken by brokers in this respect is consultancy and advice to investors, be they individual clients or institutional clients. As a follow-up of this, they also provide the services of portfolio management to big clients, institutions and NRIs. The investment consultancy firms established by brokers specialise in this portfolio management.

Thus, the activities of brokers can be set out as follows:

In the Primary Market: To act as underwriter-broker for new issue marketing — lead manager — issue manager — merchant banker — portfolio manager — adviser/consultant, etc.

In the Secondary Market: To act as dealer, broker, jobber, etc., in the trading ring, badla financier for carry forward business — arbitrageur buying and selling as between the different markets, as in Mumbai and Delhi — dealer in Government securities, bonds, etc., adviser, consultant and portfolio manager, etc.

Allied Services: Investor services like home delivery of shares, arranging for transfer of shares, safe custody of shares, etc., dealing in inter-corporate investment to act as broker for fixed deposits of companies, to operate in the money market, PSU bonds, UTI units, Mutual Fund Schemes, etc.

Brokers' Charges

Except to the charitable trusts, the broker charges brokerage to all clients, after effecting the purchase or sale and at the time of passing the contract note. The brokerage, which may range from 0.5 to 2.5%, is included in the price charged but not separately shown. The SEBI has now insisted on their showing the brokerage separately. Even a smaller brokerage may be charged depending on the volume of business and frequency of dealings put through for the client. Generally, the prices charged by the broker are higher than those officially quoted in the quotation list. This is because the broker includes the brokerage in the price and in the price band prevailing in the market on any day, the higher price is used for sale to the client and lower one for purchase as he has to buy from and sell to the jobber, who quotes in the reverse order, namely, buy low and sell high. This is the general practice of brokers, and this can be mistaken by the clients as if the broker is overcharging them. Brokers are also collecting from clients the service charge of 5% on the brokerage income, which they pay to govt., and which is shown separately in the Contract Note.

Delivery/Payment

The broker takes the cheque for purchase first and delivers the shares later in a purchase deal. He pays by cheque later but takes delivery of shares first for a sale transaction. This is explained by the settlement procedure of the stock exchanges, which has fixed the pay-in day and delivery dates first. All the members have to pay money or deliver shares first to the clearing house. On a later day fixed for pay-out, the clearing house pays by cheque and delivers the shares to the members. These transactions of members with the clearing house can be effected only when their clients in turn first pay-in and send the cheques or deliver shares and later get the cheques from them or shares delivered later on the pay-out day.

If the shares are not available with the selling brokers as there were short sales and the buyer insists on the delivery, the buyer member can ask the stock exchange for auction of those shares and get them from any member for delivery. This process takes a few more days and leads to delays in the settlement and clearing process. It is, therefore, possible that the buyer can get shares only after 40 to 50 days in the case of Group A shares and 15 to 30 days in the case of Group B shares. Similarly, the seller receives his cheque for payment after 45 to 60 days after the sale is put through in the case of Group A and 30 to 40 days in the case of Group B, on the B.S.E. which are now reduced due to weekly settlement. Due to Demat form of trading and quicker settlement and clearing through electronic mode, the time periods are very much reduced.

Settlement Procedure

The settlement procedure of the stock exchange is to be understood to comprehend why such delays take place. The Settlement Committee of the exchange fixes the schedules of trading and settlement for each group separately (A, B Groups). In these schedules, for each settlement, there will be 5 to 15 trading days (Saturdays, Sundays, and holidays excluded) after which three days would be set apart for effecting squaring up and carry forward (Badla). There will be one or two days for correcting errors and omissions and secure a final settlement of each member's position *vis-a-vis* others in respect of all scrips. Taking both sales and purchases scrip-wise, the net position is arrived and payment to be made or received is determined accordingly. Then a pay-in day is fixed for delivering cheques or shares to the clearing house by those who are due to give. There will be the first pay-in day and after a couple of days, a final pay-in day to help clear up all payments due. Then finally pay-out day is fixed with a gap of a day or two for the clearing house to make all payments out or delivery for shares to members. With the introduction of National Settlement System (NSD) deliveries are effected within a few days.

Auctions

Auctions are arranged for scrips which could not be delivered even on the final day. These auctions are tenders for sale of the desired scrips in the quantities purchased but not delivered so that delivery can be effected to the buyers. Auction in Group A is automatic when the seller fails to deliver on the appointed day and at the request of the buyer in the case of Group B. Auctions are arranged by the stock exchange by inviting bids from other members to buy the shares on behalf of the member who could not deliver the shares.

Clearing Procedure

Daily after trading is completed, members submit to the exchange their soudas (memos of purchases and sales scrip-wise). On the next day, if there are any objections or corrections, they are submitted in the form of wandha memos (objections). This process goes on daily for all the 5 to 10 trading days. These memos are fed to the computer and the daily net position is arrived at. If the stock exchange authorities impose any margins, they are collected from members and deposited in the clearing house. At the end of the settlement, the overall net position of a member is arrived at after taking into account the dealings, squared up and those to be carried forward. During the three days, set apart for badla settlement, members' squaring up position and carry forward position is known. Any objections or errors are recorded and corrections carried out. Then the final corrected position of members is arrived at. At this stage, the carry over margins, if imposed, are collected. This forms the basis for asking the members to pay-in or deliver the shares on the pay-in day. The entire process involves time varying from 30 days to 60 days, mainly due to the large trading volume and secondly, due to the large component of speculative trading and carry forward transactions on the BSE. Now, with electronic clearing system, the time taken was reduced to a few days, or less than a week.

Recent Trends

The recent trends on stock exchanges are increased volumes due to electronic form of trading, higher volatility in prices, and larger role played by FIIs, and institutional players. Due to liberalisation and discretion to banks to lend to capital market, credit flowing from banks has also increased. Despite the fact that new issues market is depressed for some years, stock market activity has continued to be active, particularly during 2003-07.

The new economy stocks in the form of those of I.T. companies, Telecommunications, multi-media, software and bio-tech companies have become more popular during 1999-2001 and their price changes were very high due to the international forces and trends in Nasdaq and Wall Street, and due to expected high earnings per share. But with disappointments in their earnings, their share prices fell but due to bear hammering and a speculative scam, prices fell to new lows involving losses to investors on a large-scale, during 2001 to 2003. The stock markets picked up in 2004 to 2007 on reports of good fundamentals of the economy, corporate results and upswing in the international markets, reaching a peak level at end Dec. 2007.

Trading Pattern in the Markets

The trading turnover in the NSE is more than in the BSE, because of larger volume of trade in high net worth companies listed and the larger volume of trade by FIIs and FIs and MFs and other high net worth investors on the NSE. The market capitalization on the other hand, is higher on the BSE due to larger number of companies listed and their higher net worth.

The market capitalization as a percentage of GDP at current prices was almost one hundred per cent as in March 2005, when the sensex was at 6,493 level, but in July 2007 when the sensex had reached an all time peak of 15,800, almost double of that in 2005, the MC should have gone to more than the value of the GDP at current prices. This reflects the growth in importance of the equity markets in the economy, strong fundamentals of the corporate sector and of the stock market as an index of the state of the economy.

The trading value was about ₹16 lakh crore in 2005 in the cash market, which has gone up to three times or more on the futures and options markets, although it was started only recently in 2000 and 2001. Futures are more popular than the options in F&O segment. Besides, the interest rate futures although permitted by the RBI has not taken off on the NSE. During 2005-06, the turnover in the cash segment was about ₹16 lakh crore on the NSE while the same in the F&O segment it was ₹48 lakh crore – about three times that in the cash market – which indicates the growth in importance of the F&O segment in the stock market due to the operations of foreign institutions and foreign investors. In 2006-07, when the turnover in the cash market was ₹19-20 lakh crore and that in the derivative segment had gone up to ₹74 lakh crores. In 2010-11, the turnover of cash market on BSE was only ₹11,03,467 crore, while the same on NSE was ₹35,77,412 crore. The turnover in the derivative market on the NSE was ₹315.330 crore in the year 2012-13 in respect of index options which is nearly five times that in the cash market (on the NSE cash turnover was ₹27,08,380 crore in the same year).

There are two inferences from the above discussion. One is that the NSE is more prominent in the derivative market than the BSE. Second, the derivative markets have by themselves become more significant in trading in the Indian financial markets than the cash market.

✠ ✠ ✠

DEBT (GILTED SECURITIES) MARKET

39

Introduction

Debt securities are of two categories, namely, that of government and corporate debt. As trading in gilted debt constitutes the bulk in this market, attention is concentrated on Government securities. In India, trading in corporate debt is in an infant stage and has yet to be developed. Attempts are being made now to develop corporate debt trading also on the NSE but it has still to takeoff to deserve any worthwhile discussion on it.

Trading in government securities is referred to as the gilt-edged market. This is mostly over the counter market and trading is confined to banks, financial institutions and PFs. The role of brokers is to intermediate as between the above institutions through their contacts with the money managers in the banks. The government sector is a major borrower in India and government securities represent government debt to the other sectors of the economy. The government sector includes the Central and State governments, local and municipal bodies and semi-government bodies, whose securities are guaranteed by the Central or State Governments. These agencies or bodies borrow every year from the capital market in the form of new loans and bonds floated. Besides, their old securities are also traded in the stock market.

Emergence of Public Debt

The government spends more than its income by borrowing from various sources to meet the growing needs of defence, social services and planned development. The borrowing in the form of market loans in rupees is the internal debt of the government and borrowing from external agencies in other currencies is its external debt. Since 1951, the importance of public borrowing as a source of financing government expenditure has increased enormously and public debt began to grow by leaps and bounds due to the increasing planned expenditure under the various five-year plans. The ratio of market borrowing to plan outlay was fairly steady at around 10-12 per cent up to the Third Plan period, but rose to 17.6 per cent in the Fourth Plan, 15.9 per cent in the Fifth Plan and about 20 per cent in the Sixth Plan. Market borrowing in the Seventh Plan period was planned at 17 per cent of the total plan outlay, but is was higher due to the shortfall in resources raised from tax and non-tax sources. In more recent years, the amount of Central Government borrowings from the market rose from ₹73,431 crore in 2000-01 to ₹1,09,504 crore in 2007-08 and ₹5,58,000 crore in 2012-13. The outstanding internal debt of the Centre and States worked out to around 30% to 40% of the total revenue expenditure Interest payments constituted around 13% of total GDP.

External vs. Internal Debt

The debt of the Government of India consists of two components internal and external. At the end March 2011, internal debt and the external debt worked out to of 60-70% of GDP.[@] Of the total internal liabilities, a part of if it is in the form of unfunded debt. Some Treasury bills held by the RBI are also converted into dated securities. In fact the bulk of the public debt, namely, more than 90 per cent in the form of Treasury bills, is held by the RBI and the rest by banks and financial institutions. There is, however, no developed market for Treasury bills. It is only the marketable internal debt of the government which has a respectable turnover and a market worth the name in the stock exchanges.

Management of Public Debt

In terms of the provisions of the Public Debt Act, 1944, replaced by Government Securities Act (2005), the administration of public debt of the Centre and the States is entrusted to the RBI. The actual administration is carried out by the Public Debt offices of the RBI in Mumbai, Bangalore, Chennai, Kolkata, Guwahati, Hyderabad, Kanpur, Nagpur, New Delhi, Patna, etc. The government business and their accounts are looked after in these centres. Besides, the items of government work are also entrusted to the SBI and nationalised banks in addition to the treasury offices with currency chests in the district headquarters. These offices report their transactions to the Central Accounts Section at the Nagpur Office of the RBI, which consolidates these accounts.

Public debt management is concerned with the raising of finance for the government through market loans, Treasury bills and other methods. The required finance in any year is governed by the budgetary considerations of their revenue and expenditure. The amount of finance to be raised, the time, the rate of interest and terms of loans are all decided by the Ministry of Finance in consultation with the RBI. The RBI acts as an underwriter for government loans, and uses its moral influence on the market to see that full subscription takes place for the loans floated.

The role of RBI in debt management is (*i*) to keep the cost of financing to the minimum consistent with the offer of market-related interest rates on govt. securities; (*ii*) to maintain the market stable and smooth; (*iii*) to meet the portfolio requirements of all investors to the extent possible; and (iv) to maintain a minimum level of activity in the market with a view to providing liquidity to the securities in the market for the purpose of developing the market.

Open Market Operations

As part of the debt management policy of the RBI, it operates in the gilt-edged market to buy and sell government securities on cash/switch basis. These operations directly affect the reserve base of the banks through an increase or decrease in the cash with banks or the public. These operations are designed to bring about a proper change in the size, composition, ownership and distribution of the marketable debt of the government, as well as to influence the prices and yields on these securities in tune with the interest rate and credit policies of the government and the RBI. Although these operations have a monetary import, they are not used for the support of monetary policy as such. But they help adjustment of the liquidity position in the market and indirectly help the operation of monetary policy. The government debt requirements and the cost of such operations influence the debt management policy in India. The open market operation in 2006-07 were very subdued at ₹5,124 crore of net sales, as against net purchase of ₹514 crore in 1995-96.

@ RBI Annual Report at end March 2014.

The Centre raised through market loans an amount of ₹73,431 crore in 2000-01 and ₹9,74,976 crore in 2013-14. The State Governments have raised gross amount of ₹13,300 crore in 2000-01 and ₹1,03,910 crore in 2010-11 on a gross basis. The public sector undertakings mobilised funds through bonds of ₹10,325 crore in 2006-07 and ₹50,865 crore in 2013-14.

In India, open market operations were conducted only in selected Central Government securities, whose stocks with the RBI are adequate for these operations to be conducted. The reason for confining these operations to the central securities is that these are held by the RBI on its own investment account and can be used as backing for the issue of currency. Very few are conducted on cash basis while the majority are on a switch basis. The general trend is that there are more sales of securities than purchases to help curtail the liquidity with the banks and financial institutions as part of the anti-inflationary drive of the monetary policy. Only in a few exceptional years, there were net purchases which helped the augmentation of reserves with the banks and liquidity in the economy.

Banks vs. Gilt-edged Market

Banks are required by law to invest a proportion of their deposits as determined by the statutory liquidity ratio, which is at present 24%. The contributions to the new securities, trusts, PFs, etc., who have surplus funds are required by law to invest in these securities. Due to the controlled rates of interest on these securities, these are not attractive for the general public to invest or hold. There is, therefore, no secondary market in the government securities. But banks, financial institutions and PFs trade in these securities to take advantage of the differences in prices between the primary and secondary markets, and to gain in yields or to secure a maturity distribution that they desire to have. Repo deals are struck by banks with RBI to optimise return on surplus funds. Repos are allowed by RBI to DFHI, STCI, banks, etc., for 1 to 4 days to control the supply and demand maladjustments in the money market.

The portfolio requirements of investors are determined by the maturity pattern and yield pattern of their existing securities. They operate in the market to take advantage of the price and yield differentials. The price differential exists due to the adjustments taking place between the primary and secondary markets in securities representing trading at wholesale and retail levels. The price differentials may also be due to the distance factor, as between centres or due to the regional disparities in industrial development. The registration charges or stamp duties in each State in respect of government securities are different. Besides, regional disparities may exist in industrial development leading to differences in PF accruals and hence in the demand for government securities as between the states.

Brokers and the Market

Brokers did not enter the initial issues market as the issue of government securities is underwritten in a monopolistic manner by the RBI until 1995. But now some primary dealers are licensed to operate and underwrite in this market. Secondly, most brokers do not act as dealers in government securities due to lack of financial backing to hold these securities. They mostly act as intermediaries between trading banks, financial institutions and PFs etc., in the secondary market. The brokers can deal with the RBI as per the prices fixed in their buying and selling lists. Bilateral and triangular switches are put through with the banks by the RBI for which brokers act as intermediaries. The RBI fixes quota for each bank for these switch deals, with a view to preventing the banks from unloading low-yielding bonds on the RBI. The financial institutions and PFs are permitted to buy from the RBI their requirements of securities in terms of maturity and yields. There is selected list of brokers called approved list of brokers of the RBI in each centre, with which the RBI deals in government securities. The approved list is very restrictive in the sense that only a few with a proven record of government business and a large turnover in addition to their reputation for creditworthiness and having SGL Accounts with the RBI, are enrolled as approved brokers. Their profit margins are restricted due to the limited market and due to the captive nature of the market with the RBI and banks as major holders of these securities. But they make their profits on a larger turnover in government securities.

RBI and the Gilt-edged Market

The RBI plans in consultation with the government and prospective subscribers the amounts to be floated, the timing and terms of new issues, such as coupon rates, maturity of loans, etc. The policy matters relating to the new issues are attended to by the Secretary's Department in the RBI. The Public Debt Offices of the Banking Department of the RBI arrange for the subscription, payment of interest, renewal, etc., of these securities. The Securities Department deals with the purchase and sale of securities on behalf of government departments, agencies and the RBI and is responsible for the safe custody of these securities. The centralisation and co-ordination of the public debt accounts of the Central and State Governments and making arrangements for new loan floatations are carried out by the Central Debt Section of the Department of Government and Bank Accounts. Each Public Debt Office works as an independent unit and is responsible for attending to transactions relating to the public debt matters within its territorial jurisdiction. The matter of servicing of loans registered in its office is the responsibility of the PDO of the RBI under the present system of decentralised servicing. Only in respect of some bonds, such as compensation and rehabilitation bonds, the accounts are maintained in the Central Office where the centralised system operates.

The Central Accounts Section (CAS) in Nagpur exercises accounting functions for the government and co-ordinates these accounts of all offices. The principal functions of the CAS are maintenance of deposit accounts of the Central Government departments, including the Railways, P & T and the State Governments, keeping a watch on the minimum balances to be maintained by government, grant and recovery of advances from the State Governments, investment of surplus funds of governments, issue of Treasury bills, *ad hoc* Treasury bills, remittance facilities, etc. for the government. All these accounts are now computerised and all regional offices are connected through the internet.

The Secretary's Department of the RBI is entrusted with the conduct of open market operations in addition to the policy matters relating to the floatation of new loans, Treasury bills, creation and cancellation of *ad hoc* Treasury bills, etc., ways and means advances to Centre and State Governments and all matters to liaison with these governments.

Investment Criteria of Banks

Commercial banks manage their investment portfolio with the following objectives:

1. to provide a steady income and reduce risk
2. to optimise the return; and
3. to obtain capital gains, or record capital losses.

Generally, the portfolio management of commercial banks involves a compromise between the maximising of return and minimising of risk. The investment portfolio of the banks is influenced by the various economic factors such as monetary policy, credit regulations, the outlook of the interest rates, etc. Banks are generally unwilling to hold securities of long-dated maturities as they are sensitive to the risk of the fall in the capital value although, in more recent years, they are holding them for yield consideration. If interest rates are likely to rise, banks will shift from medium to short and *vice versa*. From the banks' point of view, long-dated loans are not an ideal type of investment, as they are likely to have greater fluctuations in the capital values. Banks give support to long-dated loans although they may disinvest them soon after in favour of high-yielding loans. But PFs, Pension Funds, LIC, Insurance Companies, etc., prefer investment in the long-dated loans for yield purposes. They acquire them as and when funds accrue to them by purchasing them from the banks in the open market or the RBI.

Reforms in the Gilt-edged Market

The Reserve Bank has been taking steps since 1968 to activate the gilt-edged market. It has widened the range and scope of open market operations and State Governments were also assured of success in their loan operations although the Reserve Bank does not invest in the State Government securities on its own investment account. The practice of banks accepting a margin account from the State Governments either directly or indirectly for subscribing to State loans has been stopped by the Reserve Bank. These measures have imparted a spirit of confidence to the market and the State Government securities have since then become more attractive to banks due to higher yields in the range of short and medium-dated maturities in which the banks are mostly interested. In general, the marketability of all government securities has been made more easy since 1968 by the measures taken by the Reserve Bank and by its own willingness to do open market operations in a larger number of securities than hitherto.

The Government of India have also taken a significant step amending the rules governing the provident fund investment, whereby the provident funds are able to invest up to 45% of their monthly provident fund accumulation in government-guaranteed bonds. This has helped the sentiment in the gilt-edged market and in particular in the guaranteed bond market. As referred to earlier, the banks have also been keeping a part of their excess funds in government-guaranteed bonds in view of their higher yields. This is in addition to their SLR investments.

Following the securities scandal of 1991-92, some further reforms were introduced in 1992. Bank Receipts (BR) in Government securities are not permitted where the SGL facility is available. In cases where BR is permitted, it is only for ready deals. Ready forward deals through BRs are prohibited in Government securities, Treasury bills etc.

Effective from June 22, 1992, RBI issued new guidelines for dealings in Government securities for banks and brokers. All inter bank ready forward deals are prohibited in Government securities, P.S.U. bonds, U.T.I. units. Where SGL facility is available, all deals should be put through the SGL only. Bank receipts in lieu of physical certificates are not allowed, where SGL facility is available. BRs should be used only for ready deals under certain specific conditions such as delivery from another centre, or where allotment advice is there but certificates are not issued, etc. Where there are no stocks with the SGL, no deals are allowed and banks should make sure of their position in the SGL No ready forward or double ready forward deals are permitted in any securities or bonds even for a client's account or in Portfolio Management System. The operations in SGL, the transfer forms and the procedures have been streamlined and computerised to eliminate all malpractices of short sales or wrong entries, and to improve transparency. The system of delivery versus payment is imposed on all operations.

The Banks have been advised to strengthen their internal Control System. The Reporting and monitoring has to be supervised by qualified inspectors and auditors. The top management is held responsible for inspection and monitoring. Similarly, restrictions have been imposed on the deals to be put through the brokers and business is to be distributed through as many brokers as possible.

The rates on Government securities were enhanced to make them market related rates since 1985. With a view to developing an active market in Government securities, the dependence of the Government on the market is increased and its dependence on RBI and banks is reduced. The system of auctioning of Government securities was introduced in 1992 to allow the rates to reflect the true market conditions. The Central Government securities were sold on auction basis in respect of 5 years and 10 years loans in June and August 1992 respectively and this practice is now continued.

The more recent reforms, affecting the Govt. securities market, as also other markets are listed briefly here:

(*i*) The Board for Financial Supervision was set up in Nov. 1994, with the Governor of RBI as its Chairman, to oversee the whole financial system, through proper monitoring and inspection of banks, financial institutions and non-bank financial companies.

(*ii*) The Securities Trading Corporation of India (STCI) was set up in May 1994 to operate and promote Secondary market trading, in Govt. securities, to supplement the activities of DFHI.

(*iii*) A new Dept. of Supervision (DOS) was started in RBI in December 1993, and this Dept. provides the operational support to B.F.S. This Dept. was bifurcated into two, namely, Dept. of Banking Supervision and Dept. of Non-banking Supervision in 1997, to improve operational efficiency.

(*iv*) Starting of a new cadre of primary dealers in Govt. securities market to help RBI operations and act as market makers, etc.

(*v*) Streamlining the whole system of operations in Govt. securities, on spot basis (DVP), SGL deals, NSE deals, Broker deals, etc., and imparting transparency to them.

The work and nomenclature of various departments in RBI have been changing from time to time.

Recent Reforms

Auctions of Central Government securities and Treasury bills were introduced in 1992-93, which resulted in market determined yields on these instruments. The RBI has discontinued the issue of *ad hoc* Treasury bills to make the monetary policy independent of government debt management. New instruments of debt were issued like Zero Coupon Bonds, Floating Rate Bonds and Capital Indexed Bonds, etc.

The issue of and development of Repos in all Gilt-edged securities was initiated in 1997. This was also extended to Treasury bills for providing the liquidity adjustment facility to all banks and primary dealers, who were enlisted with RBI since 1995. Compulsory holding of all Government securities in Demat form and their trading on screenbased trading system on the stock exchanges were provided for during 2002-03. The market in Government securities was opened to Mutual Funds and FIIs, to make it more broad-based. In systems and procedures, delivery *versus* payment and real time gross settlement of all payments electronically were introduced in 2004 after setting up of negotiated dealing system and Clearing Corporation of India in 2002. Retail trading in Government securities and government debt, buyback scheme were successfully implemented. In addition to PDs and banks, the Repo market was thrown open to non-banks.

Over the years, the turnover in government bond market has become more than 200% of GDP. Primary dealers share in turnover is the largest at 65%-70% of the total. The need for more debt of government and semi-government bodies for infrastructure bonds and those of banks and state sponsored bodies is likely to increase further in the coming years.

There was thus widening and deepening of the Government securities market along with strengthening of institutional structure and systems and procedures. These reforms brought about application of latest technology, better work management and quicker settlement and clearing of payments and better regulatory framework.

Types of Loans

The Central Government loans are of two kinds: (a) Direct loans and (b) Indirect loans. Direct loans include funded loans and non-funded loans issued by the Central Government. Indirect loans are those guaranteed by the Central Government but issued by various government agencies such as IFCI, IIBI, FCI, NABARD, NHB etc. Among the funded loans, there are terminable (dated) and non-terminable loans. The latter have been repaid. The rest of the funded loans are dated loans. The unfunded loans include Treasury Savings Deposit Certificates, Defence Deposit Certificates and Annuity Certificates. The RBI has gradually withdrawn or repaid all non-terminable loans, with the result that there are now only dated loans in the market in addition to 364 days Treasury Risks.

Switch Deals

The sale/purchase of one security against purchase/sale of another security of an equal amount is called a switch operation. These are undertaken for re-arranging the yield pattern and/or the maturity pattern without disturbing the overall portfolio structure of investments. Timely switch operations might help gain in returns or avoid possible capital losses.

Washed Sales

A washed sale is the sale of a security and immediate repurchase of the same for the purpose of registering a realised capital gain/loss for tax purposes, while recording the re-acquisition at the new cost. Sales for registering capital loss are subject to the condition that the same security may not be purchased thirty days before or after the sale.

Current Yield

Coupon rate is the rate at which the bond carried interest. This is the nominal yield payable on the face value of the bond regularly and remains unaltered, say, for example, the 6-1/4% Central loan 1996. The State loans carry a higher coupon rate than the Central loan for comparable maturity to compensate for the larger risk involved in the former.

$$\text{The current yield} = \frac{\text{Coupon rate} \times \text{face value (100)}}{\text{Cost (Market price)}}$$

The short-term investors and banks generally look into current yields of Govt. securities in their investments. The yields curve should then depict the current yields or coupon rates if they are first issued maturity-wise. When banks invest in primary market, what they compare are the yields on various maturities in the Primary market, as they are issued by the govt. The maturity wise yields are set out in the chart below, for 1995 only for illustration of yield curve:

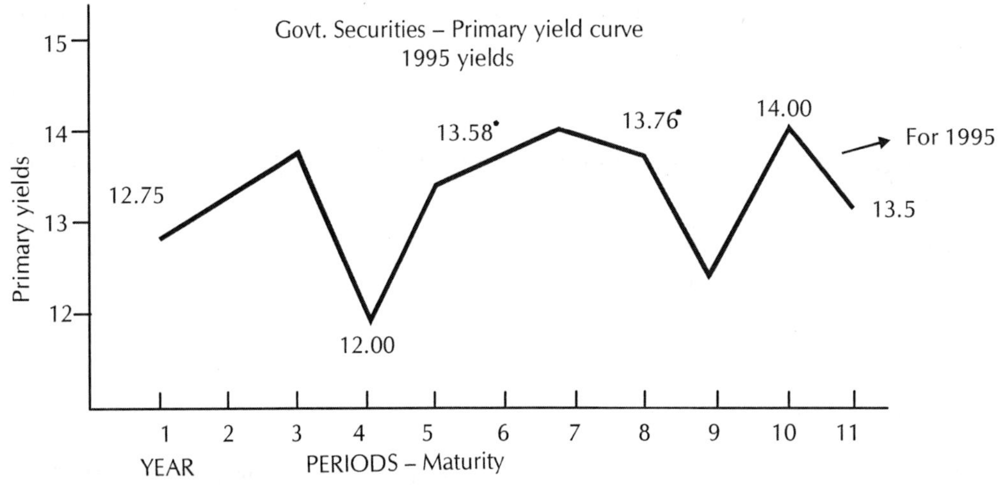

Some maturities showed lower yields and there is no consistent upward trend in the curve, due to differences in the demand and coupon rates, issued in various years. Banks are interested in current yields in the secondary market. In 2000-01, the cut off yields were lower and ranged from 9.47 to 11.61% in respect of government fresh borowings. They were declining year after year later on and stood at a range of 5.8 to 7.2% in September 2004. The primary market cut off yields in 2006-07 were in the range of 7.06% to 8.72%.

Redemption Yield

This takes into account the price paid for the bond, length of the time to maturity and the coupon rate of the bond. This is the yield which the holder gets per annum if he holds it until maturity and is the same as current yield if the bond is purchased at par (₹100). Redemption yield = Current yield + or – (minus) average annual capaital gain or loss (for the bond purchased at a discount or premium as the case may be).

The gilt-edged yields have no role in determining the amount of funds borrowed or on the responsiveness of the public to the borrowing programme. For, the former depends on the projected outlays of the government in the various annual plans and the latter on liquidity requirements imposed on banks. As the gilt-edged market is an isolated and captive market, the linkage of these rates to other interest rates in the economy is indirect and weak. The dichotomy in rates in the Government securities and other securities cannot be stretched too far as it will constitute a levy on the holders of government debt for the benefit of others and loss on such investments have to be made good by higher rates to the non-government sector. There is thus no feasibility of insulating completely the gilt-edged market from the rest of the money market. Only since 1992, the gilt-edged rates have been freed to approach the market rates through a system of auctioning of securities. The yield spread between government debt and corporate debt has narrowed down more recently. Redemption yields on Central Government securities varied from 6.06% for 5-year bonds to 8.39% on bonds maturing after 10 years as in 2010.

Experience in Other Countries

In the U.S.A., U.K. and developed Western countries, Government securities markets are well developed although they are mainly traded in over-the-counter market. The brokerage firms and discount houses in the U.S.A. and security dealers in U.K. deal in this market both as buyers and sellers. There is also an Open Market Committee in the U.S.A. to decide on policy matters of day-to-day operations in the market. In some countries, these open market operations are carried on not only in Government securities and Treasury bills but in private commercial bills of exchange, foreign exchange, gold, etc. In India, although the RBI is authorised to buy and sell Central and State Government securities or securities of local authorities or Treasury bills, commercial bills of exchange, etc., it operates in practice only in a selected list of Central Government securities. Thus, the experience in foreign countries is different from that in India, both in respect of RBI operations in the market and the nature of the market itself. There is thus vast scope for development of this market in India.

Principal Forms of Government Securities

There are three forms in which Government securities are held: *(i)* Stock or Book Debt, *(ii)* Promissory Notes, and *(iii)* Bearer Bonds.

(i) Stock Certificates: When the debt is held in the form of stock, the owner is given a certificate to the effect that the owner is the holder of a stock (loan or loans) registered in the books of PDO of RBI, as to its rate of interest, dates when interest is payable and its maturity. This Stock Certificate is not transferable by mere endorsement as the execution of a transfer deed is necessary for its transfer. Stocks can be held jointly by more than one person but these will have to be transferred by all the surviving joint holders. Stock certificates need not be presented for interest payment but interest warrants are sent by the PDO to the holders on the due dates. These certificates are the only form of Government security which can be held by Trustees of specified Trusts or holders of offices other than public offices. The officials holding the office can negotiate and sign for their respective offices in respect of these certificates. These stocks can also be held in the form of Subsidiary General Ledger Accounts (SGL) with the PDO of the RBI. This form of holding in SGL is restricted to institutions, agencies, banks and those with a corporate status having regular dealings with the RBI.

(ii) Promissory Notes: This is a promise by the Government, Central/State, to a person named therein, to pay a specified amount at a specified date and to pay interest at a fixed rate at periodical intervals at a particular office of the RBI. It is a negotiable instrument payable to the order of a specified person and transferable by endorsement.

(iii) Bearer Bonds: A bearer bond certifies that the bearer is entitled to a certain sum specified in rupees on the date indicated in accordance with the terms of a particular loan to which the bond relates. Printed

coupons for interest payable to bearer are attached to the bond. The interest is paid to the holder of the coupon and the bond is discharged on the due date of the loan to which it relates by physical presentation of the bearer. A change of ownership is effected by simple delivery of bonds by the transferor to the transferee. Examples are prize bonds and premium prize bonds. More recently, this form of loan issue was stopped by the government.

The Stock Certificates are the best of the three forms of holdings from the point of view of security and convenience of big holders of government debt. As between promissory notes and bearer bonds, the former are more secure but the latter are more easy to transfer, and get interest and repayment with the least difficulty. Thus a promissory note stands in between stock certificates and bearer bonds, from the point of view of security, on the one hand, and the ease and convenience for transfer on the other. Transactions in the stock exchange take place mainly in the form of these promissory notes as these can be transferred by endorsement and are a good delivery against contracts under the stock exchange rules.

Role of Yields

The yields on Government securities should normally be in tune with the spectrum of interest rates prevailing in the economy and to conform to the rationale of risk-return formula and inflationary expectations. But these principles do not apply to the gilt-edged market in India. Only up to 1964-65, the yield on long-term government bond was in tune with and around the bank rate. Since then, the bond yields were broadly lower than the bank rate, indicating the deliberate policy of keeping the cost of government financing low. Only in the eighties again the coupon rates on government loans were raised substantially to approximate to the market rates. Thus the long-term bond coupon rate was raised from 6-7% in the seventies to 11-11.5% during the eighties. Not only the yields on Government securities lower than those in private securities of comparable maturity but long-term yields were many times lower than those of medium and short-term yields. But this pattern is also being changed in more recent years with the coupon rates on long-term bonds rising substantially over those of short- and medium-term bonds. The trend is in tune with the policy of the government to make the gilt-edged rates to conform to the market rates and make them more attractive for the public and individuals to hold. The yields on semi-government bonds or government-guaranteed bonds are higher than those on Central and State Government bonds. As between the Centre and States, the yields on the State loans are higher than those on the Central loans in tune with the degree of their creditworthiness. In the nineties, the coupon rates were further raised to 13.5% and 14.0% for Central and State loans respectively. In India, the yield curve behaves erratically due to quick changes in liquidity, temporary imbalances in money market and forex market and different short-term and long-term expectations. During the early year of new millennium, the yields have again fallen in tune with the market trends.

Maturity Pattern

Out of the total outstanding internal debt of the Central Government, about 26% relates to the short-term debt. Out of the marketable rupee loans (other than Treasury bills), early in fifties about 11% belonged to the maturity of 5 years and below, 6% to those of 5 years to 10 years and 83% above ten years. This position has changed considerably since 1992 reforms. The proportion of debt on the long end has risen considerably over the years which shows an increasing burden of interest in the future years. The prudency of this pattern of financing is questionable, as the present burden is being increasingly passed on to the future generations. Thus, in 1970, nearly 36% of the rupee debt was in the form of loans up to 5 years, while 43% belonged to debt above 10 years. In 1987, the proportion of short-term debt (up to 5 years) went down to 10% while that of long-term (above 10 years) increased to 80%. The nature of the market has also undergone changes accordingly. The transactions in switch have gone up considerably to make adjustment in the maturity and yield pattern of the portfolio of investors, now in the form of Repos of RBI with other trading partners like banks. In March 2012, short-term debt rose to 29% and long-term debt of above 10 years fell to 31%, as part of policy of government for more balanced maturity pattern of debt for better fiscal and debt management.

Ownership of Government Debt

The market also depends on the pattern of ownership of government debt. The combined ownership of Central and State Government securities is published annually in their reports by the RBI. This pattern shows that in 1975 the RBI, banks and the government together held about 64 per cent of the debt, while "others" including private corporate bodies and individuals held only 3 per cent. More recently, the holdings of banks, RBI and the government had in fact gone up to 75% in 1999, but declined to 54% by Dec. 2006, indicating a large captive nature of the market, wherein the role of the public is almost negligible. The trend is changing as the securities and Treasury bills of the govt. were sold on auction basis, now, with "others" rising to 4% of the toal debt in 2007. By 2012, RBI and banks together held 60%. Insurance, PF, MF held 29% and the rest was held by FII, corporates, others, etc.

Trading in Secondary Market

The Government securities market is a part of the overall stock market, although trading does not take place in the trading ring of the exchange. The market is a captive market confined to banks, FIs, PFs, etc. The RBI is the leader in the market and is an underwriter for Central loans and manages the government debt by holding a large chunk of Central loans. The RBI conducts open market operations to stabilise the market and help the institutions, banks, etc., operating in the market. Only since the 80s the interest rates in this market have been raised to more realistic levels in tune with the market trends. The operations in the market still continue to be confined to banks and FIs either directly with the RBI or through brokers in the market. Even today, the market is limited in terms of the number of players and the brokers who act as intermediaries.

In the management of this market, the RBI, in addition to its traditional tools, adopted a mixture of non-traditional tools, like auctions of securities of various maturities, funding of Treasury bills, and zero coupon bonds, to reduce the costs and improve the operational efficiency. The tool of Repos as an instrument of operations is used to regulate liquidity and facilitate trade in Govt. securities, without undue fluctuations in yield. The system of fixed coupon rates is still in vogue for State Govt. securities.

The NSE has started trading in Govt. securities since June 1994 but operations were small in magnitude. So, since June 1994, the Securities Trading Corporation of India (STCI) set up in May, 1994, started operations, immediately to provide depth to the market. The market turnover on NSE rose from ₹4,147 crore in 1994-95 to ₹31,230 crore in 1996-97, and rose steeply to ₹6 lakh crore in 1999-2000 in the debt segment and further to ₹9 lakh crore in 2004-05 and ₹35 lakh crore in 2010-11.

FIIs are permitted to invest 30% of their total investment in debt instruments in gilted securities in 1997-98; they were permitted to operate in Govt. securities market since January 1997.

Operations of STCI

The focus of operations of STCI is only on dated Govt. securities, with a view to promote the market, facilitate the operations and help the RBI liquidity management. Its turnover during June 15, 1994 to March 31, 1995 (since its starting) was ₹39,631 crore, which has grown in time with its gaining experience and control on the market. Its operations are supported by the Discount and Finance House of India (DFHI) and extend to call money market and related activities. The debt market segment of NSE, trading in Central Govt. securities showed a turnover of ₹27,053 crore during 1996-97, which rose to ₹3,04,216 crore in 1999-2000 and roughly ₹26 lakh crore in 2010-11.

To develop the institutional set up in the secondary market, in these securities, the RBI initiated the following measures which are implemented since 1995-96:

(*i*) Enlistment of primary dealers in this market since March 1995, to help placement of securities, trading in the secondary market as market makers and to act as a conduit pipe of RBI's operations and to give signals to the market, regarding the policy changes of RBI. Six PDs were operating in 1997-98 and 18 PDs in 2006-07. They were paid underwriting commission and liquidity support.

(*ii*) A Delivery versus Payment System (DVP or spot deals) was started in July 1995 for cash and delivery of these securities to avoid risk in settlement.

(*iii*) RBI extended the Repos facility to DFHI and STCI.

(*iv*) Publication of SGL deals by RBI on a daily basis to impart transparency to deals in Govt. securities.

YTM fixed by RBI

The YTM curve is set out for all banks to adjust their investment portfolio of Government securities to market value as at end March of each year. For 1997-98 for example, banks were required to value at least 60% of their investment portfolio at market prices the current category. Each bank has to bifurcate investment portfolio into current category consisting of short and medium-term securities and permanent category comprising long dated securities. The banks are expected to trade and operate on securities in the current category and mark to market yields or prices at the end of the financial year. All private sector banks are directed to mark to the market values the whole of investment portfolio, unlike the public sector banks (PSBs) which have to mark 60% of its investments to the market value. This ratio was set to grow each year, until the whole of their investment portfolio is marked to the market prices.

The gilt-edged yields up to ten years, namely, yields to maturity of zero to 10 years are given by the RBI, for the banks to adjust the market value of portfolio for booking profits or losses, every year. For the year 1997-98 the YTM data were given as follows which serves an illustration purpose: For the year 2000-01 yields have gone down further to 9 to 11% for different maturities, and to 5 to 6.5% in the year 2004-05. The range of YTMs at primary issues in 2006-07 stood at 7.58 to 8.64%. The range of maturities of new loans in 2011-12 was 6 years to 30 years.

Year	*YTM*
0 =	9.43
1	10.50
2	10.83
3	11.09
4	11.28
5	11.40
6	11.57
7	11.73
8	11.88
9	12.02
10	12.15

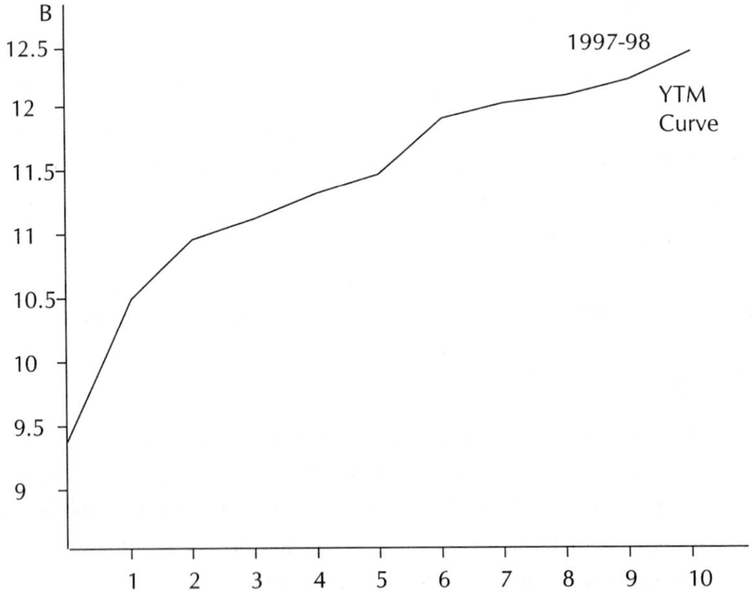

Graph of Yield Curve

The above system was replaced by market to market, value of all Government securities, held by banks both private and public, in the early years of 21st century. The yields varied from day-to-day and depend on the nature of security, maturity and time of issue in the primary market or time of transactions in the secondary market.

Redemption yields of Central Government security 10.79% 2015 are given below for the period 2005 to 2014 for illustration.

Year	*YTM*
2005-06	7.22%
2006-07	7.65%
2007-08	8.02%
2008-09	8.37%
2009-10	7.75%
2013-14	8.5% to 9.5%

✠ ✠ ✠

PART VII

MARKET INDICATORS AND PORTFOLIO MANAGEMENT SERVICS

SECURITY MARKET INDICATORS

40

Introduction

Security markets are those financial markets in which securities, like shares, bonds, debentures, etc., are issued and traded. The constituents in these markets include broker firms, financial institutions, banks, investment companies and many others including mutual funds which actively participate in the market as dealers, traders or as intermediaries. The demand emanates from investors while the supply comes from the issuers of securities. These issuers may be government, semi-government bodies, public undertakings, private corporate sector, financial institutions, etc. In the case of old securities, demand and supply may emanate from the buyers and sellers. In the case of new issues, these are issued direct to savers and investors including households, companies, institutions, PFs, etc.

Different types of securities and financial instruments are traded, purchased and sold in these markets. These instruments may be of ownership nature like equities and preference shares or of debt nature like debentures, bonds, etc. Bulk of the trading in the stock market is in these corporate securities, equities, which are traded in the trading ring. However, there are some instruments issued by the Government, Central or State, or by government bodies, municipalities, local bodies, etc., in which case they are called government and government-guaranteed bonds or semi-government bonds. The section of the market in which these are traded is also a part of the stock market and is called gilt-edged market. These markets and their indicators are set out, in this book, as financial services are provided in them.

Functions and Activity

These markets perform some basic functions and activity in the markets reflects these functions. The activity in turn is represented and measured by some leading indicators. Therein lies the importance of these indicators. These indicators would throw light on the degree and extent of the activity and trends in the market and reveal the importance of the market.

Basically, the functions of these markets are:

1. Provision for securitisation of the debt or capital issued, which promotes savings mobilisation through new capital issues.

2. Extending facilities for trading (buying and selling) in these securities so as to impart liquidity to these instruments so that investors can disinvest while new savers can invest and enter the market. This will facilitate the reallocation of funds as between securities or companies.
3. Making a quotation for a share available to the investors and companies so that their net asset values are known and they can be used for tax purposes.
4. This market also enables the companies to raise more capital from the capital market than is possible without these facilities for disinvestment, trading and liquidity.
5. For the economy as a whole, these markets help mobilisation of savings for financing of corporate and government investment in order that economic growth and rise in incomes of the people can take place on a continuing basis.

These markets have thus a vital role to play for investors at the micro level and for the economy at the macro level. For investors, it provides a venue for use of their savings for earning an income, capital appreciation and returns. For the economy, it facilitates savings mobilisation for capital formation which is necessary for economic growth.

The constituents of the markets are:

1. issuers of securities like companies and government;
2. investors or traders who buy and sell securities; and
3. intermediaries like brokers, merchant bankers, etc., who mediate between issuers and investors and as between buyers and sellers.

Segments of the Markets

Fig. 40.1 describes the segments of the security markets.

The investors in the primary issues or new issues would be only buying in the primary market but cannot sell there. They will be dealing in buying and selling in the secondary market only. Investors or institutions and buyers and sellers would deal in the secondary market through the intermediaries or brokers. The issuers of securities are the corporate units, government and semi-government bodies and public sector undertakings. The public, savers, investors and institutions, etc., can invest in both the primay and secondary markets. Their investments would be the sources of funds for the issuers of securities.

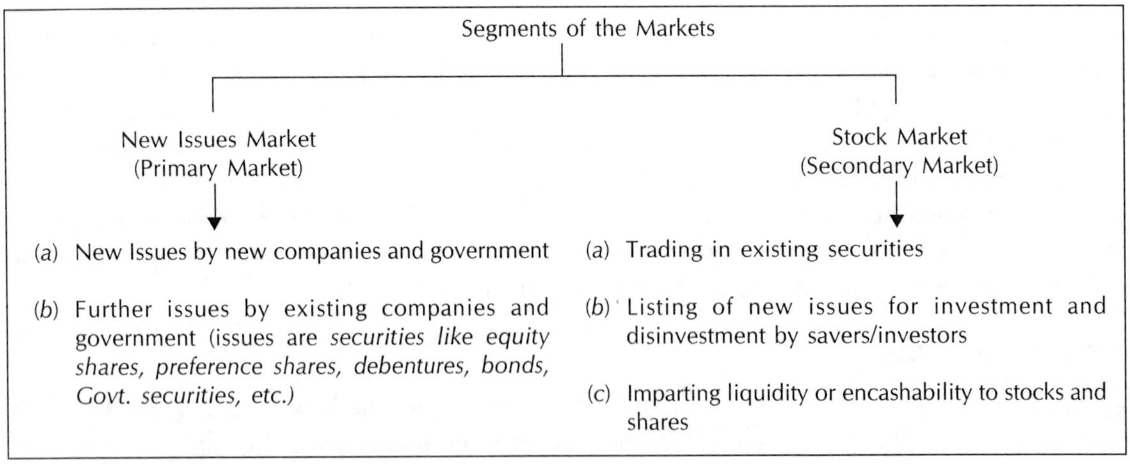

Fig. 40.1

The primary market is called new issues market or the capital market while the secondary market is called the stock market. In the primary market, the government and the public sector undertakings as well as corporate units borrow funds or issue capital in the form of securities, shares, bonds, etc. The activity here refers to raising capital of ownership or debt nature. In this market, the primary savers or investors can keep their funds for a return. In the secondary market, they can both buy and sell existing securities, invest and disinvest or rechannel funds from one company into another or one type of security into another.

The secondary market is thus an important adjunct of the primary market. The activity in these two markets is inter-linked and the indicators are also related although separate in themselves and the starting link is listing of issues on the stock markets.

The new issues, which are floated in the primary market, are permitted to be issued to the public by a nod of SEBI at price which is at par (face value) in the case of new companies or at a premium or par in the case of existing companies. The Capital Issues Controller as the authority to regulate was abolished. But in the secondary market the SEBI, the Ministry of Finance, and the stock exchange division control and regulate the stock markets and the stock exchange authorities. The stock markets are directly regulated by their own board of directos, namely, the stock exchange authorities, with the consent and approval of the government. The stock exchanges are recognised bodies to trade and deal in securities through their members who are brokers. The stock exchange authorities are self-regulatory bodies under the overall supervision of the SEBI and stock exchange division of the government.

The new issues of companies are in the form of shares — equity and preference shares — debentures, etc. The securities issued by the companies and government are listed on the stock markets after they are floated and issued to the public. So far as the Government and the semi-Government securities are concerned, they are automatically listed for trading without any conditions or fees but in the case of corporate securities, the companies have to approach the respective stock exchanges where their registered office is located for the purpose of listing. A listing agreement is entered into containing all the rules and regulations governing the conduct of the companies in respect of shares listed and the relations between the stock exchange and listed companies. The listed shares can be bought and sold and traded which will lead to price formation for shares. The resultant price may be at par or face value or at a premium or discount of the face value depending upon the demand for and supply of these shares. These demand and supply forces may in turn depend on the physical and financial performance of the companies in question and their future prospects, etc. Trading before listing is called the grey market, which is not controlled.

Sub-markets of Government Securities

In the securities market, an important segment is the gilt-edged market which comprises the Central and State Government securities, bonds of local bodies and semi-government organisations. The Reserve Bank arranges for the issue of these securities through banks and financial institutions and acts as the manager and underwriter of the issues, particularly with respect to Central Government securities. As a part of its functions, the RBI acts as a banker to the Central and State Governments and as manager of the public debt of the Central Government. In this context, it arranges for the accepting of subscriptions to the Central loans, issue of securities, servicing of these securities, repayment of loans, etc. As a part of the RBI credit control policy, the banks have to invest 25%* of their total and incremental deposits in the Central and State Government securities and other approved securities. Besides financial institutions, LIC, GIC, etc., have also to invest a part of their funds in Government securities as a statutory obligation. But in view of the lower interest rates on these securities than those on other instruments of the corporate sector, the public and individuals are not much interested in these securities. Thus, the market in government securities is a captive one and of a limited nature. The secondary market in these securities is also limited to transactions as between the banks and the RBI and among banks and financial institutions.

The market in these securities is over-the-counter (OTC), through telephones, personal contact, telex, etc., and hence the data on prices and yields, etc., are not properly reported to the stock exchange where they are quoted. But as the manager of the public debt of the government and through the operations

* Effective from October 1994, the S.L.R. on aggregate deposits was reduced to 31.5%, and thereafter to 24% in 2013 and CRR stood at 5% in 2014.

undertaken in the open market (called open market operations), the RBI collects all information on prices and compiles data on yields. The prices and yields on Government securities are thus compiled and published by the RBI regularly in their monthly and annual publications.

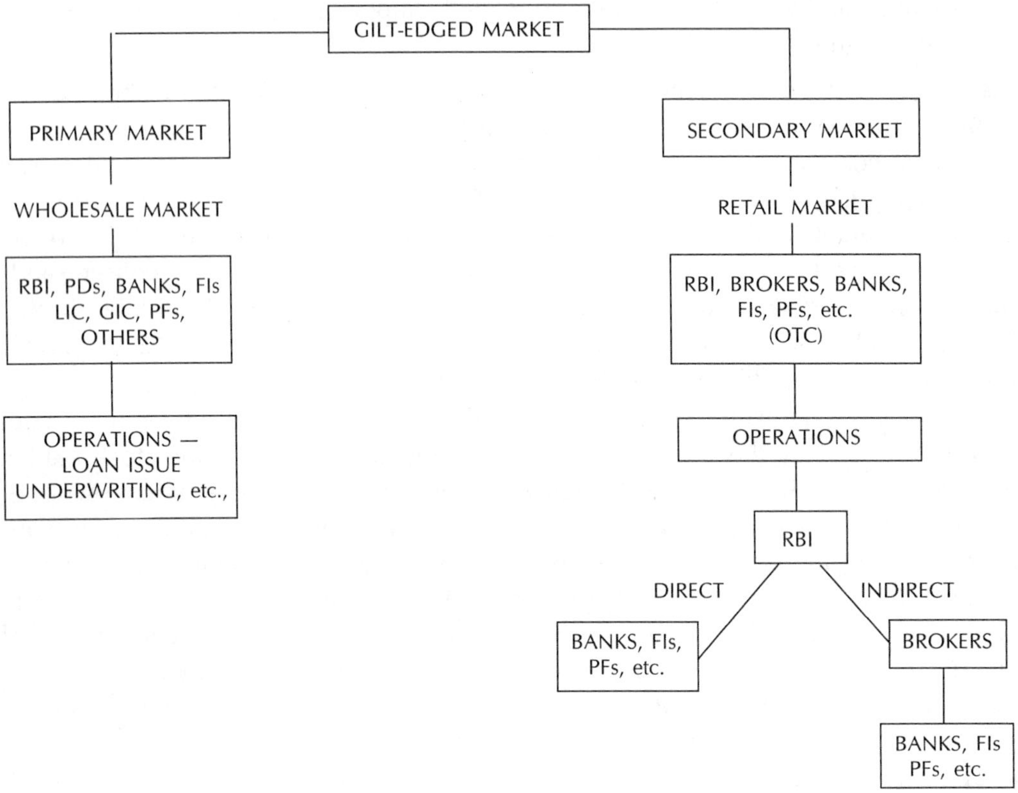

Fig. 40.2

Fig. 40.2 presents a picture of sections within the gilt-edged market, namely, primary and seconday sections, representing the issue of Government securities, wholesale and trading in retail respectively. The players in the market are RBI, banks, FIs and brokers. The RBI is the main lead manager and underwriter with respect to Central Government securities and a major holder of these securities which it now carries on through authorised primary dealers (PDs). The banks and financial institutions, PFs and companies deal in these securities with or without the help of brokers.[@] The RBI conducts open market operations of purchase and sale directly with banks and financial institutions or with the help of brokers. New securities are now sold through auctions.

Yield Curve

To give an example of the use of yields, Fig. 40.3 presents the yield curve of the Central Government securities of various maturities. The securities are loans carrying fixed coupon rates such as 7½% maturing in 2001 or 11.37% maturing in 2002, etc. The figure shows that in 1994-95, the yields varied from about 11% to 14% depending upon the maturity period of the loan, demand and supply factors, attactiveness of loans in terms of rate of interest payment and date of redemption, etc. These yields are worked out on a daily basis and are used for making decisions by banks and FIs for purchases and sale deals and reshuffling of their portfolios of Government and semi-Government securities with the objective of maximising returns and booking capital gains or losses for tax purposes. The yield had gone down significantly due to fall in interest

@ The RBI has announced a scheme of licensing primary market dealers in Govt. securities in March 1995. They act as market makers and help placement of these securities, develop secondary market and act as conduit for open market operations of RBI.

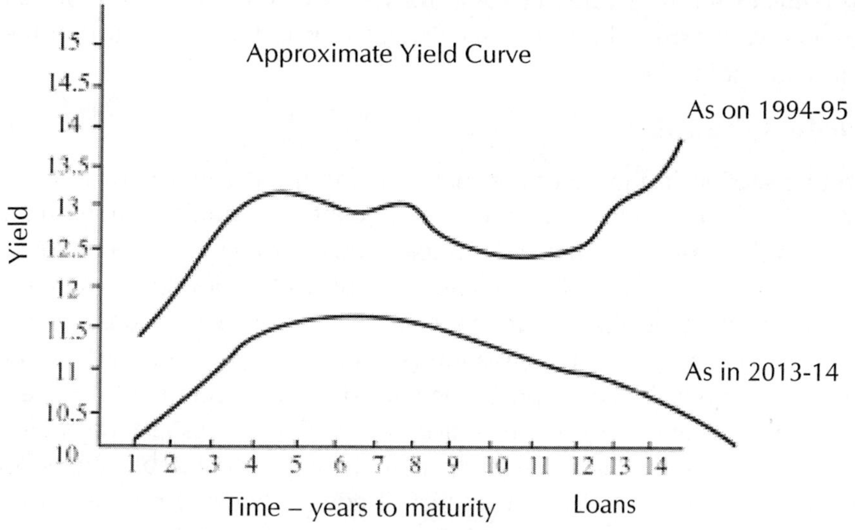

Fig. 40.3

rates in general after 1999 to 4.50% in 2004-05, but has gone up again to 7 to 8.5% by 2007-08 and further to 9% to 12% in 2013-14. The interest rates are mostly decontrolled and hence the yields change daily, monthly and yearly.

Indicators

The main indicators in the section of Government securities are:

1. Volume of turnover, on which data are colleced or published by NSE and RBI.
2. Prices of these securities which are collected by the RBI and reported to the stock exchange by the brokers from time to time.
3. Yields on these securities — current yields and redemption yields[1] compiled and published by the RBI from time to time.

The available indicators in this segment of the market are thus only prices and yields. The data on the total volume of trade turnover are not available as there is no good reporting system here as the market is over-the-counter and on prices and yields in respect of various Government and Semi-govenment bonds/ securities are, however, reported with a time lag to the stock exchanges and the RBI also collects these data, as they are also directly involved in this market under open market operations, under which they buy and sell Central Government securities to stabilise the market and the structure of yields. NSE has also been publishing these data since 1994-95. YTMs are available in RBI publications.

The data on prices are reported and published by the RBI under three heads as shown below, in the form of indices:

(*a*) Central Government Security price indices.

(*b*) State Government Security price indices.

(*c*) semi-Government Security price indices.

These data are published in the publications of the RBI and NSE. Those of State and Semi-government papers were discontinued later on. The security price indices reflect the pressures of demand and supply for the securities. The yields are the returns on these investments expressed in terms of income as a percentage of purchase price. Yields are compiled mainly in respect of fixed interest securities. As the purchase prices of these securities vary depending on the supply and demand pressures but interest rates (or coupon rates)

1. Auction prices and yields of TBs-G-securities are now available in RBI publications.

on them are fixed in terms of the face value (₹100), the yields vary from the coupon rates depending upon how much purchase price varies from the face value. Yields thus reflect the return on these instruments and influence the demand and supply forces.

Corporate Securities Section

The other important section in the securities market is the trading in securities issued by the corporate sector in the form of equity shares, preference shares and debentures. In this section, the most actively traded securities are equities in respect of which prices (or price indices), volume of trading (or turnover), yields and spread of fluctuations in prices, etc., are all available in respect of major stock exchanges like Mumbai. In respect of debentures and preference shares, trading is less active for two reasons. One is that they are held mostly by financial insitutions and public participation is poor. Secondly, these are not attractive enough for investors who want capital appreciation, as these are only fixed income securities. In respect of these securities, only prices and yields are available. The price indices and yields in respect of equity (variable dividend industrial securities), are published by the RBI in their monthly and annual publications (Monthly Bulletin and Report on Currency and Finance of the RBI). In respect of equity shares, a number of market indicators are available. The price indices of various types are available on a daily, weekly and monthly basis from many sources, as referred to later. (Refer to Handbook of Statistics on the Indian Economy, RBI).

Main Indicators

In addition to the prices, the other main indicators of securities markets may be set out as follows:

1. No. of companies quoted of which —
   (*a*) Those most actively traded daily and placed in Group A or specified group (eligible for carry forward business);
   (*b*) Those less actively and less frequently traded and placed on a cash list (not allowed to be carried forward but for delivery only) called Group B. In this section, B_1 and B_2 are separately available. Besides, there are "T" and "Z" sections which are referred to earlier.
2. No. of issues/scrips available for trading in:
   (*a*) Equity issues; (*b*) Preference shares; (*c*) Debentures.
3. Paid-up capital of companies listed in Stock Exchange
   Equity issues available paid-up capital.
4. Market value of companies (or market capitalisation) listed in respect of:
   Equity issues is available.
5. Value and volume of trading or turnover daily (or number of shares or transactions and their value) indicating the extent of activity in the market.
6. Volatility of price changes daily, weekly or monthly (indicating the stability of price behaviour or the range of spread of prices in the market), or coefficient of variation.
7. Breadth of the market, namely, daily gainers or losers among scrips indicating the extent of bullishness or bearishness in the market (No. of scrips rising in price and falling in price), advances and declines.
8. Market price as a ratio to earning per share of each scrip or for all traded scrips in the market also called P/E ratio, indicating the relationship of market behaviour to the performance of companies.
9. Velocity of price changes or rate of change of prices of each scrip or for the market index, indicating how fast or quickly the price, representing the price behaviour and likely reversal of the trend or acceleration or deceleration of market activity.

10. Yields or returns on investments at the current market prices, and current market yields on equities and at the time of maturity if the securities are bonds, debentures or preference shares (also called fixed income securities).
11. Badla rates for carry forward of shares in the specified shares (Group A) which tell about the technical position in the market, whether the market is overbought or oversold in scrip and the extent of overheating in the market and the availability of finance for badla and the money market conditions. These badla rates are no longer published after T+1 settlement was introduced on the major stock exchanges in India.

SECURITY PRICE INDICES

RBI Index of Industrial Security Prices

As noted earlier, the RBI has been compiling since 1949 indices of security prices under the following heads. These are revised from time to time by shifting the base year and enlarging the coverage.

1. Government and Semi-government securities.
2. Debentures of joint stock companies.
3. Ordinary shares.

The present RBI series is with base 1980-81 = 100. The price indices are compiled on a weekly basis and the average of weeks for months/years, etc. These are presented on an all-India basis and on a regional basis for the five regions, namely, Mumbai, Kolkata, Chennai, Ahmedabad and Delhi. However, the compilation of index numbers of prices for debentures and preference shares was discontinued with effect from December 1979, for the reason that these were not actively traded and their price quotations were not up to date.

Among the ordinary shares, only 338 are included in this series with the following regional distribution: Mumbai 32%, Kolkata 26%, Chennai 17%, Ahmedabad 10%, Delhi 15%. The selection of individual scrips in each industry group was made on the basis of —

1. size of the average market value of the share capital of the company during the base year; and
2. the activity of the scrip as indicated by the number of price changes during the base year.

The number of sample scrips selected at each centre has been so fixed taking into account the total number listed and their paid-up capital and taking care to see that the sample scips accounted for 60-70% of the aggregate market value of scrips in each centre.

The weights given to each company and to each industry groups are proportional to their share in the aggregate average market value of share capital of total companies quoted on each stock exchange. The regional market weights for group and sub-group indices of ordinary shares were proportional to the aggregate average market value of share capital of all the scrips belonging to the group or sub-group and quoted on the respective stock exchanges as on the base date, namely, March 31, 1981. The all-India weights in respect of various group/sub-group indices were proportional to their respective shares of their average market value to total market value of all scrips in the concerned groups/sub-groups quoted at all centres, counting only once the average market value of scrips quoted at more than one centre. The all-India index is thus secured from the regional groups.

The method of compilation is such that the weekly average price of each sample is obtained as the arithmetical average of daily closing quotations in the week. The price relative for a scrip during a particular week is worked out as the ratio of the average price for the current week to the base year average price of that scrip. The price relative to a sub-group at each region is obtained as the unweighted geometric mean of price relatives of scrips selected in that sub-group. Since 1999, RBI has discontinued their own series and is publishing the BSE Sensex and National Index and Nifty of NSE.

BSE Sensitive Index

The Stock Exchange, Mumbai, had started its own price index since January 1, 1986, called the BSE Sensitive Index of Equity Prices. It had 30 scrips which were actively traded, many of which were in Group A (specified group) and a few in Group B (non-specified group). It had a base year 1978-79 = 100 and represent all the major industries quoted on the exchange. These indices were published on a daily, monthly and yearly basis since April 1979. These were available in the daily papers and in the publications of the BSE.

The selection of the base year was made only on the basis of its price stability and its proximity to the current period. The year 1978-79 was selected for this purpose as it had shown relative price stability and proximity to the latest years.

Scrip Selection

The selection of scrips has been made on the basis of market activity in these scrips and for giving representation to all major industrial groups. All the 30 scrips chosen are actively traded on a daily basis on the BSE. The 15 out of 30 scrips have been replaced by new and more representative scrips in August 1996, which still maintains the continuity and its representative character. Subsequently, there were minor changes in the composition of this basket.

Methods of Compilation

The index for a day is calculated as the percentage of the aggregate market value of the equity shares of all companies in the sample on that day to the average market value of the equity shares of the same companies during the base period. This method of compilation enables the necessary flexibility to adjust for arbitrary and non-market related price changes caused by the issue of rights and bonus shares.

Weightage

The weightage given to each scrip is according to the number of shares outstanding in that scrip. The current market value for any share in the list is obtained by multiplying the price of the share by the number of shares outstanding, so that it would influence the index of price in proportion to the market importance of each scrip.

Other Adjustments

When bonus or rights issues are made or when consolidation or splittting of shares takes place or mergers are efffected or when convertible debentures are converted into equity, necessary adjustment are made and a new weighting factor is arrived at after taking the number of shares outstanding, its face value and its market value after the event has occurred. If by the issue of right share or merger, the total paid-up capital is changed, necessary changes are made in both the base year and current year. When the bonus issue is made, the number of shares will increase but not the paid-up capital. When rights are issued, the number of shares and paid-up capital will change. In such cases, base year weights are changed accordingly to make them comparable to the current period.

BSE National Index

This series of BSE National Index has been started by the Bombay stock exchange in 1988-89 with the base year 1983-84 = 100. This series has 100 scrips, including also the 30 scrips belonging to the BSE Sensitive Series. These 100 scrips have been chosen from almost all industrial groups which represent the listing on the major stock exchanges, namely, Mumbai, Kolkata, Chennai, Delhi and Ahmedabad. The method of compilation and other details are almost similar to the compilation of BSE Sensitive Series. Adjustments are also made from time to time for the bonus issues, right issues, conversion of debentures, etc.

Of these 100 scrips, 22 are quoted in Mumbai only while 72 scrips are quoted on the BSE besides other stock exchanges, while the remaining six scrips are quoted only on the other stock exchanges. Thus, nearly 95% of the issues covered are quoted and traded on the BSE.

The National Series is compiled from April 1984 while the Sensitive Series has been available from April 1979. A comparison of these two series shows that the National Index is more broad-based and has been showing a relatively more stable picture of price trends as compared with the BSE Sensitive Series. Although percentage changes in prices over a long period correspond to each other in both the series, the Sensitive Series is more fluctuating and more sensitive to changes in prices of a few scrips, which are highly speculative. These two series are, therefore, complementary and are compiled and published on a daily basis by the Bombay stock exchange.

The choice of the base year 1983-84 is due to its price stability and relative proximity. The weightage pattern and method of compilation are similar to those adopted in the case of BSE Sensitive Series. The price of each component share in the index is weighted by the number of shares outstanding so that it will influence the index in proportion to its respective market importance. The current market value for any share is obtained by multiplying the price of the share by the number of shares outstanding. The index for a day is calculated as the percentage of the aggregate market value of the equity shares of all the companies in the sample on that day to the average market value of the equity shares of the same companies during the base period.

As in the case of Sensitive Series, adjustments are made for bonus issues, rights issues, conversion of debentures into equity or loans into equity by financial institutions, mergers, etc., where necessary as in the case of rights or debenture conversion. When paid-up capital will change, the base year average is suitably adjusted on the basis of ex-right or ex-conversion price of the equity share.

Base year changes are in effect proportional adjustments in the base year average market value to offset price changes in the market values upon which the index is based. The formula is

$$\text{New Base Year Average} = \text{Old Base Year Average} \times \frac{\text{New Market Value}}{\text{Old Market Value}}$$

For example, a company issues rights to raise capital by ₹100 crore. Its base year average is, say, ₹2,450 crore, its old market value is ₹4781 crores and by the addition of rights, its new market value is ₹4,781 + 100 = ₹4,881.

$$\text{The new base year average} = \frac{2{,}450 \times 4{,}881}{4{,}781} = 2{,}501.24$$

The figure of 2,501.24 will be used on the base year average for calculating the index number from then onwards till the next base change becomes necessary.

BSE 200 and Dollex

Two move indexes were compiled by BSE since 1993, with base year, 1989-90 = 100. Both include very actively traded scrips from Group A and Group B, accounting for about 73% of total market capitalisation. BSE 200 is in rupee terms while the Dollex is dollar terms.

Economic Times Price Indices

The Economic Times (ET) introduced its first series of share prices index on May 18, 1961, with base 1959-60 = 100. The second series with base 1969-70 = 100 was started on October 20, 1972. This had 61 scrips spread over both the specified and non-specified groups and quoted on the major stock exchanges. This revision was made to bring the index to a more realistic representation of the actual market trading pattern.

The last series of share price index of *ET* is with a base of 1984-85 = 100 published since 1985. The choice of the base year is based on the relative stability of prices in the recent past. The series covers shares traded on 8 major stock exchanges, namely, Mumbai, Kolkata, Chennai, Delhi, Ahmedabad, Pune, Bangalore and Kanpur. Of these, separate indices are compiled for the 5 major stock exchanges, namely, Mumbai, Kolkata, Chennai, Delhi, Ahmedabad and the other three stock exchanges, namely, Bangalore, Pune and Kanpur, have been clubbed together under the term "Other" and a separate index is compiled for them. The number of scrips selected was based on the total number quoted on each stock exchange, the number in each industry group and their paid-up values. Those scrips which are actively traded and sensitive to market conditions, as judged by the frequency of price changes and the magnitude of price changes, are included in the sample.

Altogether 72 shares have been selected for inclusion in this new series. These shares are actively traded in the markets and act as a sensitive barometer of the fluctuations in the market prices. The price relatives for each day are obtained by dividing the daily quotations by the corresponding average prices of the base year. For this purpose, the average base year prices are derived by taking a simple arithmetical average of daily quotations of the selected scrips for that year. No further weightage is given to the price relatives.

The latest *ET* index is the broadbased *ET*-100 which was started in March 2005 with base Jan., 1, 2003 = 100 and is expected to capture the sentiment better than the BSE National 100. In earlier series, the regional and industry representation was as shown in Table 40.1 and 40.2 respectively.

Table 40.1

Share Market	*No. of Shares Selected*
Mumbai	30
Kolkata	15
Chennai	7
Delhi	9
Ahmedabad	5
Others*	6
Total	72

* Bangalore, Pune, Kanpur.

Adjustments for issue of bonus shares, rights and conversion of debentures, etc. are similar to those made by the BSE for its series.

Table 40.2

Industry Groups	*Number of Scrips*
Textiles*	6
Man-made fibres*	5
Basic metal industry	2
Transport vehicles	5
Engineering	15
Fertiliser and Chemicals	8
Pharmaceuticals	4
Cement	3
Paper*	2
Tyres and Tubes	3
Food Products	3
Plantation*	3
Others*	13
Total	72

* Includes companies with highly diversified activities.

The industry group indices are also compiled for the major industries. Table 40.1 presents the distribution of selected shares of the earlier series among the various stock exchanges. Table 40.2 presents the data on the number of selected shares of the earlier series in each industry group. The index for each industry group was a simple arithmetical average of the price relatives of all the scrips belonging to the group. The index for each stock exchange was a simple arithmetical average of the corresponding price relatives compared to the base year. Similarly, the all-India index for all shares was a simple arithmetical average of the daily quotations of selected scrips for the current period as compared to the base period.

Other Indicators

Table 40.3 presents the data on major stock market indicators, other than those of prices. Although over the last five years, the number of stock exchanges has increased by only 8, listed companies and their paid-up capital quoted on these markets had increased sharply. Market capitalisation shot up by 8 times and trade turnover by more than 8 times. The market capitalisation refers to the market price of a share multiplied by the number of shares in that company and these values are aggregated for all the companies quoted on the stock exchange. The trade turnover relates to the value of deals or number of transactions put through in the market during the official hours during all the trading days of the year. The width of activity and intensity of trading have increased substantially in these markets, reflecting the growing investment habits of the public and the expansion of the capital market in India, particularly during the last six years. The market capitalisation as a percentage of GDP is another indicator of importance of stock market.

The annual trade turnover constitutes about 50-80 per cent of the market capitalisation, which is a good performance in trading as compared with many markets in the developing world in Asia and Far East. In fact, India compares very well with even developed countries in the number of companies listed and the per hour intensity of trading.

There are a number of other market indicators, indexes of prices of some groups and other relevant data published in daily *Financial Press*. Among them the more important is NIFTY of NSE, with 50 scrips called SOP CNX Nifty with base year 1995 = 100.

Table 40.3 **STOCK MARKET INDICATORS**

1. No. of Stock Exchanges.
2. Types of Stock Exchanges National, Regional, Inter-connected stock exchanges, Electronically traded exchanges, OTCEI Network, Nse Network, Bolt, Etc. and Inter-connected stock exchange.
3. No. of Members of stock exchanges.
4. No. of Listed Companies.
5. Paid-up Capital of Listed Companies.
6. Market Capitalisation of Listed Companies.
7. Yearly or Monthly Trade Turnover or Volume of Trading.
8. Market P/E Ratio.
9. Market Price to Book Value, etc.
10. Market Price Index.
11. Velocity of Price changes or coefficient of variation, volatility of prices.

The other indices which are also available are CRISIL 500, OTCEI Index, S&P CNX 500, CNX Mid-cap 200 Skindia GDR (for foreign GDRs, quoted abroad). But the most popular Index continues to be BSE Sensex. The *ET* is publishing daily a few more sectoral indices on certain selected groups like MINDEX, LIFEX, Brandex and INSTANEX SKINDIA (for GDR and ADRs). The BSE is also publishing some sectoral indices like BSE, PSU; BSE, Capital Goods; BSE Consumer Durables, BSE IT, BSE Teck; BSE Bankex, BSE Metal, etc.

Those interested in further analysis on this subject may refer to the Authors' book on "Securities Analysis and Portfolio Management"

Some major indicators of Stock market acivity are provided below for illustration. These indicators are for the Bombay Stock Exchange which is the oldest and largest Stock Exchange in India, with the largest number of companies listed on it.

NSE has similar indicators and they are not shown in the table below. NSE has a larger turnover than on BSE, both cash and futures sections. the table shows that the market is not overvalued, as it has a moderate P/B (price to book value) of three times, and P/E multiple at 16.9, which ar not very high. The table also shows that there is scope for rise in prices, if the foreign funds are allowed to flow more freely.

TABLE ON MARKET INDICATORS (BSE) 2013-14

Price Index at end December 2014	27,500
Coefficient variation	6.4
P/E ratio	16.9
P/B ratio	2.9
Gross turnover (2014)	₹ 32,571 billion
Market capitalisation	₹ 63,879 billion

Source: RBI Annual report, 2013-14.

✠ ✠ ✠

INTEREST RATES — THEORY AND STRUCTURE

41

Introduction

The object of this chapter is to examine the conceptual and operational aspects of interest rate policy in India. The importance of this policy can be better appreciated in the background of a conceptual discussion on the mechanism of its operations and its significance to the economy. It would thus be apt to start with the role of interest rates in India.

Role of Interest Income

Conceptually, interest is a return to the capital as a factor of production. According to the traditional theory, interest is paid for abstaining from present consumption leading to savings. Savings is the basis of investment and capital formation. At the macro level, capital is a major factor of production to which interest is a reward or income just as wages, profits, rents, etc., are rewards to the other factors of production.

Inter alia, investment is a function of interest rate, and the quantum and directional flow of investment determine income. More scientifically, the impact of interest rate is both on savings and investments in the economy. In other words, the borrowings as well as lendings are influenced by the interest rates. The costs of production which depend upon the production function also include the credit costs, as credit is an input in the productive process.

In the macro sense, interest rate and interest income have a vital role in the economy, as capital, for which it is a reward, plays a significant part in the growth dynamics of the economy. Capital formation and capital accumulation are very much dependent upon the level and rate of savings and investment in the economy. Thus interest is not a simple monetary phenomenon; it is the product of interaction of the monetary system with the real system.

The savings and investment in the economy which are influenced by the interest rates are the real economic variables. The incomes and expenditures of the various sectors of the economy result in excess savings or excess investment in each of the sectors. The sectors having excess savings provide them to those with excess investment. It is these savings and investment activities of the real sector which are influenced and facilitated by the flow of funds from the financial system. Here both domestic as well as international forces operate if the economies are open. We, however, assume in our study that the economy is closed as we are studying the domestic savings rate in relation to domestic interest rates.

Relative Share of Interest Income

The importance of interest income as a factor reward has been growing in India over the last few decades. Dr. V.K.R.V. Rao has observed thus: "There is a clear indication of the increasing role of loan capital in financing the development of non-self-employed economic activity. Credit has thus played a crucial role in India's economic development" (India's National Income 1950-80, publication of 1983).

The factor income shares in the Indian economy are available from the C.S.O., published in their National Accounts Statistics for various periods. The relative importance of interest income is revealed here. At the macro level, the share of interest income in the total national income at current prices has shown a consistent rise over the past two-and-a-half decades. Sector-wise the largest rise of the interest income took place in the secondary sector comprising mining and manufacturing activity. This is attributed to the increasing use of loan capital in these activities.

Role of Interest Rates

Interest rate has diverse roles in the economy such as a reward to capital which is a factor of production, a return to saving and a cost to investment and an instrument of monetary policy for credit control. The role of interest rate mechanism in India has been the subject of controversy. In fact, even in theory, there has been a controversy from the days of Lord Keynes about the role of interest rates in the economy. In this background, it is relevant to examine the role of interest rates in India. Do interest rates influence mobilisation of savings? Do they have an allocative role in the distribution of savings as between different instruments? How far the interest rates influence deposits of banks and shift as between deposits of various maturities? These and other aspects of interest rates are relevant for policy makers.

At the macro level, interest is a reward to the capital which is a factor of production. In the developing economy, capital formation and capital accumulation are of vital importance to economic development. Interest rates influence both savings and investment in the economy and serve a vital role for the mobilisation of savings. Besides, interest rate has a role in the allocation of investment funds as between different uses. Thus, in addition to influencing their cost, and availability of funds from the supply side, interest rates also influence the quantum of investments from the demand side and thus determine the income and employment in the economy.

Despite the common belief that savings in India are interest-insensitive, our study has shown that while the overall household sector savings are mildly influenced by interest rates, household sector savings in the form of bank deposits are highly sensitive to interest rates. It would, therefore, appear that investment rates have a positive role in the savings mobilisation, particularly with regard to savings in the form of bank deposits. In addition to interest rates, personal disposable income, *per capital* income, the ratio of non-agricultural income to agricultural income and the population coverage per bank office have been found to be significantly influencing household savings in bank deposits, as revealed in our research studies.

Interest rates have also a significant role in the investment process in India. Our empirical tests have shown that domestic capital formation in India is a function of GDP, MEC@ and the cost of capital.

The costs of borrowing from banks to the corporate sector are not high, constituting as they do only about 5 per cent of the total value of production in respect of large and medium public limited companies, as revealed by the Company Finance Studies of the RBI.

The share of interest income in comparison with the shares of wages, rent and profits in the Indian economy is presented in the Fig. 41.1. It is seen that interest income constitutes about 9% of the total income and is tending to rise over the years due to the preference of the corporate sector for debt capital *vis-a-vis*

@ Marginal Efficiency of Capital Represented by Return on Investment (RoI).

ownership capital and increasing borrowings of the government for financing public investment and their expenditure. A part of mixed income may also be a return to capital.

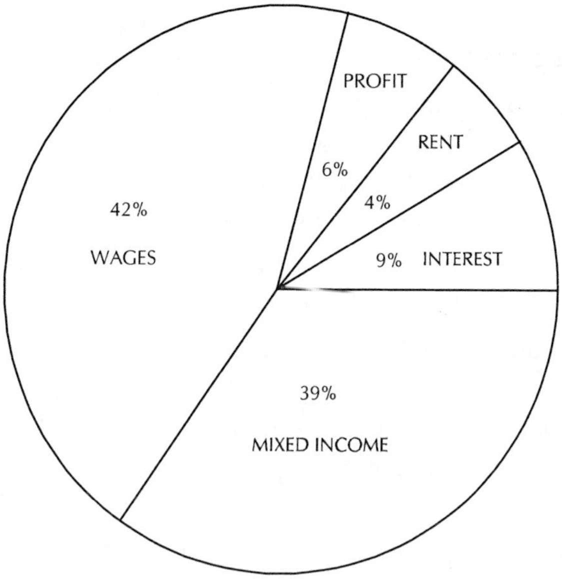

Fig. 41.1 National Income — Share of Interest

Theories of Interest Rate

The classical view of interest rate can be expressed as the loanable funds theory which postulates that interest rate is determined by the supply of and demand for loanable funds. These loanable funds are in the present-day parlance the I.O.U.s of financial institutions. The demand for and supply of these funds will determine the interest rate.

When Keynes' considered the interest rate as a monetary phenomenon, he took money as an asset with an opportunity cost, namely, the return on short-term bonds. Under the partial equilibrium approach, one can assume that the forces in the real economic system remain constant and analyse the financial factors which explain the interest rates. Under this theory, interest rate is determined by the relative supply of and demand for liquidity or money in the economy which is a function of the financial system. Keynes' motives for the demand for liquidity are well-known, namely, the transactions, precautionary and speculative motives. The last motive has been renamed as an asset motive by the neo-classical economists.

The nominal interest rates according to the neo-classical theories depended also on the expectations of the public and the rate of inflation in the economy. According to Irving Fisher, for example, interest rate is also a function of inflation as the nominal rate is affected by the expected rate of inflation. The Gibson-Wicksell proposition that interest rates and wholesale prices move together in the long run has been found to be empirically valid but the linkage co-efficient is less than unity in India. This is so if only the organised financial sector is considered. During periods of inflation, the gap between the rates in the organised financial system and those in the unorganised system widen sharply although the linkages are weak. Funds flow from the organised to the unorganised sector and *vice versa* which influence rates in both the sectors.

Structure of Interest Rates

The maturity pattern of debt is an important factor for interest rate determination. The maturity pattern is particularly relevant in the gilt-edged market, small savings schemes and deposit and lending rates of banks. The longer the maturity, the larger is the risk and hence the risk premium. The prime criterion to be looked into is the extent of liquidity premium that public is prepared to pay on money *vis-a-vis* near-money assets. The public are concerned with the real rate of return as the nominal interest paid can be eroded by the degree of inflation. The flow of savings and availability of funds would depend on positive real rates in the first place. Money has no return and to hold on to money has an opportunity cost as the alternatives to money have returns.

Factors Influencing Interest Rates

Savings flow into various physical and financial assets. Financial assets are future claims on money like bank deposits, UTI units, shares, debentures, etc. These are in the form of I.O.U.s. These financial assets have a structure of interest rates which should be rationally based on the degree of risk of ownership, uncertainty of return, period of maturity and a host of other factors.

The factors which influence interest rates on various financial investments are the nature of the instrument, maturity period, risk, tax status, marketability and liquidity. These are discussed below:

1. The return on ownership capital should be higher than on loan capital, as the risk of the former is greater than that of the latter.
2. Difference in maturity periods would influence the extent of the risk taken during the period when the lender is out of funds for varying periods of time. Ordinarily, the longer the period, the higher is the interest rate.
3. The degree of default risks or uncertainty of return would also determine the interest rates. Such risks are nil or negligible in the case of government bonds while they are higher in the case of private debt or private ownership securities or company deposits. The rate is to be higher on those which have a higher risk.
4. The tax provisions on the financial instruments or incentives or disincentives in the form of taxes on interest income or tax concessions would also influence the demand for different types of financial assets. Thus the effective rates on some postal certificates are higher due to tax concessions which would increase the effective take home rates.
5. Another factor is the marketability of financial instruments with facilities for discounting or re-discounting and/or ready saleability which thus imparts liquidity and/or ready saleability. Liquidity means convertibility of assets into cash as and when required without loss of time or money.

The normal pattern of yields is that the short-term rates are lower than the long-term rates and under normal expectations, the yields on ownership capital (risk-taking ventures) would be higher than on loan capital. Besides the interest rates on government bonds which are less risky would also be lower than those on private securities of similar maturity. It is also true that the interest rates on some securities subject to special incentives or tax concessions may be lower than on comparable other instruments. Similarly, the financial instruments which have a good marketability like units of the Unit Trust of India or the shares quoted on the stock exchange may have lower rates than those which are not so marketable and/or not quoted on the stock exchanges. It would thus be seen that a number of cognisable factors operate on the determination of interest rates. In India even now the rates are partly fixed by the government and the Reserve Bank of India, but the above basic principles of interest rate determination hold good in a free economy. The existing term structure in India is a by-product of administrative fiat and exigencies of monetary and credit policies.

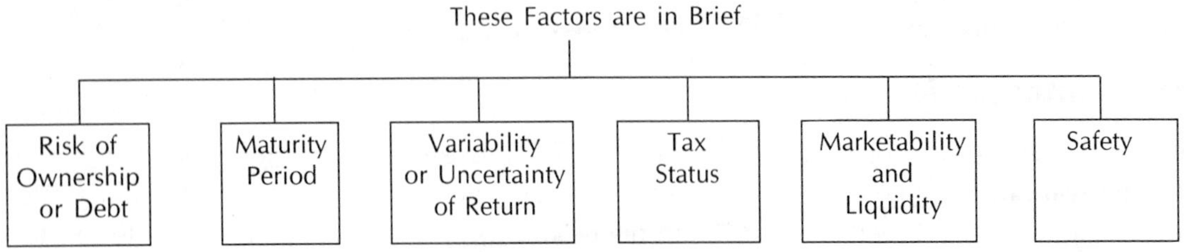

Fig. 41.2

There are drawbacks inherent in any system of partially controlled market forces with some rates fixed by the government, some rates by the Reserve Bank and a few left to the market forces. The multiplicity of controls and the agencies controlling have made the interest rate system in India complicated and distorted. This complex system prevailing even in the organised markets is made more difficult to comprehend by the generally uncontrollable interest rates charged in the unorganised and primitive markets in India. The deficiencies and anamolies in present system of partially administered rates in India are ably brought out by the Sukhamoy Chakravarthy Committee (RBI, 1985).

Interest Rates in India

Most of the interest rates in India are controlled and administratively fixed. It would, therefore, be difficult to isolate the free market forces which influence the interest rates in India. So far, interest rate policy has been used as a support to other instruments of monetary policy in India. Even under these controlled conditions, the basic postulates that interest rates are influenced by the money, liquidity and the rates of inflation, etc., hold good particularly in uncontrolled unorganised market. But where there exists some correspondence, the linkages are weak statistically.

Bank Rate and Refinance Rates

In the organised sector of the financial system for which data are available, interest rate policy is set by the actions of the Central Bank as its discount rate (viz., Bank rate) is the leader of interest rates. In India, the Bank rate is the discount rate at which the central bank of the country makes advances to the commercial and co-operative banks against eligible assets. Section 49 of the RBI Act defines Bank Rate as the standard rate at which the Bank is prepared to buy and discount bill of exchange or other commercial paper eligible for purchase under the Act. In view of the limited role of the money market and bill market in India, the Bank rate is not the real leader among the interest rates. Under Section 17 of the RBI Act, the Reserve Bank provides refinance through various windows at different rates. It is these refinance rates which are the discount rates of the central bank in India.

The weighted average rate of interest on these various types of refinance would be the effective rate of discount by the RBI. This is different from the Bank rate. The multiplicity of rates is necessitated by the social obligations of the banking system and the nature of our financial system.

Over the last two decades, the Bank rate was raised twice to keep it adjusted to the general level of interest rates in the economy, *viz.,* from 7% to 9% in July 1974 and further to 10% in July 1981. The Bank rate has been raised to 11% in July, 1991 and to 12% in October 1991 but the rate fell later and stood at 6% as in June 2008. But the cost of funds provided by the RBI would be influenced by its refinance policy. The refinance and other rates are as follows: (March 2014)

Bank rate	6%
Banks' Prime Lending Rate or Repo Rate	10 - 10.75
For Food Credit Provided by Banks	8%
For Export Credit Provided by Banks	PLR – 2.5%
Refinance to DFHI against Commercial Bills	6-8%
Term Loans of Banks FIs	8.5 - 12.5%%
RBI Refinance Rates at Bank rate and 1% above that	(Bank rate is 6% as in 2013)
(Only against Export Credit and General Refinance Limit)	(7% to 9%)

Money Market Rates

Next to the Bank rate, the other short-term rates of significance are the Treasury bills rate and Call Money rate. The 91-day Treasury bill rate has remained frozen for years at 4.6% but from January 1993 this rate was freed. This is because there is no market for Treasury bills in India and the instrument was used for the purpose of financing government expenditure. As such this rate had no significance for the general structure of interest rates. Treasury bills of 182 days sold on auction basis since 1987 bear higher rates which are more realistic and market-oriented.

As regards call money rate, it has no doubt some relevance to the money market conditions, as the stringency or otherwise of the banks' funds is reflected in this market. The ceiling rate was fixed at 10% in April 1980 but was removed in May 1989. Since then, the rates fluctuated daily depending on the demand and supply conditions.

Rates in Gilt-edged Market

In the Government securities market, interest rates are set by the government in the form of coupon rates. The yields on these securities are also influenced by the RBI through their purchase and sale operations in the market. In India, there was a captive market in the Government securities as the banks are required to invest a proportion of their funds in Government securities and other approved trustee securities as fixed by the statutory liquidity ratio (SLR). Similarly, the non-bank financial institutions, provident funds, trusts, etc., are also required to invest a proportion of their funds by law in the Government securities. From the point of view of risk, these securities are least risky and if the return is to be positive in real terms, the yield has to be higher than the actual inflation rate in the economy. The yields are also related to the maturity period and a differential is maintained as between the Centre and States and government-guaranteed bonds. As part of reforms in gilt-edged markets their rates of interest are decided through auction system, since 1987.

The auctioning system of 182 days of Treasury bills was extended to Treasury bills of 364 days since April 1992. This has become an additional money market instrument between 91 days Treasury bill and dated Government security. The Discount and Finance House of India Ltd., was allowed to operate in Government securities since April 1992, in addition to their operations in money market instruments like Treasury bills and Commercial paper and in the inter-bank call market.

Private and Government Bond Rates

Earlier there used to be a gap between the return on public debt *vis-a-vis* the return on the private debt. The interest rates on debentures and company deposits and preference shares are substantially higher at around 14-15 per cent as against the yield of 7 to 8 per cent which one might get on government debt. This anomaly dissuades one from entering the Government securities market. So there is need for two types of adjustments in gilt-edged market; firstly, the long end of the spectrum is to be made more attractive, consistent with the expected rate of inflation. Secondly, the yields on Government securities should be attractive *vis-a-vis* yields on private securities, which is reflected in gaps and reverse gaps. A gap is positive if the risk is rewarded. If it is a reverse gap, there is risk aversion in the economy which has to be corrected.

These adjustments were made over the decade of the eighties with result that the gap between them is narrower at around 2 percentage points. The coupon rates offered in the gilt-edged market during the eighties and nineties have been jacked up to bring them to realistic levels of the expected rate of inflation. Besides, this has improved the earnings of banks and made them more attractive to banks and non-bank investors.

Rates of Borrowings and Lendings by Commercial Banks

In view of the limited role of the interest rate policy in India and the weak linkages as between the various segments in the market, it has become necessary for the RBI to resort to direct controls on banks' lending and borrowing rates. Minimum lending rates of scheduled commercial banks were first fixed in 1960 and the maximum lending rates in 1964. Similarly, interest rates on deposits have been fixed by the Reserve Bank of India since September 1969. The control encompasses almost all categories of borrowers and different maturities of deposits.

The Reserve Bank of India derives its authority to fix interest rates of banks under Sections 21 and 35 (A) of the B.R. Act. These provisions have been used by the Reserve Bank in a flexible manner since 1960.

The rationale of direct controls on interest rates may be briefly set out here. Firstly, in view of the weak linkages between the Bank rate and/or refinance rate of the RBI with other money market rates, the effectiveness of monetary and credit policy can only be ensured by the direct fixation of various categories of interest rates. Secondly, the banking structure of India is such that there is uneven competition amongst the banks, namely, as between the weaker and smaller banks and dominant bigger banks. It is, therefore, necessary that competition in matters of interest rates has to be regulated by the Reserve Bank. Thirdly, with the acceptance of social obligations by the Banking system following the nationalisation of banks in 1969, the multiplicity of lending rates has become necessary to encourage lending to priority sectors, neglected segments of the economy and backward classes of people. The geographical and sectorial credit gaps have to be filled in through price and non-price incentives. Lastly, the developmental needs of the country have to be met at the lowest possible costs by the banking system through bank credit to government borrowings through bonds, treasury bills, etc. This has also necessitated the differential interest rate system in India.

The Sukhamoy Chakraborty Committee (1985), has opined that the administered interest rate system has adverse effects on the financial system and the economy due to the complexity introduced by it. The number of administered rates were brought down since then.

The same policy of fixing the interest rates was followed for the co-operative banks as well. However, in respect of co-operative credit societies, the RBI has permitted the payment of additional interest of 1/4 to 1 per cent per annum on deposits over and above those allowed for commercial banks. Similarly, the RBI stipulations on lending rates were also made applicable to co-operative banks.

The data on interest rates prevailing on term credit by banks and the IDBI show that they are generally kept lower to facilitate long-term investment in capital assets by borrowers and promote capital formation in the corporate sector. The bank lending rates were freed from control of RBI in October 1990. There is no minimum lending rates for limits above ₹2 lakh. The controls on deposit rates were also removed to those above one year since 1996-97.

Interest Rates on Small Savings

Interest rates on saving deposits, cumulative time desposits and other categories of deposits in post offices are fixed from time to time by the government in consultation with the Reserve Bank. These rates are marginally higher than those offered by commercial and co-perative banks in order to attract the small savers and to encourage the flow of savings into the government sector. Similarly, interest rates on various categories of national savings certificates, social security certificates, etc., are fixed higher, as they are for lump sum investments and meant for small savers.

Interest Rates on Non-resident Accounts

Since 1975, the Government of India has been encouraging the inflow of foreign currency funds and non-resident Deposit Accounts. The FCNR deposits scheme was introduced in November 1975 for non-resident Indians to keep their accounts in time deposits of one to five year duration in US $ and Pound Sterling with remittances from abroad. Till March 1982, interest rates under FCNR deposits were the same as those applicable to domestic deposits. However, from March 1982, the deposits under Non-resident External (NRE) Rupee Accounts were offered at 2% higher interest rates than those on domestic deposits.

Interest rates under FCNR Accounts continued to be higher than those offered in international currency markets on European deposits but there is no cover for exchange fluctuations. This incentive of additional interest has attracted the non-resident funds to India judged by the net inflow in the past, although it is no longer true now, due to fluctuating rupee rate; the rates offered on FCNR and NRE accounts are now freed by RBI and are fixed by banks, but are kept lower than the LIBOR plus to LIBOR minus to discourage the larger inflow of funds from abroad. The policy of FCNR rates depended on the exigencies of foreign exchange and the need for borrowing from abroad, and in general linked to LIBOR. NRE (Rupee accounts are no longer allowed by banks.

Export Credit

Interest rates on export credits have been subject to a ceiling with a view to encouraging exports from India. These rates have been uniformly lower than those applicable to domestic creditors. Term credits and those on deferred payments arrangements are kept still further lower. The ceiling rates on export credit stood at a range of 8% to 10% depending upon the nature of goods and period of credit. While the interest rate on credit under deferred payments is at present 8.6%, the credits by EXIM (Exports and Import Bank) Bank are given at 8.5%. Banks have been asked to provide at least 12% of their total advances to exports and to reduce the interest rate by one percentage point, but the philosophy of subsidised credit to exports was given up. In the latest policy of April 2001, export credit was made available at lowest rates, lower by 1.5% over the normal PLR. In 2007-08, these are at 2.5 percentage points below the PLR of banks now.

Structure of Rates

Table 41.1 shows that interest rates are adjusted by the government and RBI from time to time in tune with the requirements of the economy. The table compares the rates in 1996 with those in 1980 and in 2007. There are some which were raised while others were lowered. The ceiling of 10% on call money rate was removed in May 1989. Similarly, in October 1990, the banks were given freedom to charge rates for lending at their own discretion in respect of non-priority sector advances. The government policy of lending at concessional rates to priority sectors like agriculture, SSIs, weaker sections of society, etc., however, continued to be operative; but the slabs are brought down from 4 to 3.

New Treasury bills of 182 days were sold on an auction basis since 1986-87 and their interest rates are determined by the market forces. The short-term deposit rates varied from 9 to 12% in 1998. The auction of 182 TBs was stopped in May 2001. The yields on Government securities were raised over the period in a significant way so as to make them attractive to investors and to bring them nearer to the free market rates. The recent liberalisation of interest rate policy in respect of banks' lending rates is also in tune with the policy of financial deregulation followed by the government and recommended by the committee, to review the working of Monetary Policy (Chakrabarthy Committee1985). The term-lending rate was for the purpose of encouraging long-term investment raised lower while the other rates were raised more. But the rate of rise was neither consistent throughout nor was it offsetting the fall in the value of money through inflation. In fact, the rate payable on company deposits was lowered to 11% by 2003-04 along with a similar cut in the rate on debt capital of debentures and on ownership capital of preference shares. The only significant rise in interest rates is seen in the case of those on Government securities as they were kept at artificially lower rates for a long time and hence the need for readjustment in an upward direction. The rate on company deposits is 11% and the rate on debentures was freed from controls in 1992. During 1999-2001, interest rate policy was administered in a free and flexible manner to suit prevailing economic and financial conditions and market forces.

The level and structure of interest rates in India is thus a product of *ad hoc* policies pursued from time to time. The rates do not reflect the true value of capital, risk element and the maturity period of the instrument. The free market forces are not operating in India. Only in limited spheres is the liberalisation process implemented and that too on an *ad hoc* basis. While some controlled rates still continue some free market rates are now available. Similarly, the changes in rates are affected to suit the changing conditions in the economy and in tune with the monetary policy, but in the interest of hedging the household savers against fall in the value of rupee, the deposit rates as in 2008, should have been 9% or more, but the actual rates are in fact lower than the inflation rate of 12%.

Thus, in India, the structure of interest rates is complicated and administered by the government although there is some liberalisation in this policy in recent years following the reform process. The level in interest rates does not reflect the true market forces or the scarcity value of capital or the depreciation in the value of money as measured by inflation.

Level of Interest Rates

Leaving aside the basic postulate that there are many factors influencing interest rates in general as referred to above, we have to note that in some countries like India, the interest rates are fixed by the government or by the Central bank of the country (RBI). In such cases, the level and structure of interest rates will be determined by the policy of the government and the RBI and not by the market forces of supply and demand. The traditional theories do not apply in India.

Talking of the economy in macro terms, according to the traditional theory, the level of interest rate is determined by the supply and demand for money or loanable funds. The larger the available funds for lending, the lower is the interest rate. Similarly, the larger the demand for funds, higher is the interest rate. The level of interest rate, therefore, depends on the demand and supply pressures in the market. Looked at from a different angle, if there are more borrowers than lenders, interest rates would be high. On the other hand, if there are more lenders than borrowers, interest rates will be lower.

Assuming free market forces where demand and supply presures determine the interest rates, the level of interest rates can be depicted as shown in the following diagram. If MN is the available supply of money or funds, then the amount of demand for funds will determine the level of interest rates. Thus, when D_1-D_1, is the demand curve for funds, the interest rate will be R_1 and if the demand increases to D_2 - D_2, the interest rate will rise to R_2. Similarly, if the demand falls to D_o-D_o, the interest rate will also fall to $R_o$as shown in Fig. 41.3.

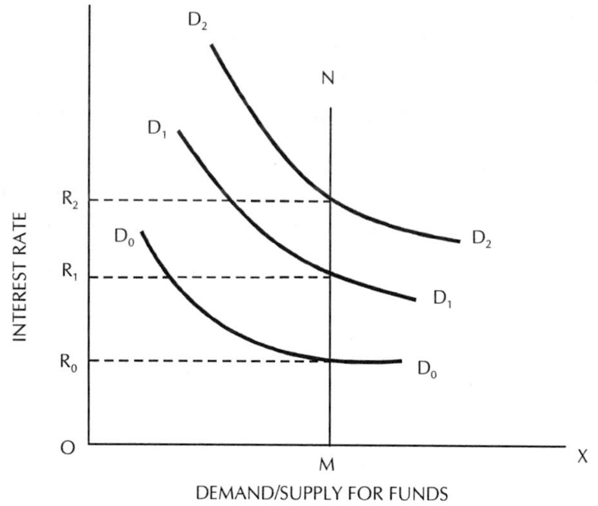

Fig. 41.3 Determination of Interest Rate

Data on Interest Rates

Leaving aside the time factor, the increase in risk in respect of banks' lending rates and the longer period involved in such lending have been reflected in the higher level of interest rates on them. As compared with the call money rates or treasury bill rates, which are for short periods, the interest rates on debentures, PSU bonds and term-lending rates by banks are higher due to the higher risk involved. Thus risk, maturity period, the safety and certainty of funds, etc., would influence the relative levels of interest rates and the structure of rates as seen from Table 41.1 which also, represents the data on the structure of rates. There are various types of instruments with varying rates of interest rates in India. These rates will depend on the characteristics of these instruments like ownership risk, variability of return, maturity period, safety, marketability, etc. The data clearly brings out the upward and downward shifts in the structure of rates depending upon the level of risk, time period of maturity and other features of the financial instruments involved.

The change in the level of interest rates as between 1980 and 2007 can also be seen from Table 41.1. The Bank rate rose, as also the banks' borrowing and lending rates and yields on government securities upto 1996. But the rate on company deposits and the term-lending rate of banks and FIs stood at around 14% respectively upto 1998. Thereafter, the interest rates became more flexible and were lowered by stages.

Table 41.1 DATA ON INTEREST RATES IN INDIA

(in percentages)

S. No.	*Types of Interest Rate*	*1980*	*1996*	*1998 (June)*	*2000 Dec.*	*2005 April*	*2007 June*	*2012 March*	*2014*
1.	Bank Rate of RBI/Repo Rate	9	12	9	8	6	6	9	6.0
2.	Auction Treasury Bill Rate (91 days) (Average)	Not applicable	12.93-12.94	7.33	8.70	4.9	7.20	8.09	8.2
3.	Auction Treasury Bill Rate (364 days) (Average)	Not applicable	12.71-13.03	7.98	9.96	5.2	7.65	8.29	8.4
4.	Call Money Rate	7.12	9-18	2-9	5-11.5	4.7	7.22	8.74	8.1
5.	Banks' Deposit Rate — Maximum	10	@12 & above	9-12	4-10	4 to6.25	4 to 9.50	9.0-9.25	6.6
6.	Banks' Lending Rate — Minimum	13.50	17-18	13-14	11.00	8 to11	12 to17.25	9.5-10.7	10.3
7.	Term Lending Rate of FIs	14.00	15.50	14.00	12.00	9-12	12 to 14.5	9.5-15	Free
8.	Rate of Preference Shares	11.00	14.00	14.00	14.00	Free	Free	Free	Free
9.	Rate on Debentures	13.50	16-18 (free rate)	14-16.0	14-16	Free	Free	Free	Free
10.	Company Deposit Rate — Maximum	15.50	15.00	15-16.0	14	11	11-14	9.45-11.50	9.2%
11.	Yields on Govt. securities — Maximum	6.44–7.49	13.50–14.00	10-12.1	10-11	5-9	8.20	8.68	8-10.3%

The 14 day auction Treasury bill was introduced in June 1996 and of 182 days Treasury bills from May 1990. But these were discontinued from April 2001.

The structure of interest rates has changed over time as between, say 1980 and 1998 and more frequently thereafter. Generally the level of interest rates has increased over time to reflect the increased cost of raising funds and degree of inflation which erodes the value of money. The interest rates were brought down during 1996 to 2003, to boost the sagging economy. They rose again during 2007 and 2008.

The rationale of regulating interest rates in India is as follows:

(*i*) It keeps the interest cost low for the government borrowings and their investment.

(*ii*) It promotes the socio-economic objectives of providing cheaper finance to weaker sections and priority sectors of the economy.

Reforms

Certain adjustments may be necessary to remove the deficiencies in the interest rate structure. Firstly, interest rates in the Indian economy are to be positive in real terms so as to promote real savings in the economy. This point has been emphasised by the Sukhamoy Chakrabarthy Committee. The implementation of this suggestion involves a projection of the expected rate of inflation and ensuring that the basic or the minimum rates are marginally above the average inflation rate. Secondly, the short-term money markets, namely, bill market, discount market and call money market, are to be further developed and broadbased. Thirdly, in the gilt-edged market, the government and the public sector bodies should be provided finance in the forms of treasury bills or of Government securities and/or loans and advances at positive real rates. This

@ Banks are allowed to pay more than 12% for deposits above 2 years since October 1995.

would ensure that the government gets its funds at the scarcity value of capital and curtail the Reserve Bank credit to the government to the minimum.

It was felt necessary to rationalise call money rates to reflect the scarcity of inter-bank funds or stringency in the resources of the banks. Thus, the then existing ceiling of 10% was removed in May 1989. The need for a ceiling was eliminated when the supply of funds was augmented by allowing non-bank financial institutions also to operate in the market, such as IDBI, IFC, etc.

In the Government securities market, the interest rate reforms were already started earlier and coupon rates were adjusted in an upward direction to reflect the scarcity value of the capital in India and to improve the attractiveness of the government bonds with the primary savers and financial intermediaries during late eighties. These reforms were carried forward to rationalise the term structure of the interest rates. The short-term debt which is of a low proportion has to be increased and long-term debt is to be reduced. The gaps between these short and long-term yields and the gap on government debt *vis-a-vis* the private debt should be rational. Between the venture (ownership) yield and debt yields, there is a reverse gap discouraging the flow of funds to the risk market. Those were attended to in the late nineties.

The existing framework of controls on bank lending and borrowing operations has been based on some justification. The reforms were in the form of reducing the various tiers of interest rate to a minimum of three or less both at the lending and borrowing ends. Interest rates on special categories like term credit, export credit, etc., may be kept out of this normal spectrum of interest rates by funding the concessionalities on them either by the government or the Reserve Bank. The fiscal and tax benefits should be kept out of the purview of these savings instruments. Unfortunately, the small savers were the worst hit, as their rate has been at an artificially low rate of 3½% or 4% when inflation rate was always higher than that at 8%.

Recent Deregulation Measures

Following the recommendations of the High Level Committee on Financial System (of Shri M. Narasimham, November 1991), some measures of deregulation were initiated in the banking and monetary system. The SLR on an incremental basis stood at 25% in 1995 and the incremental CRR of 10% was discontinued. The Committee's recommendations on capital adequacy norms, prudential norms of income recognition and provisioning for bad debts are also being implemented in stages. The recommendations aimed at improving the functional autonomy of banks and financial institutions and enhance competition, efficiency and profitability.

Interest rates are being increasingly left to market forces. In August 1991, interest rates on debentures and P.S.U. Bonds were freed from all restrictions. The system of ceiling rates for term lending institutions was replaced by a system of minimum rate of 9% to 12% in 2003-04. The ceiling rate on fixed deposits of companies was raised to 15% in January 1992 but lowered to 14% in 2001, and further to 11% in 2003-04.

The banks have been given greater autonomy in their lending operations and rates of interest charged subjected to a ceiling on deposit rates at 12%. These were replaced by flexible rates fixed by 2003-04. New financial instruments such as Participation Certificates, Commercial Paper, Certificates of Deposits, Money Market Mutual Funds and Non-Resident (Non-repartiable) Rupee Deposit Scheme are being promoted at the market related interest rates.

New guidelines were issued in June, 1992 and again in 1997 for non-bank financial institutions. The maximum interest rate payable was 14% in 2001 at monthly or quarterly interests, on a compounding basis. As in the case of shares, deposits can be accepted in joint names, not exceeding three with or without either or survivor, etc.

Premature repayment is permitted without penalty in the event of death of the depositor to surviving holder or the legal heirs of the deceased.

In respect of hire-purchase and equipment leasing companies which enjoy separate limits and conditions, it has been decided that if a company is engaged in hire purchase finance and equipment leasing activities, its business in both these lines will be taken together in determining its classification.

THE YIELD

Current Yield

Another facet of interest rate is the return on capital invested or yields. Hence a brief description of yields is relevant here.

The concept of yield relates on investment made in any security or financial instrument. Yields may be classified into different types depending on the securities. In the case of equities, the yield refers to the current yield, which means the return on investment made at the present juncture. The yield is derived by dividing the Dividend + Capital appreciation by the purchase price of share. In the case of debentures and Government securities, they are having coupon rates. Normally the coupon rate is the rate of interest payable on a face value of ₹100. It is not related to the market price or the purchase price. The current yield in the case of these fixed income securities is annual interest divided by current price or purchase price of the security. Thus, if 6% 1998 government loan was purchased at ₹95, the current yield is = 6/95 x 100, which gives 6.3% as current yield.

Redemption Yield

Redemption yield refers to yield to maturity. It is the average rate of return involving the return in the form of interest as well as appreciation or depreciation of capital over the period remaining to maturity. Thus for working out the redemption yield for a government bond or a debenture, the following steps are to be taken:

1. Compute the capital gain (or loss) if it is held up to the maturity date. If the purchase price is ₹95 and its face value is ₹100, the amount realised will be ₹100 involving a capital appreciation of ₹5 at the time of maturity.
2. Allocate a capital gain for the remaining part of the maturity or life of the security. Thus if the security has five-year maturity, an appreciation of ₹5 is to be distributed equally among all the 5 years, which means that there will be an appreciation of one rupee per year.
3. This annual appreciation is to be added to the annual interest rate paid on the security. If the coupon rate is 6%, an income distribution of ₹6 per annum is available and this is to be added to rupee one per annum as capital appreciation.
4. As a next step, add the redemption proceeds at the time of maturity and the purchase price and divide it by 2 which gives the average cost of holding the security.
5. Then divide the total return of investment, namely, (6 + 1) by the average holding cost, arrived at as above. In the example, the average cost of holding is (100 + 95) divided by 2 is equal to ₹97.5. Then the redemption yield is arrived at by dividing the total return by the average cost of holding, namely, *₹7/97.5 = 7.2%.*

It will thus be seen that the redemption yield is slightly different from other concepts. The redemption yield gives the actual return on investment in the form of Interest or Dividend + Capital Appreciation or Depreciation. The formula for deriving redemption yield is as follows:

$$V = \sum_{n=1}^{n} \frac{I_n}{(1+i)^n} + \frac{P_N}{(1+i)^N}$$

Where *V* is the value of the bond, *I* is the interest amount paid in absolute terms, *i* is the rate of interest or yield required to be derived; P_N, is the face value at maturity and *N* is the number of years to maturity.

Holding Period Yield (HPY)

Where redemption yield is not relevant, holding period yield (HPY) is used. Holding period yield brings out the possibility of purchase and sale of a security during the period of its maturity without waiting until the date of maturity. Thus one can buy a 13.5% debenture of Reliance Petro at ₹80 against its face value of ₹100. It could be sold at ₹85 after a year, without waiting up to the time of maturity, say, after 5 years. In this case, the holding period yield is relevant. The investor has purchased at ₹80 and sold at ₹85 after a year. The holding period is one year and the yield is interest at 13.5% that he receives during the year plus an appreciation of ₹5 for holding it over the year, which gives a total of 18.5%. The formula for the holding period yield is as follows: The return (18.5) is divided by the purchase price (₹80) which gives the holding period yield (23.1%).

$$\text{The formula is HPY} = \frac{(P_t - P_0) + I}{P_o}$$

where I is interest payment, P_o is price at the beginning of the holding period and P_t is price at the end of the holding period.

Real Yield

Real yield is a different concept which takes into account the depreciation in the value of money. Thus as opposed to nominal yield, which is the coupon rate as, for example, 6%, the real yield is adjusted for depreciation in the value of the rupee, namely, an increase in the prices of goods and services. If the price increase is represented by Wholesale Price Index (WPI), then the nominal yield is deflated by the rise in WPI over the period considered. Thus the nominal yield of 6% if deflated by the rise in prices of, say 5% (as in 2003-04) will give a positive yield of 1%. Thus the concept of real yield presents the picture of the real return in terms of goods and services and purchasing power of the return.

Net Yield

The above concepts of yields present the picture of general yields common to any investor, irrespective of his status such as tax status or type such as an individual or institution, etc. As such, they are gross yields — yields prior to tax payment. The net yield is that after payment of tax. As tax liability varies from individual to individual or company to company, the general tax deduction rate can be applied, say 10% or 20% of the gross yield to arrive at the net yield. Interest and dividend incomes are paid without deduction of tax at source for amounts up to ₹2,500 per annum. These tax factors become relevant for net incomes.

Maturity and Yields

Yields vary depending not only on the type of security and interest rate, coupon rate but on the maturity of the security. Thus the yields are higher, longer is the maturity. This is particularly true of Government securities, which are issued with varying maturities.

Yield Curve

If yields on any security are available on a cross section basis, a yield curve can be drawn to serve for comparative purposes or for indicating the trends and for forecasting purposes. The yield curve is mainly useful in the Government securities market where yields differ mainly on the basis of maturity. It depicts the relationship of time periods to yields, referred to earlier.

The effect of interest rate changes on value of bonds is shown below:

Example: Take one bond of 5 years maturity and another of 30 years maturity — both with a coupon rate of 6%.

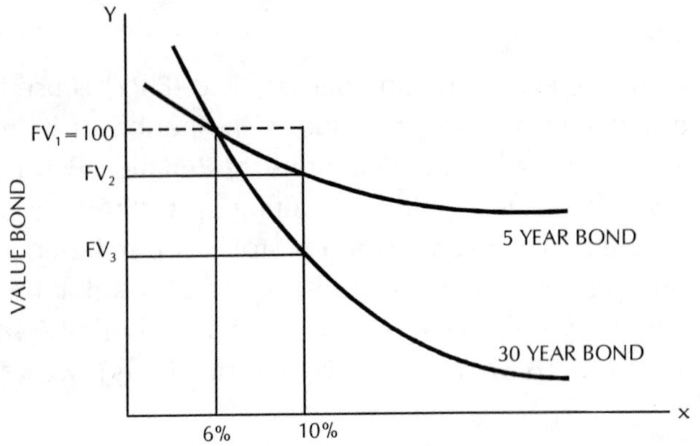

The Required Rates of Return (r) goes up to 10%, the fall in value of 30 years bond is steeper than a 5 years bond (that is FV_1 to FV_3, for 30-year bond as against FV_1 to FV_2 for 5-year bond, as shown in the chart, above.

✠ ✠ ✠

BASICS OF PORTFOLIO MANAGEMENT SERVICES

42

In India, Portfolio Management is still in its infancy as a financial service. Barring a few Indian banks, and foreign banks and UTI, no other agency had professional Portfolio Management until 1987. After the setting up of public sector Mutual Funds, since 1987, Professional Portfolio Management, backed by competent research staff became the order of the day. After the success of Mutual Funds in Portfolio Management, a number of brokers and investment consultants some of whom are also professionally qualified have become Portfolio Managers. They have managed the funds of clients on both discretionary and non-discretionary basis. It was found that many of them, including Mutual Funds have guaranteed a minimum return or capital appreciation and adopted all kinds of incentives which are now prohibited by SEBI. They resorted to speculative over-trading and insider trading, discounts, etc., to achieve their targeted returns to the clients, which are also prohibited by SEBI.

The recent CBI probe into the operations of many market dealers has revealed the unscrupulous practices by banks, dealers and brokers in their Portfolio Operations. The SEBI has then imposed stricter rules, which included their registration, a code of conduct and minimum infrastructure, experience and expertise, etc. It is no longer possible for any unemployed youth, or retired person or self-styled consultant to engage in Portfolio Management without the SEBI's licence. The guidelines of SEBI are in the direction of marking Portfolio Management, a responsible professional service to be rendered by experts in the field.

SOME ASPECTS OF PORTFOLIO MANAGEMENT

Basically Portfolio Management involves:

(A) A proper investment decision making of what to buy and sell;

(B) A proper money management in terms of investment in a basket of assets so as to satisfy the asset preferences of investors;

(C) Reduction of the risk and increase of the returns.

SEBI — Guidelines

PORTFOLIO MANAGEMENT

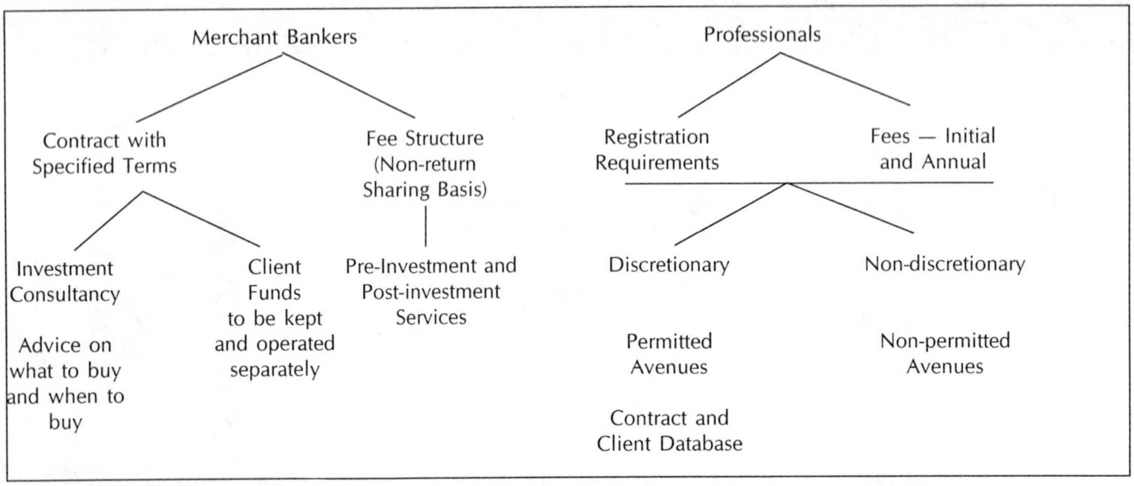

Note: The required net worth and licence fee and annual fees payable by them are fixed by SEBI and they are variable.

Rules/Regulations

(A) Client relationship with portfolio manager.

(B) Period of contract for portfolio manager to be specified.

(C) Investment strategy to be recorded.

(D) Records, accounts, and audit to be kept regularly.

(E) Inspection and power to call for returns by SEBI.

(F) Periodical reports to clients.

CODE OF CONDUCT			
Integrity Honesty and Professionalism	Contract with Client and Service Before and After Trade	Dealings with Members and Fellow Managers Fair Practices Fair Competition	Market Dealings Not to indulge in Rigging, False Market, Kerb Deals, Insider Trading

Investment Strategy

In India, there are a large number of savers, barring the 26% of the population who are below the poverty line. In a poor country like this, it is surprising that its saving rate is as high as 34% of GDP per annum and investment at 36% of GDP. But the return in the form of output growth was as low as 8% per annum over the nineties. One may ask why is it that high levels of investment could not generate comparable rates of growth of output? The answer is poor investment strategy, involving high capital output ratios, low productivity of capital and high rates of obsolescence of capital. What is true of the nation at that macro level is also true at micro level of individuals and institutions. The use of capital in India is wasteful and inefficient, despite the fact that India is labour rich and capital poor. Thus, the Portfolio Managers in India lack the expertise and experience, which will enable them to have proper strategy for investment management.

Secondly, the average Indian household saves around 45% in financial form and 55% in physical form. Of those in financial form, nearly 56% is held in cash and bank deposits, as per the latest CSO data and they have negative real returns or return less than the inflation rates. Besides, a proportion of 28% of financial savings is held in form of Insurance, P.F., Pension Funds, etc., while another 18% is in government instruments and Certificates like Post Office Deposits, N.S. Certificates, Public Provident Funds, National Saving Scheme, etc. The real returns on Insurance, P.F., etc., are low and many times lower than the average inflation rates. With the removal of many tax concessions for investments in P.O. Savings instruments, Certificates, etc., they also become less attractive to small and medium investors. The only investments, statisfying all their objectives are capital market instruments. These objectives are income, capital appreciation, safety, marketability, liquidity and hedge against inflation, and investment by average household in shares and debentures is only around 1 to 2% of the total financial savings, in early 21st century.

Objectives of Investors: The return on equity investments in the capital market particularly if proper investment strategy is adopted would satisfy the above objectives and the real returns would be higher than any other saving instruments. It is in this context, the art and science of investment and of Portfolio Management become the *sine-qua-non* of success.

All investments involve risk taking. However, some risk free investments are available like bank deposits or P.O. deposits whose returns are called risk free returns of about 4 to 9%. So the returns on more risky investments are higher than that, having risk premium. Risk is variability of return and uncertainty of payment of interest and repayment of principal. Risk is measured by standard deviation of the returns over the mean for a given period. Risk varies directly with return. The higher the risk taken, the higher is the return, under normal market conditions.

Risk and Beta

Risk is of two components — systematic market related risk and unsystematic risk or company specific risk. The former cannot be eliminated but managed with the help of Beta (β), which is explained as follows:

$$\beta = \frac{\text{\% age change of Scrip return}}{\text{\% age change of Market return}}$$

If $\beta = 1$, the risk of the company is the same as that of the market and if $\beta > 1$, the company's risk is more than the market risk. If $\beta < 1$, the reverse is the position.

Specific Risk: If risk is company specific risk, it can be reduced by diversification into different industries and companies of different types and nature and whose co-variances are different and whose performances are disparate. It is also called unsystematic risk.

TYPES OF RISK	
Unsystematic Risk	*Systematic Risk*
Company related risks due to higher costs, mismanagement, defective sales or inventory strategy, insolvency, fall in demand and company specific recession, labour problems, etc.	Market-related risk due to demand problems, interest rates, inflation, raw materials, import and export policy, tax policy etc., Business Risk, Market Risk, Financial Risk, Interest Rate Risk, Inflation Risk, etc.

Modern Portfolio Theory (MPT): This postulates that public generally are risk averse. In a perfect market, information is free and quickly absorbed by the market. Given the return, risk can be reduced by diversification of investment into a number of scrips. Each scrip has its own risk profile. The risks of any two scrips are different from the risk of a group of two companies together. Thus, if the risk of Reliance (b) is say 1.90 and that of Dr. Beck is 0.70, the total of these two units is 1.30 as the average. But the actual 'β' may be less at say 1.00, reason being that the co-variance of these two may be zero or negative (less than 1).

CAPM and SML: (Capital Asset Pricing Model and Security Market Line) CAPM postulates that in a perfect market, where shares are correctly priced, every security will give a return commensurate with its risk.

"β" is a measure of the risk. The market risk is different from the risks of individual scrips comprising the market. CML relates to the total risk of the Market. But SML refers to the risk, which is undiversifiable market-related risk. Total risk is meaured by the standard deviation, while the undiversificable risk or systematic risk is measured by Beta (β). CML, (β) is Capital Market Line and SML is Security Market Line.

Risk premium of portfolio is the excess of the expected portfolio return over the risk free return. Similar is the definition in respect of risk premium of the market, namely, expected Market Return minus Risk Free Return. CML passes through the risk free rate, which represents the true time value of money or the reward for waiting by savers.

Time Value of Money

In Portfolio Management and investment decision-making, time element and time value of money are very relevant. Savings are automatic or induced. If induced, it requires a return enough to induce them to part with liquidity. Thus, savings and liquidity will be parted by the investors if only their time preference is satisfied by proper return.

Why time preference? Why savers prefer today's return to tomorrow's return? "A bird in hand is worth two in the bush", as the adage goes.

1. More money is to be received after a year, if he has to lend to the user of funds today. He forgoes consumption which has to be compensated.
2. Money lent today can produce something more than before and hence present money is more valuable than money tomorrow. This premium is needed for waiting.
3. Money is losing in value due to rise in prices. Hence, moneylenders lose and borrowers gain in times of inflation. Premium given is to compensate the lenders against loss due to fall in value of money.

Compounding

Future Value Factor (FVF) is $(1 + r)^n$ where (r) is the rate of interest required and (n) is the period of years of waiting. P is the present value.

$Fn = P\ (1 + r)^n$, or

Future Value = (Present Value) × (Future Value Factor)

So the return required by savers is related to the waiting period, loss of consumption at present, or liquidity and risk of loss of money or variance of returns.

Discounting

If the future flow of money is known as C_1, C_2, C_3, etc., what is the present value of them and how much is he prepared to pay for them? If he deposits today ₹100, he gets ₹110 at the end of 1 year and ₹121 at the end of 2 years, if the interest rate is 10%. This process of finding the present value for future money flows is called discounting. Present value of future amounts is:

$$P = F\ (n)\ \frac{1}{1+r^n}$$

The multiplier $\left(\frac{1}{1+r^n}\right)$ is called PVF or Present Value Factor. We should know the amounts of cash flows, (Fn) number of years (n) and the required rate of return (r).

Perpetuity

When we receive a fixed sum of money every year up to infinity, it is called perpetuity. Suppose we want to receive ₹100 every year for infinity and interest rate is 10%, we have to deposit ₹1,000 and the equation is PV = $\frac{a}{r}$ where PV is Present Value of perpetuity, a is fixed periodic cash flow and r is the rate of interest.

Annuity

Annuity is a constant cash flow for a finite time period of say 5 years (n). Examples of annuity are found in the case of lease rentals, loan repayments, recurring deposits, etc.

Application to Porfolio Management

Portfolio Management involves time element and time horizon. The present value of future returns/cash flows by discounting is useful for share valuation and bond valuation. The investment strategy in Portfolio Construction should have a time horizon, say 3 to 5 years, to produce the desired results of say 20-30% return per annum.

Besides, Portfolio Management should also take into account tax benefits and investment incentives. As the returns are taken by investors' net of tax payments, and there is always an element of inflation, returns net of taxation and inflation are more relevant to tax paying investors. These are called net real rates of returns, which should be more than other returns. They should encompass risk free return plus a reasonable risk premium, depending upon the risk taken, on the instruments/assets invested.

Portfolio Construction, Revision and Evaluation

Portfolio Manager has to use all the tools of research like fundamental analysis and technical analysis in addition to Risk-Return analysis to decide on the investment, buying and selling, etc. After the design of the Portfolio Strategy, the construction and allocation of funds will lead to the building up of the Portfolio. Thereafter, the Portfolio thus built requires a constant review and revision with the result that operations on it are a continuous process. This is also called Monitoring. Finally, once in a year or half-year, the Portfolio performance has to be evaluated, for its success by comparing the actual achievements with the targets fixed. This throws light on the efficiency of the investment strategy of Portfolio Manager.This all boils down to a constant process of investment and disinvestment, trading, review and evaluation of investments and examination of the results of the Portfolio.

MPT and Dominance Concept

The Modern Portfolio Theory (MPT) is based on assumptions of *free and perfect information flow* and the *notion of dominance*. This means that if the market is able to absorb the information, fully and efficiently, price reflects the risks involved given the same return, the investor can choose the scrips with the lowest possible risk. This is possible by diversification for an individual into a number of companies of say 10 to 15, which have diverse characteristics of risk. Thus, when any two scrips behave differently to given changes in the economy and industry and when the co-efficient of correlation between them is less than 1, such scrips can be joined in a Portfolio so as to reduce the combined risk of the Portfolio.

The notion of dominance tells us that no investor should invest in one company alone and if there are two or more companies with the same risk, then he has to choose the one with higher return and if both have the same return he has to choose the one with lower risk. The investor can reduce the risk by distributing his funds in a diverse variety of companies with varying risks and returns which do not have much auto correlation. Thus the investor has not only to make proper investment decision of what to buy and when to buy, but has a proper investment strategy through diversification and choice of a proper 'β' for the scrips selected so that the total risk of Portfolio is the lowest possible. 'β' is Beta which is a measure of systematic risk.

Diversification Process

The process of diversification has various phases involving investment into various classes of assets like equity, preference shares, CDs, NCDs, P.S.U. Bonds and money market instruments like commercial paper, inter-corporate investments, deposits, etc. Within each class of assets, there is further possibility of diversification into various industries, different companies, etc. The proportion of funds invested into various classes of assets, instruments, industries and companies, would depend upon the objectives of investor, under Portfolio Management and his asset preferences, income and asset requirements.

A Portfolio with the objective of regular income would invest a proportion of funds in bonds, debentures and fixed deposits. For such investments, duration of the life of the bond/debenture, quality of the asset as judged by the credit rating and the expected yield are the relevant variables.

Retail bond market is not well developed in India but debentures, partly or fully convertible into equity are in good demand both from individuals and mutual funds. The Portfolio Manager has to use his analytical power and discretion to choose the right debentures with the required duration, yield and quality. The duration, expected inflows of funds and quantum of funds have to be well planned by the Portfolio Manager. Research and high degree of analytical power in investment management are necessary.

Another specialised area connected with Portfolio Management is Equity and Bond Market Research. The financial markets in which they render service to clients are to be juxtaposed and this is the function of the market research wing. The details of this are available in our book on Security Analysis and Portfolio Management.

The bond investments are thus equally challenging as equity investments and more so in respect of money market instruments which are complex and still developing. All these facts bring out clearly the needed analytical powers and expertise of Portfolio Manager. Bond market in India is not well developed, but efforts are being made to develop by the SEBI and RBI.

It will thus be seen that Portfolio Management is an art and requires high degree of expertise. The merchant bankers are authorised to do Portfolio Management Services, by the SEBI. Others who want to provide such services should have a minimum net worth of ₹50 lakh and expertise, as laid down by the SEBI and would have to register with the SEBI. The SEBI have set out the guidelines in this regard, in which the relations of the client *vis-a-vis* the Portfolio Manager and the respective rights and duties of both have been set out. The code of conduct for Portfolio Managers has been laid down by the SEBI. The job of Portfolio Manager in managing the client's funds, either on discretionary or non-discretionary basis has thus become challenging and difficult due to the multitude of obligations laid on his shoulders by the SEBI, in respect of their operations, accounts, audit, etc.

It is thus clear that Portfolio Management has become, a complex and responsible job which requires an in-depth training and expertise. It is in this context that the regulations of SEBI on Portfolio Management has become necessary, so that the minimum qualifications and experience are also ensured for those who are registered with SEBI. Nobody can do Portfolio Management without SEBI registration and licence.

SEBI Guidelines for Portfolio Managers

The SEBI has given permission to Merchant Bankers of category I to do Portfolio Management. As per the guidelines of September 1991 a separate category of Portfolio Managers is also licensed by SEBI for which guidelines were given in January 1993. Merchant bankers of categories II to IV were abolished by SEBI in 1996-97.

What is Portfolio Management Service?

As per the SEBI norms this service refers to professional service rendered for management of Portfolio of anybody, namely, clients or customers with the help of experts in Investment Advisory Services. Investment

Consultancy involves the advice regarding the worthwhileness of any particular investment or advice of what to buy and sell and when to buy and sell. Investment management on the other hand involves continuing relationship with client to manage investments with or without discretion for the client as per his requirements.

Method of Operation

The Professional Portfolio Manager can be approached by any individual or organisation with a minimum amount of investible funds of say, ₹ 1 lakh or ₹ 2 lakhs. If the manager is willing to accept him as his client, a contract is entered into for management of his funds either on discretionary basis or non-discretionary basis, specifying the objectives, risk to be tolerated, composition of assets/securities in the Portfolio and their relative proportion, fees payable and time period of management, as per the preference of the client, etc. The client's database is collected, namely, his available income and assets, his needs, his risk preferences, his choice for income or growth or both and host of personal details of the client so as to enable him to design a proper investment strategy for him.

SEBI Norms on Operations

SEBI has prohibited the Portfolio Manager to assume any risk on behalf of the client. Portfolio Manager cannot also assure any fixed return to the client. The investments made or advised by him are subject to risk which the client has to bear. The investment consultancy and management has to be charged at rates which are fixed at the beginning and transparent as per the contract. No sharing of profits or discounts or cash incentives to client is permitted.

The Portfolio Manager is prohibited to do lending, badla financing and bills discounting as per SEBI norms. He cannot put the clients' funds in any investment, not permitted by the contract, entered into with the client. Normally, investments can be made in both capital market and money market instruments.

Client's money has to be kept in a separate account with the public sector bank and cannot be mixed up with his own funds or investments. All the deals done for a client's account are to be entered in his name and Contract Notes, Bills, etc., are all passed in his name. A separate ledger account is maintained for all purchases/sales on client's behalf, which should be done at the market price. Final settlement and termination of contract is as per the contract and for the time period agreed upon. Notice of termination of contract is also as per the contract. During the period of contract, Portfolio Manager is only acting on a contractual basis and on a fiduciary basis. No contract for less than a year is permitted by the SEBI.

Who can be a Portfolio Manager?

Only those who are registered and pay the required licence fee are eligible to operate as Portfolio Managers. An applicant for this purpose should have necessary infrastructure with professionally qualified persons and with a minimum of two persons with experience in this business and a minimum net worth of ₹ 50 lakh. The certificate once granted is valid for three years. Fees payable for registration are ₹ 2.5 lakh every year for two years and ₹ 1 lakh for the third year. From the fourth year onwards, renewal fees per annum are ₹ 75,000. The fees payable are subject to change by the SEBI.

The SEBI has imposed a number of obligations and a code of conduct on them. The Portfolio Manager should have a high standard of integrity, honesty and should not have been convicted of any economic offence or moral turpitude. He should not resort to rigging up of prices, insider trading or creating false markets, etc. Their books of accounts, are subject to inspection and audit by SEBI. The observance of the code of conduct and guidelines given by the SEBI are subject to inspection and penalties are imposed for violation. The Manager has to submit periodical returns and documents as may be required by the SEBI from time to time.

✠ ✠ ✠

Part VIII

INTERNATIONAL MARKETS

FOREIGN EXCHANGE MARKETS

43

Foreign Exchange operators do a financial service to the exporters, importers and for the flow of funds across the borders. Dealers in foreign markets help in joint ventures abroad, mergers and acquisitions and a host of other services, relating to international markets in which foreign exchange and foreign currencies are dealt with. India's economic growth depends on that and Indian markets are influenced by financial markets abroad. Hence, the importance of foreign exchange services and thus it is included in this book.

Definition

Foreign exchange as a subject deals with the means and methods by which rights to income and wealth in one country's currency are converted into similar rights in terms of another country's currency. It involves the investigation of the methods by which the currency of one country is exchanged for that of another, the causes which render such exchange necessary, the forms in which exchange may take place and the ratios or equivalent values at which such exchanges are effected.

Such exchange may be in the form of one currency to another or of conversion of credit instruments denominated in different currencies such as cheques, drafts, airmail transfers, fax and telegraphic transfers, cable transfers, bills of exchange, trade bills, bankers' bills or any promissory notes. It is through these instruments and foreign currency accounts of banks that the banks are able to effect such exchange of currencies or claims to currencies.

Every exchange of goods and services is having a corresponding exchange of remittances involving two currencies, as depicted in chart below.

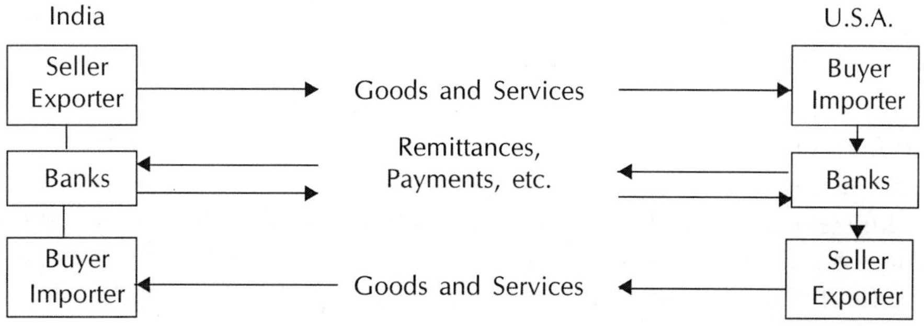

No currency will be physically exchanged as it is not legal tender in any country other than in the issuing country. So exchanges take place through book entries and/or through credit instruments by banks. The instruments through which exchanges of currencies take place are Telegraphic Transfers (TTs), Mail Transfers (MTs), Demand Drafts (DDs), Cheques, Bills of Exchange, etc. In the absence of banks, the buyer-importer who has to pay in dollars has to hunt for an exporter-seller who received an equivalent amount of dollars from the foreign importer. Banks facilitate such transactions by acting as intermediaries between buyers and sellers or importers and exporters.

International Financial System and Foreign Exchange Market

One of the important components of the international financial system is the foreign exchange market. The various commercial and financial transactions as between countries result in receipts and payments as between them. The items of balance of payments leading to receipts and payments are trade, travel, transportation, royalties, fees, investment income, unilateral transfers, short-term and long-term capital receipts and payments, etc. Such receipts and payments involve exchange of one currency for another. Thus, rupee is a legal tender in India, but an exporter in UK will have no use for these rupees. He, therefore, wishes to receive from the importer in India only in pounds sterling. Then the importer will have to convert such rupees into pounds in that transaction. The foreign exchange market provides facilities for such operations. The demand for goods and services from one country to another is the basis for demand for currencies in the exchange market. Such merchandise and invisible trade items constitute nearly 70-80 per cent of the total transactions in the market. Conversion of currencies is also necessary for short-term capital flows or long-term investment in financial or physical assets of another country. It will thus be seen, that the services of the exchange market are necessary not only for trade transactions but for any financial receipts or payments as between countries. Any receipt and payment of foreign cash, coins, claims in currencies or credit instruments involve a foreign exchange transaction.

Foreign Sector and Foreign Exchange Market

Each economy has a foreign sector representing that economy's external transactions. All such external transactions are either economic and commercial or financial transactions. These result in receipts into and payments out of the domestic economy. Such receipts and payments involve exchange of domestic currency as against all foreign currencies of countries with which domestic economy has dealings. Such exchange transactions are put through in the exchange market for that currency. For each nation, therefore, there is an exchange market for that country's currency *vis-a-vis* other currencies. These national foreign exchange markets are components of the international financial system.

There is thus, as for any other currency, a market for the rupee. If an Indian bank buys dollars, it will pay rupees for dollars and if it sells dollars, it will receive rupees for dollars. The origin of these transactions is an export or an import, inward or outward remittances or any similar transactions between Indian residents and foreign residents. An exporter in India receives dollars from say, USA and he surrenders the bill of exchange along with other documents to his bank. The bank would have bought that currency from the exporter. The bank has since been on the lookout for selling those dollars in the foreign exchange market for those in need of dollars. Let us say an importer in India importing from the USA is in need of dollars to cover up his position from the former bank.

Thus, basically demand for and supply of foreign currencies arises from exporters or importers or the public having some receipts from or payments to foreign countries. These receipts or payments may give rise to foreign credit instruments which the banks buy or sell at specified rates. There are different rates for buying and selling in which an interest element is included and quoted by the banks if the bill or promissory note or any instrument of exchange is not a demand or sight bill but a usance note involving some period to run to maturity for payment. Even in the case of sight bills, some grace period of 2 days and transit period of 10 to 20 days are allowed as fixed by the Foreign Exchange Dealers' Association, depending upon the place on which it is drawn and interest element for these periods is also included in the rate quoted by banks.

Banks generally cover up these positions in currencies by corresponding purchases or sales from other banks. Such a market as between banks is called inter-bank market. There are reputed brokers who act as intermediaries for banks in these transactions.

Bank's Purchase and Sale

Every foreign exchange transaction involves a two-way conversion — a purchase and a sale. Conversion of rupees into dollars involves purchase of dollars and sale of rupees or *vice versa* depending upon the angle from which we are looking. If it is looked at from the country having rupees (India), then the transaction looks as follows:

(*a*) Sale of rupees for dollars (importer) — conversion of home currency into foreign currency.

(*b*) Purchase of rupees for dollars (exporter) — conversion of foreign currency into home currency.

As an Indian banker has to keep his accounts in rupees, he buys and sells foreign currencies like any commodity for money (Indian rupee).

Instruments of Credit Traded

In addition to conversion of foreign currency notes and cash for domestic currency notes/coin, a number of instruments of credit are used for effecting conversion of one currency into another. These instruments are discussed below:

(1) Telegraphic Transfers (TT)

A TT is a transfer of money by telegram or cable or telex or fax from one centre to another in a foreign country. It is a method used by banks with their own codes and correspondent relations with banks abroad for transmission of funds. As it involves the payment of funds on the same day, it is the quickest means of transmission of funds. As there is no loss of interest or capital risk in this mode, it enjoys the best rate for the value of receipts.

(2) Mail Transfers (MT)

It is an order to pay cash to a third party sent by mail by a bank to its correspondent or branch abroad. It is issued in duplicate — one to the party buying it and the other to the banker — correspondent or agent abroad. The amount is paid by the agent bank to the third party mentioned therein in the transferee country by its own cheque or by crediting the party's account. As the payment is made after the mail advice is received at the other end, which will take a few days, the rate charged to the purchaser is cheaper to the extent of the interest gain to the seller-bank. MT rates are cheaper than TT rates.

(3) Drafts and Cheques

Draft is a pay order issued by a bank on its own branch or correspondent bank abroad. It is payable on sight but there is always a time lapse in the transit or in post between the payment by the purchaser of the draft to his bank and the receipt of the money by the seller in the foreign centre. As in the case of MT, there is risk of loss of the draft in transit, delay in effecting payment to the beneficiary and loss of interest during the intervening period. The rate charged by the bank for this is less advantageous to the buyer of the draft than in other modes.

(4) Bills of Exchange

It is an unconditional order in writing addressed by one person to another, requiring the person to whom it is addressed to pay a certain sum on demand or within a specified date. If it is payable on demand, it is a sight bill and if it is payable after a period, it is a long bill or a usance bill. Such bills can be banker bills or trade bills. Banks bills are drawn on a bank abroad. While the bank bills carry better rates due to their greater security, the trade bills drawn on private parties may not fetch good rates. Sight bills are paid on sight but allow a transit period of 10 to 20 days on which interest is lost. In the case of usance bills, the purchase price is adjusted on the basis of maturity date of the bill for the interest lost, adjusted in the rate quoted for such a bill. So, the sight bills carry a better rate than usance bills.

Foreign Exchange Market Components

There are three major components of this market, depending upon the level at which transactions are put through:

(1) Firstly, transactions between the public and the market at the base level involve receipts from any payments to the public or purchases from and sales to public.

(2) Secondly, transactions as between the banks dealing in foreign exchange involving conversion of currencies taking place in the same centre or as between centres in the same country (inter-bank market) or as between countries involving the correspondent or agent banks abroad or branches of the domestic banks abroad.

(3) Thirdly, transactions between banks and central bank involving purchase and sale of foreign currencies for cover or final disposal of excess foreign balances. The central banks may in turn deal with the foreign central banks or foreign governments.

Basically, the above exchanges involve no physical exchange of currencies except in small dominations when travellers and tourists carry them across national borders, but through exchange of credit instruments or book entries in the books of banks in various centres. The banks are linked together by phone, cable, telex, post or other means of communication. The transactions are put through directly by the banks or through the brokers located at various centres where these transactions are concentrated like Mumbai, Kolkata, Chennai, etc. All the dealer banks in foreign exchange in India have an Association called Foreign Exchange Dealers' Association of India.

Exchange Rate Mechanism

As in the case of any commodity, there is a price for any purchase or sale of a currency. Such a price in the exchange market is called the exchange rate. This is defined as the number of units of one currency that will be exchanged for a unit of another currency. The exchange rate of any currency can be expressed in two ways — one unit of domestic currency. Thus ₹100 = £ 1.4164 as indirect method and the other method, namely, in direct method, it is £ 1.00 = ₹70.600. And in terms of dollars, U.S. $1 = ₹42.2600 in the direct method on Sept. 15, 1998, and US $ = ₹46.85 on April 20, 2001, and $1 = ₹63.36 at end December 2014.

It is pertinent to ask what factors normally determine the exchange rate in the market. *Prima facie,* if the market is free and rates are allowed to fluctuate, the exchange rate would depend on the supply of and demand for a currency. Thus, taking dollars *vis-a-vis* rupees, the rate is determined by the demand for dollars and supply of dollars in relation to the rupee. Those who demand dollars are primarily importers from the USA to India who have to pay the US exporters in dollars or those having remittances or payments to make to USA. Similarly, those who supply dollars are primarily the exporters to USA who are paid in dollars by importers in USA.

The rate of exchange is determined at any moment by the forces of demand for and supply of a currency which in turn depends on the demand for and supply of commodities and services as between India and the USA and inflation rates in those countries. They also depend on arbitrage and interest rate speculation, currency speculation and short-term capital flows if these are permitted. This can be represented diagrammatically as follows:

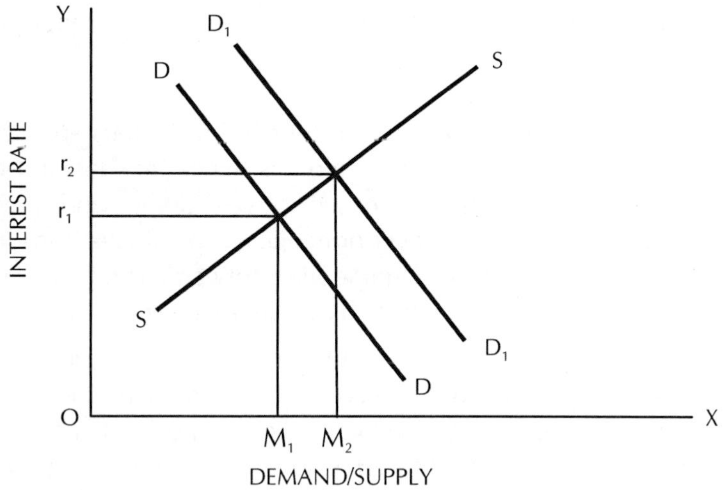

Fig. 43.1

Given the supply (SS), if the demand increases from DD to D_1D_1 the rate will rise from r_1 to r_2 and *vice versa*. A rise in the rate for rupee means more foreign currency units are given for given unit of domestic currency.

The basic factors which determine the exchange rates are the intrinsic purchasing power of the currencies in their own domestic economies. In the era of paper currencies, which are not backed by gold exchange standard, currencies of different countries are not based on their intrinsic worth in terms of gold, but in terms of what Prof. Gustav Cassell, the renowned classical economist, called the Purchasing Power Parity Theory. According to this theory, exchange rates are determined by what each unit of a currency can buy in terms of real goods and services in its own country. The rate of exchange is the amount of currency which would buy the equivalent basket of goods and services in its own country. The rate of exchange is the amount of currency which would buy the equivalent basket of goods and services in both the countries. Such an exercise in real world is based on comparisons at two periods of time, with one year as the basis of comparison, but no absolute comparison as between two currencies is possible as the pattern of goods and services produced varies from country to country. It is assumed that the base year prices in both the countries are at equilibrium and the exchange ratio at that time represents the ratio of their purchasing powers. Thus, if the base period exchange rate is 1:1 a doubling of prices in the domestic economy of B with A's prices remaining constant, would lead to a new exchange rate of 1:2. This ratio would set the bounds or limits to day-to-day fluctuations in the exchange rates, based on the supply or demand forces for each currency.

This theory of Gustav is criticised on the ground that the quality of goods and services in both the countries is not the same and that a comparison of them is not realistic. The markets are not free due to trade and payments restrictions such as tariffs, quotas, etc. Besides the base period exchange rate may not be the equilibrium rate which distorts the comparison of their purchasing power parties at the current period. The index number technique used for such comparison is also criticised as defective due to changes in the composition of goods, their qualities over a period of time, etc.

Under the exchange rate system prevailing in the world, before 1971, under the aegis of the IMF, exchange rates were fixed in terms of gold or US dollar and a fluctuation on either side by 1 per cent was permitted. Any changes in exchange rate parity, as fixed with the Fund, could be changed up to 10 per cent by consultation with the Fund. Any change beyond 10 per cent is to be justified on grounds of fundamental disequilibrium in the parities. The system prevailing after the breakdown of the Bretton Woods system in August 1971 is one of a wider band of margins and floating currencies with varying degrees of controls on such floating rate system which was set up by IMF in 1972, favoured stable but adjustable par values and fixation of par values of currencies in terms of SDR which is represented by a basket of currencies and intervention in the exchange markets in terms of a multi-currency approach.

Spot and Forward Rates

If an importer is paying on receipt of documents, then he can buy dollars spot and the bank sells him spot dollars. But if the importer agrees to pay three or six months hence, his demand for dollars might arise only after three or six months hence. These dollars are called forward dollars and the market is the forward market. The existence of a forward market provides cover or hedge against fluctuations in exchange rates. This exchange risk falls on the banks who are buying or selling dollars forward. The banks in turn can pass on the risk to the central bank of the country or to a foreign bank at another centre.

Just as banks are buying and selling spot, they also do business in forward currencies. Corresponding to the spot rate of exchange, there is a forward rate for various periods. If any bank succeeds in matching forward purchases with forward sales of the same currency, it avoids "taking a position" and assumes no risk. If they do not match, the bank may have an uncovered position which it may cover with another bank which has a contrary position. If it fails to cover with a bank, it may still do so with the central bank of the country or with a correspondent bank abroad. If a bank takes a position uncovered it takes risk of position against a spot deal or against a future sale or purchase.

Currencies purchased or sold in forward would be subject to the influences of interest rates at home and abroad. A forward currency will be at premium (higher than the spot expressed in foreign currency per domestic unit quoted as ₹100 = $ 4.7555), as at end June 1991. Later rates were quoted as $ 1 = ₹31.3283 in June 1993, and $ 1 = ₹43.66 in mid-March 2005, if interest rates abroad are higher than at home.The rupee dollar exchange rate depreciated from a high of ₹22.69 in 1991 at the time of initiation of economic and financial reforms to a low of ₹48.59 in 2002, before appreciating again to ₹43.75 in June 2008 (Averages). The premium or discount will depend on interest rates and expectations of interest rates and exchange rates. Forward premia for U.S. dollar is 8-10 paise per month on September 15, 1998. Quoted in terms of percentage per annum basis the premiums varied around 2-3 per cent per annum during June 2004 and at 1.60 per cent per annum in Aug. 2007. Quotations are given up to 6 months forward on a daily basis. The above quotations are only for illustration. The premium stood at a high of 6.99% in June 2011.

Speculation

Speculation and hedging operations are taking place in free markets to take advantage of interest rate and exchange rate differentials. In the case of India, such hedging and speculation are possible to a limited extent, due to continued capital account controls and banks are not allowed to take position in any currency beyond the minimum working balances to be kept in various centres. In a free foreign exchange market, short-term capital flows take place to take advantage of interest rate differentials and will be quickly reversed, leading to instability in the exchange rates. One-sided speculation is also very destabilising which generally the central bank of a country would not allow unchecked. Controls on capital account, particularly to counter such destabilising short-term flows, are in tune with the spirit of the International Monetary Fund. Speculation on a limited scale and if it is on both sides of purchase and sale is healthy and welcome to keep the balance in the market and absorb the excesses of demand/supply of currencies in the foreign exchange market.

Arbitrage

When foreign exchange markets are free to fluctuate, the exchange rate of a currency should be the same in almost all the centres. Thus, if the dollar rate per sterling is different in New York and Frankfurt, then funds would flow in either direction to take advantage of the rate differential. It is, however, possible that slight differentials might be still there due to carrying costs of moving funds from one place to another. Such operations in terms of movements of funds from one centre to another are called arbitrage operations.

Such operations can take place only if there are no exchange controls in both the countries and if funds are free to move. Thus, if either New York or Frankfurt is subject to exchange restrictions involving central bank supervision of funds inflow and outflow and ban on free movements, arbitrage cannot take place and differentials in rates between two countries might exist.

Arbitrage is not limited to two centres or two currencies alone. Three-point and multi-point arbitrage can also take place if the respective currencies are free. Thus, in a three-point arbitrage, the dollar-sterling rate and the dollar-franc rate are considered and the cross rate between sterling and franc should be in conformity with the above two rates. Otherwise, three-point arbitrage can take place by moving funds from dollar to franc and franc to sterling and back to dollar from sterling. Suppose the dollar-sterling rate is £ 1 = $ 2.80 and franc 350 = $1 and £ = 1020 francs. Starting with $100, one can buy up pounds, move from pounds to francs and thence to dollars back, making a gain of about $ 4 per $ 100 in the above example. Thus, arbitrage can take place as between centres or currencies at more than two centres and currencies at a time. Such arbitrage operations may be for gain in exchange rate differential or in interest rate differential as between centres. The former are called currency arbitrage and the latter interest arbitrage. An operation of simultaneous purchase and sale in each of the two markets to take advantage of interest differential is called interest arbitrage. Such deals are put through swaps or forward deals.

The operations in the foreign exchange market are exposed to a number of risks which are difficult to foresee and forecast. These risks may be credit risks arising out of lending to a foreign borrower whose credit rating is not known for certainty. Secondly, there may be currency risks of trading in a currency whose political and economic strength is weak and is uncertain. Thirdly, there are risks of fluctuating interest rates in various currencies in the inter-bank market and anticipations may sometimes go wrong. Fourthly, there are risks of illiquidity due to mismatch between current assets and current liabilities with the result there may be sudden need for borrowing and difficulties may arise in securing funds at short notice. Lastly, the dealers sometimes take risks by exceeding the limits of prudent trading in a currency with the result that they may find it difficult to cover the transactions and incur losses in such a position. Such risks are more marked in international lending and borrowing and in foreign exchange and currency markets. Further details of risk are discussed in a separate chapter.

For a country like India, with a wide network of controls, arbitrage operations were not possible. Indian rupee was insulated from world free currency markets as the banks' operations in India were strictly controlled and monitored by the Reserve Bank of India, until 1992, when the trend to freely convertible rupee was started.

INDIAN FOREIGN EXCHANGE MARKET

In India there are many commercial and co-operative banks who are authorised to deal in foreign exchange called Authorised Dealers and are eligible to operate in the foreign exchange market. However, not all co-operative banks are authorised to deal in foreign exchange. These banks cover their open positions in currencies in London through their correspondents or branches abroad or in India in the inter-bank market. There are no published figures as thousands of crores of foreign trade, are put through and crores of foreign remittances and a host of other purchases and sales take place. However, the data on monthly turnover in foreign markets both in merchant banking and inter-bank trading are available in the Handbook of

Statistics of RBI, separately for purchases and sales. In the process of such purchases and sales directly with the public, the authorised dealers would have various currencies which they try to dispose of by matching demand with supply in the inter-bank market. It is only the unmatched net requirements that are purchased from the RBI, or excess sold to the RBI.

Exchange Dealers

The foreign department of every bank draws up a position sheet for each currency daily in which purchases and sales of the currency are recorded. As the banks generally avoid taking any exchange risk by keeping uncovered balance and are not permitted to do so under the previous regulations, they try to cover their position by the end of the day. When the purchases exceed sales, the credit balance is plus (or long) and overbrought. This is to be covered by equal sales of that currency. When the sales exceed purchases, the debit balance is minus, short or oversold position and is to be covered by equivalent purchases. These sales and purchases would include both spot and forward, import bills or export bills negotiated or purchased, clear sales or purchases (other than through bills, namely, by TT, MT, cheques, drafts) BC sales or OD sales, etc.

Before entering into the inter-bank market, the banker decides how much to cover and what is the outstanding balance position in his books. Banks operate in the inter-bank market through the foreign exchange brokers. In every important market centre, some brokers operate in these dealings. The banker keeps some minimum balances in all his Nostro accounts to meet the customer-needs as they accrue. Nostro accounts are our balances abroad kept in foreign centres. The more exactly he synchronises the delivery dates of his purchases and sales, the greater is his profit. The finer the rates he quotes, the better is his position. The better he foresees the trends in exchange rates and interest rates in various centres, the more efficient he is and the better is his profitability.

In the inter-bank market, banks put through the dealings of purchase and sale of currency through authorised brokers. Brokers in each centre are in contact with other centers in India and in foreign countries for effecting matching transactions in various currencies. In all centres, export bills, import bills and various remittances are daily purchased and sold by banks. Imports give rise to payments abroad and purchase for foreign currencies. As the bulk of the imports in India is on government account and the SBI keeps the account of the public sector undertakings and of the government, the SBI enters the foreign exchange market mostly as a buyer of foreign currencies. Exports are more concentrated in the private sector, in which all banks are involved in varying degrees. Hence, sales of foreign currencies in the exchange market are more evenly spread among the banks in India. Many times, brokers cannot match in the local centres for odd currencies like Austrian Shilling or Nigerian naira or Libyan dinar, which are to be put through in a more sophisticated market like London or Singapore.

In India, some financial centres are more developed than others in the foreign exchange market. Thus, Mumbai, Kolkata and Chennai are more developed than others. Some of the foreign exchange transactions being seasonal, the markets are also seasonal.

RBI and Exchange Market

The RBI operates in the market as the last recourse agency. The RBI purchases and sells sterling spot and buys and sells forward sterling up to six months but since June 1966, forward sales have been stopped. Since the abandonment of convertibility of the US dollars in 1971, the forward cover for a longer period was felt necessary due to greater exchange risks and it was provided by the RBI up to 9 months at a rate of 0.0075 per month for the extended period.

The other currencies in which the RBI started operations during the seventies are dollars, D.M. and Yen. The RBI started purchases spot and forward dollars from July and August 1966 respectively, and with brief interruptions from August 1971 to October 1972 and February 1973, the RBI continued to purchase spot and forward dollars. Similar purchases of DM and of Yen were started from March and May 1974 respectively.

The period of forward cover was up to three months initially but was extended upto six months from September 1975. Thus, the RBI provided cover for 4 currencies which are our major trading partners, namely, sterling, dollar, DM and Yen. The Bank purchased and sold spot, buys forward sterling and bought dollar, DM and Yen both spot and forward.

The RBI was operating in four major currencies, namely, UK, US $, Japanese Yen and DM. Early in 1987, the RBI has started selling spot US dollars with the result that it used to buying and selling two currencies, UK £ and US $, in addition to its purchases of DM and Japanese Yen. It has also adopted recently the practice of changing the rates quoted by it in the course of the day if the conditions in the market warranted it. The RBI used to quote both the spot and forward rates in the currencies it transacts with the banks and in ACU on a daily basis. But now, the RBI operates through intervention by U.S. dollar and Euro purchases and sales.

The RBI was providing cover for a fairly long period of up to 10 years in respect of long-term contracts for engineering exports and construction projects. Since November 1975, the RBI has also offered the cover to ADs against exchange rate fluctuations in respect of deposits received in foreign currency from non-residents. Most of the facilities which the RBI offered are intended for exporters in terms of cover or purchase and sale. This is justified in view of the national importance attached to exports. But they have not offered similar facilities for importers for two reasons. Firstly, the bulk of the imports into India is by the government or public sector agencies who do not need such facilities. Secondly, the inter-bank market is designed to develop to provide cover as and when needed by the importers in this regard. The RBI is maintaining itself as a last resort institution in foreign exchange as in domestic finance. The policy of RBI in this regard is very flexible and designed to promote self-reliance by banks and greater resort to the inter-bank market. The RBI has, however, responded to emerging situation in the foreign exchange market quickly and promptly. Since rupee convertibility was launched in March 1992, RBI is publishing a reference rate around which it operates in the market to stabilise the rate of exchange of rupee in terms of US dollar. These are open market operations by RBI, done on a daily basis.

Exchange Rate System in India

India was a formal member of the sterling area from September 1939 to June 1972, during which period the external value of the rupee (exchange rate) was kept stable in terms of sterling. Since the establishment of IMF, of which India was a founder member, the external value of the rupee was declared in terms of gold and US dollar (₹1 = 0.2688601 grams of fine gold or ₹1 = US $ 0.3022) and its value was maintained stable in terms of sterling by purchases and sales of sterling by the RBI (the sterling rupee rate was ₹1 = 1 S. 6d). Rupee was devalued twice, namely, in September 1949 by 30.5 per cent and June 1966 by 36.5 per cent to maintain parity with sterling. Since June 1966, the new rate has been ₹1 = 13.3 US cents. This link with sterling which was maintained by keeping the rupee stable in terms of sterling and using the sterling as intervention currency was justified on the ground that the bulk of India's trade was either with the sterling area or was denominated in sterling and that India's foreign interests lie with sterling which was considered at that time a stable and strong reserve currency.

With the breakdown of the Bretton Woods system in August 1971, and the floatations of various major currencies, the Indian rupee was temporarily kept pegged to the US dollar at ₹7.5 per US $ 1, and this rate was kept stable by intervention in the market by purchases and sales of sterling. Rupee-dollar peg was used to determine the rupee-sterling rate. This position continued up to December 1971, when under the Smithsonian agreement, the exchange rate of sterling was fixed in terms of US dollar and the rupee was again linked to sterling thereafter. This sterling link proved shortlived up to June 1972 when sterling and other major currencies started floating. Between June 1972 and September 1975, rupee was kept stable in terms of sterling but was allowed to fluctuate against all other currencies. During this period, rupee was effectively devalued against all major currencies other than sterling by as much as 18-20 per cent, while it was depreciating by 29 per cent. Since the effect of such depreciation was not favourable to India, with her inelastic supplies of export goods and growing debt burden, along with the rising import bill, India decided to delink itself with sterling completely in September 1975. Since then, the external value of rupee was determined by the market value, as quoted in London, of a basket of currencies. The currencies included in the basket and the relative currency weights as well as the method of compilation of the exchange rate were kept confidential. Since then the rupee valuation has been based on a mix of international currencies with which India has trade relations and this has resulted in changes in its value very frequently and a net depreciation in terms of sterling. Since September 1975, the value of rupee has been maintained stable within a wider margin of 2.25 per cent on either side up to 30th January, 1979 and 5 per cent thereafter. A middle rate, as between selling and buying rates is fixed in terms of sterling which continued to be an intervention currency. The cross rates for the rupee against other currencies are calculated and fixed by banks in terms of the cross quotations in London. Whenever there is a change in the market value of the units of the currencies in the basket by more than 2¼ per cent against the standard unit of account, namely, SDR, the rupee-sterling rate is altered suitably. The external value of rupee was kept relatively stable within the permitted band of 5 per cent on either side of the middle rate. Minor fluctuations on either side evidence the fact that India does not need the support of any currency, namely, sterling or dollar. But there was, however, a net depreciation in terms of sterling. The wisdom of using the sterling as an intervention currency was doubted and advocates were not wanting in demanding the use of dollar for the purpose, at that time.

Floating vs. Fixed Exchange Rates

In the post-Smithsonian era, the currencies have been on various types of floating systems due to the abandonment of the convertibility of US dollar into gold. Single float, joint float, managed float, etc., are examples of such floats. The system of fixed exchange parities (par values) was given decent burial following the breakdown of the Bretton Woods system in August 1971.

Floating rate is a rate which is allowed to fluctuate freely according to supply and demand forces. Such float is a free float, if no intervention takes place by the central bank of the country. In the real world, some degree of intervention exists which leads to a managed float. Such managed floats are either single or joint. Dollar, sterling and Yen were floating with varying degree of intervention within a band of 2.25 per cent on either side and they are single floats. The European Common Market countries (West Germany, France, Belgium, Netherlands, Luxembourg and Ireland, Denmark and Sweden) were under a joint float within a narrow band called "Snake in the Tunnel". The new IMF policy was to keep relatively stable exchange rates within a wider band of fluctuations. Indian rupee kept relatively stable with the help of a basket of currencies, up to July 1991, when the rupee was devalued and 'LERMS' was adopted later.

Advantage of Basket Currencies

With the then existing system of exchange controls in India, a free floating rupee was out of question in the eighties. The rupee was not strong enough to withstand the speculative onslaughts. Our trade would have suffered. Alternatives left to the monetary authorities in India were, therefore, to link it with $, or a combination of some major currencies like the SDR. Since both $ and £ were having their own problems, the choice has fallen on a basket of currencies but unlike the 166 major currencies in the case of the SDR, at that time only 5 major currencies having good trade connections with India have been chosen. SDR would have been unrealistic for India as some of the currencies represented in SDR have no relations with India's trade. The basis of SDR valuation was itself changed to a bag of five currencies in 1981. It was felt that it would be advantageous for India to link the rupee to a mix of currencies properly weighted as this would give greater stability and more certainty so that India's trade and investment abroad would not suffer. The import bill and debt servicing burden are heavy for India and it would be necessary to have relative stability in the exchange rate. The fact that moderate depreciation took place in effect as against $, DM, etc., would have probably helped our export trade in particular.

Present Exchange Rate System

With the initiation of economic and financial reforms, in July 1991, far-reaching changes were introduced in the foreign exchange policy and exchange rate management. FERA was diluted and banks have been allowed greater freedom. Lending and lending rates have also been freed. Foreign exchange release is mostly left to the banks, for many purposes, subject to an upper limit for each purpose. Rupee was made partially convertible first in 1992 followed by full convertibility on trade account in 1993 and thereafter full convertibility on current account, inclusive of invisible account in 1994. The era of controls on foreign exchange has ended with these reforms. FERA is now replaced by Foreign Exchange Management Act (FEMA), which was passed by the Parliament in 1999.

In times of turbulent conditions as during foreign exchange crisis in Asian markets and weakening of the rupee, say during major part of 1998, forward premium ruled high. Spot rupee weakened from a rate of ₹31.6538 (average) for March 1995 to ₹35.8095 in June 1998 (average). Subsequently it fell to a low ₹43.20 in mid-August before recovering to ₹42.52 in mid-September 1998. The forward premium at this time was as high as 8.6% (Sept. 15, 1998) as against 3.47% in June 1997 (3 month forward premia), which depended on the operators' perception of exchange rate stability of the rupee. The RBI had to intervene in the market many times during the later period to ease undue gyrations in the rates, both spot and forward. In April 2001, the rupee dollar rate was ₹46.8 per dollar, and the same in May 2004 was ₹45.96 and there was further appreciation of Rupee after that during 2004-05.

RBI Policy Applied to Banks

RBI continued to delegate more powers to ADs in dealing in the forex market and in effecting receipts and payments.

RBI has been publishing the Reference Rate of rupee against dollar on a daily basis. The RBI is dealing in buying and selling of rupee for the dollar only both spot and forward. On the basis of the RBI's Refinance rate, Foreign Exchange Dealers Association (FEDAI) is giving the rates for banks, both for buying and selling separately but banks are free to adjust their rates depending upon their currency positions. RBI also gives the Reference rate for the Euro on a daily basis.

$1 = in Rupees

EXAMPLES OF RBI AND FEDAI RATES

	RBI rate	*FEDAI Rate*
June 30, 1995	31.3940	31.3930
Sept. 30, 1996	35.7600	35.7550
July 1997 (End)	35.7100	35.7150
June 1998 (End)	42.4700	42.4800
March 2000	43.6200	43.6100
End-December 2004	43.5800	43.5900
End-June 2005	43.5100	43.5200
End-June 2007	40.7550	40.7650
June 30, 2011	44.7256	44.7350
End-June 2012	56.3090	56.4600
End-Dec. 2014	63.3600	63.4600

In the forward exchange market, RBI allowed free functioning following the current account convertibility of the Rupee since March 1994, particularly after deregulation of lending rates in Oct. 1994. The swap premia seemed to adjust to real interest rates, *i.e.,* interest rates adjusted for inflation rates. Another factor affecting the swap premia is the call money rates in the respective countries.

RBI has been pursuading banks to develop forward market in India by dealings with interbank, and in foreign market. There is however need to develop foreign exchange derivatives for providing hedge through forward contracts, swaps and cross currency options. It is possible to develop rupee based options if international quotes for rupee are available which is not the case at present.

Currency Deals

The principle the banker follows is to give two way quotes — based on "give less and take more". The spread between the buying and selling rates is the banks' profit. The interest component for any period is shown separately from the currency position, the spread depends on the cable cost brokerage cost and administrative cost leaving only a small margin of profit to the banker.

If the quotation $1 = ₹35.750 – 35.780, then the banker is prepared to buy dollars at ₹35.750 and sell dollars at ₹35.780. Here the principle is buy low and sell high. Let us take a quote of $ to pounds say pound = $ 1.4200 – 10, the quoting bank wants to sell sterling $ 1.4210 and buy at $ 1.4200. The price of dollar to D.M. at $ 1.5810/20 means that for every dollar, the quoting bank will pay 1.5810 DM and would receive 1.5820 DM for dollar. In the quotation, the bank always wants to gain.

In some banks the dealing rooms are located also in Chennai and Bangalore. In fact, foreign banks concentrate their deal mostly in Mumbai, while SBI has its Central Dealing room at Kolkata. The largest component of inter-banks market operations is concentrated in Mumbai.

Rate Quotations

The exchange rate is quoted in two different methods in the foreign exchange markets. In some markets, the quotation is direct method called direct quotes. In other markets, the quotation is given in indirect method called Indirect quotes. In direct quotes, the number of units of foreign currency are given for one unit of domestic currency, say fo one rupee (or for 100 rupees) or 100 Yen, etc. The examples for Indian rupees are given below for illustration:

(for March end 2005)
₹100 = U.S. $ 2.29
₹100 = UK £ 1.21
₹100 = Euro 1.78

In Indirect method of quoting, the number of units of domestic currency are given for one unit of foreign currency say US $, UK £, or Euro. The examples, in the case of Indian rupees are given as:

£1 = ₹85.5938
US $1 = ₹43.5950 for March end-2007 for illustration
Euro 1 = ₹58.1515

SPOT TRADING OPERATIONS

Thus bank has classified the trading operations as shown below:

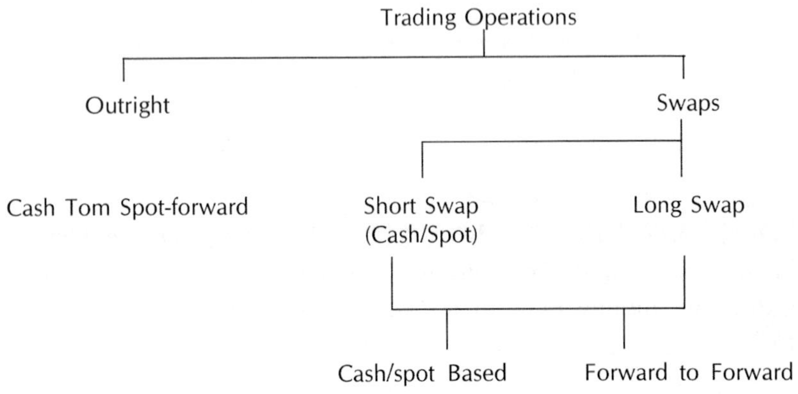

Spot is settled in the same day (cash), value tomorrow (tom) and forward (beyond spot date); spot deals are less risky while forwards are more risky. The forwards may be for a few months.

Spot trading has two types of deals:

1. *In and Out Trading:* The number of deals are many but the profit/loss in each is minimal. Minimal exposure and minimum risk is involved in this.

2. *Position Trading:* There will be fewer deals with large exposure being held for sometime for profit to be booked.

The portfolio dealer in foreign currency has to go in for a judicious mix of these two strategies. Examples of these two strategies of the trader in Mumbai is given below. For in and out trading, the exposure is pound 1 million.

1 million pounds about @ U.S. $1.5270, sold 1.5272, profit: 2 pips

1 million pounds about @ U.S. $1.5274, sold 1.5277, profit: 3 pips

and so on; he made 10 deals, each with a profit of 1 to 10 pips. For 10 transactions of million 1 pound, he has made a profit of say 20 pips, exposure is only pound 1 million total.

In position trading, the trader takes a big exposure of $ 5 million hoping DM will improve against dollar. He sells $ 3 million first at DM 1.5840 and if the trend assumed is correct, he sells another $ 2 million at DM 1.5780. When the DM rises to 1.5700, he sells all the DM for dollars back to make profit of his total position. Say the average sale price of dollars is 1.5780 and purchase price is 1.5700. He made a profit of 80 points for dollar, which is a large amount, for deals involving, millions of dollars.

Cross Currency Deals

Dealing in Forex market depends on the availability of rupee funds as also the foreign funds. Therefore, the surplus funds or floating funds of the banks are used for the dealing *vis-a-vis* the foreign currencies.

In India, premium or discount depends on the demand and supply position and not much on the interest rates. Movements in the spot currency rates also influence the forward premium or discount. Suppose, a large import payment in dollars is due 3 months hence, the premium for 3 months is higher than 6 months premium because of demand and supply factors, although in terms of interest rate gain, 6 months premium should be higher than 3 months premium as per normal interest rate structure.

Let us take a simple crude example:

Suppose the pound and dollar to rupee rates are as follows:

	$ - ₹	₹ - pound	pound - $
Spot	31.25 - 28	47.50 - 53	1.5260 - 70
1 month,	15-20 points,	13-16 points	36-32 points

Suppose you have a deficit in pound, what is the best way to cover it? Rupee is at discount over pound. If we buy pound or sell pound, we receive less (13 paise). Instead of going directly to sterling, if we go through $, we gain 15 paise by this method. We bought spot $ and dollar to pound on dollar one, we gain 15 paise by this method. We brought spot $ at 31.28 and sold one month forward at 31.43 (discount added 32.28 + 15). Then take the pound — $ forward 36-32 pound is at a discount and dollar at premium. Here we sell spot dollar at 1.5270 and bought one month forward dollar at 1.5234 (36 points deducted from spot rate (1.570-36).

Combining the above two deals we brought $ at 31.28 and sold it at $ 1.5270 to acquire pound. The Spot pound at ₹47.7645 (31.28 × 1.5270). We sold forward $ at 31.43 and bought forward $ at 1.5234 for one pound. We sold one month forward pound at ₹47.8804 (31.43 × 1.5234).

Thus, we brought spot pound for ₹47.7645. We sold one month forward pound at ₹47.8804 We gained 12 paise in this swap deal, whereas we would have lost in direct deal as the rupee was at a discount on pound.

Mismatch — Need for Matching

In export and import deals and other purchase and sale deals, the dealer gets short dollar purchase 1,000 million — not covered. Forward dollar sold 2,000 million — not matched. If the purchases and sales of the same currency and the same maturity are done on the same day, they are said to be matched. Otherwise marching is to be done through inter-bank deals or with foreign branches and foreign correspondents abroad, so that open position is minimal. The uncovered open position in any currency overnight should not exceed a maximum amount as per the banks' own guidelines. The cover can be through swap — Spot to forward or forward to forward. However, risk matching or risk reduction has to be adopted by the dealers through any derivative products.

When you expect premium to go up or swap differentials to rise, pay now and receive later — sell now and buy later. When you expect premium to come down in any currency, buy now and sell later.

Forex Management

If we have extra Nostro funds, keep them in call market, in that currency and earn some interest abroad. If German interest rate (6%) is higher than in US rate of 4%, buy DM spot and keep in the call market at the higher rate of 6%, in Frankfurt and convert back to dollar by selling forward DM one month to three months hence. Here the currency rate expectations play a major role. If the DM is becoming dearer and its interest rate (6%), higher than in New York (4%) then the above operation in funds management will earn profit. Such operations should maximize profits with minimum risk.

Similarly, payments are due to come to India in dollars three months hence from US. Three months dollars will be in demand. So buy spot dollar and keep earning interest in Europe at 6%, more than in US and sell them to those needing dollars three months hence.

There are a host of other methods of gaining in Forex market due to interest rate differentials and expectations regarding them and exchange rate changes and their expectations or cross rate differentials in exchange rates.

Derivative Products

One of the methods of risk coverage by the Treasury Manager is the use of derivatives, either in the Bond market or in the Forex market. The risk in the cash market can be hedged in the derivative market. An example of such deals in the Forex Market is the forward contract to cover the risk of currency fluctuations in the spot contract. Swaps and options are other examples of risk covering instruments.

Forward Contracts

Forward Contract is a contract for delivery of foreign currency at a specified future date at a fixed exchange rate. Only genuine trade and invisible transactions can be covered in India, as per the RBI guidelines. These forward contracts for foreign currency can be delivered at a fixed date or within a specified range of dates and penalty provisions may be laid down for breach of contract by either party. These depend on the terms of the approved contracts, usage and practice.

Swaps

A swap is a deal in which a bank buys a specified foreign currency and sells the same at different maturity dates, like simultaneous purchase of dollar on spot and sale of forward dollars of the same amount. Here the risk is possible adverse movement in exchange rate which is covered by prior fixing of the rates.

Forward to forward deal is the purchase of two months dollars, followed by a sale of three months dollars. Swap deals are used as a tool to cover arbitrage operations, namely, buy in Frankfurt and sell in London of the same currency (dollars); swaps are also required to cover a mismatch in forex deliveries to the genuine clients of the bank. Use of swaps or even Repos for speculative purposes are not permitted by the RBI. Arbitrage of risk cover or genuine matching of demand with supply are permitted by RBI. Repos are repurchase agreements, which are encouraged by the RBI for liquidity adjustment in both domestic and foreign currency markets.

Options

Currency options are contracts with a right to buy or sell a stated currency without any obligation, at a fixed rate on a future date. If the future rate moves against expected line the holder of the option can exercise the right to buy or sell.

Futures

While forward contracts can be entered into by any parties outside the stock exchange or in any organised system, the futures contracts are regulated by a proper authority with fixed terms, involving an obligation to buy and sell or give and take delivery. Delivery is compulsory in futures. A currency future contract is an agreement to buy or sell a foreign currency at a fixed amount at a stated price or rate at a specified future time. The obligations rest on both the parties and their deals are regulated and supervised by a properly constituted authority. The holder of the option can exercise the right to buy or sell. For this right to cover the risk, the party has to pay a price called premium. Under the American options, the customer can exercise the option at any time during the currency of the contract but under the European contract, the option has to be exercised only at a specified date mentioned. As it is only a right, but no obligation it need not be based on genuine transactions and no delivery may be there and may lead to speculation.

Sodhani Committee Report (1995)

This Committee has come out with two reports one on the details on various schemes and incentives available to NRIs and the other for development of active exchange market system. The major recommendations are set out below.

NRI investments are not freely flowing in due to the following constraints, which have to be removed, namely, administrative red tape, tax hurdles, government interference, rampant corruption, infrastructure and inadequate access to bank credit to NRIs. The time taken for allotment of new issues to NRIs is very long; despatch of certificates or statements should be faster and there should be quick transfer of shares from one to other and for payment of dividends, etc. The issue of shares to NRIs by company is to be left free without prior permission of RBI but the companies have to report to stock exchange, RBI and SEBI, the holdings of NRIs and the details of these holdings as per the committee's recommendations.

NRIs should be free to buy not only in new issues but from existing shares from Indians directly. Only the ADs should have the powers to scrutinise and effect the payments. There should be no lock-in period for shares, in sick units acquired by NRIs, OCBs and they should be brought in on par with all FFIs. Most of these recommendations are implemented in stages since October 1996.

As regard the measures for the development of Forex Market, the following are given as a few examples:

1. To increase the number of participants by inclusion of companies, and merchant exporters.
2. To allow the ADs to lend and invest or borrow abroad and to allow them to keep cross currency positions abroad.
3. To allow developments of modern products and derivatives such as future, options, etc., in foreign currencies and interest rates.

4. To develop proper accounting practices and disclosure standards for such operations.
5. Companies and exporters can keep funds abroad and take positions.
6. The RBI and tax authorities should clearly bring down their requirements and relax these controls and formalities regarding the abolition of withholding tax on derivative transactions.
7. Legal and regulatory framework should be simplified and even reduced.
8. Risk management techniques should be expanded and developed through the introduction of futures and other derivative products.
9. RBI's attitude should change from regulatory angle to development angle.

Although the wording of the Sodhani's report is different from the words used above, the substance of the Report's recommendations is set out here. The most important pre-requisite for developments of the Forex Market in India is the reduction of controls and restrictions, delegation of more powers to ADs and expertise in RBI and banks to be improved and banks to be empowered to deal with risk management techniques and for development of derivative markets. The government and tax authorities should be either liberal or free such foreign transactions with a long withholding tax of not more than 10% as applicable to FFIs in some respects at present. The treatment given to NRIs by banks has to be improved and OCBs and NRIs should be treated on par which is now implemented. The role of the Treasury Manager in banks and companies, therefore becomes critical, needing a multi-disciplinary expertise, in the forex market, as it is more volatile and complicated by national and international factors. With the changing scenario, these practices changed over time with regard to treatment for tax and regulatory purposes.

Forward Rate Agreement (FRA)

Major foreign banks are offering FRAs to depositors and borrowers. Here the bank guarantees the depositor or borrower the difference between the agreed rate and the LIBOR. If the six months LIBOR under the FRA is say 9% but the actual rate happens to be 10%; the difference will be reimbursed by the bank to the customer of a premium or price. If the actual rate of LIBOR is 8%, the customer will have to pay 1% to the bank. Under the agreement, this is a type of hedge measure provided by the bank.

Forward and Future Contracts

The difference between forward contracts and future contracts is as follows:

In forward contracts, the delivery is compulsory but not in futures. In forward contracts the amount and maturity periods are flexible but in futures it is organised trading in the exchange with standard contracts, standard maturity dates and contracts trading is regulated by the authorities through down payment margins and other margins which are marked to market. Forward contracts are traded over the counter, telex, telegram, etc. These can be contracts for various amounts and periods of maturity, say, 1 month to 12 months, and are not tradeable in an organised manner.

Currency and Interest Rate Swaps

Swap is simultaneous sale and purchase of identified amounts of one currency against another for different maturities, for different interest rates (from fixed rate to LIBOR and *vice versa*). It is a finance transaction in which two parties agree to exchange streams of payments or cash flows over time. These are three main types of swaps: (1) Coupon Swaps. Fixed for floating rates. (2) Basis swaps — exchange of one benchmark for another — say from LIBOR to Treasury bill rate. (3) Cross Currency Swaps — flows from one currency to another currency.

✠ ✠ ✠

EURO-CURRENCY MARKETS

44

Euro-dollar or Euro-currency markets are the international currency markets where currencies are borrowed and lent. Each currency has a demand and a supply in these markets. Thus, dollar deposits outside USA or sterling deposits outside UK are called offshore funds and have a market so long as they are convertible and readily usable in international transactions. Convertible currency is defined as one which is widely accepted in international payments and whose country does not have current account controls under Article VIII of the I.M.F. Agreements. Thus, Euro-currency market is a market principally located in Europe for lending and borrowing the world's most important convertible currencies, namely, dollar, sterling DM, French franc, yen, etc. On the same basis, the Asian currency market or the African currency market can also be defined.

International Money and Capital Markets

In general, international money and capital markets are for lending and borrowing money or claims to money in various currencies in demand outside the country of origin. By far the most important of such money markets are located in Europe called the Euro-currency markets. Next in importance comes the Asian currency market located in the East. Although US dollars are most frequently traded in these markets, any internationally convertible currency which has a demand and supply can also be traded.

As in the case of international money markets represented by Euro-currency markets or Asian currency markets, there are international capital markets as well, represented by Euro-bond or Asian-bond markets, which reflect the lendings or borrowings at the long-end of the liquidity spectrum of five years and above. While such international money markets have developed in the fifties, the corresponding capital markets have grown in the sixties.

Both the money and capital markets of this type for offshore funds were of recent vintage, when the old sources of funds under the pre-war system of borrowing from the domestic money and capital markets of New York and London, etc., had dried up. Domestic money markets in the post-war world were greatly insulated from foreign money markets in most cases due to the prevailing exchange controls in the interest of pursuit of independent domestic monetary policy, but the interactions and effects of one on the other could not be completely ruled out. Trading in these currencies both for short-term and long-term and in any of the currencies which are convertible is termed Euro-currency market. The bonds or certificates can be denominated in any convertible currency in which the borrower and the lender have confidence in terms of the stability of the currency, its future value and intrinsic strength of the economy.

Exchange Markets vs. Currency Markets

The international currency markets are an adjunct of the foreign exchange markets. In the latter, one currency is exchanged for another currency at a rate of exchange which is the price in terms of the number of units of the currency exchanged for one unit of the latter. On the other hand, in the former, currencies are borrowed and lent; the price paid for borrowing or lending a currency in the international currency market is the rate of interest. The purpose for which currencies are exchanged in the foreign exchange market or borrowed in the international currency market may be the same, namely, for meeting trade and payment requirements, or for short-term or long-term investment in working capital or fixed capital or for meeting debt or other obligations.

These two markets are inter-related in the sense that operations in the one impinge on the operations in the other and that arbitrage and speculation take place in both and that exchanges of currencies in the exchange market are involved in most of the operations in the international currency markets. When a currency is borrowed, it is possible that this currency is exchanged for another before it is used for payments or a loan may be granted with a multi-currency clause with the result that a number of currencies are borrowed in the same transaction and one is exchanged for the other.

Origins of the Euro-currency Markets

After the Second World War, a number of European and US banks used to take deposits out of USA to place them in free centres in Europe like London, Zurich, Frankfurt, etc. These US dollar deposits with the outside banks were used for short-term lending to the countries in need of dollars for balance of payments purposes or for investment. Such activity in dollar deposits gathered momentum with the sterling crisis in 1957, which encouraged European and British banks to depend more upon dollars. More particularly, the introduction of non-resident convertibility throughout Western Europe in the early sixties gave a fillip to the use of dollars in the financing of world trade. The imposition of controls in the domestic economies on interest rates on time deposits (Regulation 'Q' in USA) and on free flow of funds across national boundaries and on US banks' operating in these markets for offshore funds such as those imposed on the domestic money markets and absence of any reserve requirements for these international deposits and lendings of the type of domestic deposits enabled these Euro-banks to operate at least cost and at lowest margins. These factors led to highly competitive rates being offered by Euro-banks compared to national banks. Thus, Euro-banks are more competitive and their rates for deposits and lending are relatively finer as compared to domestic money rates, as the former work on lower margins. Finally, the surplus dollars flowing through persistent deficits in balance of payments of the USA gave lifeblood to this market. The foreign owners of these dollars got a good investment outlet in these markets. The domestic monetary and foreign exchange controls in some countries aided the development of the market for offshore funds.

Dealers in the Market

International banks or multinational banks and foreign branches of domestic banks, private banks, merchant banks and other banks are the main dealers in this market. In fact, most of the US banks deal in this market. The market is of a wholesale nature, highly flexible and competitive and well-connected in the world over by a wide network of brokers and dealers. London is the focal centre for the Euro-dollars as Singapore is the focal centre for Asian-dollars. There are a number of centres in both West and East, namely, Zurich, Luxembourg, Paris, Tokyo, Hong Kong, Manila, etc. London has grown in importance because of its historical connections with international banks, its link between European and American interests, its expertise in banking field and freedom from controls in their dealings. On a similar basis, Singapore has developed as a centre in the East due to its geographical strategic position in between the London market and Tokyo market. When London is still working, Singapore opens and as such this market provides a link to their dealings, particularly in the inter-bank dealings.

Besides, Singapore has other advantages like an excellent telecommunication system, a tradition for free banking, representation for all nationalities, expertise in banking services and positive incentives from the government for its growth in the sixties and seventies.

Market Features

1. Both investors and borrowers are well known names in the international market.
2. These loans are unsecured and no government guarantee either. Only creditworthy borrowers are generally approaching this market.
3. Country's credit rating and borrowing party's credit rating rate are being looked into; ratings by Standard and Poor or Moody's are popular for assessing the creditworthiness of the borrower, and his country.

Regulations

The market is functioning outside the countries and is offshore in nature. No regulation of any national and international nature exists. SROs regulate the investment industry. Thus, the market practices in the secondary market trading are based on the rules laid down by Association of International Bond dealers.

Some parent companies and some foreign governments do guarantee the interest and payment of principal. The interest payment is provided in the agreement itself and stricter controls are exercised in the collection of interest, although these rates are lower than those on national bonds of any country. Many countries notably U.S. and Germany removed the withholding tax to attract bond market to the national level. But Euro-bond market has been kept out of the jurisdiction of any nation.

Magnitude and Terms of Issue

The maturity period ranges from 5 to 7 years and an Indian Company (Reliance) issued a 100-year bond in this market long ago. Issues of 10 to 20 years are normally possible and popular issues are for about 5 years. The size of the bond issue varies from a few millions to a few billions of dollars.

Bearer Status

These bonds are negotiable and transferable as they have the bearer status. There are no restrictions on transfers, and the right to receive interest and payment of principal is for the bearer of the bond. The bonds are printed on special security printing paper and terms and conditions are printed on the back of the paper. There is also authentification of the individual bonds by the staff of lead manager. The security and safe custody of the bond and avoidance of fake certificates are all the responsibilities of Managers to the issue and banks dealing in this market.

Instruments Issued and Traded

1. *Fixed Rate Bonds:* Here the company gets a 10% coupon bond for a maturity of 5 years.
2. *Convertibles:* Issuers of bonds are eligible for conversion into shares of the company after a date, at a fixed conversion price.
3. *Floating Rate Notes:* This coupon is changed every 3/6 months depending on the LIBOR or any other standard rate, as laid down in the agreement.
4. *Swaps:* Interest rate swaps — borrowing at fixed rate but swapping for floating rate or *vice versa.*

Currency swaps can be depicted as shifting of one bond of dollars into some other currency either at fixed rate or at a floating rate.

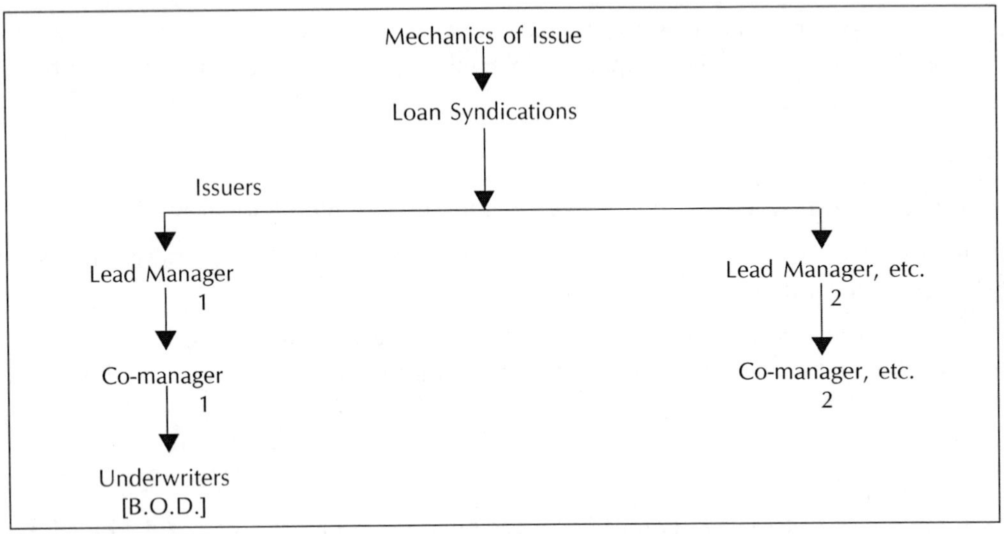

Boughtout deals occur when the lead manager offers to launch the issue at a specified price. There will be trustees and paying agents in different countries and appointed in various commercial centres in different countries.

Lawyers and Auditors

Lawyers and auditors are needed for proper documentation of offer circulars and prospectus and preparation of the agreement and signing of the same before the money is released to the borrowers — Issue of Tombstone in the press at the end of the issue. The fees are payable to all these parties lead manager, co-manager, underwriter, solicitors, lawyers, auditors, etc.

Euro-bond Clearing and Settlement System

Buyer and seller exchange the notes on what they owe each other, the buyer the number, securities and the seller the money he is due. All the trades are automated and transactions in primary and secondary markets are kept in the form of bookkeeping entries in the books of traders. Before automation, contract notes were issued to the parties to the trade. They are checked manually and transferred to computer system for matching and confirmations.

ACE System

ACE = Automated Confirmation Entry

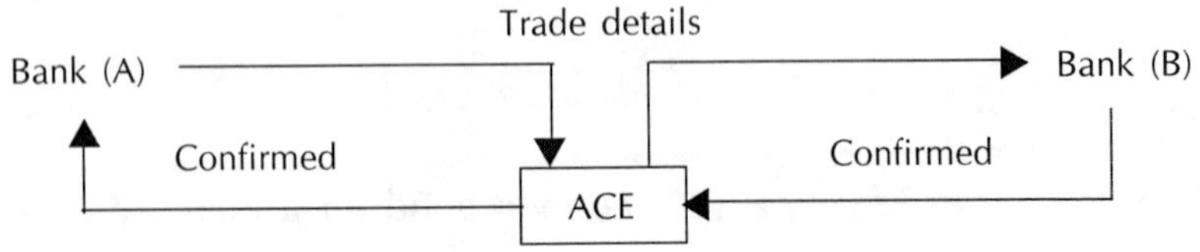

Rules of AIBD or Association of International Bond Dealers and their code of conduct will apply to these entries.

ASIAN CURRENCY MARKET

Just as Euro-dollars have been popular in the currency markets in the sixties, Asian dollars have come into prominence in the seventies. Asian dollars are the same current account supplies in dollars used in the Asian continent. Singapore has developed as the centre for this market, particularly after 1968.

This market facilitates the use of dollar balances in the Asian continent for balance of payments purposes as well as for investment in development projects. It is imparted greater liquidity for the Asian economies whereby larger trade and larger investment became possible in this region. There was also greater co-operation in economic and financial matters as a result of the Asian dollar market in many centres in the region such as Hong Kong, Sydney and Manila.

Singapore acts as a bridge between the Asian market in Tokyo and Hong Kong and the Western market in London, Paris and Frankfurt. Singapore has both time and locational advantages in keeping contact with the Western and eastern markets. Besides its strategic geographical location, Singapore has the necessary financial infrastructure, expertise and the facilities for developing into an international currency market.

The scheme of market operations and the techniques used by the agents and operators as well as banks in the market are the same either in the Euro-market or the Asian-market. The rates of interest on various maturities, the pattern of financing, etc., may vary. The demand and supply forces operated in the Asian zone are different from those in the European zone. The socio-economic factors and the political forces are also different in Asia and the resulting market forces and the operations are, therefore, different. Although the markets are all inter-linked, the Asian dollars are thus distinguished as a separate entity.

The growth of offshore syndication, offshore funds management and the financial futures are the main developments in the Singapore Asian dollar market more recently.

The financial future markets has resulted in the establishment in 1984 of the Singapore International Monetary Exchange (SIMEX). It started with four contracts traded on SIMEX, namely:

1. The gold contracts;
2. The Euro-dollar time deposits;
3. The interest rate contracts; and
4. The multi-currency contracts involving U.S. dollars, Yen, D.M., etc.

Petro-dollar Market

One of the important developments in the international currency markets in the last three decades has been the hike in the oil prices in 1973 which led to a larger flow of funds into these markets. Many petroleum-producing countries have since started accumulating foreign funds due to current account surpluses in their balance of payments. The second price hike in 1979 had also considerably augmented the current account surpluses leading to a larger increase in their foreign assets. The free market prices of crude petroleum rose sharply again from \$ 40 a barrel to \$ 140 a barrel during 2007 and 2008 and there was a turmoil in the international financial markets and again balance of payments position of oil importing countries have become more adverse. The current account balances of OPEC came out with huge surpluses again. These offshore funds of the oil-producing countries have been designated as petroleum dollars and the market in such currencies as a petro-dollar market.

In more recent years, the deregulation of domestic banking and removal of restrictions on the capital accounts of many countries like Switzerland, France and Japan and the repeal of the withholding tax on interest income of non-residents in the USA, Germany and France in 1984 have given a further fillip to the international currency markets and attracted petro-dollars into these markets. There has been an increase in the number of financial instruments, and the methods of floating the instruments have also been diversified. These developments have increased the competitiveness in the international currency markets.

Petro-dollars flowed first into the traditional financial centres as offshore funds such as the USA, West Germany, UK, Japan, and France. In more recent years, Switzerland, Beirut, Singapore and Hong Kong have also attracted these funds in the active manner. The recent removal of restrictions on the capital account in Switzerland and the existence of banks' secrecy and political neutrality aided the development of the international financial centre in Switzerland in the early eighties. The geographical position of this country in the middle of Europe and the well-developed banking system in the country have also added attractiveness to this financial centre.

The initial hike in oil prices has resulted in a large inflow of funds into the industrialised countries for investment. Some of the surpluses have been used by the Arab countries to purchase luxury consumer goods and essentials from the international markets. Subsequent flows began to move into the physical assets, dams, railways, etc., inside the country and real estate inside and outside these countries. Later, there was investment in short-term or long-term assets of a financial nature. The rest of the current account surpluses has found a place in the international financial centres. These funds were kept with foreign banks or national banks as offshore funds, and have given rise to petro-dollars which are recycled for purposes relending, investment and use in various developed and developing countries of the world for growth.

The oil-producing countries referred to as "OPEC countries" in the BIS data, include Iraq, Syria, Oman, Libya, Kuwait, Algeria, Ecuador, Gabon, Indonesia and Venezuela. The liabilities to oil-producing countries (OPEC) reported by banks to the BIS have increased from 44 billion US dollars in 1974 to 160 billion dollars in a decade. Of this, the share of Swiss Banks has been about 14 per cent.

The petro-dollar market has started developing since 1974. In addition to the use of the current account surpluses for current consumption and imports, assets have been built abroad by these countries. The use of currencies of these petroleum-producing countries has also been increasing since them. Thus, since 1978, there has been an increase in the share of their currencies in the total identified financial holdings of foreign exchange of the countries from a mere 4.3 per cent in 1978 to 11 per cent at the end of 1984. The second oil price hike in 1979 has given a further boost to the use of their currencies in international financial markets and the increase in their assets abroad. Thus, net assets of the oil-exporting countries rose from US dollars 257 billion at the end of 1979 to US dollars 380 billion at the end of 1983 according to the Bank of England estimates.[1] Of the assets held in industrialised countries, about 60 per cent of the oil-producing countries' assets are held in UK, USA and Germany and the rest are distributed among the other industrialised countries. These were initially concentrated in liquid assets such as bank deposits and short-term money market instruments and later diversified into long-term investments such as bonds, equities and loans.

European centres like London, Paris, Frankfurt, and Beirut in addition to New York have been the main centres attracting petro-dollars since 1974. Subsequent to the second hike in oil prices in 1979, there has been an increase in financial flows to Asian centres like Singapore, Hong Kong and Tokyo. However, after 1984, the current account surpluses of these oil-producing countries have dwindled due to the consistent fall in oil prices and this resulted in deficits or reduced surpluses of these countries in foreign accounts. The major industrialised countries continue to be the main suppliers of savings to the financial centres.

The petro-dollars like other Euro-currencies affect the volume and geographical pattern of capital flows among countries. These in turn influence the interest rates in the markets and exchange rates as between the currencies: A large flow of short-term capital across borders could be destabilising sometimes. On the other hand, a higher degree of capital mobility might have facilitated the functioning of floating rate system. These funds have also eased the balance of payments pressures of deficit countries like the oil-importing countries. The long-term capital flows on account of Euro-dollars for investment and for correcting the balance of payments disequilibria. During the latter half of seventies when petro-dollars flooded the markets, a larger volume of development finance had flowed to the developing countries. A part of these oil surpluses has been

1. *Bank of England Quarterly Bulletin,* March 1985, BIS, International Banking Statistics, 1978-83.

multilateralised through regional and international institutions for assistance to the LDCs. IMF oil facility is an example of how petroleum-producing countries aided the oil-importing countries to correct their balance of payments imbalances. Such larger flows of funds for investment in the seventies have in fact given rise to debt repayment problems in respect of LDCs.

Impact on Exchange Markets

The impact of Euro-currency markets on the foreign exchange markets is multi-dimensional. Not only the demand and supply of various currencies are influenced through pressures from the Euro-currency markets, but the exchange rates are altered by speculation and hedging in currencies. Larger international capital mobility due to the operations in the currency market, influences the volume and geographical pattern of capital flows. These flows can be both stabilising and destabilising depending upon the conditions. The geographical asset preferences of nations also influence the exchange rate variations and the role of the financial intermediaries in the currency markets rather than of the final economic agents became more important. The impact can be either positive or negative or neutral. The impact has to be analysed from the point of view of both sources and uses. As sources, new types of outflow in the form of deposits or investments are possible by lending to Euro-currency markets. This outlet has another dimension in that funds (dollars) can be kept outside the US system. As uses, it is now easier to borrow in dollars as also to obtain dollar credits from banks outside the US. Taking the above points into account, if there is a net capital outflow from the country, the impact on the exchange market is negative. If there is net capital inflow, the effect is positive and in all other cases the impact is neutral.

Segments of the Market

The business in Euro-dollars starts with the acceptance of dollar deposits of any maturity with fine rates for each maturity. These are two segments in this market, namely, inter-bank and non-bank public. In terms of the number of transactions and amounts involved, the bulk of them, namely, about 80 per cent, is accounted for by inter-bank transactions. Firstly, banks use this market as a buffer — to absorb the excesses of supply and demand — in their transactions of deposits and lendings with the non-bank public. Secondly, this inter-bank market is a means of adjusting their liquidity position to the requirements. Thirdly, banks do arbitrage and speculation in the market depending upon their view of how the future movements of interest rates and exchange value of currencies would be. Apart from these, the basic purpose of banks' involvement in the Euro-currency markets is to satisfy the genuine demand for currency in the commercial operations of the borrowers which is the market for non-bank public.

Sources and Uses

The main sources of funds for the market came from varied groups, individuals, corporations, commercial banks, international institutions, multinationals, the central banks, the governments, etc. In view of the controls in the domestic market, many respectable corporations, banks, etc., keep their deposits abroad. Thus, a part of the dollar deposits is owned by the US banks and US nationals. Besides the official agencies, governments and central banks also keep their deposits in this market which not only gives an official stamp of approval but an encouragement to the market. Originally, the market had grown without any official favour and as an off-shoot of pure private enterprise. Subsequently, when it reached a state of significant dimensions which no single nation could control, all governments and international institutions began to consider it respectable and partake in its operations. Borrowers and lenders in the market are only banks in so far as the inter-bank segment is concerned. Among the non-bank public, companies in export and import business or in investment business or multinationals in need of funds and governments or central banks for balance of payments purposes figure prominently in the non-bank markets. Among borrowings, bulk of it is for commercial operations by non-bank public and business corporations.

The Euro-currency market has no geographical limits or a common market place. Business is done by telex, telephone and other communication systems. Internationally-reputed brokers put through the transactions for the banks. Deposits are secured for the banks operating in the market by the general guarantee of its parent or holding company and in some cases, by its central bank and/or the government of the concerned country. Similarly, loans to commercial parties are guaranteed by their respective governments. Deposits and loans to banks are, however, not guaranteed except by the banks' parent companies or their exchange control authorities.

The amounts of loans and the periods of maturity vary over a wide range from a few thousands to millions of dollars and from call loans to maturities extending up to 10-15 years. Some of the loans may be syndicated and jointly sponsored by a number of banks. There are also varied interest rates or floating rate notes.

The purposes for which loans are taken from this market are varied — from balance of payments requirements of governments or monetary authorities to commercial short or long-term investments in the private sector. The market has very little scope for follow-up of the end-use of credits. But terms and payments schedules are tight so that strict financial discipline is imposed on the borrower with penalty clauses. The syndicated loans have a leading bank as the manager, who assesses the worthwhileness of the project financed and insist on a time schedule of drawals and repayments which impose a sense of discipline on the borrower.

Size and Growth of the Market in Euro-dollars

The Euro-currency market has grown enormously since its inception in 1958. The principal agencies for collection of data on operations in this market are the Bank for International Settlements and the Bank of England. Starting with less than $ 1 billion in 1958, the market has grown to $ 100 billion (net size) by 1972 and further to a few thousand billion early in nineties.[2] The bulk of the rise was accounted by the OPEC and developed countries.

About two-thirds to three-quarters of these funds are in dollars and the rest in various other convertible currencies. In the seventies, the relative importance of non-dollar currencies had increased due to the decline in confidence in dollar and the abandonment of the old Bretton Woods System. The importance of the bond market has also been growing in recent years. Loans of more than 3 years now constitute a large portion of total loans.

Techniques of Operations

Deposits of currencies are made against a certificate given by the bank. These certificates of deposits are in bearer bonds and transferable by endorsement and a market has been developed in them. This is the secondary market which imparts liquidity to the depositors as these certificates can be discounted with the banks dealing in this market.

The loan operations are concluded mostly for short-term duration and if necessary on a revolving basis. Some loans are transacted on a floating interest clause which enables the rate to be varied depending upon the daily interest rates prevailing in the market or on a quarterly or six monthly interest rate review. The long-term loans or bond issues are facilitated by the introduction of revolving credit nature. The increased use of floating rate of interest clause and revolving credit facility and improved performance of the US dollar in the foreign exchange market were responsible for the increase in bond issues in recent years. Multi-currency clause and floating interest rate clauses afford protection to both the borrowers and lenders in the market against a sharp fall or rise in interest rates as well as exchange rates in any currency which influences the Euro-currency market. Basically, short-term funds in the form of deposits are converted into term loans in this market.

2. Total foreign Currency Positions or Liabilities of BIS reporting banks. *Source:* BIS Annual Report.

Internationally reputed brokers are constantly in touch with the banks dealing in Euro-currencies. Their quotations for borrowing and lending rates of interest in each currency are advised to the banks early at the start of the trading hours of the day. These quotations given separately for each of the maturities and for each currency are the starting point for offer and bids in the inter-bank market which is the centre piece of Euro-currency market mechanism and which accounts for 80 per cent of the total transactions in the market. The commercial market consisting of loans to the public — both short and medium-term — is arranged on a syndicated or a consortium basis if the loan is for large amounts. The syndicated loans have become an important segment of the market in more recent years.

In addition to the revolving credit facilities, fixed term facility extending up to 5 or more years has subsequently developed. In such cases, banks are mostly intermediaries taking in deposits for the same maturity as fixed term loans which they are offering to borrowers. Many times banks take a view of the likely trend of interest rate in various currencies before granting such term loans.

Another type of facility granted by banks is standby facility which gives the borrower greater flexibility. Companies in need of funds at a future date can negotiate such a line of standby credit. The borrowers pay a commission of ½ per cent to 1 per cent for such a commitment. These are called the Notes Issuance Facilities (NIFs).

Such large scale credit arrangements are made possible by banks operations in the inter-bank market — one bank helping the other banks — or by the syndicated or consortium arrangements among banks. The bulk of growth of the Euro-dollar market must be attributed to the revolving nature of the credits and the gearing ratio on which banks operate.

With the growth of sophistication in operation and rising competition in the market, the margins between the lending and borrowing rates have been reduced considerably in recent years. The margins are anything from 3/4th per cent to 1½ per cent and in some cases, they are as low as 5/8 per cent to ½ per cent. The fact that these margins are low reflects the efficiency of their operations and the high degree of competition in the markets.

The interest rate in the market is the London inter-bank offer rate (LIBOR) which is the average of rates offered by the major lending banks in the inter-bank market in London. The lending rate is adjusted up to 1/8th of one per cent on the LIBOR along with a margin to the bank for lending to the non-bank public. The margin or spread depends upon the market conditions of demand and supply and the interest rates in various centres ruling and expectations.

In addition to interest charges, the borrowers have to incur incidental expenses in the form of charges for syndication, management of the issue, negotiation charges, commitment fees, etc. These fees would aggregate to anything from ½ per cent to 3 per cent of the amounts borrowed. The fees which the banks collect also influence the spread they keep between their borrowing and lending rates.

The more recent developments are a lengthening of the maturity period, lowering of margins, growing competition and increased size of loan operations. If the reputation of borrowers is high, no security is taken. Many times it is against a government guarantee and the cases where this security is not taken may be few, mainly accounted for by the reputed multinational corporations. Although the credit risks are rising and costs of management of the Euro-currency department are growing and inflation is further eroding into their margins, the increasing size of the market and the growth of the deposit and lending operations along with sound banking practices have been responsible for keeping the margins low. The Euro-currency market is thus developing fast in the international financial scene on healthy competitive lines.

Importance of the Market

The growth of Euro-currency market has produced far reaching effects on the international financial system and the monetary scene. Firstly, these floating funds have augmented the official international liquidity and helped the financing of deficits in the balance of payments of countries. Secondly, these Euro-currency funds are found useful for private corporate investments and for working capital purposes. Thirdly, the quick and efficient source of funds provided by this market has helped the easing of pressures on the international monetary system, particularly on the dollar and other currencies under strain. Fourthly, it has provided a channel for profitable investment for excess funds of governments, central banks and business corporations. This market has finally opened up avenues for greater international monetary co-operation and integration. Lastly the interest rates here are lower than in domestic markets.

India and Foreign Currency Markets

The operation of Indian banks in the international currency markets has been allowed since 1969, particularly in Singapore and Hong Kong. In the seventies, the State Bank of India was permitted to enter the market. Over the past few years, the SBI has raised funds for the public sector units such as the Shipping Corporation of India and later for units in the private sector also (Orissa Aluminium Project). So far loans raised in these markets were well within $ 50 billion such as for purchase of aircraft by Air India or drilling equipment by ONGC. The SBI has also been instrumental in raising loans for the Birlas for their project in Indonesia and for the Tisco from the US and UK banks. In 1980, a $ 680 million Euro-dollar loan was raised for the Orissa Aluminium Project. It is thus clear, that private parties and banks in India are increasingly allowed to either borrow from this market or operate in this market. The recent decline in flow of funds from IBRD and other world bodies had an added impetus to the growth of these operations.

Euro-dollar loans were raised for the Bombay High for its fourth and fifth stages (200 million dollars). The rate at which the recent loan of $ 680 million was raised for Orissa Aluminium was 17 per cent — slightly above the prevailing London inter-bank offer rate of 16.5 per cent. This rate could float up or down depending upon the LIBOR. But even so, it is cheaper than that at which some countries have borrowed (Brazil for example) namely, at 2 per cent above the LIBOR.

The fact is that we have refrained from resorting to this market for a long time because of its high cost and the commercially going rate charged therein. In addition to the high cost of borrowing in it, India was deterred from this market because of uncertainty of interest cost due to its variability every six months, under floating interest rate clause and shorter maturities on Euro-loans unsuitable to developmental need of India. We continued to enjoy until recently the benefit of soft loans from IDA, IBRD and IMF. But by early in the nineties, a stage is reached when we have almost exhausted these resources, as their own funds were getting attenuated. Then the only alternative appears to be to allow the private sector to borrow from these markets, compete with their counterparts abroad effectively in both the output markets and input markets as much as in financial markets. When private companies borrow at commercial rates, they have to make enough foreign exchange earnings to pay for the servicing charges on them. The projects must then be of long life but a short gestation period and investment should lead to productive asset creation and enlarge the export potential of the country to repay instalments due on the loans. India has also problems of identifying projects with a short gestation but a long life duration and commercially viable projects. Besides the commercial discipline of time-bound utilisation of funds, stringent commitment fees and strict adherence to schedules of repayment, etc., were the further deterring factors.

The Indian banks and ICICI have been borrowing international capital markets and from financial bodies abroad for commercial and industrial purposes. The Government of India has been encouraging more recently the use of Euro-dollar funds in a flexible and yet discretionary manner for commercial enterprises such as Orissa Aluminium. Rastriya Chemicals, etc. A number of companies such as Gujarat Narmada Fertilisers, Telco, Tata Power, J.K. Synthetics, etc., were able to raise funds from non-residents or foreign capital markets. The government has permitted the IDBI, ICICI and other financial institutions to raise foreign resources through syndicated loans in Euro-currency markets. After making rupee convertible since March 1992 on trade account, a number of private sector companies like Reliance and Essar, have been allowed to borrow in these markets abroad.

International Financial Centre in India

Can India host an international financial centre? What are its repercussions on the domestic economy? The financial centres at Singapore, Hong Kong, London, etc., have been evolved historically by natural advantages, convenient locations and deliberate planning. Questions are often asked about the feasibility of developing such centres in India. Efficient manpower and competent bankers, network of communications, computer facilities and other infrastructural facilities are necessary for the development of a financial centre. India has to go ahead further with its reforms to develop such facilities and a set of dedicated secondary markets in broker firms, discount houses, bill market, etc., before such a financial centre can be set up.

The other essential pre-requisites are:

1. Reducation in rigours of exchange restrictions so as to free the current account transactions. This has been done.
2. Allow free inflow and outflow of funds at least for genuine-investment and not for speculation which was also initiated.
3. Rupee to be strengthened further by greater cost-consciousness of producers, greater efficiency and productivity of factors.
4. Rupee holdings abroad to be liberalised and allowed freer trading in it. A start can be made by allowing GDRs to be traded in Indian stock exchanges.
5. Necessary fiscal concessions, exemptions and simplification to be made in corporate income-tax, withholding tax on income earned by non-residents etc., which are in the process of being done through ongoing structural reforms.

The following conditions have to be observed for developing an offshore centre in India.

As in 2012-13, inflation has to be brought down to 8% Economic growth rate to be accelerated to 9% fiscal discipline has to be imposed and fiscal deficit to be kept at 4%. Current account/deficit has to be cut down and rupee to be strengthened.

India's Reliance on Euro-market

During 1996-97, Indian corporates could mobilise larger amounts from the Euro-market through FCCB and GDRs, due to sluggish domestic capital market. Thus the issues were floated in 1996-97 to raise an aggregate amount of ₹5,594 crore as compared to only 4 issues for an aggregate amount of ₹1,297 crore in 1995-96. The dependence on Euro-market fell after 1997-98 due to weak rupee and lower country credit rating for India due to turbulent conditions in the foreign exchange market. During 1999-00, six issues were made by Indian corporates for a total amount of ₹3,847 crore. During 2001 to 2005, there was a net capital outflow due to amortisation of ECBs, GDRs, etc., but no net borrowing from abroad including ADR, GDR, etc. But foreign capital investment inflows stood at U.S 50 billion in 2009-10 and U.S. $ 41.6 billion in 2010-11.

Euro Issue — Operational Aspects

The international markets which are free for borrowings are U.S.A., U.K., Germany and Japan. Capital market controls are relatively more in Japan than in other countries in the list above. Bulk of international borrowing is therefore in U.S. dollars (30-40%), followed by Pound Sterling, Japanese Yen and D.M. in that order.

Controls in Euro-markets are less than in domestic markets. Whatever is the centre, be it London, Frankfurt, Singapore or Hong Kong, there are no controls on Euro-issues, either in terms of interest rates, reserve requirements or exchange controls of the govt.

Sequence in bond issues is presented below in terms of the steps to be followed:

1. Decide on the rate of issue, maturity and terms — choice of T.B. rate, govt. bond rate, LIBOR-related rates, Floating rate — Quarterly or half-yearly or yearly interest payments — Guarantees, if any — Repayment schedule — Bullet repayment. Equal instalment repayment accelerated payments maturity period — Bonds in perpetuity or 100 years are rare, long-term bonds of 30 to 50 years, medium-term of 5 to 30 years or short-term bonds. Foreign currency Notes, or Note issuance facilities can also be resorted to.
2. Decision on the mode of Issue — Syndicated loan arrangement, private placement, offer of sale or publicly placed issue with the prior sanction of SEC (USA), SIB (UK) or govts. in many countries.
3. Tapping the Investment Bankers/Merchant bankers of international standing for consultations, regarding the amount, terms/mode of issue and timing, etc.
4. Appointment of Group Managers or Lead Managers and assignment of responsibilities.
5. Appointment of underwriters.
6. Entering into written agreements with managers and underwriters to the issue.
7. Completion of all legal and regulatory requirements with SEC, Stock Exchanges or govts. of host countries, etc.
8. Documentation needed for the above steps such as documents to be submitted to the regulatory agencies or agreements, entered into with various intermediaries involved in the issue process.
9. Pricing of the issue and actual terms of issue to be fixed.
10. Actual issue and allotment of letters of acceptance.
11. Loan Agreement, Guarantee Agreement, etc., are all entered into.
12. Tombstone — An advertisement regarding the issue made and its closure.
13. Post-issue formalities to be followed.
14. Complying with the requirements of the govt. of domestic country, regarding the issue.
15. Listing formalities, payment of tax, etc., for making the issue like GDRs' tradeable.

Junk Bonds/Securitised Bonds

If bonds are raised in U.S.A., they are called Yankee bonds, and if raised in Japan they are called Samurai bonds. Offshore bonds and country funds are raised in more than one country or currency. In the case of PSUs and sick undertaking, they have no access to the regular markets except through Junk bonds by securitising the book debts, non-performing assets, etc., and selling them at heavy discounts. This has a number of advantages for the issuing company.

Conclusion

India has already moved to current account convertibility and is in the process of moving to capital account convertibility. It is time to develop offshore banking in India on the lines of a Euro-currency market with one or two centres in the special economic zones, where the domestic controls and taxes do not apply. Rupee can be developed as an international convertible currency with an independent market for the rupee in the international markets. The SEZ policy is being pursued by the government in this context.

EXCHANGE RISK MANAGEMENT

45

Introduction

All financial services involve some risks associated with them. They vary from service to service and foreign exchange and foreign currency markets involve more risks than their domestic counterparts, due to many international unpredictable factors and uncertain variables, which are part of these services.

With the Indian rupee being convertible, since March 1994, the risks in the foreign exchange market have become more pronounced and the need to take risk or protect oneself from these risks has become evident. Many countries have already made their currencies convertible and some are in the process of doing so particularly in Asia and Africa. In the context of such scenario of free foreign exchange markets, uncertainty of currency rates and their volatility has made it imperative for the dealers in foreign exchange to expose themselves to the risk. Risk is inherent in the foreign dealings due to the following reasons:

1. Trade across countries involve dealings with parties — exporter or importer — who are unknown and whose creditworthiness is uncertain.
2. Foreign dealings also involve countries whose credibility and creditworthiness is not certain.
3. Currency rates and exchange rates fluctuate more widely.
4. Foreign and domestic interest rates influence the exchange risk more in a complex and unpredictable manner.

Many countries are having political and economic problems, racial, and communal riots or other disturbances and there is no certainty about their economic and financial policies and their willingness and capacity to repay the loans or service them, through their exports and inward remittances. Fundamentals in the economy may be in doubt and inflation and other problems of the country, such as unemployment, poverty, low rates of growth or no growth in the economies etc., may be plaguing the country, when they may default in their external obligations, as in the case of some African and Latin American countries. Their capacity to borrow on commercial lines will be then poor and they depend on donations, gifts and concessional aid from Governments and international bodies. They are not able to service and repay the debts to foreigners.

Exchange risk is due to fluctuations in the rate of exchange in conversion of one currency into another and likely changes in conversion of one currency into another and likely changes in interest rates which might effect the forward rates. Forward cover of any currency which the banks provide will take into account the possible changes in interest rates, inflation rates and the intrinsic strength of country and the currency. Exchange risk will basically depend on the economic strength of the country and its foreign exchange reserves, as the volatility of the exchange rate depends on them.

Strength of Currency

Exchange risk depends on the strength or weakness of currency which in turn is a reflection of the strength of the economy. Thus, a country whose productivity is low and its competitive strength in international markets is poor, cannot export enough of the domestic products abroad and its foreign exchange earnings will be poor due to current account deficits. Such a country will have a weak currency and its rate of exchange will be uncertain.

A strong country like U.S.A. or Japan will have good export performance resulting in trade surplus and good inflow of foreign funds for investment, leading to high rates of growth of output, employment and income. So economy, its strength and its rate of growth and its competitive strength along with a host of other factors will influence the currency rates. The exchange risk is thus dependent upon an array of economic and extra economic factors which will lead to an unpredictable rate of exchange. The risk and uncertainty of exchange rate is a multi-dimensional phenomena and requires an expert to fend and manage the risks involved. Genuine trade and investment require a stable and fixed exchange rate which is not possible in free and competitive world without current account controls, where trade and receipts and payments abroad are all free and market determined. There is thus need for risk management for all dealings in foreign exchange, particularly so for exporters and importers.

Exchange Risk Defined

Exchange risk simply means that the rate at which a currency is exchanged for another currency may be uncertain and volatile and the amount that an exporter receives in domestic currency or an importer has to pay in terms of domestic currency will be unpredictable and uncertain. Similarly, if funds are transmitted from one country to another, the amounts to be sent or to be received will not be certain, if exchange rates are not fixed. But in the present global economy, free market forces operate to determine the exchange rates depending upon the supply and demand for the currency. This will lead to fluctuating rates, which may result in profits or losses to the holders of foreign currency.

The fluctuating rates result in uncertainty and risk, which will have to be managed by the genuine traders and investors in foreign countries and dealers in foreign exchange and banks. Under free market forces operating, no individual dealer in foreign exchange can influence its prices, but the supply and demand pressures for any currency in total lead to its appreciation or depreciation. The totality of receipts either for exports or inward remittances or inflows of funds will decide the demand pressure while the supply pressures emanate from those who have to make payments outside for imports, outward remittances or outflow of funds, etc. Such demand and supply pressures influence the exchange rates on a daily and hourly basis and from time to time and lead to uncertainty, in exchange rates.

Factors Affecting Exchange Rates

Foreign exchange rates, being freely determined, the following factors influence the exchange rates and enhance the risk in particular:

1. Hot money flows as between countries and currencies will take place to take advantage of short-term economic and political factors or disturbances or fears of such developments leading to changes in currency rates and interest rates.

2. Speculative attacks on currencies in anticipation of exchange rate changes and interest rate changes through short-term flows of funds.
3. Exchange rate volatility emerges out of erratic funds flows as between countries, short-term flows of funds in either direction and inflows of funds followed by immediate reversals, etc.
4. Freely fluctuating exchange rates across countries do sometimes lead to erratic movements of rates on either side, unless counterveiled by central bank of the country to offset such excesses.
5. Present international monetary system under the IMF imposes the burden of adjustment on the deficit countries to change their exchange rates rather than on the surplus countries. In the absence of adjustment on both sides, balance of payments adjustment is delayed and partial with the result that exchange rates remain uncertain and fluctuating and sometimes unpredictable, in the deficit countries.
6. Limited powers of IMF to discipline the surplus countries also lead to partial adjustment or lack of adjustment as between currencies of countries with the result that exchange rates continue to be fluctuating and sometimes even unpredictable.

Basically exchange rates as between two currencies should reflect the true fundamentals of the concerned countries, such as domestic purchasing powers, relative strength or weakness of the economies, in terms of their productive power and trends in output, employment and income. In the absence of stabilised and equilibriated rates, the actual prevailing rates may fluctuale widely which will lead to uncertainty and risk. In order to avoid such destabilising fluctuations in rates, many developing countries maintain exchange and trade controls to reduce such risk and promote trade and investment in their own countries.

India has also moved to current account convertibility in March 1994, with the result that rupee exchange rate is now freely fluctuating in either direction. But to reduce wider fluctuations the RBI has been announcing a reference rate for rupee in terms of dollars and the Foreign Exchange Dealers Association (FEDA) has been fixing the major currency rates in terms of rupees for banks to adopt them to the extent possible, as warranted by the foreign funds position. Even so, the risk and uncertainty is not eliminated in the foreign exchange market in India. It is still the demand and supply pressures on rupee that determines its exchange rate.

Types of Risk

The risks in foreign exchange market in India are of the following nature and include transactions in both trade and non-trade items of balance of payments:

1. Risk of creditworthiness of the other party in trade in concerned countries.
2. Risk of credit control and exchange control rules in countries.
3. Risk of economic and political policy changes in the other country.
4. Risk of interest rate changes in the respective countries.
5. Risk of loss of goods shipped in transit or theft, damage, or destruction.
6. Risk of market changes in the concerned countries or changes in the costs or in duties or levies imposed by the trading partners on others.
7. Risk of war or epidemics, or riots or any untoward events affecting trading relations as between the trading partners.
8. Risk and uncertainty of exchange rates of one currency against another.
9. Risk and uncertainty due to changes in forward rates for the currency following the changes in interest rates as between countries.
10. Risk of changes in cross currency rates for any unpredictable changes in the currency markets and in foreign exchange markets.

Foreign exchange markets are very sensitive and volatile as they are influenced by all and sundry developments in economic, political, business, social and financial factors among the countries. Events across borders and domestic and international forces operate on the markets to force volatility in rates and attendant risks in the exchange markets.

Exchange Rate Management in India

The rupee was devalued twice in July 1991 and the depreciation of the rupee continued in the free market thereafter. The rupee dollar rate was ₹17.1274 in March 1990 which fell to ₹32.6456 in Feb. 1993, and thereafter it stabilised around ₹31.3727 since March 1994 when current account convertibility was introduced by the government. Exchange rate movements were already referred in an earlier chapter.

After the structural reforms undertaken since July 1991, the rupee exchange rate management assumed all the importance and attention from the RBI and the government. The Liberalised Exchange Rate Management System (LERMS) introduced in March 1992 is a step in that direction of a freely convertible rupee at a future date. Under this system, rupee can be freely converted at free market rate up to 60% of exports, while official rate still prevailed for the 40% or rest of the exports. This system called Liberalised Exchange Rate Management System (LERMS) helped to stabilise the rupee and the official rate remained unchanged except for a downward adjustment of 1.12% in the rate effected by December 4, 1992. The market determined rate remained also stable and the spread between the official rate and the market rate remained in a narrow range except for short and extraordinary periods.

The experiment with limited convertibility was successful and the government was emboldened to launch the full convertibility on trade account in March 1993. Since then there was unification of the dual exchange rate into a single floating rate which imparted considerable strength to the rupee. Now the external value of the rupee is determined by market forces fully. As this is on the trade account, it only meant that the ADs did not have to surrender to the RBI the exchange proceeds at fixed rate as before. The exporters can sell their earnings at the free market rates to the banks and the importers have to buy the same from banks at the prevailing market rates from time to time.

Since mid-January 1995, the RBI has banned the rollover of forward contracts, and as a step in the direction of liberalisation, allowed the customers to book forward contracts in any permitted currency. Now the companies will have to book forward contracts matching with their foreign exchange exposure. This facility to hedge in any currency will permit the corporates to take positions in currencies and develop the foreign exchange market and the forward market in particular.

Full Convertibility of Rupee

The convertibility on trade account was launched on March 1993 and exports have become convertible at free market rates up to 100% of them. The experiment on convertibility on trade account proved a success in the sense that no untoward fluctuations in the rupee rate were noticed during 1993-94 with the result that the government has announced in March 1994 the full convertibility on current account also which means that all invisible receipts and payments have to be effected at market related rates. Thus, not only trade items but all invisible items or services are paid and received at the free market rates since March 1994.

The Government of India have announced a package of further measures to promote and facilitate exports from time to time. Exporters are allowed to retain 25% of the foreign exchange earned in dollar denominated accounts abroad. Export Oriented Units (EOUs) are permitted to retain even upon 50% of their exchange earnings in dollar terms abroad. These measures would help reduce conversion costs in payments abroad for their import requirements and other service payments. The export promotion measures and the subsidy on exports were cut short during the reforms after 1996.

The foreign exchange receipts and payments are now freer than before under all current account items, particularly for travel, tourism, medical expense and education. The government have introduced amendments to the FERA to do away with many controls on foreign investments in India, inflow of foreign technology, employment, etc. India is now on a path of full convertibility of the rupee on both current and capital account. Preparatory to that, foreign investment in equity of Indian companies is permitted up to 51%. Much of this investment which requires to be cleared by the government, Ministry of Finance, Investment Division has been flowing into priority sector industries. Foreign direct portfolio investment has been freely allowed without limit and foreign financial institutions and foreign security firms have been permitted by the SEBI to operate in the Indian stock and capital market.

Multilateral Investment Guarantee Agency

The MIGA is an international agency set up in 1988 for the purpose of promoting and encouraging the flow of foreign direct investment. It offers investment insurance and advisory services for foreign direct investment in developing countries. It provides protection to international investors against losses arising out of non-commercial risk of currency transfers, expropriation, war and civil disturbances. It provides promotional and advisory role to governments in framing and implementing foreign investment policy. India signed the MIGA convention in fiscal 1992 and with this the member countries who signed this convention increased to 85. India has also opened up bilateral negotiations for extending the investment guarantee with other countries for promoting the foreign direct investment in India. Thus, it has entered into bilateral guarantees with many countries, including the U.S.A., Russia, among others. This is intended to reduce risks in foreign Investments.

FERA Liberalisation

FERA companies which are companies incorporated in India but in which non-resident interest is more than 40% have now got freedom from many restrictive provisions under Sections 26 (7), 28, 29 and 32 FERA.

FERA companies are now permitted to do the following:

1. To borrow money or accept deposits from persons resident in India.
2. To acquire any undertaking, carry on any trade, commerce or industry, or purchase shares of any company.
3. To allow trade marks of theirs to be used by any person or company.
4. To accept any appointment as agent or technical or management advisers.
5. To acquire hold, transfer any immovable property in India.

Trade and Exchange Risk

In dealing with international currencies, risk is inherent in both trade and finance. These risks arise out of dealings as between countries: (1) in terms of exchange of goods for money, (2) in terms of sale of services and payment thereof in foreign currencies, (3) lending and borrowing in foreign currencies, and (4) capital inflows and outflows from foreign countries. Risks arise out of all these transactions and due to unpredictable market related forces which determine the supply and demand pressures on foreign currencies and speculative forces. Demand and supply for currencies emanate from corresponding demand and supply for goods and services and needed receipts and payments to and from abroad.

The instruments involved in foreign trade and in foreign exchange dealings have also a component of risk in them. Briefly, these instruments are: (1) Currency dealt with in small quantities and involved loss or theft or cheating for counterfeit notes, etc. (2) M.T., T.T, D.D. cheques, etc., — risk is in transit loss, time in transit and delays involved, etc., (3) Commercial and trade bills: bills of exchange and other foreign trade bills and documents have risks involved in the parties, drawer, drawee, banker and the goods involved in these bills. Sight bills are having a grace period to maturity of 30 to 180 days usually. These bills and documents are given to banks for collection or for outright purchase, which are again full of risks. The risks arise out of defective documents, time for waiting, problems with goods in transit, shipping or airfreight, etc., is addition to party risk and country risk and risk of default or non-payment. Besides, there is the currency risk during the conversion of foreign currency into domestic currency and *vice versa*.

The exporters and importers have to bear some risks. Some risks like party, country and currency risks are passed on to the banks, ECGC and EXIM Bank. Insurance agencies cover some risks like those in transit time, shipping and air freight, etc. Banks in turn pass on some risks to Central Bank of the country, or cover them with foreign correspondents, international markets or inter-bank market.

Exchange Rate and Currency Risk

Exchange rate is determined by free flow of demand and supply forces for one currency against another. Receipts and payments on trade account, for services and capital flows would influence the demand and supply forces which are in turn determined by the following factors: (1) Relative quantum of exports and imports and other remittances; (2) Cost and price differences in goods and services as well as their quality; (3) Relative purchasing power parity of domestic currency *vis-a-vis* foreign currency; (4) Interest rates at home and abroad; and (5) Inflation rates at home and abroad. Some currency risks due to interest rate changes, speculation changes in expectations, etc., cannot be insured, but can be covered or hedged in the derivative markets.

Spot rate is decided by the demand and supply pressures, which are influenced by the above factors. Besides, the demand for a currency is also influenced by the hedge and speculative forces. The forward rates are at discount or at premium depending on the current interest rates and expectations about them, present rates of exchange and expectations about their movements, future arbitrage and hedge deals and short-term speculative flows of funds, etc. Some discussion on forward rates is also found later in this chapter and in other chapters.

Types of Exchange Rates

The exchange risk depends on the type of rate. In this context, it is relevant to know the types of rates which are common in the foreign exchange market. The major types are set out below: (1) *Spot Rate:* The rate for immediate exchange of currency or receipts. Thus, the rate for exchange of currency notes, TTs, MTs, cheques, and DDs which are clean and unaccompanied by documents is called the spot rate; (2) *Short Rates:* The rates for short periods of 30 to 90 days; (3) *Long Rates:* The rates for long periods of 90 days and above; (4) *Telquel Rates:* The rates for broken periods of 15 days or 45 days, etc. The risk varies with the rate dealt with. The longer the period of rate, the larger is the risk. The telquel rates are generally higher than for rounded periods of one/two/three months due to more administrative work. Short rates for those with documents carry higher risk than clean credits or instruments, for the same reason. Similarly, the forward rates are having more risk than spot rates.

Risk also varies with the country and the currency, in which the instruments are drawn. The political and economic factors, stability or otherwise of the political system and economic policies and a host of non-economic factors play a role in deciding the degree of risk and the rate charged.

Forward rate is generally at a premium due to larger risk involved in it. It is assumed here that the rate is quoted in direct method say $ 1: 1.58 D.M. The forward premium will indicate the larger number of D.M. per dollar to be given in each transaction. Applying the principle of "buy high and sell low" for the indirect method of quotation, as in the case of rupee, the forward rate for the rupee will be at a premium in the sense that more rupees are to be given for a dollar. Take an example. Say $ 1: ₹31.2100 for TT buying spot. The forward premium for one month is 10 points which means that the rate will be $ 1: ₹31.2110 for one month forward and so on. That means you have to give ₹31.2110 for buying a dollar forward, one month as against ₹31.2100 for spot buying. If you are selling dollars, you will only get ₹31.2090 for dollar forward.

Arbitrage and Speculation

In addition to the financing of the genuine trade and payments on merchandise and invisible trade account, banks do finance capital flows of both short-term and long-term. Funds move in and move out for hedging and speculation as between currencies. While sometimes the hedging transactions help stabilise the rates, the same cannot be said of the speculative flows of short-term nature. Speculative deals are made only to book profits and they are short-term flows of funds with only profit motive and they serve no other purpose.The excesses of such flows destabilise the exchange market and lead to violent fluctuations in exchange rates. The greater the volatility, the larger is the risk in foreign exchange market and premiums on forwards will go up abnormally. Arbitrage is dealing in foreign exchange to take advantage of the differences in cross rates as between centres or currencies or as between quotations in two or more centres. Thus, if dollars are cheap in one centre and dear in another centre, arbitrage takes place to buy in the cheap centre and sell in dear centre with the result that rate quotations will tend to get equalised as between centres. Thus, to an extent, arbitrage has a stabilising influence on the foreign exchange market.

Types of Risk in Foreign Exchange

There are different types of exchange risks in the foreign exchange market which are set out briefly below:

1. *Credit Risk of Customer:* Credit rating by international banks and international credit rating agencies will help reducing this risk. In India, ECGC and banks do take this risk for the exporters.

2. *Country Risk:* This is different slightly from the currency risk and arises out of the policies of economic and political nature and their external payments position and their export earnings to service the foreign creditors, convertibility or otherwise of their currencies, etc.

3. *Currency Risk:* This risk arises out of the volatility or otherwise of the currency and its strength or weakness in terms of other currencies and interest rates and relative degrees of inflation in the respective countries which influence the exchange rates. It also depends on hot money flows and speculative short-term flows as between countries which will destabilise the exchange rates. The currency risk is generally covered by banks on the guarantee of the ECGC. The country risk may be covered by the ECGC in some cases or by the EXIM Bank.

4. *Market Risk:* Risks of commodities, their quality and the change of government policies of taxation, etc., in respect of those commodities are borne by the exporters or the ECGC in some cases. It will thus be seen that some risks cannot be avoided or passed on by the exporters and in fact many more risks are to be borne by the importers, as the government policy in India wants to encourage the exports from the country.

Coverage of Risks

In India both exporters and importers face risks of foreign exchange market, referred to above, but risk coverage to exporters is more than to importers. The reason is that the Indian government has to enable exporters to compete effectively with their foreign counterparts, where exporters get many facilities, particularly credit at low rates of interest and lower tax rates.

The RBI cannot impose controls in foreign exchange market as hitherto as FERA has been liberalised but it has been entering the market to stabilise the rate and more recently it has been announcing a reference rate for its operations, to stabilise the market. FEDA is fixing the rates for major currencies around which banks are free to operate in the Indian foreign exchange market. Banks continue to cover the currency risk and EXIM Bank provides the credit and country risk cover for long duration export contracts, deferred payment contracts, project and consultancy exports and capital goods exports. ECGC extends the risk coverage by country insurance and party credit insurance — for banks to lend to parties of unknown credit rating. But banks and firms are allowed to keep funds abroad and take risk in currencies and even trade in foreign currency markets.

They can hedge, swap currencies enter into arbitrage deals, secure/provide cover abroad, and even take open positions in currencies. Options and futures in the derivative markets are also open to banks and firms to cover their risks and trade in the markets for hedge purposes.

Market Makers in Foreign Exchange Market

A market maker is one who takes the risk and gives a two-way quotation for any currency — bid and offer rates — and deals in given currencies. As the RBI deals only in dollars, the banks who act as market makers, which are generally foreign banks, concentrate and primary dealers on deals in dollar but quote cross-currency rates such as dollar to sterling or dollar to yen etc. The market makers are generally prone to take positions or hold uncovered currency holdings in strong currencies such as dollar, yen or D.M. as their rate fluctuations are minimal and risk is lower. The risk manager in a company or in a bank, plans his holdings of uncovered currencies into a diversified portfolio, to reduce risk and maximise returns. He may invest in short-term assets or money market instruments of countries whose currencies are strong. Such currencies are unlikely to fluctuate violently and are stable, but returns may be lower, due to lower interest rates. The risk manager has a trade off between risk and return. If he takes a higher risk, he gets higher returns. Both interest rate volatility and exchange rate volatility are to be taken into account to take a risk cover or hedge in derivative markets.

A market maker has to forecast not only the currency rates but the interest rates in the respective countries, which will influence the forward rates. He may cover the risk in some currencies but keep open positions in others. He takes calculated risks to maximise his returns. Leaving the uncovered positions, he may cover the rest by the following methods:

(1) Swap forward to spot, (2) Swap forward of one maturity to another maturity, (3) Swap one currency against another of same maturity or a different maturity, (4) Buy spot for future liability, (5) Buy strong currency and sell weak currency, (6) Buy forward of one maturity against sale of another maturity or of another currency and a host of other techniques.

Market makers in foreign exchange market are authorised dealers, and the Reserve Bank in the case of India. In markets well developed the Central Bank intervention is minimal and the market making is left to reputed foreign exchange dealers and international banks.

Risk in Forward Market

As refered to earlier forward exchange rates are more risky than spot rates. These refer to rates which are quoted for the currencies for delivery in one month to six months ahead. During 1991 to 1994 the exchange markets were undergoing many changes due to the ongoing reforms in India.

During major part of 1994 following the full convertibility of rupee on current account, forward markets turned more volatile and listless conditions prevailed in the spot market.

The forward exchange market is generally influenced by many factors, in addition to spot market conditions, like:

(*a*) Perception regarding U.S. dollar rate and Indian Non-resident Rupee exchange rate against dollar and in general currency markets.

(*b*) Current position and forecast of domestic and foreign money market conditions.

(*c*) Arbitrage, hedge and speculative deals effecting the market.

(*d*) Currency risk manager's strategies of the proportion of forward cover effected to total exposures.

Forward market cover was as high as 18% in 1992 just at the time of introduction of partial convertibility of the rupee in February 1992, but fell to less than 10% by February 1994, when the rupee gained in strength.

The exporters and importers are able to cover their forward risk with the banks for their receipts and payments, but in times of currency stability such covers are less in demand and the traders choose to take some risk themselves. Similarly, the currency risk manager will also keep some open positions. Since January 1995 firms are allowed to trade in currencies and in forward exchange as referred to earlier. The currency risks of short-term of 3 to 6 months are generally lower. The currency risks, involved in medium and long-term foreign exchange exposures of companies are unpredictable and difficult to cover. But these risks are high in India at present. The earlier practice of covering such risks by EXIM Bank and ECGC will have to be turned into developing a long and medium-term forward market. Now banks as well as firms can keep foreign currencies abroad and trade with the attendant risks. The RBI policy is to encourage a well developed forward market in foreign exchange.

The factors of interest rates and money market conditions are important determinants of forward market. The banks started covering their positions of exposure under FCNR(A) Scheme, when the market was volatile. The market has become more stable since 1994-95. FCNR(A) Scheme is being phased out due to the currency risk coverage it involves on the RBI which is not necessary under the free market system.

The risk of currency manager is higher or lower depending on a host of factors. The proportion of risk covered by him to total exposure will depend on his perception of money market rates in India and abroad and volatility of the currency market and number of financial and non-financial factors. When the U.S. dollar interest rates are high, exporters prefer to keep their earnings abroad. If the rupee dollar rate is stable, exporters can take a view on the future exchange rate and lock in a forward to forward Swap arrangement with banks to obtain a better cover on their receivables. The forward market is however illiquid beyond 6 months as the banks find it difficult to foresee the coming trends.

The risk that the currency manager takes will vary from manager to manager and from the conditions in the money market and currency market. He generally covers his risk by taking forward to forward cover by adopting appropriate Swap techniques and calculated risk management through diversification and proper investment strategies. The currencies in which he takes a position should be stable as U.S. dollar or D.M. or yen. The same can be said of the currencies held abroad by firms and companies in India.

Hedge cover of exchange risk for the trader is common. Besides, banks resort to currency Swaps, options and futures in foreign currencies to cover their exchange risk. The risk manager generally keeps an open position only in strong currencies, which are likely to be less volatile. Highly volatile currencies are generally less traded, and their risk is invariably covered. But the cover rates are higher. The terms of hedge, Swaps and options as applied to foreign exchange markets are part of the derivative market operations.

The recent attempts of the RBI to develop a rupee exchange market and a forward exchange market were already referred to. The companies are in a position to trade in the market and take position in currencies which need not be in the currency in which their foreign trade contract lies. They can keep foreign exchange earned abroad and trade in the currencies permitted by the RBI. The foreign currency option market is also expected to be developed well due to these measures, taken recently by the RBI, as also the forward exchange market in India.

Portfolio Management in Foreign Assets

Banks keep their foreign funds in various forms: cash on hand, balances with other banks, deposits with banks of various maturities, foreign government bonds, Treasury bills, short-term commercial bills and Treasury paper etc. These assets are of various maturities and risks. The maturities may vary from ready cash in foreign currencies to various durations of short and medium nature.

Management of the above assets involve the same principles of risk and return, as applicable to domestic assets. Risk is more in foreign assets than in domestic assets. The foreign currency and funds managers have to plan to maximise the returns and minimise the risk through proper diversification into country and currency combinations and the use of Beta for long-term assets. The currency manager has to choose a proper coverage of risk and reduce his risk in currency positions, through various options open to the trader in foreign exchange market.

In general, the principles of portfolio management in domestic market will apply to management of foreign assets as well. The special risks to be covered in the foreign markets were referred to earlier.

Risk management by proper hedge and cover of risk is necessary for the investment operations. It is in this context that investment function becomes more critical for finance and investment companies. For, manufacturing companies, financing function is relatively more important as the cost of finance has to be kept low and profit margins have to be increased. Broadly both investment and finance functions need to be taken care by the company.

Investment and Trading

Investment is purchase of securities or any financial instrument or claims of money. Companies keep some investments in short-term, some in medium-term and also in long-term assets. The investment and trading activities should be distinguished. As cash is required at short notice, investment in Treasury bills, bills of exchange, commercial paper or other short-term credit instruments is necessary. Inter-corporate deposits or investments for a few days to a few months in UTI Units, PSU bonds, etc., are examples of medium-term investments. Long-term investments are in equity shares, debentures, bonds, etc., including those in its subsidiary companies.

Trading is investment and disinvestment in above categories for the purpose of making capital gains or appreciation. Speculation is such trading for short-term gains. When some manufacturing companies are not making adequate profits, the finance manager will try to find alternatives of raising income. The funds manager or treasury manager will be given a role of profit generating centre in funds management or in treasury function in such cases. Some manufacturing companies combine manufacturing with trading. Normally, manufacturing companies do not actively trade but keep investments of both short-term and long-term nature in the portfolio, to enable the company to improve its profits and generate cash at short notice from the existing investment portfolio.

Basically, treasury function involves both investment and trading. Taking open position in trading in stock market and in trading in forex market are examples of active trading, which is also called speculation. Investment aims at long-term gains and take less risk while speculation is trading for short-term gain and most are risky. Both investment and trading expertise are necessary for treasury manager to operate in those markets.

Financial Engineering (Derivative Markets)

Treasury manager has to be conversant with financial engineering as a means of financing and as a mode of risk management. Financial engineering is a multidisciplinary approach to the management of risk and return in treasury management or portfolio management. This involves the use of derivative financial products to decompose the standard financial transactions into their elements and then synthesise them into innovative cross structures to suit the requirements of the parties and preference of investors and the issuers.

Financial engineering is thus the by-product of several factors which have grown in importance in recent years, namely —

1. Development of many financial new products and OTC derivatives.
2. Revolution in information technology.
3. Financial deregulation and liberalisation.

4. Increasing volatility of the markets and need for risk coverage.
5. Growing sophistication of risk management Techniques and their application to financial field.
6. Application of scientific and advanced management techniques.

Financial Engineering Involves

(*a*) Multidisciplinary approach comprising engineers, mechanics and scientists.

(*b*) Adoption of derivative products like Swaps, Repos, and option and futures, options on futures, and futures on options, etc.

(*c*) Decomposition into elements and recomposition of elements and

(*d*) Synthesis of new elements.

Recent Innovations Introduced

A Balance Sheet — Price risk transfers:

(*a*) Adjustable rate mortgages.

(*b*) Floating rate notes.

(*c*) Back to back loans.

Credit Transfers (examples)

Loan Swaps.

Asset sales without recourse.

Securitised assets.

Transferable loan contracts.

Liquidity Enhancing Transfers (examples)

Securitised Asset Instruments.

Securitised Debt Instruments.

Swap Accounts.

Credit Enhancing Transfers (examples)

Junk Boards.

Zero Coupon Bonds.

Money Market Mutual Funds.

Equity Participating Financing (examples)

PCD, FCD, and Convertibles, Warrants, Loyalty Coupons, etc.

Off Balance Sheet Instruments (examples)

Futures, Options, Loan caps, Swaps, Repos, Forward Rate Contracts.

Letters of Credit (examples)

Note Issuance Facilities, Guarantees, Sureties, Contingent liabilities.

INTEREST RATE RISK MEASURES

1. Gap or Mismatch Risk

This gap will arise when assets and liabilities will fall due for repricing at different times. A floating rate issue will reduce the risk to zero, as there is no gap or time for repricing. Mismatched repricing the periods of assets and liabilities is a form of risk.

2. Net Interest Position Risk

If a bank has more assets, on which interest is earned than liabilities on which it pays interest then the bank has net interest position which leads to risk. But, when interest rates rise, the bank's positive net interest position will gain.

3. Basis Risk

Interest rates of any two instruments will not change by the same degree or percentage. But borrowing rate and lending rate will not change in the same degree or proportion, which causes risk. This is the change in interest rates by basis points which will vary from instrument to instrument. The differences in basis point changes will lead to an additional risk. Thus, rates on deposits of all maturities will change, while some lending rates only are changed.

4. Repayment or Withdrawal Risk

If interest rates fall, there is a possibility of some borrowers repaying the high interest loans and if interest rates rise on deposits, old deposits may be withdrawn and new deposits are kept at high interest rates. As interest rates rise and fall, the banks are exposed to some degree of risk as customers exercise the embedded options, inherent in their deposits and loan contracts. The larger the interest rate changes in quantum and more frequent these changes are, the greater will be the risk to the bank.

Yield and Price Changes

With change in interest rates, yields and price of fixed income securities change in inverse relation. Prices fall when yields rise and *vice versa*. A bank having a large component of long-term loans, a rise in yield will lead to fall in prices and hence depreciation and loss of capital value. Yields curve risk arises when the yield curve varies as between different securities and of differing maturities. Changes in yields result in price changes and such frequent changes upset the planning for income and profits. Price risk along with reinvestment risk should be looked into. The differences in the timing of interest cash flows for reinvestment between assets and liabilities may create a further risk.

How to Cope with Interest Risk?

Obviously it is better for the bank to manage its balance sheet items to have less interest sensitive assets and liabilities. They have to resort to floating rate liabilities and flexi-debt instruments. Bankers can also vary the gap in tune with interest rate changes on the basis of forecasts.

The portfolio composition should be constantly reviewed and changed in tune with the change in interest rates. The one method of doing it is to get the duration of its loans to match with the duration of deposit or match the cash inflows with outflows as exactly as possible.

The banks have to reduce asset sensitivity, after maximising the discretionary funds.

Extend investment portfolio maturities, increase short-term deposits and borrowings to suit to lending or investment pattern, increase fixed rate leaning of long-term or adjustable rate loans.

The banks have to reduce sensitivity of liabilities.

Increase longer term deposits and borrow on flexi-rate basis but sell fixed rate loans.

More recently banks and financial institutions are opting for flexible rate loans or loans adjustable to basic deposit rate of one year and above. Banks can adopt strategies like matching long-term assets by equity own funds and match repriceable assets with similar repriceable liabilities and resort to options, futures, and various combinations of them to hedge interest rate risk by Swaps for principal as well as flows of interest payments. More important, banks have to scrutinize the credit delivery system, improve the quality of assets and reduce the NAP (Non-performing Assets).

Asset Liability Management (ALM)

Asset liability management can be defined as the process of adjusting liabilities to meet loans and asset demand, liquidity needs and safety requirements. It should take care to ensure the following:

(*a*) an active management of liabilities or deposits.

(*b*) ensuring bank profitability.

(*c*) securing the long-term operating viability.

ALM is management of funds, wherein the discretionary elements are properly used, by increase or decrease in the interest sensitive funds. It should ensure that bank rates are competitive on both liabilities and assets. Besides regulatory factors should be favourable to enable the company to change the composition of assets and liabilities. These factors require a good secondary market, interest rate deregulation, and competitive market free scenario.

Instruments for ALM

1. Use of CDs and active primary and secondary market in them; the interest rates on them are freed.
2. Another instrument for use, where interest rates are freed is call and notice money which banks can use.
3. Since 1988, inter-bank participations certificates are used for adjusting liabilities with flexibility of rates offered and minimum costs and maximum return.
4. Float or liability in the process of collection or cash and credit in the process of collection.
5. Refinance from RBI and IDBI, etc.

Banks discretionary funds should be maximum in order to enable them to make proper ALM Bank-wise data showed that SBI and its associate banks are having maximum discretionary funds.

Objectives of ALM

1. To maximise the income, and control risk exposure.
2. Liquidity should be ensured and the spread between return and costs should be maximum.
3. Bank interest income minus interest expense should be termed as gap which should be maximised.

Spread Management

RBI may fix a minimum rate or maximum rate on deposits and loans and subject them to these guidelines. The banks should have a large component of interest sensitive assets and liabilities which is possible with big size banks. If a small bank has predominantly retail deposit mix of fixed interest rates, it needs to aim at fixed rate earning assets and maintain as much spread as possible between return and costs.

Disintermediation reduces the low cost funds for bank's deregulation of interest rates, puts pressure on banks and spreads may be reduced. Liquidity pressures due to deregulation and disintermediation can be managed effectively by big sized banks. Interest sensitivity is measured by changes in interest rate on the concerned assets or liability divided by the change in RBI refinance rate. GAP = RSA – RSL, where RSA is in the rate sensitive assets, RSL is the rate sensitive liability.

Traditional Gap Management

Banks first fix the length of the plan horizon, of say 3 months, then the estimates of return and risk for pursuing various alternative programmes of borrowing and lending should be set and finally the bank chooses that programme with a stable net interest income. The gap is the excess of interest sensitive assets over interest sensitive liabilities; incremental gap is worked out by taking one year, divided into quarters and maximum insulation of net interest income is achieved by making the incremental gap equal to zero. Under the traditional approach, banks would have their net interest income immunised from interest rate changes.

Examples of interest sensitive assets are short-term investments in securities, Treasury bills, CP and CD, etc.

Examples of interest sensitive liabilities are instruments of CDs and ICD and volatile call money, notice money term deposits, short-term debts are all rate sensitive.

Rate Adjusted Gap

Different parts of assets and liabilities will respond differently to change in interest rates. Each asset and liability item of balance sheet should be multiplied by its corresponding rate change ratio, namely, RSA/RSL. After those adjustments if the rate adjusted gap is zero, then interest income of a bank is considered to be fully immunised to market rate changes.

Maturity mismatches can be offset by lengthening or shortening either assets or liabilities. Liquidity problem can arise at any point period. Hence it is necessary to be prepared to adjust continuously both — the assets and liabilities.

Liquidity needs of banks arise due to:

1. Meeting the contingent liabilities.
2. Non-receipt of expected funds inflows.
3. Non-renewal of deposits or withdrawal of funds.
4. Profits may change either in investments or in advances side.

The source of liquidity may arise from any one or more items both in assets and liabilities. Banks should be prepared to adjust on both sides of the balance sheet, to meet the proper risk management requirements.

Conclusion

As banks and non-bank financial institutions provide the financial services, the risk management techniques discussed are mostly confined to them, but are relevant to all corporates. The RBI gave some guidelines for risk management, but the Bank Boards have to shoulder this responsibility. The chapter provides thus the basics of risk management techniques, available in general terms for the students and the readers to grasp with ease.

✠ ✠ ✠

EXCHANGE MANAGEMENT IN INDIA

46

Introduction

Controls on foreign exchange dealings involving foreign receipts and payments are an adjunct to the controls on foreign trade. These controls were first resorted to during the Second World War for the purpose of conserving limited foreign exchange reserves and mobilising them for war effort. The war-time controls were put on a statutory basis soon after the war, by the Foreign Exchange Regulation Act of 1947. This Act was replaced by a more comprehensive legislation "Foreign Exchange Regulation Act of 1973" (FERA) incorporating wider powers of control to the RBI and better enforcement through Inspecting Officers and Enforcement Directorate, with a view to plugging all the loopholes or leakages noticed in its working since 1947. But the basic framework of controls remains the same under the new Act as under the old. As a member of the IMF, India is under an obligation to collaborate with the Fund to ensure orderly exchange arrangements and to promote stable exchange rate. Although current account controls are not permitted by the Fund, India secured their permission under Article XIV to keep these controls as transitional measure. In March 1992, limited convertibility of rupee was launched and on the basis of experience gained, full convertibility of rupee on trade account was announced in March 1993, followed by full convertibility of rupee on current account since March 1994. Now India is under Article VIII of IMF Articles of Agreement.

RBI as the Exchange Control Authority

One of the important central banking functions of the RBI is maintenance of external value of the rupee. As such it has been given the custody of foreign exchange reserves and sole agency for administration of exchange controls in India. All receipts and payments in and out of India require general or special permission of the RBI. The dealings in foreign exchange and foreign securities in India, payments to persons resident outside and export and import of currency notes, bullion or precious stones, etc., are subject to general or special permission of RBI or are prohibited. The administration of controls is carried on by the RBI with the help of ADs, and money changers.

The types of transactions which are controlled by the RBI and the government are, in general, those having international financial implications and include *inter alia* the following important items. Many of them are liberalised and some of them withdrawn since 1991 economic reforms.

1. Purchase and sale of and other dealings in foreign exchange and maintenance of balances at foreign centres by residents.
2. Procedure for realisation of proceeds of exports of goods and services.
3. Payment to non-residents or to their accounts in India for imports and others.
4. Transfer of securities as between residents and non-residents and acquisition and holding of foreign securities.
5. Foreign travel (with or without foreign exchange).
6. Export and import of currency, cheques, drafts, travellers' cheques and other financial instruments, securities, gold, jewelleries, etc.
7. Trading, commercial and industrial activities in India of foreign firms and companies (including branches of foreign firms and companies) and foreign nationals as well as acquisition of business undertakings or holding of shares in Indian companies by such firms, companies and persons.
8. Appointment of non-residents and foreign nationals and companies as agents or as technical and management advisers in India.
9. Employment, profession etc., undertaken in India by foreign nationals.
10. Acquisition, holding and disposal of immovable property in India by foreign nationals and companies.
11. Acquisition, holding and disposal of immovable property outside India by persons resident in India.

Government as Controlling Authority

Foreign investment in India and Indian investment abroad require the authorisation of the Ministry of Finance, in addition to that of RBI. FFI and FIIs and activities of Foreign Security Firms are all authorised and controlled by the SEBI, on behalf of the govt. Besides, all capital account transactions of the balance of payments, of India such as dealings with International bodies, Foreign govts., Foreign Currency loans, Joint ventures, Collaborations, Technological inflows and outflows require the permission of the Govt. of India for sanctions and the RBI for corresponding receipts and payments. RBI has therefore only concurrent jurisdiction along with the govt. with respect to some of the Exchange Controls and RBI/SEBI act as agents of the Govt. Within the govt., the ministries concerned with them are the Ministry of Finance, Ministry of Industry and the Ministry of Commerce, and the Foreign Investment Promotion Board constituted for this purpose.

Authorised Dealers (ADs)

Authorised dealers are the scheduled commercial and co-operative banks who are authorised by the RBI to deal in foreign exchange which include all scheduled commercial and co-operative banks at present. The regulations under the FERA governing the banks are contained in the Exchange Control Manual and in the various circulars and notifications issued thereunder by the RBI. The ADs can deal in foreign currencies and for that purpose open and maintain accounts abroad in such currencies, approve applications from the residents for purchase of foreign currencies and maintain rupee accounts in the names of non-residents and pass debits and credits to such accounts. The ADs can deal directly with the public and the RBI with the ADs in putting through these transactions.

The ADs have an association called Foreign Exchange Dealers' Association (FEDA) which fixes the rates for dealings in sterling with rupees on the basis on RBI's declared rates for buying and selling and the middle rates. The ADs are free to quote their own rates for other currencies on the basis of cross rates quoted in London as between sterling and other currencies and on the basis of RBI's buying rates for D.M., the US dollar and yen. The RBI buys and sells sterling under Section 40 without limit, while it buys only \$, DM and yen under Section 17 (3) of the RBI Act. The RBI has also started selling US \$ from February 1987. Since 1992,

RBI is quoting a Reference Rate in terms of US $ and Euro and intervenes in the market to stabilise the rupee in terms of dollar.

As agents of the RBI, ADs have to scrutinise applications from the public and implement the rules and regulations of exchange control under powers delegated to them by the RBI. They have to satisfy themselves that all receipts and payments are in accordance with the Exchange Control Manual. It is obligatory for ADs under Section 74 of FERA to comply with all general or special directions and instructions given by the RBI. They can keep Non-resident Accounts (Nostro and Vostro) and operate on them subject to the overall control and reporting to RBI. They can deal in permitted methods of receipts and payments, keep minimum working balances in foreign centres, operate in the inter-bank market and maintain a square or near square position in each currency which means that their purchases (spot and forward) and sales should be matched as far as possible. The RBI has delegated the powers of taking position in any currency and the prudential limits for trading to be decided by the Boards of individual banks since the reforms were started. ADs can provide hedge in foreign markets, trade in options and futures and in other derivative products, subject to some limits.

Money Changers

Money changers are authorised by the RBI to deal in foreign currencies and coins. Restricted money changers can only purchase while others can do both purchases and sales in foreign currencies and coins. Some hotels, firms and establishments, etc., have been given licences by the RBI to act as money changer.

Permitted Methods

All exporters have to get a code number from the RBI for which an application in Form CNX has to be made in duplicate. This code number has to be quoted in all subsequent correspondence with banks and RBI. The inward remittances are freely permitted except that they are to be reported to the RBI. The export receipts are to be declared in the prescribed form and should represent the full export value of the goods and the transactions should be put through the ADs. The method of receipt should be in permitted currencies (listed in the Exchange Control Manual) and in approved forms. The proceeds should normally be realised within six months and in the case of Pakistan and Afghanistan within three months (extended six months in October 1985), except in the case of exports of engineering goods under deferred payment arrangements when permission is generally given for extended periods of receipt. Trade discounts and agency commissions are permitted normally up to 5 per cent of the invoice value.

The object of control in respect of exports is to ensure that the export earnings are duly and promptly repatriated back to India in full, within the stipulated time and in the currency of the importing country or a convertible currency. No underinvoicing or overinvoicing or any measure to earn foreign exchange, with a view to keeping it abroad is permitted. Blanket exchange permits and exchange release for sales promotion are permitted up to certain limits. Exporters and EOUs are now permitted to keep some part of their earnings abroad, to facilitate future transactions.

The prescribed methods of receipt and payment are as follows:

(A) External Group Countries: Include all countries who are not in Group 'B'- Bilateral Group. Export receipt should be in the currency of importing country or of any country in this group. Import payment from India should be in rupees to the account of the resident of the exporting country or of any country in this group.

(B) Bilateral Group Countries: Include Czechoslovakia, East Germany, Poland, Rumania and Russia. Any receipts or payments in respect of these countries should be in non-convertible rupees or as per the relative agreement on which ADs are advised from time to time.

In respect of Nepal and Bhutan the receipts and payments are to be effected in rupees without reference to the Exchange Control formalities.

Other Receipts

All receipts whether current or capital are to be channelised through ADs. Any unauthorised use of foreign exchange is not permitted. The foreign exchange earned should be repatriated home at the earliest possible time through the ADs into the official channels. The purpose of remittance and the beneficiary of remittance and other details are to be recorded and reported to the RBI by the ADs. All inward remittances for investment of foreign capital in India should be made to the Ministry of Commerce and Industry, while those for repatriation after such clearance are to be made to the RBI. All flows on current account are now free while those on capital account are liberalised.

Payment for Imports

Authorised dealers are permitted to open letters of credit or make remittances abroad for imports, if they are covered by import licences or are under OGL. If the goods are covered under deferred payment terms, prior approval of RBI is also necessary for opening of letters of credit or giving a bank guarantee. The method of payment should be in terms of permitted currencies and advance payments require prior approval of RBI and are granted in respect of engineering goods or capital goods. Payment to bilateral account countries should be in non-convertible rupees, as per the relative trade agreements. Payments are freely allowed and at free market rates of exchange since March 1992, once the corresponding licence is there or the goods are on OGL.

Other Payments

Payments for travel, education, medical treatment, etc., are permitted as per scales laid down by the RBI from time to time, depending upon the purpose and the country of visit. These payment restrictions are advised to the ADs from time to time and have been fairly liberalised more recently due to comfortable foreign exchange position of India. Remittances of freight, profits, dividends, insurance, etc., are permitted to actual beneficiaries abroad. Family remittances of foreign nationals are permitted but not of Indian nationals or Indian residents for maintenance of their families abroad. Similarly, transfer of assets by Indian nationals emigrating abroad is also not allowed except in small quantities or in special circumstances. Some of these items of flow of funds on current account are now freed, and ADs are now authorised to grant the necessary permits and provide the permitted exchange to the parties but they have to report them to RBI periodically.

All applications for transfer of funds for investment abroad are to be made to the Ministry of Commerce and Industry for clearance first and then to the Ministry of Finance and RBI. These are now granted freely in view of comfortable foreign exchange position and liberalised policy.

Delegation to ADs

ADs have been delegated some powers to approve and to make remittances for dividends, profits, subscription to magazines, membership fees, correspondence course frees, examination fees, up to prescribed limits without reference to the RBI. Similarly, remittances out of income for family maintenance abroad for non-nationals are permitted up to some limits. Payments for samples for trade and laboratory testing up to some limits of value are permitted by the ADs. But prior permission is required in case of reduction in proceeds over invoice value, change in terms of sale or penalties, quality claims or any other deductions in invoice value. Since 1992 FERA was diluted very much and many controls were removed.

Forward Covers

Exchange control permits ADs to enter into forward sales and purchases with customers for genuine trade transactions provided they are in permitted currencies and in prescribed methods and corresponding foreign country's exchange control does not prohibit such transactions. The ADs can in turn cover them in an inter-bank market in India or abroad or with the RBI. The AD has to satisfy himself that the importer has an import licence with an exchange control copy, except when the imported goods are on OGL. The customer must have also entered into a purchase contract, opened a letter of credit or produced other documentary evidence in that direction. Banks can normally enter into sale contracts up to six months except in the case of deferred payment imports in which case RBI's permission for longer periods is secured. Where an export is made on consignment basis, a forward sale is given only after shipment is effected and up to the extent of the value declared in the shipping bill. The contract should be based on the value expected to be received minus agency commission. Any extension of contract beyond six months normally requires prior permission of RBI. Cancellation of forward contracts should also be referred to RBI for approval. The RBI has introduced many changes in December 1985 to expand the spectrum of forward cover facilities such as for overseas projects, contracts, commissioning charges, consultancy fees, cross-currency deals, etc. Banks are now permitted to cover such risks in foreign markets. In 1994-95, RBI has permitted banks and companies to trade freely in the forward market and stopped giving the cover.

Securities

There are no restrictions on import of securities, Indian or foreign, export of securities is prohibited except with the prior approval of the RBI. Similarly, issue and transfer of securities to non-residents requires the general or special permission of the RBI as also the Foreign Investment Board of the Ministry of Industrial Development. Indian residents require prior permission to hold foreign securities or export or send out of India, Indian securities. Now these transfers are freely permitted and both direct and portfolio investments are now permitted by NRIs and FFIs.

Foreign Currency Accounts

The RBI has granted general permission to persons resident but not domiciled in India to maintain and operate foreign currency accounts. Such of the accounts of residents as existed before 1947 were continued but fresh credits to such accounts are to be approved by RBI before hand. Normally, residents of India are not permitted to open or maintain such accounts in foreign currency abroad except those permitted in connection with technical collaboration or joint collaboration agreements. Indians who are resident outside India had to close such accounts when they return to India on a permanent basis, but it is not necessary at present due to recent liberalisations. The present Exchange Control Manual is being replaced by a new one and the existing law (FERA) has been redrafted as Foreign Exchange Management Act (FEMA) with deletion of emphasis on controls in 1999.

Non-resident Accounts

The terms resident and non-resident have been defined in the Foreign Exchange Regulation Act of 1973. A non-resident is one who resides outside India for the whole or a substantial part of the year, Indians who are working abroad, and offices and branches abroad of Indian or foreign companies in India (excluding residents of Nepal and Bhutan). Two types of non-resident accounts are clearly discernible.

1. Private non-resident accounts (of individuals, firms, companies and organisations).
2. Non-resident bank accounts.

The Private Non-resident Accounts

The private non-resident accounts are again of three categories:

(1) Ordinary non-resident (rupee) accounts (NRO) are opened without reference to RBI in respect of non-Indians and Indians residing abroad but holding a passport of a country other than that of India with funds from abroad but others require prior permission of RBI.

(2) National Defence Remittance Scheme Special Accounts were opened during 1965-66 with the rupee proceeds of inward remittance received under the NDR scheme from non-resident Indians abroad. These

funds are not repatriable from India under any circumstances but can be converted into rupee accounts and used in India, if the circumstances of the accountholder warranted it.

(3) Non-resident (External) Accounts Rules 1970 permit the opening of such accounts (FCNR) in the names of persons of Indian origin or Indian nationality but resident abroad provided the funds are transferred into India from abroad through banking channels. Such funds can be paid back in foreign currency for repayment of principal and interest without prior approval of the RBI after the maturity of fixed deposits. Non-resident (ordinary) accounts can be converted into non-resident (external) accounts or transfers from one to the other are permitted. The operation on these accounts are no longer subject to earlier controls.

In more recent years, foreign investment in India is encouraged. Non-residents of Indian origin are given liberal facilities for investment in shares, debentures and units of the U.T.I., both on repatriation basis and non-repatriation basis. There are provisions for non-resident investment in new issues up to 40 per cent in the case of some industries and up to 74% or 49% in some cases and even 100 per cent in respect of a few priority industries such as hospitals and hotels, which are foreign exchange-earners and in sick units. Funds have thus flown in through the non-resident accounts for remittances and investment. Foreign investment in Indian companies is now permitted up to 51% of equity capital.

Non-resident (Banks) Accounts

All accounts kept in India by foreign banking companies, including foreign branches of Indian banks, are designated non-resident bank accounts. ADs can open accounts in Indian rupees for their correspondents, branches, agents, etc., abroad subject to the advice to the RBI. The operations (credits and debits) on these accounts have to be reported to the RBI. They have the same implication as operation in foreign currency accounts kept by Indian banks abroad with their agents, correspondents and branches. The operation on these accounts are freely allowed now.

Loans and Overdrafts

ADs can grant temporary loans and overdrafts to their agents, correspondents and branches, etc., abroad other than from bilateral group without prior approval of RBI up to a limit. They can also receive similar financial assistance from abroad. Such facilities are for current operations and of working capital nature and not for investment in term capital and loans to private parties. Such operations are to be reported to the RBI.

Blocked Accounts

An account is blocked if operations on it are not permitted without the prior approval of the RBI. Any account of a person, firm or company, resident abroad may be opened as blocked or may be declared as blocked by the RBI under the Exchange Control Rules. Thus, assets in India, including bank accounts and securities, etc., of Indians emigrating to foreign countries, are set out as blocked accounts. Balances in blocked accounts can, however, be invested with RBI's permission in fixed deposits with banks, or other approved categories of shares, debentures, etc. The rules governing the blocked accounts are laid down in the Exchange Control Manual and have been liberalised more recently allowing more liberal use of these funds for local payments or investments by accounts having less than ₹ 50,000. The operations on such accounts are normally governed by rules of the RBI and subject to scrutiny of RBI and to be reported to it in Form A-4. Blocked accounts have disappeared with the liberalisations in FERA and permission given to free use of all such funds, since 1992-93.

The Table below presents balances of NRIs in India, under the currently available schemes:

Table 46.1 OUTSTANDING BALANCES OF NRIs

(in US $ million)

Various Schemes	1997 end March	1998 end March	1999 end March	2004 end March	2005 end March	2007 March	2008 March	2012 March	2013 March	2014 March
FCNR (A)	2,306	36	Phased out	—	—	—	—	—	—	—
FCNR (B)	7,496	8,467	8323	10,961	11,490	15,129	14,168	14,968	15,188	41,823
NR(E)RA	4,983	5,637	6220	20,559	21,109	24,495	26,716	31,408	45,924	52,908
NR(NR)RD	5,604	6,262	6258	1,746	271	—	—	—	—	—
NRO	—	—	—	—	—	1,616	2,788	12,232	9,719	9,714

Source: RBI Annual Report.

Only FCNR(A) deposits are declining as this scheme was phased out by the RBI, by 1997-98 NR (NR)D were also phased out by 2004-05.

LIBERALISATION OF EXCHANGE CONTROL

Since 1992, deregulation and liberalisation were pursued by the government and the RBI in respect of foreign exchange and exchange controls. The basic framework of controls remained, except for liberalisation in some directions; rupee was freed on trade account in 1993 and on current account in 1994. Consequential and supplemental to these measures the RBI has diluted many provisions in FERA.

ADs were given more powers, through delegation of authority in respect of both Trade Account and Invisible Account. ADs were allowed to export surplus stocks of foreign currency notes and coins, keep balances and short-term investment abroad for their working requirements. The ceiling of ₹ 15 crore, imposed in 1995, on AD's overnight position was removed in January 1996. ADs can use their discretion in releasing foreign exchange for foreign travel for business seminars, conferences, medical treatment and studies. Banks have to maintain Tier I capital funds at 5% of foreign exchange open position.

Exporters were permitted to keep Exchange Earner Foreign Currency accounts (EEFC) to utilise them for all purposes connected with trade promotion and other current account purposes. ADs were given freedom to fix their own Aggregate Gap Limit (AGL) for more efficient management of their assets and liabilities. They were also allowed, if they have the expertise, to initiate positions overseas in cross currency dealings. They can give forward cover to overseas investors on account of dividends due or returns on foreign investment in India or to shipping companies in respect of foreign collections.

ADs are allowed to offer hedges, interest rate swaps, currency swaps, caps/collars, and forward rate agreements to corporates, without prior permission of RBI or government. RBI has been providing single window clearance (under fast track) within 21 days for proposals of joint ventures and foreign investment by Indian companies up to a limit of U.S.$ 4 million.

Inter-bank deals account for about 80-85% of total transaction in forex market and the RBI has initiated the process of setting up clearing house facilities for settlement and clearance for the operations of ADs. The RBI has set-up a Market Intelligence cell to study and monitor the developments in Forex Market, on a daily basis.

Sodhani Committee Recommendations

Following the recommendations of this committee the RBI implemented the following measures:

1. General permission for sale of shares, required under Portfolio Investment Scheme, given to NRI was extended to OCBs.

2. NRIs and not OCBs have been permitted to invest in MMMFs, set up for money market operations in India.
3. General permission to NRIs for subscribing to Articles of Association of Indian Companies engaged in Industrial activities to cover other companies engaged in other permissible activities.
4. Granting of housing loans to NRI staff of Indian companies.
5. ADs are permitted to remit sale proceeds of shares kept under pledge for liquidation of loan outstandings.
6. General permission for crediting interest on delayed refunds of share application money.
7. Extending the scope of safe custody of securities on behalf of NRIs to institutional custodians.

In short, consideration was given to NRIs for more liberal treatment of their repatriation and operations of them under Portfolio Management. Funds mobilised by banks through the NRI deposits (FCNR, EFFC and RFC) can be invested abroad by banks in short-term investment, in addition to their lending at home.

ADs can effect remittances up to U.S.$ 10,000 or its equivalent for importers to settle disputes abroad on trade account. Hotels and Airline companies are allowed to receive payment in Indian rupees from foreign tourists without insisting on their encashment certificates.

Software exports were permitted, since September 1995 without receipt of advance payment and software exports are put on par with any other exports. Since Oct. 1995, RBI has stopped announcing dollar buying and selling rates, but specific quotes are given for a deal with RBI, by any AD. Since Nov. 1995, ADs are allowed to provide US $ 5,000 or less in any year to the close relatives abroad for their maintenance by any resident Indian if the beneficiary abroad is a permanent resident abroad and has insufficient income and unable to return to India. Authorised dealers are permitted since February 1996, to effect remittances towards import of designs and drawings, up to ₹25 lakh on production of suppliers' invoice, postal wrappings and exchange control copy of bill of entry as documentary evidence in support of import.

Norms for investment abroad were eased in May 1997. Indian companies are now allowed to freely invest in overseas market up to $ 15 million raised through GDR or EEFC without RBI prior permission, provided they are invested in overseas projects. Corporates are allowed since June 1997 to raise funds abroad up to $ 15 million as short-term finance useful for even rupee expenditure on their projects, if they are export earners and EPCG licence holders. Other corporates are allowed to raise up to $ 3 million for their foreign currency requirements or for their rupee expenditure. Residents are allowed to invest abroad up to $ 25,000 in permitted listed companies, or those with investments in listed Indian companies.

Exchange Rate Management

Since 1994, when the rupee has declared convertible, exchange control in the strict sense was not operated. What the RBI did is better called Exchange Rate Management (ERM). FERA was replaced by FEMA in 1999.

The RBI policy in this regard was guided by market conditions, current account deficit, and capital inflows/outflows. Excess demand and supply pressures of rupee versus dollar were absorbed by RBI intervention. The Rupee value was maintained within a narrow range between ₹36 to 40 per US $ at end Dec. 1997. The RBI had to maintain a delicate balance, between price stability or control of inflation and the required Exchange rate stability. Even at ₹36, per US dollar, rupee depreciated by about 15% during the Eighth Plan period (1992-97). From March 1993, there was a temporary appreciation of the rupee due to the adoption of convertibility on trade account followed by convertibility on current account in March 1994.

There was relative stability of the rupee during 1994-95 and in 1995-96. The RBI allowed the rate to fall from ₹31 to ₹35 and started supporting it between ₹35 to 36. It has stabilised around ₹36 by May-

June 1996. The RBI intervention in the Forex market since October 1995 helped the rupee rate to remain around ₹35-36, until Nov. 1997 when it fell to ₹39. The rupee depreciated to ₹46.7 per dollar in April, 2001 and reached a low of ₹49 per dollar early in 2002 before appreciating to ₹43.7 by end March 2005. RBI has purchased dollars, when there are large inflows into the country and also sold when there is large demand for dollars, from its foreign exchange assets. Excluding gold and SDRs, India's foreign currency assets rose from a low of $ 29 million in March 1991 to a peak of US $ 42 million in April 2001 and rose further to 114 billion by June 2004. These foreign currency assets stood at US $ 206 billion as at end June 2007 and US $ 260 billion at end March 2012 and $ 276 billion at end March 2014. This sharp rise in exchange reserves was due to foreign confidence in Indian Economy and large foreign inflows of funds from abroad. This enabled India to repay some of its foreign debt obligations and the RBI to intervene in the forex market to stabilise the rupee, which is necessary for sustained growth of our exports.

MARKETING OF FINANCIAL SERVICES

47

Introduction

This chapter is not a loose ended standalone piece, in this part on international markets. This chapter is kept here deliberately to provide integration of foreign markets with domestic markets through one of the channels, namely, marketing, which is most vital for all activities. Domestic and foreign markets are linked through inputs and outputs and inter-flows as between them. But for all markets, *marketing* is the key link providing the *Master Key* to all financial activities.

In India, service sector constitutes nearly 60% of GDP at present and its rate of growth, is also higher at 8 to 9% as against 2-3% in the case of agriculture and around 6-8% in the case of manufacturing sector. Service sector has a stable demand as against fluctuating fortunes in the case of agriculture and recession and boom conditions in manufacturing sector. With increasing specialisation in all fields, this trend has a tendency to proliferate in services also, as hiring of services is more economical than to undertake their own services. Many companies give franchise for providing some services to others and they hire mailing and advertising agencies, instead of undertaking them by own agencies. So is packing and forwarding and a host of other services in the financial field. But the particular features for special treatment of this subject lay in its unique features different from that of product marketing, and the changing customer profile, demanding these services, with sophistication and quality consciousness. Hence, the importance of the service marketing and as this book deals with the financial services, the importance of marketing and the treatment of this subject need no special mention.

Firstly, service marketing has more human element in it, and hence personal skills, attitudes and motivation play a greater role, than in product marketing. Secondly, service marketing needs a more fortified, cohesive and interactive organisation and hence the needed organisational skills for service marketing are different. Thirdly, the personal touch and quality are more important in the service sector. Fourthly, service being specific to customer and customer to be treated as the king, his satisfaction is paramount particularly in banking, stock and capital markets.

Marketing of Financial Services

After the recent liberalisation measures from 1992 onwards, involving deregulation, privatisation and globalisation, the financial sector has witnessed a deepening and widening of its services. Expansion and diversification became the hallmarks of banking and non-banking financial sector. There was a mushroom growth of NBFCs. The problems in this transition period were many such as emergence of various spurious companies, increased competition with the weak and inefficient finding it difficult to survive and many malpractices in the stock and capital market. Some of these problems like malpractices are being tackled by the SEBI through its directives, inspection and audit of all the capital market intermediaries and by the RBI through its increased powers of registration, directives, inspection, etc., of the NBFCs. In the process, many merchant bankers and some other capital market intermediaries closed their business due to lack of sufficient business, tough competition and the need for higher net worth, which they could not muster. Similarly, many NBFCs below ₹25 lakh net worth, inefficient ones and corrupt units which were refused licence from the RBI had to close their doors.

In this new competitive environment and globalised trading practices, the marketing of financial services assumed greater significance. Today's financial services market require new strategies to survive and continue to operate. They have to adopt new marketing strategies and tactics which enable them to capture the minimum opportunities with the lowest risks in order to enable them to survive and meet the tough competition from global players of domestic and foreign origin.

New Challenges

The challenges posed to the financial sector in the marketplace are the following:

(1) Deregulation, (2) Advanced Information technology, (3) Globalised markets and growing volumes of financial transactions, (4) Volatility of the markets and (5) Increased customer demands and sophistication of markets and customers.

Many of the existing units could not cope with this new environment. Most of them sought to strengthen themselves by mergers and acquisitions, diversification or closure of some business lines which are uneconomical. Others have met the challenges by better management talent, adoption of the new organisational structure, strengthening of the information system and technology and drastic changes in their marketing strategies. Adoption of all risk management strategies, soundly formulated business plans, acquiring new innovative talents, SWOT analysis, and correction of weaknesses and threats while making full utilisation of their strengths and opportunities.

Special Features of Service Marketing

1. Services are intangibles and cannot be standardised or reproduced in the same form. They are customer need based and unique.
2. Both suppliers of services and consumers should have a rapport, willingly understand each other and co-operate through meaningful dialogue and effective communications.
3. Services are dominated by human element and quality counts. But quality cannot be homogenised, "It will vary with time, place and customer to customer".
4. Inventories cannot be created. Services are immediately consumed and marketing and operation are closely inter-linked.
5. Branding and designing in a standardised manner is not possible in service sector particularly in the financial field, except in generic form.

Vendors of services should have a track record of integrity, reputation for quality and timeliness of delivery. More than media advertisement, the best advertisement for them is the mouth to mouth word of satisfied customers, and building of corporate image of the vendors, rather than their presentations, oral assurances to the vendees. The first best market strategy is thus a satisfied customer. The second strategy is to maintain quality, human approach, appearances and courtesies of the personnel and the available infrastructural facilities for them. Thirdly, service counts in terms of how it is priced and how much it is cost effective for the customer and for the vendor each.

Basic Bricks for Marketing Strategies

To enable a finance company to formulate its unique marketing strategy to meet the challenges of the financial market scene, it has to be familiar with the various laws, environment constraints, its potential customers and their requirements, its competitors and their charges, etc. Some of the key elements which are the basis for formulating the strategies are as follows:

(1) Customer Focus: That customer is the king and his requirements are to be satisfied in full is the basic tenant of any marketing strategy. This customer focus is to be incorporated in marketing, management and back office operations that have immediate access to customer. There is need for effective innovative schemes suitable to customers and the company should provide timely delivery of services that the customer has asked for and meets with his requirements.

(2) Capturing the Growth Opportunities: In a competitive world, information technology is available to note what the competitors offer. To gain upper hand, any smart business unit should identify the new business opportunities and realistically anticipate the demand or create a demand, which is easily and convincingly saleable to potential customers, after analysing the risk-return scenario of the project realistically associated with each opportunity before deciding on the choice of pursuing it or not.

(3) Successful Differentiation: Success in a competitive world demands a unit's ability to create a different product image in the minds of target customers. The product offered by the company should be rated as different and superior to others in the line and should have been priced competitively. As in the case of products, differentiation of the service rendered counts and its can be built in the minds of customers through assiduous efforts of communication, direct letters, display of their special features through presentations and effective mouth to mouth communications either from the company or its satisfied customers or their votaries.

(4) Innovativeness and Management Ability: Ultimately, the success of a firm's marketing strategy depends on whether it is innovative and the extent of its innovativeness. For this the ability and expertise of the management is all that matters. They should be able to prove creative and innovative and with ability to operate with new and unfamiliar customers and marketplaces.

(5) Quality and Professionalism: Much more than in the product markets, service markets are prone to depend on subjective factors of image, reputation, quality of service and professionalism in management. The customers are enlightened and quality conscious and are highly demanding in the present day competitive environment. Service quality, delivery system and process and timeliness and conformity with specifications are the pre-requisites for a successful marketing strategy. Skills, training and education of all the human factors at various levels in the firm is a vital necessity for any marketing strategy to succeed. In the financial service sector, human factor, skills and quality are all vital to success, for which the adopted technology and skills count very much.

(6) Concept Selling: Some concepts like retail banking and home banking or internet trading or e-mail transfers are examples of concept building and selling of services. I.T. and T.V. can be used as a media for this purpose.

The likely determinants of service quality may be briefly set out as follows:

1. Reliability which includes timely performance and dependability of the service.
2. Responsiveness of the management to the needs of customers, to effect any necessary changes or incorporate new ideas, etc.

3. Competence and skills of the personnel in the vendor firm counts for dependability of quality.
4. Courtesy and effective communication with the client by the firm and consistency in their approach counts for infusing confidence in the customer.
5. Understanding the requirements of the customer and knowing them fully well also helps the firm meet the quality requirements and the demands to satisfy the customer completely.
6. Credibility involving trustworthiness, honesty and integrity of the company providing services will add to its name and reputation to provide the quality service required.
7. Security and freedom from any risk or uncertainty for the customer from the company in respect of timeliness and quality of service is equally important.
8. Most important of all, management skills, their professionalism in approach, their easy access to the clients, and willingness to help and amend with positive attitudes will infuse confidence in the customers on the competency of management to deliver the quality service as required and within time limit.

The quotation from J.P. Morgan, who successfully emerged as the leading Banker in the above respect is apt in this context. "Situations will arise that can be solved by bright people backed by uncompromised capital strength." This would imply that the role of management, skills, ideas, innovation accompanied by sufficient networth, are the *sine-qua-non* of success in the financial world of highly competitive and global environment.

To sum up, services are different and that too financial services are more different from products. Here consumer-oriented are the services and these are more specific to consumer and time. These cannot be standardised and are not easily reproducible. Human element in these services is more prominent and hence management talent and personnel skills count. Sometimes, roadside shows, incentives, gifts and treats will help attract customer base, but the quality is the enduring factor for expanding the base. Each service activity needs a different type of market strategy and hence generalisation is risky.

Banking Field

In commercial banking, marketing strategy has to meet the challenges by strengthening themselves by mergers or diversifications such as going to national from regional and from national to global level playing. They have to have a dynamic management team, modified value systems, suitable to the requirements of customers and a market thrust to meet the challenge of competitors. There is need for diversification of product range such as introduction of credit cards or debit cards, 24-hour banking, ATM and other computerised services, banking from home through the website of the internet, electronic transfer of funds and dematerialisation of all physical certificates. Banks may be prepared to service the customers as they desire, say by arranging Portfolio Management, Tax Payment, consultancy and personal investments. These are all called market responsive management practices and customer-oriented services.

What is true of commercial banks is also applicable to Co-operatives and investment banks. Diversified loan portfolios, new avenues such as home banking, personal consumer finance, new deposit mobilisation techniques and designing innovative schemes of lending and entering with global services, say Euro-markets and foreign borrowing and lending. Customers are now demanding and they want to deal with people who are empathetic, knowledgeable, responsive, caring, open and communicative and professionalised. What is wanted in consumer finance is how a loan product is explained and delivered rather than simply interest rate or terms which are generally common to all companies.

Mutual Funds

Selling by mutual funds is also different. As per SEBI norms, they can neither promise a fixed return nor indulge in prohibited practices such as speculative trading. Many mutual funds in India have underperformed partly due to lack of expertise, stringent investment norms of SEBI and poor market conditions. In this scenario, their marketing strategies have limited alternatives. They can offer hope, although their past is blank. They can offer service, which may still fall short of the expectations of customers. They can at best promise safety of funds buyback arrangements and trustworthiness. In fact, while mutual funds, venture funds, and offshore funds are amenable to proper sales strategies like roadshows, advertisement and hoardings, but not so in the case of stock brokers and bankers, who cannot advertise their products as intermediaries. In the case of other intermediaries, like merchant bankers, registrars, collecting bankers, etc., they can be customer-friendly, meet the challenges by quick adaptive methods and, management skills to adjust to the requirements of customers quickly and timely delivery and a serious commitment to quality. Their customers are companies and individuals and their requirements are specific.

Insurance

Unlike the above, services, life insurance and general insurance require a different kind of marketing strategy, namely, a diversified product range, a mix of products suitable to meet varying needs of consumers, combining life with endowment, or a combination of accident, health and unemployment, etc. Their approach and their talents are more powerful than the attributes of product range. This is direct selling. Letters to potential customers, personal approach through telephone, agents, visits, etc., are also a part of the marketing strategy.

Many times, employees are approached through the employers for group insurance and like mass banking, mass insurance policies are also sold. Many insurance needs are met in India by monopoly agencies. But now that insurance has opened up, their competence to meet competition, the strength of human element and management skills to organisational adoption and marketing strategies make a difference for their performance. Pre-sales and after-sales service are equally important in insurance.

Need for Meeting Global Competition

One of the marketing strategies to meet globalisation and increased competition for banks, mutual funds and many other financial intermediaries is to expand to international business through alliances with foreign counterparts, joint ventures, collaborations or by opening branches or offices and subsidiaries in the selected countries abroad. International business should help strengthen the institution, expand business and profits. It may be worthwhile to enter such business only if it helps diversification, reduce risks and improve profitability. The enterprises that may enter this business should be already dominant domestically, inherently profitable already, and the entry into international business should positively contribute to the organisational strength, improve the overall firm's performance, against the present objectives. For this, an organised M.I.S., careful choice of centres to be entered and the selection of the expert staff needed for the purpose and the marketing strategies adopted for this purpose are all important. There should also be favourable external environment contributing to the success of the entry into international business. Evaluation of the international business is generally based on the cost-benefit analysis of that unit as well as its contribution to the success of the organisation, as a whole.

Financial restructuring and organisational adaptation are the key words for the management to meet the emerging challenges arising out of globalisation, deregulation and free market economy. The organisation has to change its corporate governance strategies, arrange for adaptation to new technology, and strengthen the organisation financially by internal structural changes and external forces through mergers, acquisitions and divestments. For these purposes, the organisation has to build a database which becomes part of the M.I.S., comprising the information on customers, potential and actual, and the market factors to be reckoned and chalk out alternative strategies of which cost-effective, low risk and high return scenarios are accepted in the order of ranking laid down by O and M Group of the corporate unit. There is need for proper data collection, analysis and interpretation of all the relevant data through appropriate research techniques. The final objective is to arrive at the proper marketing strategies which will influence consumer behaviour through strategic decision making. The major strategies are: (1) Direct approach to customers. (2) Advertisement of their cost and quality features.(3) Innovation and Introduction of new financial products more suitable to consumer needs. (4) Strive to achieve excellence in quality. (5) Demand determined forces and market feasible research base will help design and develop those products which meet the requirements of consumers. Technology and research (R & D) should be a tool and not a master in this process. (6) Emphasis should be on human elements and personal skills in selling services. (7) Sales through various modes such as advertisement on T.V., internet websites, personal phone calls, letters of mutation, recommendations of satisfied customers and through many other methods, feasible technologically.

(8) Finally financial institutions, selling their products have to be dynamic, result-oriented: they must have highly skilled staff, efficient systems and practices, a useful M.I.S. and non-traditional structures in their organisation. Strategic and organisational changes along the lines discussed above should place the firm in a unique position in Product Management and market-driven strategies should promote sales and profits.

There is need to promote after sales service in the form of attending to complaints, redressal of their grievances, particularly lacking in banking, insurance and registrars to corporate issues and a few other capital and stock market intermediaries. The follow-up service and customers' full satisfaction are as vitally important as the quality and the timeliness of service. In financial services, good customer relations and their satisfaction is the single major factor contributing to the success of an organisation.

Customer Satisfaction

The elements of implicit promotion of service are the customer satisfaction, image building for the quality and timeliness and a reputation as a leader in any line. Similarly, the elements of explicit promotion are the advertisement and publicity, which are transmitted via mass media and the personal selling and direct response contact with potential customers through mail, telex, phone, etc.

Banks are service organisations whose customer service is poor and need a lot of organisational and personnel skills. So is the case of the life and general insurance, whose reputation for quality and delivery of service is probably poorer than that of banks. This has been the result of protracted market monopoly and semi-monopoly elements in the market and poor quality of human element and personal skills, which are the basic bricks for service marketing. Both in banking and insurance, whose customer base is as wide as the whole household sector, customer is not treated as the king and their marketing strategies are weak. The pre-requisites for customer satisfaction are the following:

1. identification of customer needs for financial and non-financial services.
2. develop appropriate plans and schemes for them.
3. price them reasonably on a cost plus basis in a competitive spirit and not on monopoly basis. After sale, service is equally important.
4. strategies for marketing through personal contact, letters, advertisement through agents as in the case of insurance and in media.
5. use of development officers, R and D and customer based research for schemes and policies, which are innovative and need based.
6. servicing with quality and time consciousness of depositors, customers and policyholders.

So far as leasing, hire-purchase and related non-bank financial services are concerned, they should evince competitive differentiation of their service, quality and timeliness and productivity. Their planning for marketing programmes should consist of:

(*a*) Product strategy or product-mix.

(*b*) Pricing strategy or cost factors.

(*c*) Direct marketing and personal selling.

(*d*) Distribution strategy for non-bank financial services including channels of service flow.

(*e*) Promotion of business strategy which includes emphasis and specialisation in the areas where it has competence and strategies for highlighting them and divesting of the areas, where it is weak.

As referred to earlier, service quality is another important aspect of marketing of services, which include design development process, marketing strategies and delivery process. Sometimes, after-sales service is also a critical factor as in the case of banks, insurance companies and non-bank financial services. The image and reputation for service depends among others on the following factors:

Reliability, responsiveness, competence of staff, courtesy and communication skills of personnel, credibility, security or risklessness and customer satisfaction. Quality achievement, quality maintenance and quality improvement.

In marketing of services, attention has to be given to selection of personnel, their education and training, their special skills, motivation and attitudes of the organisation and its personnel. There should be feedback from customers for attending to customer complaints and their effective and quick redressal and ultimately aim at unique customer satisfaction.

The recent development is Business Process Outside (BPO) services in another country. This activity is expanding in the areas of I.T., multimedia, telecommunications, etc. This involves the use of expert staff for specific services, like R&D work, testing, programming, call centres, etc. This is advantageous only if the costs are lower for the same or better quality service. Here the parties to the contract come to an understanding, without much need for marketing strategy. The human resource endowments and the efficiency and costs, are the only criteria for the choice of this service.

✠ ✠ ✠

SELECT BIBLIOGRAPHY

1. Chandratre, K.R.: *Report of Working Group on Redrafting of Companies Act, 1995-96.*
2. Dave Committee: *Report on Infrastructure for Capital Market, 1995-96.*
3. SEBI: Report of the Committee on Derivatives.
4. Alan Shapiro: *Multinational Financial Management*, Prentice-Hall of India Pvt. Ltd.
5. Avadhani V.A.: *Theory and Practice of Central Banking in India*, Somaiya Publications, 1978.
6. Avadhani V.A.: *Studies in Indian Financial System*, Jaico Publishing House, 1979.
7. Joshi Vijay and IMD Little: *Indian Economic Reforms*, 1991-2001, O.U.P. (1996).
8. Jalan, Bimal: *India's Economic Policy — Preparing for the Twenty-first Century,* Penguin Books (1996).
9. Cox J.C. and M. Rubansten: *Options Markets,* Englewood Cliffs, N.J. Prentice-Hall, 1985.
10. Farrel, J.I. Jr.: *Guide to Portfolio Management,* New York, McGraw-Hill, 1983.
11. Joseph L.M. Massive: *Essentials of Management,* Prentice-Hall of India Pvt. Ltd. 1979.
12. RBI : Reports on Currency and Finance.
    : Trend and Progress of Banking in India.
    : Annual Reports and monthly Bulletins of RBI.
    : website of RBI.
13. Smith Roy, C. and Ingowalter: *Global Financial Services*, New York, Harper.
14. Standard and Poor's Corp: *Credit Overview: Corporate and International Ratings*, New York, 1992.
15. Wodmsley Julian: *The New Financial Instruments,* John Wiley and Sons.

JOURNALS FOR REFERENCE

Journal of Finance
Financial Services Review
Financial Analysts Journal
Journal of Portfolio Management
Journal of American Economic Review
Journal of Futures Markets
Journal of Company Secretaries.
Indian Journal of Economics

✠ ✠ ✠